THE
KING ARTHUR FLOUR
COOKIE
COMPANION

The Essential Cookie Cookbook

The Countryman Press
Woodstock, Vermont

An Invitation to the Reader
If you like this book, you'll love the James Beard Foundation's 2004 KitchenAid® Cookbook of the Year, *The King Arthur Flour Baker's Companion;* and King Arthur's bimonthly baking newsletter, *The Baking Sheet*. For information or to subscribe, call *The Baker's Catalogue* at 1-800-827-6836. Also, if you have questions about the recipes in this book, call the Baker's Hotline at 802-649-3717.

Library of Congress Cataloging-in-Publication Data
The King Arthur Flour cookie companion : the essential cookie companion.
    p. cm.
  Includes index.
  ISBN 0-88150-659-1
    1. Cookies. I. King Arthur Flour (Firm)

TX772.K565 2004
641.8'654--dc22

                                            2004050162

Interior design and composition by Susan McClellan
Cover design by Joseph Kantorski
King Arthur Flour logo fabricated in icing by Helen Raffels and Slobodan Saramandic
Recipe and instructional illustrations by Laura Hartman Maestro
Cover and food photography by H/O Photographers, Inc., Hartford, Vermont
Tool photography by Brenda Hickory
Editing by Joan Whitman and Julie Stillman
Index by Joan Whitman

Published by The Countryman Press, P.O. Box 748, Woodstock, Vermont 05091

Distributed by W. W. Norton & Company, Inc., 500 Fifth Avenue, New York, New York 10110

Printed in the United States of America

10 9 8 7 6 5 4 3 2

Acknowledgments

The longest journey begins with a single step. And this long journey began with The Countryman Press, whose editor, Kermit Hummel, and colleagues Jennifer Thompson and Clare Innes, provided valuable advice on the book's outline and content, then supported us in myriad ways through the ensuing months of work. Our thanks, also, to W. W. Norton editor Maria Guarnaschelli, whose sage counsel right at the outset of the project helped design this book's compelling architecture.

Our thanks to the many King Arthur Flour bakers, past and present, whose treasured family recipes grace these pages: Pierre Bourque, Carol Colby, Michelle Diamond, Joan Dunn, Cindy Fountain, Sue Gray, Jeffrey Hamelman, Bonny Hooper, Kate Hookway, Jane Korhonen, Jennifer Korhonen, Janet Matz, Kelly Mousley, Tracy Peer, Robin Rice, Brinna Sands, Robyn Sargent, Ali Scheier, Beth Spaulding, Mary Tinkham, and Patti Vaughan.

Cookbook author, teacher, and longtime King Arthur friend Lora Brody stepped in to save the day with some much-needed expertise and a pocketful of recipes, when it

The King Arthur Flour bakers

seemed this book would never get done. And Nik Hamel spent countless evenings tightening up and enlivening headnotes.

The photos and illustrations are truly what make the *Cookie Companion* sparkle. King Arthur Flour test kitchen director Sue Gray spent days baking perfect cookies; art director Janet Matz made sure each cookie setup was an exquisite jewel; and studio photographer John Sherman used a seasoned eye to bring everything together in a series of delicious pictures. Back at the test kitchen, King Arthur photographer Brenda Hickory, Susan Reid, and Jen Korhonen spent months photographing tips and techniques, and supervising their illustration.

King Arthur baker Robby Kuit, who test-baked (and test-baked again) the vast majority of recipes in this book, never faltered in her pursuit of cookie perfection. Whether it meant rising at 4 AM to bake cookies at home before coming in to work, mixing up batches of dough on Sunday night to be ready for Monday morning, or just being a good sport when we asked her to "Try that crunchy oatmeal cookie just one more time, pretty please?" Robby was always there when we needed her. This book wouldn't have happened without Robby.

The King Arthur Flour publications team, led by Toni Apgar, visualized a cookie book, and then made it happen. Author Susan Reid's imagination and playful creativity is evident in such recipes as Midnights and Rocky Road No-Bakes. When she wasn't writing or plotting out the order of illustrations in each chapter, Susan cheerfully pitched in and helped with the test-baking. To Toni fell the job of pulling together bakers, writers, editor, publisher, and photographers to produce a book that's cogent, compelling . . . and completed on time. And finally, author P. J. Hamel parked herself at her computer in the late summer of 2003, and emerged nine months (and thousands of words) later with this book, an extraordinary testament to the teamwork that makes The King Arthur Flour Company a very special place.

We'd like to dedicate this book to longtime King Arthur Flour owners Frank and Brinna Sands, whose tireless pursuit of excellence has for years provided America's bakers with the best flour in the world. Brinna's baking expertise, her love of culinary history, and her stubborn refusal to let American baking fade away has earned her the admiration and love of fellow bakers everywhere. Frank's enthusiasm for flour, his unwaveringly ethical business practices, and his knowledge of wheat and the milling industry made King Arthur a great company. And in 1996, their re-creation of the business as an employee-owned company paved the way for the ensuing energy and hard work that have inspired King Arthur's growth ever since.

—The King Arthur Flour Company, Inc.

Contents

Introduction   8

GETTING STARTED   10

THE ESSENTIALS   41

     Chocolate Chip Cookies   42

     Sugar Cookies   53

     Oatmeal Cookies   73

     Molasses Cookies   84

     Peanut Butter Cookies   95

     Shortbread   109

     Biscotti   132

     Brownies   154

     Decorated Cookies   168

BARS & SQUARES   187

DROP COOKIES   249

ROLL-OUT COOKIES   323

SHAPED COOKIES   353

BATTER COOKIES   407

NO-BAKE COOKIES   441

THE FINISHING TOUCH   455

INGREDIENTS   475

Index   497

Introduction

Of all of the people in the world, those in the United States are by far the biggest bakers (and consumers) of cookies. Most of us shell out money in the supermarket for cookies, at least occasionally. Over $550 million is spent by the American consumer annually just on Oreos, the snack industry's top-selling cookie. Nevertheless, more than 90 percent of us who still bake at home, bake cookies. There are more cookies coming out of America's home ovens than any other kind of baked good.

Clearly, the cookie has incredible allure for Americans, and it's an attraction that starts very young. When you first toddled across the kitchen and plopped down on the linoleum next to your mom's feet, did she reach down and lovingly hand you a piece of pie? In elementary school, when you opened your lunch box, did you find blueberry buckle tucked alongside your bologna sandwich? And what did you bring to the swim team bake sale? Breadsticks? Cookies are a constant companion throughout our lives, and for good reason: they're simple to make, easily transported, and they're every dessert-lover's notion of the perfect comfort-food sweet.

There are plenty of cookies—good cookies, cookies you'd eagerly pair with a glass of milk and enjoy—for sale at the supermarket. But there are even more—many, many, *many* times more—available to you when you bake at home. Here in America we have a cookie recipe tradition stretching back to our original Dutch and English settlers. By the 1800s, cookie recipes were being published in cookbooks—usually at the end of the cake chapter, as they were considered small cakes, rather than an entity in their own right. This long tradition has yielded hundreds of thousands of recipes, making the decision of which ones to include in this book challenging. But we've met the challenge, and we offer you here a selection of some of the best cookie recipes America has enjoyed over the years, from the simple snickerdoodle to the lovely linzer.

The heart of this book is the chapter called The Essentials: (Chocolate Chip Cookies, Sugar Cookies, Oatmeal Cookies . . .). We've identified nine particular cookies that have generated so much buzz down the years, and so many recipes encompassing so many hundreds of variations in taste, texture, and ingredients, that each deserves more than just one simple recipe. Thus we've done extensive research and testing to develop brownies that are dense and fudgy; brownies that are light and nearly cakelike; and brownies that straddle the fence between those two extremes. Why do some brownies have a light-colored, crisp, and shiny top—and how can I get that top on *my* brownies? And what about those brownies with the layer of mint in the middle, or the ones with the cheesecake swirl? We offer a variety of brownie recipes that diverge from the essential recipe—so that you can enjoy the brownie texture you want with the flavor, filling, or add-in of your choice.

Likewise, sugar cookies come in a wide range of types, from cakey-soft, palm-sized vanilla rounds to snapping crisp, buttery diamonds. Some sugar cookies are soft in the middle and crunchy around the edges; others are bendy-chewy; and some are just solid, delightful crunch from one side to the other. Once you choose your favorite texture, join us as we add cherries or pecans, amend their taste with butter-pecan flavor or lemon oil, stuff them with raisin filling, or ice them with thick chocolate ganache. Cookie bakers are clearly an imaginative lot, and we've tracked down plenty of variations (plus created many of our own) that are sure to make it onto your list of favorite recipes.

Surrounding these Essential recipes are hundreds of others, ranging from ethnic favorites such as *Pizzelle,* to tart-sweet Lemon Bars, to crackly-topped Chocolate Crinkles, and crisp Butterscotch Thins. We've divided them into families based on how they're made, from the very simplest no-bake and drop cookies, to those that are shaped or molded, and even filled.

We invite you now to settle into a comfortable chair, wander through this book, and then go into the kitchen and bake cookies. You'll be a part of an American baking tradition that's as old as shortbread and as new as the cookies your budding 8-year-old baker invents on a rainy Saturday afternoon. Create, enjoy and, most of all, share: both the cookies and the recipes they're made from. Because that's what baking—especially cookie baking—is all about.

—P.J. Hamel, Susan Reid, and the bakers at King Arthur Flour

Getting Started

Before you begin . . .

While baking is art as well as science, the science isn't something science-phobes (you?) can simply ignore. Measuring accurately is important. And the ingredients you use—specifically, using what's called for in the recipe—are also critical. When following recipes in this book, please use the ingredients called for, in the amount indicated. Straying from these indicated ingredients can yield results quite different from what was intended.

That said, let us specify some of the common ingredients you will find in this book.

Eggs	large eggs
Butter	unsalted butter, 80% butterfat
Salt	table salt
Unbleached all-purpose flour	protein level: 11.7%
Cake flour	bleached, protein level: 8.0%
Sugar	cane sugar
Brown sugar	light or dark, your choice, unless specified
Vegetable oil	vegetable, canola, safflower, or sunflower oil
Shortening	hydrogenated all-vegetable shortening, plain or butter-flavored
Chocolate chips	semisweet chocolate chips, unless otherwise indicated
Coconut	shredded sweetened coconut
Raisins	Thompson or golden, your choice
Baking powder	double-acting baking powder
Extracts and flavors	extra-strong flavors, less-strong extracts, as indicated
Spices	ground spices
Cocoa	unsweetened natural or Dutch-process, as indicated
Milk	1%
Yogurt	low-fat or full-fat (not nonfat)
Cream cheese	reduced fat (Neufchâtel) or full-fat
Molasses	unsulfured golden or dark (not blackstrap)
Rolled oats	old-fashioned (not quick-cooking) rolled oats

A Note on Measuring • • • • • • • •

We take measuring pretty seriously. We know lots of bakers who "throw things together" and never measure, often with spectacular results. Trouble is, those results can't be repeated with any regularity. So we make every effort to measure correctly and write down the results. That's because we run a test kitchen that is expected to turn out consistent results time and again. We also think that's a good way to learn what works and what doesn't, and we're passionate about teaching bakers—experienced or not—how to take their baking to a more satisfying level.

There are two principal ways to measure ingredients in baking: by weight (ounces, grams) and by volume (teaspoons, cups). Small amounts of ingredients, such as baking soda, vanilla extract, or salt, are usually measured in volume amounts. For these you need a set (or two) of measuring spoons, ranging from ⅛ or ¼ teaspoon to 1 tablespoon (see page 34). Larger ingredient amounts can be measured by either weight or volume, with weight being the more accurate of the two choices. For that reason we encourage you to buy a kitchen scale, preferably an electronic one, which calibrates best. If you don't have a kitchen scale, here are some basic rules to keep in mind when measuring; these will ensure your recipes turn out well.

Use the proper type of measuring cup for the ingredient you're working with. Liquid measuring cups are designed for wet ingredients. They're usually clear, with markings on the side so you can see when the amount you need has been reached, and have a pour spout. Some angled liquid measuring cups allow you to read amounts from above.

Dry measuring cups are designed with a flat rim so the ingredients being measured can be leveled off with a straight edge.

Think before you measure!

First step: Make sure, before you measure, that you know what you're supposed to be measuring, for example, 1 cup of pecans, chopped, or 1 cup of chopped pecans. The former is pecan halves weighed first, then chopped; the latter is pecans that have been chopped first, then weighed. Yes, it does make a difference!

Curing the stickies

Honey, corn syrup, maple syrup, and molasses are easier to measure if you coat the inside of your measuring cup with nonstick spray before filling.

Using a metric scale?

Most scales shift easily between American (ounce) and metric (gram) measurements. However, if you're doing the mental conversions yourself, 1 ounce = 28.35 grams.

Stir the flour to fluff it up . . .

. . . sprinkle it into the measuring cup . . .

. . . and sweep off the excess with the straight edge of the scoop.

MEASURING BY VOLUME

Flour is perhaps the most important ingredient in a baking recipe, and the easiest to measure incorrectly. Flour can absorb moisture from the air, as well as compact during shipping. Add to these factors the common practice of digging into a compacted container of flour and pressing it down to make a level cup, and it's very easy to use too much flour in your recipe. Too much flour means dry, crumbly, disappointing results. A properly measured cup of flour should weigh close to 4¼ ounces per 1 cup of volume.

Other dry ingredients: For dry ingredients such as granulated sugar or cornstarch, fill the measuring container above its rim and sweep off the excess with a straight edge drawn across the rim.

Liquid ingredients: To read the amount in a liquid measure, set it on a flat surface with the markings at eye level, either by crouching down or by placing the cup on an eye-level shelf. Pour liquid into the cup until the level reaches the measurement you need.

Brown sugar: Measure brown sugar by firmly packing it into a dry measuring cup until it's level with the top edge.

Solid fats: To measure a solid fat (butter or vegetable shortening) or peanut butter, try the displacement method. Use a measuring cup that is significantly larger than the amount you want to measure (for instance, a 2-cup measure, to measure ½ cup of vegetable shortening). Fill the 2-cup measure up to the 1 cup mark with cold water. To measure ½ cup of shortening, scoop shortening into the water, allowing it to float freely until the water reaches the 1½ cup mark. You now have ½ cup of shortening. Drain the water and use the shortening in your recipe.

MEASURING BY WEIGHT

Weighing ingredients is a more accurate way of determining amounts than measuring by volume. When it comes to volume measurements, there are many variables that can affect actual amounts. Measuring cups and spoons can vary significantly (we've discovered this over and over in our test kitchen). Cooks everywhere use varying techniques, and one person's idea of "full" or "packed" is usually different from the next person's.

Ingredient weights also can vary, depending on storage and weather conditions. The following chart gives average weights for amounts commonly given in recipes. It can help you plan your shopping, and it's handy if you want to convert recipes to larger or smaller amounts.

WEIGHTS IN OUNCES FOR RECIPES

28.35 GRAMS PER OUNCE

Item	Measurement	Weight in Ounces
Almonds, chopped	1 cup	5
Almonds, sliced	½ cup	2
Almond flour	1 cup	3¼
Almond paste	1 cup	9
Apples, dried, diced	1 cup	3
Apples, peeled, sliced	1 cup	4
Apricots, dried, diced	½ cup	3
Baking chips, all flavors (butterscotch, peanut butter, cherry, etc.)	1 cup	6
Baking powder	1 tablespoon	½
Bread crumbs, fresh	1 cup	2¼
Butter	½ cup, 1 stick	4
Buttermilk, yogurt	2 tablespoons (⅛ cup)	1
Caramel, 14 to16 individual pieces	½ cup	5
Carrots, grated	1 cup	3½
Cashews	1 cup	4
Chocolate, chopped	1 cup	6
Chocolate chips	1 cup	6
Cocoa, unsweetened, regular or Dutch process, unsifted	2 tablespoons	⅜
	¼ cup	¾
	⅓ cup	1
	1 cup	3
Coconut, grated, unsweetened	1 cup	4
Coconut, sweetened flakes	1 cup	3
Cornmeal	1 cup	4⅞
Corn syrup	1 cup	11
Cornstarch	¼ cup	1
Cranberries, dried	½ cup	2
Currants	1 cup	5¼
Dates, chopped	1 cup	5¼
Espresso powder	1 tablespoon	⅛
Flour, cake	1 cup	4
Flour, King Arthur unbleached all-purpose	1 cup	4¼
Flour, whole wheat/graham	1 cup	5¼
Semolina	1 cup	5¾
Ginger, crystallized	½ cup	3¼
	⅓ cup	2¼
Graham crackers, crushed	1 cup	5
Hazelnuts	1 cup	4
Honey	1 tablespoon	¾

WEIGHTS IN OUNCES FOR RECIPES (CONTINUED)

Item	Measurement	Weight in Ounces
Instant Clearjel	1 tablespoon	⅜
Jam or preserves	¼ cup	3
	⅔ cup	7¾
Lemon juice	½ cup	4
Macadamia nuts, chopped	1 cup	4¾
Maple sugar	½ cup	2¾
Maple syrup	½ cup	5½
Marshmallow creme	1 cup	3
Marshmallows, miniature	1 cup	2
Meringue powder	¼ cup	1
Milk	1 cup	8
Molasses	¼ cup	3
Oats, rolled	1 cup	3½
Oil, vegetable	1 cup	7
Peanut butter	½ cup	4¾
Peanuts, dry-roasted, salted	1 cup	5
Pecans, chopped	1 cup	4
Pecan meal	1 cup	3½
Pineapple, dried	½ cup	2½
Pine nuts	½ cup	2½
Pistachio nuts	½ cup	2
Pumpkin, canned	1 cup	9½
Raisins, loose	1 cup	5¼
Raisins, packed	1 cup	6
Sesame seeds	½ cup	2½
Sour cream	1 cup	8
Sugar, granulated	1 cup	7
	⅔ cup	4¾
Sugar, confectioners', unsifted	2 cups	8
Sugar, coarse or pearl	½ cup	4⅜
Sugar, dark or light brown, packed	1 cup	8
Sugar, Demerara	1 cup	7¾
Toffee chunks	1 cup	5⅛
Vegetable shortening	½ cup	3¼
Walnuts, whole	½ cup	2¼
Walnuts, chopped	1 cup	4
Water	⅓ cup	2⅝
	⅔ cup	5⅜
Yeast, instant	2¼ teaspoons	¼
Zucchini, shredded, lightly packed	1 cup	8

TIPS ON TECHNIQUES ● ● ● ● ● ● ● ●

Many bakers who are just getting started have questions about phrases commonly used in recipes. If you weren't lucky enough to grow up with Grandma in the kitchen, where these things were lovingly explained, you may have questions about what we mean when we say, "cream butter and sugar," "scrape down the bowl," or "cut fat into the flour mixture." Even if you're familiar with this baking vocabulary, it can be helpful to know why these techniques are important. What follows is a guide to common baking terms and phrases, arranged alphabetically, for bakers of all skill levels to use as a reference.

Adding eggs, one at a time: After creaming together butter and sugar (see page 17), the next ingredient in many cookie recipes is eggs. They should be added one at a time, each one thoroughly beaten in before the next is added, to allow the creamed butter/sugar mixture to retain its trapped air most effectively. Be sure to scrape the sides of the bowl so all of the butter/sugar mixture is incorporated.

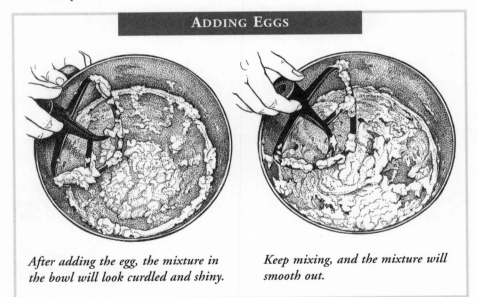

ADDING EGGS

After adding the egg, the mixture in the bowl will look curdled and shiny.

Keep mixing, and the mixture will smooth out.

Baking in batches: After you've removed a cookie sheet from the oven and transferred the baked cookies to a cooling rack, be sure the pan has cooled to room temperature before putting more cookie dough on it. Putting dough on hot pans will cause it to spread or lose its shape before it gets into the oven, increasing the risk of burned edges and flat cookies. If you want to continue scooping or shaping while your first pan of cookies is baking, deposit the rest of the dough on sheets of parchment, then lift the parchment onto the cooled sheets when they're ready.

BEATING EGG WHITES

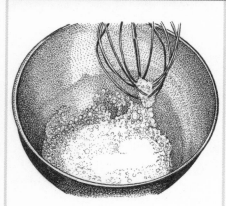

As you beat the egg whites, the liquid will become opaque, forming many more, smaller bubbles.

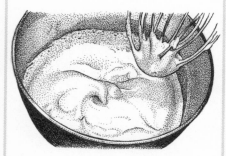

If a point forms and then falls over immediately, the egg whites are at a soft peak.

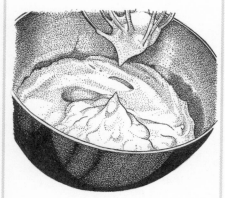

From here, several more seconds will bring you to a medium peak, and another several seconds to stiff peaks.

Beating egg whites: Beating egg whites properly is the key to creating certain extra-light cookies, such as meringues or ladyfingers. Three things to remember: the bowl and beaters must be clean and grease-free. Use a stainless steel, ceramic, or glass bowl, not plastic. Egg whites will whip more fully if they're at room temperature before beating.

When beating egg whites, at first you'll have a puddle of clear liquid with some large bubbles in it.

Continue beating, and soon the whisk will begin to leave tracks in the bowl. To test the character of your whites, pull your whisk or beaters straight up out of the foam.

It's extremely easy to go too far. When you start to see grainy white clumps, you're beyond stiff peaks, and every stroke of the whisk or beater is tearing apart the network of air, water, and protein you've worked so hard to create. You'll also see a pool of clear liquid under the foam. The good news is that the foam still on top of the liquid essentially will still work. The bad news is that you can't really fix what's happened, other than to start over with new egg whites.

Boiling: When bringing liquid to a boil over a burner, the first sign of that impending boil is very small bubbles atop the liquid at the edge of the pan; if you're heating milk, this is called scalding the milk. Next, bubbles will begin to rise from the interior of the pan, popping on the surface. These bubbles are small and spaced apart; this is called a simmer. If directed by your recipe to simmer the liquid in the pan, adjust the heat so that these bubbles continue to form and break at intervals, not constantly. To bring liquid to a boil, keep heat high until so many bubbles are erupting across the surface that you can't distinguish one from another. This is called a full, or rolling, boil.

Chilling: After mixing cookie dough, chilling firms up the fat and gives the flour time to absorb liquid evenly. This allows dough to roll out more evenly, without sticking as much, and to hold its shape while being cut and transferred to a baking sheet.

CHILLING DOUGH

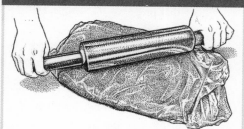

Place dough to be chilled inside a plastic bag and flatten it a bit with a rolling pin. This will allow dough to chill quickly and give you a head start on rolling it out later.

Cooling cookies: When baking drop cookies, especially if you like chewy ones, leave the cookies on the baking sheet for 5 minutes after you take the pan out of the oven. This gives the cookies a chance to firm up a bit before you slide a spatula underneath them. After 5 minutes, transfer the cookies to a cooling rack to finish cooling. We prefer a cooling rack that has a grid pattern with half-inch holes, to give fragile cookies support while they're cooling.

Bar cookies should cool in their baking pans on a rack. Don't cut them while they're warm; you'll make bars with very ragged edges, and they're much more likely to fall apart when you're taking them out of the pan.

Batter cookies that need to be shaped after baking should be transferred while still warm to whatever shaping device you're using: a dowel, custard cup, cone, etc. Some cookies may be shaped while warm by simply rolling them into a tube shape around the handle of a wooden spoon.

Whatever type of cookies you're making, be sure they're entirely cool before you wrap them up to store. Wrapping a still-warm cookie will cause it to steam inside its container, which could yield soggy, stuck-together results.

Creaming: Creaming is responsible for creating the texture of cookies, particularly crisp ones. It's the process that begins many cookie recipes; where sugar and fat are beaten together to form and capture air bubbles, bubbles that form when the edges of sugar crystals cut into fat molecules to make an air pocket. When you first start beating sugar and fat together, the mixture is thick and somewhat lumpy. As you continue to beat, the mixture becomes creamier in texture, more uniform, and lighter in color as air is beaten in.

Cutting in: This technique combines fat and flour in a way that preserves shards of fat in the mixture. These shards create a flaky, tender texture in the baked cookie by getting between the layers of flour/liquid in the dough and keeping them separate as they bake. Cutting in can be accomplished with your fingers, a pastry fork, two knives, a pastry blender, a mixer, or a food processor, pulsed gently.

COOLING COOKIES

Use a spatula to transfer cookies to a cooling rack.

CREAMING

The fat and sugar mixture has a fluffy texture when creamed properly, as shown.

CUTTING IN

Flattened chunks of fat the size of your thumbnail will yield the flakiest results.

Cutting into bars: Most bar cookies are baked in a square or rectangular pan. The simplest way to divide these cookies evenly is by cutting the sheet of baked dough in half, then cutting the halves in half again. When using uncoated metal pans, we've found a bench knife (see page 31) is a wonderful cutting implement for bar cookies. The handle on top allows you to cut right to the edge of the pan, an awkward proposition when you're using a regular knife. For pans with nonstick coating, plastic cutting implements are a better choice. Or use your nylon spatula (see page 38).

CUTTING INTO BARS

Bars in 9 x 9-inch pans are cut four across and four down to yield 16 squares.

Bars in 7 x 11-inch pans are cut three down and eight across to yield 24 rectangles.

Bars in 9 x 13-inch pans are cut four down and six across, to yield 24 squares.

A 10 x 15-inch jellyroll pan yields 35 squares, when cut five down and seven across.

Bars baked in 18 x 13-inch (half-sheet) pans can be cut four down and six across, to yield 24 large squares; or eight down and six across to make 48 rectangles. For small squares, cut eight down and 12 across, for a total of 96 squares.

Docking: Pricking holes in a short dough (one that's high in fat and has a flaky or crisp texture after baking, such as shortbread or the crust of some bar cookies), helps to vent the steam created in the oven while baking. You can use a fork or a dough docker (see page 33) to prick small holes all over the surface of the dough. By venting the steam, docking keeps the dough from billowing or heaving as it bakes. It's an important step for crisp cookies or those that are baked in a single sheet and not cut up until they come out of the oven.

DOCKING

Vent holes for steam can be made with a fork or a dough docker.

Doneness: How do you know when your drop or shaped cookies are done? Cookies will continue to set from the heat of the pan after being removed from the oven, so how do you know when to take them out? Open the oven door and insert the edge of a turner or spatula under the edge of one cookie. Lift gently. If the cookie stays flat across the bottom and doesn't bend or break in the middle, it's ready to come out of the oven, as shown below.

DONENESS

This cookie doesn't hold together when lifted off the baking sheet, a sign that it needs more baking time.

This cookie holds its shape when lifted off the baking sheet. It's ready to come out of the oven.

When ready to take out of the oven, bar cookies will pull away from the edge of the pan just slightly, and batter cookies will be golden brown at their edges.

Drop the dough by the tablespoonful: A typical drop cookie recipe directs you to drop the dough by either the teaspoonful or the tablespoonful onto prepared baking sheets. What does this really mean? Do you have to measure out an exact teaspoon or tablespoon of dough? No. These measurements are idiomatic, and date back to the time bakers used a soup spoon (tablespoon) or regular spoon (teaspoon) to scoop out and deposit their cookie dough. In order to make cookies the same size as the original recipes intended, the modern baker can rely on a cookie scoop (see pages 32–33). The tablespoon cookie scoop, which mimics the original soup spoon, holds a level, scant 2 tablespoons (5 teaspoons) of dough; the teaspoon scoop holds a level 2 teaspoons of dough. So, when the recipes in this book call for "dropping dough by the tablespoonful," it's expected you'll make a ball of dough, either with a cookie scoop or a spoon, that measures about 2 tablespoons (about the size of a table tennis ball). To "drop dough by the teaspoonful," make a ball of dough that measures about 2 teaspoons (about the size of a large gumball). This will yield the size cookies, and thus the yield, the recipe intends.

Filling cookies: Soft fillings, such as marshmallow or sandwich cookie fillings, can be scooped onto the flat side of a cookie with a teaspoon-sized cookie scoop. Firmer fillings can be spread with an offset spatula or a table knife.

Filling a pastry bag: Most people wish they had three hands when it comes to filling a pastry bag. Here are some hints to make it easier:

A tall, narrow container with a heavy base (such as a flower vase) is a great holder to steady and support the bag as you fill it, so your hands are free to put frosting or batter into the bag.

Be sure to fill the bag no more than three quarters full. Overfilling the bag makes it hard to close and hard to control. It should fit comfortably in your hands.

A twist tie is a big help to keep the top of the bag closed, so icing doesn't back up onto your hand when you squeeze the bag. See pages 176–177 for more information.

Folding: Ingredients with air beaten in, such as beaten egg whites or whipped cream, are combined with the rest of a recipe's ingredients in a way that preserves as many of the air bubbles as possible. We like to use a whisk for this, because the many wires of the whisk combine the two mixtures effectively in just a few strokes. This results in a light texture in the finished product.

FOLDING

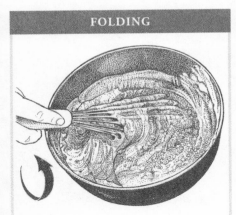

Sifted dry ingredients are being folded into beaten egg whites with a whisk. Draw the whisk down through the bowl and back up in a circular motion.

Freezing cookie dough and baked cookies: This is one of our favorite hints: Cookie dough can be made in advance of baking and frozen for up to 3 months. An effective way to do this is to form it into logs for slice-and-bake cookies (see page 26). Freeze the logs in a large zip-top plastic bag, and don't thaw the cookie dough before baking. Simply use a bench knife or sharp knife to cut as few or as many slices as you like, place them on a greased or parchment-lined baking sheet, and let them thaw while the oven is heating.

FREEZING COOKIE DOUGH

Rolled cookie dough keeps well when stored inside a zip-top freezer bag. Use a drinking straw to suck the air out of the bag before closing.

Drop cookie dough can be scooped, or rolled into balls, and frozen on a lightly greased baking sheet. Once the unbaked cookies are frozen, they can be stored in a zip-top storage bag in the freezer. When you're ready to bake, thaw as few or as many as you like while your oven heats.

Most baked cookies are good candidates for up to 3 months of freezer storage (with the exception of cookies filled with freshly whipped cream, which should be enjoyed immediately). Place completely cooled cookies in a zip-top bag, remove as much air as possible (using a drinking straw, as illustrated on page 20), and freeze.

Greasing a pan: Preparing your baking pan properly before filling it can save a lot of heartbreak (and cookie-break). We recommend using a nonstick pan spray for quick, effective coverage, but a thin coat of vegetable shortening also does the trick.

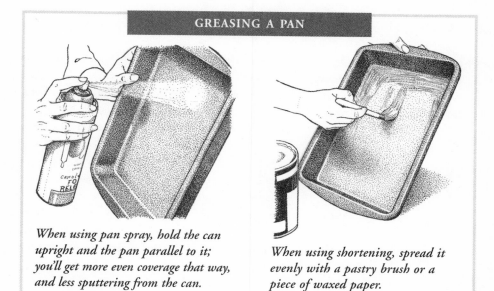

GREASING A PAN

When using pan spray, hold the can upright and the pan parallel to it; you'll get more even coverage that way, and less sputtering from the can.

When using shortening, spread it evenly with a pastry brush or a piece of waxed paper.

Leveling (smoothing) the crust: When baking layered or bar cookies, it is very important to have the crust, filling, or batter level before the pan goes into the oven. Uneven batter will bake unevenly; one section may be burned, while the other is underdone.

Lining a pan: Lining with parchment is by far our favorite technique for cookie baking. Parchment is coated with silicone, so cookies don't stick to it; it can be reused again and again. Simply line the pan with parchment that stretches as close to the edge of the pan as possible.

Silicone mats are another popular option. They're more durable than parchment and can be used thousands of times. Be careful not to cut anything on a silicone baking mat, as the mat can be damaged. For baking cookies, a thin silicone mat is preferable to a thick mat (often sold as a "kneading mat").

LEVELING

The top pan of brownies was properly smoothed out; the bottom pan was unevenly filled.

HIGH-ALTITUDE BAKING

Because cookies bake for a shorter amount of time than breads or cakes, and are relatively low in water and high in fat content, they're much less susceptible to the vagaries of high-altitude baking. The principal adjustments recommended for cookies baked at higher altitudes (generally considered to be above 3,500 feet) are to increase the water slightly to help the dough come together, and to decrease the amount of chemical leaveners (baking powder, baking soda) used. Experienced high-altitude bakers know to bake at a slightly higher temperature, with a shortened baking time. The tables below give guidelines for baking cookies at high altitude.

WHAT TO CHANGE	HOW TO CHANGE IT	WHY
Oven temperature	Increase 15 to 20 degrees F; use the smaller increase when making a recipe that's largely chocolate, like brownies or chocolate crinkles.	Since leavening and evaporation proceed more quickly, the idea is to use a higher temperature to "set" the structure of baked goods before they over-expand, spread too much, or dry out.
Baking time	Decrease by 1½ to 2 minutes per 10 minutes of baking time.	Baking at a higher temperature means cookies are done sooner.
Liquid	Increase by 1 to 2 tablespoons at 3,500 feet. Increase by an additional 1½ teaspoons for each additional 1,000 feet over 3,500. You can also use extra eggs as part of this liquid in recipes with a tender crumb, like bar cookies or batter cookies (such as madeleines).	Extra liquid helps high-fat doughs come together, and keeps cookies from drying out at higher baking temperatures and accelerated evaporation rates.

ADJUSTING CHEMICAL LEAVENERS

Baking powder, soda, or other leavener in original recipe	3,500 to 6,500 ft.	6,501 to 8,500 ft.	8,501 ft. and above
1 teaspoon	⅞ tsp.	⅞ to ¾ tsp.	¾ tsp.
1½ teaspoons	1⅜ tsp.	1⅜ to 1⅛ tsp.	1⅛ tsp.
2 teaspoons	1¾ tsp.	1¾ to 1½ tsp.	1½ tsp.
2½ teaspoons	2⅛ tsp.	2⅛ to 1⅞ tsp.	1⅞ tsp.
3 teaspoons	2⅝ tsp.	2⅝ to 2¼ tsp.	2¼ tsp.
3½ teaspoons	3 tsp.	3 to 2⅝ tsp.	2⅝ tsp.
4 teaspoons	3½ tsp.	3½ to 3 tsp.	3 tsp.

Melting chocolate: Chocolate scorches easily and can seize (become hard and unmixable) if it comes in contact with water when melting. We recommend melting chocolate at medium power in the microwave, in a heatproof container. One cup of chocolate chips melted at half power should be heated for 1½ to 2 minutes, depending on the power of your microwave.

Chocolate can also be melted in a double boiler set over simmering water, tightly covered so steam doesn't come in contact with it.

Piping: Piping is a basic technique that can add a lot of polish to the look of your baked goods. See Filling a Pastry Bag on page 20, for hints on getting set up. Stop squeezing before lifting the bag as you pipe, to make a cleaner separation point.

Rolling into a ball: Some cookies, like Snickerdoodles (see page 60), are shaped into balls before being rolled in sugar to coat them evenly. This process is made easier with a cookie scoop (see pages 32–33), which portions roughly spherical amounts to start with.

Rolling out: This process involves using a rolling pin to flatten chilled dough to an even thickness, to be cut into shapes before baking. Dusting the work surface and your rolling pin with flour is an important first step. It's a good idea to have a large, thin spatula (See page 38) and a ruler or tape measure on hand before you begin. The spatula helps you pick up the dough frequently, to keep it from sticking, and the measuring tools help you keep track of the dough's dimensions and thickness as you work. Roll from the center of the dough to the edges, not back and forth, which tends to toughen the dough's gluten. If the dough is soft or sticky, it's helpful to place a layer of plastic wrap between the dough and your rolling pin, and to place the dough on parchment before rolling.

MELTING CHOCOLATE

It's preferable to melt the chocolate three-quarters of the way, then let carryover heat finish the melting process while you stir the chocolate to smooth it out.

PIPING

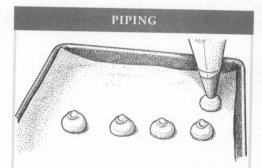

Squeeze from the top of the bag toward the tip as you go, gathering the slack in the palm of your hand to maintain pressure.

ROLLING INTO A BALL

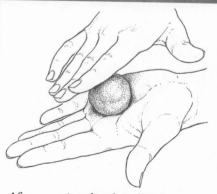

After scooping dough, roll it between your hands to finish rounding it.

SCOOPING COOKIE DOUGH

Fill a spoon halfway with stiff dough. Using another spoon of the same size, scrape the dough off the first spoon onto the baking sheet.

Scoop the dough against the side of the bowl, using the lip of the bowl to level off the bottom, then squeeze the scoop's handle to release the dough onto a baking sheet. When dough begins to stick in the scoop, rinse scoop with water.

Scooping cookie dough: There are two widely used methods to do this: using two spoons or a cookie scoop (also known as a disher). The cookie scoop (see pages 32–33) results are more consistent, and it's a quicker way to get the job done.

Scraping the bowl: Recipes that combine creamed fat and liquids can be difficult to mix thoroughly, because the butter/sugar mixture sticks to the sides of the bowl. The only sure remedy for this is to stop mixing partway through and scrape the sides and bottom of the mixing bowl.

SCRAPING THE BOWL

It's important to use a spatula to scrape the sides of the bowl during mixing, to ensure the ingredients are evenly combined.

Separating eggs: It's easier to separate the whites from the yolks when eggs are cold. If you need help, try one of the many types of egg separators found in any kitchen store.

Shaping batter cookies: When batter cookies are still warm, they can be shaped using any number of kitchen items. *Tuiles* can be draped over the handle of a rolling pin, or over the back of a custard cup to make a small, edible bowl to hold ice cream, pudding, or berries. *Krumkake* are traditionally rolled

SEPARATING EGGS

Crack the shell and use it to pass the yolk from one side to the other as the white drips down into a bowl. An egg separator (bottom) does the same thing.

around a cannoli form (a hollow tube), and lace cookies wrap nicely around the handle of a wooden spoon. See the Batter Cookies chapter (pages 407–408), for illustrations of these shapes being created.

Shipping cookies: There are two types of cookies that ship well: bar cookies and crisp cookies. Bar cookies are fairly moist; they can be cut into convenient squares or rectangles, and they stay fresh longer than other types of cookies, so long as they're wrapped well. Crisp cookies have a low water content and should be well wrapped to keep them from absorbing moisture. See page 26 for some hints for sending your creations to someone you care about.

Sifting flour: Sifted flour has been passed through a strainer or screen to aerate it, sometimes in concert with other dry ingredients. Sifted flour is usually folded in with wet ingredients, in recipes where the desired result is a light, spongy texture.

Slice and bake: Shaped cookie doughs are often rolled into a log shape and sliced before baking. Any stiff drop cookie dough can be treated the same way; thick slices of dough will make a chewier cookie, and thin slices will create crisper ones.

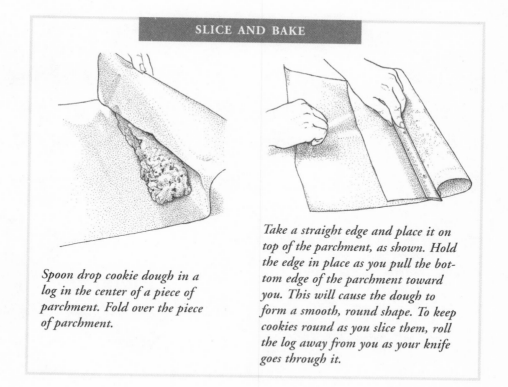

SLICE AND BAKE

Spoon drop cookie dough in a log in the center of a piece of parchment. Fold over the piece of parchment.

Take a straight edge and place it on top of the parchment, as shown. Hold the edge in place as you pull the bottom edge of the parchment toward you. This will cause the dough to form a smooth, round shape. To keep cookies round as you slice them, roll the log away from you as your knife goes through it.

CREATING PACKAGES OF COOKIES WITH CARE

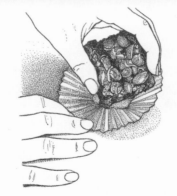

Choose a sturdy corrugated box or large tin to ship your cookies. Line the bottom with soft, food-safe packing material, such as plastic bubble wrap or unbuttered popped popcorn.

Small paper baking cups are an attractive way to package individual cookies. They also protect the cookies.

Place heavy cardboard in the bottom of a zip-top freezer bag.

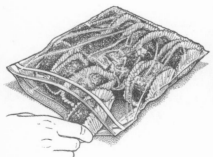

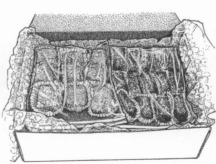

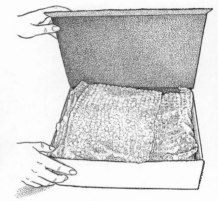

Place cookies in a single layer, covering the bottom of the bag completely. The more snugly the cookies fit, the less they'll shift as they travel.

Cushion each layer of cookies with a layer of packing material.

Fill the remaining space in the box with more packing material to ensure a snug fit.

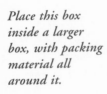

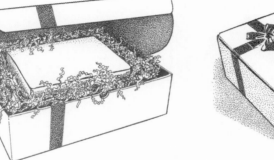

Place this box inside a larger box, with packing material all around it.

Close the box, seal, label, and ship.

Stir: Many cookie doughs and batters need no more than a bowl and spoon to prepare. Wetter batters, like brownies, are good candidates for stirring, since overmixing with a machine can make them tough.

Storing cookies: The first thing to keep in mind when storing cookies is that they need to be completely cool before you put them away, otherwise they'll steam, soften up, and stick to each other. Cookies usually can be stored at room temperature, in airtight containers, for up to a week. Appropriate containers can be cookie jars or tins, screw-top plastic jars or snap-top plastic boxes, or tightly closed plastic bags. Bar cookies with lots of fruit or dairy ingredients should be refrigerated, well wrapped. If you plan to store cookies for more than a week, we advise wrapping them so air can't get to them and freezing for up to 3 months.

Straining unsweetened cocoa: Unsweetened cocoa contains cocoa butter, which can cause it to clump. To make sure it combines evenly with the rest of the dry ingredients in your recipe, it's best to strain it.

Toasting nuts and coconut: Toasting nuts enhances their flavor. Since nuts are high in fat, they can scorch easily. Always toast nuts in a shallow container in a single layer. A low to moderate oven (300° to 325°F) is best. Check at 8 minutes for smaller or sliced nuts. Larger nuts may take 10 to 15 minutes. The nuts are done when you can smell their aroma and they've become golden brown. Remove them from the oven when their color is just a shade lighter than what you're looking for, as they'll continue to cook a bit as they cool. Transfer the nuts to a cool surface immediately, to minimize this carryover cooking. If you're toasting sweetened coconut, remove it from the oven and stir it on the baking pan every 5 minutes to ensure even browning.

STIR

After whisking together the dry ingredients, add them to the wet ones, stirring until the mixture is evenly combined.

STRAINING UNSWEETENED COCOA

Push the cocoa powder through a strainer, after measuring it and before adding it to your recipe.

TOASTING NUTS

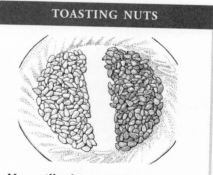

Nuts will take on a deeper color when toasted. On the left, untoasted pine nuts. On the right, toasted pine nuts.

TOOLS TO MAKE THE JOB EASIER ● ● ●

For many people, cookies are their first baking adventure. As with many skills, one starts with the basics and branches out from there. For any baker, the quality of the tools you use can mean the difference between a rewarding experience and unnecessary frustration. But it can take time and some wrong turns before you know what to avoid when choosing baking equipment. That's where we can help.

We put baking pans, tools, and gadgets of every description through their paces every day in our test kitchen. We've already encountered the awkward zesters, flimsy, warped cookie sheets, and the sticks-no-matter-what pans out there. We've also found plenty of utensils, pans, and tools that are a joy to work (and play) with. What follows is an overview of cookie-baking equipment. Here's what to look for and how each item is used, so you can choose tools that will become reliable partners in your baking adventures to come.

BAKING PANS

8-inch round cake pan: We like to use 8- or 9-inch round cake pans for shortbread recipes, since they hold the same amount of dough as most embossed shortbread molds. If you want a quick way to make nice, even shortbread wedges, just press the dough into the pan, then decorate the top by docking it in a pretty pattern with a fork. Bake the shortbread and cut it into wedges with a serrated knife while still warm.

8" round

8 x 8-inch square pan: An 8-inch square pan holds roughly half the volume of a 9 x 13-inch pan. If you find a brownie recipe that calls for a 9 x 13-inch pan, and you want to make a smaller batch, cut the ingredient amounts in half and use an 8 x 8-inch pan. You'll want to check on the brownies 10 minutes sooner than the baking time calls for, just to be sure they don't overbake.

9" square

9 x 9-inch square pan: Perfect for many bars and squares recipes, 9 x 9-inch pans are a pantry staple. Some 9-inch square pans come with removable bottoms, which can be a convenient feature. Choose a light-colored metal pan with accurate dimensions (it's a good idea to measure any pan before buying, no matter what the label says). Measure from the inside of one edge to the inside of the opposite edge: your ruler should say 9 inches, not 8¼ or 9½.

8" square

*9" x 13"
bar pan*

*7" x 11"
bar pan*

7 x 11-inch bar pan: Measuring 7 x 11 inches and usually 1½ inches deep, bar or brownie pans are an old-fashioned size, but beloved by many bakers. If you need a substitute for this pan, you can use a different size pan by figuring out how much surface area the recipe needs. Bar pans measure 77 square inches (7 times 11); a 9 x 9-inch pan is an acceptable substitute, at 81 square inches.

9 x 13-inch pan: Commonly called for in larger bar cookie recipes, a 9 x 13-inch pan should be of light-colored metal, and be sturdy enough to hold itself without flexing when you pick it up from one end. This is a popular size for heatproof glass pans, but we find they're heavier to lift, take longer to heat, and retain heat longer once they're up to temperature. All of these characteristics can change the results you're expecting from your bar cookie recipes, so we save glass pans for casseroles instead of using them for bars.

18" x 13" half-sheet pan

10" x 15" jellyroll pan

10 x 15-inch pan: This size is known as a jellyroll pan, but can also be put to use for bar cookie recipes. In a pinch, a 10 x 15-inch pan can do double duty as an extra cookie sheet.

Cookie sheets: There's an abundance of choices here: light, dark, or nonstick finishes, textured or smooth, sides or no sides, air cushioned or not. In general, we recommend light finishes for baking cookies. Cookie doughs have a lot of fat, which can mean very fast browning when baked on a dark surface. We usually choose cookie sheets with raised sides, because they're easier to pick up, the cookies won't slide off, and we can flip them over and use the backs for things that are cut out with a template, like construction gingerbread.

Half-sheet pan: Made of sturdy aluminum with a steel band that reinforces the rim, half-sheet pans measure 18 x 13 inches. Their sides are 1 inch tall. Half-sheet pans are excellent for baking cookies and bars; we use them more than any other pan in our kitchen. Their light color encourages even browning, and their sturdy construction stands up to all manner of abuse. The size we've based our recipes on is a 18 x 13-inch half-sheet pan, which comfortably holds a dozen 2-inch cookies.

Madeleine pan: Madeleines are a cross between a sponge cake and a cookie, and are baked in pans with indentations that are reminiscent of seashells. Full-size madeleines are 3¼ inches long, 2⅛ inches wide, and take 2 tablespoons of batter in each form; small madeleines are 1¼ by 1 inch, using 1½ teaspoons of batter apiece. Madeleine pans can be made of metal or silicone; look for one with pronounced ridges in the wells.

Saucepan: The ideal saucepan has a flat, heavy bottom and sides, with no "hot spots" in the corners, and a securely attached handle that stays cool. Look for pans with sturdy handles and good balance: they shouldn't rock or tip when empty. Stainless-steel-lined pans with aluminum cores give the best combination of a nonreactive, durable surface next to the food, backed up by the excellent conductivity and heat transfer of aluminum. As a rule, you want to use the smallest sized saucepan that will comfortably hold your ingredients, to lessen the risk of scorching. Nonstick or not is largely a matter of preference. Nonstick saucepans are easier to clean but require more care when reaching for a utensil to stir with.

Madeleine pan

BOWLS

Mixing bowl: From Grandma's heavy stoneware bowl to the one that came with your mixer, there are hundreds of mixing bowls available, in a complete range of sizes. Most stand mixers come with their own stainless steel bowls. A handle on these is a desirable feature. If you use a hand mixer in a large bowl on the counter, your bowl should have a stable base and walls that are high enough and steep enough to keep the contents of the bowl moving back down toward the beaters as you're mixing. If you're mixing a recipe by hand, rigid plastic bowls with flat lips you can grab on to are a good choice, since they're sturdy without being too heavy. Some plastic mixing bowls have a handle molded into the rim and a pour spout opposite; these are very handy for mixing and pouring wet ingredients or batter. Stainless steel bowls are useful, since they're nonreactive and can be placed over a water bath to melt butter or chocolate. Avoid bowls that have ridges or seams inside the bottom.

Plastic

Stand mixer

Stainless steel

Melting bowl: We prefer heat-proof glass bowls to melt butter or chocolate. They can be put in the microwave, you can see from the side if everything is melted, and the glass holds enough heat to keep melted ingredients liquid for a longer time.

TOOLS

Baker's bench knife: A 6-inch rectangle of stainless steel with a handle on one side, a bench knife is indispensable for cutting bar cookies, chunks of butter, scooping up piles of chopped nuts, and scraping down countertops.

Baker's bench knife

Bowl (dough) scraper: Usually made of somewhat flexible plastic, bowl scrapers have a curved edge to follow the contour of a mixing bowl. They can assist with mixing heavy doughs, and are the most efficient tool to get all of a sticky or heavy dough out of a bowl quickly. Their shape is comfortable in your hand, and we also use them for portioning dough and patting it into shapes, particularly if it's a sticky one like biscotti.

Bowl (dough) scraper

Cake tester: Checking for doneness used to be accomplished with toothpicks, clean straws from a broom, or a paring knife. If it came out clean, your baked good was done. Today we have cake testers, which are made of wood or metal, and are used to test the doneness of brownies or other thick bars or some soft cookies. Choose one that's about the same diameter as a piece of raw spaghetti; you want it to be thick enough that you can easily see if there's moist batter sticking to it, and thin enough so as not to leave a big hole in the brownie where it was inserted.

Cake tester

Candy thermometer: Designed to clip on the side of a saucepan and register temperatures from 100°F to 400°F, this tool is useful not only for making candy, but for deep-frying, and making dips, toppings, or fillings for cookies. Look for a clip that doesn't slide up and down the thermometer's body too easily, and numbers that can be easily read. Some candy thermometers have flagged location indicators on their temperature scale for various candymaking stages: soft ball, hard ball, hard crack. Try to find a thermometer that will submerge the bulb in liquid at least half an inch away from the edge of the pan.

Candy thermometer

Cannoli forms: These are stainless steel tubes, roughly half an inch in diameter and 4 inches long. Cannoli dough is rolled, cut, and wrapped around these tubes before deep-frying. Warm batter cookies can also be wrapped around them after baking, so they cool into a tube shape.

Cannoli forms

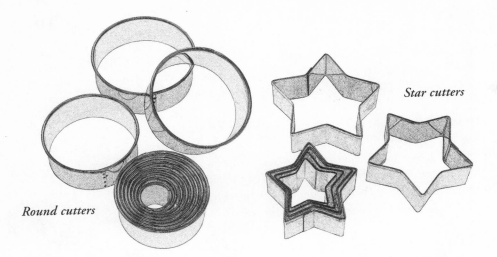

Star cutters

Round cutters

Cookie cutters: There are hundreds of shapes and silhouettes to chose from with cookie cutters, but no kitchen is complete without a good set of graduated round cutters. These should be sturdy, with one rolled or wide edge for pressing down, and a sharper edge for cutting. There are lots of small cutter shapes that can be used in conjunction with round cutters, to make a linzer-style sandwich cookie, or a windowpane cookie. When choosing silhouette cutters, look for a smooth vertical seam where the metal overlaps, and an easy gripping surface on the top edge. It's also best to look for cutters without closed backs so you can see where you're cutting.

Cookie molds, stamps, and plaques: Many traditional European cookies get their distinctive shapes from beautifully designed molds and stamps. *Springerle* and *speculaas* are two types of cookies that are pressed into molds before baking. The molds are carved in decorative relief patterns; the pattern is transferred to the dough, and the mold removed before baking. Stoneware plaques with raised patterns (such as shortbread molds) can be filled with dough, which is then baked in the plaque before being cut into individual cookies afterward. Many people collect different cookie mold designs to display.

Speculaas *mold*   Springerle *plaque*

Cookie press: Ideal for making shaped cookies such as stars, wreaths, and flowers, cookie presses come in manual and electric versions. Both types use a screw press mechanism to push cookie dough through a template to form shapes. Look for one that's easy to refill without undoing the die plate. A cookie press should be lightweight without being flimsy, and fit your hands comfortably while you're operating it.

Cookie scoops: We don't know how we'd get along without our cookie scoops. We use two sizes most of the time, both of which do a good job of consistently portioning the amounts that in days past were dished out with the spoons from the kitchen drawer: a *teaspoon scoop* (which actually holds about 2 teaspoons), and a *tablespoon scoop* (which actually holds a scant 2 tablespoons). Cookie scoops are faster and more accurate than using two flatware spoons. For oversized cookies, we use a scoop that holds ¼ cup of dough or batter.

Cookie scoops

Cooling rack: Made of sturdy wire mesh, look for a rack that has at least four feet to keep it steady on the counter and holes no bigger than ½ inch across. Cooling racks come in nonstick finishes, but we haven't found them to behave significantly better than a regular stainless steel rack. If a cookie will stick to a standard rack, it will stick to a coated one. Larger capacity is always a plus for the cookie baker. Cooling racks come in expandable versions that telescope out for more cooling surface area, then retract to take up less storage space. You can also find tiered holders to put your racks on, to save on counter space.

Cracker crisper (moisture absorber): A perforated disk with moisture-absorbing silica crystals inside, a crisper is stored in a closed container with any baked good that you want to keep crisp. When the silica has absorbed as much water as it can, it changes color. To restore its absorbent qualities, the crisper is baked in the oven to dry it out before being put back to use.

Dough docker

Dough docker: This mini-rolling pin with spikes pricks dough in an even pattern, making holes to release steam. This ensures that the dough will stay flat as it bakes. This step is a must when you're making shortbread, graham crackers, or any other cookie that begins life as one flat sheet of dough and is intended to be crisp after baking.

Flour sifter: Essentially a cylinder with a screen on the bottom, sifters have a mechanical device to push flour through the screen and break up lumps in dry ingredients like baking soda and confectioners' sugar. Flour sifters come in electric, hand crank, and squeeze-handle types. Smaller versions hold 2 cups of material at a time, larger ones can hold as much as 12. Choose one that feels comfortable in your hand, with a screen with medium-gauge mesh.

Box grater

Graters: For a quick tablespoon of zest to add to a recipe, we love these hand graters. The more traditional box-style grater is handy for grating chocolate or frozen butter.

Hand grater

Knives: If you could have only three knives in the kitchen, they should be a paring knife, a chef's knife, and a serrated knife (see illustrations, next page). The *paring knife* should fit your hand comfortably, with a blade between 2½ and 4 inches long. You can use it to peel, trim, cut around stencils, decorate, and slice.

A *chef's knife* is an all-around kitchen workhorse. The tip is good for fine work, the middle of the blade slices and chops, and the heel will do the heavy work. The side of the blade will help you crush things, then scoop them up off the board. Look for a chef's knife that's well balanced (you should be able to hold the knife behind the heel of the blade, balanced on one finger like a

Serrated knife

Chef's knife

Paring knife

teeter-totter). A quality knife will be made of high-carbon stainless steel and will have a full tang (end of the blade) visible through the end of a handle held together with rivets. Look for a blade that's the most comfortable fit for your hands; chef's knives come with blades from 5 to 12 inches long.

For cutting crisp cookies like shortbread or biscotti, a *serrated knife* is the right tool. Some have offset blades, which can keep your knuckles out of the way when making a straight, vertical cut. The teeth of a serrated blade work like a saw, so when using a serrated knife don't push down as much as pull it back and forth. That way the teeth on the knife do the work.

In addition to these three workhorses, the everyday *table knife* plays many roles. It's the right tool for loosening baked goods from the edge of their pans while cooling, it's handy for leveling the top of dry ingredients in their measuring cups, and it's the first thing you reach for when you need to cut a few tablespoons from a stick of butter.

Plastic knives are handy for slicing high-fat, moist, or dense baked goods, like fudgy brownies or moist bar cookies. They're also a nice thing to have around if you like to bake in nonstick pans, since they won't mar the finish.

Krumkake **iron:** *Krumkake* are thin (less than a quarter-inch-thick), waffle-like cookies that can be molded around a form or spoon or cooled flat (see pages 430–431). The iron works like a waffle iron, with a handle that clips together. This presses the stiff dough into the forms evenly. Look for an iron that has a clip that snaps closed with a reassuring click, but is simple to open when the cookies are done.

Measuring cups: Measuring cups come in two types: dry and liquid. Dry measuring cups should have flat rims, sturdy handles, and be accurate (we've found that the volume of different manufacturers' cups can vary significantly). Liquid measuring cups should have lines you can read clearly either through the side of the cup of from above. To test the accuracy of either a dry or liquid 1 cup measure, place it on a scale you trust, hit "tare" or zero, and pour in water until the scale reads 8 ounces. If the level of the water reaches the rim or line, your cup is accurate. If the cup overflows or has room left in it, the cup is inaccurate. Most sets of measuring cups come in ¼, ⅓, ½ and 1 cup increments. Odd-sized sets (2 tablespoons, ⅔, ¾, 1½ and 2 cups) are also available, and can be big time-savers.

A *Wonder Cup* is another kind of measuring cup, consisting of a clear, round sleeve with a sliding solid base set within. It's wonderful for measuring sticky ingredients like shortening, molasses, and peanut butter.

Measuring spoons: Available in plastic and stainless steel, we rely on stainless measuring spoons, because they don't hold on to sticky liquids, and they stand up well to constant trips through the dishwasher. When you're baking a lot, it's helpful to use two sets of measuring spoons: one to measure wet ingredients such as vanilla extract, one to measure dry ingredients such as baking powder. Standard sets come in ¼, ½, 1 teaspoon, and 1 tablespoon amounts. Odd-sized sets may include pinch, dash, ⅛ teaspoon, and ½ tablespoon amounts.

Mixers: *Hand mixers* are good for batters, whipping cream and egg whites, and for single batches of softer cookie doughs. Hand mixers have limited power, since they need to be light-weight enough to be easily maneuvered. *Stand mixers* are the baker's true workhorse, with the advantages of more power, more capacity, and the ability to leave your hands free to measure and add ingredients while the mixer is running. In either case, look for sturdy construction, the most powerful motor you can afford, and ease of cleaning. Many stand mixers have a variety of attachments or extra mixing bowls that can be added to the base unit.

Parchment Available in precut sheets or on a roll, parchment is treated with silicone to make it nonstick. We find it indispensable for rolling out cookies, then removing excess trimmed dough and transferring the cookies, parchment and all, to a baking sheet. It's also perfect for lining a baking sheet, providing both nonstick release of the cookies, and easy cleanup. Parchment can be reused repeatedly, until it becomes brittle, burned, or gets overly sticky or greasy.

Pastry bags: These cone-shaped bags are the first step to making piped cookies look their best. Pastry bags come in a variety of sizes, from 12 inches tall to 18 inches or more. They can be made of canvas, coated synthetic fabric, or disposable plastic. For most cookie-making pur-poses, the smaller end of the range is best, and heavyweight disposable plastic bags are our test kitchen favorite. Choose a bag that fits in your hands comfortably, and don't fill it more than three quarters full.

Pastry blender or fork: These tools have tines or blades used to "cut in" shortening or other fat. By placing the fat on top of a recipe's dry ingredients and pressing down, the tines break up the fat into flat pieces. These pieces create a flaky texture when baked. Look for a pastry blender that is sturdy enough to press down on firmly without its wires or blades bending or shifting. A pas-try fork should be stainless steel, have ¼ inch of space between the tines, and have tines that are at least 1½ inches long.

Pastry blender

Pastry fork

Bristle pastry brush

Pastry brushes: For spreading an even coat of egg white over a crust, greasing a pan with shortening, or putting a thin film of frosting on a batch of bar cookies, a pastry brush is the appropriate tool. Look for bristles that are firmly mounted to the handle; silicone bristle brushes are dishwasher safe.

Pastry tips and couplers: Pastry tips are metal cones that come with an infinite variety of openings, each creating a distinctive shape. The most commonly used are the star tip and simple round; both types come in various diameters. A large star tip is good for piping whipped cream or fillings, a smaller one for more detailed decorations like ruffled borders, stars, and seashells. A simple round opening is equally versatile: A smaller round is used for piping letters or making dots, a larger one shapes blobs of meringue or makes rectangular ladyfingers. Plastic couplers allow you to change the pastry tip from one shape to another quickly and easily.

Star tip

Coupler

Round tip

Pastry wheel: This device looks like a wavy pizza wheel. The fluted edge of a pastry wheel gives a distinctive look to cutout cookies.

Pastry wheel

Pizza wheel: Pizza wheels make short work of cutting strips of dough for a lattice, diamonds, squares, sticks, or any rectangular shape. Look for one with a comfortable handle, whose blade doesn't wobble back and forth when it spins.

Pizza cutter

Pizzelle **maker:** This looks like a half-sized waffle iron, but with much shallower indentations. The batter is put on the embossed section, then the top is put down and clipped tight to spread out the batter. Most *pizzelle* makers have combinations of ready lights and thermostat controls; none of these enhancements is particularly effective. If you want to know when the *pizzelle* is done, check the first one periodically to establish a baking time; then time the remainder.

Plastic bags: This may seem like an odd item to mention in a collection of baking tools, but we use plastic bags to make all kinds of jobs easier. Zip-top styles are the perfect impromptu pastry bag—just fill, close, and snip off one corner. Larger plastic bags are perfect for holding roll-out cookie dough. You can flatten the dough right inside the bag with a rolling pin, which gives you a head start on rolling out the dough later. A plastic bag makes a great improvised mitten, for patting sticky dough into place. (We use them to store things, too.)

Plastic wrap: This humble pantry staple can help your baking more often than you might realize. The most frequent use for plastic wrap in our test kitchen is to cover sticky or soft roll-out doughs before rolling, so they won't stick to the rolling pin. You can see through the plastic while you're working, and it's easy to pick up and reposition the plastic as the dough gets bigger.

Potholders: Potholders can be made of cloth, silicone, leather, or wool. It's important to keep in mind that cloth potholders are very dangerous if used when wet: the heat from the pan can create enough steam inside a wet potholder to scald you, and you won't know you're in trouble until you already have a hot, heavy object in midair. Whatever potholder you choose, make sure it's thick enough to protect your hands yet flexible enough to give you a good grip. Some bakers like the protection of an oven mitt, which covers the back of the hand as well as the wrist.

Pastry pin

Rolling pins: Rolling pins can be made of wood, marble, stainless steel (a favorite of ours), even glass. Most pins have a barrel that's about 10 inches wide, with ball bearings that allow the barrel to spin freely while you hold on to the handles. A good pin has some heft to it, so the weight of the pin does most of the work. The handles should be able to sustain some downward force without bending, and the pin should roll easily without any grinding sensation.

Rolling pin

Springerle *pin*

There are lots of variations with rolling pins. Some are embossed so they can transfer a pattern or design to the dough, for *springerle* and some Scandinavian cookies. There are pastry pins, with tapered ends, that are good for rolling round pieces of dough with thinner edges. There are even specialty rolling pins, like the plastic ones designed for rolling out fondant without sticking.

Rosette iron: Available in any number of decorative shapes, these irons are placed in hot oil to preheat, dipped into batter, then returned to the oil to fry the cookie. The rosette heads can be made of aluminum or cast iron and are screwed onto a handle before being dipped. Rosette irons should have a secure, screw-on connection to a handle that's at least 12 inches long. Newer versions of rosette irons come with nonstick coatings, to make releasing the finished cookie easier.

Rosette irons

Ruler: We measure the dimensions of pans, doughs, and cookie shapes with our rulers. Choose rulers with smooth, food-safe surfaces, such as stainless steel or plastic, so they can be cleaned after being used. We recommend keeping one 12-inch and one 30-inch ruler on hand (for larger projects).

Scale: A good kitchen scale should have clear readouts, be easy to clean, and able to register in grams or ounces (in ⅛-ounce increments). Look for a scale that has a long shutoff time, you don't want to start all over if you have to take 30 seconds to let the dog out. A two-minute shutoff time is a good benchmark to look for. The platform on the scale should be big enough to hold a large bowl without obscuring the readout, and be stable enough so whatever you place on it doesn't wobble. Most home kitchen scales have a capacity between 4 and 11 pounds.

Shortbread mold: Circular or square in shape and roughly 8 inches in diameter, shortbread molds are deeply embossed to transfer a decorative pattern to the cookie dough. Most shortbread molds are made of ceramic or stoneware, so the dough can be baked in the form.

Shortbread mold

Silicone pan liners (mats): These nonstick pan liners are reusable, sturdy, and save a lot of time on cleanup. They're particularly helpful for sticky batters like lace cookies, and can do double duty as a nonstick kneading surface. An extra-thick silicone liner may not be appropriate for cookies, as it actually provides too much insulation and the cookie bottoms won't brown; choose thinner silicone, or silicone-coated, flexible fiberglass instead.

Slotted spoon: A larger spoon with holes in it, slotted spoons are handy for scooping fried cookies out of hot fat. They'll also do a quick job of evenly mixing dry ingredients before adding them to a recipe.

Spatulas: Flexible spatulas have thin blades, which are good for getting under things. Flexible *metal spatulas* (turners) are useful for removing thin cookies such as *tuiles* from a sheet pan. Flexible *nylon spatulas* are particularly effective for scraping sticky ingredients off the sides of a mixing bowl.

Look for sturdy joints between blades and handles. *Giant spatulas* are used to move large, rolled-out pieces of dough or crusts. They also can collect many cookies at a time for transfer to a cooling rack. *Icing spatulas* have a straight blade that can be rounded or tapered at the end, to create different effects in the finished texture of icing. *Offset spatulas* come in sizes ranging from 3-inch to 14-inch blades. The angle of the blade near the handle allows you to smooth frosting or batter to a level surface from above, without dragging your hand through it.

Combining the scraping abilities of a spatula with the scooping abilities of a spoon, **spoonulas** are handy for transferring lots of batter or dough from one place to another. They're also helpful when trying to get stiff icing into a pastry bag.

Giant spatula

Nylon spatula

Offset spatula

Strainer: It's helpful to have two strainers on hand: one with a fine mesh for catching tiny seeds, and one with larger spaces between the wires, to make quicker work of straining the lumps out of confectioners' sugar and cocoa.

Sugar softener: Made of terra cotta, these disks (or other shapes) are soaked in water, then drained and placed in a container with brown sugar. The slow release of water from the disk helps to keep the sugar soft.

Thermometers: For taking the guesswork out of baking, thermometers are indispensable. If you want to know if your custard is fully cooked (165°F), or your oil for fried cookies is hot enough (375°F), you need a thermometer. Instant-read types are preferable for baking, since it's not very comfortable to stand in front of an open oven waiting for a thermometer to register, and it's not very good for what you're baking, either.

Instant-read thermometers come in both digital and mechanical versions. Digital is generally easier to read, but requires a battery. *Mechanical thermometers* are less expensive. Be sure to find

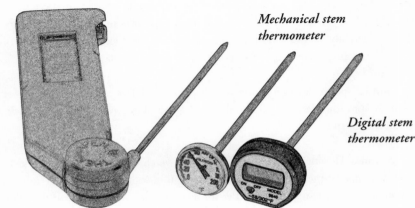

Instant-read digital thermometer

Mechanical stem thermometer

Digital stem thermometer

out where the thermometer's sensor is; mechanical *stem thermometers* have a dimple on the shaft that has to be inside whatever is being measured to get an accurate number. More expensive instant-read thermometers have the sensor at the end of the probe.

We recommend an *oven thermometer,* too. Look for one that can hang from an oven rack or stand on top of it. Many ovens have "hot spots," and the temperature probe for your oven's thermostat reads only one place inside your oven.

Timers: Like scales and thermometers, timers come in both mechanical and battery-powered digital versions. We prefer digital timers, not just because they're more accurate, but because we've never found a mechanical timer with a ring longer than about 8 seconds, and that's not long enough for the busy baker who might have stepped out of the kitchen for 10 seconds.

Depending on how many things you're trying to accomplish at once, you may want a timer that hangs around your neck, clips to your apron, or fits in your pocket. Most digital timers have magnets on the back so they can attach to your oven or refrigerator; if you like that style, be sure the magnet is strong enough to withstand a few door openings and closings without flying off. Look for a large readout, long ringing time (1 minute is good), and a range that goes from 1 second to 99 minutes.

Tongs: For reaching into hot oil or over a hot surface, tongs are indispensable. We use them to turn cookies over when frying, and for lifting them out of the hot oil.

Whisk: A whisk consists of a number of wires attached to a handle, forming a collection of loops that draw air through egg whites or combine dry ingredients swiftly. The wires of your whisk should be sturdy yet flexible, and mounted securely to the handle. Whisks are an excellent tool for folding egg whites into other ingredients.

Zester: Consisting of several small circular cutting edges mounted to a handle, zesters are designed to cut thin strips of citrus rind, leaving the bitter pith behind.

Zester

The Essentials

Chocolate Chip Cookies 42

Sugar Cookies 53

Oatmeal Cookies 73

Molasses Cookies 84

Peanut Butter Cookies 95

Shortbread 109

Biscotti 132

Brownies 154

Decorated Cookies 168

Chocolate Chip Cookies

Chocolate chip cookies. What joy those three little words bring to the baker's heart! When you think of the quintessential cookie, you think chocolate chip, and for good reason: the chocolate chip cookie is so popular because it tastes so good. A buttery, sweet, mild-flavored cookie brimming with bits of assertive (semisweet, not milk) chocolate, tender and crunchy or soft and chewy (take your pick), studded with toasty-tasting pecans or walnuts (or macadamias)—what's not to like? And, like chocolate cake, chocolate chip cookies are the perfect complement to ice-cold milk, the ideal drink of childhood. We're talking cookie as a cultural icon here.

By some statistics, 80 percent of the cookies baked in American homes are chocolate chip cookies. We're not surprised; there have probably been more words written and read on the chocolate chip cookie than any other confection you could name. When Ruth Wakefield added chopped chocolate to her butter cookie recipe at The Toll House restaurant in Whitman, Massachusetts, back in the 1930s, little did she know she was creating American culinary history. The 1948 edition of Wakefield's *Toll House Recipes Tried and True* includes a range of Toll House specialties, with Toll House Chocolate Crunch Cookies (nestled securely between Toll House Biscuits and Toll House Chocolate Icebox Cake) holding no particular place of honor. No asterisk, no bold type in the index denotes that this is the paradigm of cookie recipes, the future focal point of a campaign standoff between American presidents' wives, the model on which books will be written, lawsuits filed, and backyard fence battles fought.

Our families and friends think we have the best job in the world—creating and testing chocolate chip cookie recipes. Then testing more recipes, and then more, until THE perfect chocolate chip cookie is born. It isn't as easy as it seems. There are some pretty good chocolate chip cookie recipes out there, and improving on some of the classics proved to be a challenge. When you add in the element of personal taste—some like 'em crunchy, some like 'em chewy—our testers had to be quite discerning. But we were up to the task, and we've created two Essential Chocolate Chip Cookie recipes—one light and crunchy, one soft and chewy—from which you'll be able to take many paths, one of which is bound to lead to your own personal chocolate chip cookie nirvana. Break out the cold milk!

Does it matter how heavily I grease my baking sheets?

In the case of cookies—yes! Cookies, with their high ratio of both fat and sugar, tend to spread as they bake. A heavily greased pan exacerbates this spreading; instead of picking up resistance from the pan as the cookie bakes and spreads, it glides right over that grease and spreads too far. The result? Thin edges, with a tendency to burn. So when the directions say to grease the pan lightly, use an easy hand with the vegetable shortening or nonstick vegetable oil spray. And remember, the best solution of all is parchment. It doesn't add any more fat to your cookies, helps protect their bottoms from burning, and allows them to slide right off the pan onto the cooling rack.

essential recipe

The Essential Chewy Chocolate Chip Cookie

Golden brown, **craggy** from a surfeit of chips, these moist cookies bend, then reluctantly break to reveal a lava flow of melted chocolate. Truly—if you're a chewy chocolate chip cookie lover, it just doesn't get any better than this. The surprise ingredient? Vinegar. The small amount of vinegar accomplishes two things: it tempers the sweetness of the sugar just a bit, allowing the flavors of the chocolate and butter to shine through, and it reacts with the sodium bicarbonate in the leavener, giving the cookies a little extra lift in the oven. Try it, you'll like it.

Yield: 4 dozen cookies ● *Baking temperature: 375°F* ● *Baking time: 10 minutes*

¾ cup (1½ sticks, 6 ounces) unsalted butter
⅔ cup (5¼ ounces) dark brown sugar
⅔ cup (4¾ ounces) granulated sugar
2 tablespoons (1¼ ounces) light corn syrup
1 tablespoon cider vinegar or white vinegar
2 large eggs
1 tablespoon vanilla extract
½ teaspoon salt
½ teaspoon baking powder
¼ teaspoon baking soda
2¼ cups (9½ ounces) unbleached all-purpose flour
3 cups (18 ounces) semisweet chocolate chips

● Preheat the oven to 375°F. Lightly grease (or line with parchment) two baking sheets.
● In a medium-sized mixing bowl, cream together the butter, sugars, corn syrup, and vinegar, then beat in the eggs. Beat in the vanilla, salt, baking powder, and baking soda. Stir in the flour and chocolate chips.
● Drop the dough by the tablespoonful onto the prepared baking sheets. Bake the cookies for 10 minutes, until they're just set; the centers may still look a bit underdone. Remove them from the oven, and transfer to a rack to cool.

Nutrition information per serving (1 cookie, 29 g): 124 cal, 6 g fat, 1 g protein, 5 g complex carbohydrates, 12 g sugar, 1 g dietary fiber, 17 mg cholesterol, 40 mg sodium, 60 mg potassium, 31 RE vitamin A, 1 mg iron, 11 mg calcium, 25 mg phosphorus, 7 mg caffeine.

Classic Crunchy Chocolate Chip Cookies

Ah, heaven! This light, golden cookie, heady with the taste and aroma of brown sugar and chocolate, has a crisp-crunchy texture that makes even the most jaded chocolate chip cookie diehards roll their eyes in blissful satisfaction. Look no further: this is the quintessential crunchy (as opposed to chewy) chocolate chip cookie.

Yield: 4½ dozen cookies ● *Baking temperature:* 350°F ● *Baking time:* 12 to 14 minutes

½ cup (1 stick, 4 ounces) unsalted butter
½ cup (3¼ ounces) vegetable shortening
1 cup (8 ounces) brown sugar
½ cup (3½ ounces) granulated sugar
2 teaspoons vanilla extract
¾ teaspoon salt
1 tablespoon cider vinegar or white vinegar
1 large egg
1 teaspoon baking soda
2 cups (8½ ounces) unbleached all-purpose flour
3 cups (18 ounces) semisweet chocolate chips

● Preheat the oven to 350°F. Lightly grease (or line with parchment) two baking sheets.
● In a large mixing bowl, cream together the butter, shortening, sugars, vanilla, salt, and vinegar. Beat in the egg, then the baking soda and flour. Stir in the chocolate chips.
● Drop the dough by the tablespoonful onto the prepared baking sheets. Bake the cookies for 12 to 14 minutes, until they're golden brown. Remove them from the oven and transfer to a rack to cool.

Nutrition information per serving (*1 cookie, 25 g*)*:* 120 cal, 6 g fat, 1 g protein, 5 g complex carbohydrates, 10 g sugar, 1 g dietary fiber, 9 mg cholesterol, 56 mg sodium, 48 mg potassium, 18 RE vitamin A, 1 mg iron, 5 mg calcium, 17 mg phosphorus, 4 mg caffeine.

Mega-Chippers

This cookie is sized to impress—wrap these individually to sell at a bake sale, or pack them for a hike.

Yield: *2 dozen cookies*

1 recipe Essential Chocolate Chip Cookies (Chewy, page 44 or Crunchy, page 45)

● Prepare the cookie dough of your choice. Drop the dough by ¼-cupfuls onto prepared baking sheets, leaving 2 inches between them. Bake the chewy cookies for 14 minutes, the crunchy cookies for 18 minutes. Remove the cookies from the oven and allow them to cool on the pan for 10 minutes. Transfer them to a rack to cool completely.

Chocolate Chip Cookies with Nuts

Some like 'em, some think they're excess baggage: "Why would anyone ever think of taking away chocolate chips to add nuts?!" If you're in the former camp, and savor the interplay between the toasty, rich flavor of nuts and chocolate's dark sweetness, you'll enjoy these.

Yield: *About 4 dozen cookies*

1 recipe Essential Chocolate Chip Cookies (Chewy, page 44 or Crunchy, page 45)
1½ cups (6 ounces) chopped pecans or walnuts, toasted (see page 27)

● Prepare the cookie dough of your choice, substituting the nuts for 1½ cups of the chocolate chips in the recipe. Bake the cookies as directed in the recipe you've chosen.

Butterscotch-Granola Chippers

Some of us gravitate to butterscotch just as avidly as we do to chocolate. If you're a butterscotch fan, you'll enjoy these oat-enriched, buttery cookies.

Yield: About 4 dozen cookies

1 recipe Essential Chocolate Chip Cookies (Chewy, page 44 or Crunchy, page 45)
1 cup (4 ounces) granola
1½ cups (9 ounces) butterscotch chips

● Prepare the cookie dough of your choice, reducing the flour in the recipe by ¼ cup and adding the granola. Substitute the butterscotch chips for 1½ cups of the chocolate chips. Bake the cookies as directed in the recipe you've chosen.

Deluxe White Chocolate—Macadamia Cookies

White chocolate and light-colored macadamia nuts give a different, blonder look to these luxurious cookies. If you're not a fan of white chocolate, feel free to leave it out and go with all semisweet or bittersweet chocolate chips or chunks.

Yield: About 4 dozen cookies

1 recipe Essential Chocolate Chip Cookies (Chewy, page 44 or Crunchy, page 45)
1 cup (6 ounces) white chocolate chips or chunks
1 cup (4¾ ounces) chopped salted macadamia nuts

● Prepare the cookie dough of your choice, substituting the white chocolate or chunks and the macadamia nuts for 2 cups of the semisweet chips. Bake the cookies as directed in the recipe you've chosen.

Orange-Pistachio Milk Chocolate Chippers

Those among us whose taste runs to milk chocolate rather than semisweet love these cookies. The pistachios and hint of orange strike just the right balance with milk chocolate's sweeter, milder flavor.

Yield: About 4 dozen cookies

1 recipe Essential Chocolate Chip Cookies (Chewy, page 44 or Crunchy, page 45)
2 teaspoons almond extract
4 teaspoons grated orange rind (zest)
1½ cups (9 ounces) milk chocolate chips
1½ cups (6 ounces) whole pistachios, salted or unsalted

● Prepare the cookie dough of your choice, substituting the almond extract for the vanilla, and adding the orange zest at the same time. Substitute the milk chocolate chips and pistachios for the 3 cups semisweet chocolate chips in the recipe. Bake the cookies as directed in the recipe you've chosen.

Gianduja Delights

Gianduja (jahn-DOO-yah) is an ultrasmooth blend of hazelnuts and chocolate, used widely in Italian candies and pastries. We took the liberty of naming these hazelnut-studded cookies after that classic specialty chocolate of Piedmont.

Yield: About 4 dozen cookies

1 recipe Essential Chocolate Chip Cookies (Chewy, page 44 or Crunchy, page 45)
2 to 3 teaspoons hazelnut extract, or ¼ to ½ teaspoon strong
    hazelnut flavor, to taste
1 cup (4 ounces) chopped hazelnuts, toasted (see page 27)
1 cup (6 ounces) white chocolate chips or chunks (optional)

● Prepare the cookie dough of your choice, substituting the hazelnut extract for the vanilla. Substitute the hazelnuts for 1 cup of the semisweet chips. If desired, substitute the white chocolate chips for another cup of the semisweet chips in the recipe. Bake the cookies as directed in the recipe you've chosen.

Candy Bar Cookies

Nuts, caramel, and chocolate are the main ingredients in our favorite candy bar, Snickers. Replicating those flavors in a cookie was easy and delicious.

Yield: About 4 dozen cookies

1 recipe Essential Chocolate Chip Cookies (Chewy, page 44 or Crunchy, page 45)
1 cup (5 ounces) chopped lightly salted peanuts
1 cup (5⅛ ounces) toffee bits

● Prepare the cookie dough of your choice, substituting the peanuts and toffee bits for 1½ cups of the semisweet chips. Bake the cookies as directed in the recipe you've chosen.

Cherry-Almond Chocolate Chip Cookies

Cherry and almond are a match made in heaven; cherry and chocolate are similarly divine. Put them all together and what have you got? Your ticket to chocolate chip cookie nirvana. Note that adding white chocolate makes this a very sweet cookie. If you don't love white chocolate, leave it out and retain 1 cup of the semisweet chips.

Yield: About 4 dozen cookies

1 recipe Essential Chocolate Chip Cookies (Chewy, page 44 or Crunchy, page 45)
½ teaspoon almond extract
1 cup (4 ounces) slivered almonds, toasted (see page 27)
1 cup (5 ounces) dried cherries
1 cup (6 ounces) white chocolate chunks or chips (optional)

● Prepare the cookie dough of your choice, substituting the almond extract for the vanilla. Substitute the almonds, dried cherries, and white chocolate for the semisweet chips. Bake the cookies as directed in the recipe you've chosen.

Butter-Nut Chocolate Chip Cookies

Butterscotch + chocolate + pecans . . . bring on the vanilla ice cream! While this combination may sound like your favorite sundae, it translates equally well to a warm-from-the-oven cookie.

Yield: About 4 dozen cookies

1 recipe Essential Chocolate Chip Cookies (Chewy, **page 44** or Crunchy, **page 45**)
2 to 3 drops butterscotch flavor or butter-rum flavor (optional)
1 cup (6 ounces) butterscotch chips
1 cup (6 ounces) white chocolate chips or semisweet chocolate chips
1 cup (4 ounces) chopped pecans or walnuts, toasted (see page 27)

● Prepare the cookie dough of your choice, substituting the butterscotch flavor for the vanilla, and the butterscotch chips, white or semisweet chocolate chips, and nuts for the semisweet chips. Bake the cookies as directed in the recipe you've chosen.

The chocolate grating challenge

While the recipe on the following page calls for 8 ounces of chocolate, grated, we were finding it a challenge to actually grate the chocolate. Trying to grind it in the food processor produced a soft, oily mush; the chocolate also melted when we tried grating it by hand on a box grater. Using a small rotary grater worked, but was very slow. The solution? Grind the chocolate and oats together. The oats keep the chocolate from becoming oily, and the chocolate disperses nicely through the oats, making it easier to mix evenly into the cookie dough. We suggest processing the oats very briefly, then adding the chocolate and processing briefly again. The oats should be finely ground, and the chocolate should appear as finely diced chunks within the oats. Note that this step will make the cookies a bit dark and chocolaty looking. Would we trade taste for appearance? Never. But if you're set on baking a cookie that has the typical golden-brown, chocolate chip cookie look, leave out the grated chocolate.

Good-as-Store-Bought Cookies

If you're an aficionado of those big, soft chocolate chip cookies you find at the mall, or being sold from a kiosk at the airline terminal, give these a try. Loaded with chocolate and nuts, with the mild, nutty flavor of oatmeal, these cookies are also similar to those sold in fancy department stores (which is why we often refer to them as "those fancy department store cookies.") One taste-tester proclaimed these "better than any store-bought cookie I've ever had—the *perfect* bake-at-home cookie!"

Yield: 6½ dozen cookies ● *Baking temperature:* 350°F ● *Baking time:* 12 minutes

2½ cups (8¾ ounces) rolled oats, finely ground (see sidebar, page 50)
8 ounces, semisweet, bittersweet, or milk chocolate
1 cup (2 sticks, 8 ounces) unsalted butter
1 cup (8 ounces) brown sugar
1 cup (7 ounces) granulated sugar
2 large eggs
2 teaspoons vanilla extract
2 cups (8½ ounces) unbleached all-purpose flour
1 teaspoon salt
1 teaspoon baking powder
1 teaspoon baking soda
1 tablespoon espresso powder
2 cups (12 ounces) semisweet chocolate chips
1½ cups (6 ounces) chopped walnuts or pecans

● Preheat the oven to 350°F. Lightly grease (or line with parchment) two baking sheets.
● Grind the oats and 8 ounces of chocolate together in a food processor (see sidebar, opposite). Set the mixture aside.
● In a large mixing bowl, cream together the butter, sugars, eggs, and vanilla. In a separate bowl, whisk together the flour, salt, baking powder, baking soda, espresso powder, and the reserved oat/chocolate mixture. Add the dry ingredients and stir to combine. Stir in the chocolate chips and nuts.
● Use a tablespoon cookie scoop (see page 33) to drop the dough onto the prepared baking sheets, leaving about 2 inches between them so they can spread. Bake for 12 minutes; don't overbake, or they'll be hard. Remove them from the oven and transfer to a rack to cool.

Nutrition information per serving (1 cookie, 25 g): 118 cal, 6 g fat, 2 g protein, 6 g complex carbohydrates, 9 g sugar, 1 g dietary fiber, 12 mg cholesterol, 53 mg sodium, 56 mg potassium, 25 RE vitamin A, 1 mg vitamin C, 1 mg iron, 9 mg calcium, 34 mg phosphorus, 5 mg caffeine.

VARIATION

● For real mall-sized cookies, drop the batter by the ¼-cupful onto the prepared baking sheets. Bake the cookies for 15 to 18 minutes (the shorter time for a soft cookie, the longer time for a crunchy cookie). Yield: 27 large (3½-inch) cookies.

Chocolate-Peppermint Snaps

Though dissimilar in appearance, on the first bite of this cookie you'll think Girl Scout Thin Mints! And that's just what they taste like. For a special treat, make a sandwich out of these with mint chocolate chip ice cream.

Yield: 6 dozen cookies ● *Baking temperature:* 350°F ● *Baking time:* 12 to 15 minutes

1½ cups (3 sticks, 12 ounces) unsalted butter
1 cup (8 ounces) brown sugar
1 cup (7 ounces) granulated sugar
2 large eggs
2 teaspoons vanilla extract
2 teaspoons peppermint extract, or ⅛ to ¼ teaspoon peppermint oil, to taste
3 cups (12¾ ounces) unbleached all-purpose flour
½ cup (1½ ounces) unsweetened natural cocoa powder
2 teaspoons baking soda
½ teaspoon salt
2 cups (12 ounces) semisweet chocolate chips

● Preheat the oven to 350°F. Lightly grease (or line with parchment) two baking sheets.
● In a large bowl, cream together the butter and sugars. Add the eggs one at a time, beating well after each addition. Mix in the vanilla and peppermint extract.
● Add the flour, cocoa, baking soda, and salt, beating to combine. Stir in the chocolate chips.
● Drop the dough by the tablespoonful onto the prepared baking sheets. Bake the cookies for 12 to 15 minutes, until they're slightly darker around the edges. Remove them from the oven, and transfer to a rack to cool.

Stick-free scooping

If you're using a cookie scoop and the dough starts to stick in the scoop, simply rinse the scoop in cold water, wiping off any dough. A clean, wet scoop will deposit cookies onto the baking sheet absolutely stick-free.

Nutrition information per serving (1 cookie, 23 g): 104 cal, 5 g fat, 1 g protein, 4 g complex carbohydrates, 8 g sugar, 16 mg cholesterol, 54 mg sodium, 48 mg potassium, 38 RE vitamin A, 1 mg iron, 7 mg calcium, 20 mg phosphorus, 6 mg caffeine.

Sugar Cookies

Are you an aficionado of nuance, of the haunting aroma that's barely there, of the compelling flavor you can't quite identify? Do you embrace a cookie that's pure and simple, rather than one that's complex and fussy? Then the sugar cookie —light and crunchy, thick and chewy, thin and crisp, or any of its myriad incarnations— is for you.

Sugar cookies are always high on the list of America's most popular cookies. And for good reason: there's simply nothing in a sugar cookie not to like. Think about it: sugar, butter, and flour, maybe an egg, some salt, vanilla, perhaps a touch of nutmeg or lemon, a little bit of leavening for texture . . . these are the basic elements of cookie baking, uncluttered by any other assertive ingredients.

The clean profile of a sugar cookie makes it the ideal palette for a colorful world of dips, decorations, and fillings. Alternatively, a plain sugar cookie served with fresh berries or the first ripe peaches of summer is a delicious dessert that's striking in its simplicity. Whichever direction you take it, classic or fancy, the sugar cookie will be right at home.

The three Essential Sugar Cookie recipes in this chapter—chewy, crunchy, and crisp—are followed by a number of recipes that start life as sugar cookie dough, then morph into everything from big, soft, Pennsylvania Dutch-style sugar "cakes," to crunchy sugar diamonds, thin and crisp as a cracker. Most sugar cookies are drop cookies; you make them simply by beating cookie dough and dropping it from a spoon onto a baking sheet. Some sugar cookies, the ones you shape into stars and angels at Christmas, or hearts for Valentine's Day, are made from dough that's rolled out before being cut. But all sugar cookies have one key element in common: sugar. Essence of sweetness, beloved taste of us all, even babies, sugar is the heart and soul of sugar cookies. And an ambrosial soul it surely is.

Beating the spread

Why do some cookies flatten out as they bake (indeed, turn to molten puddles on the cookie sheet), while others stand firm, and leave the oven looking exactly as they did going in? In large part, it's the liquid in cookies that makes them flatten out as they bake. Liquid in the dough ingredients—in the egg, the butter, the milk, or any other liquid—is "freed" by the oven's heat, and causes cookies to "flow"—i.e., flatten. In addition, some dry ingredients (such as sugar) become liquid at high heat, adding to the spread. Cookies made with a liquid sweetener, such as corn syrup, honey, maple syrup, or molasses, tend to spread more than cookies made with a dry sweetener, as these sweeteners are already a liquid.

There are a number of other reasons why cookies may flatten more than you like as they bake. Here are a few tips for avoiding this "cookie collapse."

First, be sure to use shortening in recipes that call for it. Substituting butter, margarine or oil will result in cookies that spread, because these fats have a lower melting point than shortening does. If a recipe calls for butter, and the spreading is excessive, try using shortening instead. Butter-flavored shortening is a good substitute.

Other reasons cookies may spread:

- A cool oven. Baking cookies in a too-cool oven allows the fat to melt before the rest of the cookie "sets up."
- An overgreased cookie sheet. Most cookies need but a touch of oil to keep them from sticking, so don't overdo it.
- A hot cookie sheet. This allows the shortening to melt before the cookies are even in the oven.
- Too much sugar. Sugar is hygroscopic, which means it attracts water. Water molecules in your cookie dough, rather than be absorbed by the flour, are attracted by the sugar (which doesn't absorb the water, but simply attracts it; kind of like flirting, with no marriage). The dough remains soft and "liquid," and spreads as it bakes. By cutting back on the sugar, you're increasing the amount of water that will be absorbed by the flour, thus stiffening the dough and preventing spread. Try cutting the sugar in your recipe back by ¼, and see what happens.

The Essential Chewy Sugar Cookie

Some like 'em crisp. Some like 'em crunchy. But for those of you who think a chewy cookie beats a crisp or crunchy one hands down, this recipe is a winner. The cookie's crackly surface, glittering with coarse sugar, lends panache to its appearance.

Yield: 3 dozen cookies ● *Baking temperature:* 375°F ● *Baking time:* 10 minutes

¾ cup (1½ sticks, 6 ounces) unsalted butter
¾ cup (5¼ ounces) granulated sugar
½ cup (4 ounces) brown sugar
¼ cup (2¾ ounces) light corn syrup
2 teaspoons vanilla extract
¼ teaspoon nutmeg, or ¼ teaspoon lemon oil (optional, your choice)
1½ teaspoons baking powder
½ teaspoon baking soda
½ teaspoon salt
1 large egg
2½ cups (10½ ounces) unbleached all-purpose flour
¼ cup (2¼ ounces) coarse or granulated sugar, for coating

● Preheat the oven to 375°F. Lightly grease (or line with parchment) two baking sheets.
● In a large mixing bowl, beat together the butter, granulated and brown sugars, corn syrup, vanilla, nutmeg, baking powder, baking soda, salt, and egg. Stir in the flour.
● Place the coarse sugar in a shallow dish. Drop the dough by the tablespoonful (a tablespoon cookie scoop works well here, see page 33) into the sugar, rolling the balls to coat them. Place them on the prepared baking sheets.
● Bake the cookies for 10 minutes, until the edges are just barely beginning to brown, they'll look soft. If you bake these cookies too long, they'll be crunchy, not chewy. Remove them from the oven and cool on the baking sheet for 5 minutes, then transfer them to a rack to cool completely.

Nutrition information per serving (1 cookie, 25 g): 100 cal, 4 g fat, 1 g protein, 6 g complex carbohydrates, 9 g sugar, 16 mg cholesterol, 74 mg sodium, 24 mg potassium, 38 RE vitamin A, 1 mg iron, 16 mg calcium, 16 mg phosphorus.

The Essential Crunchy Sugar Cookie

Like many old-time New England favorites, these sturdy, crunchy, golden-hued cookies are plain and simple. We theorize that frugal Yankee housewives saw no sense in using more sugar than was absolutely necessary, to say nothing of adding "fancy" ingredients, like butter, when lard would do. However, being New Englanders but not *old-time* New Englanders, we "fancied" these up just a bit with the addition of vanilla and nutmeg, a combination that simply sings "sugar cookie." And lard isn't in our cookie repertoire; shortening and butter have taken its place.

We like the degree of sweetness in these cookies: less sweet than a normal cookie, but still plenty sweet enough to plainly say "cookie." We tried making them with even less sugar—½ cup, instead of ⅔ cup—but found their appearance started to suffer. Instead of being nicely rounded and very lightly cracked on top, they became gnarly looking, spreading unevenly and developing deep cracks. This is an example of what a difference sugar makes in cookie spread and texture. Our original recipe called for a cup of sugar, and those cookies spread to become very flat, and their texture was chewy. When we reduced the amount of sugar to ⅔ cup, they spread less, the texture was more substantial, and they were crunchy-crumbly rather than chewy.

Yield: 26 cookies ● *Baking temperature: 325°F* ● *Baking time: 20 minutes*

¼ cup (1⅝ ounces) vegetable shortening
4 tablespoons (½ stick, 2 ounces) unsalted butter
⅔ cup (4¾ ounces) sugar
¼ cup (2 ounces) milk (regular or low fat, not nonfat)
1 teaspoon white vinegar or cider vinegar
1 tablespoon vanilla extract
¼ teaspoon nutmeg
2 cups (8½ ounces) unbleached all-purpose flour
½ teaspoon baking soda
Heaping ¼ teaspoon salt

● Preheat the oven to 325°F. Lightly grease (or line with parchment) two baking sheets.
● In a large mixing bowl, cream together the shortening, butter, and sugar until smooth. In a liquid measuring cup, stir together the milk, vinegar, and vanilla; add this to the butter mixture, beating until well combined. The mixture will look curdled, which is okay.
● Add the nutmeg, flour, baking soda, and salt and beat until the mixture forms a cohesive dough.
● Drop the dough by the tablespoonful onto the prepared baking sheets (a tablespoon cookie scoop works well here, see page 33). Using the the bottom of a drinking glass dipped in sugar, flatten the balls to ¼ inch thick.

● Bake the cookies for 20 minutes, or until they're a light gold color and just beginning to brown around the bottom edges. Remove them from the oven and transfer to a rack to cool. As they cool, they'll become crisp. If you want them to remain crisp, store in an airtight container when they're totally cool. If you want them to get a bit chewy, store in a bag with a slice of apple or a sugar softener.

Nutrition information per serving (1 cookie, 21 g): 83 cal, 3 g fat, 1 g protein, 7 g complex carbohydrates, 5 g sugar, 5 mg cholesterol, 46 mg sodium, 16 mg potassium, 17 RE vitamin A, 1 mg vitamin C, 1 mg iron, 3 mg calcium, 11 mg phosphorus.

VARIATION

● To make big, bake sale–sized (4-inch) cookies, drop the dough by ¼ cupfuls onto the prepared baking sheets. Flatten them and bake as directed above. Yield: About ten 4-inch cookies.

The fancy factor

If you just can't resist gussying up your favorite crunchy or chewy sugar cookie, here are some ideas for add-ins. Add 2 cups of any of the following to the cookie dough just before shaping:
● M&M's or other small candies
● Pistachio nuts (or the chopped nuts of your choice)
● Diced apricots or other diced dried fruits
● Diced crystallized ginger
● Butterscotch chips, cinnamon chips, or the flavored chips of your choice
● A combination of shredded coconut (unsweetened preferred) and diced dried pineapple

The Essential Crisp Sugar Cookie

These cookies remind us of the bakery-case frosted cookies we used to ooh and aah over as children. (Or, if your point of reference is more European, they're very close to a French *sablé*.) There was something about being on eye level with the gorgeous creations in the glass case that gave them enormous cachet. These golden cookies are very crisp, very light (yet still sturdy enough to decorate), and not too sweet, which makes them the ideal candidate for a flavored icing or glaze; check out our favorites on pages 457–464. Our thanks to Amy Persons, the baker behind this recipe.

Yield: 8½ dozen 2-inch cookies ● *Baking temperature: 375°F* ● *Baking time: 8 minutes*

1 cup (2 sticks, 8 ounces) unsalted butter
1½ cups (6 ounces) confectioners' sugar
1 large egg
1 teaspoon vanilla extract
½ teaspoon almond extract
2½ cups (10½ ounces) unbleached all-purpose flour
1 teaspoon baking soda
1 teaspoon cream of tartar
¼ teaspoon salt

● In a large bowl, cream the butter and sugar together, beating until fluffy. Beat in the egg until smooth, then add the vanilla and almond extracts.
● In a separate bowl, whisk together the dry ingredients, then add to the butter mixture, mixing until the dough is smooth. Refrigerate the dough for 2 to 3 hours (or overnight).
● Preheat the oven to 375°F. Lightly grease (or line with parchment) two or three baking sheets.
● Transfer the dough to a floured work surface and roll it ¼ inch thick. This dough is fairly soft, so put a piece of plastic wrap over it while you roll it out. Cut out shapes with your favorite cutters and transfer them to the prepared baking sheets.
● Bake the cookies for 8 minutes, until set and just slightly colored around the edges. Remove the cookies from the oven, let them cool on the baking sheet for 2 minutes to firm up, then transfer to a rack to cool completely.

Nutrition information per serving (1 cookie, unfrosted, 14 g): 65 cal, 4 g fat, 1 g protein, 4 g complex carbohydrates, 3 g sugar, 14 mg cholesterol, 35 mg sodium, 18 mg potassium, 35 RE vitamin A, 2 mg calcium, 7 mg phosphorus.

King Arthur's Special Roll-Out Sugar Cookies

Often sugar cookies are fat and soft, the cumulus clouds of cookiedom. But when you roll out the dough, rather than drop it from a spoon, you reach the other extreme: thin and snapping-crisp. Make them just a bit thicker, and you've got crunchy. These golden cookies, with their comforting vanilla flavor, pair nicely with ice cream or fresh fruit. The dough is also sturdy enough to be cut into fanciful shapes and decorated (see Decorated Cookies, pages 168–184).

Yield: 42 cookies ● *Baking temperature:* 350°F ● *Baking time:* 10 to 12 minutes

1 cup (2 sticks, 8 ounces) unsalted butter
1 cup (7 ounces) sugar
¾ teaspoon salt
1½ teaspoons baking powder
2 teaspoons vanilla extract
½ teaspoon almond extract (optional)
1 large egg
¼ cup (2 ounces) heavy cream or sour cream
3 tablespoons (¾ ounce) cornstarch
3 cups (12¾ ounces) unbleached all-purpose flour

Flattening the dough into thick rounds before wrapping it in plastic wrap allows it to chill more quickly. When you're ready to roll, it's already partly flattened and will become pliable quickly and evenly.

- In a medium-sized bowl, beat the butter, sugar, salt, baking powder, vanilla, and almond extract until light and fluffy. Add the egg and beat well. Add half the cream, all of the cornstarch, and half the flour; beat well. Add the remaining cream and flour, mixing just until all of the ingredients are well incorporated.
- Divide the dough in half, flatten into rounds, and wrap well. Refrigerate for 1 hour or more, to facilitate rolling.
- Preheat the oven to 350°F. Lightly grease (or line with parchment) two baking sheets.
- Transfer the chilled dough to a lightly floured work surface and place a piece of plastic wrap over it while you roll it out to keep it from sticking to the rolling pin. Roll the dough to ⅛ to ¼ inch thick. Cut it into the shapes of your choice and transfer to the prepared baking sheets.
- Bake the cookies for 10 to 12 minutes, until they're set but not browned. Remove them from the oven and let cool for 5 minutes on the baking sheet before transferring to a rack to cool completely. Use a metal spatula to pick up one cookie; if it seems fragile or breaks, let the cookies continue to cool until you can handle them easily.

Nutrition information per serving (1 cookie, 31 g): 134 cal, 7 g fat, 2 g protein, 10 g complex carbohydrates, 7 g sugar, 26 mg cholesterol, 81 mg sodium, 21 mg potassium, 69 RE vitamin A, 1 mg vitamin C, 1 mg iron, 18 mg calcium, 22 mg phosphorus.

Making cutout cookies

Here are a few easy steps to make your cutout cookies a success:

- Once the dough is thoroughly chilled, lightly dust both sides with flour. If you've just taken it out of the refrigerator, let it rest at room temperature for 5 to 10 minutes. When you pinch a piece of dough, it should feel pliable, not break off in a chunk. Trying to roll ice-cold dough is like trying to flatten an ice-cold stick of butter; it's more likely to crack and break into pieces than to roll flat and smooth.

- Transfer the dough to a lightly floured, clean work surface. Try to use as little flour as possible; the more you use, the more the cookie dough will absorb, and the tougher and harder the cookies will be. Starting in the middle and rolling out toward the edges, roll the dough into a circle ⅛ to ¼ inch thick. Thinner cookies will be crisper, thicker cookies will be sturdier (and appropriate for sandwiching around a scoop of ice cream).

- Use a cookie cutter to cut the dough into shapes, spacing them as close together as possible. Using a metal turner, pick up individual cookies and place them on the prepared baking sheets. Here's how: edge the turner under the cookie, lift slightly, pull away the scraps around the edge, then give your hand a gentle jerk to slip the cookie onto the baking sheet. This is the same motion you'd use for sliding a pancake onto a plate or a hamburger onto a bun.

- Gather all the dough scraps into a ball and reroll and cut them. You'll find that by the third go-around, the dough may be getting pretty rubbery and hard to roll. Just refrigerate it for 15 minutes, and it should behave again.

Snickerdoodles

Think crunchy sugar cookie. Think cinnamon, everyone's favorite baking spice. Put them together and what have you got? A snickerdoodle, that whimsically named, crisp-crunchy cinnamon sugar cookie that's one of the absolute stalwarts of the genre. Around the turn of the century, when snickerdoodle recipes first appeared in print, they included dried fruit and nuts. Over the years they've gradually become simpler, and now rely solely on their wonderful texture and cinnamon topping for character.

Yield: 7 dozen cookies ● *Baking temperature: 400°F* ● *Baking time: 8 minutes*

DOUGH
½ cup (3¼ ounces) vegetable shortening
½ cup (1 stick, 4 ounces) unsalted butter
1½ cups (10½ ounces) sugar
1 teaspoon vanilla extract
2 teaspoons baking powder

> 2 large eggs
> ¾ teaspoon salt
> 2¾ cups (11½ ounces) unbleached all-purpose flour
> COATING
> ½ cup (3½ ounces) sugar
> 2 teaspoons cinnamon

- Preheat the oven to 400°F. Lightly grease (or line with parchment) two baking sheets.
- **To make the dough:** In a medium-sized bowl, cream together the shortening, butter, sugar, vanilla, and baking powder, beating until smooth. Add the eggs, again beating until smooth, stopping to scrape the bowl once. Add the salt and flour, mixing slowly until combined.
- **To make the coating:** Mix the sugar and cinnamon together in a shallow bowl (or in a large plastic bag).
- Using a cookie scoop or your fingers, dip out 1 level tablespoon of dough (a teaspoon cookie scoop, generously filled, works well here) and roll it into a ball. Place the ball in the bowl or bag of cinnamon sugar. When you've got five or six dough balls in the sugar, gently shake them until they're completely coated. Place them on the prepared baking sheets, about 1½ inches apart. Using the bottom of a glass, flatten each cookie to about ½ inch thick. Repeat with the remaining dough.
- Bake the cookies for 8 minutes, or until they're golden brown around the edges. Remove them from the oven and transfer to a rack to cool.

Nutrition information per serving (1 cookie, 12 g): 51 cal, 2 g fat, 1 g protein, 3 g complex carbohydrates, 5 g sugar, 8 mg cholesterol, 25 mg sodium, 7 mg potassium, 12 RE vitamin A, 1 mg vitamin C, 7 mg calcium, 8 mg phosphorus.

Snickerdoodles, Jolly Boys, and Tangle Breeches

Around the turn of the twentieth century, New England cookbooks began to feature cookies with names that were . . . whimsical? silly? Despite the best efforts of food historians, none has been able to pin down exactly why, where, or how Jumbles, Cry Babies, or Kinkawoodles (to say nothing of Snickerdoodles) were born. Our favorite theory, of the many espoused? These words are just plain fun to say. After all, why not wrap your tongue around a charming combination of vowels and consonants before wrapping it around the cookie itself?

Vanilla Dreams

The texture of these cookies—ultratender, ethereally light, melt-in-your-mouth—is unlike anything you can get using baking powder or baking soda. The secret? Baker's ammonia, a.k.a. ammonium carbonate (see page 488), possibly available at your local pharmacy, and certainly available via mail order. Note that you may smell a strong ammonia odor while these cookies are baking, but never fear—by the time they come out of the oven the odor will be gone. Can these cookies be made without baker's ammonia? Sure, substitute 1½ teaspoons baking powder for the baker's ammonia. Just be aware their texture won't even come close to what we've just described.

Yield: 34 cookies ● *Baking temperature: 300°F* ● *Baking time: 25 to 30 minutes*

1¼ cups (8¾ ounces) sugar
1 cup (2 sticks, 8 ounces) unsalted butter
1 teaspoon salt
2 teaspoons vanilla extract
2 cups (8½ ounces) unbleached all-purpose flour
¼ teaspoon baker's ammonia
Coarse or granulated sugar, for coating

● Preheat the oven to 300°F. Lightly grease (or line with parchment) two baking sheets.
● In a medium-sized bowl, beat together the sugar, butter, salt, and vanilla. Add the flour and baker's ammonia and beat until the dough almost comes together, scraping the bowl once. The dough will seem quite dry at first, but keep beating, eventually it will clump up and become cohesive. This could take up to 5 minutes.
● Squeeze the dough together, gather it into a ball, and break off pieces about the size of a large gumball (about ¾ ounce). Roll the pieces into balls, and then roll them in the coarse sugar. Place them on the prepared baking sheets and use the bottom of a glass, dipped in sugar if necessary to prevent sticking, to flatten the balls to about ¼ inch thick.
● Bake the cookies for 25 to 30 minutes, until they're a very light golden brown around the edges. Remove them from the oven and transfer to a rack to cool.

Nutrition information per serving (1 cookie, 22 g): 102 cal, 5 g fat, 1 g protein, 5 g complex carbohydrates, 8 g sugar, 15 mg cholesterol, 85 mg sodium, 11 mg potassium, 50 RE vitamin A, 14 mg calcium, 12 mg phosphorus.

Brown-Edge Cookies

The name describes these sugar cookies quite aptly. Golden yellow with a deeper brown edge, they're delicate and elegant. A plate of these cookies is a good-looking (and good-tasting) addition to any tea table.

Yield: 4½ dozen cookies ● ***Baking temperature:*** *375°F* ● ***Baking time:*** *10 to 12 minutes*

1 cup (2 sticks, 8 ounces) unsalted butter
1 cup (7 ounces) sugar
1½ teaspoons vanilla extract
1 large egg
2 cups (8½ ounces) unbleached all-purpose flour
½ teaspoon salt
Heaping ½ cup (2½ ounces) pecan halves

● Preheat the oven to 375°F. Lightly grease (or line with parchment) two baking sheets.
● In a medium-sized bowl, cream together the butter, sugar, and vanilla until light and fluffy. Add the egg and beat well.
● In a separate bowl, whisk together the flour and salt and beat it gradually into the butter mixture. Drop the dough by the teaspoonful onto the prepared baking sheets. Nestle a pecan half atop each cookie.
● Bake the cookies for 10 to 12 minutes, or until their outside edges are golden brown. Remove them from the oven and transfer to a rack to cool.

Nutrition information per serving *(1 cookie, 15 g):* 70 cal, 4 g fat, 1 g protein, 3 g complex carbohydrates, 4 g sugar, 13 mg cholesterol, 21 mg sodium, 13 mg potassium, 34 RE vitamin A, 1 mg vitamin C, 2 mg calcium, 10 mg phosphorus.

Sugar Puffs

This featherlight cookie has the buttery taste of shortbread, but its texture will remind you of a puff of cotton candy—once the first light-and-crunchy bite passes your lips, the cookie practically dissolves in your mouth.

Yield: 20 cookies ● *Baking temperature: 300°F* ● *Baking time: 25 minutes*

½ cup (2 ounces) confectioners' sugar
¾ cup (1½ sticks, 6 ounces) unsalted butter
½ teaspoon salt (extra-fine preferred)
1½ teaspoons vanilla extract
½ cup (2 ounces) cornstarch
1 cup (4¼ ounces) unbleached all-purpose flour

● Preheat the oven to 300°F. Lightly grease (or line with parchment) two baking sheets.
● In a medium-sized mixing bowl, cream together the sugar, butter, salt, and vanilla. Add the cornstarch and flour, stirring to make a cohesive dough. Drop the dough by the tablespoonful onto the prepared baking sheets.
● Bake the cookies for 25 minutes, until they're a light golden brown. Remove them from the oven, let cool for 5 minutes on the baking sheet, then transfer to a rack to cool.

Nutrition information per serving (*1 cookie, 21 g*)*:* 106 cal, 7 g fat, 1 g protein, 7 g complex carbohydrates, 3 g sugar, 19 mg cholesterol, 55 mg sodium, 10 mg potassium, 64 RE vitamin A, 2 mg calcium, 8 mg phosphorus.

Pass the (extra-fine) salt, please

In cookies with only a few ingredients, such as shortbread and certain sugar cookies, occasionally the salt in the recipe won't dissolve fully; you may actually taste individual grains of salt. Extra-fine salt blends with the rest of the ingredients much more easily than regular table salt. You can find national brands of extra-fine salt (such as Diamond Crystal) in the salt section of your supermarket.

Light-as-Air Sugar Cookies

Light, airy, and crunchy are the three adjectives that spring to mind when you first bite into these tender cookies. The combination of vanilla and almond extracts gives them a subtle, sophisticated flavor. Note that ¼ teaspoon almond extract lends the merest hint of almond to these cookies. If you're someone who just can't get enough of that almond flavor, increase it to ½ (or even ¾) teaspoon.

Yield: 5½ dozen cookies ● *Baking temperature: 350°F* ● *Baking time: 10 minutes*

½ cup (2 ounces) confectioners' sugar
½ cup (3½ ounces) granulated sugar
½ cup (1 stick, 4 ounces) unsalted butter
½ cup (3½ ounces) vegetable oil
1 large egg
1 teaspoon vanilla extract
¼ to ½ teaspoon almond extract
½ teaspoon salt
2 teaspoons baking powder
2½ cups (10½ ounces) unbleached all-purpose flour

● Preheat the oven to 350°F. Lightly grease (or line with parchment) two baking sheets.
● In a large bowl, cream together the sugars, butter, and oil until smooth and light-colored. Beat in the egg, vanilla and almond extracts, salt, and baking powder, then mix in the flour.
● Roll the dough into 1-inch balls and place them on the prepared baking sheets. Using the bottom of a drinking glass dipped in granulated sugar, flatten the balls to ¼ inch thick.
● Bake the cookies for 10 minutes, until they're a very light brown around the edges. Remove them from the oven and transfer to a rack to cool.

Nutrition information per serving (1 cookie, 11 g): 51 cal, 3 g fat, 1 g protein, 3 g complex carbo-hydrates, 2 g sugar, 7 mg cholesterol, 31 mg sodium, 7 mg potassium, 14 RE vitamin A, 9 mg calcium, 9 mg phosphorus.

Crystal Diamonds

The inspiration for this recipe came from cookbook author John Thorne. We've made some slight changes, and think it's just about the most delicious roll-out sugar cookie we've ever enjoyed. These crisp, buttery, caramelized sugar wafers are, surprisingly, made with yeast, an interesting twist for a cookie. If you don't have coarse sugar, use regular granulated; the cookies won't be quite as crunchy but will be just as tasty.

   Pair these cookies with a dish of blueberries or blackberries (or the fresh local berry of your choice) for a simple end to a summer meal or picnic.

Yield: About 5 dozen 2-inch cookies ● *Baking temperature:* 275°F ● *Baking time:* 45 to 50 minutes

> 1½ cups (6¼ ounces) unbleached all-purpose flour
> ½ cup plus 1 tablespoon (4½ ounces) whole milk
> 1 drop lemon oil*
> 1 teaspoon instant yeast
> ¼ teaspoon salt
> ½ cup (1 stick, 4 ounces) unsalted butter, cut into 8 pieces
> 1½ cups (13 ounces) coarse sugar, for rolling

● Using an electric mixer, beat together the flour, milk, lemon oil, yeast, and salt until well combined. Beat in the pieces of butter one at a time, beating for 1 full minute after each piece is added. The dough will be very smooth and elastic. Remove the dough from the mixer, place it in a small bowl, cover, and refrigerate it for 2 hours, or as long as overnight.

● Preheat the oven to 275°F. Sprinkle your work surface heavily with coarse sugar (white or Demerara, see page 480).

● Divide the dough in half. Working with one half at a time (and keeping the other half refrigerated), roll out the dough on the sugar-covered surface as thin as possible, adding additional sugar to the work surface and sprinkling it atop the dough as necessary. Halfway through the rolling process, turn the dough over and sprinkle the work surface with more sugar, so that both top and bottom surfaces end up heavily coated with sugar. The dough should be about 1/16 inch thick, almost translucent in spots.

● Using a rolling pizza wheel or sharp knife, cut the dough into diamonds. Try to cut pieces about 2½ inches in size. They'll shrink a bit, and by the time they're finished baking, they'll be about 2 inches, a nice size for this cookie. (If you make them too large, the edges brown way before the middle; the goal is an evenly browned cookie.) Transfer the diamonds to ungreased, unlined baking sheets. Repeat with the remaining dough.

* Yes, a drop of lemon oil. You want just the merest hint of citrus here; it should be almost unidentifiable, just enough to make people wonder what they're tasting.

● Bake the cookies for 45 to 50 minutes. They should be a deep golden brown, but not burned. The closer you get to deep brown, the better they'll taste. Remove them from the oven and transfer to a rack immediately to cool, otherwise they may stick to the pan.

Nutrition information per serving (*3 cookies, 36 g*)*:* 131 cal, 5 g fat, 1 g protein, 7 g complex carbohydrates, 14 g sugar, 13 mg cholesterol, 77 mg sodium, 29 mg potassium, 45 RE vitamin A, 9 mg calcium, 20 mg phosphorus.

Make sure the dough is heavily sugared on both sides. Sugar is doing the work of flour here, keeping the dough from sticking to the work surface or your rolling pin. Use a rolling pizza wheel to cut the dough into diamond shapes.

Soft Sugar Cakes

These soft, moist cookies, scented with both nutmeg and vanilla, are a specialty of the farmers' markets in Pennsylvania Dutch country. They're very light and soft in texture, quite cakelike, and are wonderful served with fresh fruit, particularly berries. Freshly grated nutmeg will produce a tastier and more authentic cookie, but if you don't have a nutmeg grater, you can use ground nutmeg.

Yield: 24 large cookies ● *Baking temperature: 400°F* ● *Baking time: 8 minutes*

½ cup (4 ounces) sour cream (regular or low fat; not nonfat)
½ teaspoon baking soda
½ cup (1 stick, 4 ounces) unsalted butter
¾ cup (5¼ ounces) sugar
1 large egg
¾ teaspoon salt
¾ teaspoon freshly grated nutmeg
2 teaspoons vanilla extract
1½ teaspoons baking powder
1½ cups (6¼ ounces) unbleached all-purpose flour
Coarse sugar, colored sugar, or sprinkles, for decoration (optional)

● In a small mixing bowl, whisk together the sour cream and baking soda. Set aside. In a large mixing bowl, cream together the butter, sugar, egg, salt, nutmeg, vanilla, and baking powder. Add the sour cream mixture and blend well. Add the flour, blending until well combined. Cover the bowl and refrigerate overnight.

● Preheat the oven to 400°F and lightly grease (or line with parchment) two baking sheets.

● Drop the dough by the tablespoonful (a tablespoon cookie scoop works well here, see page 33) onto the prepared baking sheets, at least 2 inches apart. Sprinkle with coarse sugar, colored sugar, or sprinkles, if desired. Refrigerate any remaining dough while the first batch of cookies bakes.

● Bake the cookies for 8 minutes. They should look barely done—still very pale, almost white. (if they're golden brown, they've baked too long). Remove the cookies from the oven and leave them on the cookie sheets for 3 minutes to finish baking. Using a thin, flexible spatula, carefully remove the cookies from the baking sheet and transfer to a rack to cool completely.

● These cookies keep well in airtight containers, or wrapped individually and frozen in a tin. However, don't try to stack them without wax (or parchment) paper in between the layers, as they'll stick together.

Nutrition information per serving (1 cookie, 26 g): 104 cal, 6 g fat, 1 g protein, 6 g complex carbohydrates, 6 g sugar, 11 mg cholesterol, 128 mg sodium, 19 mg potassium, 13 RE vitamin A, 1 mg vitamin C, 24 mg calcium, 21 mg phosphorus.

Lemon Drops

These very light, soft cookies are pleasantly lemony. The lemon doesn't knock your socks off because these are, after all, sugar cookies; but it does assert itself in a gentle, happy way.

Yield: 5½ dozen cookies ● *Baking temperature:* 350°F ● *Baking time:* 18 minutes

DOUGH
½ cup (1 stick, 4 ounces) unsalted butter
1¼ cups (8¾ ounces) sugar
1 cup (8 ounces) sour cream (regular or low fat, not nonfat)
½ cup (4 ounces) freshly squeezed lemon juice
1 to 2 tablespoons grated lemon rind (zest)
2¼ cups (9½ ounces) unbleached all-purpose flour
1 teaspoon baking soda
1 teaspoon salt

TOPPING
½ cup (3½ ounces) sugar
1 drop Fiori di Sicilia, 1 to 2 drops lemon oil, or ½ teaspoon lemon extract
Yellow food coloring (optional)

● Preheat the oven to 350°F. Lightly grease (or line with parchment) two baking sheets.

● **To make the dough:** In a large bowl, cream together the butter and sugar. In a small bowl, combine the sour cream, lemon juice, and zest, then stir this into the butter mixture. Mix in the flour, baking soda, and salt, beating to make a smooth, soft dough.

● Drop the dough by the tablespoonful onto the prepared baking sheets. Bake the cookies for 18 minutes, until they're a very light gold around the edges. Remove them from the oven and transfer to a rack to cool.

● **To make the topping:** In a small food processor or blender, process together the sugar, lemon, and a few drops of food coloring. Add additional food coloring until the sugar is the tint you want. Sift this sugar over the cooled cookies just before serving.

Nutrition information per serving (1 cookie, 17 g): 55 cal, 2 g fat, 1 g protein, 3 g complex carbohydrates, 5 g sugar, 5 mg cholesterol, 53 mg sodium, 13 mg potassium, 20 RE vitamin A, 1 mg vitamin C, 5 mg calcium, 7 mg phosphorus.

Tea Sandwiches

If you're a fool for creamy filling, or chocolate or nuts—or all three!—then you'll want to bookmark this recipe. Crisp, flat sugar cookies sandwich the filling, and a rolled edge of chocolate and nuts makes the whole rather impressive-looking. Still, they really aren't fussy to make, especially if you bake the cookies one day and then make the filling and decorate the next.

Yield: 27 sandwich cookies ● *Baking temperature: 325°F* ● *Baking time: 15 minutes*

DOUGH
- 1 cup (2 sticks, 8 ounces) unsalted butter
- 1 cup (7 ounces) sugar
- 1 egg yolk
- 1 teaspoon vanilla extract
- 2 cups (8½ ounces) unbleached all-purpose flour

FILLING
- 1 cup (4 ounces) confectioners' sugar
- 4 tablespoons (½ stick, 2 ounces) unsalted butter
- 1½ teaspoons vanilla extract
- 1 tablespoon (½ ounce) milk (regular or low fat, not nonfat)

FROSTING
- ⅓ cup (2 ounces) chocolate chips
- 2 tablespoons (1 ounce) unsalted butter
- ½ cup (2 ounces) finely crushed almonds, hazelnuts, or walnuts

● **To make the dough:** In a medium-sized mixing bowl, cream together the butter and sugar. Beat in the egg yolk, vanilla, and flour to make a cohesive dough. Cover the bowl with plastic wrap and chill the dough for 2 hours.

● Preheat the oven to 325°F. Lightly grease (or line with parchment) two baking sheets.

● Break off 1-inch pieces of dough and roll them into balls. Flatten the balls to ¼ inch with the bottom of a glass dipped in sugar. Bake the cookies for 15 minutes, until their edges are slightly brown all around. Don't overbake. Remove the cookies from the oven and transfer to a rack to cool.

● **To make the filling:** In a small bowl, cream together the confectioners' sugar and butter. Beat in the vanilla and milk; add additional milk if necessary to make a spreadable filling. Spread the filling very thin on half the cookies, using a scant teaspoon for each. Place the remaining cookies on top of the filling to make sandwiches.

● **To make the frosting:** In the microwave, or the top of a double boiler, heat the chocolate chips and butter just until melted. Transfer the frosting to a shallow dish.

● Roll the edges of each sandwich first through the chocolate mixture, then through the nuts. Transfer the sandwiches to racks for the chocolate to set.

Nutrition information per serving (1 cookie, 38 g): 185 cal, 11 g fat, 2 g protein, 7 g complex carbohydrates, 13 g sugar, 1 g dietary fiber, 33 mg cholesterol, 2 mg sodium, 37 mg potassium, 91 RE vitamin A, 1 mg vitamin C, 1 mg iron, 11 mg calcium, 27 mg phosphorus, 2 mg caffeine.

Old-Fashioned Raisin Sugar Cookies

Raisin lovers, unite! There are those who are merely lukewarm about raisins (or, worse, even turn up their noses), but if you love this sweet, chewy fruit with its distinctive flavor, you'll appreciate these cookies. The nicely assertive hint of vanilla in the finish is an added plus. Bake these cookies so they're crisp outside, soft and chewy at the center; or crisp all the way through—it's just a matter of juggling the baking temperature and time.*

Yield: 26 cookies ● *Baking temperature:* 425°F ● *Baking time:* 9 minutes

½ cup (1 stick, 4 ounces) unsalted butter
¾ cup (5¼ ounces) sugar
2 teaspoons vanilla extract
¼ teaspoon baking powder
½ teaspoon salt
1 large egg
1½ cups (6¼ ounces) unbleached all-purpose flour
2 cups (12 ounces) raisins or currants

● Preheat the oven to 425°F. Lightly grease (or line with parchment) two baking sheets.
● In a large bowl, beat together the butter, sugar, vanilla, baking powder, and salt. When smooth, beat in the egg. Add the flour and raisins, stirring until well combined.
● Drop the dough by the tablespoonful onto the prepared baking sheets. Using the bottom of a glass dipped in sugar, flatten the dough to a scant ½ inch thick.
● Bake the cookies for 9 minutes, until they're barely set and just starting to brown around the edges. Remove them from the oven, let them rest on the pan until you can move them without them breaking, then transfer to a rack to cool.

* For crisp cookies, bake in a preheated 350°F oven for 13 to 15 minutes, until the cookies are starting to brown around the edges.

Nutrition information per serving (1 cookie, 32 g): 120 cal, 4 g fat, 1 g protein, 15 g complex carbohydrates, 6 g sugar, 1 g dietary fiber, 18 mg cholesterol, 50 mg sodium, 110 mg potassium, 37 RE vitamin A, 1 mg vitamin C, 1 mg iron, 11 mg calcium, 24 mg phosphorus.

Brown Sugar Cookies

Maybe some of us have the enormous patience required to decorate cookies in painstaking detail, but there are probably many more who would rather just get the job done and move on to the next project. That's where these cookies come in. First of all, the silky-smooth shortbread-like dough, made with brown sugar for extra flavor, is a joy to work with; there's no tedious rolling. Then there's the easy decorating. The result is a beautiful batch of buttery, sugary, choco-laty cookies, gussied up with as little or as much garnish as you see fit—all created without working up a sweat!

Yield: 55 cookies ● *Baking temperature:* 375°F ● *Baking time:* 10 to 12 minutes

DOUGH
¾ cup (1½ sticks, 6 ounces) unsalted butter
1 egg yolk
⅔ cup (5⅜ ounces) light brown sugar
1½ teaspoons vanilla extract
½ teaspoon salt
2 cups (8½ ounces) unbleached all-purpose flour

TOPPING
1 cup (6 ounces) chocolate chips
2 tablespoons (1 ounce) unsalted butter
3 tablespoons (2 ounces) light corn syrup
Colored jimmies, colored nonpareils, finely chopped nuts, or other sugar decorations

● **To make the dough:** In a large bowl, beat together the butter, egg yolk, brown sugar, vanilla, and salt until well combined. Mix in the flour. Cover and chill the dough for at least 1 hour.

● Preheat the oven to 375°F. Lightly grease (or line with parchment) two baking sheets.

● Break off teaspoonfuls of dough and form them into balls. Place on the prepared baking sheets and flatten to ¼ inch thick with the bottom of a glass dipped in granulated sugar.

● Bake the cookies for 10 to 12 minutes, until they're lightly browned. Remove them from the oven and transfer to a rack to cool.

● **To make the topping:** In a small bowl in the microwave, or in a small saucepan set over very low heat, melt the chocolate chips and butter together, stirring until smooth. Stir in the corn syrup.

● When the cookies are cool, use a flat butter knife or small icing spatula to cover half of each cookie with the topping, so you're looking at a cookie that's half iced, half bare. Then make small piles of whatever garnishes you use—it's fun to mix and match—and dip the choco-late-coated side into the decorations. Nonpareils and colored jimmies are fun. Toasted, finely chopped nuts are tasty. Refrigerate the cookies in a single layer on a baking sheet until the chocolate sets, about 1 hour.

Nutrition information per serving (1 cookie, 15 g): 72 cal, 4 g fat, 1 g protein, 3 g complex carbo-hydrates, 5 g sugar, 12 mg cholesterol, 3 mg sodium, 26 mg potassium, 29 RE vitamin A, 5 mg calcium, 10 mg phosphorus, 2 mg caffeine.

Oatmeal Cookies

Were we to choose just one cookie to represent America—the All-American Cookie—it would be chocolate chip. But the humble oatmeal cookie would finish a strong second. When you think comfort food cookies, and you can get your mind beyond the allure of the chocolate chip, it's oatmeal cookies—warm and chewy, studded with raisins and nuts—that come to mind.

Oats have a long and storied history in cooking and baking, particularly in Scotland, where bannocks—flat oatcakes—are noted as early as the fourteenth century. But the oatmeal cookie got a big push at the turn of the last century, when the Quaker Oats Company was formed in Chicago, from three smaller, regional companies. Quaker Oats, in the familiar red and blue canister we still see today, kicked oats into the American mainstream. Legend has it that Quaker Oats was the first mass-marketed product in America. Cooks everywhere began to think of oats as more than a breakfast porridge, adding them to favorite dishes like meatloaf, making them into muffins and bread, and, of course, baking oatmeal cookies.

Today, we celebrate National Oatmeal Month (January), and even National Oatmeal Cookie Day (April 30). But we hardly need a designated month, or even a day, to remind us how satisfying these cookies are. The nutty flavor and "nubby" texture oatmeal gives cookies is as distinctive as the crumbly-crunchy "bite" of a peanut butter cookie. The Essential Oatmeal Cookie is crunchy or crisp, soft or chewy; whatever your preference, you'll find it here. And if ever you were to add raisins to a cookie, this is the place; raisins and oats truly are a marriage made in heaven.

The Essential Chewy Oatmeal Cookie

This flat cookie has a lovely crisp edge, but bends before it breaks—unlike crunchy cookies, which snap cleanly in two. Raisins both enhance the cookie's flavor, and add additional moistness, and nuts lend their own distinct, toasty taste.

Yield: 45 cookies ● *Baking temperature:* 375°F ● *Baking time:* 11 minutes

½ cup (1 stick, 4 ounces) unsalted butter
½ cup (3¼ ounces) vegetable shortening
½ cup (3½ ounces) granulated sugar
1 cup (8 ounces) brown sugar
2 teaspoons vanilla extract
¼ teaspoon almond extract
¾ teaspoon cinnamon
⅛ teaspoon ground cloves
¼ teaspoon nutmeg
1 teaspoon salt
1 teaspoon baking soda
1 large egg
6 tablespoons (4⅛ ounces) light corn syrup
2 tablespoons (1 ounce) milk (regular or low fat, not nonfat)
3 cups (10½ ounces) quick-cooking oats (or old-fashioned rolled oats pulsed in a
    food processor, to make smaller, thinner flakes)
1½ cups (6¼ ounces) unbleached all-purpose flour
1 cup (5¼ ounces) raisins
1 cup (4 ounces) chopped pecans or walnuts

● Preheat the oven to 375°F. Lightly grease (or line with parchment) two baking sheets.
● In a large bowl, cream together the butter, shortening, sugars, extracts, spices, salt, and baking soda, beating until fairly smooth. Beat in the egg, scraping the bowl, then beat in the corn syrup and milk. Stir in the oats, flour, raisins, and nuts.
● Drop the dough by the tablespoonful onto the prepared baking sheets. Bake the cookies for 11 minutes, until they're a light golden brown. Remove them from the oven and transfer to a rack to cool.

Nutrition information per serving (1 cookie, 39 g): 156 cal, 6 g fat, 2 g protein, 15 g complex carbohydrates, 9 g sugar, 1 g dietary fiber, 10 mg cholesterol, 84 mg sodium, 75 mg potassium, 22 RE vitamin A, 1 mg vitamin C, 1 mg iron, 9 mg calcium, 29 mg phosphorus.

The Essential Crunchy Oatmeal Cookie

This oatmeal cookie is crumbly-crunchy, the lightest textured of all the oatmeal cookies we tested. If you're not a raisin lover, leave them out, but we feel both raisins and nuts give a plain oatmeal cookie pizzazz.

Yield: 4 dozen cookies ● *Baking temperature:* 325°F ● *Baking time:* 20 minutes

¾ cup (6 ounces) brown sugar
¾ cup (5¼ ounces) granulated sugar
½ cup (1 stick, 4 ounces) unsalted butter
½ cup (3¼ ounces) vegetable shortening
1 teaspoon salt
1 teaspoon baking powder
½ teaspoon cinnamon
¼ teaspoon nutmeg
⅛ teaspoon ground cloves
2 teaspoons vanilla extract
1 large egg
3 cups (10½ ounces) rolled oats
1 cup (4¼ ounces) unbleached all-purpose flour
1 cup (6 ounces) raisins, packed (optional)
1 cup (4 ounces) chopped pecans or walnuts (optional)

● Preheat the oven to 325°F. Lightly grease (or line with parchment) two baking sheets.

● In a large mixing bowl, cream together the sugars, butter, shortening, salt, baking powder, spices, and vanilla, beating until smooth. Beat in the eggs. Stir in the oats and flour, then the raisins and nuts.

● Drop the dough by the tablespoonful onto the prepared baking sheets. Using the flat bottom of a drinking glass dipped in sugar, flatten each ball of dough to about ¼ inch.

● Bake the cookies for about 20 minutes, until they're golden brown; these are supposed to be crunchy, so don't underbake them. Remove them from the oven and transfer to a rack to cool.

Nutrition information per serving *(1 cookie, 26 g):* 114 cal, 6 g fat, 2 g protein, 8 g complex carbohydrates, 7 g sugar, 1 g dietary fiber, 10 mg cholesterol, 58 mg sodium, 69 mg potassium, 21 RE vitamin A, 1 mg vitamin C, 1 mg iron, 16 mg calcium, 50 mg phosphorus.

The Essential Crisp Oatmeal Cookie

A bit darker in color than most due to its dark brown sugar, this cookie retains its crisp texture even when raisins are added. Solid and sturdy, it's a good traveler, whether in your backpack going up a mountain trail or at the bottom of your brown-bag lunch.

Yield: 45 cookies ● *Baking temperature: 350°F* ● *Baking time: 14 minutes*

6 tablespoons (2½ ounces) vegetable shortening
⅓ cup (2¾ ounces) unsalted butter
1 cup (8 ounces) dark brown sugar
½ cup (3½ ounces) granulated sugar
1 large egg
¼ cup (2 ounces) water
1½ teaspoons vanilla extract
¼ teaspoon almond extract
½ teaspoon cinnamon
⅛ teaspoon ground cloves
¼ teaspoon nutmeg
1 teaspoon salt
1 teaspoon baking soda
3 cups (10½ ounces) rolled oats
1¼ cups (5¼ ounces) unbleached all-purpose flour
1 cup (5¼ ounces) raisins (optional)
1 cup (4 ounces) chopped pecans or walnuts (optional)

● Preheat the oven to 350°F. Lightly grease (or line with parchment) two baking sheets.
● In a large bowl, cream together the shortening, butter, sugars, egg, water, extracts, spices, salt, and baking soda. Stir in the oats, then the flour. Add the raisins and nuts last, and stir to combine.
● Drop the dough by the tablespoonful onto the prepared baking sheets. Bake the cookies for 14 minutes, or until they're a light golden brown. Remove them from the oven and transfer to a rack to cool.

Nutrition information per serving (1 cookie, 26 g): 114 cal, 6 g fat, 2 g protein, 8 g complex carbohydrates, 7 g sugar, 1 g dietary fiber, 10 mg cholesterol, 58 mg sodium, 69 mg potassium, 21 RE vitamin A, 1 mg vitamin C, 1 mg iron, 16 mg calcium, 50 mg phosphorus.

The Essential Soft Oatmeal Cookie

Shaped in a soft mound rather than a flattened round, this cookie not only has great flavor, but it's also wonderfully soft and tender. If your taste runs to melt-in-your-mouth crumbly—rather than chewy, crisp, or crunchy—this one's for you.

Yield: 45 cookies ● *Baking temperature:* 350°F ● *Baking time:* 12 minutes

½ cup (1 stick, 4 ounces) unsalted butter
2 tablespoons (⅞ ounce) vegetable oil
1 cup (8 ounces) brown sugar
1 large egg, beaten
6 tablespoons (3 ounces) sour cream or yogurt (regular or low fat, not nonfat)
2 teaspoons vanilla extract
1 cup (5¼ ounces) currants or raisins (optional)
2 cups (7 ounces) rolled oats
½ teaspoon baking soda
½ teaspoon cinnamon
½ teaspoon salt
1½ cups (6¼ ounces) unbleached all-purpose flour
1 cup (4 ounces) chopped pecans or walnuts (optional)

● Preheat the oven to 350°F. Lightly grease (or line with parchment) two baking sheets.
● In a large bowl, cream together the butter, oil, and sugar. Add the egg, beating until fluffy, then beat in the sour cream and vanilla. Stir in the currants and the oats.
● In a separate bowl, mix together the baking soda, cinnamon, salt, and flour. Add this mixture, a cup at a time, to the oat mixture, beating well after each addition. Stir in the nuts. Let the dough rest for 15 to 30 minutes.
● Using a tablespoon cookie scoop (see page 33), drop the dough onto the prepared baking sheets. Bake the cookies for 12 minutes, or until they're light brown. Remove them from the oven and transfer to a rack to cool.

Nutrition information per serving (1 cookie, 26 g): 105 cal, 5 g fat, 2 g protein, 9 g complex carbohydrates, 5 g sugar, 1 g dietary fiber, 11 mg cholesterol, 43 mg sodium, 82 mg potassium, 26 RE vitamin A, 1 mg vitamin C, 1 mg iron, 14 mg calcium, 41 mg phosphorus.

VARIATIONS

Chocolate Chip–Oatmeal Cookies

Add 1 cup semisweet chocolate chips to the Essential Oatmeal Cookie recipe of your choice.

Very Vanilla Oatmeal Cookies

Add 1 vanilla bean, finely ground, to the Essential Oatmeal Cookie recipe of your choice. This will add an assertive hit of pure vanilla to your cookies.

Trail Mix Jumbles

Prepare the Essential Oatmeal Cookie recipe of your choice, substituting 1 cup dried cranberries for the raisins, and adding ⅔ cup chocolate chips or candy-coated chocolates and ⅓ cup flaked coconut, unsweetened preferred.

Cranberry Chews

Prepare the Essential Oatmeal Cookie recipe of your choice, substituting 1½ cups dried cranberries and ½ cup chopped walnuts for the raisins and nuts. Add ¼ teaspoon orange oil, or 1 tablespoon grated orange rind.

Oat Scotchies

Prepare the Essential Oatmeal Cookie recipe of your choice, substituting 1 cup butterscotch chips for the raisins, and using chopped pecans. Add a few drops of strong butterscotch or butter-rum flavor, if desired.

Mocha Chip Oatmeal Cookies

Prepare the Essential Oatmeal Cookie recipe of your choice, adding ½ teaspoon espresso powder to the dough, and substituting 1 cup semisweet or bittersweet chocolate chips for the raisins and 1 cup chopped macadamia nuts for the pecans or walnuts.

Coconutties

Prepare the Essential Oatmeal Cookie recipe of your choice, adding a few drops of strong coconut flavor to the dough, and substituting 2 cups shredded unsweetened coconut for the raisins and nuts. If you use sweetened coconut, reduce the sugar (either brown or granulated) in the recipe by 2 tablespoons.

Piña Colada Cookies

Prepare the Essential Chewy Oatmeal Cookie recipe or the Essential Soft Oatmeal Cookie recipe. If you're making the Chewy Oatmeal Cookies, omit the milk; if you're making the Soft Oatmeal Cookies, omit 2 tablespoons of the sour cream. Substitute one 8-ounce can crushed pineapple, thoroughly drained, and 1 cup shredded sweetened coconut for the raisins and nuts. Add a few drops of strong pineapple flavor and/or strong coconut flavor to the dough, if desired.

Date-Stuffed Oatmeal Sandwiches

Like raisins, dates are a natural in oatmeal cookies. In this recipe, we sandwich cookies around a smooth filling of cooked dates.

FILLING
> 1½ cups (8 ounces) chopped dates
> ¼ cup (2 ounces) brown sugar
> ½ cup (4 ounces) water
> ⅛ teaspoon salt
> 2 teaspoons lemon juice

DOUGH
> 1 recipe Essential Oatmeal Cookies (Choose Chewy, page 74; Crunchy, page 75; or Crisp, page 76; not Soft)

● **To make the filling:** In a small saucepan set over medium heat, gently cook the dates, sugar, water, salt, and lemon juice for about 7 minutes, stirring frequently, until it thickens.

● Preheat the oven as directed in the recipe you've chosen.

● Prepare the cookie dough recipe of your choice, omitting the raisins and nuts. Bake the cookies as directed in the recipe you've chosen.

● When the cookies are cool, spread half the cookies generously with the filling. Top with the remaining cookies, pressing down to compact the filling.

Oatmeal is oatmeal, isn't it?

Au contraire! Oats come in a number of different grinds, and not all are suitable for cookies.

The coarsest grind of oats is steel-cut, which means the actual oat grains have been cut into several pieces. These extremely hard oat nuggets are great for porridge, but don't use them in your cookies.

If the oat berries are steamed and then rolled flat, they become rolled oats, often called old-fashioned oats. If the berries are first cut into several pieces before being steamed and rolled, the result is a smaller-particle rolled oat, called quick-cooking oats. Rolled (old-fashioned) oats and quick-cooking oats can be used in any of these recipes; be aware that quick-cooking oats will give you a cookie with a more uniform texture, while old-fashioned oats produce a craggier cookie.

Instant oatmeal, the kind you buy in individual packets, has been precooked and isn't suitable for any of these recipes. Using it will produce a sticky-textured cookie with little character. Save it for a quick breakfast.

Old-Fashioned Oatmeal Cookies

These big, dark brown, lusty rounds bear little resemblance to the light tan, chunky-looking cookies anyone would immediately identify as oatmeal. Grinding the oats makes these cookies smoother in appearance; grinding the raisins also evens out their texture and adds wonderful moistness and flavor. And molasses lends that old-fashioned taste. We like to make these cookies bigger than normal, using ¼ cup batter for each. The result: a big (3½-inch), "dunkable" cookie, somewhere in between crisp and chewy, and perfect with coffee or milk.

Yield: 16 cookies ● *Baking temperature: 325°F* ● *Baking time: 18 minutes*

½ cup (1 stick, 4 ounces) unsalted butter
¼ cup (1⅝ ounces) vegetable shortening
1¼ cups (10 ounces) brown sugar
¼ cup (3 ounces) molasses
1 large egg
2 teaspoons vanilla extract
3 cups (10½ ounces) rolled oats
1 cup (4¼ ounces) unbleached all-purpose flour
1½ cups (8 ounces) raisins
1¼ teaspoons salt
½ teaspoon baking powder

● Preheat the oven to 325°F. Lightly grease (or line with parchment) two baking sheets.
● In a large bowl, cream together the butter, shortening, brown sugar, molasses, egg, and vanilla. Beat until light-colored and smooth.
● In a food processor or blender, process the oats, flour, raisins, salt, and baking powder for about 30 seconds, or until both the oats and raisins are chopped, yet still in recognizable pieces.
● Beat the oat mixture into the butter mixture until smooth. Using a ¼-cup measure or large cookie or muffin scoop, drop the dough onto the prepared baking sheets, leaving 3 inches between cookies; they'll spread as they bake. Moisten your fingers and gently flatten each cookie into a 2 ½-inch round that is ½-inch thick.
● Bake the cookies for 18 minutes, or until they're a medium golden brown. Remove them from the oven and let rest on the baking sheets for 1 minute, then transfer to a rack to cool completely. The cookies will be soft and delicate when they come out of the oven, but will get firmer as they cool.

Nutrition information per serving (1 cookie, 18 g): 306 cal, 10 g fat, 5 g protein, 29 g complex carbohydrates, 22 g sugar, 3 g dietary fiber, 29 mg cholesterol, 203 mg sodium, 269 mg potassium, 61 RE vitamin A, 1 mg vitamin C, 2 mg iron, 49 mg calcium, 124 mg phosphorus.

Flourless Oatmeal Drops

Chewy, sticky, almost candylike, these golden, shiny cookies are all oats, all the time.

Yield: 2 dozen cookies ● *Baking temperature:* 375°F ● *Baking time:* 10 minutes

⅓ cup (2¾ ounces) unsalted butter
⅞ cup (7 ounces) brown sugar
½ teaspoon salt
½ teaspoon cinnamon
¼ teaspoon nutmeg
⅛ teaspoon ground cloves
½ teaspoon baking powder
1½ teaspoons vanilla extract
2 teaspoons white vinegar or cider vinegar
2 large eggs
2½ cups (8¾ ounces) rolled oats

● In a medium-sized bowl, beat together the butter, sugar, salt, spices, baking powder, vanilla, and vinegar until light and fluffy. Add the eggs one at a time, beating well after each addition. Stir in the oats. Cover the bowl and refrigerate the dough for 1 hour.
● Preheat the oven to 375°F. Lightly grease (or line with parchment) two baking sheets.
● Remove the dough from the refrigerator and drop it by the tablespoonful onto the prepared baking sheets. Moisten your fingers and flatten the cookies to ¼ inch thick.
● Bake the cookies for 10 minutes, or until their edges are lightly browned; they won't look completely done in the center, but that's okay. Remove them from the oven and let rest on the baking sheets for 5 minutes before transferring to a rack to cool completely.

Nutrition information per serving (*1 cookie, 25 g*): 94 cal, 4 g fat, 2 g protein, 6 g complex carbohydrates, 8 g sugar, 1 g dietary fiber, 25 mg cholesterol, 64 mg sodium, 65 mg potassium, 33 RE vitamin A, 1 mg vitamin C, 1 mg iron, 21 mg calcium, 52 mg phosphorus.

Salty Oatmeal Cookies

Salt and sweet is a flavor combination that's quite appealing: think honey-roasted peanuts, or white chocolate–covered pretzels. These cookies add the nuttiness of oats to that salt/sweet combo to make a delightful, rather eccentric cookie. Note that this is a grownup kind of cookie: no raisins, no butterscotch chips, just a tender round packed with the comforting, tweedy texture of oats. While the salty surprise at first bite is an eye-opener, it's practically impossible to eat just one.

Yield: 3 dozen cookies ● *Baking temperature:* 375°F ● *Baking time:* 10 to 12 minutes

½ cup (3¼ ounces) vegetable shortening
½ cup (1 stick, 4 ounces) unsalted butter
1 cup (7 ounces) sugar
1 large egg
1½ cups (6¼ ounces) unbleached all-purpose flour
½ teaspoon salt, plus more for sprinkling
½ teaspoon baking soda
1 teaspoon vanilla extract
3 cups (10½ ounces) rolled oats

● In a large mixing bowl, cream together the shortening, butter, and sugar until light. Beat in the egg. In another bowl, whisk together the flour, salt, and baking soda and stir into the sugar/shortening mixture. Mix in the vanilla and oats. Cover the bowl and chill the dough for 30 minutes.
● Preheat the oven to 375°F. Lightly grease (or line with parchment) two baking sheets.
● Remove the dough from the refrigerator and roll it ¼ inch thick on a lightly floured work surface. Cut it into shapes with your favorite cutter, or simply cut it into squares or diamonds, using a pizza wheel or a sharp knife. Lightly sprinkle the surface of the dough with salt.
● Bake the cookies for 10 to 12 minutes, until they're just lightly colored at the edges. Remove them from the oven, let rest on the baking sheets for 5 minutes, then transfer to a rack to cool completely.

Nutrition information per serving (1 cookie, 26 g): 116 cal, 6 g fat, 2 g protein, 9 g complex carbohydrates, 6 g sugar, 1 g dietary fiber, 13 mg cholesterol, 50 mg sodium, 37 mg potassium, 27 RE vitamin A, 1 mg iron, 6 mg calcium, 46 mg phosphorus.

Anzac Biscuits

These crunchy cookies, redolent of both oats and coconut, are perhaps the all-Australian cookie. During World War II, Australian women baked these cookies and sent them off to the "Anzacs"—soldiers—in care packages. As they keep well for a very long time and contain no eggs, which were in short supply back then, Anzacs were the perfect cookie for the job. Anzacs could be compared to America's Oreo cookies in popularity, and they go just as well with a long, cold glass of milk.

Yield: 4 dozen cookies ● *Baking temperature:* 350°F ● *Baking time:* 15 to 20 minutes

> 1 cup (3½ ounces) rolled oats
> 1 cup (4¼ ounces) unbleached all-purpose flour
> ¾ cup (5¼ ounces) sugar
> ¾ cup (2¼ ounces) shredded sweetened coconut
> ½ cup (1 stick, 4 ounces) unsalted butter
> 2 tablespoons (1½ ounces) golden syrup*
> 1½ teaspoons baking soda
> 2 tablespoons (1 ounce) boiling water

● Preheat the oven to 350°F. Lightly grease (or line with parchment) two baking sheets.

● In a large bowl, mix together the oats, flour, sugar, and coconut. Place the butter and syrup in a small saucepan and cook over medium heat until the butter has melted and the syrup is bubbling.

● In a small bowl, combine the baking soda and water and stir this into the butter mixture. The mixture will foam up as you stir it. Stir this mixture into the dry ingredients and mix until well combined.

● Drop the dough by the heaping teaspoonful onto the prepared baking sheets, allowing room for spreading. Bake the cookies for 15 to 20 minutes; they should be a rich golden brown in color. Remove them from the oven and transfer to a rack to cool; they'll become crunchy as they cool.

* Australian golden syrup has rich caramel flavor with a hint of burnt sugar. The English variety is somewhat more like a corn syrup in taste, and quite a bit lighter in color. It's an acceptable substitute, and can be purchased in many specialty food shops. If you're unable to obtain either, try a dark table syrup with a high percentage of cane sugar, such as King's table syrup. Or, if all else fails, use dark corn syrup.

Nutrition information per serving (1 cookie, 13 g): 54 cal, 2 g fat, 1 g protein, 4 g complex carbohydrates, 4 g sugar, 5 mg cholesterol, 44 mg sodium, 15 mg potassium, 18 RE vitamin A, 2 mg calcium,14 mg phosphorus.

VARIATION

● Add ½ to ¾ cup chopped dried apricots and/or ½ cup crystallized ginger.

Molasses Cookies

Molasses, one of the world's ancient foods, has long been a staple of American cooking and baking. Its history stretches back to at least 600 BC, with proof that it was produced in Persia and India. It has also played a huge role in American history—the infamous trade triangle of molasses, rum, and slaves was a major part of the American economy in the seventeenth century. And in the eighteenth century, the Molasses Act of 1733 helped precipitate the American Revolution. In the twentieth century, one of the strangest disasters of all time occurred in Boston, when a vat of molasses exploded and flooded streets along the waterfront with over two million gallons of sticky syrup, killing twenty-one people.

Gingerbread, baked beans, Indian pudding, doughnuts, shoofly pie, taffy, cakes, and cookies all took their sweetness and flavor from molasses, which until the 1920s was America's most popular sweetener. The drop in sugar prices after World War I made white sugar affordable to all, and the use of molasses waned. But a certain patriotic nostalgia for America's earliest baked goods, paired with molasses' rich, complex taste, means it has never disappeared entirely from the culinary scene. Today, most of us experience molasses in connection with cookies.

Molasses cookies, mentioned in print as early as 1830, are surely the most ubiquitous cookie in any New England cookbook. More venerable than those newcomers, Toll House (chocolate chip) cookies (which, after all, are only about seventy years old), molasses cookies come in two basic varieties: soft and crisp. We give a recipe for each (as well as one in the middle, for you fence-sitters), and you can do your own taste test and come down on one side or the other of a debate that's been raging here in New England for centuries, namely, which molasses cookie is better—hard or soft?

Measuring molasses

This messy task can be made easier by first lightly spraying the inside of your measuring cup with a vegetable oil spray. This works with other sticky sweeteners or peanut butter as well. Here in our test kitchen, we measure molasses in a dry measuring cup instead of in a liquid measuring cup; if you spray the inside of the cup with oil, it flows out pretty easily.

A different kind of measuring cup that works great on messy liquids and sticky ingredients is a clear, round sleeve with a sliding base set within it. You'll see these under the brand name Wonder Cup (see page 34).

Soft Molasses Cookies

What is a great soft molasses cookie like? Rich with spices, piquant and sweet at the same time, and wonderfully chewy. These are perfect with a cold glass of milk or a hot cup of tea.

Yield: 44 cookies ● *Baking temperature: 350°F* ● *Baking time: 10 minutes*

1 cup (2 sticks, 8 ounces) unsalted butter
1 cup (7 ounces) sugar, plus more for coating the dough
½ cup (6 ounces) molasses
2¼ teaspoons baking soda
1 teaspoon salt
1¼ teaspoons cinnamon
1¼ teaspoons ground cloves
¾ teaspoon ground ginger
2 large eggs
3½ cups (14¾ ounces) unbleached all-purpose flour

● In a large mixing bowl, cream together the butter and sugar until light and fluffy. Add the molasses while mixing at slow speed, then the baking soda, salt, and spices. Add the eggs one at a time, beating well after each addition. Scrape down the sides of the bowl to make sure everything is incorporated. Stir in the flour. Cover the bowl and refrigerate the dough for 1 hour.

● Preheat the oven to 350°F. Lightly grease (or line with parchment) two baking sheets.

● Shape or scoop the dough into 1½-inch balls; a tablespoon cookie scoop (see page 33) works well here. Roll them in granulated sugar and put them on the prepared baking sheets, leaving about 2 inches between them.

● Bake the cookies for 10 minutes. The centers will look soft and puffy, which is okay. As long as the bottoms are set enough to lift partway off the cookie sheet without bending or breaking, they're ready to come out of the oven. Cool the cookies on the pan for 10 minutes before transferring them to a rack to cool completely.

Nutrition information per serving (*1 cookie, 25 g*)*:* 103 cal, 4 g fat, 1 g protein, 7 g complex carbohydrates, 8 g sugar, 10 mg cholesterol, 121 mg sodium, 34 mg potassium, 4 RE vitamin A, 1 mg vitamin C, 1 mg iron, 6 mg calcium, 14 mg phosphorus.

Crisp Molasses Cookies

Sometimes **known as molasses crinkles,** in the oven these sugar-dusted cookies puff up, crack across the top, then fall, and become thin and ultracrisp as they cool. With its sugary, crackly crust, the resulting cookie is both attractive and delicious. The spices and molasses combine for a cookie that's snapping-crisp and light (rather than hard), the perfect accompaniment to afternoon coffee or tea.

Yield: 5½ dozen cookies ● *Baking temperature:* 350°F ● *Baking time:* 13 minutes

¾ cup (1½ sticks, 6 ounces) unsalted butter
1 cup (7 ounces) sugar, plus more for coating the dough
¼ cup (3 ounces) molasses
1 large egg
2 cups (8½ ounces) unbleached all-purpose flour
1 teaspoon baking soda
¼ teaspoon salt
1 teaspoon ground cloves
1 teaspoon cinnamon
½ teaspoon ground ginger

● In a medium-sized mixing bowl, beat together the butter and sugar until well combined, then add the molasses and egg, beating until smooth.

● In a separate bowl, whisk together the flour, baking soda, salt, and spices. Add this mixture to the wet ingredients, beating until smooth. Cover and refrigerate the dough for 1 hour, or until it's stiff enough to roll into balls.

● Preheat the oven to 350°F. Lightly grease (or line with parchment) two baking sheets.

● Shape the dough into 1-inch balls (or use a teaspoon cookie scoop to scoop off 1-inch balls of dough) and roll them in granulated sugar. This is most easily accomplished by placing some sugar in a bag and adding the balls of dough, six or eight at a time, then shaking gently to cover them with sugar. Transfer the balls to the prepared baking sheets.

● Bake the cookies for about 13 minutes, or until they crack on top and flatten out. Remove the cookies from the oven and transfer them to a rack to cool completely.

Nutrition information per serving (1 cookie, 11 g): 48 cal, 2 g fat, 1 g protein, 3 g complex carbohydrates, 4 g sugar, 9 mg cholesterol, 30 mg sodium, 13 mg potassium, 21 RE vitamin A, 1 mg vitamin C, 3 mg calcium, 6 mg phosphorus.

On-the-Fence Molasses Cookies

These thin, crisp-chewy cookies pack some punch with the addition of black pepper and allspice. Their texture isn't crisp, neither is it soft; it's more what we call "bendy," thus their "on-the-fence" moniker. They're very gingery and hot-spicy, so be sure to have a tall pitcher of something cold handy when serving these.

Yield: 3 dozen cookies ● ***Baking temperature:** 350°F* ● ***Baking time:** 13 minutes*

1 cup (2 sticks, 8 ounces) unsalted butter
⅓ cup (4 ounces) molasses
2¼ cups (15¾ ounces) sugar, plus more for coating the dough
1 teaspoon salt
2 teaspoons ground ginger
1 teaspoon ground allspice
1 teaspoon ground black pepper
3 cups (12¾ ounces) unbleached all-purpose flour
1 teaspoon baking soda
1 large egg

● Heat the butter, molasses, sugar, and salt in a saucepan over low heat, or in a bowl in the microwave, stirring until the butter melts and the sugar and salt dissolve. Remove from the heat and stir in the spices. Transfer the mixture to a large mixing bowl.

● In a separate bowl, whisk together the flour and baking soda. Beat half the flour mixture into the melted butter mixture, then beat in the egg. Stir in the remaining flour. Cover and refrigerate the dough for 1 hour, or until it's firm.

● Preheat the oven to 350°F. Lightly grease (or line with parchment) two baking sheets.

● Shape or scoop the dough into 1½-inch balls; a tablespoon cookie scoop (see page 33) works well here. Roll the dough balls in granulated or coarse sugar to coat. Transfer the balls to the prepared baking sheets.

● Bake the cookies for 13 minutes; they will still look soft and won't have changed color much. Remove them from the oven and let cool for 5 minutes on the pan before transferring them to a rack to cool completely. They'll become crisper as they cool.

Nutrition information per serving (1 cookie, 16 g): 59 cal, 2 g fat, 1 g protein, 4 g complex carbohydrates, 6 g sugar, 9 mg cholesterol, 39 mg sodium, 38 mg potassium, 18 RE vitamin A, 1 mg vitamin C, 10 mg calcium, 17 mg phosphorus.

Joe Froggers

The addition of rum to these spicy cookies helps keep them soft, and also earns them their special name. Legend has it that an old man named Joe, who lived by a frog pond in Marblehead, Massachusetts, was famous for his chewy molasses cookies. One day, in thanks to a neighbor for the gift of a jug of rum, he added some of that spirit to a batch of his molasses cookie dough, then gave the cookies to the generous neighbor. Eureka! A rum-laced molasses cookie was born, one that quickly earned a great reputation around town and was christened with the name of its creator.

These cookies are chewy, with a beautiful, smooth, dark brown crust, and a craggy inner crumb. Their strong molasses flavor is perfect for those who are fans of this particular sweetener. To keep Joe Froggers soft, we recommend storing them in an airtight container (a plastic bag is fine) as soon as they're just barely warm. Add a couple of slices of cut apple if you plan on keeping them around long (an unlikely scenario).

Yield: 16 large (3½-inch) cookies ● *Baking temperature: 375°F* ● *Baking time: 11 minutes*

2 cups (8½ ounces) unbleached all-purpose flour
1½ teaspoons ground ginger
½ teaspoon ground cloves
½ teaspoon nutmeg
¼ teaspoon allspice
½ teaspoon salt
¼ teaspoon baking soda
½ cup (1 stick, 4 ounces) unsalted butter
½ cup (4 ounces) brown sugar
⅔ cup (8 ounces) molasses
3 tablespoons (1½ ounces) dark rum (or use apple juice or water)

● Preheat the oven to 375°F. Lightly grease (or line with parchment) two baking sheets.
● In a medium-sized mixing bowl, whisk together the flour, spices, salt, and baking soda.
● In a saucepan set over low heat, or in the microwave, melt together the butter, sugar, molasses, and rum. Stir the molasses mixture into the flour mixture; the dough will be wet and sticky. Cover and refrigerate the dough, for 30 minutes or longer; it will become quite firm.
● Using an overstuffed tablespoon cookie scoop (see page 33), scoop out 2-inch balls of dough, somewhere in size between a table tennis ball and a golf ball. Place the balls on the prepared baking sheets, leaving 2 inches between them. Flatten them slightly.
● Bake the cookies for 11 minutes, until they appear set (but not dark brown) around the edges. Remove them from the oven and transfer to a rack to cool.

Nutrition information per serving (1 cookie, 46 g): 181 cal, 6 g fat, 2 g protein, 11 g complex carbohydrates, 18 g sugar, 1 g dietary fiber, 16 mg cholesterol, 109 mg sodium, 115 mg potassium, 54 RE vitamin A, 1 mg vitamin C, 2 mg iron, 24 mg calcium, 23 mg phosphorus.

VARIATION

● Add 1 cup sweetened flaked coconut to the dough.

Extra-Spicy Date-Ginger Cookies

It's easy to take the basic Joe Frogger recipe and soften it up even further with moist candied ginger and dates. This cookie is for those of you who believe "the softer and moister, the better."

Yield: 16 large (3½-inch) cookies ● *Baking temperature: 375°F* ● *Baking time: 12 minutes*

> 1 recipe Joe Froggers (page 89)
> ¼ cup (1½ ounces) diced crystallized or soft ginger
> ¾ cup (3¾ ounces) chopped dates

● Follow the Joe Frogger recipe, combining the flour, spices, salt, and baking soda in the work bowl of a food processor. Add the ginger and dates and process until both are finely and uniformly chopped. Add the flour mixture to the molasses mixture and shape the cookies as directed in the recipe.

● Increase the baking time by 1 minute (to 12 minutes), and bake as directed in the recipe.

Nutrition information per serving (1 cookie, 55 g): 208 cal, 6 g fat, 2 g protein, 16 g complex carbohydrates, 20 g sugar, 1 g dietary fiber, 16 mg cholesterol, 111 mg sodium, 160 mg potassium, 54 RE vitamin A, 1 mg vitamin C, 2 mg iron, 27 mg calcium, 26 mg phosphorus.

Which kind of molasses should I use?

When sugar cane or sugar beets are refined and their sugar crystals extracted, the remaining dark, sweet liquid is molasses. Light molasses is liquid from the first boil of the syrup; dark molasses is from the second boil. In England, the syrup from either of these boils is referred to as light treacle. Light molasses is lighter colored, sweeter, and not as assertively flavored as dark molasses. Use either light or dark molasses in these cookie recipes, depending on your fondness for molasses' distinctive taste.

Blackstrap molasses comes from the syrup's third boiling, and it's heavy, thick, and much less sweet than either light or dark molasses. In England, blackstrap molasses is called dark treacle. It's unsuitable for cookie baking.

And what about sulfured vs. unsulfured molasses? In days gone by, sulfur dioxide was used in the sugar refining process and the resulting molasses was said to be sulfured. These days sulfur is seldom used, and nearly all molasses is labeled unsulfured.

Sugar & Spice Drops

A deep, rich brown color, and marked with a crisscross on top, these cookies offer the best of both worlds: they're crisp on the outside but soft in the middle. They have a wonderful, assertive spice flavor, and lots of molasses "bang for the buck."

Yield: 2 dozen cookies ● *Baking temperature:* 350°F ● *Baking time:* 10 minutes

½ cup (3½ ounces) vegetable oil
½ cup (4 ounces) brown sugar
½ cup (6 ounces) molasses
1 teaspoon baking powder
1 teaspoon baking soda
½ teaspoon salt
1 teaspoon cinnamon
1 teaspoon ground ginger
½ teaspoon nutmeg
¼ teaspoon ground cloves
1⅔ cups (7 ounces) unbleached all-purpose flour
Granulated sugar, for coating the dough

● Preheat the oven to 350°F. Lightly grease (or line with parchment) two baking sheets.
● In a medium-sized bowl, beat together the oil, brown sugar, molasses, baking powder, baking soda, salt, and spices. Mix in the flour.
● Shape or scoop the dough into 1½-inch balls. A tablespoon cookie scoop (see page 33) can be used to portion the dough. Roll the balls in granulated sugar and place them on the prepared baking sheets. Use a fork to press a crisscross pattern into the top of each.
● Bake the cookies for 10 minutes, or until they're set. Remove them from the oven and transfer to a rack to cool.

Nutrition information per serving (*1 cookie, 26 g*): 112 cal, 4 g fat, 1g protein, 7 g complex carbohydrates, 10 g sugar, 129 mg sodium, 129 mg potassium, 1 mg vitamin C, 1 mg iron, 24 mg calcium, 17 mg phosphorus.

Molasses Snaps

If you've ever had a brandy snap, you'll recognize these parchment-thin, ultracrisp cookies. Made with just enough flour and oats to give the sugar, butter, and molasses some structure, these big (3½-inch) cookies pair well with vanilla ice cream. The cookies are very deep brown in color, even before they're fully baked, so you may want to bake one test cookie to ascertain the exact baking time. Bake it, remove it from the oven, and let it cool for 10 minutes. Does it taste good? Is it starting to become crisp? You've nailed the baking time. Go ahead and bake the rest of the dough.

Yield: 4 dozen cookies ● *Baking temperature: 350°F* ● *Baking time: 10 to 12 minutes*

½ cup (1 stick, 4 ounces) unsalted butter
½ to ¾ teaspoon salt
1¼ cups (10 ounces) brown sugar
¼ cup (3 ounces) molasses
1 teaspoon ground ginger
¼ teaspoon cinnamon
½ teaspoon grated lemon rind (zest), or ¼ teaspoon lemon oil
1 tablespoon brandy or rum (or 1½ teaspoons vanilla extract)
¾ cup (3 ounces) unbleached all-purpose flour
½ cup (1½ ounces) oat flour, or very finely ground rolled oats

● In a large saucepan, gently melt the butter with the salt, brown sugar, molasses, spices, and lemon zest over low heat. Remove the mixture from the heat and stir in the brandy and the flours. Let this mixture cool and thicken while you preheat the oven to 350°F and lightly grease (or line with parchment) two baking sheets.
● Use a teaspoon cookie scoop (see page 33) to deposit 1-inch balls of dough (it will be quite thin); on the prepared baking sheets, leaving about 3 inches between them.
● Bake the cookies for 10 to 12 minutes, until they're a deep mahogany brown, but not even close to being burned. Remove the pan from the oven and place it on a rack. When the cookies have solidified enough to move, transfer them to a rack to cool and crisp completely.

Nutrition information per serving (1 cookie, 15 g): 64 cal, 2 g fat, 1 g protein, 2 g complex carbohydrates, 8 g sugar, 6 mg cholesterol, 44 mg sodium, 41 mg potassium, 20 RE vitamin A, 1 mg vitamin C, 9 mg calcium, 10 mg phosphorus.

VARIATION

● For maple snaps, substitute ¼ cup maple syrup for the molasses.

Ginger Crisps

Ginger cookies are found in most Scandinavian cultures, and you'll see them at Christmastime in unusual shapes, often decorated with an egg-white and confectioners' sugar piped icing. Ginger-bread houses form a backdrop for gingerbread men and women, gingerbread kids, farm animals, hearts, stars, and other traditional Christmas shapes. This ginger cookie is somewhat lighter in color, thinner, and more delicate than the usual American ginger cookie. Flavored with orange as well as classic gingerbread spices—cinnamon, ginger and cloves—it's a great addition to a cookie gift tin.

Yield: 5 dozen cookies ● *Baking temperature: 350°F* ● *Baking time: 8 to 10 minutes*

1 cup (2 sticks, 8 ounces) unsalted butter
1½ cups (10½ ounces) sugar
1 large egg
2 tablespoons grated orange rind (zest)
¼ teaspoon orange oil (optional, for increased orange flavor)
¼ to ½ teaspoon ground black pepper (optional, for "heat")
2 tablespoons (1½ ounces) molasses
1 tablespoon (½ ounce) water
3¼ cups (13¾ ounces) unbleached all-purpose flour
2 teaspoons baking soda
¾ teaspoon salt
2 teaspoons cinnamon
1 teaspoon ground ginger
½ teaspoon ground cloves or allspice

● In a large mixing bowl, cream together the butter and sugar. Beat in the egg, orange zest, orange oil, and pepper, then the molasses and water.

● Add the flour, baking soda, salt, and spices. Beat until everything is well combined and the mixture has formed a stiff dough. Divide the dough into two pieces, shape each piece into a disk, wrap in plastic wrap, and refrigerate for several hours, or overnight.

● Preheat the oven to 350°F. Lightly grease (or line with parchment) two baking sheets.

● Remove the dough from the refrigerator and let it rest at room temperature for 5 to 10 minutes, until it's soft enough to roll easily. Working with one piece at a time, roll the dough into a circle ⅛ inch thick. Use a 2- to 3-inch cookie cutter to cut shapes close together, getting as many cookies from the first roll-out as you can. Transfer the cookies to the baking sheets, leaving 1 inch between them. Gather the scraps together, reroll, and cut again, continuing the procedure until you've used all the dough. Re-rolling toughens the dough a little and will make the cookies a bit heavy, so try to be as economical as possible when you cut your cookies. Repeat with the remaining piece of dough.

● Bake the cookies for 8 to 10 minutes, until they're just beginning to turn golden brown around the edges. Remove them from the oven and transfer to a rack to cool completely.

Nutrition information per serving (1 cookie, 17 g): 71 cal, 3 g fat, 1 g protein, 5 g complex carbohydrates, 9 mg cholesterol, 80 mg sodium, 14 mg potassium, 31 RE vitamin A, 14 mg calcium, 7 mg phosphorus.

Raisin-Filled Ginger Crisps

These spicy ginger cookies surround a surprise in the middle—a sweet, moist filling of golden raisins and ginger.

Yield: 26 cookies ● *Baking temperature: 350°F* ● *Baking time: 10 to 11 minutes*

DOUGH
> 1 recipe Ginger Crisps (page 93)

FILLING
> 1 cup (6 ounces) golden raisins
> ½ cup (3¼ ounces) diced crystallized ginger
> 2 tablespoons (½ ounce) unbleached all-purpose flour
> ½ teaspoon ground ginger
> ½ cup (3½ ounces) sugar
> ¼ teaspoon salt
> 1 cup (8 ounces) water
> 1 large egg, lightly beaten

● Prepare the Ginger Crisps cookie dough as directed.

● **To make the filling:** In a small saucepan set over medium heat combine all the ingredients except the egg. Bring the mixture to a boil, reduce the heat, and simmer for 15 minutes, until it has thickened. Remove from the heat and let cool.

● Preheat the oven to 350°F. Lightly grease (or line with parchment) two baking sheets.

● Remove one piece of dough from the refrigerator and roll it into a round about ⅛ inch thick. Cut the dough into 3-inch circles using a large cookie or biscuit cutter, or a clean, empty can. Transfer the circles to the prepared baking sheets. Brush each circle with some of the beaten egg, then top with 1 scant tablespoon of the filling.

● Remove the other piece of dough from the refrigerator and roll, cut out, and brush with egg as directed above. Center these circles atop the filled circles (egg-brushed side up), pressing the edges together with the tines of a fork. Use the fork to prick the top of each cookie, so steam can escape.

● Bake the cookies for 10 to 11 minutes, until they're set and beginning to brown. Remove them from the oven and transfer to a rack to cool.

Nutrition information per serving (1 cookie, 25 g): 49 cal, 1 g fat, 1 g protein, 6 g complex carbohydrates, 6 g sugar, 8 mg cholesterol, 26 mg sodium, 55 mg potassium, 4 RE vitamin A, 1 mg vitamin C, 7 mg calcium, 12 mg phosphorus.

Peanut Butter Cookies

If peanut butter was a welcome part of your diet growing up—PB&J sandwiches, peanut butter and crackers, peanut-buttered toast—then for nostalgic reasons, at least, you'll carry a certain fondness for peanut butter with you for the rest of your days. But as an adult, it's kind of . . . well, embarrassing to eat peanut butter sandwiches when all your colleagues at work are scarfing down Caesar salads or Thai chicken wraps. Enter the peanut butter cookie. That familiar deep-tan cookie with the crisscross top is sure to elicit smiles from your coworkers. And the smiles will grow wider if you've brought an entire batch of cookies, to share.

While it may feel as if peanut butter cookies have been around forever, their ascendancy to the level of Essential began only at the turn of the last century, when George Washington Carver promoted peanuts as an insect-resistant replacement for the American South's cotton crop. Carver published a book of recipes in 1916 that included crushed peanut cookies. But it wasn't until 1930—following the introduction of the first national brand of peanut butter, Peter Pan, in 1928—that the inaugural peanut butter cookie recipe, with its distinctive crisscross top, appeared in print.

Since then, peanut butter cookies have taken their place among the royalty of the cookie world. Some versions are soft, rather than crunchy; many pair peanut butter with chocolate, and some even go beyond the bounds of simple drop cookie, to roll-out or shaped. But no other version of peanut butter cookie can stand next to that original criss-cross version: the Essential Peanut Butter Cookie.

Store-bought is better

All of the cookies in this chapter have been tested using regular store-bought peanut butter—not low fat, not unsweetened, not all-natural or freshly ground or organic. Feel free to experiment with alternate types of peanut butter, but be aware that they may not give you the same results as we experienced.

THE ESSENTIALS

The Essential Peanut Butter Cookie

An all-time favorite (a.k.a. Peanut Butter Crisscrosses), this cookie is marked by its tic-tac-toe patterned top. These crunchy-tender cookies, whose peanut butter taste is enhanced by the occasional melting nugget of dark brown sugar, are best enjoyed with a glass of cold milk.

Yield: 4½ dozen cookies ● *Baking temperature: 350°F* ● *Baking time: 10 minutes*

1 cup (6½ ounces) vegetable shortening
1 cup (7 ounces) granulated sugar
1 cup (8 ounces) dark brown sugar
2 large eggs
1 teaspoon vanilla extract
2 teaspoons baking soda
½ teaspoon salt
1 cup (9½ ounces) creamy or crunchy peanut butter*
3 cups (12¾ ounces) unbleached all-purpose flour

● Preheat the oven to 350°F. Lightly grease (or line with parchment) two baking sheets.
● In a medium-sized bowl, cream together the shortening, sugars, eggs, vanilla, baking soda, salt, and peanut butter. Add the flour, stirring to combine.
● Drop the dough by the tablespoonful onto the prepared baking sheets. Press down each cookie with a fork to make a crisscross design. Bake the cookies for 10 minutes, or until they're lightly browned. Remove them from the oven and transfer to a rack to cool.

* See the sidebar on page 85 for a tip on measuring sticky ingredients.

Nutrition information per serving (1 cookie, 25 g): 113 cal, 6 g fat, 2 g protein, 5 g complex carbohydrates, 8 g sugar, 1 g dietary fiber, 8 mg cholesterol, 92 mg sodium, 56 mg potassium, 3 RE vitamin A, 1 mg iron, 4 mg calcium, 25 mg phosphorus.

The all-important crisscross

Though many cookie recipes call for you to flatten each ball of dough with the bottom of a drinking glass before baking, there are a select few that ask you to use the tines of a fork; the well-loved crunchy peanut butter cookie is foremost among these.

When flattening peanut butter cookie dough, lay the fork across the middle of the ball of dough and press down firmly, until it's about ⅓ inch thick. Remove the fork, rotate your hand 90 degrees, and press down across the cookie again, to make a tic-tac-toe pattern. If the fork starts to stick, just dip it in water. There are those who use a potato masher for this task, but we prefer the original fork method; why monkey with a proven good thing?

Peanut Butter Chews

Nicely soft and chewy, with just the faintest crunch around the edges, these cookies balance peanut butter flavor with the wonderful caramelized taste of dark brown sugar.

Yield: 5½ dozen cookies ● ***Baking temperature:*** *325°F* ● ***Baking time:*** *15 minutes*

1 cup (2 sticks, 8 ounces) unsalted butter
1 cup (8 ounces) dark brown sugar
½ cup (3½ ounces) granulated sugar
¼ cup (2¾ ounces) dark corn syrup
¾ teaspoon baking soda
1 teaspoon salt
2 teaspoons vanilla extract
2 large eggs
2 cups (19 ounces) creamy peanut butter
2 cups (8½ ounces) unbleached all-purpose flour

● Preheat the oven to 325°F. Lightly grease (or line with parchment) two baking sheets.
● In a medium-sized bowl, cream together the butter, sugars, corn syrup, baking soda, salt, and vanilla. Add the eggs one at a time, beating well after each addition. Add the peanut butter, beating until the mixture is light and fluffy. Stir in the flour.
● Drop the dough by the tablespoonful onto the prepared baking sheets. Bake the cookies for 15 minutes, until they're a light golden brown around the edges. Don't overbake or they'll be crisp, not soft. Remove them from the oven and transfer to a rack to cool.

Nutrition information per serving (1 cookie, 22 g): 104 cal, 7 g fat, 2 g protein, 3 g complex carbohydrates, 6 g sugar, 1 g dietary fiber, 13 mg cholesterol, 85 mg sodium, 68 mg potassium, 27 RE vitamin A, 4 mg calcium, 31 mg phosphorus.

Corn syrup: dark vs. light

Did you know that corn syrup—the thick, sticky syrup used in some cookies to keep them moist—is actually made from cornstarch? A multistep process converts cornstarch into a series of liquid sugars, which are then processed further and blended with other ingredients, including water and vanilla, to make the familiar light corn syrup. Dark corn syrup is simply light corn syrup to which some refiner's syrup or molasses (or, in some cases, caramel color) has been added; it has a light molasses flavor.

Which should you use? Does it make a difference? In cookies, not really, dark corn syrup will give your cookie a darker color. But seldom do you use enough of it in a cookie to add any distinct flavor.

When you're making chewy or soft cookies, and they're just not quite as soft and chewy as you'd like, try substituting 2 tablespoons corn syrup for 1½ tablespoons of the sugar in the recipe. The corn syrup helps prevent crystallization of the sugar in the cookie and also retains moisture, both of which will help keep cookies soft.

Old-Fashioned Peanut Cookies

Made with peanuts, as well as peanut butter, these cookies don't spread very much. Instead, they bake into tall, gently crunchy mounds, nicely flecked with the ground peanuts.

Yield: 3 dozen cookies ● *Baking temperature:* 350°F ● *Baking time:* 12 minutes

½ cup (1 stick, 4 ounces) unsalted butter
½ cup (4¾ ounces) peanut butter, crunchy or creamy
1 cup (8 ounces) brown sugar
2 teaspoons baking powder
2 teaspoons vanilla extract
½ teaspoon salt
2 large eggs
2 cups (8½ ounces) unbleached all-purpose flour
1 cup (5 ounces) salted peanuts, ground

● Preheat the oven to 350°F. Lightly grease (or line with parchment) two baking sheets.
● In a large bowl, cream together the butter, peanut butter, sugar, baking powder, vanilla, and salt. Beat in the eggs, then stir in the flour and peanuts.
● Drop the dough by the tablespoonful onto the prepared baking sheets. Bake the cookies for 12 minutes, until they're set and lightly browned. Remove them from the oven and transfer to a rack to cool.

Nutrition information per serving (1 cookie, 22 g): 91 cal, 4 g fat, 2 g protein, 5 g complex carbohydrates, 6 g sugar, 18 mg cholesterol, 76 mg sodium, 55 mg potassium, 28 RE vitamin A, 1 mg iron, 21 mg calcium, 29 mg phosphorus.

Peanut Butter Cutouts

Peanut butter cookie dough, when dropped onto a baking sheet, becomes fat and crunchy cookies. But when you roll out the dough, rather than drop it from a spoon, you reach the other extreme: thin and crisp. Roll them out just a bit thicker, and you've got crunchy again—but delicately crunchy, not the big, thick crunch of a drop cookie.

This mildly flavored peanut butter cookie is wonderful sandwiched around Chocolate Creme Filling (see page 470) or Peanut Butter Filling (see page 466). Or make sandwiches with your favorite complementary flavor of ice cream.

Yield: 5½ dozen cookies ● *Baking temperature: 350°F* ● *Baking time: 10 to 12 minutes*

½ cup (1 stick, 4 ounces) unsalted butter
½ cup (4¾ ounces) creamy peanut butter
1 cup (7 ounces) sugar
¾ teaspoon salt
½ teaspoon baking soda
2 teaspoons vanilla extract
1 large egg
¼ cup (2 ounces) heavy cream or sour cream (regular or low fat)
3 tablespoons (¾ ounce) cornstarch
3 cups (12¾ ounces) unbleached all-purpose flour

● In a medium-sized bowl, beat the butter, peanut butter, sugar, salt, baking soda, and vanilla until light and fluffy. Add the egg and beat well. Add half the cream, all of the cornstarch, and half the flour; beat well. Add the remaining cream and flour, mixing just until all the ingredients are well incorporated. Divide the dough in half, flatten each half slightly, and wrap well. Refrigerate for 1 hour or longer to facilitate rolling.
● Preheat the oven to 350°F. Lightly grease (or line with parchment) two baking sheets.
● Lightly dust both sides of the chilled dough with flour. If you've just taken it out of the refrigerator, let it rest at room temperature for 5 to 10 minutes.
● Transfer the dough to a lightly floured work surface. Roll each piece into a circle ⅛ to ¼ inch thick. Thinner cookies will be crisper, thicker cookies will be sturdier. Cut the dough into circles or shapes and transfer them to the prepared baking sheets.
● Bake the cookies for 10 to 12 minutes, until they're set but not browned. Remove them from the oven, and let them cool for 5 minutes on the baking sheet, then transfer to a rack to cool completely.

Nutrition information per serving (1 cookie, 14 g): 60 cal, 3 g fat, 1 g protein, 4 g complex carbohydrates, 3 g sugar, 8 mg cholesterol, 44 mg sodium, 22 mg potassium, 18 RE vitamin A, ! mg vitamin C, 1 mg calcium, 13 mg phosphorus.

Peanut Butter Spritz Cookies

Peanut butter cookies don't have to have a fork-tine crisscross on top. And spritz cookies don't have to be plain vanilla. These cookies are crisp and crunchy when piped into small shapes, chewy when made larger.

Yield: 7 dozen small cookies ● *Baking temperature: 375°F* ● *Baking time: 9 minutes*

½ cup (1 stick, 4 ounces) unsalted butter
1 cup (9½ ounces) creamy peanut butter
1 cup (8 ounces) brown sugar
¼ teaspoon salt
½ teaspoon baking soda
1 teaspoon vanilla extract
1 large egg
1¾ cups (7¼ ounces) unbleached all-purpose flour
Chocolate chips, nonpareils, and/or chocolate kisses, for decorating

● Preheat the oven to 375°F. If desired, for easier cleanup line two baking sheets with parchment (they don't need to be greased). If you're using a cookie press, place your baking sheets in the refrigerator or freezer while making the dough. Your cookies will deposit more easily onto a cold surface.
● In a large bowl, cream together the butter, peanut butter, sugar, salt, baking soda, and vanilla, scraping the bottom and sides of the bowl. Beat in the egg, then the flour.
● Place the dough in the barrel of a cookie press fitted with a large or small flower disk, and pipe it onto the prepared baking sheets. If you're not using a cookie press, drop the dough by the teaspoonful (a teaspoon cookie scoop works well here) onto the prepared baking sheets, then flatten it slightly with your fingers.
● Bake the cookies for 9 minutes, until they're set. Remove them from the oven and place your decoration of choice in the center of each cookie. Let the cookies cool on the pans for 5 minutes, then transfer them to a rack to cool completely.

Nutrition information per serving (1 cookie, 11 g): 49 cal, 3 g fat, 1 g protein, 2 g complex carbohydrates, 3 g sugar, 6 mg cholesterol, 32 mg sodium, 35 mg potassium, 12 RE vitamin A, 3 mg calcium, 15 mg phosphorus.

VARIATION

● For PB&J cookies, prepare the cookie dough and drop it by the teaspoonful onto the prepared baking sheets. Bake the cookies for 9 minutes, until they're set. Remove them from the oven and immediately use the top of an extract bottle (or other small, round bottle top) to press an indentation into each cookie. When cool, fill each indentation with a scant ½ teaspoon jelly or jam.

Peanut Blossoms

Peanut butter and chocolate is definitely one of our favorite flavor combinations. And not only do these cookies pair those flavors delightfully, they also look great, with their perky chocolate candy "caps."

Yield: 4 dozen cookies ● *Baking temperature:* 375°F ● *Baking time:* 10 minutes

½ cup (1 stick, 4 ounces) unsalted butter
¾ cup (7⅛ ounces) creamy peanut butter
⅓ cup (2¼ ounces) granulated sugar, plus more for coating the dough
⅓ cup (2¾ ounces) brown sugar
1 large egg
2 tablespoons (1 ounce) milk (regular or low fat, not nonfat)
1 teaspoon baking soda
½ teaspoon salt
1 teaspoon vanilla extract
1½ cups (6¼ ounces) unbleached all-purpose flour
48 chocolate kisses (7 ounces)

● Preheat the oven to 375°F. Lightly grease (or line with parchment) two baking sheets.
● In a large bowl, beat the butter and peanut butter together until well blended. Add the sugars and beat until light and fluffy. Add the egg, milk, baking soda, salt, and vanilla and beat well. Gradually mix in the flour.
● Shape the dough into 1-inch balls and roll them in granulated sugar. Place the balls on the prepared baking sheets.
● Bake the cookies for 10 minutes, until they're a very light golden brown. Remove them from the oven and immediately place one chocolate kiss atop each cookie, gently pressing it in. Transfer the cookies to a rack to cool completely.

Nutrition information per serving (1 cookie, 14 g): 64 cal, 4 g fat, 1 g protein, 2 g complex carbohydrates, 4 g sugar, 7 mg cholesterol, 53 mg sodium, 41 mg potassium, 14 RE vitamin A, 1 mg vitamin C, 8 mg calcium, 23 mg phosphorus, 1 mg caffeine.

Triple Play Peanut Butter Cookies

These cookies highlight the tempting flavor combination of salty peanuts and sweet brown sugar. And with peanuts, peanut butter, and peanut butter chips, we've got all the bases covered as far as America's favorite sandwich filling goes.

Yield: 6 dozen cookies ● *Baking temperature: 350°F* ● *Baking time: 14 minutes*

1 cup (2 sticks, 8 ounces) unsalted butter, very soft
1 cup (8 ounces) dark brown sugar
1 cup (7 ounces) granulated sugar
1¼ cups (11⅞ ounces) peanut butter, creamy or chunky
½ teaspoon baking powder
½ teaspoon baking soda
½ teaspoon salt
2 large eggs
2⅔ cups (11¼ ounces) unbleached all-purpose flour
1¼ cups (6¼ ounces) chopped, dry-roasted salted peanuts
1⅓ cups (8 ounces) peanut butter chips or chocolate chips

● Preheat the oven to 350°F. Lightly grease (or line with parchment) two baking sheets.
● In a large bowl, cream together the butter, sugars, peanut butter, baking powder, baking soda, and salt. Add the eggs one at a time, beating well after each addition. Stir in the flour, peanuts, and chips.
● Drop the dough by the tablespoonful onto the prepared baking sheets. Bake the cookies for 14 minutes, until they're set and brown around the edges. Remove them from the oven and cool on the pan for 5 minutes, then transfer to a rack to cool completely.

Nutrition information per serving (1 cookie, 22 g): 108 cal, 7 g fat, 2 g protein, 4 g complex carbohydrates, 5 g sugar, 1 g dietary fiber, 13 mg cholesterol, 67 mg sodium, 72 mg potassium, 26 RE vitamin A, 1 mg iron, 8 mg calcium, 34 mg phosphorus, 2 mg caffeine.

Scout's Honor PB Sandwiches

Seldom do you hear the words "Girl Scout" without "cookies" following shortly thereafter. And for good reason: American Girl Scouts have been selling their wonderful cookies since 1917. One of our favorites has always been the peanut butter–oatmeal sandwich cookie; here's our homemade rendition.

Yield: 32 sandwich cookies ● *Baking temperature: 350°F* ● *Baking time: 8 minutes*

DOUGH
- ⅓ cup (2¾ ounces) unsalted butter
- ⅔ cup (6¼ ounces) creamy peanut butter
- ⅓ cup (2¼ ounces) granulated sugar
- ⅔ cup (5¼ ounces) brown sugar
- ½ teaspoon baking soda
- ¼ teaspoon baking powder
- ½ teaspoon salt
- 1 teaspoon vanilla extract
- 1 large egg
- ¾ cup (3 ounces) unbleached all-purpose flour
- 1 cup (3½ ounces) rolled oats

FILLING
- 1 cup (9½ ounces) creamy peanut butter
- 1 tablespoon honey
- ¼ cup (1 ounce) confectioners' sugar

● Preheat the oven to 350°F. Lightly grease (or line with parchment) two baking sheets.
● **To make the dough:** In a large bowl, cream together the butter, peanut butter, sugars, baking soda, baking powder, salt, and vanilla. Add the egg, beating until light and fluffy. Stir in the flour and oats. Drop the dough by the heaping teaspoonful (a teaspoon cookie scoop works well here) onto the prepared baking sheets. Use the bottom of a drinking glass, lightly greased, to press each cookie to about ¼ inch thick.
● Bake the cookies for 8 minutes, or until they're a very light golden brown. Remove them from the oven and transfer to a rack to cool.
● **To make the filling:** In a small bowl, cream together the peanut butter, honey, and confectioners' sugar until smooth.
● **To assemble the cookies:** When the cookies are cool, spread half of them with the filling, or if you have a teaspoon cookie scoop, use it to drop the filling into mounds atop half the cookies. Top the filling with the remaining cookies, pressing together gently.

Nutrition information per serving (1 cookie, 32 g): 150 cal, 9 g fat, 4 g protein, 5 g complex carbohydrates, 10 g sugar, 1 g dietary fiber, 12 mg cholesterol, 122 mg sodium, 116 mg potassium, 22 RE vitamin A, 1 mg vitamin C, 1 mg iron, 9 mg calcium, 62 mg phosphorus.

How much filling?

Okay, you've made these great cookies and think they'd be over the top if you sandwiched them around, say, some chocolate ganache or vanilla cream filling. But how do you know how much filling to make?

First, count your cookies, then divide by two; remember, it takes two to make a sandwich. Then assess how much filling you want to use in each. A half-teaspoon of filling, on a typical 2- to 2½-inch diameter cookie, is probably the minimum you want; 1 teaspoon is average, and more than that is overstuffed. (To help in deciding, try making a sample sandwich cookie using peanut butter as filling, measuring the amount that seems right to you.)

Next, multiply what you've decided on (half-teaspoon, 1 teaspoon, 2 teaspoons) by the number of sandwiches you're making. Finally, look at the yield for the filling recipe and adjust it accordingly to match what you need.

Here's an example: You've made 48 cookies. You want to create 24 sandwich cookies, each stuffed with 1½ teaspoons filling. Multiply 24 times 1½ teaspoons to get 36 teaspoons. Divide 36 teaspoons by 3 to yield 12 tablespoons. Twelve tablespoons = ¾ cup, and that's how much filling you need (unless, of course, you need to make a little extra for "sampling").

Peanut-Chocolate Half-Moons

These tender, chewy-crunchy peanut butter cookies rise to new heights when gilded with rich chocolate icing.

Yield: 3 dozen cookies ● *Baking temperature: 375°F* ● *Baking time: 8 to 10 minutes*

DOUGH
½ cup (1 stick, 4 ounces) unsalted butter
1 cup (8 ounces) brown sugar
¼ teaspoon salt
1 teaspoon vanilla extract
½ teaspoon baking soda
1 large egg
½ cup (4¾ ounces) peanut butter, creamy or chunky
1 cup (4¼ ounces) unbleached all-purpose flour
1 cup (6 ounces) peanut butter chips, butterscotch chips, or chocolate chips, or a combination

ICING
1 cup (6 ounces) semisweet or bittersweet chocolate chips
2 tablespoons (1 ounce) unsalted butter
3 tablespoons (2 ounces) light corn syrup

● Preheat the oven to 375°F. Lightly grease (or line with parchment) two baking sheets.
● **To make the dough:** In a medium-sized mixing bowl, cream together the butter, brown sugar, salt, vanilla, and baking soda. Add the egg and beat until light and fluffy. Add the peanut butter, beating until well blended. Stir in the flour and chips, mixing slowly until the dough is cohesive.
● Drop the dough by the tablespoonful onto the prepared baking sheets; then flatten it slightly with your fingers. Bake the cookies for 8 to 10 minutes; they'll be soft, but will become crisp/chewy as they cool. Be careful not to overbake; they burn easily. Remove the cookies from the oven and transfer to a rack to cool completely.
● **To make the icing:** In a small bowl in the microwave, or in a saucepan set over low heat, melt the chocolate and butter, stirring until smooth. Stir in the corn syrup.
● Dip half of each cookie into the chocolate (to make a half-moon effect) and return the cookies to the cooling rack to set.

Nutrition information per serving (1 cookie, 29 g): 134 cal, 7 g fat, 2 g protein, 3 g complex carbohydrates, 12 g sugar, 14 mg cholesterol, 53 mg sodium, 77 mg potassium, 31 RE vitamin A, 1 mg iron, 9 mg calcium, 28 mg phosphorus, 7 mg caffeine.

Peanut Butter Pick-Me-Ups

Peanut butter and oats, dried fruit and nuts—these cookies pack a nice amount of fiber into a tasty little package. Take them on your next hike; they'll help generate the energy you need to climb that daunting 4,000-footer, or maybe even that 14,000-footer!

Yield: *34 cookies* ● **Baking temperature:** *350°F* ● **Baking time:** *12 minutes*

⅓ cup (2¾ ounces) unsalted butter
⅔ cup (5¼ ounces) dark brown sugar
½ cup (4¾ ounces) chunky peanut butter
½ teaspoon baking powder
½ teaspoon cinnamon
½ teaspoon ground ginger
½ teaspoon salt
1 large egg
½ cup (2 ounces) unbleached all-purpose flour
2 cups (8 ounces) granola
½ cup (2½ ounces) dry-roasted salted peanuts, very coarsely crushed
½ cup (3 ounces) raisins, dried cranberries, or dried cherries*

● Preheat the oven to 350°F. Lightly grease (or line with parchment) two baking sheets.
● In a large bowl, cream together the butter, brown sugar, peanut butter, baking powder, cinnamon, ginger, and salt. Add the egg, beating the mixture until it's smooth and fluffy. Stir in the flour, then the granola, nuts, and dried fruit.
● Drop the dough by the tablespoonful onto the prepared baking sheets, then flatten slightly with your fingers. Bake the cookies for 12 minutes, until they're lightly browned. Remove them from the oven and transfer to a rack to cool.

*Add dried fruit only if there isn't any in the granola.

Nutrition information per serving *(1 cookie, 26 g):* 120 cal, 7 g fat, 3 g protein, 8 g complex carbohydrates, 5 g sugar, 1 g dietary fiber, 11 mg cholesterol, 76 mg sodium, 116 mg potassium, 20 RE vitamin A, 1 mg vitamin C, 1 mg iron, 16 mg calcium, 59 mg phosphorus.

1-2-3-4 Peanut Butter Cookies

As in 1-2-3-4 ingredients, and 1) mix, 2) scoop, 3) bake, and 4) enjoy! These super-simple, super-fast cookies pack a powerful peanut butter punch. (And no, we're not missing an ingredient here—there's *no* flour in this recipe.)

Yield: 4 dozen cookies ● *Baking temperature:* 375°F ● *Baking time:* 10 minutes

> 1 cup (9½ ounces) creamy or chunky peanut butter
> 1 large egg
> 1 cup (7 ounces) sugar
> 1 teaspoon baking soda

● Preheat the oven to 375°F. Line two baking sheets with parchment (for easiest cleanup, but sheets can be left unlined, and ungreased, if you prefer).

● In a medium-sized bowl, beat together the peanut butter, egg, sugar, and baking soda until smooth. Drop the dough by the teaspoonful onto the prepared baking sheets.

● Bake the cookies for 10 minutes, or until they appear set. Remove them from the oven and cool on the pan for 5 minutes before transferring them to a rack to cool completely.

Nutrition information per serving (1 cookie, 11 g): 50 cal, 3 g fat, 2 g protein, 1 g complex carbohydrates, 5 g sugar, 4 mg cholesterol, 53 mg sodium, 37 mg potassium, 2 RE vitamin A, 1 mg calcium, 19 mg phosphorus.

Shortbread

Back to basics often connotes something plain,

unadorned and, frankly, boring. In this case, going back to basics takes us to the soul of cookiedom: shortbread. Composed solely of the building blocks of virtually every cookie (flour, sugar, butter, and salt), shortbread is a distillation of all that's delightful about cookies—their sweet, buttery taste and their distinctive texture (in this case, crisp and light).

Shortbread was born in Scotland, where it was made with oats and traditionally served at Christmas and New Year's. It was eventually embraced by Tudor England, whose bakers replaced the oats with wheat flour to make a cookie much like what we know today. Shortbread came to this country with the Colonists and has been a staple of the baker's kitchen ever since, appearing everywhere from the original 1896 Fannie Farmer cookbook, to shortbread Girl Scout cookies, the earliest flavor sold door-to-door by the Scouts.

Shortbread is a wonderful starting point for all kinds of sweet adventures: top it (with nuts, chocolate, jam, cinnamon), flavor it (with lemon, chocolate, ginger), or do both (cappuccino with a mocha ganache drizzle, anyone?). Then again, if you're a "make mine vanilla, please" kind of person, leave it alone; it can stand on its own in perfect simplicity.

The Essential Shortbread

Shortbread is one of the best proofs we know of the maxim "the whole is greater than its parts." Butter, sugar, salt, and flour, in just a few short steps, become crunchy, tender, delicious cookies through the alchemy of baking chemistry and oven heat. These cookies are truly effortless to prepare. With a bowl, a couple of cake pans, and about 45 minutes, you can have beautiful shortbreads, ready to serve. Bring on the Earl Grey!

Yield: 2 dozen shortbread wedges ● *Baking temperature: 300°F* ● *Baking time: 35 to 40 minutes*

1 cup (2 sticks, 8 ounces) unsalted butter
1 teaspoon salt
¾ cup (5¼ ounces) sugar
1 teaspoon vanilla extract (optional)
2⅓ cups (10 ounces) unbleached all-purpose flour

● Preheat the oven to 300°F. Lightly grease two 9-inch round cake pans.

● In a medium-sized bowl, cream together the butter, salt, sugar, and vanilla, then beat in the flour. The dough will be stiff. Divide the dough in half (each half will weigh about 12 ounces), and press it into the prepared pans, smoothing the surface with your fingers or the bottom of a measuring cup, as shown. Prick the dough with a fork in an attractive pattern.

The dough will feel stiff, but just keep pressing on it until you've covered the bottom of the pan.

A flat-bottomed measuring cup will help you smooth out the dough.

essential recipe

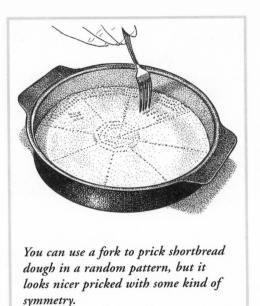

You can use a fork to prick shortbread dough in a random pattern, but it looks nicer pricked with some kind of symmetry.

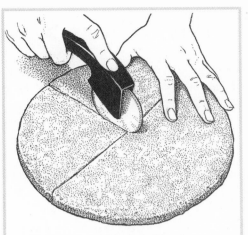

A rolling pizza wheel is the easiest, fastest way to cut warm shortbread into wedges.

- Bake the shortbread for 35 to 40 minutes, until it's golden brown around the edges. Remove it from the oven and loosen the edges with a heat-resistant plastic knife or table knife. Wait 5 minutes, then carefully turn the shortbread out onto a clean work surface, all in one piece.
- Using a pizza wheel, baker's bench knife, or sharp knife, cut each round into 12 wedges. (Do this while the shortbread is still warm; if you wait until it's cool, it won't cut easily.) Transfer the wedges to a rack to cool.

Nutrition information per serving (1 wedge, 28 g): 132 cal, 8 g fat, 1 g protein, 8 g complex carbohydrates, 6 g sugar, 21 mg cholesterol, 90 mg sodium, 17 mg potassium, 71 RE vitamin A, 1 mg iron, 2 mg calcium, 12 mg phosphorus.

Why is shortbread traditionally baked in a round pan?

In ancient Scotland, the winter solstice—the shortest day of the year—was marked by bonfires and the baking of round cakes, notched around the edges to symbolize the sun's rays. These cakes were a sweet entreaty to the sun to return and light up the cold, dark world. As time went on the cakes evolved into flat, crisp cookies—shortbread—that were still baked in the same shape as those original cakes. Nowadays, shortbread is baked as drop cookies, in square molds, or even rolled out and cut into fanciful shapes, but we like to honor its origins by baking it in a round cake pan and cutting it into triangular wedges. As always, there's a certain beauty in simplicity.

Go-Anywhere Shortbread

Of all the cookies in the cookie pantheon, shortbread is probably the best candidate for flavoring to your own taste. It's the perfect blank palette, awaiting the addition of your own favorite flavor, be it lemon, coffee, almond, or butter-rum!

Yield: 2 dozen shortbread wedges ● *Baking temperature: 300°F* ● *Baking time: 35 to 40 minutes*

1 cup (2 sticks, 8 ounces) unsalted butter
1 teaspoon salt
¾ cup (5¼ ounces) sugar
⅛ to ¼ teaspoon strong flavor, or 1 to 2 teaspoons extract, to taste
2⅓ cups (10 ounces) unbleached all-purpose flour

● Preheat the oven to 300°F. Lightly grease two 9-inch round cake pans.

● In a medium-sized bowl, cream together the butter, salt, sugar, and flavor or extract, then beat in the flour. Start with the smaller amount of flavor and add it to taste. The flavor will mellow somewhat with baking.

● Divide the dough in half, and press it into the prepared pans, smoothing the surface with your fingers. Prick the dough with a fork in an attractive pattern.

● Bake the shortbread for 35 to 40 minutes, until it's golden brown around the edges. Remove it from the oven and loosen the edges with a heat-resistant plastic knife or table knife. Wait 5 minutes, then carefully turn the shortbread out onto a clean work surface, all in one piece.

● Using a pizza wheel, baker's bench knife, or sharp knife, cut each round into 12 wedges. (Do this while the shortbread is still warm; if you wait until it's cool, it won't cut easily.) Transfer the wedges to a rack to cool.

Nutrition information per serving *(1 wedge, 28 g):* 132 cal, 8 g fat, 1 g protein, 8 g complex carbohydrates, 6 g sugar, 21 mg cholesterol, 90 mg sodium, 17 mg potassium, 71 RE vitamin A, 1 mg iron, 2 mg calcium, 12 mg phosphorus.

Chocolate Shortbread

But of course! Just because shortbread is the quintessential golden, buttery cookie doesn't mean that we can't make it in a chocolate version, too. These crisp chocolate cookies are wonderful as is, or ice them with Chocolate Ganache (page 460) for a killer chocolate treat.

Yield: 2 dozen shortbread wedges ● *Baking temperature: 300°F* ● *Baking time: 35 to 40 minutes*

> 1 cup (2 sticks, 8 ounces) unsalted butter
> 1 teaspoon salt
> 1 cup (7 ounces) sugar
> 1 teaspoon vanilla extract (optional)
> ⅓ cup (1 ounce) Dutch process cocoa
> ½ teaspoon baking powder
> 1¾ cups (7¼ ounces) unbleached all-purpose flour

● Preheat the oven to 300°F. Lightly grease two 9-inch round cake pans.

● In a medium-sized bowl, cream together the butter, salt, sugar, and vanilla, then beat in the cocoa, baking powder, and flour.

● Divide the dough in half and press it into the prepared pans, smoothing the surface with your fingers. Prick the dough with a fork in an attractive pattern.

● Bake the shortbread for 35 to 40 minutes, until it appears done around the edges. Remove it from the oven and loosen the edges with a heat-resistant plastic knife or table knife. Wait 5 minutes, then carefully turn the shortbread out onto a clean work surface, all in one piece.

● Using a pizza wheel, baker's bench knife, or sharp knife, cut each round into 12 wedges. (Do this while the shortbread is still warm; if you wait until it's cool, it won't cut easily.) Transfer the wedges to a rack to cool.

Nutrition information per serving (1 wedge, 26 g): 126 cal, 8 g fat, 1 g protein, 7 g complex carbohydrates, 6 g sugar, 1 g dietary fiber, 21 mg cholesterol, 101 mg sodium, 33 mg potassium, 71 RE vitamin A, 1 mg iron, 10 mg calcium, 21 mg phosphorus, 3 mg caffeine.

Chocolate Chip Shortbread

Chocolate and vanilla—let's get down to basics here, shall we? This elegant version of a chocolate chip cookie is subtle and understated, with the cookie playing the star's role while the chips are supporting actors.

Yield: 2 dozen shortbread wedges ● *Baking temperature:* 300°F ● *Baking time:* 35 to 40 minutes

> 1 cup (2 sticks, 8 ounces) unsalted butter
> 1 teaspoon salt
> ¾ cup (5¼ ounces) sugar
> 1 teaspoon vanilla extract (optional)
> 2⅓ cups (10 ounces) unbleached all-purpose flour
> 1 cup (6 ounces) chocolate chips

● Preheat the oven to 300°F. Lightly grease two 9-inch round cake pans.

● In a medium-sized bowl, cream together the butter, salt, sugar, and vanilla.

● Combine 1 cup of the flour and the chocolate chips in the workbowl of a food processor and process until the chocolate is chopped (you want the chocolate pieces to be small enough that they don't poke out of the dough, as they would in chocolate chip cookies, but large enough that you can still discern them as individual bits). Beat the remaining 1⅓ cups flour and the flour/chocolate mixture into the butter/sugar mixture until well combined.

● Divide the dough in half and press it into the prepared pans, smoothing the surface with your fingers. Prick the dough with a fork in an attractive pattern.

● Bake the shortbread for 35 to 40 minutes, until it's golden brown around the edges. Remove it from the oven and loosen the edges with a heat-resistant plastic knife or table knife. Wait 5 minutes, then carefully turn the shortbread out onto a clean work surface, all in one piece.

● Using a pizza wheel, baker's bench knife, or sharp knife, cut each round into 12 wedges. (Do this while the shortbread is still warm; if you wait until it's cool, it won't cut easily.) Transfer the wedges to a rack to cool.

Nutrition information per serving (1 wedge, 35 g): 168 cal, 10 g fat, 2 g protein, 9 g complex carbohydrates, 10 g sugar, 21 mg cholesterol, 90 mg sodium, 38 mg potassium, 71 RE vitamin A, 1 mg iron, 5 mg calcium, 20 mg phosphorus, 5 mg caffeine.

VARIATIONS

● Substitute the flavored chip of your choice for chocolate chips.

● Follow the Chocolate Shortbread recipe (page 113), adding chocolate chips.

Butter-Pecan Shortbread

Toasted pecans and a hint of butterscotch add great flavor to these cookies.

Yield: 2 dozen shortbread wedges ● ***Baking temperature:** 300°F* ● ***Baking time:** 35 to 40 minutes*

> 1 cup (2 sticks, 8 ounces) unsalted butter
> 1 teaspoon salt
> ¾ cup (5¼ ounces) sugar
> ⅛ to ¼ teaspoon strong butterscotch or butter-rum flavor, to taste
> 2⅓ cups (10 ounces) unbleached all-purpose flour
> 1 cup (4 ounces) chopped pecans, toasted (see page 27)

● Preheat the oven to 300°F. Lightly grease two 9-inch round cake pans.
● In a medium-sized bowl, cream together the butter, salt, sugar, and flavor. Start with ⅛ teaspoon of flavor and add it to taste. The flavor will mellow somewhat with baking. Beat in the flour and the pecans.
● Divide the dough in half and press it into the prepared pans, smoothing the surface with your fingers. Prick the dough with a fork in an attractive pattern.
● Bake the shortbread for 35 to 40 minutes, until it's golden brown around the edges. Remove it from the oven and loosen the edges with a heat-resistant plastic knife or table knife. Wait 5 minutes, then carefully turn the shortbread out onto a clean work surface, all in one piece.
● Using a pizza wheel, baker's bench knife, or sharp knife, cut each round into 12 wedges. (Do this while the shortbread is still warm; if you wait until it's cool, it won't cut easily.) Transfer the wedges to a rack to cool.

Nutrition information per serving (1 wedge, 32 g): 163 cal, 11 g fat, 2 g protein, 9 g complex carbohydrates, 6 g sugar, 1 g dietary fiber, 21 mg cholesterol, 90 mg sodium, 35 mg potassium, 72 RE vitamin A, 1 mg vitamin C, 1 mg iron, 4 mg calcium, 26 mg phosphorus.

Lemon Essences

For those of you whose taste runs to citrus, the snapping-fresh flavor of these cookies will brighten your day. Using the lesser amounts of lemon zest and lemon oil will give your short-bread a mild hint of lemon; the greater amount is more assertive. And you real lemon lovers can ice the cookies with Lemon Glaze (page 459), if desired.

Yield: 2 dozen shortbread wedges ● *Baking temperature:* 300°F ● *Baking time:* 35 to 40 minutes

1 cup (2 sticks, 8 ounces) unsalted butter
1 teaspoon salt
¾ cup (5¼ ounces) sugar
2 to 3 tablespoons grated lemon rind (zest)
3 to 5 drops lemon oil (optional)
2⅓ cups (10 ounces) unbleached all-purpose flour

● Preheat the oven to 300°F. Lightly grease two 9-inch round cake pans.
● In a medium-sized bowl, cream together the butter, salt, sugar, lemon zest, and lemon oil, then beat in the flour.
● Divide the dough in half and press it into the prepared pans, smoothing the surface with your fingers. Prick the dough with a fork in an attractive pattern.
● Bake the shortbread for 35 to 40 minutes, until it's golden brown around the edges. Remove it from the oven and loosen the edges with a heat-resistant plastic knife or table knife. Wait 5 minutes, then carefully turn the shortbread out onto a clean work surface, all in one piece.
● Using a pizza wheel, baker's bench knife, or sharp knife, cut each round into 12 wedges. (Do this while the shortbread is still warm; if you wait until it's cool, it won't cut easily.) Transfer the wedges to a rack to cool.

This really cuts it . . .

Whoops! You took the shortbread out of the oven and then the phone rang, you got busy . . . and you forgot to cut it while it was warm. No problem—simply slip the shortbread back into its pan or mold and bake it in a 350°F oven for 2 to 3 minutes. It will soften right up again, and cut without crumbling.

Nutrition information per serving (1 wedge, 28 g): 132 cal, 8 g fat, 1 g protein, 8 g complex carbohydrates, 6 g sugar, 21 mg cholesterol, 90 mg sodium, 18 mg potassium, 71 RE vitamin A, 1 mg vitamin C, 1 mg iron, 3 mg calcium, 13 mg phosphorus.

VARIATION
● For orange wedges, substitute orange zest and orange oil for the lemon zest and lemon oil.

Sweet Oatcakes

The nutty flavor of oats, enhanced with the mellow sweetness of brown sugar, enrich this twist on classic oatcakes. These cookies closely resemble a Scottish confection called flapjacks; slightly chewy when warm, they become nicely crumbly as they cool. Their deep-gold color and buttery aroma are reminiscent of butterscotch.

Yield: 2 dozen shortbread wedges ● *Baking temperature: 300°F* ● *Baking time: 35 to 40 minutes*

> 1 cup (2 sticks, 8 ounces) unsalted butter
> 1 teaspoon salt
> ¾ cup plus 2 tablespoons (7 ounces) brown sugar
> 1 teaspoon vanilla extract (optional)
> ¼ teaspoon baking soda
> 1½ cups (6¼ ounces) unbleached all-purpose flour
> 1 cup (3½ ounces) rolled oats, coarsely ground in a small food processor

● Preheat the oven to 300°F. Lightly grease two 9-inch round cake pans.

● In a medium-sized bowl, cream together the butter, salt, brown sugar, and vanilla. Beat in the baking soda, flour, and oats.

● Divide the dough in half and press it into the prepared pans, smoothing the surface with your fingers. Prick the dough with a fork in an attractive pattern.

● Bake the shortbread for 35 to 40 minutes, until it's golden brown around the edges. Remove it from the oven and loosen the edges with a heat-resistant plastic knife or table knife. Wait 5 minutes, then carefully turn the shortbread out onto a clean work surface, all in one piece.

● Using a pizza wheel, baker's bench knife, or sharp knife, cut each round into 12 wedges. (Do this while the shortbread is still warm; if you wait until it's cool, it won't cut easily.) Transfer the wedges to a rack to cool.

Nutrition information per serving (1 wedge, 23 g): 113 cal, 8 g fat, 1 g protein, 8 g complex carbohydrates, 1 g sugar, 1 g dietary fiber, 21 mg cholesterol, 104 mg sodium, 29 mg potassium, 72 RE vitamin A, 1 mg iron, 5 mg calcium, 28 mg phosphorus.

Filled Double Shortbread

Though it's quite a bit fussier to make than regular shortbread wedges, filled shortbread is both tasty and good-looking. Choose your favorite thick fruit jam or preserve for filling (raspberry or apricot are our favorites); if you're an almond lover, almond paste is a nice option (see variations).

Yield: 2 dozen filled shortbread wedges ● ***Baking temperature:*** *300°F* ● ***Baking time:*** *40 to 50 minutes*

1 cup (2 sticks, 8 ounces) unsalted butter
1 teaspoon salt
¾ cup (5¼ ounces) sugar
1 teaspoon vanilla extract (optional)
2⅓ cups (10 ounces) unbleached all-purpose flour
6 tablespoons (4½ ounces) jam or preserves

● Preheat the oven to 300°F. Lightly grease two 8-inch round cake pans.

● In a medium-sized bowl, cream together the butter, salt, sugar, and vanilla, then beat in the flour.

● Divide the dough into four pieces, each about 6 ounces. Stretch a piece of plastic wrap to cover the outside bottom of an 8-inch round cake pan. Press one of the pieces of dough onto the plastic until it covers the bottom of the pan entirely (see box below, left). Remove the plastic and dough, fold the plastic to cover the dough, and refrigerate it while you repeat the process with a second piece of dough. Refrigerate the second piece, too.

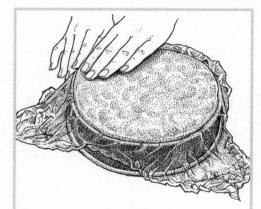

Gently press shortbread dough to cover the bottom of the plastic-wrapped pan.

Turn the dough over so the plastic is on top, and you're cradling it in your hand. Slide it onto the filled dough in the pan, peeling off the plastic.

● Press the remaining two pieces of dough into the bottoms of the prepared cake pans. Spread the dough in each pan with about 3 tablespoons of the jam or preserves, leaving a ½-inch bare border around the edges. Take a circle of the chilled shortbread dough and position it atop the shortbread in the pan (see box opposite, right). Gently push down around the edges to seal. Using a fork, pierce through all three layers—shortbread, filling, shortbread—in several places, to allow steam to escape as the shortbread bakes. Repeat with the remaining dough and jam.

- Bake the filled shortbread for 45 to 50 minutes, or until it's golden brown. Remove it from the oven and loosen the edges with a heat-resistant plastic knife or table knife. Let cool in the pan for 10 minutes. Turn the shortbread out of the pan onto a clean work surface, all in one piece, and cool for an additional 5 minutes before cutting into wedges. Transfer the wedges to a rack to cool.

Nutrition information per serving (*1 wedge, 32 g):* 143 cal, 8 g fat, 1 g protein, 9 g complex carbohydrates, 9 g sugar, 21 mg cholesterol, 92 mg sodium, 20 mg potassium, 71 RE vitamin A, 1 mg vitamin C, 1 mg iron, 3 mg calcium, 13 mg phosphorus.

VARIATIONS

- For almond-filled shortbread, use about 1 cup almond paste. Knead it gently to soften and divide it in half. Dust a clean work surface and rolling pin with flour and roll each piece of paste into a 7½-inch circle. Lay one circle atop the shortbread dough in each pan. Bake as directed above, decreasing the baking time by 5 minutes, to about 40 minutes.
- Fill one shortbread with jam, the other with almond paste. Or try two different flavors of jam. Since you're making two pans of shortbread anyway, there's no use wasting the opportunity to experiment with different flavor combinations.

Freckled Fruit Shortbread

This lovely speckled shortbread features the tang of dried fruit, a nice complement to the cookie's buttery sweetness. Because of the moistness of the fruit, this cookie is nicely chewy, rather than crisp.

Yield: 2 dozen shortbread wedges ● *Baking temperature: 300°F* ● *Baking time: 35 to 40 minutes*

> 1 cup (2 sticks, 8 ounces) unsalted butter
> 1 teaspoon salt
> ¾ cup (5¼ ounces) sugar
> 1 teaspoon vanilla extract (optional)
> 2⅓ cups (10 ounces) unbleached all-purpose flour
> ⅔ cup (3½ ounces) dried fruit of your choice (cranberries, apricots, dates, raisins, cherries, etc.)

● Preheat the oven to 300°F. Lightly grease two 9-inch round cake pans.

● In a medium-sized bowl, cream together the butter, salt, sugar, and vanilla. Combine 1 cup of the flour and the dried fruit in the bowl of a food processor equipped with the steel blade. Process until the fruit is finely minced; this may take up to 1 minute. Add this mixture and the remaining 1⅓ cups flour to the butter/sugar mixture, beating until well combined.

● Divide the dough in half and press it into the prepared pans, smoothing the surface with your fingers. Prick the dough with a fork in an attractive pattern.

● Bake the shortbread for 35 to 40 minutes, until it's golden brown around the edges. Remove it from the oven and loosen the edges with a heat-resistant plastic knife or table knife. Wait 5 minutes, then carefully turn the shortbread out onto a clean work surface, all in one piece.

● Using a pizza wheel, baker's bench knife, or sharp knife, cut each round into 12 wedges. (Do this while the shortbread is still warm; if you wait until it's cool, it won't cut easily.) Transfer the wedges to a rack to cool.

Nutrition information per serving (1 wedge, 32 g): 143 cal, 8 g fat, 1 g protein, 11 g complex carbohydrates, 6 g sugar, 1 g dietary fiber, 21 mg cholesterol, 93 mg sodium, 56 mg potassium, 89 RE vitamin A, 1 mg iron, 4 mg calcium, 15 mg phosphorus.

VARIATION

● For ginger shortbread, substitute 1 teaspoon ground ginger for the vanilla extract, and use ⅔ cup finely chopped crystallized ginger in place of the dried fruit.

Maple Shortbread

If maple's a flavor you gravitate toward, try these shortbreads; maple not only perfumes the dough, but also adds crunch and flavor to the top and bottom crusts.

Yield: 2 dozen shortbread wedges ● *Baking temperature: 300°F* ● *Baking time: 35 to 40 minutes*

¾ cup (4 ounces) maple sugar (see page 480)
1 cup (2 sticks, 8 ounces) unsalted butter
1 teaspoon salt
¼ cup (1¾ ounces) granulated sugar
1 to 2 teaspoons maple extract, or ⅛ to ¼ teaspoon strong maple flavor, to taste
1 teaspoon vanilla extract (optional)
2⅓ cups (10 ounces) unbleached all-purpose flour

● Preheat the oven to 300°F. Lightly grease two 9-inch round cake pans. Sprinkle each pan with 1 tablespoon of the maple sugar.
● In a medium-sized bowl, cream together the butter, salt, granulated sugar, ½ cup of the maple sugar, maple extract, and vanilla, then beat in the flour.
● Divide the dough in half and press it into the prepared pans, smoothing the surface with your fingers. Sprinkle each round with 1 tablespoon of the remaining maple sugar, pressing it in gently. Prick the dough with a fork in an attractive pattern.
● Bake the shortbread for 35 to 40 minutes, until it's golden brown around the edges. Remove it from the oven and loosen the edges with a heat-resistant plastic knife or table knife. Wait 5 minutes, then carefully turn the shortbread out onto a clean work surface, all in one piece.
● Using a pizza wheel, baker's bench knife, or sharp knife, cut each round into 12 wedges. (Do this while the shortbread is still warm; if you wait until it's cool, it won't cut easily.) Transfer the wedges to a rack to cool.

Nutrition information per serving (1 wedge, 30 g): 136 cal, 8 g fat, 1 g protein, 8 g complex carbohydrates, 7 g sugar, 21 mg cholesterol, 90 mg sodium, 32 mg potassium, 71 RE vitamin A, 1 mg iron, 7 mg calcium, 13 mg phosphorus.

VARIATION

● For maple-walnut shortbread, add ⅔ cup chopped walnuts to the shortbread dough, along with the flour.

Chai Shortbread

Chai, a heady blend of spices (typically including cinnamon, anise, cloves, ginger, and vanilla, plus honey and tea) makes a hot brew with lots of flavor. That same flavor translates beautifully to shortbread.

*Yield: 2 dozen shortbread wedges ● **Baking temperature:** 300°F ● **Baking time:** 35 to 40 minutes*

> 1 cup (2 sticks, 8 ounces) unsalted butter
> 1 teaspoon salt
> ¼ cup (1¾ ounces) sugar
> ½ cup (3½ ounces) dry chai drink mix
> 1 teaspoon vanilla extract (optional)
> 2⅓ cups (10 ounces) unbleached all-purpose flour

● Preheat the oven to 300°F. Lightly grease two 9-inch round cake pans and sprinkle 1 tablespoon of the chai mix in the bottom of each.

● In a medium-sized bowl, cream together the butter, salt, sugar, ¼ cup of the chai mix, and vanilla, then beat in the flour.

● Divide the dough in half and press it into the pans; sprinkle each round with 1 tablespoon of the remaining chai mix. Prick the dough with a fork in an attractive pattern.

● Bake the shortbread for 35 to 40 minutes, until it's golden brown around the edges. Remove it from the oven and loosen the edges with a heat-resistant plastic knife or table knife. Wait 5 minutes, then carefully turn the shortbread out onto a clean work surface, all in one piece.

● Using a pizza wheel, baker's bench knife, or sharp knife, cut each round into 12 wedges. (Do this while the shortbread is still warm; if you wait until it's cool, it won't cut easily.) Transfer the wedges to a rack to cool.

Nutrition information per serving (1 wedge, 28 g): 132 cal, 8 g fat, 1 g protein, 8 g complex carbohydrates, 6 g sugar, 21 mg cholesterol, 90 mg sodium, 17 mg potassium, 71 RE vitamin A, 1 mg iron, 2 mg calcium, 12 mg phosphorus.

Tweed Cakes

These chewy, golden cookies, generously studded with dark toffee bits, will remind you of brown tweed (in appearance only). The caramelized sugar in the toffee is delightful when played out against the plain, buttery goodness of the cookies.

Yield: 2 dozen shortbread wedges ● *Baking temperature:* 300°F ● *Baking time:* 35 to 40 minutes

> 1 cup (2 sticks, 8 ounces) unsalted butter
> 1 teaspoon salt
> ¾ cup (5¼ ounces) sugar
> 1 teaspoon vanilla extract (optional)
> 2⅓ cups (10 ounces) unbleached all-purpose flour
> 1½ cups (7⅝ ounces) crushed toffee bits

● Preheat the oven to 300°F. Lightly grease two 9-inch round cake pans.

● In a medium-sized bowl, cream together the butter, salt, sugar, and vanilla, then beat in the flour and toffee bits.

● Divide the dough in half and press it into the prepared pans, smoothing the surface with your fingers. Prick the dough with a fork in an attractive pattern.

● Bake the shortbread for 35 to 40 minutes, until it's golden brown around the edges. Remove it from the oven and loosen the edges with a heat-resistant plastic knife or table knife. Wait 5 minutes, then carefully turn the shortbread out onto a clean work surface, all in one piece.

● Using a pizza wheel, baker's bench knife, or sharp knife, cut each round into 12 wedges. (Do this while the shortbread is still warm; if you wait until it's cool, it won't cut easily.) Transfer the wedges to a rack to cool.

Nutrition information per serving (1 wedge, 37 g): 182 cal, 11 g fat, 2 g protein, 9 g complex carbohydrates, 11 g sugar, 1 g dietary fiber, 26 mg cholesterol, 118 mg sodium, 44 mg potassium, 71 RE vitamin A, 1 mg iron, 7 mg calcium, 17 mg phosphorus, 1 mg caffeine.

Fancy, bite-sized shortbread cookies

Want to turn shortbread dough into a plateful of festive-looking, bite-sized cookies? Simply break off teaspoon-sized pieces of the dough and roll them into balls about ¾-inch in diameter. Dip each in an egg white wash (made from 1 egg white whisked with 1 tablespoon cold water). Then roll the balls in finely chopped nuts, cinnamon sugar, ginger sugar (ground ginger mixed with granulated sugar, to taste), chocolate sugar (cocoa powder mixed with granulated sugar), or shredded coconut. Place the cookies on lightly greased or parchment-lined baking sheets and flatten them to ¼ inch thick with the bottom of a drinking glass. Bake them in a preheated 300°F oven for 25 minutes, until they appear set and are brown on the bottom. Remove them from the oven and cool on a rack.

Brickle 'Bread

This recipe uses toffee bits as a topping, rather than an integral part of the dough. You'll find these cookies have stronger flavor, and a "crisp cookie, chewy topping" texture, rather than chewy all the way through, as are the Tweed Cakes on the previous page.

Yield: 2 dozen shortbread wedges ● Baking temperature: 300°F ● Baking time: 35 to 40 minutes

> 1 cup (2 sticks, 8 ounces) unsalted butter
> 1 teaspoon salt
> ¾ cup (5¼ ounces) sugar
> 1 teaspoon vanilla extract (optional)
> 2⅓ cups (10 ounces) unbleached all-purpose flour
> 1½ cups (7⅝ ounces) crushed toffee bits

● Preheat the oven to 300°F. Lightly grease two 9-inch round cake pans.

● In a medium-sized bowl, cream together the butter, salt, sugar, and vanilla, then beat in the flour.

● Divide the dough in half, and press it into the prepared pans, smoothing the surface with your fingers. Prick the dough with a fork in an attractive pattern.

● Bake the shortbread for 15 minutes. Remove the pans from the oven and generously cover the top of the dough with a ¼-inch layer of crushed toffee bits, pressing them in gently. Return the shortbread to the oven and bake until it's a light golden brown at the edges, about 20 minutes. Remove it from the oven and loosen the edges with a heat-resistant plastic knife or table knife. Wait 5 minutes, then carefully turn the shortbread out onto a clean work surface, all in one piece.

● Using a pizza wheel, baker's bench knife, or sharp knife, cut each round into 12 wedges. (Do this while the shortbread is still warm; if you wait until it's cool, it won't cut easily.) Transfer the wedges to a rack to cool.

Nutrition information per serving (1 wedge, 37 g): 182 cal, 11 g fat, 2 g protein, 9 g complex carbohydrates, 11 g sugar, 1 g dietary fiber, 26 mg cholesterol, 118 mg sodium, 44 mg potassium, 71 RE vitamin A, 1 mg iron, 7 mg calcium, 17 mg phosphorus, 1 mg caffeine.

VARIATION

● Bake the shortbread for 35 minutes and turn it out of the pan. Turn it right side up and sprinkle with the toffee bits, pressing them in gently. This will make a cookie that's crisp all the way through.

Black and White Shortbread

If your usual behavior at the Christmas cookie exchange is to make a beeline for the chocolate, you'll love these cookies. With white chocolate icing on one side, dark on the other, they're pretty to look at, as well as delicious.

Yield: 2 dozen shortbread wedges ● *Baking temperature: 300°F* ● *Baking time: 35 to 40 minutes*

1 cup (2 sticks, 8 ounces) unsalted butter
1 teaspoon salt
¾ cup (5¼ ounces) sugar
1 teaspoon vanilla extract (optional)
2⅓ cups (10 ounces) unbleached
    all-purpose flour
Chocolate Ganache (page 460)
White Chocolate Ganache (page 461)

● Preheat the oven to 300°F. Lightly grease two 9-inch round cake pans.

● In a medium-sized bowl, cream together the butter, salt, sugar, and vanilla, then beat in the flour.

● Divide the dough in half, and press it into the prepared pans, smoothing the surface with your fingers. Prick the dough with a fork in an attractive pattern.

● Bake the shortbread for 35 to 40 minutes, until it's golden brown around the edges. Remove it from the oven and loosen the edges with a heat-resistant plastic knife or table knife. Wait 5 minutes, then carefully turn the shortbread out onto a clean work surface, all in one piece.

● Using a pizza wheel, baker's bench knife, or sharp knife, cut each round into 12 wedges. (Do this while the shortbread is still warm; if you wait until it's cool, it won't cut easily.) Place the wedges on a rack set on a piece of parchment paper.

● Spread the chocolate ganache on one side of the cookies and place them on the rack to set. When the chocolate has hardened enough for you to handle the cookies easily, spread the white chocolate ganache on the other sides and return to the rack to set.

Nutrition information per serving (1 wedge 44 g):
207 cal, 13 g fat, 2 g protein, 10 g complex carbohydrates, 11 g sugar, 1 g dietary fiber, 30 mg cholesterol, 93 mg sodium, 48 mg potassium, 101 RE vitamin A, 1 mg vitamin C, 1 mg iron, 7 mg calcium, 27 mg phosphorus, 4 mg caffeine.

No matter what shape you're in...

Shortbread is lovely baked in a patterned stoneware shortbread mold. An 8-inch round or square shortbread mold will hold the same amount of dough as a 9-inch round cake pan; follow the baking directions that come with the mold. Shortbread dough also can be rolled into 1½-inch balls, placed on lightly greased (or parchment-lined) baking sheets, and flattened to ¼-inch with the bottom of a drinking glass, or pressed with a cookie stamp. Bake the cookies in a preheated 350°F oven for 10 to 12 minutes, until they're barely beginning to brown around the edges.

Use a cookie stamp to gently press each ball of dough to about ¼ inch. The imprint will remain in the dough as it bakes.

Demerara Shortbread

Demerara sugar, a coarse, golden brown, large-crystal raw sugar native to Guyana, gives these cookies both sparkle and rich taste. If you can't find it in your supermarket, Demerara (or other coarse-crystal brown sugars) can often be found with coffee supplies in gourmet shops. It's also available via mail order.

Yield: 3½ dozen shortbread cookies • *Baking temperature:* 300°F • *Baking time:* 20 minutes

1 cup (2 sticks, 8 ounces) unsalted butter
1 teaspoon salt
¾ cup (5¼ ounces) granulated sugar
1 teaspoon vanilla extract (optional)
2⅓ cups (10 ounces) unbleached all-purpose flour
1 large egg white, lightly beaten with 1 tablespoon water
¼ cup (2 ounces) Demerara sugar

- In a medium-sized bowl, cream together the butter, salt, sugar, and vanilla, then beat in the flour.
- Shape the dough into a log that is 1½ inches in diameter. Brush the log all over with the beaten egg white and roll it in the Demerara sugar. Wrap the log and chill it until firm, at least 1 hour.
- Preheat the oven to 300°F. Lightly grease (or line with parchment) two baking sheets.
- Remove the dough from the refrigerator and slice it into ¼-inch-thick rounds. Bake the cookies for 20 minutes, or until they're a light golden brown around the edges. Remove them from the oven and transfer to a rack to cool.

Nutrition information per serving (1 cookie, 42 g): 80 cal, 4 g fat, 1 g protein, 5 g complex carbohydrates, 5 g sugar, 12 mg cholesterol, 53 mg sodium, 15 mg potassium, 41 RE vitamin A, 2 mg calcium, 7 mg phosphorus.

VARIATION

- For a more substantial cookie, slice the dough ½ inch thick and bake the cookies for 30 minutes.

Toasted Pecan—Fudge Shortbread

The cookie equivalent of candy's toffee buttercrunch, this shortbread is topped with a thick drizzle of deep dark chocolate and a shower of toasted nuts.

Yield: 2 dozen shortbread wedges ● *Baking temperature:* 300°F ● *Baking time:* 35 to 40 minutes

DOUGH
- 1 cup (2 sticks, 8 ounces) unsalted butter
- 1 teaspoon salt
- ¾ cup (5¼ ounces) sugar
- 1 teaspoon vanilla extract (optional)
- 2⅓ cups (10 ounces) unbleached all-purpose flour

GLAZE
- 1½ cups (9 ounces) chocolate chips or chopped bittersweet chocolate
- 2 tablespoons (1¼ ounces) light corn syrup
- ½ cup (4 ounces) heavy or whipping cream
- ½ cup (2 ounces) chopped pecans, toasted (see page 27)

● Preheat the oven to 300°F. Lightly grease two 9-inch round cake pans.
● **To make the dough:** In a medium-sized bowl, cream together the butter, salt, sugar, and vanilla, then beat in the flour.
● Divide the dough in half and press it into the prepared pans, smoothing the surface with your fingers. Prick the dough with a fork in an attractive pattern.
● Bake the shortbread for 35 to 40 minutes, until it's golden brown around the edges. Remove it from the oven and loosen the edges with a heat-resistant plastic knife or table knife. Wait 5 minutes, then carefully turn the shortbread out onto a clean work surface, all in one piece.
● Using a pizza wheel, baker's bench knife, or sharp knife, cut each round into 12 wedges. (Do this while the shortbread is still warm; if you wait until it's cool, it won't cut easily.) Transfer the wedges to a rack to cool.
● **To make the glaze:** In a microwave-safe bowl, or in a saucepan set over low heat, combine the chocolate, corn syrup, and cream, stirring until the chocolate has melted. Remove from the heat source and continue to stir until the mixture is very smooth. The chocolate may seem to be an unmanageable blob at first; that's okay, just keep stirring.
● Spread the glaze on one side of each shortbread wedge, and immediately sprinkle with the toasted pecans. Allow the chocolate to set before wrapping the shortbreads for storage.

Nutrition information per serving (1 wedge, 47 g): 225 cal, 14 g fat, 2 g protein, 11 g complex carbohydrates, 12 g sugar, 1 g dietary fiber, 27 mg cholesterol, 93 mg sodium, 59 mg potassium, 91 RE vitamin A, 1 mg vitamin C, 1 mg iron, 6 mg calcium, 33 mg phosphorus, 4 mg caffeine.

Petticoat Tails

There's some argument about the origin of the name for this traditional Scottish shortbread. One school says it derives from the way the cookies are shaped, like a petticoat with a hoop. Another, remembering Scotland's old alliance with France, says that the name is a corruption of *petite gatelles,* meaning small cakes. Wherever the whimsical name sprang from, the cookies themselves—buttery, not overly sweet, and attractively shaped—add European panache to any dessert buffet. They pair especially well with fresh fruit.

Note that caraway seeds are very often called for in older recipes for petticoat tails. If you're not a caraway fan, we recommend using 2 teaspoons vanilla extract instead.

Yield: 20 shortbread cookies ● *Baking temperature: 325°F* ● *Baking time: 20 to 25 minutes*

¾ cup (1½ sticks, 6 ounces) unsalted butter
1 cup (4 ounces) confectioners' sugar
1 teaspoon salt
2½ cups (10½ ounces) unbleached all-purpose flour
2 tablespoons (1 ounce) milk (regular or low fat)
1 tablespoon caraway seeds (optional)

● In a large mixing bowl, cream together the butter, sugar, and salt. Add the flour gradually, scraping the bowl down at least once. The mixture will look crumbly in the bowl. Add the milk and caraway seeds and continue mixing until the dough comes together; this will take about 90 seconds. Once the dough forms, take it out of the mixing bowl, pat it into a disk, wrap it, and refrigerate for 1 hour.

● Remove the dough from the refrigerator and preheat the oven to 325°F. Lightly grease (or line with parchment) two baking sheets.

● Roll the dough into a circle about ¼ inch thick and 12 inches in diameter. To shape cookies in their traditional manner, flute the outside rim of the circle as you would the edge of a pie crust, with your fingers, so it looks like the ruffled edge of a petticoat. Cut out a circle about 4½ inches in diameter from the center of the dough, and set it aside. (See top illustration, opposite.)

● Using a long, sharp knife cut the large circle into quarters, then cut each quarter into four wedges. Transfer the cookies to the prepared baking sheets. Flute the edge of the small reserved circle, and either place it whole, or cut into quarters, on the baking sheet with the rest of the dough (see bottom illustrations, opposite).

● Bake the cookies for 20 to 25 minutes, until they're golden brown. Remove them from the oven and transfer to a rack to cool.

Nutrition information per serving (1 cookie, 31 g): 136 cal, 7 g fat, 2 g protein, 11 g complex carbohydrates, 6 g sugar, 1 g dietary fiber, 19 mg cholesterol, 108 mg sodium, 27 mg potassium, 65 RE vitamin A, 1 mg vitamin C, 1 mg iron, 6 mg calcium, 18 mg phosphorus.

SHAPING AND CUTTING PETTICOAT TAILS

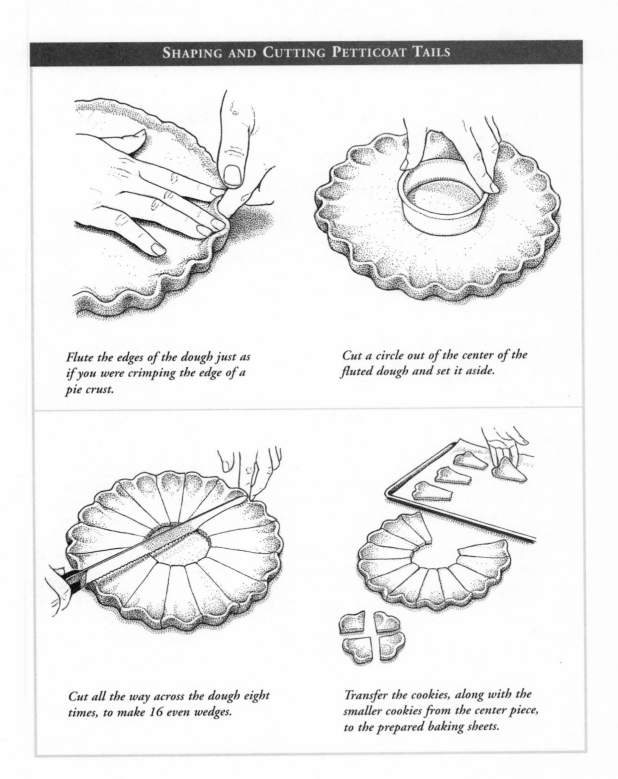

Flute the edges of the dough just as if you were crimping the edge of a pie crust.

Cut a circle out of the center of the fluted dough and set it aside.

Cut all the way across the dough eight times, to make 16 even wedges.

Transfer the cookies, along with the smaller cookies from the center piece, to the prepared baking sheets.

Cinnamon-Caramel Swirl Shortbread

Cinnamon and caramel, together? They laughed when we set these down on the test kitchen table . . . but simply smiled when they tasted this unusual, but perfectly matched combination of flavors.

Yield: 2 dozen shortbread wedges ● *Baking temperature:* 300°F ● *Baking time:* 35 to 40 minutes

> ¼ cup (1¾ ounces) cinnamon sugar
>
> DOUGH
>
> 1 cup (2 sticks, 8 ounces) unsalted butter
> 1 teaspoon salt
> ¾ cup (5¼ ounces) sugar
> 1 teaspoon vanilla extract (optional)
> 2⅓ cups (10 ounces) unbleached all-purpose flour
>
> TOPPING
>
> 14 to 16 (5 ounces) vanilla caramel candies
> 1 tablespoon cream or milk (regular or low fat)

● Preheat the oven to 300°F. Lightly grease two 9-inch round cake pans. Sprinkle the bottom of each pan with about 1 tablespoon cinnamon sugar.

● **To make the dough:** In a medium-sized bowl, cream together the butter, salt, sugar, and vanilla, then beat in the flour. Divide the dough in half, and press it into the prepared pans, smoothing the surface with your fingers. Sprinkle the top of both rounds of dough with the remaining cinnamon sugar. Prick the dough with a fork in an attractive pattern.

● Bake the shortbread for 35 to 40 minutes, until it's golden brown around the edges. Remove it from the oven and loosen the edges with a heat-resistant plastic knife or table knife. Wait 5 minutes, then carefully turn the shortbread out onto a clean work surface, all in one piece.

● Using a pizza wheel, baker's bench knife, or sharp knife, cut each round into 12 wedges. (Do this while the shortbread is still warm; if you wait until it's cool, it won't cut easily.) Transfer the wedges to a rack to cool.

● **To make the topping:** Heat the caramels and milk in a microwave-safe bowl, or in a saucepan set over low heat. Stir until the caramels melt and the mixture is smooth. Drizzle the topping over the cooled shortbread wedges. If it becomes too thick to drizzle, reheat briefly. Allow the caramel to set before wrapping the shortbreads for storage.

Nutrition information per serving (1 wedge, 36 g): 161 cal, 8 g fat, 2 g protein, 9 g complex carbohydrates, 12 g sugar, 1 g dietary fiber, 21 mg cholesterol, 105 mg sodium, 33 mg potassium, 72 RE vitamin A, 1 mg vitamin C, 1 mg iron, 18 mg calcium, 20 mg phosphorus.

Your Favorite Jammies

Though reminiscent of a linzer cookie, those jam-sandwiched holiday cutouts, these cookies are much easier to make. When selecting your jam or preserve, make sure it's fairly stiff and substantial; grape jelly isn't a good choice.

Yield: 22 shortbread wedges ● *Baking temperature:* 300°F ● *Baking time:* 35 to 40 minutes

> 1 cup (2 sticks, 8 ounces) unsalted butter
> 1 teaspoon salt
> ¾ cup (5¼ ounces) sugar
> 1 teaspoon vanilla extract (optional)
> 2⅓ cups (10 ounces) unbleached all-purpose flour
> 1¼ cups (14½ ounces) jam or preserves

● Preheat the oven to 300°F. Lightly grease two 9-inch round cake pans.

● In a medium-sized bowl, cream together the butter, salt, sugar, and vanilla, then beat in the flour. Divide the dough in half, and press it into the prepared pans, smoothing the surface with your fingers. Prick the dough with a fork in an attractive pattern.

● Bake the shortbread for 35 to 40 minutes, until it's golden brown around the edges. Remove it from the oven and loosen the edges with a heat-resistant plastic knife or table knife. Wait 5 minutes, then carefully turn the shortbread out onto a clean work surface, all in one piece.

● Using a pizza wheel, baker's bench knife, or sharp knife, cut each round into 12 wedges. (Do this while the shortbread is still warm; if you wait until it's cool, it won't cut easily.) Transfer the wedges to a rack to cool.

● Crumble two of the shortbread wedges into a small bowl and set aside. Spread the remaining wedges with a thick layer of jam. Sprinkle the reserved crumbs lightly over the jam.

Nutrition information per serving (1 wedge, 43 g): 175 cal, 8 g fat, 1 g protein, 10 g complex carbohydrates, 14 g sugar, 1 g dietary fiber, 23 mg cholesterol, 103 mg sodium, 28 mg potassium, 78 RE vitamin A, 1 mg vitamin C, 1 mg iron, 5 mg calcium, 15 mg phosphorus.

Biscotti

Ah, biscotti—the darling of Starbucks! These fat, crusty, flattened crescent moon cookies were an also-ran in America's cookie popularity race for years, a foreign entry with a steady but limited following. Suddenly, we all began drinking "Italian" double lattes with caramel cream, and Italy's favorite cookie—biscotti—rode coffee's coattails right up to the top.

From the Latin *bis coctum,* "twice baked," one of the earliest mentions of biscotti was in second-century Rome, where the term referred to a hard, dry, unsweetened cracker known for its extra-long keeping qualities. Thirteen centuries later, northern Italian bakers were serving a richer, sweeter (but just as hard) version of biscotti with *vin santo* (a sweet wine). Since then, biscotti have worked their way around the world, usually turning up in company with coffee (though in its native land biscotti are still enjoyed just as often with wine).

Biscotti, like shortbread, are a blank slate waiting to be drawn upon. Use the recipes in this chapter to fire your imagination and create your own personal favorite. We offer two basic recipes, and many variations. Most of the variations can be made with either basic recipe, though in some we've specified our preferences. Finished biscotti are delicious served as is. Or dust them with confectioners' sugar, drizzle them with caramel, dip in chocolate (dark or white) . . . see The Finishing Touch Chapter (pages 455-473), for further inspiration. Meanwhile—start brewing the coffee!

Italian or American?

Want to make up your own biscotti recipe? Which version of dough you begin with—the denser, harder Italian, or the lighter, crunchier American—is up to you. You'll find, however, that some recipes are better suited to one version than the other, depending on the types of add-ins. Since the Italian recipe starts out with a fairly dry dough, it's difficult to add 2 cups of dry ingredients, like chips, nuts, dried fruit, or granola; there's simply not enough moisture in the recipe to allow the dough to accept these ingredients easily. If you're determined to try it anyway, add 2 tablespoons of vegetable oil or water to the dough when you're beating the eggs; this should help.

On the other hand, if you want to use more than ¼ cup of added liquid (juice, syrup, honey), the American-style recipe is already so soft that, unless the liquid is accompanied by a fairly substantial amount of extra dry ingredients, the biscotti will spread too much as they bake. So if you're making an American-style biscotti with a significant amount of added liquid, be sure you also add 1½ to 2 cups of dry add-ins, to help "carry" that liquid.

Once you've mixed the dough, it's easy to see whether it's an acceptable consistency. If it isn't, don't worry, it's fixable. If you've made Italian-style dough without added liquid and are trying without success to mix in 2 cups of chips and nuts, simply sprinkle in 1 to 2 tablespoons water or vegetable oil. The dough will seem slimy at first, but keep beating, and eventually it will absorb the add-ins and become softer. If you've made the American-style dough that flows easily from the beater rather than forming a cohesive mass, add some bulk in the form of nuts or flavored chips, or even rolled oats. This will help stiffen the dough. As a last resort, add flour by the tablespoonful until the dough is stiff enough to cling to an overturned spoon without dripping off.

Here are a few more guidelines for successful biscotti:

- The more moist or melting add-ins you include, the longer biscotti will need to bake to become dry. Dried fruit and chocolate, if added in a combined quantity of 1½ cups or more, will add 5 minutes to biscotti's initial bake, and 5 to 10 minutes to its second bake.
- Think about sugar content. Biscotti are mildly sweet to begin with; adding 2 cups of butterscotch chips may push them over the top. Instead, consider adding a cup of butterscotch chips and a cup of toasted pecans, for balance.
- If you've baked biscotti, removed them from the oven, let cool completely, and they're softer than you'd like, simply put them back in a 250°F oven until they attain the degree of crunchiness you're after. Alternatively, if the weather is dry, let them sit, uncovered, on the cooling rack overnight; they'll continue to dry out.

Italian-Style Biscotti

These biscotti reflect their ancient origin as the ideal traveling companion, whether over land by caravan, or across the ocean in ships; legend has it that both Marco Polo and Christopher Columbus carried biscotti with them on their journeys. Quite dry and hard, like the ship's biscuits they're descended from, biscotti may prove a challenge for those who aren't partial to things like crunchy breadsticks or the hard crust on a baguette. But these biscotti are the perfect texture for dunking—in coffee or, as the original fifteenth-century Tuscan biscotti bakers did, in wine.

Yield: 14 to 16 biscotti ● *Baking temperature:* 350°F, then 325°F ● *Baking time:* 50 minutes

> 2 large eggs
> ⅔ cup (4¾ ounces) sugar
> ½ teaspoon baking powder
> ½ teaspoon salt
> 1 teaspoon vanilla extract
> 2 cups (8½ ounces) unbleached all-purpose flour

● Preheat the oven to 350°F. Lightly grease (or line with parchment) a large (about 18 x 13-inch) baking sheet.

● In a medium-sized bowl, beat the eggs, sugar, baking powder, salt, and vanilla until creamy looking; the mixture will be light-colored and as thick as pancake batter (see #1, below). Lower the mixer speed and add the flour, beating gently just until it's totally incorporated.

● Transfer the dough to the prepared baking sheet, and shape it into a rough log about 14 inches long. It will be about 2½ inches wide and about ¾ inch thick. Smooth the top of the log with a wet dough scraper (see #2 and #3, below).

When the egg/sugar mixture is properly beaten, it will be thick, lemon-colored, and drop in a ribbon from the beater.

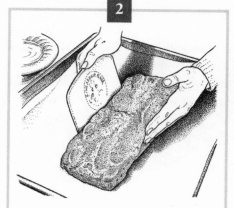

To shape the dough, wet your fingers and a dough scraper, and pat and smooth it into a rectangle about 14 inches long on a parchment-lined baking sheet.

Use the wet dough scraper to smooth the top of the dough.

essential
recipe

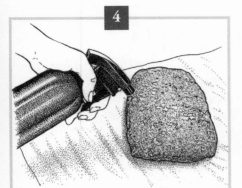

4

Spraying the biscotti dough after its first bake will make slicing it much easier, with less crumbling.

● Bake the dough for 25 minutes. Remove from the oven and let cool on the pan for 5 to 25 minutes. Five minutes before cutting, use a spray bottle of room-temperature water to lightly but thoroughly spritz the log, making sure to cover the sides and the top. Softening the crust just this little bit will make slicing the biscotti much easier (see #4, left).

● Reduce the oven temperature to 325°F. Wait another 5 minutes, then cut the biscotti into ½- to ¾-inch slices. How thick you slice them depends on a number of factors. This recipe, without nuts or add-ins, is easy to slice thin. Once you add chips, almonds, raisins, and other chunky ingredients, a ¾-inch slice is more realistic. When slicing, be sure to cut straight up and down. If you cut biscotti wider at the top than at the bottom, they'll topple over during their second bake (see #5, #6 and #7, right and below).

● Set the biscotti upright on the prepared baking sheet (see #8, below). Bake for 25 minutes. Remove from the oven and transfer to a rack to cool. Store the biscotti in an airtight container, to preserve their texture. If they aren't as hard as you'd like (and the weather is dry), store them uncovered, overnight, to continue drying. Biscotti can be stored at room temperature for 2 weeks; for longer storage, wrap airtight and freeze.

Nutrition information per serving (1 biscotti, 29 g): 91 cal, 1 g fat, 2 g protein, 11 g complex carbohydrates, 8 g sugar, 27 mg cholesterol, 90 mg sodium, 26 mg potassium, 12 RE vitamin A, 1 mg iron, 12 mg calcium, 27 mg phosphorus.

5

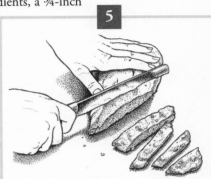

Slice the baked dough on the diagonal, into ½- to ¾-inch-wide strips. The steeper the angle of the diagonal, the longer the biscotti. Cutting the log into crosswise strips, rather than on the diagonal, will yield the shortest biscotti.

6

When cutting the biscotti, keep the knife from tilting off center, as shown.

7

Cutting the biscotti with the knife kept straight up and down will give you slices that can stand up for the second bake.

8

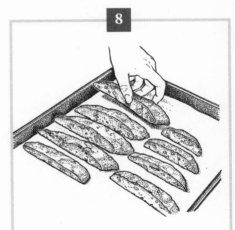

Place the sliced biscotti ½ inch apart, so air can circulate around them as they bake for the second time.

American-Style Biscotti

The cookies we know and love in America—the chocolate chip, oatmeal, peanut butter and sugar cookies that line the shelves of the supermarket cookie section, and whose recipes and variations fill our cookbooks—are far removed from traditional Italian biscotti. The cookies most of us grew up with are softer, more tender, crunchier, and lighter. American-style biscotti, likewise, are lighter and more tender than their Italian counterparts. Though not particularly suited to dunking in coffee or wine, they're appreciated by kids, or anyone whose idea of a cookie runs more toward a delicate cutout gingerbread cookie than a teething biscuit. Extra fat (in the form of butter) and extra leavening, for lighter texture, make the difference.

Yield: 14 to 16 biscotti ● *Baking temperature:* 350°F, then 325°F ● *Baking time:* 50 minutes

> 6 tablespoons (¾ stick, 3 ounces) unsalted butter
> ⅔ cup (4¾ ounces) sugar
> ¼ teaspoon salt
> 1 teaspoon vanilla extract
> 1½ teaspoons baking powder
> 2 large eggs
> 2 cups (8½ ounces) unbleached all-purpose flour

● Preheat the oven to 350°F. Lightly grease (or line with parchment) a large (about 18 x 13-inch) baking sheet.

● In a medium-sized bowl, beat the butter, sugar, salt, vanilla, and baking powder until the mixture is smooth and creamy. Beat in the eggs; the batter may look slightly curdled. Lower the mixer speed, add the flour, and mix until smooth. The dough will be quite soft and sticky, but should hold its shape when you drop it from a spoon.

● Transfer the dough to the prepared baking sheet, shaping it into a rough log about 14 inches long (see illustrations 2 and 3 on page 134). It will be about 2½ inches wide and about ¾ inch thick.

● Bake the dough for 25 minutes. Remove it from the oven and let cool on the pan anywhere from 5 to 25 minutes; just work it into the schedule of whatever else you're doing in the kitchen. Five minutes before cutting, use a spray bottle filled with room-temperature water to lightly but thoroughly spritz the log, making sure to cover the sides as well as the top. Softening the crust just this little bit will make slicing the biscotti much easier (see illustration 4, page 135).

● Reduce the oven temperature to 325°F. Wait another 5 minutes, then cut the biscotti into ½- to ¾-inch slices. How thick you slice them depends on a number of factors. This recipe, without nuts or any add-ins, is easy to slice thin. Once you start adding chips, almonds, raisins, and other chunky ingredients, a ¾-inch slice is more realistic. When you're slicing, be sure to cut straight up and down, if you cut at an angle, biscotti may be thicker at the top than the bottom, and they'll topple over during their second bake. (See illustrations 5-7, page 135.)

- Set the biscotti upright on the prepared baking sheet (see illustration 8, page 135). Bake for 25 minutes. Remove from the oven and transfer them to a rack to cool.
- Store the biscotti in an airtight container, to preserve their texture. If they aren't as crunchy as you'd like (and the weather is dry), store them uncovered, overnight, to continue drying. Biscotti can be stored at room temperature for 1 week; for longer storage, wrap airtight and freeze.

Nutrition information per serving (*1 biscotti, 35 g*)*:* 131 cal, 5 g fat, 2 g protein, 11 g complex carbohydrates, 8 g sugar, 39 mg cholesterol, 88 mg sodium, 27 mg potassium, 54 RE vitamin A, 1 mg iron, 30 mg calcium, 35 mg phosphorus.

Changing a plain biscotti's taste, texture, or crust

Adding nut flour—ground nuts, most typically almonds, hazelnuts, or pecans—to your American-Style biscotti recipe adds tenderness (from the nut oils), and heightens taste. We suggest adding up to 1 cup nut flour for optimal results; more than that, and biscotti may become too crumbly.

Substituting 1 cup semolina, a bright gold, coarse form of milled durum wheat, for 1 cup of the flour in the recipe gives biscotti a warm color and a bit of extra crunch. Due to its relatively large particle size, semolina takes longer to absorb liquid and form a cohesive dough. For that reason, we suggest combining the semolina with the eggs and sugar (or, in the American-Style recipe, with the eggs, sugar, and butter), and letting the mixture rest for 30 minutes. If you skip this step, the dough won't come together well.

Semolina biscotti tend to brown a bit faster than those based entirely on flour. To protect biscotti from overbrowning, either tent them loosely with aluminum foil midway through the second bake, or turn off the oven midway through the second bake, allowing the biscotti to remain in the turned-off oven until they're cool.

To give biscotti a shiny top crust, whisk together 1 egg white and 1 tablespoon water. Brush this mixture on the biscotti's top crust after its first bake, before slicing.

Pistachio-Cherry Biscotti

Golden-green, mildly salty pistachios and deep red, sweet and tangy dried cherries complement each other beautifully, both in color and flavor.

Yield: 16 to 18 biscotti ● *Baking temperature:* 350°F, then 325°F ● *Baking time:* 50 to 60 minutes

> 1 recipe Essential Biscotti (Italian-Style, page 134 or American-Style, page 136)
> 2 drops strong cherry flavor, to taste (optional)
> 1 cup (4 ounces) chopped pistachios
> 1 cup (4⅝ ounces) sweet or sour dried cherries

● Preheat the oven to 350°F. Lightly grease (or line with parchment) a large (18 x 13-inch) baking sheet.

● Prepare the biscotti dough of your choice, substituting the cherry flavor for the vanilla, if desired. Stir in the pistachios and cherries. Shape and bake the biscotti as directed in the recipe you've chosen. If the cherries are very fresh and moist, the biscotti may be fairly soft at the end of the baking time. For crunchier biscotti, bake for an additional 5 to 10 minutes.

Mexican Mocha Biscotti

The different flavors in these biscotti play in harmony like the instruments in an orchestra, and the resulting symphony of taste is sublime.

Yield: 16 to 18 biscotti ● *Baking temperature:* 350°F, then 325°F ● *Baking time:* 50 to 55 minutes

> 1 recipe Essential Biscotti (Italian-Style, page 134 or American-Style, page 136)
> 1 tablespoon espresso powder, or 1½ tablespoons instant
>   coffee granules
> ½ teaspoon cinnamon
> ⅔ cup (4 ounces) chocolate chips
> ⅔ cup (4 ounces) cinnamon chips
> ⅔ cup (2¾ ounces) chopped pecans, toasted (see page 27)

● Preheat the oven to 350°F. Lightly grease (or line with parchment) a large 18 x 13-inch baking sheet.

● Prepare the biscotti dough of your choice, substituting the espresso powder and cinnamon for the vanilla. If you're making the Italian recipe, add 2 tablespoons water or vegetable oil to the egg and sugar mixture. Shape and bake the biscotti as directed in the recipe you've chosen.

Gianduja Biscotti

Chocolate and hazelnut are a classic Italian pairing; in fact, the flavor has its own name, *gianduja* (jahn-DOO-yah). The hazelnut (like the pistachio) has quite a different flavor when you compare the actual nut to the flavor we identify as hazelnut in coffee or ice cream. If you're a fan of this assertive hazelnut flavor, enrich the taste of biscotti by adding a little (⅛ teaspoon) to a lot (¼ teaspoon) of strong hazelnut flavor.

Yield: 16 to 18 biscotti ● *Baking temperature:* 350°F, then 325°F ● *Baking time:* 50 to 55 minutes

> 1 recipe Essential Biscotti (Italian-Style, page 134 or American-Style, page 136)
> ⅛ to ¼ teaspoon strong hazelnut flavor, to taste (optional)
> 1 cup (4 ounces) chopped hazelnuts, toasted (see page 27)
> 1 cup (6 ounces) chopped bittersweet chocolate or semisweet
>   chocolate chips

● Preheat the oven to 350°F. Lightly grease (or line with parchment) a large (18 x 13-inch) baking sheet.

● Prepare the biscotti dough of your choice, substituting the hazelnut flavor, if desired, for the vanilla, and stirring in the nuts and chocolate along with the flour. Shape and bake the biscotti as directed in the recipe you've chosen.

VARIATION

● For white chocolate–hazelnut biscotti, increase the hazelnuts to 1½ cups. Dip one end of each finished biscotto in melted white chocolate. Place the dipped biscotti on a rack set over a piece of parchment or plastic wrap (to catch drips), and allow the chocolate to set before serving.

Butter-Pecan Biscotti

Toasted pecans and rich butterscotch pair wonderfully in ice cream—and do likewise in biscotti.

Yield: 15 to 17 biscotti ● *Baking temperature:* 350°F, then 325°F ● *Baking time:* 50 to 55 minutes

> 1 recipe Essential Biscotti (Italian-Style, page 134 or American-Style, page 136)
> ¼ teaspoon butterscotch or butter-rum flavor
> ⅔ cup (2¾ ounces) chopped pecans, toasted (see page 27)
> ⅔ cup (4 ounces) butterscotch chips

● Preheat the oven to 350°F. Lightly grease (or line with parchment) a large (18 x 13-inch) baking sheet.

● Prepare the biscotti dough of your choice, substituting the butterscotch flavor for the vanilla and stirring in the nuts and chips along with the flour. Shape and bake the biscotti as directed in the recipe you've chosen.

What's the best way to chop add-ins for biscotti?

While it's tempting to use whole nuts, extra-large chips or chocolate chunks, or large pieces of dried fruit in biscotti—they just look so impressive—it's challenging to slice biscotti for their second bake with these obstacles stopping the knife and knocking it off course. We've found the best solution is to chop nuts coarsely. And the most effective way to do this is as follows: place nuts in a heavy-duty zip-top plastic bag; close the bag, forcing out as much air as possible; and gently tap the nuts with a heavy rolling pin until they crack apart. Using a food processor will result in big chunks of nuts mixed with finely chopped nuts; a nut grinder will grind nuts into small dice. A rolling pin gives you the most control.

We suggest chopping large chocolate chunks coarsely, and snipping dried fruit into pieces no larger than a raisin.

Cranberry-Orange Biscotti

This classic muffin and quick bread flavor pairing translates beautifully to biscotti. These make a lovely dessert at Thanksgiving, if you can tear folks away from the pumpkin pie. Measure the orange zest into the tablespoon without packing it. It takes about half a large orange to yield a tablespoon of zest.

Yield: 16 to 18 biscotti ● *Baking temperature:* 350°F, then 325°F ● *Baking time:* 50 to 55 minutes

1 recipe Essential Biscotti (Italian-Style, page 134 or American-Style, page 136)
2 tablespoons (1 ounce) orange juice
1 tablespoon grated orange rind (zest)
1 cup (4⅝ ounces) dried cranberries
1 cup (4 ounces) chopped walnuts, toasted (see page 27)

● Preheat the oven to 350°F. Lightly grease (or line with parchment) a large (18 x 13-inch) baking sheet.
● Prepare the biscotti dough of your choice, adding the orange juice and zest once the egg/sugar mixture is fully beaten. Stir in the cranberries and walnuts along with the flour. Shape and bake the biscotti as directed in the recipe you've chosen.

Adding flavor

Fat is a flavor carrier, and biscotti—partly because they're low in fat—have a tendency to taste more bland than other cookies. Thus many recipes you see suggest add-ins: chocolate chips, dried cherries, toasted pecans . . . All add bold brushstrokes of strong flavor to a rather plain canvas. To increase the flavor of the dough itself, add a matching or complementary extract or strong flavor, for example, maple extract in maple-walnut biscotti, or hazelnut flavor in chocolate biscotti. The amount of flavor to add varies greatly, depending on both your own taste and the strength of the flavor you're adding. Here are some general guidelines:

● When adding orange, lemon, or lime oil, start with ¼ teaspoon. Taste and see how you like it; if it seems very weak, add more by the drop. These oils tend to have a rather raw finish if they're used to excess, so start out with less rather than more; you can always make the flavor stronger with your next batch of biscotti. Also, unlike extracts and other flavors, citrus oils retain most of their flavor through biscotti's two bakes, so again, go easy with these.

● When adding a flavor oil (such as anise oil, bitter almond oil) or a strong flavor (the kind that usually comes in a 1-ounce bottle and is generally sold as a candy-making flavor), start with ⅛ teaspoon, going up to ½ teaspoon for extra-strong flavor. For more information on these strong flavors and how to identify them, see page 490.

● When adding an extract (such as vanilla extract, peppermint extract), start with 1 teaspoon, then go up to 1 tablespoon, tasting as you go.

Pine Nut, Fennel, and Raisin Biscotti

Pasta fiorentina, a dish native to Florence, features pine nuts, golden raisins, and anchovies. We've dropped the fish and substituted another classic flavor, fennel, to make biscotti that will please anyone who's ever enjoyed the anchovy version. For a mild licorice flavor, use 1 tablespoon of the fennel seeds, for more assertive flavor, use 2 (or more) tablespoons.

Yield: 16 to 18 biscotti ● ***Baking temperature:*** *350°F, then 325°F* ● ***Baking time:*** *50 to 55 minutes*

> 1 cup (4½ ounces) golden raisins, not packed
> 2 tablespoons (1 ounce) brandy
> 1 recipe Essential Biscotti (Italian-Style, page 134 or American-Style, page 136)
> 1 cup (5 ounces) pine nuts
> 1 to 2 tablespoons fennel seeds

● Place the raisins in a bowl, sprinkle them with the brandy, and cover with plastic wrap. Microwave for 1 minute, then remove from the microwave and let rest, covered, for 1 hour. The raisins should absorb all but a few drops of the brandy.

● Preheat the oven to 350°F. Lightly grease (or line with parchment) a large (18 x 13-inch) baking sheet.

● Prepare the biscotti dough of your choice, adding the brandy-soaked raisins, nuts, and fennel seeds along with the flour. Shape and bake the biscotti as directed in the recipe you've chosen.

Granola Biscotti

Crunchy oats, seeds, toasted nuts, a bit of dried fruit—granola makes a hearty breakfast or snack, and it also adds nutty flavor to plain biscotti dough. And since the granola never really becomes integrated into the dough, it gives the finished biscotti a gentler, pleasingly crumbly texture. Due to the dryness of granola, we advise making this recipe with American-style biscotti dough.

Yield: 16 to 18 biscotti ● ***Baking temperature:*** *350°F, then 325°F* ● ***Baking time:*** *50 to 55 minutes*

> 1 recipe American-Style Biscotti (page 136)
> 2 cups (8 ounces) granola, flavor of your choice

● Preheat the oven to 350°F. Lightly grease (or line with parchment) a large (18 x 13-inch) baking sheet.

● Prepare the biscotti dough, adding the granola along with the flour. Shape and bake the biscotti as directed in the recipe.

Brown Sugar—Cinnamon Biscotti

These comforting biscotti remind us of cinnamon toast. If you can't find cinnamon chips at the supermarket, substitute butterscotch chips.

Yield: 16 to 18 biscotti ● *Baking temperature:* 350°F, then 325°F ● *Baking time:* 50 to 55 minutes

> 1 recipe Essential Biscotti (Italian-Style, page 134 or American-Style, page 136)
> ⅔ cup (4¾ ounces) brown sugar
> 2 teaspoons cinnamon
> 1 cup (6 ounces) cinnamon chips
> 1 cup (4 ounces) chopped walnuts, toasted (optional) see page 27

● Preheat the oven to 350°F. Lightly grease (or line with parchment) a large (18 x 13-inch) baking sheet.

● Prepare the biscotti dough of your choice, substituting the brown sugar for the granulated sugar. Stir in the cinnamon, cinnamon chips, and walnuts along with the flour.

● Shape and bake the biscotti as directed in the recipe you've chosen.

Dutch Chocolate—Almond Biscotti

Chocolate and cocoa combine in these tasty biscotti; they're dark as a moonless night, and as soul-satisfying as a cup of hot cocoa on Christmas Eve.

Yield: 15 to 17 biscotti ● *Baking temperature:* 350°F, then 325°F ● *Baking time:* 50 to 55 minutes

> 1 recipe American-Style Biscotti (page 136)
> ½ cup (3 ounces) chopped bittersweet or semisweet chocolate
> ¼ cup (¾ ounce) Dutch process cocoa powder
> 1 teaspoon espresso powder (optional)
> ⅔ cup (3¼ ounces) chopped almonds

● Preheat the oven to 350°F. Lightly grease (or line with parchment) a large (18 x 13-inch) baking sheet.

● In a small food processor, electric spice mill, or small electric coffee grinder, process the chocolate, cocoa, and espresso powder until the chocolate is finely ground. Prepare the biscotti dough, stirring in the ground chocolate mixture along with the flour. Stir in the almonds. Shape and bake the biscotti as directed in the recipe.

Chocolate and espresso—so happy together

Why do so many of the chocolate biscotti recipes in this chapter call for espresso powder? We've found that coffee, like vanilla, is a flavor that deepens and enriches the taste of chocolate. And espresso powder, a highly concentrated, dry coffee essence, is an easy way to highlight chocolate's flavor in biscotti without changing the liquid/flour ratio in the recipe. Leave it out if you like, or cut it back if you find it too "coffee tasting" for your preference. You can use the same amount of instant coffee granules if you can't find espresso powder, but it will be like drinking a cup of instant coffee versus savoring a deep, rich cup of *real* coffee or espresso—not really in the same league.

Creamy Orange Biscotti

The bright citrus taste of these biscotti is tempered by a dip in smooth, rich white chocolate. The effect will remind you of the Good Humor Man and his Creamsicle bars.

Yield: 15 to 17 biscotti ● ***Baking temperature:** 350°F, then 325°F* ● ***Baking time:** 50 to 60 minutes*

> 1 recipe Italian-Style Biscotti (page 134)
> ¼ cup (2 ounces) orange juice (freshly squeezed preferred)
> 2 tablespoons grated orange rind (zest) (from 1 large orange)
> 1¾ cups (10½ ounces) white chocolate chips or chunks,
>   or white confectionery coating, melted

● Preheat the oven to 350°F. Lightly grease (or line with parchment) a large (18 x 13-inch) baking sheet.
● Prepare the biscotti dough, adding the orange juice and zest along with the eggs. Shape and bake the biscotti as directed in the recipe. If the biscotti feel soft at the end of their second bake, return them to the oven for 5 to 10 minutes.
● Dip half of each finished, cooled biscotto (or the front or the back) in melted white chocolate. Place the dipped biscotti on a rack set over a piece of parchment or plastic wrap (to catch drips), and allow the chocolate to set before serving.

Orange-Cashew Biscotti

Although this may sound like a strange combination, give it a try. The orange flavor is very mild, and plays a nice background accompaniment to the salty-sweet, nutty taste of the cashews. Make sure you use salted cashews; the salt is a critical taste element in these biscotti. Taste the nuts before toasting; if they don't taste assertively salty, sprinkle on some additional salt.

Yield: 16 to 18 biscotti ● ***Baking temperature:** 350°F, then 325°F* ● ***Baking time:** 50 to 60 minutes*

> 1 recipe Essential Biscotti (Italian-Style, page 134 or American-Style page 136)
> ¼ cup (2 ounces) orange juice
> 1½ cups (6 ounces) chopped, salted cashews, toasted (see page 27)

● Preheat the oven to 350°F. Lightly grease (or line with parchment) a large (18 x 13-inch) baking sheet.
● Prepare the biscotti dough of your choice, adding the orange juice to the egg and sugar mixture. Add the cashews along with the flour. Shape and bake biscotti as directed in the recipe. If the biscotti feel soft at the end of their second bake, return them to the oven for 5 to 10 minutes.

Chocolate-Coconut Biscotti

This combination of seemingly disparate elements, inspired by a famous candy bar, takes on an even stronger candy persona when you dip the finished biscotti in melted chocolate.

Yield: 15 to 18 biscotti ● *Baking temperature:* 350°F, then 325°F ● *Baking time:* 50 to 55 minutes

> 1 recipe Essential Biscotti (Italian-Style, page 134 or American-Style, page 136)
> 1 cup (3½ ounces, packed) shredded sweetened coconut
> 1 cup (6 ounces) chocolate chips or chopped semisweet or
>   bittersweet chocolate
> 1¾ cups (10½ ounces) semisweet chocolate chips or
>   bittersweet chocolate chunks, melted, for dipping (optional)

● Preheat the oven to 350°F. Lightly grease (or line with parchment) a large (18 x 13-inch) baking sheet.

● Prepare the biscotti dough of your choice, stirring in the coconut and the 1 cup chocolate chips along with the flour. Shape and bake the biscotti as directed in the recipe you've chosen.

● Dip half of each finished, cooled biscotto (or the front or back) in the melted chocolate, if desired. Place the dipped biscotti on a rack set over a piece of parchment or plastic wrap (to catch drips), and allow the chocolate to set before serving.

Melting chocolate

For kids, melting chocolate is a problem; whether it's your chocolate ice cream cone or your candy bar that melts, it's bound to make a mess of your hands and clothes. For adults, melting chocolate can also be a challenge—as in, what's the best way to melt chocolate without scorching it?

We've found using a double boiler or the microwave are equally effective at melting chocolate safely. The double boiler is foolproof; it's impossible to scorch chocolate when it's melting gently over simmering water. The microwave is less trouble, and faster, but you have to pay more attention to what you're doing. Place chocolate in a microwave-safe bowl and heat it in short bursts. Try 45 seconds first, then 30 seconds next. Once it becomes very soft, heat it in 15-second bursts. Take the chocolate out of the microwave and stir it; it's safer to complete the melting process by stirring for a minute or so than it is to allow the microwave to do all the work, and possibly take the chocolate beyond melted to burned.

White chocolate is particularly problematic to melt; even in a double boiler, it sometimes becomes grainy or stiffens up. If you're not a complete purist, substitute white confectionery coating (also known as summer coating), found in stores offering candy-making supplies, or via mail order. It's a simple-to-melt, good-tasting "faux chocolate" (made from sugar, vegetable oil, milk solids, and flavor) that coats and dries on cookies and candy nicely.

Piña Colada Biscotti

A taste of the tropics is the perfect antidote to the tail end of winter, when it feels as if even one more flake of snow will drive you over the edge. These pineapple-coconut biscotti evoke memories of hot midsummer days and drinks on the deck after work.

Yield: 16 to 18 biscotti ● *Baking temperature: 350°F, then 325°F* ● *Baking time: 50 to 55 minutes*

> 1 recipe Essential Biscotti (Italian-Style, page 134 or American-Style, page 136)
> 1 to 2 teaspoons rum extract, or ¼ to ½ teaspoon strong rum
>   or butter-rum flavor, to taste
> 1 cup (3½ ounces, packed) shredded sweetened coconut
> 1 cup (5¾ ounces) finely diced dried pineapple

● Preheat the oven to 350°F. Lightly grease (or line with parchment) a large (18 x 13-inch) baking sheet.

● Prepare the biscotti dough of your choice, substituting the rum flavor for the vanilla, and stirring in the coconut and pineapple along with the flour. Shape and bake the biscotti as directed in the recipe you've chosen.

Very Vanilla Biscotti

When you think vanilla, do you think plain? Perish that thought! These biscotti, flecked with ground vanilla beans, have a wonderful aroma and pleasantly assertive vanilla taste. While vanilla is usually a background flavor for other ingredients, in these biscotti it has a chance to shine on its own.

Yield: 14 to 16 biscotti ● *Baking temperature: 350°F, then 325°F* ● *Baking time: 50 to 55 minutes*

> 1 or 2 whole vanilla beans
> 1 recipe Essential Biscotti (Italian-Style, page 134 or American-Style, page 136)

● Preheat the oven to 350°F. Lightly grease (or line with parchment) a large (18 x 13-inch) baking sheet.

● Snip the vanilla bean(s) into 1-inch pieces. Place them in a small food processor, or an electric spice mill, and add the ⅔ cup sugar from the recipe. Process until the vanilla bean is finely ground and incorporated with the sugar.

● Prepare the biscotti dough of your choice, using the prepared vanilla sugar in place of the ⅔ cup plain sugar in the recipe. Increase the vanilla extract to 2 to 3 teaspoons. Shape and bake the biscotti as directed in the recipe you've chosen.

Chocolate-Chocolate Chip Biscotti

A chocolate chip–filled chocolate cookie dipped in melted chocolate—it doesn't get any better than this!

Yield: 16 to 18 biscotti ● *Baking temperature:* 350°F, then 325°F ● *Baking time:* 50 to 55 minutes

> 1 recipe Essential Biscotti (Italian-Style, page 134 or American-Style, page 136)
> ¼ cup (¾ ounce) Dutch process cocoa powder
> 1 teaspoon espresso powder or instant coffee granules
> 1 cup (6 ounces) chocolate chips
> ⅔ cup (2¾ ounces) walnuts, toasted (optional)
> 1¾ cups (10½ ounces) semisweet, bittersweet, or white chocolate chips or chunks (or white confectionery coating), melted, for dipping (optional)

● Preheat the oven to 350°F. Lightly grease (or line with parchment) a large (18 x 13-inch) baking sheet.

● Prepare the biscotti dough of your choice, reducing the amount of flour by 2 tablespoons (to 1⅞ cups). Beat in the cocoa, and espresso powder. Stir in the chocolate chips, and walnuts along with the flour. Shape and bake the biscotti as directed in the recipe you've chosen.

● Dip the finished, cooled biscotti in the melted chocolate, if desired. Place the dipped biscotti on a rack set over a piece of parchment or plastic wrap (to catch drips), and allow the chocolate to set before serving.

VARIATION

● For Black Forest biscotti, substitute 1 cup dried cherries for the walnuts. Add ⅛ to ¼ teaspoon strong cherry flavor (optional).

How do I know when they're done?

Compared to most cookies, biscotti are eminently forgivable. Since they're essentially fully baked once the uncut dough has come out of the oven, it's impossible to underbake (and difficult to overbake) biscotti. For soft, cakelike cookies, simply slice the baked log and set slices on a rack to cool. These cookies aren't biscotti (since they're not "twice baked"), but are suitable for kids and others who don't care for crunchy cookies.

Once the biscotti have been sliced and then baked for the amount of time directed, take the pan out of the oven and poke the side of a biscotto. Is it firm to the touch or does it give? Is the cut crust dry or damp? If the biscotto feels soft, like a piece of cake, give it another 5 minutes in the oven. If it feels firm, but still gives a bit when you poke it, take it out for rather soft-textured but still crunchy biscotti. If it feels firm, but the cut crust is still a bit damp, take it out; this will yield biscotti that are crunchy all the way through. If it feels firm to the touch and the cut crust is dry, take it out; these biscotti will be hard and crunchy.

Classic Italian Biscotti

The combination of anise (licorice) and almond, while it may sound strange to American ears, is a hallmark of Italian baking. Take one bite of these and you'll taste the quintessential Italian biscotti. While you can make these with either style of the biscotti dough, we recommend the Italian version, for a truly authentic experience.

Yield: 15 to 17 biscotti ● *Baking temperature: 350°F, then 325°F* ● *Baking time: 50 to 55 minutes*

> 1 recipe Italian-Style Biscotti (page 136)
> 2 teaspoons almond extract
> 1 tablespoon aniseed
> 1 cup (5 ounces) chopped almonds, toasted (see page 27)

● Preheat the oven to 350°F. Lightly grease (or line with parchment) a large (18 x 13-inch) baking sheet.
● Prepare the biscotti dough, substituting the almond extract for the vanilla, and stirring in the aniseed and almonds along with the flour. Shape and bake the biscotti as directed in the recipe.

Lemon-Almond Biscotti

These biscotti are pleasantly tangy from a strong hit of lemon juice. The almonds temper the lemon's bite and add an interesting texture. You can beat in an additional ¼ cup sugar if you want sweet biscotti; we prefer the refreshingly tart taste of these biscotti without additional sugar.

Yield: 15 to 17 biscotti ● *Baking temperature: 350°F, then 325°F* ● *Baking time: 50 to 55 minutes*

> 1 recipe Essential Biscotti (Italian-Style, page 134 or American-Style, page 136)
> ¼ cup (2 ounces) freshly squeezed lemon juice
> 1 tablespoon grated lemon rind (zest), or ⅛ teaspoon lemon oil
> ¼ cup (1¾ ounces) sugar (optional)
> 1 cup (5 ounces) chopped almonds, toasted (see page 27)

● Preheat the oven to 350°F. Lightly grease (or line with parchment) a large (18 x 13-inch) baking sheet.
● Prepare the biscotti dough of your choice, adding the lemon juice and zest along with the eggs and sugar. Stir in the nuts along with the flour. Shape and bake the biscotti as directed in the recipe you've chosen.

Hazelnut-Cappuccino Biscotti

Isn't it wonderful to end dinner with a freshly brewed cup of hazelnut-flavored cappuccino? But who wants to be wide awake for hours after that satisfying meal? These coffee-and-hazelnut biscotti are a good substitute when the last thing you need is a major jolt of caffeine.

Yield: 15 to 17 biscotti ● *Baking temperature: 350°F, then 325°F* ● *Baking time: 50 to 55 minutes*

1 recipe Essential Biscotti (Italian-Style, page 134 or American-Style, page 136)
⅛ to ¼ teaspoon strong hazelnut flavor
1 tablespoon espresso powder or instant coffee granules
1 cup (4 ounces) chopped hazelnuts, toasted (see page 27)
1¾ cups (10½ ounces) semisweet chocolate chips or bittersweet
   chocolate chunks, melted, for dipping (optional)

● Preheat the oven to 350°F. Lightly grease (or line with parchment) a large (18 x 13-inch) baking sheet.

● Prepare the biscotti dough of your choice, beating the hazelnut flavor and espresso powder with the eggs, and stirring in the hazelnuts along with the flour. Shape and bake the biscotti as directed in the recipe you've chosen.

● Dip one end of the biscotti in the melted chocolate. Alternatively, pour the melted chocolate into a shallow, wide bowl and dip one whole side (front or back) of biscotti in the chocolate. Place the dipped biscotti on a rack set over a piece of parchment or plastic wrap (to catch drips), and allow the chocolate to set before serving.

To dip, or not to dip?

How do you know which of these biscotti recipes will taste good finished with a coating of chocolate? Some are naturals—vanilla, gianduja, cappuccino, there's no question these will be delightful with one end dipped in white or dark chocolate. On the other hand, pine nut, raisin, and fennel? Don't go there, unless you're heavily into fusion cuisine. If you have any doubt—e.g. butter-pecan, cranberry-orange—taste and see. Take a bite of biscotti along with a few chocolate chips; it will become immediately apparent if this is a biscotti that will play nicely with chocolate.

Now, how much chocolate do you need to melt to dip biscotti? Though biscotti vary in size, and chocolate dips (plain melted chocolate vs. chocolate ganache, for instance) differ in thickness, a good rule of thumb is 1 tablespoon melted chocolate per biscotti. A heaping 1¾ cups (about 10½ ounces) chocolate chips will yield 1 cup melted chocolate, enough to dip about 16 biscotti.

Cinnamon-Raisin Biscotti

Cinnamon-raisin toast is a great way to start the day; cinnamon-raisin biscotti, served with a cup of tea late in the afternoon or with your evening coffee, is a great way to finish it.

Yield: 15 to 17 biscotti ● *Baking temperature: 350°F, then 325°F* ● *Baking time: 50 to 55 minutes*

> 1 recipe Essential Biscotti (Italian-Style, **page 134** or American-Style, **page 136**)
> 2 teaspoons cinnamon
> 1 cup (5¼ ounces) raisins

● Preheat the oven to 350°F. Lightly grease (or line with parchment) a large (18 x 13-inch) baking sheet.

● Prepare the biscotti dough of your choice, adding the cinnamon and raisins along with the flour. Shape and bake the biscotti as directed in the recipe you've chosen.

Maple-Walnut Biscotti

When Vermonters tap their sugar maple trees in February and sugarhouses start to turn out their yearly crop of maple syrup, the smell of maple from the boiling sap drifts over the land like a sweet cloud. The aroma of these biscotti as they bake reminds us of a Vermont spring day.

Yield: 15 to 17 biscotti ● *Baking temperature: 350°F, then 325°F* ● *Baking time: 50 to 55 minutes*

> 1 recipe Essential Biscotti (Italian-Style, **page 134** or American-Style, **page 136**)
> ⅔ cup (3 ounces) maple sugar (see page 481)
> ¼ teaspoon strong maple flavor
> 1 cup (4 ounces) chopped walnuts, toasted (see page 27)
> Maple Glaze (see page 459), optional

● Preheat the oven to 350°F. Lightly grease (or line with parchment) a large (18 x 13-inch) baking sheet.

● Prepare the biscotti dough of your choice, substituting the maple sugar for the granulated sugar, and adding the maple flavor when you're beating the sugar and eggs. Stir in the walnuts along with the flour. Shape and bake the biscotti as directed in the recipe you've chosen.

● Dip the ends of the finished, cooled biscotti in Maple Glaze (page 459), if desired.

Mini-biscotti

To make small, three-bite biscotti, simply divide the dough initially into three pieces, instead of shaping the entire log at once. Shape each of the three pieces of dough into a 1½- to 2-inch-wide log. Since these logs are fairly short, they can all fit nicely, side by side, on a half-sheet (18 x 13-inch) baking pan. Once the dough is baked, slice it crosswise, rather than on the diagonal; this will yield the smallest biscotti.

Gingerbread Biscotti

Gingerbread can come in more shapes than just men and houses. These crunchy, spicy biscotti make a great addition to any holiday cookie gift tin.

Yield: *15 to 17 biscotti* ● ***Baking temperature:*** *350°F, then 325°F* ● ***Baking time:*** *50 to 55 minutes*

> 1 recipe Essential Biscotti (Italian-Style, page 134 or American-Style, page 136)
> ⅔ cup brown sugar
> 4 teaspoons ground ginger
> 1 teaspoon cinnamon
> ½ teaspoon nutmeg
> 1 cup (6½ ounces) finely diced crystallized ginger

● Preheat the oven to 350°F. Lightly grease (or line with parchment) a large (18 x 13-inch) baking sheet.
● Prepare the biscotti dough of your choice, substituting the brown sugar for the granulated sugar in the recipe, and stirring in the ginger, cinnamon, nutmeg, and crystallized ginger along with the flour. Shape and bake the biscotti as directed in the recipe you've chosen.

Rum-Raisin Biscotti

This old-fashioned flavor combination traditionally (and most famously) appears in ice cream, but these days you'll find it in pudding, cake, bread . . . and biscotti.

Yield: *16 to 18 biscotti* ● ***Baking temperature:*** *350°F, then 325°F* ● ***Baking time:*** *70 minutes*

> 2 large eggs
> ⅔ cup (5¼ ounces) brown sugar
> ½ teaspoon salt
> ⅓ cup (2½ ounces) light, dark, or spiced rum
> ¼ teaspoon strong rum flavor
> 2 cups (8½ ounces) unbleached all-purpose flour
> 1 teaspoon baking powder
> 1½ cups (9 ounces) raisins

● Preheat the oven to 350°F. Lightly grease (or line with parchment) a large (18 x 13-inch) baking sheet.
● In a medium-sized bowl, beat the eggs, brown sugar, and salt together until smooth. Add the rum and rum flavor, then the flour, baking powder, and raisins, beating until smooth and cohesive.
● Shape and bake the biscotti as directed in the American-Style Biscotti recipe (see page 136), giving them 30 minutes for the first bake, and 40 minutes for the final bake.

Honey-Sesame Biscotti

Honey and sesame are ingredients usually associated with Middle Eastern cuisine, rather than Italian, but this classic flavor duo (think halvah) translates nicely to a cookie. Note that these biscotti will become a deep, golden brown, darker than most; this is due to the honey, which browns more quickly than sugar. Use dark, strongly flavored sesame oil, not light-gold sesame oil.

Yield: 14 to 16 biscotti ● *Baking temperature:* 350°F, then 325°F ● *Baking time:* 70 minutes

DOUGH
  2 tablespoons (1 ounce) butter
  2 tablespoons (⅞ ounce) sugar
  2 large eggs
  2 tablespoons (⅞ ounce) sesame oil
  ½ cup (6 ounces) honey
  2 cups (8½ ounces) unbleached all-purpose flour
  1½ teaspoons baking powder
  ¼ teaspoon salt
TOPPING
  1 egg white beaten with 1 tablespoon water, to glaze
  2 tablespoons sesame seeds

● Preheat the oven to 350°F. Lightly grease (or line with parchment) a large (18 x 13-inch) baking sheet.
● In a medium-sized bowl, beat the butter and sugar together until smooth. Beat in the eggs, sesame oil, and honey, then the flour, baking powder, and salt. Shape the biscotti as directed in the American-Style Biscotti recipe (see page 136). Brush the top with the egg white glaze, and sprinkle heavily with the sesame seeds.
● Bake the biscotti as directed in the essential recipe, but give them 30 minutes for the first bake, and 40 minutes for the final bake.

Biscotti as table ornament?

Unlike many cookies, biscotti will stay fresh at room temperature for a long time—up to two weeks, depending on the ingredients and how they're stored. Plain biscotti, without fruit or nuts, will keep the longest; and Italian-style biscotti, since they're hard to begin with, will remain the same texture longer than American-style, which will very gradually become harder. Of course, you can always freeze biscotti. Let them cool, uncovered, overnight, before wrapping in plastic wrap or in a zip-top plastic bag with the air removed.

Biscotti look absolutely delightful stored on end in a clear glass or acrylic container. If you plan on keeping the biscotti around awhile, you might want to slip a layer of plastic wrap over the top of the jar before adding its lid. This will help keep biscotti from getting soft in humid weather. If they become soft anyway, heat them in a 250°F oven, uncovered, for 10 to 15 minutes, until they're crisp again.

Brownies

Certain items in the wide world of baking seem to inspire long-range searches for "perfection." The perfect sugar cookie. Ultimate gingerbread. The ne plus ultra of devil's food cake. And, of course, the Perfect Brownie.

What's your idea of the perfect brownie? Whatever it is—moist, but not gooey, dense and fine-crumbed, an inch-thick slab of almost-liquid chocolate—it's your own preference that makes it so wonderful. Just as one person's favorite wine is an inexpensive Zinfandel, while another prefers a top-of-the-line Cabernet Sauvignon, greatness is in the eye of the beholder (and on the tongue of the taster). So don't let anyone tell you a cakey brownie isn't worthy of your adulation; in fact, it's just a fudgy brownie with extra flour, sugar, and eggs thrown in—and what could be wrong with that?

One common thread (crumb?) connecting all types of brownies is chocolate. If you love chocolate, you love brownies—period. Because a brownie is nothing more than rich, dark chocolate sweetened with sugar, bound together with eggs and flour. We like to think of brownies as just one step beyond pure chocolate. The few extra ingredients create an entirely different treat, one that handsomely salutes its essential element, yet takes it to another level of pleasure.

We made a plethora of different brownies before we decided these are the best. Well, our favorites, at least. It was hard to find consensus about what the perfect brownie should be; the discussion was ongoing for weeks here at King Arthur Flour as we staked out our strategic positions, and then held fast as the testing and tasting went on—each camp proclaiming this version the best, not that one.

In the end, we settled on three slightly different recipes covering everyone's brownie preferences: fudgy, cakey, and something between the two, a medium-rise brownie with a light, but very moist crumb. Choose your favorite type of brownie, then use that recipe as the starting point for a path that will include as many delicious twists and turns as your imagination can provide.

How can I tell when my brownies are done?

How do you tell if a cookie is fully baked and ready to come out of the oven? Usually by checking to see if it's golden brown. Clearly, that won't work with a dark brown brownie. Thus, it's important to be precise with oven temperatures and baking times. First, set the required time on your kitchen timer, going for the low end if a range of times is given. Make sure your oven is fully heated before putting in the pan of brownies. Once you put them in, immediately turn on the timer.

Like chocolate cake, the fully baked brownie can usually be identified by its aroma; all of a sudden, the smell of chocolate will permeate your kitchen, giving you an olfactory clue where a visual one isn't possible. Even if the timer hasn't gone off yet, check the brownies as soon as you can smell them. Their edges should be set, but not tough or burned; they may be pulling away from the sides of the pan very slightly. Gently touch your fingertips to the center of the brownies; they should be set on top, but should give easily, indicating they're soft underneath. Fudgy brownies will develop a very distinct, shiny top, which may crack or flake when gently touched. Finally, stick a cake tester (or clean broom straw) into the center of the pan; when you remove it, it might have a few scant moist crumbs clinging to it, but it shouldn't be coated with uncooked batter.

If you make a mistake and take the brownies out of the oven before they're fully baked, don't despair, the ones in the center will simply be softer and more gooey than you'd prefer, but then there are those whose gooeyness quotient knows no bounds.

essential recipe

Fudgy Brownies

Many of us here at King Arthur decided that our perfect brownie should be fudgy but not gooey, and rich enough to satisfy on its own. It should also be assertively flavored and able to stand up to hot fudge sauce and vanilla ice cream. Also, it needs to have a crisp top layer—as one of the kids said, "Just like ones from a box." The following recipe fills the bill. Chocolate chips will provide tiny molten pockets of chocolate within the greater brownie landscape. Add them if your desire for fudginess is limitless.

Yield: *Two dozen 2-inch brownies* ● **Baking temperature:** *325°F* ● **Baking time:** *29 to 32 minutes*

¾ cup (1½ sticks, 6 ounces) unsalted butter
2 cups (14 ounces) sugar
1 cup (3 ounces) Dutch process cocoa powder
1 teaspoon salt
½ teaspoon baking powder
1 tablespoon vanilla extract
3 large eggs
1 cup (4¼ ounces) unbleached all-purpose flour
1 cup (4 ounces) chopped walnuts or pecans (optional)
1 cup (6 ounces) chocolate chips (optional)

● Preheat the oven to 325°F. Lightly grease a 9 x 13-inch pan.
● In a medium-sized microwave-safe bowl, or in a medium saucepan set over low heat, melt the butter, then add the sugar and stir to combine. Return the mixture to the heat (or microwave) briefly, just until it's hot (110°F to 120°F), but not bubbling; it will become shiny looking as you stir it. Heating this mixture a second time will dissolve more of the sugar, which will yield a shiny top crust on your brownies.
● Stir in the cocoa, salt, baking powder, and vanilla. Whisk in the eggs, stirring until smooth, then add the flour and nuts and chips, again stirring until smooth. Spoon the batter into the prepared pan.
● Bake the brownies for 29 to 32 minutes, until a cake tester inserted into the center comes out clean, or with just a tiny amount of crumb clinging to it. The edges of the brownies should be set, but the center still soft. Remove the brownies from the oven and cool on a rack before cutting and serving.

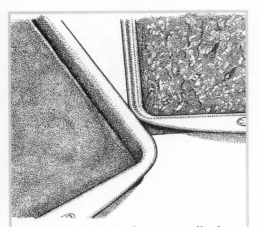

Fudgy brownies (right) are usually shiny on top, dense and moist beneath. Cakey brownies (left) have a uniform texture, and a matte surface.

Nutrition information per serving *(one 2-inch square, without nuts or chocolate chips, 39 g):* 154 cal, 4 g fat, 2 g protein, 4 g complex carbohydrates, 16 g sugar, 1 g dietary fiber, 43 mg cholesterol, 110 mg sodium, 200 mg potassium, 68 RE vitamin A, 2 mg iron, 16 mg calcium, 50 mg phosphorus, 9 mg caffeine.

Cakey Brownies

If gooey isn't a word that's high up on your list of favorite food characteristics, then this cakelike brownie is your top choice. Similar to very dense, firm chocolate cake, this brownie is an ideal candidate for your favorite chocolate-friendly icing—say, cappuccino. These brownies will have a matte-finish, rather than shiny, top crust, perfect for icing.

Yield: Two dozen 2-inch brownies ● *Baking temperature:* 350°F ● *Baking time:* 28 to 30 minutes

1 cup (2 sticks, 8 ounces) unsalted butter
2¼ cups (15¾ ounces) sugar
1¼ cups (3¾ ounces) Dutch process cocoa powder
1 teaspoon salt
1½ teaspoons baking powder
1 tablespoon vanilla extract
5 large eggs
½ cup (4 ounces) water
1½ cups (6¼ ounces) unbleached all-purpose flour
1 cup (4 ounces) chopped walnuts or pecans (optional)
1 cup (6 ounces) chocolate chips (optional)

- Preheat the oven to 350°F. Lightly grease a 9 x 13-inch pan.
- In a medium-sized microwave-safe bowl, or in a medium saucepan set over low heat, melt the butter, then add the sugar and stir to combine. Stir in the cocoa, salt, baking powder, and vanilla. Whisk in the eggs one at a time and add the water, stirring until smooth. Add the flour and nuts and chips, again stirring until smooth. Spoon the batter into the prepared pan.
- Bake the brownies for 28 to 30 minutes, until a cake tester inserted into the center comes out clean. The brownies should feel set both on the edges and in the center. Remove them from the oven and cool on a rack before cutting and serving.

Nutrition information per serving (one 2-inch square, without nuts or chips, 51 g): 197 cal, 6 g fat, 3 g protein, 7 g complex carbohydrates, 7 g sugar, 1 g dietary fiber, 66 mg cholesterol, 136 mg sodium, 255 mg potassium, 95 RE vitamin A, 2 mg iron, 31 mg calcium, 72 mg phosphorus, 11 mg caffeine.

On-the-Fence Brownies

Fudgy, cakey, fudgy, cakey . . . can't make up your mind? These brownies combine the best of both worlds—the fudge brownie's ultramoist texture, and the nice rise of a cake brownie.

Yield: Two dozen 2-inch brownies ● *Baking temperature:* 350°F ● *Baking time:* 28 to 30 minutes

> 1 cup (2 sticks, 8 ounces) unsalted butter
> 2¼ cups (15¾ ounces) sugar
> 1¼ cups (3¾ ounces) Dutch process cocoa
> 1 teaspoon salt
> 1 teaspoon baking powder
> 1 tablespoon vanilla extract
> 4 large eggs
> 1½ cups (6¼ ounces) unbleached all-purpose flour
> 1 cup (4 ounces) chopped walnuts or pecans (optional)
> 1 cup (6 ounces) chocolate chips (optional)

● Preheat the oven to 350°F. Lightly grease a 9 x 13-inch pan.
● In a medium-sized microwave-safe bowl, or in a medium saucepan set over low heat, melt the butter, then add the sugar and stir to combine. Return the mixture to the heat (or microwave) briefly, just until it's hot (110°F to 120°F), but not bubbling; it will become shiny looking as you stir it. Heating this mixture a second time will dissolve more of the sugar, which will yield a shiny top crust on your brownies.
● Stir in the cocoa, salt, baking powder, and vanilla. Whisk in the eggs, stirring until smooth, then add the flour and nuts and chips, again stirring until smooth. Spoon the batter into the prepared pan.
● Bake the brownies for 28 to 30 minutes, until a cake tester inserted into the center comes out clean. The brownies should feel set on the edges and in the center. Remove them from the oven and cool on a rack before cutting and serving.

Nutrition information per serving (one 2-inch square, without nuts or chips, 24 g): 194 cal, 9 g fat, 3 g protein, 7 g complex carbohydrates, 18 g sugar, 1 g dietary fiber, 57 mg cholesterol, 123 mg sodium, 252 mg potassium, 91 RE vitamin A, 2 mg iron, 24 mg calcium, 66 mg phosphorus, 11 mg caffeine.

BROWNIE INNOVATIONS • • • • •

"Start here, go anywhere" is the motto of a famous outdoor company, but it also sums up the innumerable variations for which brownies are perfectly suited. From add-ins such as nuts or chips, to fillings (cheesecake, peanut butter), to flavor additions, to icings, the basic brownie is a blank canvas awaiting the artist's touch.

A simple start is to drizzle brownies with melted caramel, or melted chocolate (white, milk, or dark). Another basic innovation is to sprinkle a topping—nuts, chips, crushed toffee—over the crust about 10 minutes before the end of the baking time. The brownies will be set enough that the topping won't sink in, but still have enough time in the oven for the topping to soften and melt.

Chocolate Ganache Icing

Let's start out with a very simple but ever-so-satisfying icing: chocolate ganache. Heavy cream. Chocolate. That's it. You can't go wrong. While this amount of icing is sufficient to cover a 9 x 13-inch pan of brownies with a glazelike finish, you'll want to double the ingredients to make a thickly frosted batch of brownies.

Yield: 1 cup, enough to ice a 9 x 13-inch pan of brownies

½ cup (4 ounces) heavy cream or whipping cream
1 cup (6 ounces) chocolate chips or chopped semisweet
   or bittersweet chocolate

● In a microwave-safe bowl, or in a small saucepan set over medium heat, heat the cream until it's very hot. You should see wisps of steam beginning to rise from it, and some very tiny bubbles around the edge. Add the chocolate chips to the cream and stir until smooth. Don't panic—at first, the mixture will look disarmingly soupy, but just keep stirring. Very shortly it will become a rich brown, thick, shiny spreadable icing.

Chocolate Mint Brownies

If you like Girl Scout Thin Mint cookies, you'll love these deeply chocolate, strongly mint brownies.

Yield: Four dozen 1 x 2-inch brownies

> 1 recipe Essential Brownies (Fudgy, page 156; Cakey, page 157; or
>   On-the-Fence, page 158)
> 12 thin mints or peppermint patties

● Prepare the brownie batter of your choice. Spread half of the brownie batter into a lightly greased 9 x 13-inch pan. Top with the mints, then spread with the remaining batter. Bake the brownies as directed in the recipe you've chosen.

VARIATION

If you want to make your own mint filling, here's a tasty recipe:

Mint Filling

> 4 cups (1 pound) confectioners' sugar
> ¾ cup (4¾ ounces) vegetable shortening
> ¼ teaspoon peppermint oil, or 1 to 2 teaspoons peppermint
>   extract (to taste)
> ¼ cup (1 ounce) unbleached all-purpose flour or Signature
>   Secrets Culinary Thickener*
> 6 tablespoons (3 ounces) heavy cream

● In a medium-sized mixing bowl beat all the filling ingredients together until they're cohesive; the mixture will be the consistency of stiff cookie dough. Pat the filling into a rectangle just slightly smaller than the pan; this is most easily done on a clean work surface that you've dusted with confectioners' sugar, or on a piece of plastic wrap.

● Spread half the brownie batter into the prepared pan. Top with the filling, patting it down gently. Top with the remaining batter. Bake as directed in the recipe you've chosen, adding 5 to 8 minutes to the baking time.

* Signature Secrets Culinary Thickener is a modified food starch, available by mail order, and in supermarkets soon.

Cheesecake Swirl Brownies

The creamy swirl of cheesecake in these brownies makes them a lovely looking choice for a dessert buffet.

Yield: Two dozen 2-inch brownies

1 recipe Essential Brownies (Fudgy, page 156; Cakey, page 15; or On-the-Fence, page 158)

CREAM CHEESE SWIRL

Two 8 ounce packages cream cheese, at room temperature

¾ cup (5¼ ounces) sugar

2 teaspoons vanilla extract

¼ teaspoon almond extract (optional)

¼ cup (2 ounces) heavy cream or sour cream

2 large eggs

- Prepare the brownie batter of your choice.
- **To make the cream cheese swirl:** In a medium-sized bowl beat the cream cheese until no lumps remain; add the sugar, vanilla, and almond extract, blending until smooth. Stir in the cream and eggs, mixing until everything is well combined.
- Spread three-quarters of the brownie batter into a lightly greased 9 x 13-inch pan. Spoon the cheesecake batter over the brownie batter, smoothing it out. Drop the remaining brownie batter by the tablespoonful atop the cheesecake. Draw a dull knife through the top third of the two batters, gently swirling it to make a nice design.
- Bake as directed in the recipe you've chosen, adding 5 to 10 minutes to the baking time. When the brownies are done, the top should be set and the edges puffy; they'll have much the same look as a fully baked cheesecake. Remove the brownies from the oven and cool on a rack. Chill until you're ready to cut and serve them, and refrigerate any leftovers.

To make the very best brownies, shouldn't I use the very best baking chocolate?

Many people equate expensive, often imported baking chocolate (unsweetened, solid chocolate) with optimum results when preparing chocolate baked goods. The testing we've done suggests otherwise. While each baker determines his or her own favorite nuance of flavor or aroma, we all agree that making brownies with Dutch process cocoa instead of chocolate is a good choice. Cocoa is easy to use; you don't have to fuss with melting it (and worry about scorching).

Because it's pure chocolate, with very little cocoa butter to temper it, its flavor is intense and rich. Dutch process cocoa, treated to reduce the acidic bite that often mars the flavor of solid baking chocolate, is also darker in color; people naturally tend to "eat with their eyes," and associate dark color with rich chocolate flavor. Finally, cocoa is easy to keep on hand in the pantry; you never have to worry about it melting in the summer, or "blooming" (acquiring a grayish surface cast) as it ages.

Irish Cream Cheesecake Brownies

A haunting hint of Irish Cream liqueur flavors the cheesecake swirl in these decadent brownies.

Yield: Two dozen 2-inch brownies

1 recipe Essential Brownies (Fudgy, page 156; Cakey, page 157; or On-the-Fence, page 158)

CHEESECAKE SWIRL
Two 8 ounce packages cream cheese, at room temperature
¼ cup (2 ounces) lightly packed brown sugar
¾ cup (6 ounces) Irish Cream liqueur
2 teaspoons vanilla extract
2 large eggs

- Prepare the brownie batter of your choice.
- **To make the cheesecake swirl:** In a medium-sized bowl beat the cream cheese until no lumps remain; add the sugar and liqueur, blending until smooth. Stir in the vanilla and eggs, mixing until everything is well combined.
- Spread three-quarters of the brownie batter into a lightly greased 9 x 13-inch pan. Spoon the cheesecake batter over the brownie batter, smoothing it out. Drop the remaining brownie batter by the tablespoonful atop the cheesecake batter. Draw a dull knife through the top third of the batter, gently swirling it to make a nice design.
- Bake as directed in your chosen recipe, adding 5 to 10 minutes to the baking time. When the brownies are done, the top should be set and the edges puffy, much the same look as a fully baked cheesecake. Remove the brownies from the oven and cool them on a rack. Chill until you're ready to serve them, and refrigerate any leftovers.

Toffee-Coffee Brownies

Ah, here it is: the quintessential brownie for you mocha fans. The rich espresso-laced frosting, topped with toffee chips, brings these brownies totally over the top.

Yield: Two dozen 2-inch brownies

1 recipe Essential Brownies (Fudgy, page 156; Cakey, page 157; or On-the-Fence, page 158)
1 tablespoon espresso powder

FROSTING
1 tablespoon espresso powder
1 tablespoon hot water
1½ cups (6 ounces) confectioners' sugar
1 to 3 tablespoons (½ to 1½ ounces) heavy cream or milk
½ cup (2½ ounces) toffee bits

- Prepare the brownie batter of your choice, adding the 1 tablespoon espresso powder to the batter. Bake as directed in the recipe. Allow the brownies to cool for 30 minutes before frosting.
- **To make the frosting:** In a medium-sized bowl, mix the espresso powder and hot water together. Stir in the confectioners' sugar and 1 tablespoon of the cream, adding up to 2 additional tablespoons cream to make a spreadable frosting. Spread the frosting over the bars, then sprinkle them with the toffee bits. Cool for several hours before cutting into squares.

Brownie Macaroons

Are coconut macaroons way up on your list of favorite cookies? Combine them with a brownie base for a treat that will bring to mind a chocolate-covered coconut candy bar.

Yield: Two dozen 2-inch brownies

1 recipe Essential Brownies (**Fudgy, page 156; Cakey, page 157; or On-the-Fence, page 158**)

TOPPING

⅛ teaspoon salt

2 large egg whites, at room temperature

½ teaspoon vanilla extract

¾ cup (5¼ ounces) sugar; superfine sugar preferred

3 cups (9 ounces) shredded sweetened coconut

- Prepare the brownie batter of your choice. Spread the batter in a lightly greased 9 x 13-inch pan.
- **To make the topping:** In a large bowl, beat together the salt and egg whites until the mixture forms soft peaks. Add the vanilla and gradually sprinkle in the sugar. Beat until stiff peaks form. Fold in the coconut.
- Dollop the topping onto the brownie batter; a tablespoon cookie scoop works well here. Gently press down on the dollops of topping to spread them a bit.
- Bake the brownies as directed in the recipe you've chosen, adding 6 to 8 minutes to the baking time. The topping should be light golden brown. Remove the brownies from the oven and let cool completely on a rack before cutting.

Raspberry Truffle Brownies

Chocolate and fruit flavors are sometimes difficult to pair; other times, they're a match made in heaven (think chocolate-apricot Sacher torte). This is one of those times.

Yield: Two dozen 2-inch brownies

1 recipe Essential Brownies (Fudgy, page 156; Cakey, page 157; or On-the-Fence, page 158)
1 teaspoon raspberry flavor
GLAZE
¼ cup (3 ounces) raspberry jam
¾ cup (4½ ounces) chopped semisweet or bittersweet chocolate
2 tablespoons (1¼ ounces) light corn syrup
2 tablespoons (1 ounce) unsalted butter
½ teaspoon raspberry flavor (optional)

● Prepare the brownie batter of your choice, adding the 1 teaspoon raspberry flavor to the batter. Bake the brownies as directed in the recipe. Allow the brownies to cool for 30 minutes before spreading with the glaze.

● **To make the glaze:** In a small microwave-safe bowl or in a saucepan set over low heat, combine all the glaze ingredients and cook until the chocolate and butter are melted. Stir until smooth, then spread over the cooled bars. Cool for several hours before cutting the brownies with a knife that you've run under hot water, to prevent sticking.

Peanut-Mallow Brownies

A layer of marshmallow filling with a gentle hint of peanut butter is a nice complement to the brownie's unabashed chocolatiness.

Yield: Two dozen 2-inch brownies

1 recipe Essential Brownies (Fudgy, page 156; Cakey, page 157; or On-the-Fence, page 158)
FILLING
3 cups (6 ounces) miniature marshmallows, or 1¾ cups (6 ounces) marshmallow creme or Marshmallow Fluff
⅓ cup (1⅜ ounces) confectioners' sugar
½ cup (4¾ ounces) creamy peanut butter

● Prepare the brownie batter of your choice. Spread half of it in a lightly greased 9 x 13-inch pan.

- **To make the filling:** In a microwave-safe bowl, or in a small saucepan set over low heat, stir together all the filling ingredients until they're melted and smooth. This filling is quite sticky; spray a spoon or cookie scoop with nonstick vegetable oil spray, and spoon the filling in dollops atop the brownie batter in the pan. Top with the remaining batter.
- Bake the brownies as directed in the recipe you've chosen. Cool completely before cutting.

Whoopie Brownies

The whoopie pie, a pair of flat chocolate rounds sandwiched around a thick smear of creamy white filling, is a bake sale institution in widely dispersed pockets of the country, including northern New England and Amish country in Pennsylvania. This brownie combines a topping of whoopie-pie-like filling, chocolate frosting, and dark chocolate glaze—be still, my heart!

Yield: Two dozen 2-inch brownies

1 recipe Essential Brownies (Fudgy, page 156; Cakey, page 157; or On-the-Fence, page 158)

FROSTING

½ cup (1 stick, 4 ounces) unsalted butter

1 teaspoon vanilla extract

3 to 4 tablespoons (¾ to 1 ounce) unsweetened cocoa powder, natural or Dutch process

4 cups (1 pound) confectioners' sugar

3 to 4 tablespoons (1½ to 2 ounces) milk (regular or low fat, not nonfat)

FILLING

⅔ cup (4¼ ounces) vegetable shortening

½ cup (½ stick, 2 ounces) unsalted butter

¾ cup (5¼ ounces) sugar

¾ cup (or one 5-ounce can) evaporated milk

2 teaspoons vanilla extract

Pinch of salt

GLAZE

About 1½ cups of your favorite chocolate glaze or 1 recipe Chocolate Ganache Icing (page 159)

- Prepare and bake the brownies as directed in the chosen recipe. Cool the brownies in the pan.
- **To make the frosting:** In a medium-sized mixing bowl, beat together the butter, vanilla, cocoa, sugar, and 3 tablespoons of the milk until the mixture is smooth. Add additional milk if the frosting is too stiff. Spread the frosting on the cooled brownies.
- **To make the filling:** In a large mixing bowl, combine all filling ingredients. Using an electric mixer, beat the mixture on high speed for about 13 minutes. (First it will look coagulated and as if it won't come together. But gradually it will set smoother, and be creamy.) Spread the filling evenly over the frosting.
- Prepare glaze of your choice. Allow it to cool to lukewarm. Drizzle the glaze evenly over the filling, then, using a cake spatula or rubber spatula, carefully spread it evenly over the entire surface. Let the glaze set before cutting the brownies.

Brownies with Spirit

Crème de menthe? Kahlúa? Grand Marnier? Many liqueurs add lovely flavor to brownies. For the best flavor, complement whichever liqueur you choose with a matching extract or flavor. Why can't you just add more liqueur to enhance the flavor? Because the extra liquid will change the brownies' consistency and it will make their tops a tad less shiny.

Yield: Two dozen 2-inch brownies

1 recipe Essential Brownies (Fudgy, page 156; Cakey, page 157; or On-the-Fence, page 158)
3 tablespoons (1½ ounces) liqueur
1 to 2 teaspoons flavor or extract, or ⅛ to ¼ teaspoon strong flavoring oil

● Prepare the brownie batter of your choice, adding the liqueur and flavor to the melted butter and sugar. Bake the brownies as directed in the recipe.

VARIATIONS

Grand Marnier

3 tablespoons (1½ ounces) Grand Marnier liqueur
¼ teaspoon orange oil
2 tablespoons grated orange rind (zest)

Framboise

3 tablespoons (1½ ounces) Framboise or raspberry liqueur
1 teaspoon raspberry flavor
¼ cup (3 ounces) raspberry preserves

● Heat the raspberry preserves briefly and spread them atop the baked brownies.

Kahlua

3 tablespoons (1½ ounces) Kahlúa or coffee liqueur
1 tablespoon espresso powder

● Substitute coffee-flavored or cappuccino chips for the chocolate chips in the recipe. Dust the baked brownies with cinnamon sugar.

Frangelico

3 tablespoons (1½ ounces) Frangelico or hazelnut liqueur
1 to 2 teaspoons hazelnut flavor, or ¼ teaspoon hazelnut-flavor oil
1 cup (4 ounces) toasted hazelnuts
¾ cup (4½ ounces) chocolate chips or semisweet chocolate chunks, melted
⅓ cup (3¾ ounces) praline paste

● Add the liqueur, flavor, and nuts to the batter. Bake as directed. Stir together the melted chocolate and praline paste and spread atop the baked brownies while they're still warm.

Triple Play Brownies

You knew that eventually chocolate and peanut butter had to meet along the brownie trail. Here's a three-layer brownie that will remind you of your favorite peanut butter–filled chocolate candy, in reverse.

Yield: Two dozen 2-inch brownies

FIRST LAYER
¼ cup (½ stick, 2 ounces) unsalted butter
⅓ cup (3 ounces) creamy peanut butter
¾ cup (5¼ ounces) sugar
¼ teaspoon salt
1 teaspoon vanilla extract
¼ teaspoon baker's ammonia (optional)
1¼ cups (5¼ ounces) unbleached all-purpose flour

SECOND LAYER
1 recipe Essential Brownies (Fudgy, page 156; Cakey, page 157; or On-the-Fence, page 158)

THIRD LAYER
¾ cup (4½ ounces) caramel chips, butterscotch chips, white chocolate, or white confectionery coating
¼ cup (2¼ ounces) creamy peanut butter

● Preheat the oven to 350°F. Lightly grease a 9 x 13-inch pan.
● **To make the first layer:** In a medium-sized bowl, beat the butter and peanut butter together until soft. Blend in the sugar, salt, vanilla, and baker's ammonia. Stir in the flour; the mixture will feel dry and be crumbly. Press the dough into a lightly greased 9 x 13-inch pan; using a small pastry rolling pin or a can helps, as does covering the crumbs with a piece of plastic wrap (just remember to remove the plastic wrap before baking). Bake for 8 to 10 minutes, until lightly browned at the edges.
● **To make the second layer:** Prepare the brownie batter of your choice. Spread it over the baked crust. Bake the brownies in a preheated 350°F oven for 22 to 24 minutes; when they're done, the top should be shiny and look set. Remove them from the oven and cool slightly before adding the third layer.
● **To make the third layer:** In a small saucepan or in a microwave-safe bowl, melt the chips and peanut butter over low heat, stirring often. Spread over the warm brownies. Cool completely before cutting into squares. Using a knife that's sprayed with nonstick baking spray (or warmed in hot water and wiped often) will make slicing easier.

Decorated Cookies

When you think of decorated cookies, your mind probably goes right to the December holidays—the scent of freshly cut balsam fir trees, downtown lit up like a fairyland, wrapping gifts. Well, there's more than one holiday in the year, and every single one of them can be aptly celebrated with decorated cookies, cookies that begin life as roll-out dough.

New Year's Day? Fashion some ring-in-the-new cookies in numerals indicating the new year. Valentine's Day? Hearts and cupids are an obvious slam-dunk, but how about a big pair of red lips, or a traditional heart-and-hand? St. Patrick's Day means green shamrocks, Easter is bunnies and chicks, and then we get into summer, with Memorial Day, the Fourth of July, graduations, wedding showers, birthday parties . . . when you think about it, the year is just filled with perfect occasions to make decorated cookies. (Did we mention Halloween jack-o'-lanterns and multicolored Thanksgiving turkeys?)

Thin, rolled-dough cutout cookies are easy to decorate. Much like the black-and-white pictures in a coloring book, they await your own touch of color, be it a skating rink–smooth iced coating, perfect for a handwritten message, or thick ruffles and swirls of fondant. Before you start lining up the sugar sprinkles, however, you need a base on which to put them: a cookie strong enough to be handled without breaking, yet tender enough to please even the fussiest grandma.

The following recipes—a sugar cookie, a ginger cookie, and a lightly spiced, "halfway-in-between" cookie—are the perfect place to begin your holiday cookie decorating. And remember, you don't need to wait until December to start.

MAKING THE COOKIES ● ● ● ● ●

There are several distinct stages to making decorated roll-out cookies. This makes it easy to take the process one step at a time and, depending on your schedule, those steps can be widely spaced. The cookie dough itself can be made in advance and refrigerated (for up to 1 week) or frozen (for up to 3 months). Cookies can be rolled, cut, baked, and cooled, then stored in an airtight container to be decorated at another time. Finally, decorated cookies can be frozen until you're ready to serve, or give them away. Let's get started by making cookie dough.

ROLLING AND CUTTING DECORATED COOKIES

Rolling soft cookie dough on the back of a baking sheet, or on a cookie sheet without raised edges, makes the process easier and gives better results. When cut in place on the sheet, and the scraps removed, the delicate cookies will hold their shape better because they don't have to be moved.

Cut cookies by pressing straight down with the cookie cutter. Cookies will need about ½ inch of space between them while baking. Position your cutter in a way that maximizes the number of cookies you can get from each piece of dough, as shown.

After cutting cookies, carefully peel up the scrap dough between them. Set this dough aside in a bag in the refrigerator, to be rolled again later.

If you plan to sandwich cookies together, you can cut decorative holes ("windows") in half the cookies, to allow the filling to show through. Here the tip of a pastry tube is being used to punch out holes.

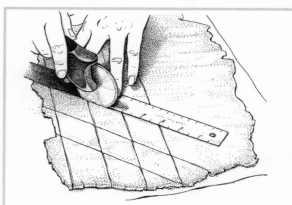

To make simple geometric shapes with no waste, use a rolling pizza wheel and a ruler to cut out squares or diamonds. If you've rolled on parchment, the cookies are easily transferred, parchment and all, to the baking sheet. After everything's safely on the baking sheet, use a thin-bladed metal turner to space the cookies properly before baking.

Decorator's Dream Cookies

Cookies for decorating should be thin, light, and crisp, sturdy enough to decorate, yet tender rather than hard. This is one of our favorite cutout cookie recipes; the *Fiori di Sicilia* ("Flowers of Sicily," a wonderful orange-vanilla flavor) adds a special bakery-style flavor to these treats. If you like an ultracrisp cookie, use the baker's ammonia.

Yield: About 4 dozen 2-inch cookies ● *Baking temperature:* 350°F ● *Baking time:* 8 to 12 minutes

> 1 cup (2 sticks, 8 ounces) unsalted butter
> 2 cups (8 ounces) confectioners' sugar
> 2 tablespoons (1¼ ounces) light corn syrup
> ¼ teaspoon *Fiori di Sicilia,* or 1 teaspoon vanilla extract or almond extract
> ½ teaspoon salt
> 1 large egg, lightly beaten with 2 tablespoons water
> 1 teaspoon baker's ammonia (optional)
> 3½ cups (14¾ ounces) unbleached all-purpose flour

● In a medium-sized bowl, cream together the butter, sugar, and corn syrup until light and fluffy. Beat in the *Fiori* or extract and salt. Add the baker's ammonia to the egg and water and stir to dissolve. Add this mixture, along with the flour, to the ingredients in the bowl and beat until smooth. Divide the dough in half, put each half in a plastic bag, and flatten each slightly. Refrigerate for 1 hour.

● Preheat the oven to 350°F. There's no need to grease the baking sheets.

● Take one piece of dough out of the refrigerator and flour a clean work surface and the dough. Roll it out as thin or thick as you like; for slightly less crisp cookies, roll it out more thickly. We roll these cookies to a ¹⁄₁₆ to ⅛-inch thickness. Sprinkle flour under and on top of the dough to keep it from sticking to the table or rolling pin.

● Alternatively, place the dough on parchment and put a sheet of plastic wrap over it as you roll, pulling the plastic to eliminate wrinkles as necessary when rolling. This will keep dough from sticking without the need for additional flour.

● Cut out shapes with a cookie cutter, cutting them as close to one another as possible.

● Transfer the cookies to the ungreased cookie sheets (or, if you've rolled right onto the parchment, remove the dough scraps between the cookies). Bake the cookies just until they're slightly brown around the edges, 8 to 12 minutes, or until they feel firm. Let the cookies cool on the baking sheets for several minutes, or until they're set. Transfer them to a rack to cool completely. Repeat with the remaining dough.

● While the cookies are cooling, prepare the icing. Choose Royal Icing (page 175) for piping decorations or Simple Cookie Glaze (page 174) for smoothing the tops of cookies before decorating with food-safe paints or markers. For a more opaque glaze, especially good with gingerbread (whose dark color sometimes shows through a normal glaze), try Hard Glaze for Cookies (page 457).

Nutrition information per serving (1 cookie, 21 g): 86 cal, 4 g fat, 1 g protein, 6 g complex carbohydrates, 5 g sugar, 15 mg cholesterol, 25 mg sodium, 14 mg potassium, 38 RE vitamin A, 1 mg iron, 2 mg calcium, 11 mg phosphorus.

essential recipe

Light Spice Cookies

Halfway between sugar cookies and gingerbread, these golden cookies are perfect for decorating.

Yield: 3 to 4 dozen 2½- to 3-inch cookies ● *Baking temperature:* 350°F ● *Baking time:* 10 to 12 minutes

½ cup (1 stick, 4 ounces) unsalted butter
½ cup (3¼ ounces) vegetable shortening
¾ cup (6 ounces) light brown sugar
½ cup (3½ ounces) granulated sugar
1½ teaspoons baking powder
1½ teaspoons cinnamon
1½ teaspoons ground ginger
½ teaspoon allspice or ground cloves
¾ teaspoon salt
1 large egg
2 tablespoons (1½ ounces) molasses
3 cups (12¾ ounces) unbleached all-purpose flour
3 tablespoons (¾ ounce) cornstarch

● In a medium-sized bowl, beat together the butter, shortening, sugars, baking powder, spices, and salt until light and fluffy. Add the egg and molasses and beat well. Stir about half of the flour into the butter mixture. When well combined, add the cornstarch and the remaining flour. Divide the dough in half, flattening each half slightly, and wrap well. Refrigerate for 1 hour (or longer), for easiest rolling.

● Preheat the oven to 350°F. There's no need to grease the baking sheets.

● Take one piece of dough out of the refrigerator and flour a clean work surface and the dough. Roll it out as thin or thick as you like; for slightly less crisp cookies, roll it out more thickly. We recommend a ⅛- to ¼-inch thickness for this cookie. Sprinkle flour under and on top of the dough to keep it from sticking to the table or rolling pin.

● Alternatively, place the dough on parchment and put a sheet of plastic wrap over it as you roll, pulling the plastic to eliminate wrinkles as necessary when rolling. This will keep dough from sticking without the need for additional flour.

● Cut out shapes with a cookie cutter, cutting them as close to one another as possible.

● Transfer the cookies to ungreased cookie sheets (or, if you've rolled right onto the parchment, remove the dough scraps between the cookies). Bake the cookies just until they're slightly brown around the edges, 8 to 12 minutes, or until they feel firm. Let the cookies cool on the baking sheets for several minutes, or until they're set. Transfer them to a rack to cool completely. Repeat with the remaining dough.

● While the cookies are cooling, prepare the icing. Choose Royal Icing (page 175) for piping decorations or Simple Cookie Glaze (page 174) for smoothing the tops of cookies before decorating with food-safe paints or markers.

Gingerbread Cookies

This molasses-dark, ginger-and-spice flavored cookie is perfect for gingerbread men. We roll it a bit thicker than usual, to give the cookies just a hint of "chew." While ginger is often thought of as a winter baking flavor, we've found that ginger pairs well with various fruits, too. Ginger and peach is an especially wonderful combination; try gingerbread cookies served with fresh sliced peaches, or a peach crumble topped with gingerbread cookie crumbs.

Yield: 3 dozen 3-inch cookies ● *Baking temperature: 375°F* ● *Baking time: 8 to 10 minutes*

¾ cup (1½ sticks, 6 ounces) unsalted butter
¾ cup (6 ounces) light or dark brown sugar
¾ cup (9 ounces) molasses
1 teaspoon salt
2 teaspoons cinnamon
2 teaspoons ground ginger
¼ teaspoon allspice or ground cloves
1 large egg
1 teaspoon baking powder
½ teaspoon baking soda
3½ cups (14¾ ounces) unbleached all-purpose flour

● In a saucepan set over low heat, or in the microwave, melt the butter, then stir in the sugar, molasses, salt, and spices. Transfer the mixture to a medium-sized mixing bowl, let it cool to lukewarm, then beat in the egg.

● In a large bowl, whisk the baking powder and soda into the flour, then stir these dry ingredients into the molasses mixture. Divide the dough in half and wrap well. Refrigerate for 1 hour or longer.

● Preheat the oven to 375°F. There's no need to grease the baking sheets.

● Take one piece of dough out of the refrigerator and flour a clean work surface and the dough. Roll it out as thin or thick as you like; for slightly less crisp cookies, roll it out more thickly. We roll these cookies, which we prefer a bit less crisp and more chewy, to a ¼-inch thickness. Sprinkle flour under and on top of the dough to keep it from sticking to the table or rolling pin.

● Alternatively, place the dough on parchment and put a sheet of plastic wrap over it as you roll, pulling the plastic to eliminate wrinkles as necessary when rolling. This will keep dough from sticking without the need for additional flour.

● Cut out shapes with a cookie cutter, cutting them as close to one another as possible.

● Transfer the cookies to ungreased cookie sheets (or, if you've rolled right onto the parchment, remove the dough scraps between the cookies). Bake the cookies just until they're slightly brown around the edges, 8 to 12 minutes, or until they feel firm. Let the cookies cool on the baking sheets for several minutes, or until they're set. Transfer them to a rack to cool completely. Repeat with the remaining dough.

continued on next page

● While the cookies are cooling, prepare the icing. Choose Royal Icing (page 175) for piping decorations or Simple Cookie Glaze (below) for smoothing the tops of cookies before decorating with food-safe paints or markers. For a more opaque glaze, especially good with gingerbread (whose dark color sometimes shows through a normal glaze), try Hard Glaze for Cookies, page 457.

Nutrition information per serving (1 cookie, 30 g): 116 cal, 4 g fat, 1 g protein, 9 g complex carbohydrates, 10 g sugar, 16 mg cholesterol, 103 mg sodium, 66 mg potassium, 38 RE vitamin A, 1 mg vitamin C, 1 mg iron, 22 mg calcium, 21 mg phosphorus.

Simple Cookie Glaze

This glaze dries hard and shiny, perfect for coating the top surface of your cookies in preparation for decorating with food-safe pens or markers. Be sure you measure accurately here—too little milk, and the glaze won't spread nicely, too much milk, and it will be thin, spotty, and develop splotches overnight. The goal is a glaze that isn't perfectly smooth when you apply it, but that settles into a smooth surface within half a minute or so. Glaze one cookie and set it aside for a minute. Has the glaze smoothed out? If so, it's the right consistency. And remember, it's easier to add more liquid than to stir in more sugar, so start with a glaze that's thicker than you think it should be, then add milk by the half-teaspoonful to adjust the consistency.

Yield: ⅔ cup (enough to cover about 2½ dozen 2-inch cookies

2¼ cups (9 ounces) confectioners' sugar
2 tablespoons (1¼ ounces) light corn syrup
1½ to 2 tablespoons plus 1 teaspoon (¾ to 1⅛ ounces) milk
Food coloring (optional)

● In a small bowl, whisk together the confectioners' sugar, corn syrup, and 1½ tablespoons of the milk. Add food coloring, if desired. Spread one cookie with glaze. If it doesn't smooth out after 1 minute, dribble in additional milk, ½ teaspoon at a time, until the glaze reaches the right consistency. Use an offset spatula or table knife to spread the glaze on the cookies.

Nutrition information per serving (1 teaspoon, 11 g): 37 cal, 9 g sugar, 2 mg sodium, 2 mg potassium, 1 RE vitamin A, 2 mg calcium, 1 mg phosphorus.

Royal Icing

Royal icing is thick, fluffy, and hard-drying, ideal for piping decorations onto cookies, or using as mortar in a gingerbread house (page 182). Meringue powder (see page 485) is available at cake decorating stores, or via mail order. For food coloring, we recommend gel or paste colors because they're so strong you only need to use a drop or two for brilliantly vibrant colors.

Yield: a generous 3 cups fluffy icing

¼ cup (1 ounce) meringue powder
¼ teaspoon salt
3 to 4 cups (12 to 16 ounces) confectioners' sugar
1 teaspoon vanilla extract
¾ to 1 cup (6 to 8 ounces) cool water
Food coloring (optional)

- In a medium-sized mixing bowl, whisk together the meringue powder, salt, and confectioners' sugar. Add the vanilla and ¾ cup cool water and stir, or beat on slow speed. The mixture will seem hard and lumpy, but the sugar will dissolve after 4 or 5 minutes and everything will smooth out.
- Once the mixture is smooth, gradually increase the mixer speed to high, taking several minutes for the transition. Beat at high speed until the icing is fluffy. Add food coloring as desired. Keep the icing covered with plastic wrap or a damp cloth to prevent it from drying out, if you won't be using it right away, or if you're tackling an extra-long project.

Nutrition information per serving (a generous 4 teaspoons coating, 14 g): 37 cal, 9 g sugar, 16 mg sodium, 3 mg potassium.

GETTING READY TO DECORATE

Once the Royal Icing is made (or the cookies are glazed), it's time to collect the tools you'll use for decorating.

If you plan to make more than one color of Royal Icing, place portions of the batch in small bowls and tint with food coloring however you like.

Decide how you're going to decorate the cookies (pipe on decorations? glaze, then paint?), then gather the appropriate tools. Here are the tools we use most often:

- A small paintbrush and a dish of water, for cleaning the brush between colors
- Cotton swabs for cleaning up mistakes
- Extra water to thin the icing
- Food coloring and small dishes in which to mix each color of icing
- Disposable pastry bags, a coupler, and piping tips
- Rolling pin
- Scissors
- Ruler
- Small nylon spatulas and thin-blade metal turners, for moving cookies around
- Rolling pizza wheel
- Parchment
- Cookie cutters
- Assorted colored sugars
- Shallow dishes for dipping and dredging
- Food-safe pens
- Garlic press

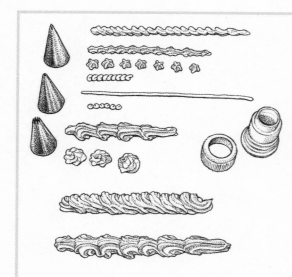

A plastic coupler can be placed in the pastry bag first. This allows you to change tip shapes without filling another bag. Different tips will give you different effects. Shown here, top to bottom, are a small star tip, used for a scalloped border and individual stars; a small straight tip, used for piping outlines; and a larger star tip, for a larger diameter shell border.

176

USING A PASTRY BAG

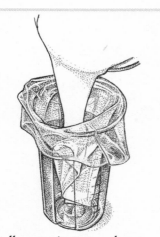

A tall measuring cup or heavy-bottomed drinking glass is a big help when filling a pastry bag. Place the bag inside the cup, folding the top back over the rim of the cup. Pour or scoop icing into the bag with the help of a spatula; don't fill the bag more than three-quarters full.

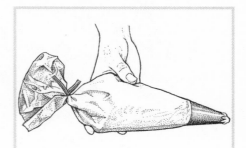

Take the bag out of the cup and twist the top (open end) to hold the frosting in. A twist tie or rubber band is helpful to keep the top of the bag closed, so icing doesn't back up onto your hand.

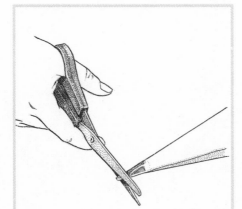

You can use the pastry bag without a tip, by snipping a very small hole at the end with a pair of scissors. If you're filling the bag with very stiff frosting, do this before putting the icing in the bag. The tiny hole will allow air to escape ahead of the icing, making the bag easier to fill.

To make a striped line of frosting, use a paintbrush to paint lines of food coloring up the inside wall of the pastry bag before filling it. The colors will mix as they come through the tube.

OUTLINING AND FILLING

One of the best ways to create a dramatic effect without much effort or fuss is to outline the edges of the cookie, then fill in the center with a contrasting icing color. When this technique is used to accent a filled cookie, the effect can be striking, as shown here.

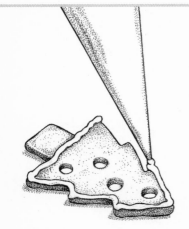

Pipe a thin bead of icing around the edge of the tree. Let it dry until stiff.

To fill in the outlined area, thin some tinted icing with water. Use a paintbrush to cover the cookie's surface inside the outline.

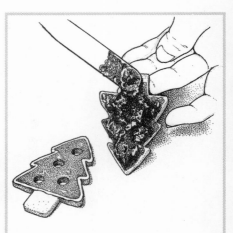

To fill cookies with jam, warm the jam in the microwave, stirring until no lumps remain. Spread the jam on the bottom cookie, covering its entire surface.

Press the top cookie onto the filling to finish your filled cookie.

A simple decoration for round cookies: Dip the edge in a shallow dish of frosting, coating it ¼ inch in toward the center, all around the outside. This works best with cookies that are at least ¼ inch thick.

To complete the decoration, while the icing is still sticky, roll the iced cookie edge, in colored sugar, nonpareils, or sprinkles.

WORKING WITH SEVERAL COLORS SIMULTANEOUSLY

Using several colors of icing on a cookie can create a stunning look. Contrasting colors can be mixed for a marbled effect, drawn through each other with a toothpick or cake tester, or mixed with a paintbrush on top of the cookie.

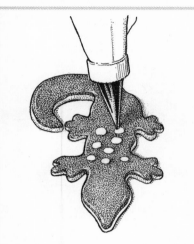

Frost the cookie with one color icing, then pipe a second color on top to create a polka-dot effect, or spots.

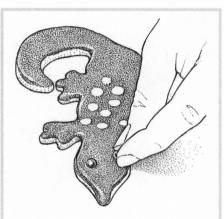

Dragées or sugar decorations are placed on the icing while it's still soft.

After piping white stripes over the base color (while the base is still soft), a toothpick, straw, or cake tester can be used to pull one color through the other. Place the toothpick at the edge of the cookie and draw it through the two colors in a straight line.

To create a marbled effect, first mix two contrasting colors in a shallow dish, leaving identifiable streaks.

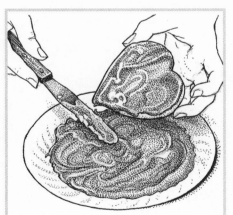

Then dip the top of the cookie into the marbled icing on the plate and use a knife or small spatula to spread it evenly over the surface.

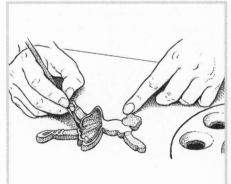

Colors can be combined right on the cookie's surface. After an area is covered with icing, it can be tinted while still soft with food coloring and a paintbrush.

ICING IN TWO STAGES

Achieve a professional look for your cookies by first coating them with a base color, allowing it to completely harden. After the base is dry, a contrasting color is piped on top. This top color can be further accented with colored sugar, sprinkles, or other sugar decorations, if you wish. Cookies that have a dry base coat of color are also perfect candidates for written inscriptions with food-safe markers.

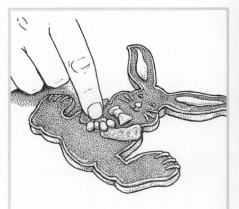

Outline an iced heart cookie with a lighter color and decorate with an inscription. To show off these features, sprinkle colored sugar over the accent frosting while it's still soft. Excess sugar can be shaken or brushed off after the top color has dried.

Accentuate both the look and flavor of cookies with warm Chocolate Ganache (page 460). A zip-top sandwich bag with one corner snipped off is a handy way to drizzle on liquid chocolate.

This bunny has two different accent colors, which show off his ears and whiskers. A food-safe marking pen has been used to draw his eyes and mouth. Egg-shaped sugar decorations are then placed in the soft frosting on his paws.

WORKING WITH FONDANT

Fondant is a stiff yet pliable icing (similar in texture to modeling clay) that can be tinted, rolled, cut out, and draped over cookies or cakes, where it dries to a smooth, hard surface (see recipe, page 462). Fondant can also be molded, or shaped into distinct textures with embossing tools. Fondant can serve as decoration on its own or be used as a base for further decoration.

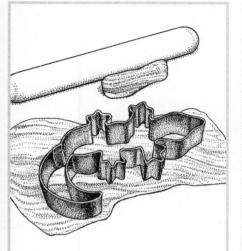

Tint the fondant with food coloring, then knead it with your hands until a marbled effect is created. Fondant is best rolled with a plastic rolling pin, to avoid sticking. To ice a cookie with fondant, roll the icing to wafer thinness, then cut it to shape with the same cutter you used to cut your cookie.

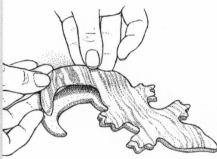

Place the fondant on top of the baked cookie, pressing it down gently to make it stick.

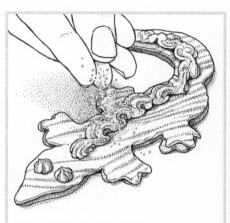

Pipe icing on top of the fondant; sprinkle sugar on top of the soft piped icing to accent.

By squeezing tinted fondant through a garlic press, strands of frosting are created that make great hair for this little girl.

A cookie cutter is used to help make a dress for the little girl from rolled fondant. Use a food marker to draw final details, such as the face, the buttons on the dress, and the ruffle on the hem.

Building a Gingerbread House

You may have seen intricate gingerbread houses created by pastry chefs and displayed at Christmas. You've probably also seen the do-it-yourself kits that include a baked house and all the decorations, ready to assemble. If you're a hands-on type (without a lot of time for anything too extravagant), you'll enjoy this just-challenging-enough gingerbread house. If you're making this with children, we suggest assembling the house beforehand, then letting them add the decorations. Their patience may wear thin if they have to wait for the house to dry fully before they can start adding the candy.

CONSTRUCTION GINGERBREAD
½ cup (3¼ ounces) vegetable shortening
¾ cup (6 ounces) light or dark brown sugar
¾ cup (9 ounces) molasses
1 teaspoon salt
2 teaspoons cinnamon
2 teaspoons ground ginger
¼ teaspoon ground allspice or ground cloves
2 large eggs
1 teaspoon baking powder
½ teaspoon baking soda
4 cups (17 ounces) unbleached all-purpose flour

● In a large mixing bowl, cream together the shortening and brown sugar. Add the molasses, salt, and spices, mixing to combine. Beat in the eggs, baking powder and baking soda, scraping the mixing bowl at least once. Stir in the flour. The dough will be quite stiff. Wrap the dough and let it rest at cool room temperature for 1 hour; this will make it easier to roll out.

● Preheat the oven to 300°F.

● Roll out the dough to a thickness of ¼ inch and cut the gingerbread pieces as illustrated at left. (Template dimensions are given opposite.) Bake the gingerbread pieces for about 20 minutes, until they're stiff and dry to the touch. Remove from the oven, cool for 10 minutes on the pan, then transfer to a rack to cool completely.

● While the gingerbread is baking, make Royal Icing, (see page 175); this will be your construction mortar.

● Follow the illustrated instructions on pages 183 and 184 for constructing and decorating the gingerbread house.

Construction gingerbread can be rolled out and baked on the back of a baking sheet. A cardboard template is helpful to cut out the shapes for walls and roof.

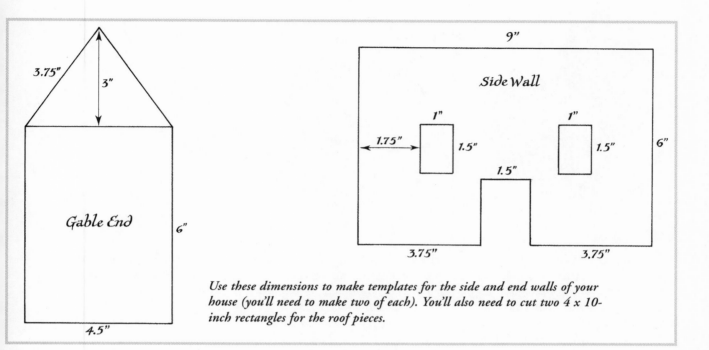

Use these dimensions to make templates for the side and end walls of your house (you'll need to make two of each). You'll also need to cut two 4 x 10-inch rectangles for the roof pieces.

After the pieces are baked, trim the edges to make them straight. This will ensure that the edges dovetail together nicely, with no gaps, when the house is assembled.

To set the first side wall, run a bead of frosting along the bottom edge and up one side. Set the wall onto a piece of cardboard and prop it up with a can or jar. Run another bead of frosting along the inside edge of the wall's base, to help support it.

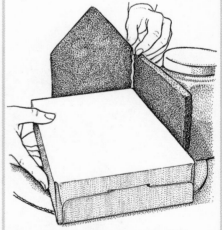

Set up the adjoining end wall the same way. Use the corner of a box to check that they're set at right angles to each other.

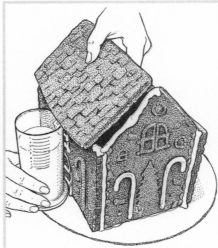

Once all four walls are in place, allow them to dry for several hours (or overnight) before adding the roof. Be sure to keep your unused royal icing tightly covered with plastic wrap while the house dries.

To put the roof on, run a bead of frosting along the top edges of the walls—side, front, and back. Place the roof panels onto the frosted walls, using props to support the lower edge of the roof while the icing sets.

After both roof panels are on, run another bead of frosting down the ridgeline of the roof.

Accent the prominent architectural features of your house with candy. The only "rule" is that everything you use should be edible, because people are bound to come along and grab a sample.

Highlight any of your house's features— windows, doors, etc.—by outlining them with frosting. Use whatever colorful candies you like to decorate.

Bars & Squares

So many cookies, so little time . . . When the bake sale, potluck, or office party looms, and you've had your mind set on baking cookies but suddenly find you've run out of time, take heart—it's bar cookies to the rescue.

Bar cookies—more commonly shortened to "bars," and known alternatively as "squares"—can be as simple as a butterscotch brownie or as complex as a multilayer extravaganza of cookie crust, chips, nuts, fruit, and a creamy topping. The origins of the bar cookie are obscure; legend has it they derived from a housewife who forgot to add leavening to her sheet cake batter. Brownies, certainly the most familiar and beloved of bar cookies, first gained acclaim in 1897, when a recipe appeared in the Sears, Roebuck catalog. They proved so popular that Sears later sold brownie mix in its *Big Book*. The rest, as they say, is history.

Bars come in two basic varieties: one-step, in which the baker mixes all the ingredients and spoons the dough or batter into a wide, shallow pan to bake; or the layered two-step, where a crust (usually prebaked) is spread with filling or topping, or both. For the truly time-pressed, one-step bars are the best solution, you can often go from basic inspiration to a pan of hot bars in less than 40 minutes. These bars, dense, moist, and often rather simple looking, are nonetheless compelling; from almond- and lemon-scented blonde brownies to spicy hermits, they're marked by simple ingredients, ease of preparation, and classic good flavor. Two-step bars, on the other hand, can bring out your inner baking artist: mix and match crusts, fillings, and toppings to your heart's content. Bring on the nuts, the chips, the dried fruit, coconut, cereal, chocolate. Two-step bars let you pull out all the stops.

So next time you find yourself assigned to bring dessert to the basketball awards dinner, or want a quick treat to take to a friend who's even more time-stressed than you are—think bars. For flavor, texture, and ease of preparation, they're one cool cookie.

ONE-STEP BARS • • • • • • • • • •

One bowl, a manageable number of ingredients, and simple techniques— usually just beating to combine—highlight these easy bars. But being easy doesn't make them dull; while uniformly moist and chewy, their flavors range from ultra-spicy to comforting peanut butter.

Ruth Wakefield's Chocolate Chip Cookie Bars

No time to make everyone's favorite, chocolate chip cookies? This dough comes together in a flash—just spread it in a pan and bake; no need to shape individual cookies. When the bars are done, cut into squares and serve to chocolate chip cookie lovers, who'll be happy to substitute this easy version for the soft, chewy-chocolaty "real thing."

We christened these bars for the inventor of the chocolate chip cookie, Ruth Wakefield, proprietor of the Toll House Restaurant in Whitman, Massachusetts. Her *Toll House Cookbook* has been a standard in the King Arthur library for years.

Yield: 35 bars ● *Baking temperature:* 350°F ● *Baking time:* 24 to 26 minutes

2¾ cups (11½ ounces) unbleached all-purpose flour
2½ teaspoons baking powder
½ teaspoon salt
⅔ cup (1⅓ sticks, 5¼ ounces) unsalted butter, melted
2¼ cups (18 ounces) brown sugar
3 large eggs
2 cups (12 ounces) chocolate chips
1 cup (4 ounces) chopped walnuts or pecans

● Preheat the oven to 350°F. Lightly grease a 10 x 15-inch jelly roll pan, a 14-inch deep-dish pizza pan, or similar sized pan.
● In a large bowl, whisk together the flour, baking powder, and salt. Set aside.
● In another large bowl, combine the melted butter and brown sugar, stirring until smooth. Allow the mixture to cool slightly. Add the eggs one at a time, beating well after each addition. Stir in the flour mixture, then the chocolate chips and nuts. Spread the batter into the prepared pan.
● Bake the bars for 24 to 26 minutes, until their top is shiny and golden. Don't overbake, or the bars will be dry; a cake tester inserted in the center will *not* come out clean. Remove the bars from the oven and cool to room temperature before cutting.

Nutrition information per serving (1 bar, 46 g): 198 cal, 9 g fat, 3 g protein, 8 g complex carbohydrates, 19 g sugar, 1 g dietary fiber, 28 mg cholesterol, 77 mg sodium, 118 mg potassium, 42 RE vitamin A, 1 mg iron, 40 mg calcium, 57 mg phosphorus, 8 mg caffeine.

VARIATIONS

● To make thicker (about ¾-inch) bars, bake the batter in a lightly greased 9 x 13-inch pan for 30 to 35 minutes.
● Substitute M&M's for the chocolate chips.

Vintage Butterscotch Bars

When someone mentions butterscotch, you think butterscotch sauce, right? Well think again: butterscotch is a flavor that easily moves from ice cream sundaes to baked confections. These bars are sweet and buttery, with the distinctive, almost smoky tang of brown sugar.

Yield: 24 bars ● *Baking temperature: 350°F* ● *Baking time: 20 to 24 minutes*

½ cup (1 stick, 4 ounces) unsalted butter
2 cups (16 ounces) brown sugar
2 large eggs
1 teaspoon vanilla extract
Scant ⅛ teaspoon butter-rum or butter-pecan flavor (optional)
1 teaspoon salt
1 teaspoon baking powder
1½ cups (6¼ ounces) unbleached all-purpose flour
1½ cups (6 ounces) chopped walnuts

● Preheat the oven to 350°F. Lightly grease a 9 x 13-inch, 11 x 11-inch, or similar-sized pan.
● Melt the butter in a saucepan set over low heat, or in a bowl in the microwave. Remove from the heat and add the sugar, mixing until well blended. Cool to lukewarm.
● Transfer the butter mixture to a medium-sized mixing bowl. Stir in the eggs, then the vanilla, flavor, salt, and baking powder. Mix in the flour and nuts.
● Spread the batter into the prepared pan. Bake the bars for 20 to 24 minutes, until the top looks shiny. Don't overbake, or they'll dry out; bake just until the edges start to pull away from

Bar cutting 101

The quickest, easiest way to cut bars is with a baker's bench knife (see page 31). First, visualize how many bars you want to make. In this chapter, almost all the bars are approximately 2 inches x 2 inches, unless noted otherwise.

If you're making bars for a bake sale, or for some reason you want them very close to one another in size, get out your ruler or tape measure and measure the bars along the sides of the pan, using a knife to make a small notch where you'll cut. This seems rather precise, but cutting bars is just like woodworking: measure twice, cut once.

For bars that are very sticky and moist, try wet-ting the blade of your knife, or spray it with non-stick vegetable oil spray. Wipe it off each time it emerges with clinging crumbs. Cutting sticky bars with a sticky knife will result in ripped and crumbled bars.

To remove the bars from the pan, slip a flexible metal spatula all around the edges of the pan, then gently lift the bars off the bottom to loosen them. Use the spatula to help you lift one bar out of the pan; it may stick and crumble, but just assume that'll be the "baker's taste" bar. Once you've got the access created by removing that first bar, slip your spatula into the space and go from there.

the sides of the pan, and a cake tester comes out almost clean, with just a few moist crumbs clinging to it. Remove the bars from the oven and cool completely before cutting.

Nutrition information per serving (1 bar, 43 g): 184 cal, 9 g fat, 3 g protein, 6 g complex carbohydrates, 18 g sugar, 1 g dietary fiber, 29 mg cholesterol, 122 mg sodium, 120 mg potassium, 48 RE vitamin A, 1 mg vitamin C, 1 mg iron, 35 mg calcium, 59 g phosphorus.

Scandinavian Blondies

Nearly as white as Scandinavia's driven snow, and almost as rich as its fresh dairy cream, these imaginative vanilla bars definitely reflect their name. Tender and cakelike, but with a bit of pleasant chew, these are a treat that's simple to make—which is a good thing, since you'll find yourself making them over and over again. These are particularly good served with a scoop of ice cream on top.

Yield: 16 squares ● *Baking temperature:* 325°F ● *Baking time:* 30 to 35 minutes

> 2 large eggs
> 1 cup (7 ounces) sugar
> ½ teaspoon salt
> 1 teaspoon almond or lemon extract
> ½ cup (1 stick, 4 ounces) unsalted butter, melted
> 1 cup (4¼ ounces) unbleached all-purpose flour
> ½ cup (2 ounces) sliced almonds (optional)

● Preheat the oven to 325°F. Lightly grease an 8 x 8-inch square or 9-inch round pan.
● In a medium-sized mixing bowl, beat the eggs well, until light colored and thick. Add the sugar and salt, continuing to beat until shiny and pale yellow. Add the extract, melted butter, and ½ cup of the flour, folding it in gently. Fold in the remaining ½ cup flour.
● Pour the batter into the prepared pan. Sprinkle with the nuts. Bake the bars for 30 to 35 minutes, until the edges are pulling away from the sides of the pan and they're a very light gold color. Remove from the oven and cool before cutting into squares.

Nutrition information per serving (1 square, 44 g): 177 cal, 8 g fat, 3 g protein, 11 g complex carbohydrates, 12 g sugar, 1 g dietary fiber, 43 mg cholesterol, 76 mg sodium, 49 mg potassium, 68 RE vitamin A, 1 mg vitamin C, 1 mg iron, 13 mg calcium, 41 mg phosphorus.

VARIATIONS

● For a more delicate flavor, use ½ teaspoon almond extract and ½ teaspoon vanilla extract.
● If you choose lemon flavor, add a tablespoon or so of grated lemon rind for added punch.

The easiest way to spread batter evenly

When you're spreading batter for bars or brownies in a pan, the easiest way to make sure it reaches all the way to the corners of the pan and is fairly smooth, is to wet your hands and use your fingers to pat and push it where you want it to go. Wet fingers work better than a spatula—they don't stick and, of course, they're user-friendly. If the batter starts to stick, simply wet your fingers again. Don't worry about dripping water atop the batter; it will evaporate as soon as the bars go into the oven.

Peanut Butter Smoothies

Who says chocolate is the only flavor that can make a fudgy, moist, must-have-right-now square? These bars are a peanut butter purist's delight. Use smooth or chunky peanut butter, to your taste, and accent with chocolate chips or lightly salted peanuts.

Yield: 16 bars ● *Baking temperature: 350°F* ● *Baking time: 30 minutes*

> 6 tablespoons (¾ stick, 3 ounces) unsalted butter
> ½ cup (4¾ ounces) peanut butter
> 1 cup (7 ounces) granulated sugar
> ¼ cup (2 ounces) brown sugar
> 2 large eggs
> 1 teaspoon vanilla extract
> 1 cup (4¼ ounces) unbleached all-purpose flour
> ¼ teaspoon salt
> 1 teaspoon baking powder
> 1 cup (6 ounces) chocolate or peanut butter chips, or lightly salted peanuts

● Preheat the oven to 350°F. Lightly grease a 9 x 9-inch pan.
● In a medium-sized bowl, cream the butter and peanut butter together until smooth. Add the sugars, beating to combine. Beat in the eggs one at a time, scraping the inside of the bowl after the first egg. Stir in the vanilla.
● In a separate bowl, whisk together the flour, salt, and baking powder and add to the peanut butter mixture, stirring until combined. Mix in the chips.
● Spread the batter in the prepared pan. Bake the bars for 30 minutes, until the edges just barely come away from the sides of the pan. Remove from the oven and cool completely before cutting.

Nutrition information per serving (1 bar, made with chocolate chips, 54 g): 237 cal, 12 g fat, 4 g protein, 29 g complex carbohydrates, 7 g sugar, 1 g dietary fiber, 39 mg cholesterol, 111 mg sodium, 114 mg potassium, 54 RE vitamin A, 1 mg iron, 28 mg calcium, 63 mg phosphorus, 8 mg caffeine.

Peanut Brittle Bars

When it comes to cookies, people seem to sort themselves along flavor and texture lines. You're a chocolate person, or a ginger aficionado, or a lemon lover. And you prefer crisp or chewy. These bars are for the crisp-texture person. They're reminiscent of peanut brittle, but you won't have to deal with any sharp edges.

Yield: 24 bars ● *Baking temperature: 325°F* ● *Baking time: 18 to 20 minutes*

½ cup (1 stick, 4 ounces) unsalted butter
½ cup (4 ounces) brown sugar
1 large egg
1 teaspoon vanilla extract
1 cup (4¼ ounces) unbleached all-purpose flour
¼ teaspoon salt
¼ teaspoon baking soda
½ teaspoon cinnamon (optional)
1½ cups (7½ ounces) chopped peanuts

● Preheat the oven to 325°F. Lightly grease a 9 x 13-inch, 11 x 11-inch, or similar-sized pan.
● In a medium-sized mixing bowl, cream together the butter and sugar. Add the egg and vanilla, mixing to combine. In a separate bowl, whisk together the flour, salt, baking soda, and cinnamon, and stir into the creamed mixture. Mix in 1 cup of the peanuts and spread the batter in the prepared pan. The batter will be stiff and barely cover the bottom of the pan. An offset icing spatula (or wet fingers) is helpful in spreading it around.
● Sprinkle the remaining ½ cup nuts on top. Spray a piece of plastic wrap with nonstick spray, cover the batter with it, and press the nuts down into the dough through the plastic. Peel off the wrap.
● Bake the bars for 18 to 20 minutes, until the dough pulls away from the edge of the pan. Remove from the oven and cut into squares or diamonds while still warm. Allow the bars to cool completely before removing them from the pan.

Nutrition information per serving (1 bar, 26 g): 128 cal, 9 g fat, 3 g protein, 10 g complex carbohydrates, 5 g sugar, 1 g dietary fiber, 20 mg cholesterol, 94 mg sodium, 87 mg potassium, 42 RE vitamin A, 1 mg iron, 12 mg calcium, 44 mg phosphorus.

Harvest Pumpkin Bars

Orange as an October sunset, these bars feature a dense, moist, cakelike base gilded with a layer of thick cream cheese icing. Add a sprinkling of diced crystallized ginger and pecans on top, for both looks and flavor.

Yield: 16 bars ● ***Baking temperature:** 350°F* ● ***Baking time:** 25 to 30 minutes*

BARS
  ⅓ cup (2½ ounces) vegetable oil
  2 large eggs
  1 cup (7 ounces) sugar
  1 cup (9½ ounces) pumpkin purée (canned pumpkin)
  1 teaspoon pumpkin pie spice, or ½ teaspoon cinnamon plus ¼ teaspoon
    each ground ginger and nutmeg
  1 teaspoon salt
  1 teaspoon baking powder
  1¼ cups (5¼ ounces) unbleached all-purpose flour

FROSTING
  ½ cup (4 ounces, half a large package) cream cheese (reduced fat [Neufchâtel]
    or full fat)
  3 tablespoons (1½ ounces) unsalted butter
  1¾ cups (7 ounces) confectioners' sugar
  1 teaspoon vanilla extract
  ¼ cup (1½ ounces) finely diced crystallized ginger (optional)
  ¼ cup (1 ounce) chopped pecans (optional)

● Preheat the oven to 350°F. Lightly grease a 9 x 9-inch or 7 x 11-inch pan.
● **To make the bars:** In a medium-sized mixing bowl, cream together the oil, eggs, sugar, pumpkin, spices, salt, and baking powder. Add the flour, stirring just until smooth. Spread the batter in the prepared pan.
● Bake the bars for 30 minutes, or until they're golden brown and a cake tester inserted into the center comes out clean. Remove from the oven and cool completely on a rack.
● **To make the frosting:** In a medium-sized mixing bowl, beat together the cream cheese, butter, sugar, and vanilla until smooth, adjusting the consistency with more sugar or a bit of milk to make it spreadable. Frost the bars and sprinkle with the ginger and pecans. Cut into bars.

Nutrition information per serving (1 square, 83 g): 292 cal, 15 g fat, 3 g protein, 9 g complex carbohydrates, 29 g sugar, 1 g dietary fiber, 51 mg cholesterol, 198 mg sodium, 72 mg potassium, 438 RE vitamin A, 1 mg vitamin C, 1 mg iron, 36 mg calcium, 46 mg phosphorus.

Chewy Date-Nut Bars

With most of us here qualifying as inveterate recipe collectors, there are many, many recipe boxes and treasured ring-bound recipe collections around the office that come from our grand-mothers' kitchens. These yellowed, stained "receipts" are mute testament to the generations of bakers who have lovingly used them. The following old-fashioned, humble-looking bars would never win a beauty contest. But they're delicious: moist and chewy, sweet and nutty, they're perfect with a cup of tea.

Yield: 16 bars ● ***Baking temperature:*** *400°F* ● ***Baking time:*** *18 to 22 minutes*

2 large eggs
1¼ cups (5¼ ounces) unbleached all-purpose flour
¼ teaspoon salt
1 teaspoon baking powder
1 cup (8 ounces) brown sugar
1 cup (4 ounces) chopped walnuts
1 cup (5¼ ounces) chopped dates
Confectioners' sugar, for dusting (optional)

● Preheat the oven to 400°F. Lightly grease a 9 x 9-inch pan.
● In a medium-sized mixing bowl, beat the eggs until they're frothy and thoroughly combined. In a separate bowl, whisk together the flour, salt, baking powder, and brown sugar. Stir the dry ingredients into the eggs. Stir in the nuts and dates.
● Spread the sticky batter into the pan. Greasing or wetting your fingers, or using an offset spatula, helps to distribute the dough evenly.
● Bake the bars for 18 to 22 minutes, until they're golden brown and shiny on top, but slightly wet looking in the center when you insert a cake tester. Overbaking will result in a crunchy rather than chewy bar. Remove the bars from the oven, and cool completely before cutting them into squares. Dust with confectioners' sugar on top, if desired.

Nutrition information per serving (1 bar, 50 g): 180 cal, 6 g fat, 4 g protein, 16 g complex carbo-hydrates, 13 g sugar, 2 g dietary fiber, 27 mg cholesterol, 77 mg sodium, 189 mg potassium, 15 RE vitamin A, 1 mg vitamin C, 1 mg iron, 41 mg calcium, 77 mg phosphorus.

Keeping the tops of your bars on an even keel

Do you ever get a tough, raised ridge around the edge of your brownies or bar cookies? There are two things you can do to prevent this. First, decrease the baking time by a minute or two. Second, run a dull knife around the outside edge of the pan as soon as the bars come out of the oven. This will release the edges so they can contract evenly as they cool, leaving an even, flat surface all the way across.

The Very Best Hermit Bars Ever

Think of the most delicious hermit bar you ever ate, the moistest, chewiest, nicely spiced bar, with a crisp shiny top and dense center. Okay? This bar beats that one, we guarantee it. If you count molasses cookies, spice cake, or gingerbread—any of the old-fashioned, dark and spicy baked goods with their long international history—among your favorites, you'll love these bars. Hermits, which have a history dating to Colonial America, came by their name honestly: like the human hermit, they're happy to be by themselves for days on end, staying chewy and fresh without any intervention from their baker. In fact, letting them rest for a couple of days allows the molasses and spice flavors to meld and mellow (a fact true of all spice cookies).

Yield: 35 bars ● *Baking temperature: 350°F* ● *Baking time: 18 to 20 minutes*

BARS
- 1⅓ cups (9¼ ounces) sugar
- ½ cup plus 2 tablespoons (4 ounces) vegetable shortening
- 4 tablespoons (½ stick, 2 ounces) unsalted butter
- ¼ cup (3 ounces) molasses
- ¾ teaspoon salt
- ¾ teaspoon ground allspice
- ¾ teaspoon cinnamon
- 1¾ teaspoons baking soda
- 2 large eggs
- 5 cups (20 ounces) cake flour
- ⅓ cup (2⅝ ounces) water
- 2 cups (12 ounces) raisins, packed

GLAZE
- 3 tablespoons (1½ ounces) milk
- 1 cup (4 ounces) confectioners' sugar

● Preheat the oven to 350°F. Lightly grease a 10 x 15-inch jelly roll pan, a 14-inch round deep-dish pizza pan, or similar-sized pan.

● **To make the bars:** In a large mixing bowl, cream together the sugar, shortening, and butter, beating at medium speed until fluffy. Add the molasses, salt, spices, and baking soda. Mix for 1 minute, then stop the mixer and scrape down the sides of the bowl. Add the eggs one at a time, beating well after each addition. Add half the flour. Once it's mixed in, add the water, then the other half of the flour. When the batter is mixed completely, add the raisins and stir until combined. Spread the batter in the prepared pan.

● Bake the hermits for 18 to 20 minutes, until the edges are light brown. They'll puff up in the oven and the top will get shiny. As soon as you see this, pull the pan from the oven. The top will fall back down and the interior of the cookies will have an almost fudgy consistency. If you leave them in the oven longer, you'll get a product that's more like a cake-type brownie, and it won't be as moist and irresistible. Remove the hermits from the oven and cool them in the pan on a rack before glazing.

● **To make the glaze:** In a small bowl, stir together the milk and confectioners' sugar until smooth; the glaze will be quite thin. Use a pastry brush to brush it on top of the hermits before cutting the bars.

Nutrition information per serving (1 bar, 52 g): 188 cal, 4 g fat, 4 g protein, 20 g complex carbohydrates, 16 g sugar, 20 mg cholesterol, 148 mg sodium, 104 mg potassium, 24 RE vitamin A, 16 mg calcium, 32 mg phosphorus.

Cookies to bars to cookies

What's the difference between, say, chocolate chip cookies and chocolate chip bars? Not much, other than their shape. Many cookie recipes can easily be transformed into bars, and some bar recipes can become cookies. The key to going from cookies to bars is to match the amount of batter to the size of the pan. A 9 x 13-inch (or 11 x 11-inch) pan, the size in which the majority of bars are made, will comfortably hold 4 to 5 cups of dough. Choose a dough that makes drop cookies. While some rolled, shaped, or batter cookie recipes may work as well, it's not as easy as using drop cookie dough. Spread the dough in the pan and bake in a 350°F oven for 20 to 30 minutes. Again, no hard and fast rules here—dough that makes moist and chewy cookies will bake longer; those made from cookie dough that produces a light, crisp cookie (such as snicker-doodle dough), will bake for a shorter amount of time. Just keep your eye on them and check doneness by poking the tip of a sharp knife or a cake tester into the center; it should come out clean, or with just a few moist crumbs clinging to it.

To go from bars to cookies, choose a bar that makes a fairly stiff dough; remember, it won't have the edges of the pan to contain it. Any bar dough that's even close to cake batter in viscosity isn't suitable for turning into cookies. Also, choose a one-step bar, one in which all the ingredients are mixed together and spooned into a pan, rather than several different combinations of ingredients being layered atop one another. Mix the dough and drop it by the tablespoonful onto lightly greased or parchment-lined baking sheets. Bake in a 375°F oven for 10 to 18 minutes, or until they're done (see "Doneness" sidebar on page 19).

Lebkuchen

These spicy gingerbreadlike bars, traditional holiday fare in Germany, contain no fat except that in the egg. They're addictive, with their hard sugar glaze and their nippy bite of crystallized ginger (a substitute for the more typical citron, unless you really like that particular ingredient). If you make the *lebkuchen* two to three days ahead, they'll taste even better. They keep very well too, especially when a piece of apple is tucked into their airtight container to soften them.

Yield: 24 bars ● *Baking temperature: 350°F* ● *Baking time: 20 to 22 minutes*

BARS

¾ cup (9 ounces) honey

½ cup (4 ounces) light brown sugar

1 large egg

2 teaspoons each chopped lemon zest and orange zest, or ¼ teaspoon each lemon oil and orange oil

2¼ cups (9½ ounces) unbleached all-purpose flour

¼ teaspoon baking soda

½ cup (2 ounces) finely chopped blanched almonds

2 teaspoons cinnamon

1 teaspoon ground ginger

1 teaspoon ground nutmeg

1 teaspoon ground cloves

3 rounded tablespoons (1¾ ounces) diced crystallized ginger, pulsed in food processor until fine

GLAZE

6 tablespoons (3 ounces) brandy or apple juice (or a combination)

1 cup (4 ounces) confectioners' sugar

● **To make the bars:** In a medium-sized saucepan, bring the honey and brown sugar to a boil, stirring occasionally. Remove the mixture from the heat and cool until it's barely warm.

● In a large bowl, beat together the cooled honey mixture, egg, and lemon and orange zest. Add the flour, baking soda, almonds, spices, and crystallized ginger and beat until well-combined. The dough will be on the stiff side, but also very sticky. Cover the bowl and refrigerate it overnight.

● The next day, preheat the oven to 350°F. Lightly grease a 9 x 13-inch or 11 x 11-inch pan.

● On a lightly floured surface, roll the dough into a 9 x 13-inch rectangle or 11 x 11-inch square. Carefully transfer it to the prepared pan, either by wrapping it around the rolling pin and then unfolding it into the pan, or by using a giant spatula. Try to fit the dough into the pan without pressing down too hard around its edges or these areas will be dense and tough.

● Bake the bars for 20 to 22 minutes, or until a cake tester inserted in the center comes out clean. Remove from the oven and immediately brush with the glaze.

● **To prepare the glaze:** While the bars are baking, stir the brandy into the confectioners' sugar, mixing until smooth. Transfer the bars to a cooling rack and immediately brush on the glaze with a pastry brush; let the glaze soak in somewhat before applying another layer.

● Let the bars cool completely, then cut them into 1 x 2-inch pieces. Store the bars in an air-tight container with a slice of apple (for its softening powers).

Nutrition information per serving (1 bar, 41 g): 137 cal, 2 g fat, 2 g protein, 9 g complex carbohydrates, 19 g sugar, 1 g dietary fiber, 9 mg cholesterol, 19 mg sodium, 60 mg potassium, 4 RE vitamin A, 1 mg vitamin C, 1 mg iron, 16 mg calcium, 28 mg phosphorus.

Café au Lait Bars

These bars have the familiar rich flavor of coffee laced with cream, and the silky texture of an uptown dessert. Dress them up with a sprinkling of chocolate chips or a dusting of confectioners' sugar. We also recommend trying these with the cinnamon-cocoa glaze on page 232.

Yield: 24 bars ● *Baking temperature:* 325°F ● *Baking time:* 30 minutes

> **3 large eggs**
> **1½ cups (10½ ounces) sugar**
> **2 teaspoons vanilla extract**
> **¾ cup (1½ sticks, 6 ounces) unsalted butter, melted**
> **2 cups (8½ ounces) unbleached all-purpose flour**
> **½ teaspoon salt**
> **¼ cup (½ ounce) instant coffee crystals, or 3 tablespoons (⅜ ounce) espresso powder**
> **¼ cup (2 ounces) heavy cream**
> **1 cup (4 ounces) chopped walnuts (optional)**

● Preheat the oven to 325°F. Lightly grease a 9 x 13-inch pan, 11 x 11-inch pan, or similar-sized pan.
● In a large mixing bowl, beat the eggs until light-colored and thick. Add the sugar, beating until glossy and stiff. Add the vanilla and melted butter, beating to combine. Stir in the flour and salt.
● Set aside 1½ cups of the batter. Stir together the coffee crystals and cream and add to the remaining batter. Spread the coffee batter in the prepared pan. Spoon the reserved batter over the top, then run a knife through the two batters to marble them. Sprinkle with the nuts.
● Bake the bars for 30 minutes, or until the sides just barely pull away from the edge of the pan and the center is set. Remove them from the oven and cool before cutting.

Nutrition information per serving (1 bar, 39 g): 154 cal, 8 g fat, 2 g protein, 7 g complex carbohydrates, 12 g sugar, 46 mg cholesterol, 54 mg sodium, 45 mg potassium, 79 RE vitamin A, 1 mg iron, 7 mg calcium, 25 mg phosphorus, 19 mg caffeine.

VARIATION

● For a "mochachino" version, sprinkle 1½ cups mini chocolate chips on top while the bars are still warm.

Tea & Spice Squares

A subtle hint of tea in the crust gives these chewy fruit squares a sophisticated taste.

Yield: 35 squares ● *Baking temperature:* 350°F ● *Baking time:* 18 to 22 minutes

FRUIT

¾ cup (6 ounces) strong black tea (not herbal) (use 2 teabags in ¾ cup boiling water)

2 cups (8 to 10 ounces) dried fruit: raisins (Thompson or golden), currants, apricots, or dates are all good choices

BATTER

1 cup (2 sticks, 8 ounces) unsalted butter

1½ cups (12 ounces) brown sugar

¼ cup (3 ounces) molasses

¼ cup (2¾ ounces) corn syrup or honey (3 ounces)

1 teaspoon salt

1 teaspoon cinnamon

1 teaspoon ground ginger

½ teaspoon ground allspice

¼ teaspoon nutmeg

¼ to ½ cup (1⅝ to 3¼ ounces) diced crystallized ginger

3½ cups (14¾ ounces) unbleached all-purpose flour

1 teaspoon baking soda

1 large egg

GLAZE

1 cup (4 ounces) confectioners' sugar

¼ cup (2 ounces) creamy liqueur (such as Irish cream), or 2 tablespoons (1 ounce) strong tea plus 2 tablespoons (1 ounce) butter, melted

● **To prepare the fruit:** In a bowl, combine the hot tea and the dried fruit. Set aside to steep. When it's cool, purée it in a food processor or blender (or use an immersion blender). You may also leave the fruit whole; the bars will simply be a bit more difficult to cut cleanly.

● **To make the batter:** Melt the butter in a medium-sized saucepan set over low heat. Stir in the brown sugar, molasses, corn syrup, salt, and ground spices. Cook the mixture for 3 to 5 minutes, until it bubbles around the edges of the pan. Add the reserved fruit and any extra liquid, then the crystallized ginger. Bring the mixture to a full boil and boil for 1 minute. Remove from the heat and cool for 30 minutes or so.

● Preheat the oven to 350°F. Lightly grease an 18 x 13-inch half-sheet pan, two 9 x 13-inch pans, or similar sized pan(s).

● In a large bowl, whisk together the flour and the baking soda. Stir into the cooled fruit mixture. Stir in the egg, mixing until smooth. Spread the batter into the prepared pan(s).

- Bake the bars for 18 to 22 minutes, just until they have puffed up and a cake tester inserted into the center comes out clean. They will fall slightly, which creates the chewy moist center. Cool for 30 minutes.
- **To make the glaze:** In a small bowl, stir together the glaze ingredients until smooth, then drizzle it over the bars. Cool the bars for several hours for easiest cutting.

Nutrition information per serving (1 bar, 55 g): 188 cal, 6 g fat, 2 g protein, 14 g complex carbohydrates, 18 g sugar, 1 g dietary fiber, 22 mg cholesterol, 117 mg sodium, 143 mg potassium, 93 RE vitamin A, 1 mg vitamin C, 1 mg iron, 19 mg calcium, 24 mg phosphorus, 1 mg caffeine.

Rocky Road Bars

Over the years, Rocky Road has become an ice cream flavor just as familiar to all of us as butter-pecan, peach, or chocolate chip. The signature elements—chocolate, marshmallow, and nuts—play off one another nicely in these moist, dense bars.

Yield: 24 bars ● *Baking temperature:* 350°F ● *Baking time:* 18 minutes

1 cup (2 sticks, 8 ounces) **unsalted butter**
½ cup (4 ounces) **brown sugar**
½ cup (3½ ounces) **granulated sugar**
2 teaspoons **baking powder**
½ teaspoon **salt**
1 teaspoon **vanilla extract**
2 large **eggs**
1⅔ cups (7 ounces) **unbleached all-purpose flour**
⅓ cup (1 ounce) **Dutch process cocoa powder**
3 cups (18 ounces) **chocolate chips**
1 cup (5 ounces) **roasted salted whole almonds, chopped**
1 cup (2 ounces) **miniature marshmallows**

- Preheat the oven to 350°F. Lightly grease a 9 x 13-inch, 11 x 11-inch, or similar-sized pan.
- Cream together the butter, sugars, baking powder, salt, and vanilla. Beat in the eggs. Stir in the flour, cocoa, 2 cups of the chocolate chips, and the almonds.
- Pat the dough into the prepared pan. Bake the bars for 15 minutes, until they're set around the edge but still soft in the center. Sprinkle with the remaining 1 cup chocolate chips and the marshmallows, and bake until they soften, about 3 minutes more. Remove from the oven and cool completely before cutting into bars.

Nutrition information per serving (1 square 63 g): 293 cal, 17 g fat, 4 g protein, 10 g complex carbohydrates, 22 g sugar, 2 g dietary fiber, 38 mg cholesterol, 139 mg sodium, 232 mg potassium, 79 RE vitamin A, 1 mg vitamin C, 2 mg iron, 56 mg calcium, 95 mg phosphorus, 21 mg caffeine.

Vermont Granola Bars

King Arthur's headquarters in Norwich, Vermont, is nestled alongside the Connecticut River, in the valley between Vermont's Green Mountains, and New Hampshire's White Mountains. Hiking is a favorite pastime. In fact, the Appalachian Trail runs smack-dab through the center of town, one of the tiny stretches of the trail that actually runs along paved road. These granola bars are an easy treat to make and take along on any journey, even if you're only walking around town doing errands.

Yield: 48 bars ● ***Baking temperature:*** *450°F* ● ***Baking time:*** *12 to 14 minutes for the granola, 6 to 8 minutes for the bars*

¾ cup (6 ounces) brown sugar
¾ cup (1½ sticks, 6 ounces) unsalted butter, melted
1 cup (11 ounces) maple syrup
½ cup (5½ ounces) corn syrup
1 teaspoon salt
4 cups (12 ounces) rolled oats
1 cup (5 ounces) chopped almonds
1 cup (4¾ ounces) sunflower seeds
1 cup (3 ounces) sweetened flaked coconut
1 cup (5¼ ounces) raisins or dried cranberries
1 cup (6 ounces) chopped dried apricots
1 tablespoon vanilla extract, or ⅛ teaspoon butternut, maple, or other strong flavor

● Preheat the oven to 450°F. Lightly grease an (18 x 13-inch) half-sheet pan or two 9 x 13-inch pans.

● Combine the brown sugar, butter, syrups, and salt in a medium-sized saucepan. Bring to a full boil and continue to boil for 5 minutes, until a candy thermometer registers 250°F.

● While the syrup is boiling, place the oats, almonds, sunflower seeds, and coconut on the prepared baking sheet. Bake for 12 to 14 minutes, stirring the ingredients on the pan every 4 or 5 minutes to prevent the edges from getting too dark. Remove the pan from the oven. Pour the oat mixture into a bowl, add the raisins and apricots, and toss to combine.

● Add the vanilla to the syrup and pour it over the oat/fruit mixture, stirring until everything is well moistened. Then transfer the mixture back into the pan, patting it flat. Press the mixture firmly into the pan; using the lightly greased back of another half-sheet pan works well.

● Bake the bars for 6 to 8 minutes. They'll bubble up a little bit around the edges and turn a light golden brown. Remove from the oven and cool on a rack for about 10 minutes. Cut into squares while still warm. The easiest way to do this is to use a baker's bench knife to cut the bars into long strips in the pan, then transfer each strip to a cutting board to cut into bars.

Nutrition information per serving *(1 bar, 37 g):* 145 cal, 6 g fat, 2 g protein, 10 g complex carbohydrates, 11 g sugar, 2 g dietary fiber, 8 mg cholesterol, 57 mg sodium, 153 mg potassium, 46 RE vitamin A, 1 mg vitamin C, 1 mg iron, 19 mg calcium, 72 mg phosphorus.

Marlita's Chocolate-Raspberry Bars

This recipe comes from Marlita Vieira of Hanover, New Hampshire, an artist, avid cookie baker, and special King Arthur friend. We've printed recipes from two of her daughters, as well; clearly this is a family that loves (and knows how) to bake! The extra-tender, nearly crumbly texture of these bars, and the delightful interplay of flavors, make them a test kitchen favorite.

Yield: 24 bars ● *Baking temperature: 350°F* ● *Baking time: 35 to 38 minutes*

> 1 cup (2 sticks, 8 ounces) unsalted butter
> ¼ cup (1⅝ ounces) vegetable shortening
> 1⅔ cups (11½ ounces) sugar
> 1 teaspoon salt
> 1 teaspoon baking powder
> ½ cup (1½ ounces) cocoa powder (natural or Dutch process)
> 2¾ cups (11½ ounces) unbleached all-purpose flour
> 1 cup (4 ounces) finely chopped walnuts
> 1 jar (10 ounces) raspberry jam or fruit spread (about 1 cup)
> 1 to 2 tablespoons chopped nuts or coarse sugar, for garnish
> Confectioners' sugar, for dusting

● Preheat the oven to 350°F. Lightly grease a 9 x 13-inch, 11 x 11-inch, or similar-sized pan.
● In a medium-sized mixing bowl, beat together the butter, shortening, sugar, salt, and baking powder until fluffy. Add the cocoa and beat until well blended. Mix in the flour and walnuts; the mixture will be quite stiff. Press about two thirds of the dough into the prepared pan and set aside for the rest.
● In the microwave or over very low heat on the stovetop, warm the jam to make it easier to spread. Spread it over the dough in the pan and crumble the reserved dough over the jam. Sprinkle with chopped nuts or coarse sugar, if desired.
● Bake the bars for 35 to 38 minutes, until the jam is bubbling around the edges of the pan. The top crumbs will still feel soft, but they'll firm up as the bars cool. Remove the bars from the oven and cool completely on a rack. Dust with confectioners' sugar just before serving.

Nutrition information per serving (1 bar, 59 g): 260 cal, 14 g fat, 3 g protein, 12 g complex carbohydrates, 21 g sugar, 1 g dietary fiber, 22 mg cholesterol, 117 mg sodium, 90 mg potassium, 77 RE vitamin A, 1 mg vitamin C, 1 mg iron, 22 mg calcium, 61 mg phosphorus, 4 mg caffeine.

VARIATION
● Marlita likes to vary the taste of these bars a bit by substituting a mixture of seedless black raspberry and cherry preserves for the raspberry jam.

TWO-STEP BARS • • • • • • • • • •

When you've got a bit more time to spare, two-step bars give you a lot of visual bang for your buck, as well as scoring high on the YUM! scale. First prepare the crust, then, while it's baking, use the same bowl (wipe it out first if you're a purist, but no need to wash it) to make the filling or topping. Return the bars to the oven for their final bake while you're cleaning up, and voilà: a picture-perfect delicious treat for the after-school (or office) cookie crowd.

Sinfully Rich Chocolate Crunch Bars

If the mere thought of bringing a mysterious potion to the hard-ball stage (or of even owning a candy thermometer) stops you, we offer here a shortcut solution. A meltingly buttery yet crisp base, slathered with a just-thick-enough layer of chocolate, and dusted with finely chopped nuts, make these "faux candy bars" a pressed-for-time baker's newfound friend.

Yield: 96 small bars ● ***Baking temperature:*** *425°F* ● ***Baking time:*** *10 to 14 minutes*

CRUST
 4½ cups (15¾ ounces) rolled oats
 1 cup (8 ounces) brown sugar
 ¾ cup (1½ sticks, 6 ounces) unsalted butter, melted
 ¾ cup (8¼ ounces) light corn syrup
 1 tablespoon vanilla extract
 ½ teaspoon salt
TOPPING
 2 cups (12 ounces) chocolate chips
 2 tablespoons (¾ ounce) vegetable shortening
 ⅔ cup (about 3 ounces) chopped nuts

● Preheat the oven to 425°F. Lightly grease a 10 x 15-inch jelly roll pan, or 14-inch round deep-dish pizza pan.
● **To make the crust:** In a medium-sized mixing bowl, stir together the oats, sugar, butter, corn syrup, vanilla, and salt. Press the mixture into the prepared pan, using your lightly greased hands (or the greased bottom of loaf pan, see page 205) to help the process along. Bake the crust for 10 to 14 minutes, or until it's a light golden brown. It will bubble up as it bakes, which is okay. Remove from the oven and cool completely on a rack.

- **To make the topping:** In a medium-sized saucepan set over very low heat, or in a microwave, melt the chocolate chips and shortening together, stirring until smooth. Spread the mixture evenly over the cooled crust and sprinkle on the nuts. Cover loosely and chill the bars in the refrigerator until the chocolate is firm.
- Remove from the refrigerator and cut into squares. The easiest way to do this is to use a chef's knife or baker's bench knife to cut the bars into long strips while in the pan, and then transfer each strip to a cutting board to cut into bite-sized pieces.

Nutrition information per serving (1 bar, 42 g): 192 cal, 10 g fat, 2 g protein, 8 g complex carbohydrates, 17 g sugar, 1 g dietary fiber, 11 mg cholesterol, 44 mg sodium, 101 mg potassium, 40 RE vitamin A, 1 mg vitamin C, 1 mg iron, 11 mg calcium, 71 mg phosphorus, 8 mg caffeine.

To press a crumbly crust evenly into the pan, grease the bottom of a loaf pan and press down.

Classic Apricot Squares

This recipe must be at least forty years old, but with new generations of bakers heading into the kitchen all the time, we can't assume that all or even most of you have already seen it. This is an ultratender, buttery, crumbly bar with a sweet-tangy fruit filling. It invariably provokes rolling eyes and groans of enjoyment from tasters.

Yield: 24 squares ● *Baking temperature:* 350°F ● *Baking time:* 14 to 16 minutes for the crust, 28 to 32 minutes for the squares

FILLING
2 cups (12 ounces) chopped dried apricots
2 tablespoons (1 ounce) brandy (optional)
½ cup (3½ ounces) sugar
1½ cups (12 ounces) water

CRUST AND TOPPING
2¼ cups (9½ ounces) unbleached all-purpose flour
1¼ cups (5 ounces) confectioners' sugar
1 teaspoon salt
1 teaspoon baking powder
1 cup (2 sticks, 8 ounces) unsalted butter
1 cup (4 ounces) chopped pecans or shredded sweetened coconut (optional)
Coarse sugar (optional)

● Preheat the oven to 350°F. Lightly grease a 9 x 13-inch, 11 x 11-inch, or similar-sized pan.
● **To make the filling:** In a medium-sized saucepan, stir together the apricots, brandy, sugar, and water and bring to a boil. Cook the mixture for 8 to 10 minutes, until the fruit is soft and has absorbed most of the water. Cool slightly, then purée it in a food processor or blender, or with an immersion blender.
● **To make the crust and topping:** In a medium-sized mixing bowl, whisk together the flour, sugar, salt, and baking powder. Using a pastry blender, your fingers, or a mixer, cut in the butter until the mixture is crumbly but will hold together when squeezed. Transfer about 1¼ cups of the mixture to another bowl, stir in the nuts, and set aside.
● Press the remainder of the crust mixture into the bottom and slightly up the sides of the prepared pan. Bake the crust for 14 to 16 minutes. Remove it from the oven.
● While still warm, spread the crust with the filling. Spread the reserved topping mixture over the filling. Sprinkle with coarse sugar, if desired. Return the pan to the oven, and bake for 28 to 32 minutes, until they're golden brown. Remove from the oven and cool on a rack. Cut into squares. These freeze very well.

Nutrition information per serving (1 square, 65 g): 215 cal, 11 g fat, 2 g protein, 17 g complex carbohydrates, 10 g sugar, 2 g dietary fiber, 22 mg cholesterol, 112 mg sodium, 225 mg potassium, 300 RE vitamin A,1 mg vitamin C, 1 mg iron, 31 mg calcium, 45 mg phosphorus.

VARIATIONS

Try using different fruit fillings in these bars. Use about 2 cups prepared fruit filling, or about 1 cup thick jam or preserves. (You need less of the jam or preserves because it spreads more than the prepared fruit filling.) Here are some of our favorites.

Fig Filling

2 to 2½ cups (14 to 17½ ounces) chopped dried figs

1 teaspoon cinnamon

¼ teaspoon nutmeg

¼ teaspoon ground allspice

2 teaspoons lemon juice

1 tablespoon grated lemon rind (zest) or ¼ teaspoon lemon oil (optional)

1½ cups (12 ounces) water

● Prepare as directed for the apricot filling. The figs will probably be sweet enough that you don't need to add any sugar, but taste and see; add ¼ to ½ cup brown sugar if you like.

Dried Cherry Filling

2 cups (9 to 10 ounces) dried cherries (sweet or sour, or a mixture)

½ cup (3½ ounces) sugar (slightly more if using all sour cherries)

¼ teaspoon almond extract, or 2 drops bitter almond oil (optional)

2 tablespoons (1 ounce) unsalted butter

2 tablespoons (½ ounce) unbleached all-purpose flour

1½ cups (12 ounces) water

● In a medium-sized saucepan, combine all of the ingredients, bring to a boil, and cook the mixture for 8 to 10 minutes, until the fruit is soft and the mixture has thickened.

Mincemeat Filling

1 cup (5¼ ounces) raisins

½ cup (2¼ ounces) coarsely chopped dried figs

1 tablespoon coarsely chopped candied orange peel

1 tablespoon coarsely chopped candied lemon peel

1½ cups (10½ ounces) peeled, cored, and coarsely chopped apples

½ cup (3½ ounces) sugar

¼ teaspoon nutmeg

¼ teaspoon ground allspice

¼ teaspoon cinnamon

⅛ teaspoon ground cloves

¼ cup (2 ounces) brandy, or 1 tablespoon cider vinegar

2 tablespoons (1 ounce) unsalted butter

1 cup (8 ounces) water

● Combine all the ingredients in a saucepan and stir them together thoroughly. Bring to a boil and boil until the fruit is soft. Set aside to cool. Do not purée.

Over-the-Top Caramel Candy Bars

Cookies and candy join forces in these devilishly rich bars. A cookie crust is topped with buttery caramel, then the top is iced with dark chocolate frosting and sprinkled with toasted almonds. To make extra-sure these bars don't stick, line the greased pan (bottom and sides) with alumini-um foil. Many cookbooks recommend this helpful step, which makes it easy to lift bars out of the pan, as well as to cut them without marring the bottom of the pan. In truth, we don't usual-ly bother with the foil. With this recipe, however, the caramel sometimes bubbles up the sides and makes the bars stick, so it's worth the effort.

Yield: 48 bars ● *Baking temperature:* 350°F ● *Baking time:* 15 minutes for the crust, 20 minutes for the bars

CRUST

1 cup (2 sticks, 8 ounces) unsalted butter

¾ teaspoon salt

½ teaspoon baking powder, or ¼ teaspoon baker's ammonia (see page 488)

¾ cup (5½ ounces) brown sugar

1 cup (4 ounces) confectioners' sugar

2 teaspoons vanilla extract

1 teaspoon almond extract, or ⅛ teaspoon almond oil

1 large egg

2¾ cups (11½ ounces) unbleached all-purpose flour

1 cup (3¼ ounces) toasted almond flour or finely ground toasted almonds

FILLING

2 cups (16 ounces) firmly packed brown sugar

1 cup (11 ounces) light corn syrup

½ cup (1 stick, 4 ounces) unsalted butter

1 cup (8 ounces) cream (light, heavy, or whipping) or evaporated milk

2 teaspoons vanilla extract

FROSTING

1 cup (6 ounces) chopped semisweet or bittersweet chocolate or chocolate chips

3 tablespoons (2 ounces) light corn syrup

3 tablespoons (1½ ounces) unsalted butter

½ cup (2½ ounces) chopped toasted almonds (see page 27)

● Preheat the oven to 350°F. Lightly grease a 9 x 13-inch, 11 x 11-inch, or similar-sized pan. Line the pan with lightly greased aluminum foil.

● **To make the crust:** In a medium-sized bowl, beat together the butter, salt, baking powder, sugars, vanilla, and almond extract until well blended. Beat in the egg, then stir in the flour and almond flour.

● Divide the dough in half. Press half the mixture into the prepared pan, saving the remaining half to use as topping. Bake the crust for 15 minutes, until it's lightly browned around the edges. Remove it from the oven and cool slightly while making the filling.

- **To make the filling:** In a large (3½- to 4-quart) heavy-bottomed saucepan, mix the brown sugar and corn syrup. If you have a large nonstick saucepan, now's the time to use it. Bring the mixture to a boil, stirring constantly. Cover the pan and boil for 3 minutes without stirring, to wash any sugar crystals off the insides of the pan. Uncover the pan, stir in the butter, and continue to boil, stirring often, until the caramel reaches the soft-ball stage, 234°F on a candy thermometer. While the syrup is boiling, gently heat the cream in the microwave or oven low heat on the stovetop until it's hot but not boiling.

- Remove the syrup from the heat and slowly stir in the hot cream and the vanilla. Return to the heat and cook until the mixture reaches firm-ball stage, 245°F to 248°F. Pour the caramel over the baked crust.

- Let the filling cool for a few minutes, mainly to keep from accidentally burning yourself while you're adding the topping. Crumble the reserved crust mixture over the hot caramel. An easy way to make even crumbs is to press the dough into a log and freeze it while making the caramel. Then use a coarse grater to grate the crumbs over the top.

- Bake the bars for 20 minutes, until the top is golden brown. Remove the bars from the oven and cool them on a rack.

- **To make the frosting:** In a saucepan set over medium heat, or in the microwave, stir together the chocolate, corn syrup, and butter, until melted. Spread the frosting over the cooled bars. Sprinkle with the almonds and let rest until the chocolate firms up, several hours or overnight. Cut into 1 x 2-inch bars.

Nutrition information per serving (1 bar, 43 g): 187 cal, 9 g fat, 2 g protein, 7 g complex carbohydrates, 19 g sugar, 1 g dietary fiber, 19 mg cholesterol, 79 mg sodium, 89 mg potassium, 51 RE vitamin A, 1 mg vitamin C, 1 mg iron, 39 mg calcium, 49 mg phosphorus, 3 mg caffeine.

VARIATION

For an easier-to-prepare filling, try the following. If you don't have a candy thermometer, this is the route to take.

> **1½ pounds caramel, cut from a block, or vanilla caramels**
> **¼ cup (2 ounces) cream (light, heavy, or whipping)**
> **2 teaspoons vanilla extract**

- In a saucepan, melt the caramel(s), cream, and vanilla together over medium heat. Bring the mixture to a boil, then pour it over the baked crust.

Lemony Almond Bars

The inspiration for these bars came from an old recipe we found in one of our "passed-down-from-grandma" recipe boxes. While the combination of almond and lemon is somewhat surprising —raspberry-almond or cherry-almond seem to be much more common pairings of flavors—it definitely works in these bars.

Yield: 24 bars ● Baking temperature: 350°F ● Baking time: 12 minutes for the crust, 20 minutes for the bars

CRUST
- 1½ cups (6¼ ounces) unbleached all-purpose flour
- ⅓ cup (2¾ ounces) light brown sugar
- ½ cup (1 stick, 4 ounces) unsalted butter
- ¼ teaspoon salt

TOPPING
- 2 large eggs
- ¾ cup (6 ounces) light brown sugar
- ¼ teaspoon salt
- ½ teaspoon baking powder
- ½ teaspoon vanilla extract
- 1 cup (3½ ounces) chopped almonds
- ¼ cup (1 ounce) unbleached all-purpose flour

GLAZE
- 1 cup (4 ounces) confectioners' sugar
- 1 tablespoon (½ ounce) unsalted butter
- ¼ cup lemon juice
- 2 to 3 teaspoons grated lemon rind (zest), or ¼ teaspoon lemon oil

● Preheat the oven to 350°F. Lightly grease a 9 x 13-inch, 11 x 11-inch, or similar-sized pan.

● **To make the crust:** In a medium-sized mixing bowl, combine the flour, brown sugar, butter, and salt using your fingers, a pastry blender, or a mixer. Pat the mixture into the prepared pan. It's a bit sticky, so grease your fingers, or cover the dough with plastic wrap before you start. Bake the crust for 12 minutes. Remove it from the oven and set aside.

● **To make the topping:** In a medium-sized bowl, beat together the eggs, brown sugar, salt, baking powder, and vanilla. Stir in the nuts and flour. Spoon the topping over the crust, smoothing it out as much as possible. Bake the bars for 20 minutes, until they appear set.

● **To make the glaze:** While the bars are baking, stir together the sugar, butter, and lemon juice and rind in a small bowl.

● Remove the bars from the oven. Spread them with the glaze while they are still hot. Allow them to cool completely before cutting.

Nutrition information per serving (1 bar, 38 g): 161 cal, 7 g fat, 3 g protein, 7 g complex carbohydrates, 15 g sugar, 1 g dietary fiber, 29 mg cholesterol, 65 mg sodium, 78 mg potassium, 49 RE vitamin A, 1 mg vitamin C, 1 mg iron, 21 mg calcium, 42 mg phosphorus.

Camelot Dream Bars

These bars, a less-sweet takeoff on a *very* sweet original that's been in our recipe archives for a good thirty years or more, strike a nice balance among their major components: brown sugar, pecans, and coconut. These may remind you of a very chewy, moist oatmeal cookie, even though there's nary an oat in sight.

Yield: 24 bars ● *Baking temperature: 350°F* ● *Baking time: 15 minutes for the crust, 20 to 25 minutes for the topping*

CRUST
>½ cup (1 stick, 4 ounces) unsalted butter
>¼ cup (2 ounces) brown sugar
>¼ teaspoon salt
>1½ cups (6¼ ounces) unbleached all-purpose flour

TOPPING
>¼ cup (1 ounce) unbleached all-purpose flour
>¼ teaspoon salt
>1 teaspoon baking powder
>2 large eggs
>2 teaspoons vanilla extract
>¾ cup (6 ounces) dark brown sugar
>1½ cups (4½ ounces) shredded sweetened coconut
>1 cup (4 ounces) chopped pecans, toasted (see page 27)

● Preheat the oven to 350°F. Lightly grease a 9 x 13-inch, 11 x 11-inch, or similar-sized pan.
● **To make the crust:** In a medium-sized mixing bowl, cream the butter, sugar, and salt. Mix in the flour, stirring just until combined. Pat the mixture into the prepared pan. Bake for approximately 15 minutes, until the edges are just beginning to brown. Remove from the oven and let cool while you prepare the topping.
● **To make the topping:** In a medium-sized bowl, whisk together the flour, salt, and baking powder. Set aside. In another bowl, beat the eggs until they're thick and lemon-colored. Add the vanilla and the brown sugar and beat until smooth. Stir in the reserved flour mixture, the coconut, and pecans.
● Pour the topping over the baked crust, spreading it evenly. Bake the bars for 20 to 25 minutes, until they're lightly browned. Remove from the oven, and cool completely before cutting.

Nutrition information per serving (1 bar, 39 g): 173 cal, 11 g fat, 2 g protein, 9 g complex carbohydrates, 10 g sugar, 1 g dietary fiber, 28 mg cholesterol, 75 mg sodium, 92 mg potassium, 45 RE vitamin A, 1 mg iron, 25 mg calcium, 48 mg phosphorus.

VARIATION
● Add 1 cup butterscotch chips to the topping ingredients.

Summer Berry Crumble Bars

Remember the classic bakery date bar, with its crunchy oatmeal bottom crust and crumbly oat-meal top sandwiched around smooth, sweet date filling? These bars substitute blueberries for the dates, and streusel topping for the oats, but it's like painting the sky cerulean instead of robin's egg blue: it's still a beautiful picture! Note that if you are using frozen fruit, don't let it thaw—it will sink into the crust.

Yield: 24 bars ● ***Baking temperature:*** *350°F* ● ***Baking time:*** *15 minutes for the crust, 40 to 45 minutes for the bars*

CRUST AND TOPPING
- 2 cups (8½ ounces) unbleached all-purpose flour
- 1 cup (8 ounces) brown sugar
- 1½ cups (5¼ ounces) rolled oats
- 1 teaspoon salt
- 1 teaspoon baking powder
- ½ teaspoon baking soda
- ½ teaspoon cinnamon, or ¼ teaspoon ground cardamom
- 1 cup (2 sticks, 8 ounces) unsalted butter, cut into pats
- ¾ cup (3¾ ounces) sunflower seeds (optional)

FILLING
- 3 cups (15 ounces) fresh or frozen blueberries or raspberries
- ¼ cup (2 ounces) light brown sugar
- 3 tablespoons (1½ ounces) lemon juice
- 1 tablespoon lemon zest (zest from 1 lemon), or ⅛ teaspoon lemon oil
- 2 tablespoons (1 ounce) butter, melted
- ½ teaspoon cinnamon, or ¼ teaspoon ground cardamom
- 3 tablespoons (¾ ounce) unbleached all-purpose flour

GLAZE
- 2 teaspoons lemon juice
- 2 tablespoons (1 ounce) unsalted butter, melted
- 2 to 3 teaspoons water
- 1 cup (4 ounces) confectioners' sugar

● Preheat the oven to 350°F. Lightly grease a 9 x 13-inch pan.

● **To make the crust and topping:** In a large bowl, whisk together the flour, brown sugar, oats, salt, baking powder, baking soda, and cinnamon. Using a mixer, a pastry blender, or your fingers, cut in the butter until the mixture is crumbly. Transfer 2 cups of the crumbs to a bowl, combine them with the sunflower seeds, and set aside. Pat the remaining crumbs into the pan. Bake the crust for 15 minutes and remove it from the oven.

● **To make the filling:** While the crust is baking, in a large bowl, mix the berries with the brown sugar, lemon juice and zest, melted butter, cinnamon, and flour. Distribute the filling over the baked crust.

- Sprinkle the reserved crust-and-seed mixture on top of the filling and return the bars to the oven. Bake for 40 to 45 minutes, until the filling is bubbly and the crumbs have browned. Remove the bars from the oven.
- **To make the glaze:** In a small bowl, whisk together the glaze ingredients. Drizzle the glaze over the bars while they're still warm. Cool completely before cutting.

Nutrition information per serving (*1 bar, 71 g*): 241 cal, 12 g fat, 3 g protein, 15 g complex carbohydrates, 16 g sugar, 2 g dietary fiber, 26 mg cholesterol, 143 mg sodium, 126 mg potassium, 92 RE vitamin A, 4 mg vitamin C, 1 mg iron,35 mg calcium, 78 mg phosphorus.

VARIATION

- 3 cups peeled, sliced apples mixed with ½ cup raisins is a nice substitute for the berry filling.

For bars that stick to the pan

Some bars, particularly those with a sweet, viscous topping that might creep between the edge of the dough and the side of the pan, tend to stick in the pan when you're trying to cut them. If you suspect (or experience tells you) that you're making a bar like this, line the bottom of the pan with parchment before spooning in the dough or batter. Once the bars are baked, slide a baker's bench knife along the edge of the pan to loosen the bars before cutting and lifting them out.

For thick bars with a crumbly and/or delicate topping, line your pan with aluminum foil. Use a piece that's longer than the length of your pan by about 6 inches. Fit it into the pan, pushing it into the corners; you should have a 1-inch "handle" at either end. Lightly grease the foil, then spoon in the batter. Once the bars are baked, use the foil handles at either end to gently lift them out of the pan. Allow to cool before cutting.

Tropical Paradise Bars

With rum, coconut, and the "tropical" fruit preserves of your choice, these bars bring a taste of the islands to your kitchen. For the fruit portion, we suggest some of the wonderful new flavor combinations: mango-pineapple, passionfruit, and guava are good choices, as is comfortable old raspberry.

Yield: 24 bars ● *Baking temperature:* 350°F ● *Baking time:* 12 to 15 minutes for the crust, 25 to 28 minutes for the bars

CRUST
¾ cup (1½ sticks, 6 ounces) unsalted butter
¾ cup (5¼ ounces) sugar
1 teaspoon baking powder
½ teaspoon salt
1 teaspoon vanilla extract
½ teaspoon coconut extract, or 4 drops strong coconut flavor (optional)
2½ cups (10½ ounces) unbleached all-purpose flour
½ cup (2¼ ounces) chopped macadamia nuts (optional)

FILLING
¾ cup (8¾ ounces) fruit preserves or jam
2 tablespoons (1 ounce) rum (optional)
2 large egg yolks

TOPPING
¼ teaspoon cream of tartar
¼ teaspoon salt
2 large egg whites
½ cup (3½ ounces) sugar
2 cups (6 ounces) sweetened flaked coconut

● Preheat the oven to 350°F.
● **To make the crust:** In a large bowl, cream together the butter, sugar, baking powder, salt, vanilla, and coconut extract. Stir in the flour and nuts, mixing until smooth. Press the crust into the bottom and ½ inch up the sides of an ungreased 9 x 13-inch, 11 x 11-inch, or similar-sized pan. Bake the crust for 12 to 15 minutes, until it is set.
● **To make the filling:** In a small bowl, gently warm the preserves to lukewarm (a microwave makes short work of this task), stir in the rum, and whisk in the egg yolks. Be sure the mixture is warm, not hot—you don't want to cook the yolks. Spread the filling over the crust.
● **To make the topping:** Beat together the cream of tartar, salt, and egg whites until foamy. Gradually add the sugar, beating until soft peaks form. Fold in the coconut. Spread the topping over the filling. Return the bars to the oven and bake for 25 to 28 minutes, until the top is golden brown and set. Remove from the oven and cool to lukewarm before cutting.

Nutrition information per serving (1 bar, 53 g): 219 cal, 11 g fat, 2 g protein, 12 g complex carbohydrates, 16 g sugar, 1 g dietary fiber, 34 mg cholesterol, 110 mg sodium, 59 mg potassium, 65 RE vitamin A, 1 mg iron, 18 mg calcium, 35 mg phosphorus.

Linzer Cookie Bars

The age-old combination of raspberry, nuts, and cinnamon is a delicious one. We tried to adapt our favorite linzer torte recipe to bars, but it didn't make the cut. The raspberry jam oozed out the sides of each piece, and the whole thing reminded us of underbaked fudge. Ding! Enter the same idea in a new form, and a much easier one, we might add.

Yield: 24 bars ● *Baking temperature: 350°F* ● *Baking time: 15 minutes for the crust, 22 to 24 minutes for the bars*

CRUST AND TOPPING
- ¾ cup (1½ sticks, 6 ounces) unsalted butter
- 1 cup (4 ounces) confectioners' sugar
- ¼ cup (1¾ ounces) granulated sugar
- ½ teaspoon salt
- 1 teaspoon vanilla extract
- 1 teaspoon baking powder
- ½ teaspoon cinnamon
- ¼ teaspoon hazelnut or almond extract, or 1 to 2 drops bitter almond oil or strong hazelnut flavoring
- 1 large egg
- 1½ cups (5 ounces) finely ground hazelnuts or almonds (or nut flour)
- 2 cups (8½ ounces) unbleached all-purpose flour

FILLING
- 1¼ cups (14½ ounces) raspberry jam
- 1 tablespoon grated lemon rind (zest), or ¼ teaspoon lemon oil, optional
- Confectioners' sugar

● Preheat the oven to 350°F. Lightly grease a 9 x 13-inch or 11 x 11-inch, or similar-sized pan.

● **To make the crust and topping:** In a medium-sized bowl, cream the butter with the sugars, salt, vanilla, baking powder, cinnamon, and hazelnut extract. Add the egg and mix well, scraping the bottom and sides of the bowl. Add the ground nuts and flour, mixing just until blended. Set aside 1 cup of the dough for the topping. Spread the remaining dough in the prepared pan. Bake the bars for 15 minutes, or until the edges are golden and the middle is set.

● **To make the filling:** While the crust is baking, heat the jam gently and combine it with the lemon zest. Remove the crust from the oven and spread it evenly with the jam. Sprinkle with the reserved dough, using your fingers to break it into crumbs.

● Return the bars to the oven and bake for 22 to 24 minutes, until the jam is bubbling around the edges and the topping looks set. The bars won't brown, except at the edges. Remove from the oven and cool on a rack. Sprinkle with confectioners' sugar before cutting into bars.

Nutrition information per serving (1 bar, 48 g): 187 cal, 9 g fat, 3 g protein, 9 g complex carbohydrates, 16 g sugar, 1 g dietary fiber, 24 mg cholesterol, 75 mg sodium, 75 mg potassium, 58 RE vitamin A, 2 mg vitamin C, 1 mg iron, 33 mg calcium, 53 mg phosphorus.

Fudgy Peanut Butter Squares

From buckeyes to peanut butter cups to peanut butter fudge pie, the chocolate/peanut connection is a strong one, particularly among kids—or those of us who've held onto our childhood passions. These squares elicited the following test kitchen response: "Rich and delicious. Possibly illegal. Certainly immoral."

Yield: 24 squares ● *Baking temperature: 350°F* ● ***Baking time:*** *8 to 10 minutes for the crust, 22 to 24 minutes for the squares*

CRUST

    4 tablespoons (H stick, 2 ounces) unsalted butter

    1/3 cup (3¼ ounces) peanut butter, smooth or chunky

    ¾ cup (5¼ ounces) sugar

    ¼ teaspoon salt

    1 teaspoon vanilla extract

    ¼ teaspoon baker's ammonia (optional; see page 488)

    1¼ cups (5¼ ounces) unbleached all-purpose flour

FILLING

    4 ounces unsweetened baking chocolate

    ½ cup (1 stick, 4 ounces) unsalted butter

    ½ teaspoon salt

    ¼ cup (2¾ ounces) light corn syrup

    1 cup plus 2 tablespoons (7½ ounces) sugar

    1 cup (4¼ ounces) unbleached all-purpose flour

    2 large eggs

    ½ cup (3 ounces) chocolate chips, peanut butter chips, or peanut butter
        candy pieces (optional)

FROSTING

    ¾ cup (4½ ounces) butterscotch chips, white chocolate chips,
        white confectionery coating disks, or a combination

    ¼ cup (2⅜ ounces) smooth peanut butter

● Preheat the oven to 350°F. Lightly grease a 9 x 13-inch, 11 x 11-inch, or similar-sized pan.

● **To make the crust:** In a medium-sized mixing bowl, beat the butter and peanut butter until soft and well blended. Stir in the sugar, salt, vanilla, and baker's ammonia. Mix in the flour; the mixture will feel dry and be crumbly. Press the dough into the prepared pan. This is best accomplished by covering the crumbs with a piece of plastic wrap and using a small pastry rolling pin (or a can on its side) to roll out the crust evenly. Bake the crust for 8 to 10 minutes, until it has lightly browned around the edges. Remove the pan from the oven.

● **To make the filling:** In a medium-sized saucepan set over low heat (or in a microwave-safe bowl), melt and stir together the chocolate, butter, salt, and corn syrup. Remove the pan from the heat and stir in the sugar and flour. Add the eggs, beating until well blended, then mix in the chips. Spread the filling onto the crust.

- Bake the squares for 22 to 24 minutes. The top should be shiny and look set. For the best chewy texture, don't overbake; a tester inserted into the center won't come out clean, but with sticky crumbs clinging to it. Remove the squares from the oven and cool to lukewarm while you make the frosting.
- **To make the frosting:** In a medium-sized saucepan set over low heat (or in a microwave-safe bowl), melt the chips, stirring often. Add the peanut butter and stir until smooth. Spread the frosting over the warm bars. Cool completely before cutting, using a knife sprayed with non-stick vegetable oil spray, or warmed in hot water, wiping it often. These squares are sinfully rich, so cut the 2-inch squares in half, if desired.

Nutrition information per serving (*1 square, 61 g*)*:* 276 cal, 15 g fat, 4 g protein, 10 g complex carbohydrates, 24 g sugar, 1 g dietary fiber, 34 mg cholesterol, 113 mg sodium, 122 mg potassium, 65 RE vitamin A, 1 mg iron, 9 mg calcium, 66 mg phosphorus, 12 mg caffeine.

Rich Pecan Pie Bars

You know the buttery/nutty, almost-but-not-quite-too-sweet taste of pecan pie? These bars match that taste, but dispense with the hassle of rolling out piecrust. If you have a jelly roll pan with very low sides, you may find yourself with excess filling. Fill the crust almost full, and bake any leftover in a custard cup (to eat when no one is looking).

Yield: 35 bars ● *Baking temperature: 425°F, then 350°F* ● *Baking time: 10 minutes for the crust, 30 minutes for the bars*

CRUST

½ cup plus 2 tablespoons (1¼ sticks, 5 ounces) unsalted butter
4 ounces (½ a large package) cream cheese (reduced fat [Neufchâtel] or full fat)
¼ cup (1¾ ounces) sugar
1¾ cups (7¼ ounces) unbleached all-purpose flour
½ teaspoon salt
½ teaspoon baking powder

FILLING

4 large eggs
¾ cup (8¼ ounces) corn syrup, light or dark, or a mixture of both
1 cup (7 ounces) sugar
4 tablespoons (½ stick, 2 ounces) unsalted butter, melted
¼ cup (2 ounces) heavy cream
2 tablespoons rum (optional)
2 teaspoons vanilla extract, or 4 drops butter-rum, butter-pecan, or butternut flavor
½ teaspoon salt
1¾ cups (7 ounces) chopped pecans

- Preheat the oven to 425°F. Lightly grease a 10 x 15-inch jelly roll pan, 14-inch round deep-dish pizza pan, or similar-sized pan.

- **To make the crust:** In a medium-sized bowl, beat the butter and cream cheese together until smooth. Add the sugar, flour, salt, and baking powder and stir until the dough is cohesive; it will be crumbly, but hold together when squeezed. Press the dough into and up the sides of the prepared pan. Bake the crust for 10 minutes and remove it from the oven. Reduce oven temperature to 350°F.
- **To make the filling:** In a medium-sized bowl, whisk the filling ingredients together. Pour the filling over the crust. Bake the bars for 30 minutes, or until the filling looks puffy and deep golden brown. Remove from the oven and cool completely before cutting.

Nutrition information per serving (1 bar, 42 g): 172 cal, 11 g fat, 2 g protein, 5 g complex carbohydrates, 12 g sugar, 1 g dietary fiber, 43 mg cholesterol, 96 mg sodium, 43 mg potassium, 76 RE vitamin A, 1 mg vitamin C, 1 mg iron, 14 mg calcium, 39 mg phosphorus.

Almond-Apricot Squares with Chocolate Ganache

We created this recipe in order to satisfy a craving for three favorite flavors: apricot, almond, and chocolate. While these are a bit time-consuming to assemble (four steps, four layers), they're so rich that they can be cut into small pieces that will go quite a long way. And they freeze well, always a plus.

Yield: 24 squares ● *Baking temperature:* 375°F ● *Baking time:* 12 to 15 minutes for the crust, 25 to 30 minutes for the squares

CRUST

1¾ cups (12¼ ounces) granulated sugar
½ cup (2 ounces) confectioners' sugar
½ cup (1 stick, 4 ounces) unsalted butter
1 teaspoon butter-vanilla flavor, or 2 teaspoons vanilla extract
¾ teaspoon baking powder
¼ teaspoon salt
2 large egg yolks (reserve the whites)
1 tablespoon (½ ounce) milk
1¾ cups (7¼ ounces) unbleached all-purpose flour

APRICOT FILLING*

1 cup (6 ounces) shredded or diced dried apricots
½ cup (4 ounces) water
¼ cup (1¾ ounces) granulated sugar
2 tablespoons (1 ounce) brandy or rum (optional)

* Use 1 heaping cup of apricot preserves in place of the apricot filling, if desired.

ALMOND FILLING

 2 cups (6½ ounces) almond flour (finely ground almonds)
 1 cup (7 ounces) granulated sugar
 ¼ teaspoon salt
 1 large egg plus 2 large egg whites
 1 teaspoon vanilla extract
 1 teaspoon almond extract
 2 tablespoons (½ ounce) unbleached all-purpose flour

GANACHE

 1⅓ cups (8 ounces) chopped bittersweet chocolate or chocolate chips
 ¾ cup (6 ounces) heavy cream

- Preheat the oven to 375°F. Lightly grease a 9 x 13-inch, 11 x 11-inch, or similar-sized pan.

- **To make the crust:** In a medium-sized mixing bowl, beat together the sugars, butter, and vanilla until fluffy. Add the baking powder, salt, egg yolks, and milk and beat well. Add the flour, mixing just until everything is smooth. Press the dough into the bottom of the pre-pared pan. Bake the crust for 12 to 15 minutes, until it is lightly browned. Remove from the oven and set aside to cool.

- **To make the apricot filling:** Mix all the ingredients together in a small saucepan or microwave-safe bowl. Bring the mixture to a boil, stirring once or twice, and then set it aside to cool slightly. If the apricots are in large pieces, use a blender or food processor to partially purée the mixture so it will spread easily.

- **To make the almond filling:** Stir all the ingredients together in a medium-sized bowl; the mixture will be fairly stiff and sticky.

- **To assemble:** Spread the apricot filling over the baked crust, then place the almond filling on top of the apricot filling. The best way to do this is with a teaspoon cookie scoop, or a very small ice cream scoop, pressing the filling down lightly. Bake the bars for 25 to 30 minutes, until they feel set—a print will remain when you lightly press the middle with your finger-tip. Remove the squares from the oven and cool for 1 hour.

- **To make the ganache:** In a small saucepan set over low heat, or in the microwave on low power, heat the chocolate and cream together, stirring frequently. Continue to stir the mix-ture until it's smooth, then spread it atop the squares. Let cool for several hours (or overnight) before cutting into squares.

Nutrition information per serving (1 square, 80 g): 304 cal, 12 g fat, 4 g protein, 13 g complex car-bohydrates, 32 g sugar, 2 g dietary fiber, 43 mg cholesterol, 73 mg sodium, 194 mg potassium, 109 RE vitamin A, 1 mg vitamin C, 1 mg iron, 44 mg calcium, 86 mg phosphorus, 7 mg caffeine.

Build-a-Bars

This type of cookie has cousins from all quarters. You'll find them in recipe-swap columns everywhere, and by the hundreds on the Internet. The names range from Hello Dollies to 7-Layer Bars, but the idea is pretty much the same: Take a bottom crust that's not too sweet, then build the bar by piling on any combination of sweet, crunchy, nutty, marshmallowy, caramely or chocolaty nuggets you desire, and pour on a sticky topping to hold everything in place. Bake just until it all comes together, then stand back and watch them disappear! It's almost like a crunchy ice cream sundae with the works, only nobody invited the ice cream.

Traditional recipes for these bars call for sweetened condensed milk as the topping, and if that's what you're comfortable with, by all means use it. We found that version to be so sweet it made our eyes cross, so here we present a more grown-up alternative.

Yield: 24 bars ● *Baking temperature:* 350°F ● *Baking time:* 15 to 18 minutes for the crust, 20 to 25 minutes for the bars

CRUST
  2 cups (8½ ounces) unbleached all-purpose flour
  ½ cup (2 ounces) walnuts or pecans
  ¾ cup (3 ounces) confectioners' sugar
  1 teaspoon baking powder
  ½ teaspoon salt
  ½ cup (1 stick, 4 ounces) unsalted butter
  2 tablespoons (1½ ounces) honey
  2 tablespoons (1 ounce) milk

FILLING (4 TO 5 CUPS TOTAL)
  Coconut
  Nuts (pecans, walnuts, peanuts, almonds)
  Chunks of caramel
  Chips (chocolate, butterscotch, peanut butter, or your choice)
  Dried fruit (raisins, chopped apricots, diced pineapple, cranberries,
       cherries, dates, fig pieces, etc.)
  Miniature marshmallows
  Crispy cereal: Rice Krispies, cornflakes, Special K, Cheerios, Golden Grahams, etc.
  Broken graham crackers

TOPPING
  4 ounces cream cheese (reduced fat [Neufchâtel] or full fat), softened
  2 tablespoons (⅞ ounce) sugar
  ¼ teaspoons salt
  1 large egg
  One 5-ounce can evaporated milk

● Preheat the oven to 350°F. Lightly grease a 9 x 13-inch, 11 x 11-inch, or similar-sized pan.
● **To make the crust:** Place ½ cup of the flour and the nuts in the bowl of a food processor

and process until the nuts are finely ground. Transfer the mixture to a large mixing bowl and whisk in the remaining 1½ cups flour, the sugar, baking powder, and salt. Cut the butter into pea-sized pieces and work it into the dry ingredients with your hands, a pastry blender, or the paddle attachment of your stand mixer, until crumbly in texture. In a small bowl, stir together the honey and milk until smooth, then pour it over the flour/butter mixture, stirring until evenly moistened. Pat the crumbs into the bottom of the prepared pan, pressing down to cover the surface in an even layer. Bake for 15 to 18 minutes, until set.

- **To make the filling:** Choose any combination of the filling ingredients listed. You'll need 4 to 5 cups total to cover the base layer. Stir your chosen ingredients together in a mixing bowl and sprinkle them in an even layer over the cooled crust.
- **To make the topping:** In a medium-sized bowl, beat together the cream cheese, sugar, and salt. Add the egg and continue beating until no lumps remain; scrape the inside of the bowl to be sure everything combines evenly. Add the evaporated milk and stir until the mixture is smooth. Pour it evenly over the filling.
- Bake the bars for 20 to 25 minutes, until the edges bubble a bit and the center is set. Remove from the oven and cool completely before cutting.

Nutrition information per serving: No nutrition information, the options are too varied.

VARIATIONS

- For a faster (though also sweeter) topping, substitute one 14-ounce can sweetened condensed milk for the topping ingredients.
- Substitute 2 cups (10½ ounces) whole wheat pastry flour for the all-purpose flour in the crust. With all the other goodies on top, this won't automatically label these bars healthy, but it's a small start!
- For a cookie-based crust, try the following:

  **1½ cups (7½ ounces) graham cracker, gingersnap, vanilla cookie,
  or chocolate cookie crumbs**
  ½ cup (1 stick, 4 ounces) unsalted butter, melted
  ¼ cup (1 ounce) unbleached all-purpose flour
  ¼ cup (2 ounces) brown sugar

  Mix together the cookie crumbs, melted butter, flour, and brown sugar in a medium bowl. Press into the bottom of the prepared pan. Bake for 10 minutes, until set.
- To jump-start your imagination, here are some favorite filling flavor combinations dreamed up by various members of our King Arthur family.

  - White chocolate chips, cranberries, and pecans
  - Diced apricots, coconut, and macadamia nuts
  - Chocolate chips, cappuccino chips, and toffee chips
  - M&M's, peanuts, and chocolate chips
  - Dried cherries, white and semisweet chocolate chips, and pecans
  - Shredded coconut and caramel bits
  - Chocolate chips, chocolate chips, chocolate chips, and chocolate chips
  - Miniature marshmallows, peanuts, and chocolate chips

continued on next page

- Dried tropical fruits and nuts, with some key lime juice in the topping
- Candied peel and pine nuts
- Black walnuts and dates, with *dulce de leche* drizzled over the top along with the topping
- Dried figs, pine nuts, and caramel bits
- Rice Krispies and cappuccino chips or butterscotch chips
- Dried sweet cherries and chopped toasted hazelnuts
- Walnuts, with maple syrup and maple flavor in the topping
- Shredded sweetened coconut and toasted almonds
- Raspberry jam and white, bittersweet, or semisweet chocolate chips
- Orange marmalade and semisweet chocolate chips (or toasted coconut)
- Dried sweet cherries and bittersweet chocolate chips
- Diced crystallized ginger and white chocolate chips

County Fair Caramel Apple Bars

Think falling leaves, county fairs, fields of bright orange pumpkins—and the sweet aroma of caramel apples. We've transformed this autumn favorite into delicious, chewy bars.

Yield: 24 bars ● *Baking temperature:* 400°F ● *Baking time:* 35 to 40 minutes

CRUST
- 1 cup (8 ounces) brown sugar
- ¾ cup (1½ sticks, 6 ounces) unsalted butter
- 1 teaspoon apple pie spice or cinnamon
- ¾ teaspoon salt
- ½ teaspoon baking soda
- 1 cup (4¼ ounces) unbleached all-purpose flour
- 1 cup (3½ ounces) pecan meal or ground pecans
- 2 cups (7 ounces) rolled oats

FILLING
- 4 large apples, peeled and sliced or chopped (3 to 4 cups, 21 to 28 ounces)
- ½ teaspoon salt
- ½ teaspoon apple pie spice or cinnamon

TOPPING
- 10 to 12 ounces soft caramel candies (about 2 cups), or Homemade Caramel (see recipe opposite)
- 3 tablespoons (1½ ounces) milk (regular or low fat, not nonfat)

- Preheat the oven to 400°F. Lightly grease a 9 x 13-inch, 11 x 11-inch, or similar-sized pan. To make sure these bars don't stick, line the greased pan, bottom and sides, with lightly greased aluminum foil.
- **To make the crust:** In a medium-sized bowl, beat together the brown sugar, butter, apple pie

spice, salt, and baking soda until well blended. Stir in the flour, pecan meal, and oats; the mixture will be crumbly. Set aside 1 cup of the crumbs. Press the remaining crumbs into the prepared pan.

- **To make the filling:** Toss the apples in a bowl with the salt and cinnamon. Spread them over the crust, pressing them in lightly.
- **To make the topping:** In a microwave-safe bowl or in a saucepan, melt the caramel with the milk. Drizzle the topping over the apples and sprinkle with the reserved crumbs.
- Bake the bars for 35 to 40 minutes, until the caramel is bubbling and the apples are tender. Remove from the oven and cool to lukewarm. Run a knife around the edge of the pan, cut the bars into squares, and arrange them on a serving plate. Allow the bars to rest until the caramel firms up before serving.

Nutrition information per serving (1 bar, 89 g): 291 cal, 14 g fat, 2 g protein, 13 g complex carbohydrates, 29 g sugar, 2 g dietary fiber, 29 mg cholesterol, 178 mg sodium, 180 mg potassium, 98 RE vitamin A, 1 mg vitamin C, 1 mg iron, 34 mg calcium, 62 mg phosphorus.

Homemade Caramel

1 cup (8 ounces) heavy cream
2 cups (16 ounces) brown sugar
¼ cup (2¾ ounces) light corn syrup
4 tablespoons (½ stick, 2 ounces) unsalted butter
1 teaspoon vanilla extract
¼ teaspoon salt

- Stir all the ingredients together in a 2-quart saucepan. Cook over medium heat, stirring constantly, to the soft-ball stage (230°F to 234°F). Remove from the heat and pour 1 cup over the apples. You'll have leftovers (it's really hard to make less than this amount). We suggest that you pour the remaining cup into a buttered 8-inch square pan. When it's cool, cut it into squares, and enjoy!

Breakfast Crunch Bars

No, not as in "have these bars for breakfast"—they're much too rich for that! But it's breakfast cereal that lends them their crunch. Be sure to use a crisp, light cereal, like Rice Krispies or cornflakes; leave the hearty whole-grain cereals for your cereal bowl.

Yield: 35 bars ● *Baking temperature: 350°F* ● *Baking time: 20 to 24 minutes*

CRUST
2¾ cups (11¾ ounces) unbleached all-purpose flour
1¼ cups (10 ounces) brown sugar
1 teaspoon salt
¾ cup (1½ sticks, 6 ounces) unsalted butter
½ cup (4¾ ounces) chunky peanut butter
1 large egg

CHOCOLATE CRUNCH
1 cup (6 ounces) chocolate chips
½ cup (4¾ ounces) chunky peanut butter
1 cup (2 to 3 ounces) Rice Krispies or cornflakes, slightly crushed

BUTTERSCOTCH CRUNCH
1 cup (6 ounces) butterscotch chips
½ cup (4¾ ounces) chunky peanut butter
1 cup (1½ ounces) Rice Krispies or cornflakes, slightly crushed

● Preheat the oven to 350°F.
● **To make the crust:** In a medium-sized mixing bowl, mix together the flour, sugar, and salt. Using a pastry blender, your fingers, or a mixer, cut or rub in the butter and peanut butter until everything is evenly crumbly. Add the egg and mix well. Press the dough into an ungreased 10 x 15-inch jelly roll pan, 14-inch round deep-dish pizza pan, or other similar-sized pan.
● Bake the crust for 20 to 24 minutes, until it has browned and looks set; a print will remain when you press your fingertip in the center. Remove the crust from the oven.
● **To make the crunch toppings:** Over low heat, in a double boiler or in the microwave, melt the chocolate chips and peanut butter, stirring until smooth. Gently stir in the cereal. Repeat the procedure with the butterscotch chips, peanut butter, and cereal.
● Spread half the warm crust with the chocolate crunch, half with the butterscotch crunch. Be sure to press the toppinsg down firmly, and do so while the bottom crust is still warm, so everything sticks together well. Let the bars cool and harden for several hours before cutting them into squares.

Nutrition information per serving (1 bar, 46 g): 222 cal, 12 g fat, 4 g protein, 10 g complex carbohydrates, 15 g sugar, 1 g dietary fiber, 17 mg cholesterol, 140 mg sodium, 146 mg potassium, 48 RE vitamin A, 1 mg vitamin C, 1 mg iron, 13 mg calcium, 59 mg phosphorus, 4 mg caffeine.

Golden Coconut Bars

With their topping of coconut and pecans, these bars are reminiscent of the luscious coconut-caramel icing found on German chocolate cake. Which, by the way, has nothing to do with Germany. The cake was named for Sam German, an employee of the Baker's Chocolate Company who developed the special sweet chocolate used in the recipe.

Yield: 24 bars ● *Baking temperature:* 350°F ● *Baking time:* 10 to 15 minutes for the crust, 25 minutes for the bars

CRUST
4 tablespoons (½ stick, 2 ounces) unsalted butter
¼ cup (2 ounces) brown sugar
Heaping ¼ teaspoon salt
¼ teaspoon baking powder
A few drops of coconut flavor (optional)
1 cup (4¼ ounces) unbleached all-purpose flour

TOPPING
1 cup (8 ounces) brown sugar
2 large eggs
Heaping ¼ teaspoon salt
1½ cups (4½ ounces) shredded sweetened coconut, lightly packed
3 tablespoons (¾ ounce) unbleached all-purpose flour
1 teaspoon vanilla extract, or a few drops of coconut flavor
1 cup (4 ounces) chopped roasted salted pecans

● Preheat the oven to 350°F. Lightly grease a 9 x 9-inch or 7 x 11-inch pan.
● **To make the crust:** In a medium-sized mixing bowl, cream together the butter, brown sugar, salt, baking powder, and flavoring, if using. Add the flour, beating to combine; the dough will be stiff. Press the dough into the prepared pan. Bake the crust for 10 to 15 minutes, until it's a light golden brown. Remove it from the oven.
● **To make the topping:** In a medium-sized mixing bowl, beat together the brown sugar, eggs, and salt, then stir in the coconut, flour, and vanilla. Spread the topping on the crust, smoothing it out the best you can. Sprinkle with the pecans.
● Return the pan to the oven and bake the bars for 25 minutes, or until the topping starts to bubble along the edge. Remove from the oven, cool slightly, and cut into bars.

Nutrition information per serving (1 bar, 52 g): 215 cal, 10 g fat, 13 g protein, 10 g complex carbohydrates, 19 g sugar, 1 g dietary fiber, 35 mg cholesterol, 145 mg sodium, 155 mg potassium, 40 RE vitamin A, 1 mg vitamin C, 1 mg iron, 38 mg calcium, 74 mg phosphorus.

Coconut-Caramel Candy Bars

If you're an aficionado of Girl Scout cookies, you'll recognize our version of their Caramel Delites (a.k.a. Samoas).

Yield: 24 bars ● *Baking temperature:* 350°F ● *Baking time:* 15 minutes for the crust, 10 to 12 minutes for the bars

CRUST
        ½ cup (1 stick, 4 ounces) unsalted butter
        1½ cups (12 ounces) brown sugar
        2 teaspoons vanilla extract
        1 large egg
        1¼ cups (5¼ ounces) unbleached all-purpose flour
        ½ teaspoon salt
        ½ teaspoon baking powder
        3 cups (9 ounces) shredded sweetened coconut, toasted (see page 27)
TOPPINGS
        1 cup (4 to 5 ounces) caramel (block/or caramel candies), cut into ¼-inch pieces
        ¾ cup (4½ ounces) chopped bittersweet or semisweet chocolate, or chocolate chips

- Preheat the oven to 350°F. Lightly grease a 9 x 13-inch, 11 x 11-inch, or similar-sized pan.
- **To make the crust:** In a large mixing bowl, cream together the butter, brown sugar, vanilla, and egg. Mix in the flour, salt, baking powder, and 2½ cups of the coconut (the remaining ½ cup is for the topping). Gently press the dough into the prepared pan. Bake for 15 minutes.
- Remove the bars from the oven, and sprinkle them with the softened pieces of caramel. Return them to the oven and bake for 10 to 12 minutes until they're medium-brown and the caramel is bubbly.
- Remove the bars from the oven and sprinkle with the chocolate. Allow the chocolate to soften for about 5 minutes, then spread it evenly over the bars. Sprinkle the reserved ½ cup coconut over the top. Set aside to cool completely. Loosen the edges of the crust with a knife, then cut into bars.

Nutrition information per serving (1 bar, 49 g): 225 cal, 11 g fat, 2 g protein, 8 g complex carbohydrates, 23 g sugar, 1 g dietary fiber, 20 mg cholesterol, 81 mg sodium, 146 mg potassium, 42 RE vitamin A, 1 mg vitamin C, 1 mg iron, 32 mg calcium, 50 mg phosphorus, 4 mg caffeine.

No crust, please

If, despite your best efforts, your bars develop a hard crust around the edge of the pan, don't worry. Simply cut just inside that hard edge all around the perimeter of the pan and lift it out in pieces. The remaining bars will have soft edges all around. And don't discard those hard crust pieces! Mix up some pudding (instant pudding is a snap), break the crust into bite-sized pieces, and stir it into the pudding; the moisture of the pudding will soften the crusts nicely. Feeling fancy? Call it a trifle.

Cape Cod Cranberry Bars

Tangy-sweet fresh cranberries pair with crisp apples, raspberries, and pecans in these buttery tasting bars. The butter-pecan flavor adds just a touch of caramel flavor . . . or is it butterscotch you taste? You can use fresh or frozen cranberries and raspberries, but if you're using frozen, do not thaw them.

Yield: 24 bars ● *Baking temperature:* 350°F ● *Baking time:* 15 minutes for
the crust, 35 to 40 minutes for the bars

CRUST
  2 cups (8½ ounces) unbleached all-purpose flour
  1 cup (4 ounces) confectioners' sugar
  ¼ cup (2 ounces) brown sugar
  ¼ teaspoon salt (extra-fine if you have it)
  1 teaspoon vanilla extract
  2 drops butter-pecan flavor (optional), the stronger the flavor, the better
  ¾ cup (1½ sticks, 6 ounces) unsalted butter
  1 cup (4 ounces) chopped pecans

FILLING
  2 cups (7 ounces) fresh or frozen cranberries
  1½ cups (10 ounces) peeled, cored, and chopped apples
  1 cup (5 ounces) raspberries
  ½ cup (3½ ounces) sugar
  2 tablespoons (½ ounce) unbleached all-purpose flour
  2 tablespoons (1 ounce) unsalted butter, melted
  Confectioners' sugar, for dusting

● Preheat the oven to 350°F. Lightly grease a 9 x 13-inch or 11 x 11-inch pan.
● **To make the crust:** In a medium-sized mixing bowl, whisk together the flour, sugars, and salt. Add the flavorings, then use your fingers, a pastry blender, or a mixer to cut in the butter, mixing until everything is crumbly. Stir in the nuts. Set aside about 1½ cups of crumbs, then press the remaining crumbs into the bottom of the prepared pan. Bake the crust for 15 minutes. While the crust is baking, make the filling.
● **To make the filling:** In a food processor, combine the cranberries, apples, raspberries, and sugar and pulse a few times to chop the cranberries. Add the flour and melted butter, pulsing briefly to combine.
● Spread the filling over the crust. Crumble the reserved crust mixture over the filling. Bake for 35 to 40 minutes, until the mixture bubbles and the crumbs on top are golden. Remove from the oven and cool completely. Dust with confectioners' sugar, and cut into bars.

Nutrition information per serving (1 bar, 56 g): 182 cal, 10 g fat, 2 g protein, 11 g complex carbohydrates, 11 g sugar, 1 g dietary fiber, 18 mg cholesterol, 24 mg sodium, 63 mg potassium, 64 RE vitamin A, 2 mg vitamin C, 1 mg iron, 8 mg calcium, 28 mg phosphorus.

Bakery Date Squares

Date squares, fig squares, raspberry squares—two layers of crumbly, crunchy, sweet oatmeal crust sandwiching a gooey layer of filling. Much of the crust inevitably crumbles away as you take each bite; at the end you can scoop up the errant crust and enjoy one final mouthful of crunch. Open any cookbook and you'll find date bars listed in the index. The problem is, those are date *bars*—a homogeneous, rather than layered, mixture of dates and oatmeal, not at all the date square of our dreams. We made up our own recipe, and hope you enjoy it as much as we do.

Yield: 36 squares ● *Baking temperature:* 350°F ● *Baking time:* 30 minutes

FILLING*
- 3 cups (15 to 16 ounces) chopped dates
- 1 cup (8 ounces) water
- Heaping ¼ teaspoon salt
- 1 tablespoon plus 1 teaspoon lemon juice
- 2 teaspoons vanilla extract

CRUST
- 1½ cups (5¼ ounces) rolled oats
- 1½ cups (6¼ ounces) unbleached all-purpose flour (or a half-and-half combination of all-purpose and whole wheat flours)
- 1 cup (8 ounces) brown sugar
- ¾ teaspoon baking soda
- ¾ teaspoon salt
- ¾ cup (1½ sticks, 6 ounces) unsalted butter, melted
- ½ cup (2 ounces) chopped walnuts or pecans

● Preheat the oven to 350°F. Lightly grease a 9 x 9-inch or 7 x 11-inch pan.

● **To make the filling:** In a small saucepan, combine the dates, water, salt, and lemon juice. Bring the mixture to a boil, reduce the heat to low, and simmer for 3 to 4 minutes, or until the water is absorbed and mixture has thickened somewhat. Remove the pan from the heat, stir in the vanilla, and set aside to cool while you prepare the crust. If the mixture is too chunky for your taste, purée some or all of it.

● **To make the crust:** In a medium-sized bowl, whisk together the oats, flour, brown sugar, baking soda, and salt. Add the melted butter, stirring until everything is well combined.

● **To assemble the bars:** Press 2½ cups of the crust mixture into the prepared pan, smoothing it out to completely cover the bottom of the pan, with no gaps showing. Spread the filling on the crust. Add the walnuts to the remaining crust mixture and sprinkle it over the filling.

● Bake the squares for 30 minutes, or until the crust is golden brown. Remove from the oven and let cool before cutting into 1½-inch squares.

* For faster preparation, you can use your favorite jam or preserves as filling.

Nutrition information per serving (1 date square, 41 g): 134 cal, 5 g fat, 2 g protein, 14 g complex carbohydrates, 6 g sugar, 2 g dietary fiber, 11 mg cholesterol, 90 mg sodium, 130 mg potassium, 39 RE vitamin A, 1 mg iron, 23 mg calcium, 33 mg phosphorus.

VARIATIONS

Fig Filling

2 cups dried Turkish or Calimyrna figs, stems removed, snipped into quarters
1 cup raisins
¼ teaspoon ground allspice
¼ teaspoon salt
2 tablespoons orange juice
1 tablespoon grated orange rind (zest), or ¼ teaspoon orange oil
1 cup boiling water

● Prepare as directed in the recipe.

Raspberry Filling

2½ cups raspberries (frozen are fine)
3 tablespoons cornstarch
¼ cup water
1 cup sugar
2 tablespoons lemon juice
1 tablespoon grated lemon rind (zest), or ¼ teaspoon lemon oil
2 tablespoons butter

● In a saucepan, crush the raspberries. Dissolve the cornstarch in the water and add to the pan with the remaining ingredients. Bring to a boil and cook until the mixture has thickened. Substitute almonds for the walnuts or pecans in the top crust, if desired.

Spreading jam smoothly

Spreading or piping jam or preserves when making a layered bar cookie can be a bit of a hassle. Here's an easy way to smooth out the lumps and bumps: heat the jam briefly in the micro-wave, then stir the warm jam until it's smooth and viscous before spreading or piping. It will flow much more easily and smoothly.

Double-Butter Bars

No, NOT double the butter—we mean a combination of the comforting flavors of peanut butter and butterscotch. These bars are similar to chocolate chip cookie bars, but with a twist: the addition of the peanut butter and butterscotch, plus a light, crunchy upper crust. When we made them in our King Arthur test kitchen the customer service reps raved over them, as did the customers in our retail store. If you like crunchy/chewy peanut butter cookies, you'll enjoy these bars.

Yield: 24 bars ● *Baking temperature: 350°F* ● *Baking time: 40 to 45 minutes*

BARS
½ cup (1 stick, 4 ounces) unsalted butter
1 cup (9½ ounces) smooth peanut butter
1 cup (8 ounces) brown sugar
1 teaspoon salt
2 large egg yolks (reserve the whites)
2 tablespoons (1 ounce) water
2 teaspoons vanilla extract
1 teaspoon baking soda
1½ cups (6¼ ounces) unbleached all-purpose flour
1½ cups (9 ounces) butterscotch chips, peanut butter chips, or chocolate chips
1 cup (4–5 ounces) chopped almonds or pecans, toasted (see page 27), or dry-roasted peanuts

TOPPING
2 large egg whites
⅛ teaspoon cream of tartar
½ cup (4 ounces) brown sugar

● Preheat the oven to 350°F. Lightly grease a 9 x 13-inch or 11 x 11-inch, or similar-sized pan.
● **To make the bars:** In a medium-sized mixing bowl, beat together the butter, peanut butter, brown sugar, and salt until well blended. Add the egg yolks, water, and vanilla, beating to combine. Gently stir in the baking soda and flour, then the chips and ¾ cup of the nuts. Spread the dough into the prepared pan, using a spatula (or wet fingers) to smooth the top.
● **To make the topping:** In a medium-sized mixing bowl, beat together the egg whites and cream of tartar until they're foamy and start to thicken. Gradually add the brown sugar and continue to beat until the mixture is thick and glossy. Spread the meringue over the dough. Sprinkle with the remaining ¼ cup nuts, pressing them in lightly.
● Bake the bars for 40 to 45 minutes, until they're golden brown. Remove from the oven and place on a rack to cool completely before serving. To cut without too much crumbling of the topping, it's helpful to wet the knife or spray it with nonstick cooking spray.

Nutrition information per serving (1 bar, 59 g): 274 cal, 16 g fat, 5 g protein, 8 g complex carbohydrates, 22 g sugar, 1 g dietary fiber, 29 mg cholesterol, 212 mg sodium, 175 mg potassium, 46 RE vitamin A, 1 mg vitamin C, 1 mg iron, 17 mg calcium, 73 mg phosphorus.

Frosted Delights

While some bars are ooey-gooey thick 'n' chewy, these rest at the other end of the scale. With a thin, light-textured, cakelike base, and fragile-crunchy, mild-flavored nut and meringue topping, they're comforting rather than outrageous.

Yield: 24 bars ● ***Baking temperature:** 350°F* ● ***Baking time:** 25 to 30 minutes*

CRUST
> ½ cup (1 stick, 4 ounces) unsalted butter
> 1 cup (7 ounces) sugar
> ½ teaspoon vanilla extract
> 1 teaspoon baking powder
> ½ teaspoon salt
> 2 large eggs
> 1½ cups (6¼ ounces) unbleached all-purpose flour

TOPPING
> 1 cup (8 ounces) brown sugar
> 1 large egg white
> Pinch of salt
> 2 cups (8 ounces) chopped pecans or walnuts

● Preheat the oven to 350°F. Lightly grease a 9 x 13-inch, 11 x 11-inch, or similar-sized pan.

● **To make the crust:** In a medium-sized mixing bowl, cream together the butter, sugar, vanilla, baking powder, and salt. Beat in the eggs, scraping the sides and bottom of the bowl and then beating until smooth. Add the flour, stirring just until smooth. Press the dough into the prepared pan.

● **To make the topping:** In a medium-sized bowl, beat together the brown sugar, egg white, and salt until smooth and somewhat lightened in color. Stir in the nuts. Spread the topping evenly over the crust.

● Bake the bars for 25 to 30 minutes, until they're golden brown. Remove them from the oven and cool on a rack before cutting.

Nutrition information per serving (1 bar, 45 g): 191 cal, 10 g fat, 4 g protein, 7 g complex carbohydrates, 17 g sugar, 1 g dietary fiber, 29 mg cholesterol, 76 mg sodium, 99 mg potassium, 48 RE vitamin A, 1 mg vitamin C, 1 mg iron, 28 mg calcium, 65 mg phosphorus.

Double-Shot Cappuccino Bars

For those who take their coffee seriously (and you have a lot of company around here!), here's a recipe that'll get you perking. The intense espresso-flavored base is topped with a creamy vanilla layer, and finished however you like—with cinnamon, chocolate, or caramel, whichever fancy coffee drink you choose to emulate.

Yield: 24 bars ● *Baking temperature: 350°F* ● *Baking time: 12 to 15 minutes for the crust, 20 to 25 minutes for the bars*

CRUST
- ½ cup (1 stick, 4 ounces) unsalted butter
- ¾ cup (5½ ounces) sugar
- 2 large eggs
- ½ teaspoon vanilla extract
- ¼ cup (½ ounce) espresso powder, or ⅓ cup (⅜ ounce) instant coffee crystals
- 1¾ cups (7¼ ounces) unbleached all-purpose flour
- ½ teaspoon salt
- 1 teaspoon baking powder

FILLING
- ¾ cup (5¼ ounces) sugar
- ¼ cup (1 ounce) unbleached all-purpose flour
- 3 large eggs
- 1 cup (8 ounces) heavy cream
- 1½ teaspoons vanilla extract

GLAZE
- 1 cup (4 ounces) confectioners' sugar
- 1 teaspoon cinnamon
- ¼ teaspoon salt
- 4 to 5 tablespoons (2 to 2½ ounces) heavy cream or milk
- 4 teaspoons (¼ ounce) unsweetened cocoa powder, regular or Dutch process (optional)

● Preheat the oven to 350°F. Lightly grease a 9 x 13-inch, 11 x 11-inch, or similar-sized pan.

● **To make the crust:** In a medium-sized mixing bowl, cream together the butter and sugar until fluffy. Beat in the eggs one at a time, scraping the bowl after each addition. Stir in the vanilla and espresso powder.

● In a separate bowl, whisk together the flour, salt, and baking powder. Add this to the butter/espresso mixture, stirring until smooth. Press the dough into the bottom of the prepared pan. Bake the crust for 12 to 15 minutes, until it's set. Remove it from the oven and cool for 15 minutes.

- **To make the filling:** In a medium-sized mixing bowl, whisk together the sugar and flour. In a separate bowl, beat together the eggs, cream, and vanilla until well combined, then add to the flour mixture, stirring until smooth. Pour the filling over the crust. Bake for 20 to 25 minutes, until the center is set. Remove from the oven and cool on a rack for 1 hour, then refrigerate until completely cool and firm.
- **To make the glaze:** In a small bowl, whisk together the confectioners' sugar, cinnamon, and salt. Add the cream gradually, whisking until no lumps remain. Drizzle the glaze over the bars. For a fancy two-tone effect, drizzle half the glaze over the bars, then add the cocoa to the remaining glaze and drizzle it on.

Nutrition information per serving (1 bar, 59 g): 176 cal, 6 g fat, 3 g protein, 56 g complex carbohydrates, 21 g sugar, 61 mg cholesterol, 127 mg sodium, 56 mg potassium, 73 RE vitamin A, 1 mg iron, 27 mg calcium, mg 41phosphorus, 19 mg caffeine.

VARIATIONS

- For caramel macchiato bars, substitute the following glaze:

  6 ounces caramel (candies, or from a block)
  4 teaspoons heavy cream

Heat the caramel and cream together, stirring until smooth. Drizzle over the cooled bars.

What does it mean to bake bars "until they're set"?

Some bar recipes indicate a baking temperature and time, then tell you to bake the bars for the indicated time, "until they're set." What does this mean, exactly? When a bar is set, it means the edges are just barely beginning to pull away from the sides of the pan; the bars appear firm from edge to the center (there's no gelatin-like jiggling in the center); and when you press your fingertip lightly into the bars in the middle of the pan, it won't break the crust, but will leave a print. To check further, use the tip of a very sharp knife to dig into the center. Examine the interior. If it's still runny and/or very wet looking, allow the bars to continue to bake. (Don't worry about the hole in the middle—that will be your piece.)

Hot & Sweet Ginger Squares

If you're one of the many folks who thinks ginger is a flavor that ranks right up there with chocolate, you'll love these squares. Their thin, chewy gingerbread with crystallized ginger and streusel on top, got an extremely high rating from both the crew of taste-testers in our customer service department, and the customers at our store. One person commented that these were "the perfect, *perfect* holiday treat."

Yield: 24 squares ● *Baking temperature: 350°F* ● *Baking time: 40 to 45 minutes*

CRUST
   1¼ cups (5¼ ounces) unbleached all-purpose flour
   2 teaspoons ground ginger
   1 teaspoon ground allspice
   ¾ teaspoon salt
   ¼ teaspoon baking soda
   ½ cup (3¼ ounces) diced crystallized ginger
   ¼ cup (3 ounces) molasses
   2 large eggs
   1⅓ cups (10¾ ounces) dark brown sugar
   4 tablespoons (½ stick, 2 ounces) unsalted butter, melted
STREUSEL
   1⅓ cups (5½ ounces) unbleached all-purpose flour
   ½ cup (1 stick, 4 ounces) unsalted butter
   Pinch of salt
   ¾ cup (6 ounces) dark brown sugar
   ½ cup (3¼ ounces) diced crystallized ginger

● Preheat the oven to 350°F. Lightly grease a 9 x 13-inch, 11 x 11-inch, or similar-sized pan.
● **To make the crust:** In a medium-sized mixing bowl, whisk together the flour, ground ginger, allspice, salt, baking soda, and crystallized ginger. In a separate bowl, stir together the molasses, eggs, brown sugar, and butter. Combine the wet and dry ingredients, beating until smooth. Spread the batter in the prepared pan.
● **To make the streusel:** In a medium-sized mixing bowl, use a pastry blender, electric mixer, or your fingers to mix together the flour, butter, salt, and brown sugar until fairly well blended; some chunks of butter can remain. Stir in the crystallized ginger. Sprinkle the streusel over the batter.
● Bake the squares for 40 to 45 minutes, until the streusel is a deep, golden brown. Remove from the oven and run a knife around the edges of the pan to loosen them. Cool to luke-warm, then cut into 1½-inch squares.

Nutrition information per serving (1 square, 55 g): 214 cal, 7 g fat, 2 g protein, 10 g complex carbohydrates, 27 g sugar, 1 g dietary fiber, 34 mg cholesterol, 115 mg sodium, 116 mg potassium, 65 RE vitamin A, 1 mg vitamin C, 1 mg iron, 29 mg calcium, 28 mg phosphorus.

Key Lime Bars in Coconut Crust

Toasted coconut in the crust adds both crunch and flavor to these tart-sweet bars. Did you know true Key lime juice is actually pale yellow, not green? Add a couple of drops of green food color to the filling if you want them to scream lime, visually.

Yield: 24 bars ● *Baking temperature: 350°F* ● *Baking time: 16 to 18 minutes for the crust, 25 minutes for the bars*

CRUST

⅔ cup (5⅜ ounces) brown sugar

1¾ cups (7¼ ounces) unbleached all-purpose flour

3 cups (9 ounces) shredded sweetened coconut, toasted (see page 27)

½ teaspoon salt

½ teaspoon coconut extract, or 3 drops strong coconut flavor (optional)

½ cup (1 stick, 4 ounces) unsalted butter, cut into cubes

FILLING

One 8-ounce package cream cheese (reduced fat [Neufchâtel] or full fat), softened

1¾ cups (12¼ ounces) sugar

Pinch of salt

3 tablespoons (¾ ounce) unbleached all-purpose flour

4 large eggs

⅓ to ½ cup (2¾ to 4 ounces) Key lime juice, or fresh lime juice, to taste

● Preheat the oven to 350°F. Lightly grease a 9 x 13-inch, 11 x 11-inch, or similar-sized pan.

● **To make the crust:** Combine all the crust ingredients in a medium-sized mixing bowl or in the bowl of a food processor. Mix or process until the mixture is crumbly. Set aside 1 cup of the crumbs, and press the remaining crumbs into the bottom of the prepared pan. Bake the crust for 16 to 18 minutes, until it's golden brown.

● **To make the filling:** In a medium-sized bowl, beat the cream cheese until soft. Add the sugar and salt and beat until well blended. Stir in the flour, then beat in the eggs one at a time, beating well after each addition. Stir in the lime juice, mixing until smooth. Pour the filling onto the crust.

● Bake the bars for 15 minutes. Sprinkle with the reserved crumbs and bake an additional 10 minutes, or until set around the edges but still slightly wobbly in the middle. Remove from the oven and cool at room temperature for 1 hour. For easiest slicing, refrigerate for several hours. Garnish with lime jelly fruit slices, if desired.

Nutrition information per serving (1 square 65 g): 235 cal, 12 g fat, 3 g protein, 10 g complex carbohydrates, 21 g sugar, 1 g dietary fiber, 57 mg cholesterol, 104 mg sodium, 101 mg potassium, 95 RE vitamin A, 2 mg vitamin C, 1 mg iron, 21 mg calcium, 51 mg phosphorus.

Lemon Squares

These lemon squares will look familiar to you if you're a habitué of bakeries, where you'll often see them shingled on a tray in the display case, their bright yellow filling peeking out from beneath a blizzard of confectioners' sugar. Delightfully tart, with a tender, crunchy bottom crust, this recipe makes the quintessential lemon square.

Yield: 16 squares ● *Baking temperature:* 350°F ● *Baking time:* 20 minutes for the crust, 25 minutes for the squares

CRUST
  1½ cups (6¼ ounces) unbleached all-purpose flour
  ¼ cup (1 ounce) confectioners' sugar
  ¼ teaspoon salt
  ½ cup (1 stick, 4 ounces) unsalted butter

TOPPING
  4 large eggs
  1¼ cups (8¾ ounces) granulated sugar
  ½ cup (4 ounces) lemon juice
  ¼ cup (1 ounce) unbleached all-purpose flour
  ½ teaspoon salt
  2 tablespoons grated lemon rind (zest), or ½ teaspoon lemon oil
  Confectioners' sugar

● Preheat the oven to 350°F. Lightly grease a 9 x 9-inch, 11 x 7-inch, or similar-sized pan.
● **To make the crust:** In a medium-sized mixing bowl, whisk together the flour, sugar, and salt. Using a pastry blender, your fingers, or a mixer, cut in the butter, mixing to form coarse crumbs. Press the crumbs into the prepared pan. Bake the crust for 20 minutes, or until it's light brown.
● **To make the topping:** In a medium-sized bowl, beat together the eggs, granulated sugar, and lemon juice until smooth. Stir in the flour, salt, and lemon zest.
● Pour the topping over the hot crust, return the pan to the oven, and continue baking for about 25 minutes, or until the top of the squares appears set. Remove from the oven and cool in the pan. Sprinkle with confectioners' sugar just before cutting and serving.

Nutrition information per serving (1 square, 58 g): 183 cal, 7 g fat, 3 g protein, 10 g complex carbohydrates, 17 g sugar, 70 mg cholesterol, 117 mg sodium, 44 mg potassium, 81 RE vitamin A, 4 mg vitamin C, 1 mg iron, 10 mg calcium, 36 mg phosphorus.

VARIATION

● For an elegant dessert, make these bars in a 10-inch round tart pan. When completely cool, spread with ¾ cup warmed raspberry jam, combined with 1 tablespoon raspberry liqueur. Don't sprinkle with confectioners' sugar, it will make the jam look cloudy.

Nanaimo Bars

This layered bar is originally from Nanaimo (pronounced nah-NIGH-moe), a city on Vancouver Island in British Columbia. It was born in 1952, when a fund-raising cookbook from the island featured three recipes for chocolate squares and slices. These recipes were reprinted under the name "Nanaimo Bars" in the *Vancouver Sun.* Canadian food companies adopted them as a convenient vehicle for their products, and they've been around ever since.

Yield: 48 bars ● *Baking temperature:* 350°F ● *Baking time:* 10 minutes

CRUST
- ½ cup (1 stick, 4 ounces) unsalted butter, melted
- ¼ cup (1¾ ounces) sugar
- ⅓ cup (1 ounce) unsweetened cocoa powder, regular or Dutch process
- 1 large egg
- 1 cup (3 ounces) sweetened flaked coconut
- ½ cup (2 ounces) chopped walnuts
- 1 teaspoon vanilla extract
- 2 cups (10 ounces) graham cracker crumbs

FILLING
- ½ cup (1 stick, 4 ounces) unsalted butter
- 2 cups (8 ounces) confectioners' sugar
- ½ teaspoon vanilla extract
- 2 tablespoons (⅞ ounce) instant vanilla pudding mix
- 2 tablespoons (1 ounce) milk (regular or low fat, not nonfat)

FROSTING
- 1 cup (6 ounces) chopped semisweet chocolate or chocolate chips
- 2 tablespoons (¾ ounce) vegetable shortening, unsalted butter, or heavy cream

● Preheat the oven to 350°F. Lightly grease a 9 x 9-inch or 11 x 7-inch pan.

● **To make the crust:** In a medium-sized mixing bowl, combine the butter, sugar, and cocoa. Mix in the egg, then stir in the coconut, walnuts, vanilla, and crumbs. Press the mixture into the prepared pan and bake for 10 minutes. Remove from the oven and allow to cool completely.

● **To make the filling:** In a medium-sized mixing bowl, cream the butter, then add 1 cup of the confectioners' sugar and the vanilla. In a small bowl, stir the pudding into the milk and add to the butter mixture. Add the remaining 1 cup confectioners' sugar and beat until the filling is smooth. Spread it over the cooled crust and refrigerate until chilled.

● **To make the frosting:** Melt the chocolate and shortening in a small saucepan set over medium heat, or in the microwave; stir until the mixture is smooth. Spread the frosting over the chilled bars and refrigerate until the chocolate is set. Cut into bars with a sharp knife.

Nutrition information per serving (1 bar, 24 g): 116 cal, 7 g fat, 1 g protein, 3 g complex carbohydrates, 9 g sugar, 16 mg cholesterol, 41 mg sodium, 35 mg potassium, 43 RE vitamin A, 6 mg calcium, 22 mg phosphorus, 3 mg caffeine.

Elegant Raspberry-Almond Bars

These layered bars, scented with almond, feature everyone's favorite berry, the raspberry. They're fancier than most; save them for an elegant afternoon tea party, a wedding shower, or someplace they'll enjoy adult attention.

Yield: 24 *bars* ● ***Baking temperature:*** *350°F* ● ***Baking time:*** *14 to 16 minutes for the crust, 25 to 30 minutes for the bars*

CRUST
- ¾ cup (1½ sticks, 6 ounces) unsalted butter
- 1½ cups (6¼ ounces) unbleached all-purpose flour
- ½ cup (2 ounces) confectioners' sugar
- 1 cup (3¼ ounces) almond flour or finely ground almonds
- 1 teaspoon almond extract, or 3 drops bitter almond oil
- ¾ teaspoon salt

FILLING
- 1 cup (9 ounces) almond paste
- ½ cup (3½ ounces) granulated sugar
- 2 large eggs
- ¼ teaspoon salt
- 2 cups (4½ ounces) fresh bread crumbs
- ¾ cup (7¾ ounces) raspberry preserves, warmed

TOPPING
- ¾ cup (3¾ ounces) chopped almonds
- ¾ cup crust mixture (reserved from crust)

● Preheat the oven to 350°F. Lightly grease a 9 x 13-inch, 11 x 11-inch, or similar-sized pan.

● **To make the crust:** In a medium-sized mixing bowl, combine all the crust ingredients, mixing until evenly crumbly. Set aside ¾ cup for the topping, then press the remainder into the prepared pan.

● **To make the filling:** In a small bowl, mix together the almond paste, sugar and 1 egg until smooth. Stir in the other egg, the salt, and the crumbs. Spread this mixture over the crust as smoothly as possible. Bake for 14 to 16 minutes, until the filling looks set. Remove from the oven. Top with the warmed preserves.

● **To make the topping:** Mix the almonds and reserved crust mixture together and sprinkle over the filling. Return the bars to the oven and bake for 25 to 30 minutes, until the edges and top are lightly browned and the preserves are just beginning to bubble. Remove from the oven and cool completely before cutting.

Nutrition information per serving *(1 bar, 63 g):* 264 cal, 13 g fat, 5 g protein, 17 g complex carbohydrates, 14 g sugar, 3 g dietary fiber, 34 mg cholesterol, 174 mg sodium, 167 mg potassium, 65 RE vitamin A, 1 mg vitamin C, 2 mg iron, 68 mg calcium, 115 mg phosphorus.

Rhubarb Dreams

These are downright fun to eat. First, the meringuelike topping goes "poof" in your mouth—a nice little surprise start—then your teeth sink into the juicy, lemon-accented rhubarb. These bars are just the ticket if you're looking for a light, sweet dessert.

Yield: 24 bars ● *Baking temperature: 350°F* ● *Baking time: 10 to 15 minutes for the crust, 40 to 45 minutes for the bars*

CRUST
- 1½ cups (6¼ ounces) unbleached all-purpose flour
- ¾ cup (3 ounces) confectioners' sugar
- ¼ teaspoon salt
- ½ cup (1 stick, 4 ounces) unsalted butter
- ¼ teaspoon lemon oil, or 2 tablespoons grated lemon rind (zest) plus 1 teaspoon fresh lemon juice

FILLING
- 4 large eggs
- ¼ teaspoon salt
- 2 cups (14 ounces) granulated sugar
- ½ cup (2 ounces) unbleached all-purpose flour
- 4 cups (1 pound) packed diced rhubarb

● Preheat the oven to 350°F. Lightly grease a 9 x 13-inch, 11 x 11-inch, or similar-sized pan.
● **To make the crust:** In a medium-sized mixing bowl, whisk together the flour, confectioners' sugar, and salt. Using your fingers, a pastry blender, or a mixer, cut in the butter until everything is evenly crumbly. Add the lemon oil. Press the mixture into the bottom of the prepared pan. Bake the crust for 10 to 15 minutes, until it's lightly browned. Remove from the oven and let cool slightly.
● **To make the filling:** While the crust is baking, make the filling. In a large bowl, beat the eggs and salt until foamy. Gradually add the sugar, beating until the mixture is thick and a light yellow color. Blend in the flour, then fold in the rhubarb.
● Pour the filling over the still-warm crust, return the pan to the oven, and bake the bars for 40 to 45 minutes, until they're lightly browned. Remove from the oven and cool for several hours for easiest cutting. The top layer separates a bit from the filling when you cut; just press it back lightly.

Nutrition information per serving (1 bar, 60 g): 127 cal, 1 g fat, 2 g protein, 8 g complex carbohydrates, 20 g sugar, 1 g dietary fiber, 36 mg cholesterol, 56 mg sodium, 82 mg potassium, 19 RE vitamin A, 2 mg vitamin C, 1 mg iron, 23 mg calcium, 27 mg phosphorus.

VARIATION
● To make strawberry-rhubarb dreams, substitute hulled, coarsely chopped strawberries for up to half the rhubarb.

Strawberry Cheesecake Bars

A swirl of bright red strawberry in a creamy layer of golden cheesecake makes this bar a winner in the good looks department. As for the flavor, if strawberry cheesecake is a favorite, you'll want to give this recipe four gold stars.

Yield: 24 bars ● *Baking temperature:* 350°F ● *Baking time:* 12 to 15 minutes for the crust, 20 to 22 minutes for the bars

CRUST

1½ cups (6¼ ounces) unbleached all-purpose flour
¾ cup (5¼ ounces) sugar
½ teaspoon salt
1 teaspoon baking powder
¾ cup (1½ sticks, 6 ounces) unsalted butter
1 cup (4 ounces) chopped pecans, toasted (see page 27)

FILLING

Two 8-ounce packages cream cheese (reduced fat [Neufchâtel] or full fat), softened
¾ cup (5¼ ounces) sugar
1 teaspoon vanilla extract
2 large eggs
¼ cup (3 ounces) strawberry jam (or your favorite jam or preserve)

● Preheat the oven to 350°F. Lightly grease a 9 x 13-inch or 11 x 11-inch pan.
● **To make the crust:** In a medium-sized mixing bowl, mix together the flour, sugar, salt, baking powder, and butter. Stir in the pecans. Press the mixture into the bottom of the prepared pan. Bake the crust for 12 to 15 minutes, until it's set. Remove it from the oven and let cool for 15 minutes.

To smooth out a sticky crust, distribute the dough evenly over the bottom of the prepared baking pan. Cover the dough with plastic wrap and use a small rolling pin to smooth it out.

An offset spatula is the best tool to spread filling evenly.

● **To make the filling:** In a medium-sized bowl, beat the cream cheese and sugar together until smooth. Gently beat in the vanilla and eggs. Spread the filling over the crust.

● Stir the jam, or warm it slightly to make it spreadable. If it's very lumpy, use a blender or food processor to smooth it out. Spoon the jam into a small plastic bag, snip off one corner, and pipe lines of jam the length of the pan, about ¾ inch apart. Use a knife to pull the jam from side to side through the cream cheese mixture at 1-inch intervals.

● Bake the bars for 20 to 22 minutes, just until the filling is set. The middle should wobble slightly. Remove from the oven and run a spatula around the edges of the pan to loosen the filling; this will help prevent it from cracking. Cool for 1 hour at room temperature, then refrigerate until completely chilled and firm.

Nutrition information per serving (1 bar, 59 g): 238 cal, 16 g fat, 3 g protein, 7 g complex carbohydrates, 15 g sugar, 1 g dietary fiber, 54 mg cholesterol, 128 mg sodium, 60 mg potassium, 145 RE vitamin A, 1 mg vitamin C, 1 mg iron, 33 mg calcium, 54 mg phosphorus.

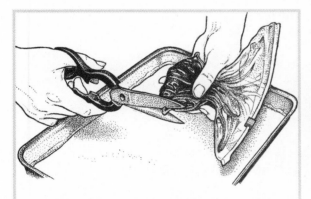

To pipe small amounts of jam, place it in a plastic bag and snip off one corner.

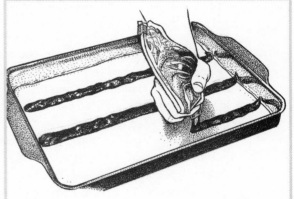

Squeeze the jam in a stripe over the cheesecake filling.

Run a knife through the stripes to pull them into a decorative pattern, changing directions with each pass.

White Chocolate–Cashew Bars

If you think white chocolate is just too sweet and bland to be in the same league with its darker brethren, think again. This rich, flavorful chocolate needs only a salty counterpart—in this case, cashews—to bring out its best qualities.

Yield: 16 bars ● *Baking temperature:* 350°F ● *Baking time:* 30 to 35 minutes

2 large eggs
¾ cup (5¼ ounces) sugar
½ teaspoon salt
1 teaspoon vanilla extract
1 teaspoon baking powder
1 cup (6 ounces) white chocolate chips or chunks
½ cup (1 stick, 4 ounces) unsalted butter
1¾ cups (7¼ ounces) unbleached all-purpose flour
1 cup (4 ounces) salted cashews, toasted (see page 27)

● Preheat the oven to 350°F. Lightly grease a 9 x 13-inch or 11 x 11-inch pan.
● In a medium-sized mixing bowl, beat the eggs until foamy. Add the sugar, salt, vanilla, and baking powder, continuing to beat the mixture until it is shiny and pale yellow.
● In a microwave-safe bowl, or in a saucepan set over low heat, melt ½ cup of the chocolate with the butter. Set aside.
● Stir the flour into the egg mixture in two additions, mixing until smooth after each addition. Beat in the reserved chocolate mixture. Spread the batter into the prepared pan. Sprinkle with the nuts and the remaining ½ cup chocolate.
● Bake the bars for 30 to 35 minutes, until they're puffed and shiny, browned around the edges, and a cake tester inserted into the middle comes out clean. Remove from the oven and cool before cutting into bars.

Nutrition information per serving (1 bar, 38 g): 174 cal, 10 g fat, 3 g protein, 8 g complex carbohydrates, 10 g sugar, 29 mg cholesterol, 118 mg sodium, 74 mg potassium, 46 RE vitamin A, 1 mg iron, 33 mg calcium, 52 mg phosphorus.

S'more Granola Bars

Sturdy enough to survive all day in the bottom of a backpack, these granola bars are topped with chocolate and golden toasted marshmallows. Quick, light the campfire!

Yield: 48 bars ● *Baking temperature: 425°F* ● *Baking time: 6 to 8 minutes for the oats, 4 to 5 minutes for the bars*

4 cups (14 ounces) rolled oats
4 cups (4½ ounces) Rice Krispies cereal
¾ cup (5¼ ounces) sugar
½ cup (1 stick, 4 ounces) unsalted butter
¼ cup (2 ounces) water
½ cup (5½ ounces) corn syrup
1 teaspoon salt
3 cups (6 ounces) miniature marshmallows
1½ cups (9 ounces) chocolate chips

● Preheat the oven to 425°F. Lightly grease a half-sheet (18 x 13-inch) pan, or two 9 x 13-inch pans.

● Place the oats on the prepared pan(s). Bake for 6 to 8 minutes, stirring frequently to prevent the edges from burning. They won't brown, but should begin to smell toasty. Remove the pan from the oven. Transfer the oats to a bowl and add the cereal.

● In a large saucepan, combine the sugar, butter, water, corn syrup, and salt. Bring the mixture to a boil and boil for 5 minutes, or until the temperature reaches 250°F on a candy thermometer. Remove the syrup from the heat and pour it over the oats and cereal, tossing to combine. Add 1½ cups of the marshmallows and stir again until well combined.

● Place the mixture on the prepared pan, patting it flat. Press the mixture into the pan; using the lightly greased back of another half-sheet pan works well. Sprinkle with the remaining 1½ cups marshmallows and the chocolate chips.

● Bake the bars for 4 to 5 minutes, until the marshmallows have puffed and are slightly brown. Remove the bars from the oven and cool for about 10 minutes on a rack. Cut into squares while still warm. The easiest way to do this is to use a baker's bench knife to cut the bars into long strips while still in the pan, then transfer each strip to a cutting board to cut into bars.

Nutrition information per serving (1 bar, 28 g): 110 cal, 4 g fat, 2 g protein, 6 g complex carbohydrates, 11 g sugar, 1 g dietary fiber, 5 mg cholesterol, 95 mg sodium, 45 mg potassium, 90 RE vitamin A, 1 mg vitamin C, 3 mg iron, 55 mg calcium, 44 mg phosphorus, 4 mg caffeine.

Fig Squares

New England has traditionally been known for its waste not, want not austerity, and some of its traditional baked goods reflect this. A case in point is fig squares. They feature a substantial bottom and top crust made of flaky pie pastry, with a thin (less than half an inch) layer of fruit filling. There's just barely enough filling to sweeten the crust, enough to create a rather severe, crust-centered pastry (ah, but there are those who love it). Found in just about every old-fashioned New England bakery, where they often share equal space with raspberry squares and lemon squares, fig squares are for the piecrust lovers of the world.

You can make your own filling or use fig filling from a jar; they're equally good. You'll need 2 to 3 cups of filling. Try lemon pie filling or raspberry pie filling if figs aren't to your taste.

Yield: 24 squares ● *Baking temperature: 425°F, then 350°F* ● *Baking time: 15 minutes for the crust, 45 minutes for the squares*

CRUST
> 3 cups (12¾ ounces) unbleached all-purpose flour
> 1½ teaspoons salt
> 1 cup (2 sticks, 8 ounces) unsalted butter
> 2 large eggs, beaten
> ¼ cup (2 ounces) ice water

FILLING
> 1 pound dried figs, chopped
> 1 cup (8 ounces) water
> ⅔ cup (4¾ ounces) sugar
> ¼ cup (2 ounces) lemon juice, fresh-squeezed preferred
> Pinch of salt
> ¼ teaspoon ground ginger (optional)

● **To make the crust:** In a medium-sized mixing bowl, whisk together the flour and salt. Using your fingers, a pastry blender, or a mixer, cut in the butter. Drizzle the beaten eggs over the mixture in the bowl and toss lightly to combine. Add the ice water 1 tablespoon at a time, stirring gently until the dough starts to clump together. Grab a fistful; if it sticks together easily, you've added enough water. Divide the pastry in half, shape each half into a flattened oval, wrap well, and refrigerate for at least 30 minutes.

● Preheat the oven to 425°F.

● Roll out one piece of the dough on a lightly floured surface into a 9 x 13-inch rectangle. You're going to be putting this pastry in a 9 x 13-inch pan, so you need to make it pretty close to the right size; make it a bit larger and trim the edges, or make it almost the right size, with the edges a bit thicker so you can stretch them once it's in the pan.

● Transfer the rolled-out dough to a 9 x 13-inch pan. If you have a giant spatula, use it. Otherwise either roll the dough around your rolling pin, then unroll it into the pan, or fold it in quarters, put it in the pan, and unfold it. Stretch the dough (or trim it) until it comes about ¼ inch up the sides of the pan all the way around. Using a dough docker or a fork, prick the crust all over.

- Bake the crust for 15 minutes, checking it about halfway through. If it's puffed up, prick it with the tip of a sharp knife. Remove the crust from the oven and let cool for 10 minutes before adding the filling. While the crust is baking, prepare the filling. After the crust comes out of the oven, lower the temperature to 350°F.

- **To make the filling:** Combine all the filling ingredients in a saucepan set over medium heat, bring to a boil, and lower the heat so the mixture simmers. Cook until the figs are soft, stirring regularly. Remove from the heat and let the filling cool. (Or open the lid on 2 to 3 cups of prepared fig pastry filling.)

- Spread the filling over the crust, leaving about a ½-inch margin all around the edges. Two cups of filling will give you squares with the merest layer of filling; 3 cups will give you squares that in New England would be considered overstuffed, the filling oozing out the sides when you cut them. Roll out the second piece of dough the same way you rolled out the first one, prick it all over, and transfer it to the pan, carefully centering it atop the filling. Press the edges of the crust together.

- Bake the squares for about 45 minutes, until the top crust and edges are beginning to brown. These won't get golden brown; they're not supposed to. Remove from the oven and cool completely before cutting. Use a baker's bench knife, a rolling pizza cutter, or a sharp knife to cut into squares.

Nutrition information per serving (1 square, 68 g): 196 cal, 8 g fat, 3 g protein, 24 g complex carbohydrates, 6 g sugar, 2 g dietary fiber, 38 mg cholesterol, 151 mg sodium, 165 mg potassium, 82 RE vitamin A, 2 mg vitamin C, 1 mg iron, 32 mg calcium, 36 mg phosphorus.

Dutch Apple Pie Bars

Looking for a picnic-portable apple pie? We've got you covered. This traditional apple pie, in user-friendly bar form, is everything apple pie should be: tangy-sweet apples touched with cinnamon, nestled in a buttery pastry crust. The streusel topping is what gives these bars their Dutch moniker.

Yield: 24 bars ● *Baking temperature:* 425°F, then 350°F ● *Baking time:* 10 to 12 minutes for the crust, 45 to 50 minutes for the bars

CRUST
1½ cups (6¼ ounces) unbleached all-purpose flour
¾ teaspoon salt
½ cup (1 stick, 4 ounces) unsalted butter
1 large egg, beaten
2 tablespoons (1 ounce) ice water

FILLING
2 tablespoons (½ ounce) unbleached all-purpose flour
½ to ¾ cup (3½ to 5¼ ounces) sugar (depending on tartness of the apples)
Pinch of nutmeg
½ teaspoon cinnamon
¼ teaspoon salt
5 to 6 cups peeled, cored, and diced apples (Granny Smith is a good choice, about 6 apples)
2 teaspoons vanilla extract
½ cup (4 ounces) heavy cream

TOPPING
1½ cups (6¼ ounces) unbleached all-purpose flour
¾ cup (5¼ ounces) sugar
¼ teaspoon salt
1 teaspoon cinnamon
½ cup (1 stick, 4 ounces) unsalted butter, melted
1 teaspoon vanilla extract
½ teaspoon almond extract

● Preheat the oven to 425°F. Lightly grease a 9 x 13-inch, 11 x 11-inch, or similar-sized pan.
● **To make the crust:** In a medium-sized mixing bowl, whisk together the flour and salt. Using your fingers, a pastry blender, or a mixer, cut in the butter. Drizzle the beaten egg over the mixture in the bowl and toss lightly to combine. Add the ice water 1 tablespoon at a time, stirring gently until the dough starts to clump together. Grab a fistful; if it sticks together easily, you've added enough water.
● Roll the dough into a generous rectangle or square to fit your pan. Place the dough in the pan, prick it all over with a fork, and bake for 10 to 12 minutes, until it's set and barely starting to harden.

- **To make the filling:** In a large bowl, whisk together the flour, sugar, spices, and salt. Add the apples, tossing to coat. Stir in the vanilla, then the cream. Spread the filling over the crust.
- **To make the topping:** In a medium-sized mixing bowl, whisk together the flour, sugar, salt, and cinnamon. In another bowl, combine the melted butter and extracts and pour over the flour mixture. Stir until the butter is absorbed and the mixture forms fairly even crumbs. Sprinkle the topping over the filling.
- Bake the bars for 15 minutes. Reduce the oven temperature to 350°F and bake for an additional 30 to 35 minutes, or until the topping is brown and the filling is bubbly. Remove the bars from the oven and cool on a rack. Allow them to cool to lukewarm before cutting.

Nutrition information per serving (*1 square 87 g*): 212 cal, 10 g fat, 2 g protein, 17 g complex carbohydrates, 12 g sugar, 1 g dietary fiber, 36 mg cholesterol, 117 mg sodium, 75 mg potassium, 98 RE vitamin A, 2 mg vitamin C, 1 mg iron, 10 mg calcium, 26 mg phosphorus.

Watch those cutting implements!

Many (most) baking pans these days come coated with a nonstick surface. Since bars are generally cut right in the pan, it's a challenge to keep that surface from getting nicked and scratched. The solution? Cut bars with plastic, acrylic, or other nonstick utensils. Unless they're extremely hard (such as completely cooled granola bars), you won't have any problem using a nonmetal cutter.

Drop Cookies

Fast. Easy. Fun. All of these terms can be applied to drop cookies, the most common type of cookie in any baker's recipe box. Beginning with a simple dough of butter, sugar, eggs, and flour, the basic drop cookie happily accommodates all manner of flavors and add-ins—Triple Chocolate Chunk Macadamia Cherry Hazelnut, anyone?—before being simply dropped, in round balls, onto a baking sheet and baked. No fancy shaping, no rolling and cutting. In fact, the only departure you might make from this basic formula is to roll the dough into balls, rather than simply drop it onto the sheet, and perhaps coat those balls with sugar or nuts.

Because drop cookies are so simple to make, they're a great way to introduce kids (or any new baker) to cookie baking. And serendipitously, many of the venerable icons of the cookie-baking world—chocolate chip, peanut butter, oatmeal, sugar, and molasses—are drop cookies (see The Essentials chapter, pages 41–184). America's most popular home-baked cookies are also the easiest to make—now how often does that happen in life?

So, leave that rolling pin in the cupboard, and put the *pizzelle* iron away for another day. All that drop cookies demand are a bowl, a spoon (or mixer), a baking sheet, and a flick of the wrist. Let's grab those cookie scoops and go!

Making the most of your baking sheet real estate

Most cookies spread as they bake; that's a fact of life. It's important to leave room between cookies on the baking sheet, so they can spread without running into their neighbors. But how much room should you leave? And what's the best way to place your cookies on the sheet, to optimize space?

Drop cookies portioned out with a tablespoon cookie scoop (approximately 2 tablespoons of dough) will usually become cookies with a 2- to 2¾-inch diameter. Leave 2 to 3 inches between unbaked cookies of this size. Cookies made with a teaspoon cookie scoop (about 2 level teaspoons of dough) will make cookies 1½ to 1¾ inches in size. Leave 1½ to 2 inches between unbaked cookies of this size. Some cookies spread more, while some barely spread at all, but use these measurements as a guide.

If you're very concerned with making perfectly round cookies (ones that don't run into each other as they bake), measure the diameter of two balls of unbaked dough, place them on the baking sheet, bake, then measure them again; you can then figure out how much clearance space that recipe needs. (You can do this with just one ball of dough, but two makes the exercise more visual, and less mathematical.)

When placing unbaked cookies on a sheet, you can optimize space by staggering rows, rather than lining all the cookies up side by side.

To optimize space, don't line cookies up in even rows on the baking sheet . . .

. . . but stagger the rows like the stars on the American flag.

Tender Toffee-Chocolate Rounds

These cookies are soft, rich, and moist, almost a brownie in cookie form. The toffee bits and chocolate chips play off one another nicely.

Yield: 30 cookies ● *Baking temperature: 350°F* ● *Baking time: 12 minutes*

> 8 ounces bittersweet chocolate, coarsely chopped
> 2 tablespoons (1 ounce) unsalted butter
> ¾ cup (6 ounces) light brown sugar
> 2 large eggs
> 2 teaspoons vanilla extract
> ½ teaspoon baking powder
> ⅛ teaspoon salt
> ¼ cup (1 ounce) unbleached all-purpose flour
> 1 cup (5⅛ ounces) toffee bits
> 1 cup (6 ounces) semisweet chocolate chips

● Preheat the oven to 350°F. Lightly grease (or line with parchment) two baking sheets.

● In the microwave, or in a saucepan set over very low heat, melt the chocolate and butter together, stirring until smooth. Set the mixture aside to cool to lukewarm.

● In a medium-sized bowl, beat together the brown sugar, eggs, vanilla, baking powder, and salt. Beat in the melted chocolate, then stir in the flour, toffee bits, and chocolate chips.

● Drop the dough by the tablespoonful onto the prepared baking sheets. Bake the cookies for about 12 minutes, or until the tops are cracked and dry but the cookies are still soft to the touch. Don't overbake these; they'll become firm as they cool. Remove the cookies from the oven and let them cool on the baking sheet for 10 minutes, then transfer them to a rack to cool completely.

Nutrition information per serving (1 cookie, 30 g): 134 cal, 7 g fat, 2 g protein, 2 g complex carbohydrates, 15 g sugar, 1 g dietary fiber, 19 mg cholesterol, 40 mg sodium, 82 mg potassium, 13 RE vitamin A, 1 mg iron, 17 mg calcium, 31 mg phosphorus, 10 mg caffeine.

Hobnails

This old New England raisin-spice cookie recipe is a chocolate chip cookie look-alike—with raisins taking the place of the chips. We found them too sweet in the first testing go-around, so we lightened the sugar a bit to come up with a dark brown, chewy cookie that's just right. Walnuts complement the raisins and spice perfectly. For a chewier, albeit sweeter cookie, increase the amount of brown sugar to 1 cup (8 ounces).

Yield: 27 cookies ● ***Baking temperature:** 375°F* ● ***Baking time:** 12 minutes*

1 cup (6 ounces) raisins, packed
3 tablespoons (1½ ounces) rum, brandy, or water
¾ cup (6 ounces) brown sugar
½ cup (1 stick, 4 ounces) unsalted butter
1½ teaspoons vanilla extract
½ teaspoon baking soda
¾ teaspoon salt
1½ teaspoons cinnamon
½ teaspoon ground ginger
1 large egg
1½ cups (6¼ ounces) unbleached all-purpose flour
⅔ cup (2¾ ounces) toasted walnuts (see page 27)

● The day before baking, toss the raisins and rum together in a small bowl. Cover the bowl and let the mixture rest at room temperature overnight.

● Preheat the oven to 375°F. Lightly grease (or line with parchment) two baking sheets.

● In a medium-sized bowl, cream together the brown sugar and butter. Beat in the vanilla, baking soda, salt, and spices, then the egg. Stir in the flour, then the raisins (and any liquid that they haven't absorbed), and the nuts.

● Drop the dough by the tablespoonful onto the prepared baking sheets. Bake the cookies for 12 minutes, until they're a light golden brown. Remove them from the oven, and cool on a rack.

Nutrition information per serving *(1 cookie, 30 g):* 120 cal, 5 g fat, 2 g protein, 10 g complex carbohydrates, 6 g sugar, 1 g dietary fiber, 17 mg cholesterol, 89 mg sodium, 97 mg potassium, 36 RE vitamin A, 1 mg vitamin C, 1 mg iron, 14 mg calcium, 31 mg phosphorus.

Butter-Pecan Fantasies

WOW! If you're a butter-pecan lover, you'll immediately move these cookies to the top of your list.

Yield: 4 dozen cookies ● *Baking temperature: 375°F* ● *Baking time: 10 to 12 minutes*

¾ cup (1½ sticks, 6 ounces) unsalted butter
1¼ cups (10 ounces) brown sugar
2 teaspoons vanilla extract
⅛ teaspoon strong butter-rum or butterscotch flavor (optional)
1 teaspoon salt
1 teaspoon baking soda
1 large egg
2¼ cups (9½ ounces) unbleached all-purpose flour
1 cup (5⅛ ounces) toffee bits
1 cup (6 ounces) butterscotch chips or the chip of your choice: chocolate, cinnamon, or white chocolate
1 cup (4 ounces) chopped pecans

● Preheat the oven to 375°F. Lightly grease (or line with parchment) two baking sheets.

● In a large mixing bowl, cream together the butter, brown sugar, vanilla, flavor, salt, and baking soda. Add the egg and beat until fluffy. Add the flour and stir until well blended. Stir in the toffee bits, chips, and pecans.

● Drop the dough by generous tablespoonfuls onto the prepared baking sheets, leaving about 2 inches between them. Bake the cookies for 10 to 12 minutes; 10 minutes will give you chewier cookies, 12 minutes, crisper. For chewy, "bendable" cookies, remove them from the oven while they still look undercooked in the center; for crisp, crunchy cookies, bake until they're an even golden brown.

● Remove the cookies from the oven and let them cool for 5 minutes on the baking sheets before transferring them to a rack to cool completely.

Nutrition information per serving (1 cookie, 26 g): 121 cal, 7 g fat, 1 g protein, 5 g complex carbohydrates, 10 g sugar, 14 mg cholesterol, 87 mg sodium, 55 mg potassium, 29 RE vitamin A, 1 mg vitamin C, 1 mg iron, 9 mg calcium, 20 mg phosphorus, 1 mg caffeine.

Chocolate Crinkles

This classic cookie is beautiful. With its Appaloosa coating of confectioners' sugar, the cracks that form in the surface as it bakes make it a miniature work of art. Nevertheless, the true reward comes in the eating. Just barely crisp at the edges, soft and almost brownie-like in the center, these cookies are sure to make a lasting impression.

Chocolate crinkles, a seeming standard in the cookie baker's repertoire, actually don't appear to have a long history. Though it feels as if they've been around forever, the earliest mention we find of them in any cookbook is 1965. This cookie is quick and easy to put together, and forgiving in the oven. If you want a slightly crisper version, bake for a few extra minutes. For a fudgier center, go with the shorter baking time.

Yield: 2 dozen cookies ● *Baking temperature:* 350°F ● *Baking time:* 12 to 14 minutes

1½ cups (6¼ ounces) unbleached all-purpose flour
1½ cups (10½ ounces) sugar
1½ teaspoons baking powder
¾ teaspoon salt
6 tablespoons (¾ stick, 3 ounces) unsalted butter, melted
¾ cup (2¼ ounces) cocoa powder, natural or Dutch process
3 large eggs
½ teaspoon vanilla extract
¾ cup (3 ounces) confectioners' sugar, for coating cookies

● Preheat the oven to 350°F. Lightly grease (or line with parchment) two baking sheets.
● In a large mixing bowl, whisk together the flour, sugar, baking powder, and salt. Set aside.
● Combine the melted butter with the cocoa in a medium-sized bowl and stir until the mixture is smooth. Cool to lukewarm. Add the eggs and vanilla, stir to combine, then add this mixture to the dry ingredients. Mix thoroughly, until the flour is evenly moistened. The dough will seem too dry at first, but keep mixing and it will become the consistency of stiff brownie batter.
● Scoop the dough into balls with a tablespoon cookie scoop (see page 32) or by the heaping tablespoon, and roll each ball of dough in confectioners' sugar to coat. Place the cookies on the prepared baking sheets.
● Bake the cookies for 12 to 14 minutes. They'll spread out and form cracks, and the insides may look a little wet, but that's okay. For a crisper cookie, leave in the oven a few minutes longer. Remove the cookies from the oven and let them cool on the pan for 5 minutes before transferring them to a rack to cool completely.

Nutrition information per serving (1 cookie, 35g): 126 cal, 4 g fat, 2 g protein, 7 g complex carbohydrates, 14 g sugar, 1 g dietary fiber, 35 mg cholesterol, 113 mg sodium, 64 mg potassium, 40 RE vitamin A, 1 mg iron, 25 mg calcium, 46 mg phosphorus, 7 mg caffeine.

VARIATION
● Add ½ cup chopped pecans to the dough.

Two-Bit Wonders

Two ingredients? Surely you jest. Actually, when one of the ingredients is sweetened condensed milk—which combines the necessary protein to set the cookie's structure, as well as sugar—the concept isn't far-fetched. The following are excellent, simple-to-make clones of coconut maca-roons; variations at the end of the recipe will point you in different directions.

Yield: *15 cookies* ● **Baking temperature:** *350°F* ● **Baking time:** *13 to 14 minutes*

½ cup (5 ounces, 1 small can) sweetened condensed milk
2 cups (6 to 8 ounces) shredded coconut, preferably unsweetened

● Preheat the oven to 350°F. Lightly grease (or line with parchment) one large or two small baking sheets.
● In a medium-sized bowl, combine the condensed milk and coconut. Drop the mixture by tablespoonfuls onto the prepared baking sheets. Bake for 13 to 14 minutes, until the cookies are set and the coconut is golden brown.
● Remove the cookies from the oven, and transfer them to a rack to cool.

Nutrition information per serving (1 cookie, 23 g): 97 cal, 6 g fat, 1 g protein, 4 g complex carbo-hydrates, 7 g sugar, 1 g dietary fiber, 3 mg cholesterol, 47 mg sodium, 80 mg potassium, 8 RE vitamin A, 1 mg vitamin C, 29 mg calcium, 38 mg phosphorus.

VARIATIONS

To ½ cup sweetened condensed milk, add 2 cups (total) of the following combinations:
● Chocolate chips and salted peanuts
● Graham cracker crumbs and chocolate chips (Note: Don't use more than 1 cup graham cracker crumbs, as the dough will become too stiff.)
● The flavored chips and/or nuts of your choice
● Minced crystallized ginger, finely diced dried pineapple, and shredded coconut
● You can also add a few drops of an extra-strong flavor to complement the add-ins you've selected.
● Drizzle Chocolate Glaze (page 459) over the finished cookies.

Monster Cookies

Our original recipe for these cookies reinforced their name: it made a monstrous amount of dough because it included 12 eggs, 2 pounds of brown sugar . . . you get the idea. We down-sized the recipe to make a more reasonable number of cookies, but considering the big crunchy cookies you make from this butterscotchy, peanut-buttery, chip- and candy-filled dough, we'd say they still earn their name: they're monstrously delicious!

Yield: 26 large (4½-inch) cookies ● *Baking temperature:* 350°F ● *Baking time:* 12 minutes

3 large eggs
1 cup (8 ounces) brown sugar
1 cup (7 ounces) granulated sugar
1 teaspoon vanilla extract
1 teaspoon corn syrup
2 teaspoons baking soda
1 teaspoon salt
½ cup (1 stick, 4 ounces) unsalted butter, melted
1½ cups (14¼ ounces) chunky peanut butter
4½ cups (15¾ ounces) rolled oats
½ cup (2 ounces) unbleached all-purpose flour
¾ cup (4½ ounces) chocolate chips
¾ cup (4½ ounces) butterscotch chips
¾ cup (5½ ounces) mini-M&M's*

● Preheat the oven to 350°F. Lightly grease (or line with parchment) two baking sheets.
● In a large mixing bowl, combine the eggs, sugars, vanilla, corn syrup, baking soda, and salt. Stir in the melted butter, then the peanut butter, oats, and flour, mixing until thoroughly combined. Stir in the chips and candy. Let the dough rest for 30 minutes so the oats can absorb some of the butter.
● Drop the dough by ¼-cupfuls onto the prepared baking sheets. Use your fingers to flatten the cookies slightly, then bake them for 12 minutes, until they're a light golden brown. Remove them from the oven and cool on a rack.

* Use mini-M&M's. If you can't find mini-M&M's, substitute ¾ cup (4½ ounces) regular M&M's.

Nutrition information per serving (1 cookie, 73 g): 328 cal, 16 g fat, 8 g protein, 13 g complex carbohydrates, 27 g sugar, 3 g dietary fiber, 35 mg cholesterol, 175 mg sodium, 228 mg potassium, 47 RE vitamin A, 1 mg iron, 25 mg calcium, 147 mg phosphorus, 4 mg caffeine.

Above: **Half-Moon Cookies** *(page 293)*

Overleaf: **Cinnamon–Caramel Swirl Shortbread** *(front left, page 130)*, **Your Favorite Jammies** *(front right, page 131)*, **The Essential Shortbread** *(back right, page 110)*, **Toasted Pecan–Fudge Shortbread** *(back left, page 127)*

Opposite: **Fudgy Brownies** *(front, bottom, page 156)*, **On-the-Fence Brownies** *(front, top, page 158)*, **Chocolate Mint Brownies** *(right, bottom, page 160)*, **Cakey Brownies** *(right, top, page 157)*, and **Cheesecake Swirl Brownies** *(back left, page 161)*

Above: **Oatmeal Whoopie Pies** *(left, page 421),* **Pumpkin Whoopie Pies** *(center, page 419),* **Chocolate Whoopie Pies** *(right, page 418)*

Center: **Americanized Chinese Restaurant Cookies** *(page 291)*

Opposite: **Lemon Tea Snaps** *(page 339),* **Faux-Reos** *(page 328)*

Above: **Rocky Road Bars** *(back, page 201),* **Ruth Wakefield's Chocolate Chip Cookie Bars** *(front, page 189)*

Right: **Vermont Granola Bars** *(page 202)*

Above: **Bakery Date Squares** *(page 228),* **Classic Apricot Squares** *(page 206),*
Bakery Raspberry Squares *(page 229)*

essential
recipe

Above: **Cherry-Nut Rugelach** *(top and right, page 372)*, **Hamantaschen** *(left, page 368)*

Opposite: **The Essential Crunchy Oatmeal Cookie** *(left, page 75)*, **Trail Mix Jumbles** *(right, page 78)*

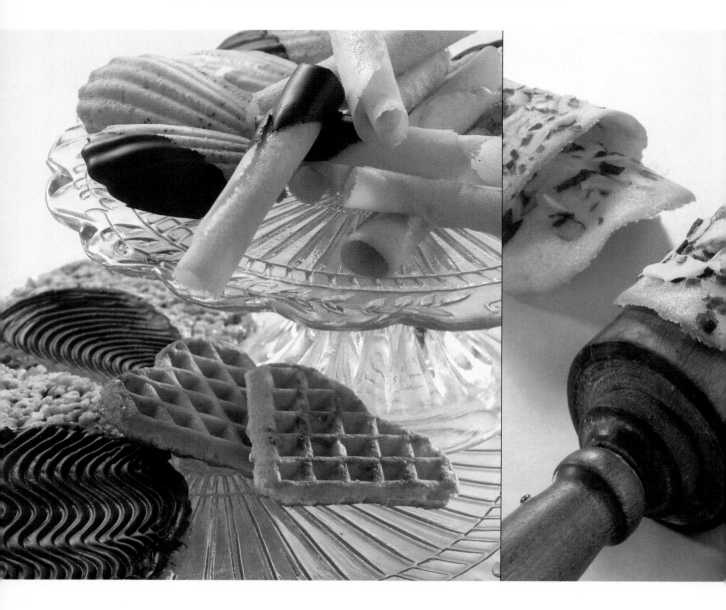

Above: **Florentines** *(page 416)*, **Belgian Sugar Waffles** *(page 438)*, **Lemon–Poppy Seed Madeleines** *(top left, page 425)*, **Cigarette Cookies** *(top center, page 415)*

Center: **Tuiles** *(page 414)*

Opposite: **Stained Glass Cookies** *(page 347)*

Center: **Easter Doughnut Cookies** *(page 374)*

Right: See page 26 for creative ways to package and ship gift cookies.

Opposite: **ESSENTIAL DECORATED COOKIES** *(pages 168–184)*

Above: **Magic in the Middles** *(back, page 359),* **Holiday Bonbons** *(front, page 356)*

Center: **Palmiers** *(page 377)*

Opposite: **Pizzelle** *(page 432)*

Left: **Peanut Butter Graham Squares** *(left, page 448)*, **Crispy Rice Treats** *(in flower pot, page 442)*, **Bird's Nests** *(page 445)*

Below: **Chocolate Dipping Sticks** *(page 335)*, **Chocolate-Caramel Dip** *(page 471)*

Opposite: **Classic Crunchy Chocolate Chip Cookies** *(front, page 45)*, **The Essential Chewy Chocolate Chip Cookie** *(back, page 44)*

Above: Left to right: **Cookie Wheels** *(page 405),* **Checkerboards** *(page 400),* **Marble Cookies** *(page 399),* **Pinwheels** *(page 398)*

Opposite: **The Essential Peanut Butter Cookie** *(in jar, page 97),* **Peanut Blossoms** *(front, page 102)*

Above: **Springerle** *(front, page 382),* **Speculaa** *(back, left, page 384)*

Opposite: **Crystal Diamonds** *(front left, page 66),* **The Essential Crunchy Sugar Cookie**, *center, page 56),* **Tea Sandwiches** *(back, page 70)*

Clockwise from 11 o'clock: **Chocolate-dipped semolina biscotti** *(see sidebar, page 137);* **Pine Nut, Fennel, and Raisin Biscotti** *(page 142);* **Granola Biscotti** *(page 142);* **Classic Italian Biscotti** *(page 149);* **Pine Nut, Fennel, and Raisin Biscotti, dipped in white chocolate** *(see sidebar, page 150);* **Granola Biscotti;** **Gianduja Biscotti** *(page 139);* **Pistachio-Cherry Biscotti** *(page 138)*
Center from left: **Italian-Style Biscotti** *(page 134);* **Pistachio-Cherry Biscotti**

Above: **Sparkling Sugar Kisses** *(left, page 260),* **St. Patrick's Day Pistachio Cookies** *(right, page 288)*

Right: **Key Lime Bars in Coconut Crust** *(left, page 235),* **Strawberry Cheesecake Bars** *(right, page 240)*

Overleaf: **Soft Molasses Cookies** *(left, page 86),* **Ginger Crisps** *(right, page 93)*

Golden Crunch Cookies

These cookies have a delightful, crunchy texture, partly from the butter (which promotes crunchiness), and partly from the "secret ingredient"—cornflakes! You can use your imagination with the chips: Try cherry, peanut butter, chocolate, or cinnamon chips, or mix and match.

Yield: 3½ dozen cookies ● *Baking temperature:* 350°F ● *Baking time:* 17 minutes

¾ cup (1½ sticks, 6 ounces) unsalted butter
½ cup (3½ ounces) sugar
1 teaspoon vanilla extract*
1 teaspoon salt
1 large egg
2¼ cups (9½ ounces) unbleached all-purpose flour
1½ cups (2⅜ ounces) lightly crushed cornflakes
2 cups (12 ounces) butterscotch chips or the flavored chips of your choice

● Preheat the oven to 350°F. Lightly grease (or line with parchment) two baking sheets.
● In a large bowl, cream together the butter, sugar, vanilla, and salt. Beat in the egg, then stir in the flour, cornflakes, and chips.
● Roll the dough into balls the size of table tennis balls (1 to 1¼ inch), and place them on the prepared baking sheets. Flatten them to about ½ inch with a fork, making a crisscross pattern. Bake the cookies for about 17 minutes, until they're golden brown around the edges. Remove them from the oven and transfer immediately to a rack to cool.

*Substitute almond extract for the vanilla if you prefer that flavor, especially if you're using cherry, white chocolate, or other chips whose flavor might go well with almond.

Nutrition information per serving (1 cookie, 25 g): 115 cal, 6 g fat, 1 g protein, 7 g complex carbohydrates, 8 g sugar, 14 mg cholesterol, 93 mg sodium, 29 mg potassium, 33 RE vitamin A, 1 mg vitamin C, 1 mg iron, 4 mg calcium, 11 mg phosphorus.

Changing the size of your cookies

Most drop cookies call for dough to be proportioned by the tablespoonful onto prepared baking sheets, which makes a cookie approximately 2½ inches in diameter. But what if you want smaller, tea-party-sized cookies, or big, palm-sized cookies for a bake sale? You can easily adjust the size of your cookies by adjusting the size of the scooped dough. A teaspoon scoop makes cookies that are about 1¾ inches across, while a ¼-cup-capacity muffin scoop will yield 4- to 4½-inch cookies. If you want something in between, just make a guesstimate as to the amount of dough and test-bake one first, then adjust up or down.

Smaller cookies will need to bake for less time than regular-sized cookies, while larger cookies will need a longer bake. Just keep your eye on them the first time, take them out when they're lightly browned, and write down the time, so you don't forget for the next batch!

Vermont Maple Cookies

Maple sugar (along with maple trees, maple syrup, and maple bowls) is plentiful here in Vermont. And these cookies are delicious made with a full cup of pure maple sugar, but to some of us—those with that old thrifty Yankee streak—it seemed extravagant to use a cup of maple sugar. We made an acceptable (though not as tasty) version cutting the maple sugar to ¼ cup, and adding ¾ cup brown sugar. We also tried a batch substituting brown sugar for the maple sugar, and relying completely on maple flavor for taste. That batch tasted sweeter and, of course, less "maple-y." We preferred the version with a full cup of maple sugar. We even tried a batch frosted with a maple glaze—certainly, on cookies made with a cup of maple sugar, an over-the-top touch.

These cookies will be tender and slightly soft if stored in an airtight container; for a crunchy cookie, leave them uncovered overnight before storing.

Yield: 3 dozen cookies ● *Baking temperature:* 400°F ● *Baking time:* 10 to 12 minutes

DOUGH
1 cup (2 sticks, 8 ounces) unsalted butter
1 cup (5½ ounces) pure maple sugar
½ cup (3½ ounces) granulated sugar
1 teaspoon cream of tartar
½ teaspoon salt
2 large eggs
½ teaspoon baking soda
½ to 1 teaspoon strong maple flavor, or 2 teaspoons maple extract, to taste
2¾ cups (11½ ounces) unbleached all-purpose flour

COATING
>   2 tablespoons (½ ounce) pure maple sugar
>   2 tablespoons (⅞ ounce) granulated sugar

GLAZE
>   1½ cups (6 ounces) confectioners' sugar
>   2 tablespoons (1⅜ ounces) maple syrup
>   1 tablespoon (½ ounce) heavy cream
>   A few drops strong maple flavor or ¼ teaspoon maple extract

- **To make the dough:** In a large mixing bowl, beat together the butter, sugars, cream of tartar, salt, eggs, baking soda, and maple flavor until fluffy. Add the flour, and beat until blended. Refrigerate the dough for about 30 minutes, to stiffen it and make it easier to shape.
- Preheat the oven to 400°F. Lightly grease (or line with parchment) two baking sheets.
- **To make the coating:** Combine the sugars in a shallow bowl or pie pan, or in a large plastic bag.
- Drop the dough by the rounded tablespoonful into the coating, gently shake the pan (or bag) to coat the balls, then roll them in your hands until they're smooth and round. Place the balls on the prepared baking sheets, about 1½ inches apart.
- Bake the cookies for 10 to 12 minutes, until they're a very light golden brown. Remove them from the oven, and after 5 minutes transfer them to a rack to cool.
- **To make the glaze:** In a medium-sized bowl, stir together the confectioners' sugar, maple syrup, cream, and flavor to make a spreadable frosting. Spread a thin layer over the cookies. Let the glaze dry for several hours before packaging the cookies for storage.

Nutrition information per serving (1 glazed cookie, 35 g): 143 cal, 6 g fat, 1 g protein, 7 g complex carbohydrates, 16 g sugar, 26 mg cholesterol, 54 mg sodium, 56 mg potassium, 55 RE vitamin A, 1 mg vitamin C, 1 mg iron, 10 mg calcium, 16 mg phosphorus.

Sparkling Sugar Kisses

Making custard? Don't throw away those leftover egg whites. Make sugar kisses—you'd never know these sweet, feather-light meringues are totally nonfat. Making egg whites into meringue is something we've always loved to do. How can a gluey blob of egg white suddenly turn into a lighter-than-air, pure white puff, a delicate, melt-in-your-mouth sweet? Well, it's the oxygen; beaten into egg whites, with a bit of acid added (cream of tartar, usually) to stabilize everything, oxygen creates both the color of the meringue and its airy texture. Add sugar and you've got meringue.

Yield: 2 dozen cookies ● *Baking temperature: 250°F* ● *Baking time: 1 hour*

2 large egg whites
⅛ teaspoon salt
¼ teaspoon cream of tartar
½ cup (3½ ounces) sugar, superfine preferred
1 teaspoon vanilla extract, or the extract of your choice
Coarse sugar

● Preheat the oven to 250°F. Line 2 baking sheets with parchment.
● In a large, very clean, nonplastic bowl, beat the egg whites until they're foamy, then add the salt and cream of tartar. Add the sugar gradually, continuing to beat until the meringue is thick and glossy, and forms stiff peaks. Beat in the vanilla at the end.
● Drop meringue by the tablespoonful* onto the prepared baking sheet. Sprinkle each with coarse (or colored) sugar. Bake for 1 hour, then turn off the oven and let the kisses cool in the unopened oven (don't peek!) for 1½ to 2 hours, or until they're dry and crisp all the way through. Remove them from the oven and store in an airtight container.

* If you use a tablespoon cookie scoop, don't heap it; level it off, to obtain the correct size and number of cookies. For fancy meringues, pipe them onto a sheet using a pastry bag and the tip of your choice.

Nutrition information per serving (1 cookie, 7 g): 18 cal, 1 g protein, 1 g complex carbohydrates, 4 g sugar, 16 mg sodium, 7 mg potassium, 1 mg iron, 1 mg calcium, 1 mg phosphorus.

VARIATIONS

● Stir in ½ to ¾ cup mini-morsel chocolate chips after the vanilla.
● For maple meringues, prepare the meringue for Sparkling Sugar Kisses (above), substituting ½ cup plus 1 tablespoon (3⅜ ounces) maple sugar for the granulated sugar, and ½ to 1 teaspoon maple extract (or ⅛ to ¼ teaspoon strong maple flavor to taste) for the vanilla extract. Sprinkle meringues with maple sugar in place of the coarse sugar.

Meringue: Oh, sweet mystery of whites

We've all enjoyed sweet, light meringues that melt on the tongue. But have we all made them? Perhaps not. There's a right way and a wrong way. Here's the right way: Start with a clean, nonplastic mixing bowl with no traces of fat in it. Any fat will coat the ends of the egg white's protein, which will greatly diminish the ability of the whites to hold air. Have the egg whites at room temperature; this gives them lower surface tension and makes it easier to incorporate air. Many recipes for beating egg whites call for salt and/or cream of tartar; these help the whites hold on to water and air.

To beat, you can use either a whisk and some elbow grease, or your electric mixer. The advantage to making meringue by hand (at least once) is that you become familiar with the stages that the whites go through. At first you have a puddle of clear liquid with some large bubbles in it. Then, as you continue beating, the liquid becomes white with many more smaller bubbles. Then the whisk begins to leave tracks in the bowl. To test the character of your whites, pull your whisk or beaters straight up out of the foam. If a point forms and then falls over immediately, you're looking at a soft peak. From here, 15 to 20 more strokes will bring you to a medium peak, and another 15 to 20 to stiff peaks.

It's very easy to overbeat meringue. When you start to see what look like grainy white clumps, you're beyond stiff peaks, and every stroke of the whisk or beater is tearing apart the network of air, water, and protein you've worked so hard to create. You'll also see a pool of clear liquid under the foam. The good news is that the foam you have on top of the liquid will still work. The bad news is that you can't really fix what has happened, other than to start over with new egg whites.

What's meringue without sugar? Sugar has two properties that affect egg whites. It will coat the ends of the proteins in the whites; and if it's added too soon, it will take much longer to make a meringue stiff enough to be piped or shaped. If you're beating egg whites by hand, don't add the sugar until you've reached the medium-peak stage. If you're using a mixer, start sprinkling sugar into the meringue after it gets to soft peaks. In a mixer, the sugar will help give you a little extra leeway with beating time; you can go longer without overbeating the whites. We advise using superfine sugar because it will dissolve faster, making the meringue less grainy.

Classic Coconut Macaroons

Coconut macaroons aren't a cookie you find very readily on the grocery store shelf; maybe that's what makes them special, because usually they're baked at home. They're easy to make: a coconut macaroon is simply sweetened shredded coconut that's bound with meringue and baked until set. These cookies are wonderful in their simple glory, but you can always dress things up by drizzling them with some melted chocolate.

Yield: 2 dozen cookies ● ***Baking temperature:*** *325°F* ● ***Baking time:*** *18 to 22 minutes*

> **2 large egg whites, at room temperature**
> **⅛ teaspoon salt**
> **¼ teaspoon cream of tartar**
> **½ teaspoon vanilla extract**
> **¾ cup (5¼ ounces) sugar, superfine preferred**
> **3 cups (9 ounces) shredded sweetened coconut**

● Preheat the oven to 325°F. Lightly grease (or line with parchment) one large or two smaller baking sheets.
● Put the egg whites in a large, clean, dry, nonplastic mixing bowl. Add the salt and cream of tartar and beat the whites until they form soft peaks. Add the vanilla, then gradually sprinkle in the sugar while continuing to beat the egg whites until they form stiff peaks. Fold in the coconut.
● Drop the batter onto the prepared baking sheets in 1½-inch mounds; a tablespoon cookie scoop works well here. Bake them for 18 to 22 minutes, until the coconut is a toasty golden brown and the crust is set; they'll still be moist inside. Remove them from the oven and let cool on the pan for 5 to 10 minutes before transferring them to a rack to cool completely. Store in an airtight container.

Nutrition information per serving (1 cookie, 20 g): 76 cal, 3 g fat, 1 g protein, 3 g complex carbohydrates, 9 g sugar, 1 g dietary fiber, 43 mg sodium, 38 mg potassium, 2 mg calcium, 11 mg phosphorus.

Toffee Crunchers

These cookies carry a big hit of toffee flavor, both from the butter and brown sugar and from the toffee bits. They're wonderful served alongside (or sandwiched around) butter-pecan or butter-almond ice cream. Their wonderful crisp-crunchy texture comes in part from two unusual sources: potato chips and crisp rice cereal.

Yield: 4½ dozen cookies ● *Baking temperature: 375°F* ● *Baking time: 10 to 12 minutes*

1 cup (2 sticks, 8 ounces) unsalted butter
1½ cups (12 ounces) light brown sugar
¼ teaspoon salt
2 teaspoons vanilla extract
½ teaspoon baking soda
½ teaspoon baking powder
2½ cups (10½ ounces) unbleached all-purpose flour
2 cups lightly (5¾ ounces) lightly crushed plain salted potato chips
2 cups (1¾ ounces) Rice Krispies
1⅓ cups (6¾ ounces) toffee bits

● Preheat the oven to 375°F. Lightly grease (or line with parchment) two baking sheets.
● In a large mixing bowl, cream together the butter, sugar, salt, vanilla, baking soda, and baking powder. Mix in the flour, then gently stir in the potato chips, rice cereal, and toffee bits.
● Drop the dough by the tablespoonful onto the prepared baking sheets, leaving 2½ inches between them; they'll spread quite a bit as they bake. Bake the cookies for 10 to 12 minutes (the lesser amount of time for a chewy, rather than crisp cookie). Remove them from the oven, cool for 5 minutes on the pan, then transfer to a rack to cool completely.

Nutrition information per serving (1 cookie, 25 g): 117 cal, 6 g fat, 1 g protein, 7 g complex carbohydrates, 8 g sugar, 12 mg cholesterol, 74 mg sodium, 83 mg potassium, 39 RE vitamin A, 2 mg vitamin C, 1 mg iron, 12 mg calcium, 17 mg phosphorus, 1 mg caffeine.

VARIATIONS

● Substitute ⅔ cup butterscotch chips and ⅔ cup chopped pecans for the toffee bits.
● Substitute 2 cups gently crushed cornflakes for the rice cereal.

Mocha Walnuts

The soft center and wafer-thin, crisp outer crust of these cookies is reminiscent of a fudgy brownie. The addition of espresso powder and walnuts complements their rich chocolate flavor.

Yield: 2½ dozen cookies ● *Baking temperature: 350°F* ● *Baking time: 13 minutes*

> 2 cups (12 ounces) chocolate chips
> ½ cup (1 stick, 4 ounces) unsalted butter
> ¼ cup (1¾ ounces) granulated sugar
> ½ cup (4 ounces) brown sugar
> ¾ teaspoon baking soda
> ½ teaspoon salt
> 1 large egg
> 2 teaspoons espresso powder, or 2 tablespoons instant coffee, dissolved in
>   2 teaspoons boiling water
> 1¼ cups (5¼ ounces) unbleached all-purpose flour
> ½ cup (2 ounces) chopped walnuts

● Preheat the oven to 350°F. Lightly grease (or line with parchment) two baking sheets.

● Melt ½ cup of the chocolate chips in a microwave-safe bowl in the microwave, or over very low heat on a burner. Set aside.

● In a medium-sized mixing bowl, cream together the butter, sugars, baking soda, and salt. Beat in the egg, then the melted chocolate and espresso powder. Stir in the flour, walnuts, and the remaining 1½ cups chocolate chips.

● Drop the dough by tablespoonfuls onto the prepared baking sheets. Bake the cookies for about 13 minutes, until they appear barely set when you poke one gently with your finger. Remove them from the oven and transfer to a rack to cool.

Nutrition information per serving (1 cookie, 30 g): 138 cal, 8 g fat, 2 g protein, 5 g complex carbohydrates, 11 g sugar, 15 mg cholesterol, 71 mg sodium, 75 mg potassium, 32 RE vitamin A, 1 mg vitamin C, 1 mg iron, 10 mg calcium, 31 mg phosphorus, 16 mg caffeine.

Brandied Cherry—Nut Cookies

Nuts and dried fruit—in this case, pecans and cherries—are flavors that sing happily together just like maple and walnut, or apple and cinnamon. These cakey-chewy, colorful cookies would look great in a holiday gift basket, but don't save the recipe for the holidays—they're equally comfortable at a June picnic. If you have difficulty finding dried cherries, dried cranberries are an apt substitute.

Yield: 4 dozen cookies ● *Baking temperature:* 350°F ● *Baking time:* 15 minutes

2 cups (9¼ ounces) dried sweet or sour cherries
2 tablespoons (1 ounce) brandy
½ cup (1 stick, 4 ounces) unsalted butter
1 cup (7 ounces) sugar
1 teaspoon almond extract
1 teaspoon salt
1 teaspoon baking soda
3 large eggs
2½ cups (10½ ounces) unbleached all-purpose flour
2 cups (8 ounces) chopped pecans or walnuts, toasted (see page 27)

● The day before baking, combine the cherries and brandy in a small bowl, tossing to coat. Cover the bowl and let the mixture rest at room temperature overnight.
● Preheat the oven to 350°F. Lightly grease (or line with parchment) two baking sheets.
● In a large bowl, cream together the butter, sugar, almond extract, salt, and baking soda. Beat in the eggs, scraping the sides of the bowl and beating until smooth. Stir in the flour, cherries (and any brandy that hasn't been absorbed), and nuts.
● Drop the dough by the tablespoonful onto the prepared baking sheets. Gently flatten the balls just a bit with the bottom of a glass dipped in granulated sugar. Bake the cookies for 15 minutes, or until they're golden brown. Remove them from the oven and immediately transfer them to a rack to cool.

Nutrition information per serving (1 cookie, 26 g): 104 cal, 5 g fat, 2 g protein, 8 g complex carbohydrates, 4 g sugar, 1 g dietary fiber, 18 mg cholesterol, 78 mg sodium, 75 mg potassium, 45 RE vitamin A, 1 mg vitamin C, 1 mg iron, 6 mg calcium, 29 mg phosphorus.

Daisies

Golden, buttery cookies with a bright dab of jam in the center, Daisies are a wonderful beginner cookie for kids. They include just a few simple ingredients, easily measured, spend 10 minutes or less in the oven, and then the kids can shape them (just a bit) and fill them. Because the shaping is done when the cookies are hot, don't involve your littlest ones in this project, but any kids coordinated enough to keep their hands safely away from the hot baking sheet will enjoy this project.

Yield: 23 cookies ● ***Baking temperature:*** *375°F* ● ***Baking time:*** *13 to 15 minutes*

⅓ cup (1⅜ ounces) confectioners' sugar
½ cup (1 stick, 4 ounces) unsalted butter
¼ teaspoon salt
1 cup (4¼ ounces) unbleached all-purpose flour
¼ cup (3 ounces) jam or preserves

● Preheat the oven to 375°F. Line two baking sheets with parchment, to aid in cleanup; there's no need to grease the pans.

● In a medium-sized bowl, cream together the sugar, butter, and salt. Beat in the flour. Roll the dough into 1-inch balls and place them on the prepared baking sheets. Flatten the cookies very slightly with a glass dipped in confectioners' sugar.

● Bake the cookies for 13 to 15 minutes, until they're golden brown around the edges. Remove them from the oven and immediately use a soft drink bottle cap, or other similar-sized cap, to make a round indentation in the center of each. Allow the cookies to cool completely on the baking sheet.

● Scoop about ½ teaspoon jam into the center of each cooled cookie.

Nutrition information per serving (1 cookie, 15 g): 67 cal, 4 g fat, 1 g protein, 4 g complex carbohydrates, 3 g sugar, 11 mg cholesterol, 25 mg sodium, 10 mg potassium, 37 RE vitamin A, 1 mg vitamin C, 2 mg calcium, 6 mg phosphorus.

Gently make a round indentation in the center of each cookie.

Pignoli Cookies

This classic Italian cookie is the essence of simplicity; chewy and rich, it packs a big almond punch along with the pine nuts.

Yield: 26 cookies ● *Baking temperature: 325°F* ● *Baking time: 22 to 24 minutes*

> 1 cup (9 ounces) marzipan
> ¼ cup (1¾ ounces) sugar
> ⅛ teaspoon salt
> 1 teaspoon almond extract, or 2 to 3 drops bitter almond oil
> 2 to 3 drops lemon oil
> ½ cup (1⅝ ounces) almond flour
> 1 large egg white
> 1½ cups (7½ ounces) pine nuts (pignoli)

● Preheat the oven to 325°F. Lightly grease (or line with parchment) two baking sheets.

● Break the marzipan in pieces into a medium-sized bowl. Stir in the sugar, salt, flavorings, and almond flour; the mixture will be crumbly. Add the egg white, beating until the mixture is smooth.

● Place the pine nuts in a shallow dish. Using a teaspoon cookie scoop, or your lightly oiled or wet hands, drop 1-inch balls of dough into the pine nuts, rolling and pressing gently to coat them thoroughly. You may also simply grab a handful of pine nuts and roll the dough between your palms, pressing in pine nuts as you go; the point is to cover the dough with nuts.

● Place the cookies on the prepared baking sheets, leaving about 1 inch between them.

● Bake the cookies for 22 to 24 minutes, until they're lightly browned. Cool them on the baking sheets for 5 minutes, then transfer to a rack to cool completely.

Nutrition information per serving (*1 cookie, 24 g*)*:* 108 cal, 8 g fat, 4 g protein, 4 g complex carbohydrates, 4 g sugar, 2 g dietary fiber, 14 mg sodium, 131 mg potassium, 1 mg vitamin C, 1 mg iron, 31 mg calcium, 97 mg phosphorus.

Almond Clouds

This delicious, bendy-chewy cookie is redolent with almond, with a hint of lemon. It's a suave accompaniment to fresh fruit, or sandwich it with prepared hazelnut-chocolate spread for a real treat.

Yield: 4 dozen cookies ● *Baking temperature:* 350°F ● *Baking time:* 10 to 12 minutes

> 5 large egg whites
> 1½ cups (10½ ounces) sugar
> ¼ teaspoon salt
> 1 cup (2 sticks, 8 ounces) unsalted butter, melted and cooled
> 1½ cups (6¼ ounces) unbleached all-purpose flour
> ¾ cup (2½ ounces) almond flour
> 1 teaspoon almond extract
> 1 tablespoon (½ ounce) lemon juice, freshly squeezed
> 1 teaspoon grated lemon rind (zest)

● Preheat the oven to 350°F. Lightly grease (or line with parchment) two baking sheets.

● In a large bowl, beat together the egg whites, sugar, and salt for 2 or 3 minutes, until the sugar has dissolved and the egg whites are thick and opaque. Beat in the melted butter and then gently fold in the all-purpose flour, almond flour, almond extract, lemon juice, and zest.

● Drop the dough by the tablespoonful onto the prepared baking sheets, leaving 2 inches between them. Bake the cookies for 10 to 12 minutes, until they're a very pale gold. Remove them from the oven.

● Using a spatula, lift the cookies off the baking sheet to a cooling rack soon after they come out of the oven. They are somewhat reluctant to part company with the sheet once they have thoroughly cooled.

Nutrition information per serving (*1 cookie, 20 g*): 81 cal, 5 g fat, 1 g protein, 3 g complex carbohydrates, 6 g sugar, 10 mg cholesterol, 17 mg sodium, 22 mg potassium, 36 RE vitamin A, 1 mg vitamin C, 5 mg calcium, 13 mg phosphorus.

Your main squeeze

To get the most juice out of a lemon, first run it under hot water, or microwave it very briefly (less than 30 seconds). Then roll it around on the counter with your hand, putting on a fair amount of pressure. This helps to release all those tiny cells of juice inside. If you're going to grate it for zest, do that before you warm and soften it.

Thumbprint Cookies

These cookies are a bit like tiny fruit tarts. They're fun to make with children (give them several choices of jam, so they can pick their favorite), and elegant enough to serve for tea.

Yield: 5 dozen cookies ● *Baking temperature:* 325°F ● *Baking time:* 12 to 16 minutes

> 1 cup (2 sticks, 8 ounces) unsalted butter
> ½ cup (3½ ounces) granulated sugar
> ½ cup (4 ounces) brown sugar
> 2 large eggs, separated
> 1 teaspoon vanilla extract
> ½ teaspoon salt
> ½ cup (1⅝ ounces) almond flour, hazelnut flour, or pecan meal
> 2½ to 3 cups (10½ to 12¾ ounces) unbleached all-purpose flour
> ½ cup (2 ounces) finely chopped nuts, or ½ cup (1½ ounces)
>   shredded sweetened coconut
> ¾ cup (8¾ ounces) raspberry jam, pineapple preserves,
>   or the jam or preserve of your choice

● In a large bowl, cream the butter and sugars together until very light. Beat in the egg yolks, vanilla, and salt. Add the almond flour and 2½ cups of the all-purpose flour, stirring until well blended. If the dough seems too sticky, add just enough additional flour to make it workable. Cover and chill the dough for 1 hour.

● While the dough chills, cover the egg whites and leave them out of the refrigerator to warm to room temperature.

● Preheat the oven to 325°F. Line two baking sheets with parchment, or use a nonstick baking sheet; greasing the pans isn't sufficient to prevent sticking.

● In a small bowl, whip the egg whites until they're foamy. Break off pieces of the dough and roll them between your palms to form 1-inch balls. Dip the balls into the egg whites, then roll them in the nuts or coconut.

● Place the cookies about 2 inches apart on the prepared baking sheets. Make a deep thumbprint in the center of each cookie (hence their name).

● Bake the cookies for 12 to 16 minutes, until they're golden brown. Remove them from the oven and transfer them to a rack to cool. Fill the thumbprint with jam or preserves, using about ½ teaspoon for each.

Nutrition information per serving (1 cookie, 20 g): 82 cal, 4 g fat, 1 g protein, 5 g complex carbohydrates, 6 g sugar, 15 mg cholesterol, 23 mg sodium, 32 mg potassium, 32 RE vitamin A, 1 mg vitamin C, 8 mg calcium, 19 mg phosphorus.

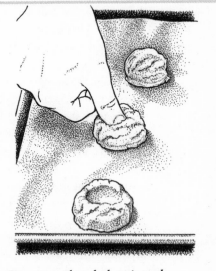

Press your thumb deep into the center of each cookie.

Sherry Cookies

When late afternoon rolls around and you just can't decide between a cup of tea or a glass of sherry, have both: these sherry-scented and -glazed cookies pair wonderfully well with tea. These cookies are definitely a grown-up treat; serve them with a cheese course at the end of your next chic dinner party. Our thanks to cookie baker extraordinaire Marlita Vieira of Hanover, New Hampshire, for this recipe.

Yield: 45 cookies ● *Baking temperature: 350°F* ● *Baking time: 10 to 12 minutes*

DOUGH
1½ cups (6 ounces) dried sweetened cranberries or dried cherries
½ cup (4 ounces) cream sherry
1 cup (2 sticks, 8 ounces) unsalted butter
1½ cups (12 ounces) light brown sugar
½ teaspoon baking soda
1 teaspoon baking powder
1 teaspoon salt
2 large eggs
3 cups (12¾ ounces) unbleached all-purpose flour
1 cup (4 ounces) chopped pecans or walnuts

GLAZE
1¼ cups (5 ounces) confectioners' sugar
3 tablespoons (1½ ounces) cream sherry
1 tablespoon (½ ounce) water

● The day before baking, combine the cranberries with the sherry in a small bowl. Cover the bowl and let the fruit soak overnight.

● Preheat the oven to 350°F. Lightly grease (or line with parchment or a silicone baking mat) two baking sheets.

● **To make the dough:** In a large bowl, cream together the butter, brown sugar, baking soda, baking powder, and salt. Beat in the eggs, then the flour. Stir in the cranberries (and any remaining sherry) and the nuts.

● Drop the dough by the tablespoonful onto the prepared baking sheets. Bake the cookies for 10 to 12 minutes, until they are just beginning to brown around the edges. Remove them from the oven and cool on a rack.

● **To make the glaze:** Stir together the confectioners' sugar, sherry, and water, adding additional water or sugar to make a smooth, spreadable glaze. Using a pastry brush (or a butter knife or icing spatula), spread the glaze over the cooled cookies.

Nutrition information per serving (1 cookie, 37 g): 143 cal, 6 g fat, 1 g protein, 9 g complex carbohydrates, 10 g sugar, 1 g dietary fiber, 20 mg cholesterol, 82 mg sodium, 91 mg potassium, 62 RE vitamin A, 1 mg vitamin C, 1 mg iron, 17 mg calcium, 26 mg phosphorus.

Crispy Chip Cookies

And the secret ingredient is (drum roll) . . . potato chips! Variations on this theme—chocolate–potato chip cookies, peanut butter–potato chip cookies—have been lurking in the dark recesses of cookiedom's annals for years. While they may sound strange at first, think about it: the crisp, salty chips play against the cookie's sweet, faintly caramel flavor much like salted peanuts in a butterscotch sundae do.

Yield: 2 dozen cookies ● *Baking temperature:* 350°F ● *Baking time:* 15 minutes

½ cup (3¼ ounces) vegetable shortening
½ cup (3½ ounces) granulated sugar
½ cup (4 ounces) brown sugar
½ teaspoon salt
1 teaspoon baking powder
1 teaspoon vanilla extract
1 large egg
1 cup (3½ ounces) rolled oats
1 cup (4¼ ounces) unbleached all-purpose flour
1 cup (2¾ ounces) gently crushed (not pulverized) plain salted potato chips

● Preheat the oven to 350°F. Lightly grease (or line with parchment) two baking sheets.

● In a medium-sized bowl, cream together the shortening, sugars, salt, baking powder, and vanilla. Beat in the egg, then stir in the oats and flour, mixing until cohesive. Gently fold in the potato chips. The dough will be stiff.

● Drop the dough by the tablespoonful onto the prepared baking sheets. Bake the cookies for 15 minutes, until they're beginning to brown around the edges. Remove them from the oven and transfer to a rack to cool.

Nutrition information per serving (1 cookie, 28 g): 120 cal, 5 g fat, 2 g protein, 8 g complex carbohydrates, 9 g sugar, 1 g dietary fiber, 9 mg cholesterol, 85 mg sodium, 82 mg potassium, 4 RE vitamin A, 1 mg vitamin C, 1 mg iron, 19 mg calcium, 38 mg phosphorus.

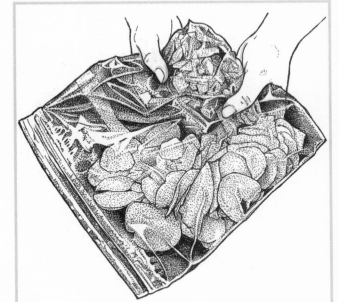

The easiest, best way to gently crush potato chips (or cereal) for cookies is to place them in a zip-top plastic bag, force the air out, then gently flatten them with your hands or a lightly wielded rolling pin.

Carrot Drops

You never heard of using vegetables as a cookie ingredient? Well, think Lemon-Zucchini Drops (page 280) and these soft, cakelike cookies, flecked with golden bits of carrot. The ginger gives these lemon-scented cookies a pleasant bite; stick to the smaller amount if you're not a fan of ginger's heat.

Yield: 30 cookies ● *Baking temperature: 350°F* ● *Baking time: 17 minutes*

¾ cup (5¼ ounces) sugar
¾ cup (4¾ ounces) vegetable shortening
2 teaspoons baking powder
1 teaspoon vanilla extract
¾ teaspoon salt
A few drops lemon oil, or ½ teaspoon lemon extract
1 large egg
1¼ cups (4½ ounces) grated raw carrots
¼ to ½ cup (1½ to 3 ounces) finely minced crystallized ginger (optional)
2 cups (8½ ounces) unbleached all-purpose flour

● Preheat the oven to 350°F. Lightly grease (or line with parchment) two baking sheets.
● In a large bowl, cream together the sugar, shortening, baking powder, vanilla, salt, and lemon oil. Beat in the egg, then beat in the carrots, ginger, and flour until the dough is smooth and cohesive.
● Drop the dough by the tablespoonful onto the prepared baking sheets. Bake the cookies for 17 minutes, or until they appear set and are just beginning to brown around the edges. Remove them from the oven, let cool on the pan for 5 minutes, then transfer them to a rack to cool completely.

Nutrition information per serving (1 cookie, 28 g): 102 cal, 5 g fat, 1 g protein, 7 g complex carbohydrates, 7 g sugar, 1 g dietary fiber, 7 mg cholesterol, 92 mg sodium, 30 mg potassium, 143 RE vitamin A, 1 mg vitamin C, 1 mg iron, 22 mg calcium, 19 mg phosphorus.

Brown Sugar Crinkles

The white confectioners' sugar topping and dark crust of these cookies lend a patchwork-quilt look to their rich, brown-sugary taste. Leave that simple flavor alone, or point it up with butter-scotch or butter-rum flavor, and/or an infusion of salted pecans.

Yield: 4 dozen cookies ● *Baking temperature:* 350°F ● *Baking time:* 12 minutes

DOUGH

1½ cups (12 ounces) dark brown sugar

½ cup (1 stick, 4 ounces) unsalted butter

2 teaspoons vanilla extract, or a few drops strong butterscotch flavor or strong butter-rum flavor

2 large eggs

¾ teaspoon baking soda

½ teaspoon salt

2½ cups (10½ ounces) unbleached all-purpose flour

1 cup (4 ounces) salted, toasted pecans (see page 27)*

¼ cup (1 ounce) confectioners' sugar, for coating

● In a large mixing bowl, cream together the sugar, butter, and vanilla. Add the eggs one at a time, beating well after each addition. Beat in the baking soda and salt, then stir in the flour and pecans, until the mixture is smooth. Cover the bowl and refrigerate the dough for 1 hour, or until it's firm enough to handle.

● Preheat the oven to 350°F. Lightly grease (or line with parchment) two baking sheets.

● Break off tablespoon-size chunks of dough and roll them into balls. Place the confectioners' sugar in a shallow dish, such as a pie plate, and roll the balls of dough in the sugar to coat. Place them on the prepared baking sheets, leaving 2 inches between them.

● Bake the cookies for 12 minutes, until they've spread and cracked on the top. Remove them from the oven, let cool on the baking sheets for 5 minutes, then transfer to a rack to cool completely.

* Before toasting the pecans, spritz them lightly with water and sprinkle with fine table salt.

Nutrition information per serving (1 cookie, 21 g): 86 cal, 4 g fat, 1 g protein, 5 g complex carbo-hydrates, 8 g sugar, 14 mg cholesterol, 66 mg sodium, 44 mg potassium, 22 RE vitamin A, 1 mg vitamin C, 1 mg iron, 8 mg calcium, 18 mg phosphorus.

Nora's Date-Stuffed Cookies

Tender brown-sugar cookies with a soft, sweet date filling—what's not to love? These mimic the old-fashioned date-stuffed cookies you find in a plastic-wrapped package on your supermarket shelf. The recipe dates back eighty years or more, to Nora Greenwald of Daleyville, Wisconsin.

Yield: 3½ dozen large cookies ● *Baking temperature: 350°F* ● *Baking time: 12 to 15 minutes*

DOUGH

2 cups (16 ounces) brown sugar
½ cup (3¼ ounces) vegetable shortening
½ cup (1 stick, 4 ounces) unsalted butter
1 teaspoon baking soda
½ teaspoon salt
1 teaspoon vanilla extract
2 large eggs
1 cup (3½ ounces) rolled oats
3 cups (12¾ ounces) unbleached all-purpose flour

FILLING

1½ cups (8 ounces) chopped dates
¼ cup (2 ounces) brown sugar
½ cup (4 ounces) water
⅛ teaspoon salt
2 teaspoons lemon juice

● **To make the dough:** In a large bowl, cream together the sugar, shortening, butter, baking soda, salt, and vanilla until smooth. Beat in the eggs, then stir in the oats and flour. Cover the bowl and chill the dough for 1 hour.

● **To make the filling:** In a small saucepan set over medium heat, cook the dates, sugar, water, salt, and lemon juice gently for about 7 minutes, stirring frequently, until thick.

● Preheat the oven to 350°F. Lightly grease (or line with parchment) two baking sheets.

● Roll the dough into chestnut-sized (1-inch) balls, placing them on the prepared baking sheets. Flatten half the balls of dough. Dollop a heaping teaspoon of filling atop each flattened cookie. Flatten the remaining balls of dough, then center them atop the date-topped cookies. Press the edges together with the tines of a fork (see illustration, opposite).

● Bake the cookies for 12 to 15 minutes, until they're a light golden brown. Remove them from the oven and transfer them to a rack to cool.

Nutrition information per serving (1 cookie, 40 g): 141 cal, 5 g fat, 2 g protein, 12 g complex carbohydrates, 12 g sugar, 1 g dietary fiber, 16 mg cholesterol, 76 mg sodium, 100 mg potassium, 25 RE vitamin A, 1 mg vitamin C, 1 mg iron, 15 mg calcium, 28 mg phosphorus.

Place a dollop of filling into the center of each flattened cookie. A partially filled teaspoon cookie scoop works well here.

Place the remaining flattened cookies on top, pressing the edges together with the tines of a fork.

Anise Chews

These bite-sized chewy cookies have a pleasantly mild flavor on their own; but add aniseed, and you can make them as assertive (or gentle) as you like. Bottom line: if you like black licorice, you'll love these cookies.

Yield: 4½ dozen ● *Baking temperature: 375°F* ● *Baking time: 8 to 9 minutes*

> ½ cup (1 stick, 4 ounces) unsalted butter
> ⅔ cup (5¼ ounces) light brown sugar
> 1 large egg
> ¼ teaspoon baking soda
> ¾ teaspoon salt
> 2 to 4 tablespoons (½ to 1 ounce) aniseed
> 1½ cups (6¼ ounces) unbleached all-purpose flour

● Preheat the oven to 375°F. Lightly grease (or line with parchment) two baking sheets.
● In a medium-sized bowl, cream together the butter and sugar, then beat in the egg, baking soda, salt, and aniseed. Mix in the flour.
● Drop the dough by the teaspoonful onto the prepared baking sheets. Bake the cookies for 8 to 9 minutes, until they're brown around the edges. Remove them from the oven and transfer to a rack to cool.

Nutrition information per serving (1 cookie, 10 g): 40 cal, 2 g fat, 1 g protein, 3 g complex carbohydrates, 3 g sugar, 9 mg cholesterol, 38 mg sodium, 23 mg potassium, 18 RE vitamin A, 1 mg vitamin C, 7 mg calcium, 8 mg phosphorus.

Maple-Walnut Crisps

Being from Vermont, we have a special affinity for maple—the gorgeous explosion of color that is sugar maples in the fall, the sweet scent of boiling sap turning to syrup in the spring, and maple-flavored baked goods year-round. Maple and walnut have paired together happily for years, and they do so once again in this cookie.

Yield: 40 cookies ● *Baking temperature: 375°F* ● *Baking time: 12 minutes*

1 cup (7 ounces) granulated sugar
½ cup (2¾ ounces) maple sugar or ½ cup (4 ounces) brown sugar
1 teaspoon baking soda
1 teaspoon salt
½ teaspoon strong maple flavor, or 2 teaspoons maple extract, to taste
½ cup (3¼ ounces) vegetable shortening
1 large egg
¼ cup (2¾ ounces) maple syrup
3 cups (12¾ ounces) unbleached all-purpose flour
2 cups (8 ounces) chopped, toasted walnuts (see page 27)

● Preheat the oven to 375°F. Lightly grease (or line with parchment) two baking sheets.
● In a large bowl, beat together the sugars, baking soda, salt, maple flavor, and shortening. Beat in the egg and maple syrup, then stir in the flour. Add the nuts, stirring to combine.
● Roll the dough into table tennis–sized balls and place them on the prepared baking sheets. Flatten each ball with the bottom of a glass that has been dipped in sugar.
● Bake the cookies for 12 minutes, until they're golden brown. Remove them from the oven and transfer to a rack to cool.

Nutrition information per serving (1 cookie, 29 g): 123 cal, 5 g fat, 2 g protein, 7 g complex carbohydrates, 9 g sugar, 1 g dietary fiber, 5 mg cholesterol, 88 mg sodium, 56 mg potassium, 4 RE vitamin A, 1 mg vitamin C, 1 mg iron, 8 mg calcium, 37 mg phosphorus.

VARIATIONS

● For a soft, chewy cookie, bake for 8 minutes.
● For a cookie that's crisp on the outside and soft in the center, don't flatten the balls of dough on the baking sheet. Bake the cookies for 10 to 12 minutes.

Flavor to taste

The wide range of flavors available to bakers can present a problem because many of them vary greatly in strength from manufacturer to manufacturer. So it's smart to add flavor several drops at a time if you're using what you know is a strong flavor—(see page 490 for more information), tasting the dough after each addition. If you're using something labeled "extract," then it's safe to add it to your cookie dough by the half-teaspoonful, as extracts are less strong than flavors.

If you're squeamish about eating raw cookie dough, bake one cookie, taste it, and add more flavor, if desired, to the remaining dough. This is a longer process, but is a good precautionary measure for those concerned with special health issues.

Almond Pennies

These cookies feature a minor note of almond, and a major cantata of chewiness. They begin as balls of dough, but flatten as they bake to become big, 3½-inch cookies—round and golden as a new copper penny.

Yield: 26 cookies ● *Baking temperature: 350°F* ● *Baking time: 13 to 15 minutes*

1 cup (8 ounces) **light brown sugar**
½ cup (1 stick, 4 ounces) **unsalted butter**
½ teaspoon **almond extract**
½ teaspoon **salt**
¼ teaspoon **baking soda**
1 large **egg**
⅔ cup (2¼ ounces) **almond flour, toasted or plain**
1 cup (4¼ ounces) **unbleached all-purpose flour**

- Preheat the oven to 350°F. Lightly grease (or line with parchment) two baking sheets.
- In a medium-sized bowl, cream together the brown sugar and butter. Beat in the almond extract, salt, baking soda, and egg. Mix in the almond flour and all-purpose flour.
- Roll the dough into table tennis–sized balls (a tablespoon cookie scoop works well here, to portion the dough) and place them on the prepared baking sheets, leaving 2 inches of space between them. Use the bottom of a drinking glass dipped in sugar, to press them to a thickness of ¼ inch.
- Bake the cookies for 13 to 15 minutes, until they're a light golden brown. Remove them from the oven and transfer to a rack to cool.

Nutrition information per serving (1 cookie, 81 g): 319 cal, 5 g fat, 1 g protein, 4 g complex carbohydrates, 66 g sugar, 18 mg cholesterol, 83 mg sodium, 261 mg potassium, 37 RE vitamin A, 1 mg vitamin C, 2 mg iron, 66 mg calcium, 36 mg phosphorus.

Harvest Moons

These big, soft, deep-golden-orange cookies are chewy-cakey, and taste nicely of pumpkin. They remind us of a fat orange moon, the kind you often see rising over our Vermont mountains in September. The chocolate chips are an option for chocolate lovers, and for those who enjoy that old favorite, pumpkin–chocolate chip quick bread; but frankly when these are made without the chocolate chips, the pumpkin really shines through and we like the purity of that flavor. Another choice is to spread the baked cookies with Chocolate Glaze (see page 459).

Yield: 2 dozen large cookies ● *Baking temperature: 350°F* ● *Baking time: 20 to 25 minutes*

DOUGH
1 cup (2 sticks, 8 ounces) unsalted butter
1 cup (8 ounces) brown sugar
1 cup (7 ounces) granulated sugar
1 teaspoon vanilla extract
1 teaspoon cinnamon
½ teaspoon baking soda
1 teaspoon salt
1 large egg
1 cup (3½ ounces) rolled oats
2 cups (8½ ounces) unbleached all-purpose flour
1 cup (9½ ounces) pumpkin purée (canned pumpkin)
2 cups (12 ounces) chocolate chips (optional)

GLAZE
2 cups (8 ounces) confectioners' sugar
½ teaspoon pumpkin pie spice, or ¼ teaspoon cinnamon
    plus ⅛ teaspoon each ground ginger and nutmeg
¼ cup (2 ounces) milk or cream (enough to make a spreadable glaze)
½ cup (2 ounces) chopped pecans (optional)

● Preheat the oven to 350°F. Lightly grease (or line with parchment) two baking sheets.
● **To make the dough:** In a large bowl, cream together the butter, sugars, vanilla, cinnamon, baking soda, and salt. Beat in the egg, then the oats. Add the flour alternately with the pumpkin. Stir in the chocolate chips.
● Drop the dough by ¼-cupfuls onto the prepared baking sheets. Bake the cookies for 20 to 25 minutes, until they're set and a very light golden brown around the edges Remove them from the oven and transfer to a rack to cool.
● **To make the glaze:** In a medium-sized bowl, stir together the sugar, spice, and enough milk or cream (about ¼ cup) to make a spreadable glaze.
● Spread or drizzle each cookie with the glaze. Top with a sprinkle of pecans, if desired.

Nutrition information per serving (1 cookie, 82 g): 320 cal, 14 g fat, 3 g protein, 12 g complex carbohydrates, 35 g sugar, 1 g dietary fiber, 30 mg cholesterol, 124 mg sodium, 140 mg potassium, 285 RE vitamin A, 1 mg vitamin C, 2 mg iron, 26 mg calcium, 64 mg phosphorus, 11 mg caffeine.

Benne Wafers

Benne wafers, ethereally light, snapping-crisp sesame cookies, are native to the "low country" of South Carolina. Sesame, a plant with a long history of cultivation, was probably first grown in Africa; West Africans, brought to this country as slaves in the seventeenth and eighteenth centuries, called sesame "benne" and legend had it that eating sesame seeds brought good luck. Middle Easterners also called sesame seeds "benne"; there must have been trade routes that brought together buyers from the Middle East with African sellers. Food, as usual, seems to have been a key component in bringing cultures together.

Yield: 44 cookies ● *Baking temperature: 350°F* ● *Baking time: 13 to 15 minutes*

½ cup (1 stick, 4 ounces) unsalted butter*
¾ cup (6 ounces) light brown sugar
½ teaspoon salt
¼ teaspoon baking soda
1 teaspoon vanilla extract
1 large egg
1 cup (4¼ ounces) unbleached all-purpose flour
1 cup (4⅝ ounces) toasted sesame seeds

● Preheat the oven to 350°F. Lightly grease (or line with parchment) two baking sheets.
● In a large mixing bowl, cream together the butter, sugar, salt, baking soda, vanilla, and egg. Add the flour and mix until smooth. Beat in the sesame seeds.
● Drop the dough by the teaspoonful (a teaspoon cookie scoop works well here) onto the prepared baking sheets. Leave at least 2 inches between them; they spread quite a bit as they bake.
● Bake the wafers for 13 to 15 minutes, until they're a deep golden brown. For a chewy, rather than crisp cookie, bake for 9 to 11 minutes. Remove them from the oven, let cool for 1 minute on the baking sheet, then transfer them to a rack to cool completely.

* For added sesame flavor, substitute 1 tablespoon strong-flavored sesame oil for 1 tablespoon of the butter.

Nutrition information per serving (1 cookie, 14 g): 64 cal, 4 g fat, 1 g protein, 3 g complex carbohydrates, 4 g sugar, 1 g dietary fiber, 10 mg cholesterol, 35 mg sodium, 35 mg potassium, 22 RE vitamin A, 1 mg iron, 39 mg calcium, 28 mg phosphorus.

Lemon-Zucchini Drops

These tender-crunchy rounds are flecked with fresh shredded zucchini, which gives them both an interesting look and added moistness. Frosted with a lemon glaze, they disappeared quickly from the test kitchen "sampling" table. And, while they don't make that much of a dent in any overflow of zucchini you might have on hand, at least it's a start.

Yield: 5 dozen cookies ● *Baking temperature:* 375°F ● *Baking time:* 10 to 12 minutes

DOUGH
¾ cup (1½ sticks, 6 ounces) unsalted butter
1½ cups (10½ ounces) sugar
1 teaspoon baking powder
½ teaspoon baking soda
1½ teaspoons ground cinnamon
½ teaspoon salt
2 large eggs
1½ cups (12 ounces) unpeeled grated zucchini
3¼ to 3½ cups (13¾ to 14¾ ounces) unbleached all-purpose flour
2 tablespoons grated lemon rind (zest)
1½ cups (8 ounces) raisins
1½ cups (6 ounces) chopped walnuts

GLAZE
2 cups (8 ounces) confectioners' sugar
2 tablespoons (1 ounce) lemon juice, freshly squeezed
3 to 4 tablespoons (1½ to 2 ounces) light or heavy cream

● Preheat the oven to 375°F. Lightly grease (or line with parchment) two baking sheets.

● **To make the dough:** In a medium-sized mixing bowl, cream together the butter, sugar, baking powder, baking soda, cinnamon, and salt until light and fluffy. Add the eggs one at a time, beating well after each addition, then stir in the zucchini.

● Beat the flour, lemon zest, raisins, and walnuts into the creamed mixture. Drop the dough by tablespoonfuls onto the prepared baking sheets. Note: Because the moisture content varies considerably in zucchini, we suggest you bake one test cookie, adding more flour to the batter if the cookie spreads more than you'd like it to.

● Bake the cookies for 10 to 12 minutes, until they spring back when touched lightly in the center. Remove the cookies from the oven. Let them cool on the baking sheet for 3 minutes, then transfer to racks to cool completely.

● **To make the glaze:** Place the sugar in a small mixing bowl, and stir in the lemon juice, then add the cream, a little at a time, to achieve the consistency you like. Use more liquid for a thin, clear glaze, less for a thicker, whiter-looking glaze. Spread the cookies with the glaze and let them set for an hour or so before wrapping.

Nutrition information per serving (*1 cookie, 33 g*): 113 cal, 4 g fat, 2 g protein, 9 g complex carbohydrates, 9 g sugar, 1 g dietary fiber, 15 mg cholesterol, 40 mg sodium, 66 mg potassium, 31 RE vitamin A, 1 mg vitamin C, 1 mg iron, 12 mg calcium, 30 mg phosphorus.

Don't toss those potato chip canisters!

You know those foil-lined cardboard canisters that come packed with nesting, stacked potato chips? When the chips are gone, rinse the canister briefly, dry thoroughly, and store it (with its plastic lid) for the next time you want to ship cookies. A stack of typical-size drop cookies (about 2½ inches in diameter) will nestle very nicely in the canister. A wadded-up paper towel at each end will help cushion the cookies as they travel; and for best freshness, seal the top with plastic wrap before snapping on the plastic lid. If it's holiday time and you're feeling imaginative, wrap a sheet of festive paper around the sides of the canister (see photo in color insert).

Walnut Butterballs

These melt-in-your-mouth balls of butter, honey, and walnuts have a rich, nutty flavor; they pair well with small, fudgy brownie squares in a holiday gift tin.

Yield: 25 cookies ● *Baking temperature: 300°F* ● *Baking time: 15 to 18 minutes*

½ cup (1 stick, 4 ounces) unsalted butter
2 tablespoons (1½ ounces) honey
1 cup (4¼ ounces) unbleached all-purpose flour
Heaping ¼ teaspoon salt
1 teaspoon vanilla extract
1 cup (4 ounces) finely chopped walnuts
Confectioners' sugar

● In a small bowl, cream together the butter and honey. Combine the flour and salt and add it to the butter mixture. Beat in the vanilla and stir in the walnuts. Chill the dough for 1 hour or more.

● Preheat the oven to 300°F. Lightly grease (or line with parchment) two baking sheets.

● Remove the dough from the refrigerator and break off pieces the size of a small chestnut (1 inch); a teaspoon cookie scoop works well here. Roll the pieces into 1-inch balls and transfer them to the prepared baking sheets.

● Bake the cookies for 15 to 18 minutes, until they're lightly browned. Remove them from the oven and sprinkle heavily with confectioners' sugar while still hot; a flour sifter or a small sieve both work well here. Transfer them to a rack to cool.

Nutritional information per cookie (1 cookie, 15 g): 77 cal, 5 g fat, 1 g protein, 4 g complex carbohydrates, 1 g sugar, 11 mg cholesterol, 114 mg sodium, 23 mg potassium, 37 RE vitamin A, 12 mg calcium, 32 mg phosphorus.

Pecan Puffs

These cappuccino-colored cookies, light as a wisp of smoke, shatter delightfully in your mouth at the first bite. The crisp outer shell contrasts nicely with a slightly chewy center and, though quite sweet, they're saved from being overly so by the toasted nuttiness of the pecans.

Yield: 3 dozen 2½-inch cookies ● *Baking temperature:* 300°F ● *Baking time:* 20 minutes

> 3½ cups (14 ounces) chopped pecans, toasted (see page 27)
> 3 large egg whites
> 2 cups (16 ounces) light brown sugar
> ¼ teaspoon salt
> 2 teaspoons vanilla extract, or a few drops (to taste) pecan or
>   pralines & cream flavor

● Preheat the oven to 300°F. Lightly grease (or line with parchment) two baking sheets.

● Whirl the nuts in a food processor until they're very finely chopped. Be careful—don't over-do it, because they'll turn to paste.

● In a large bowl, beat the egg whites until they hold a soft peak. Beat in the sugar, then the salt and flavor. Fold in the nuts.

● Drop the dough by tablespoonfuls onto the prepared baking sheets. Bake the cookies for about 20 minutes, until they're a very light brown. Remove them from the oven and transfer to a rack to cool.

Nutrition information per serving (1 cookie, 27 g): 124 cal, 8 g fat, 1 g protein, 2 g complex carbohydrates, 12 g sugar, 1 g dietary fiber, 24 mg sodium, 92 mg potassium, 1 RE vitamin A, 1 mg vitamin C, 1 mg iron, 15 mg calcium, 36 mg phosphorus.

Lavender Cookies

Imagine a late afternoon in June, the lazy drone of bees in the garden, and lavender-perfumed ladies enjoying tea and cookies on the veranda. Perhaps though, rather than the scent of lavender water, it's the cookies you're smelling? Lavender's distinctive floral aroma pairs surprisingly well with both chocolate and cookies, and is especially appealing in these crisp, buttery rounds. You'll find dried lavender flowers in the spice section of better supermarkets, particularly those with a selection of bulk spices; or check for them at www.penzeys.com.

Yield: 4 dozen cookies ● *Baking temperature: 375°F* ● *Baking time: 10 minutes*

1 to 3 teaspoons finely chopped dried lavender flowers*
½ cup (1 stick, 4 ounces) unsalted butter
1 cup (7 ounces) sugar
¼ teaspoon salt
½ teaspoon vanilla extract
2 teaspoons baking powder
2 large eggs
1½ cups (6¼ ounces) unbleached all-purpose flour
2 teaspoons baking powder

● Preheat the oven to 375°F. Lightly grease (or line with parchment) two baking sheets.
● Crumble the lavender between your fingers into a medium-sized mixing bowl. Add the butter, sugar, salt, vanilla, and baking powder and beat until the mixture is light and fluffy. Beat in the eggs, then beat in the flour.
● Drop the dough by the teaspoonful onto the prepared baking sheets. Bake the cookies for 10 minutes, or until they're lightly browned at the edges. Cool the cookies on the baking sheet for a minute or two, then transfer them to a rack to cool.

* 1 teaspoon yields the faintest floral aroma; 3 teaspoons is much more assertive. Start with 1 teaspoon and taste the raw dough (or bake one cookie, and taste that); adjust the amount if desired. For an interesting combination, try mixing various amounts of lavender and dried lemon thyme, or lavender and rose water.

Nutrition information per serving (1 cookie, 13 g): 49 cal, 2 g fat, 1 g protein, 7 g complex carbohydrates, 3 g sugar, 14 mg cholesterol, 34 mg sodium, 8 mg potassium, 22 RE vitamin A, 13 mg calcium, 12 mg phosphorus.

Cardamom-Almond Cookies

These cookies are tender and flaky, with a subtle cardamom flavor.

Yield: 4½ dozen small cookies ● *Baking temperature: 350°F* ● *Baking time: 20 minutes*

> 1 cup (2 sticks, 8 ounces) unsalted butter, chilled
> ¾ cup (3 ounces) confectioners' sugar
> ¾ teaspoon almond extract
> ½ teaspoon ground cardamom
> ½ teaspoon salt
> 1⅞ cups (8 ounces) unbleached all-purpose flour
> ½ cup (2½ ounces) finely chopped almonds
> Cinnamon-sugar for sprinkling (optional)

● In a large mixing bowl, cream together the butter, sugar, almond extract, cardamom, and salt until light and fluffy. Add the flour and nuts and stir until the mixture forms a cohesive dough. Chill the dough, covered, for 1 hour.

● Lightly grease (or line with parchment) two baking sheets.

● Roll the dough into 1-inch balls (scooping off portions with a teaspoon cookie scoop, then rolling them in your hands works well), and transfer the balls to the prepared baking sheets. Let the cookies rest at room temperature for 20 minutes, while you preheat the oven to 350°F.

● Bake the cookies for about 20 minutes, or until they're golden brown. Remove them from the oven and sprinkle with cinnamon-sugar, if desired. Transfer them to a rack to cool.

Nutrition information per serving (1 cookie, 11 g): 57 cal, 4 g fat, 1 g protein, 3 g complex carbohydrates, 2 g sugar, 9 mg cholesterol, 20 mg sodium, 14 mg potassium, 32 RE vitamin A, 1 mg vitamin C, 4 mg calcium, 10 mg phosphorus.

Almond Crisps

These almond-flavored brown-sugar cookies are so thin and crisp they look as if they were rolled out and cut with a cutter. But they're actually an easy-to-make drop cookie. The roasted almonds on top lend a nice touch of salt to this sweet treat.

Yield: 2½ dozen cookies ● **Baking temperature:** *325°F* ● **Baking time:** *17 minutes*

½ cup (1 stick, 4 ounces) unsalted butter
¼ cup (2 ounces) light brown sugar
2 tablespoons (⅞ ounce) granulated sugar
½ teaspoon salt
1 tablespoon (½ ounce) water
2 teaspoons almond extract
1¼ cups (5¼ ounces) unbleached
    all-purpose flour
½ cup (2½ ounces) roasted salted whole
    almonds

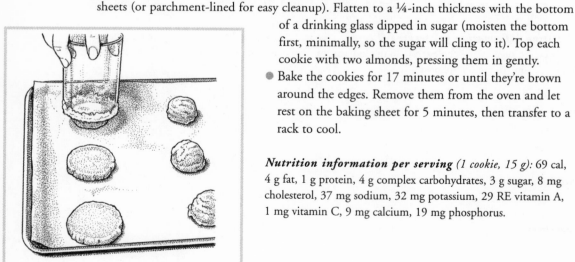

Wipe the flat bottom of a drinking glass with a wet paper towel, then dip it in sugar. You'll probably only need to moisten the bottom of the glass for the first cookie; sugar will cling to the glass of its own accord after that.

● Preheat the oven to 325°F.
● In a medium-sized bowl, cream together the butter, sugars, salt, water, and almond extract. Add the flour, stirring to make a stiff dough.
● Drop the dough by the teaspoonful onto ungreased baking sheets (or parchment-lined for easy cleanup). Flatten to a ¼-inch thickness with the bottom of a drinking glass dipped in sugar (moisten the bottom first, minimally, so the sugar will cling to it). Top each cookie with two almonds, pressing them in gently.
● Bake the cookies for 17 minutes or until they're brown around the edges. Remove them from the oven and let rest on the baking sheet for 5 minutes, then transfer to a rack to cool.

Press the cookie to the thickness indicated in the recipe.

Nutrition information per serving (1 cookie, 15 g): 69 cal, 4 g fat, 1 g protein, 4 g complex carbohydrates, 3 g sugar, 8 mg cholesterol, 37 mg sodium, 32 mg potassium, 29 RE vitamin A, 1 mg vitamin C, 9 mg calcium, 19 mg phosphorus.

Wedding Cookies

Russian Wedding Cookies, Mexican Wedding Cookies, Teacakes . . . these tender, crumbly cookies, full of ground almonds and covered with a blizzard of confectioners' sugar, go by many names. But one thing is constant: their melt-in-your-mouth texture and distinctive, attractive appearance: round and white as a cumulus cloud.

Yield: 5 dozen cookies ● *Baking temperature: 325°F* ● *Baking time: 15 to 20 minutes*

DOUGH
1 cup (2 sticks, 8 ounces) unsalted butter
½ cup (2 ounces) confectioners' sugar
1½ teaspoons vanilla extract
1 teaspoon salt
¾ cup (2½ ounces) almond flour
2¼ cups (9½ ounces) unbleached all-purpose flour

TOPPING
½ cup (2 ounces) confectioners' sugar

● In a large bowl, cream together the butter, sugar, vanilla, and salt. Beat in the almond flour, then the all-purpose flour. Cover the bowl and chill the dough for 1 hour.

● Preheat the oven to 325°F. Lightly grease (or line with parchment) two baking sheets.

● Break off chestnut-sized (1-inch) pieces of dough, using a teaspoon cookie scoop if desired, and roll them into balls. Place them on the prepared baking sheets, leaving 1 inch between them. Bake the cookies for 15 to 20 minutes, until they appear set and are just beginning to brown.

● Sprinkle the topping sugar in a shallow bowl. Remove the cookies from the oven and transfer them, a few at a time, to the bowl. Roll them in the sugar to coat, then transfer to a rack to cool.

● When the cookies are cool, roll them in confectioners' sugar again; they should be thoroughly coated and snowy white.

Place the confectioners' sugar in a bowl. Add 4 or 5 cookies, and gently roll them in the sugar to coat.

Nutrition information per serving (1 cookie, 12 g): 57 cal, 4 g fat, 1 g protein, 4 g complex carbohydrates, 2 g sugar, 8 mg cholesterol, 36 mg sodium, 15 mg potassium, 29 RE vitamin A, 1 mg vitamin C, 4 mg calcium, 11 mg phosphorus.

St. Patrick's Day Pistachio Cookies

In the wide world of baking there are very few green-colored goodies, thus few truly festive-looking St. Patrick's Day treats. These cookies qualify. Soft and sweet, packed with pistachio flavor (which in reality bears little resemblance to the taste of actual pistachio nuts), these cookies are a delight. Note that some store brands of pistachio pudding mix will lend minimal color to your cookies; for the richest green, spend the extra few cents on one of the national brands.

Yield: 53 cookies ● *Baking temperature:* 350°F ● *Baking time:* 15 minutes

½ cup (1 stick, 4 ounces) unsalted butter
½ cup (3½ ounces) sugar
¼ cup (1¾ ounces) vegetable oil
¼ cup (2 ounces) water
1 large egg
Two 3.4-ounce packages pistachio instant pudding mix
1 teaspoon vanilla extract
½ teaspoon salt
1 teaspoon baking powder
2 cups (8½ ounces) unbleached all-purpose flour
½ to ⅔ cup (2 to 2¾ ounces) chopped pistachio nuts (optional)

● Preheat the oven to 350°F. Lightly grease (or line with parchment) two baking sheets.
● In a medium-sized bowl, beat together the butter, sugar, oil, water, egg, pudding mix, vanilla, salt, and baking powder until smooth. Add the flour and nuts, beating until everything is well combined. The dough will be stiff.
● Roll or scoop the dough into chestnut-sized (1-inch) balls; a teaspoon cookie scoop yields the right size. Roll them in granulated sugar, if desired, and place them on the prepared baking sheets, leaving 1 to 2 inches between them. Press the cookies down gently with the bottom of a drinking glass, dipped in sugar if necessary to prevent sticking.
● Bake the cookies for 15 minutes, until they're just barely beginning to brown around the edges and are golden brown on the bottom. Remove them from the oven and transfer to a rack to cool completely.

Nutrition information per serving (*1 cookie, 17 g*): 74 cal, 4 g fat, 1 g protein, 4 g complex carbohydrates, 5 g sugar, 9 mg cholesterol, 83 mg sodium, 28 mg potassium, 18 RE vitamin A, 1 mg vitamin C, 8 mg calcium, 47 mg phosphorus.

VARIATIONS

● This recipe is flexible; just pick your favorite pudding flavor, then go for it. If you like, match the extract/flavor and add-ins to the flavor of pudding. For instance, butter-rum flavor and chopped pecans with butterscotch pudding; coconut or banana flavor and white chocolate chips with coconut cream pudding; espresso powder and cappuccino chips with chocolate pudding, and so on. Use about ⅛ teaspoon of a strong flavor, or ½ to 1 teaspoon of more typical strength "supermarket" flavors or extracts.

Marmalade Morsels

They say beauty is only skin deep—thank goodness, because these earthy-looking cookies definitely aren't the most attractive thing you'll ever bake. Inside their ugly-duckling exterior, however, lies a wealth of flavor, neatly packed into a moist, soft (homely) cookie.

Yield: 4 dozen cookies ● *Baking temperature:* 325°F ● *Baking time:* 18 minutes

> 1 cup (2 sticks, 8 ounces) unsalted butter
> ½ cup (3½ ounces) sugar
> 1 teaspoon salt
> 1 cup (12 ounces) orange marmalade
> ⅛ teaspoon *Fiori di Sicilia* flavor* (optional)
> 1½ cups (6 ounces) finely chopped pecans
> 2 cups (8½ ounces) unbleached all-purpose flour
> Confectioners' sugar

● Preheat the oven to 325°F. Lightly grease (or line with parchment) two baking sheets.

● In a large bowl, cream together the butter, sugar, and salt. Beat in the marmalade and *Fiori di Sicilia*, then stir in the pecans and flour.

● Drop the dough by the tablespoonful onto the prepared baking sheets, spacing the cookies 2 inches apart. If there are any shreds of orange peel sticking off the edge of the cookie, remove them, or press them in; otherwise they'll become unpleasantly hard as the cookies bake.

● Bake the cookies for 18 minutes, or until they're set. Remove them from the oven and transfer to a rack to cool. Dust with confectioners' sugar just before serving, if desired.

* Available via mail order. *Fiori di Sicilia*, a combination of citrus and vanilla flavors, complements any other fruit flavor, and also adds a welcome hit of vanilla (see page 490).

Nutrition information per serving (1 cookie, 21 g): 92 cal, 6 g fat, 1 g protein, 5 g complex carbohydrates, 6 g sugar, 10 mg cholesterol, 48 mg sodium, 21 mg potassium, 36 RE vitamin A, 1 mg vitamin C, 4 mg calcium, 14 mg phosphorus.

Chinese Restaurant Almond Cookies

Made without any adornment save a whole blanched almond in the center, these cookies are reminiscent of those crunchy, almond-scented rounds brought to the table at the end of the meal in many old-fashioned, American-style Chinese restaurants. The fat that you use in this cookie makes a big difference, in both the flavor and the texture. Using vegetable shortening makes a crumbly-crisp cookie, with a texture similar to the restaurant version. Using half butter and half vegetable shortening makes a cookie that's less "sandy" in texture, but still very crisp. Using all butter changes the flavor and texture, but makes a very tasty cookie—just not exactly a "Chinese restaurant cookie."

Yield: 2 dozen 3- to 4-inch cookies ● *Baking temperature:* 325°F ● *Baking time:* 16 to 18 minutes

> 2¾ cups (11½ ounces) unbleached all-purpose flour
> 1 cup (7 ounces) sugar
> ½ teaspoon salt
> ½ teaspoon baking soda
> 1 cup (2 sticks, 8 ounces) cold unsalted butter, lard, or vegetable shortening
>   (6½ ounces)
> 1½ teaspoons vanilla extract
> 2 teaspoons almond extract
> 1 large egg plus 1 egg yolk
> Whole blanched almonds (optional)

● Preheat the oven to 325°F. Lightly grease (or line with parchment) two baking sheets.

● In a medium-sized mixing bowl, whisk together the flour, sugar, salt, and baking soda. Cut the cold butter into cubes, then cut the cubes in to the dry ingredients until the mixture is evenly crumbly. In a separate bowl, combine the vanilla and almond extract with the egg and yolk and stir together.

● Sprinkle the egg mixture over the flour mixture, then stir together until the dough is cohesive when squeezed. Roll the dough into 1½-inch balls, then place them on the prepared baking sheets. Or use a tablespoon cookie scoop (overfill it, to yield a 3½- to 3-inch cookie) to deposit balls of dough onto the sheets. Flatten the balls to about ½-inch thickness. Press an almond in the center of each cookie, if desired.

● Bake the cookies for 16 to 18 minutes, until they feel set (a fingerprint will remain if pressed in the center). If you bake the cookies until they're totally set (your fingerprint will spring back), they'll be crispy to the point of rock-hardness. Remove the cookies from the oven and transfer to a rack to cool completely.

Nutrition information per serving (1 cookie, 35 g): 153 cal, 8 g fat, 2 g protein, 10 g complex carbohydrates, 9 g sugar, 39 mg cholesterol, 75 mg sodium, 23 mg potassium, 79 RE vitamin A, 1 mg iron, 4 mg calcium, 21 mg phosphorus.

Americanized Chinese Restaurant Cookies

Long ago and far away, in a village by the sea, there was a bakery selling a tender, melt-in-your-mouth, golden cookie with edges rolled in chopped nuts, and whose center sported a thick blob of rich, soft chocolate. Called Chinese Cookies, they were the bakery's signature cookie and one of its best-selling treats. The bakery has since disappeared, but this variation on the Chinese Restaurant Cookie lives on. Our thanks to the vanished Camden Home Bakery in Camden, Maine, for the inspiration that produced this recipe.

> 1 recipe Chinese Restaurant Almond Cookies, baked without the whole almond in the center
> CHOCOLATE FROSTING AND TOPPING
> 1¼ cups (7½ ounces) chocolate chips
> 5½ tablespoons (2¾ ounces) unsalted butter
> 2 tablespoons (1⅜ ounces) corn syrup
> 1 teaspoon vanilla extract
> 1 cup (5 ounces) chopped toasted almonds

● **To make the frosting:** In the top of a double boiler or in the microwave, melt the chocolate chips and butter together slowly. Add the corn syrup and vanilla, stirring until well blended.

● **To finish the cookies:** Frost all around the edge of each cookie, making a band of frosting about ½ to ¾ inch wide from the outer edge toward the center. An easy way to do this is to place the chocolate in a shallow dish, so it's about ½- to ¾-inch deep. Place the nuts in another shallow dish. Grasp a cookie in the center (between thumb and forefinger, then roll it through the chocolate, and roll it through the nuts, just as if you were rolling a wheel along the ground. Put a 1-inch dollop of chocolate into the center of each cookie. Allow the chocolate to set before storing the cookies in an airtight container.

Nutrition information per serving (1 cookie, 52 g): 246 cal, 15 g fat, 3 g protein, 11 g complex carbohydrates, 14 g sugar, 1 g dietary fiber, 46 mg cholesterol, 78 mg sodium, 81 mg potassium, 104 RE vitamin A, 1 mg vitamin C, 1 mg iron, 21 mg calcium, 56 mg phosphorus, 5 mg caffeine.

Cinnamon-Raisin Rounds

If you're a raisin "apprecionado," you'll love these moist, cinnamony cookies. The corn syrup makes them chewy, while the vegetable oil makes them crisp. They are soft just out of the oven, then become crisp around the edges and stay chewy in the center as they cool. For crisper cookies, bake them a bit longer. These cookies are particularly good sandwiched with vanilla ice cream.

Yield: 4 dozen cookies ● *Baking temperature:* 375°F ● *Baking time:* 14 minutes

4 cups (21 ounces) raisins
2 cups (8½ ounces) unbleached all-purpose flour
6 tablespoons (¾ stick, 3 ounces) unsalted butter
¾ cup (5¼ ounces) brown sugar
1 large egg
⅓ cup (2⅜ ounces) vegetable oil
¼ cup (2¾ ounces) light corn syrup
1 teaspoon vanilla extract
1½ teaspoons cinnamon
1 teaspoon salt
1 teaspoon baking soda
1 cup (4¼ ounces) unbleached all-purpose flour

● Preheat the oven to 375°F. Lightly grease (or line with parchment) two baking sheets.
● In a food processor or blender, process 1 cup of the raisins with 1 cup of the flour. Set aside.
● In a medium-sized mixing bowl, cream together the butter and brown sugar until smooth, then beat in the egg, oil, corn syrup, vanilla, cinnamon, salt, and baking soda. Don't worry if the mixture appears curdled; it will all straighten out in the end. Stir in the reserved raisin-flour mixture, then the remaining 1 cup flour and 3 cups raisins, mixing until well combined.
● Scoop out 1-inch balls of dough (approximately the size of table tennis balls) and drop them on the prepared baking sheets. Bake the cookies for 13 minutes, or until they're a light golden brown. Remove them from the oven and transfer to a rack to cool.

Nutrition information per serving (*1 small cookie, 28 g*): 102 cal, 3 g fat, 1 g protein, 15 g complex carbohydrates, 4 g sugar, 1 g dietary fiber, 8 mg cholesterol, 78 mg sodium, 122 mg potassium, 16 RE vitamin A, 1 mg vitamin C, 1 mg iron, 11 mg calcium, 21 mg phosphorus.

VARIATIONS

● To make big, palm-sized cookies, scoop out 2-ounce balls of dough (about the size of an overgrown golf ball, 2 inches in diameter) and space them about 2 inches apart on the prepared baking sheets. This will make 16 palm-sized cookies, a good size for a bake sale.
● Toss the raisins with ¼ cup rum or brandy, cover the bowl, and let them rest overnight before using.

Half-Moon Cookies

These jumbo-sized cookies (a.k.a. Black and Whites, Half and Halfs) are soft and cakelike, and would be quite plain save for their faint hint of lemon and the assertive vanilla and chocolate icings on top. Their distinctive taste (and look) seems to be a great attraction to many kids . . . and, truth be told, their parents as well. Informal research tells us these cookies are New York City natives. In fact, we've seen a recipe titled New York Black and White Deli Cookies; and the corner deli is where you'll most likely find them in the Big Apple, as the sweet counterpoint to a pastrami on rye and a half-sour.

Yield: 2 dozen 3½-inch cookies ● *Baking temperature:* 400°F ● *Baking time:* 11 minutes

DOUGH

1 cup (2 sticks, 8 ounces) unsalted butter

⅛ teaspoon lemon oil, or 1 teaspoon grated lemon rind (zest)

1½ teaspoons salt

2 teaspoons vanilla extract

1 tablespoon baking powder

1½ cups (10½ ounces) sugar

3 large eggs

4½ cups (19 ounces) unbleached all-purpose flour

1 cup (8 ounces) milk (regular or low fat, not nonfat)

WHITE ICING

½ cup (3 ounces) white confectionery coating or white chocolate pieces

2 cups (8 ounces) confectioners' sugar

2 tablespoons (1⅜ ounces) light corn syrup

¼ cup (2 ounces) hot water

½ teaspoon vanilla extract

CHOCOLATE ICING

½ cup (3 ounces) semisweet or bittersweet chocolate chips

2 cups (8 ounces) confectioners' sugar

2 tablespoons (1⅜ ounces) light corn syrup

¼ cup (2 ounces) hot water

½ teaspoon vanilla extract

● Preheat the oven to 400°F. Lightly grease (or line with parchment) two baking sheets.

● **To make the dough:** In a large mixing bowl, cream together the butter, lemon, salt, vanilla, and baking powder. Beat in the sugar, then the eggs, one at a time, beating well after each addition. Stir in the flour alternately with the milk, beginning and ending with the flour. Do this gently; there's no need to beat the batter.

● Using a muffin scoop or a ¼-cup measure, drop the dough onto the prepared cookie sheets. With wet fingers, icing spatula, or the greased bottom of a drinking glass, flatten each mound of dough to a circle about 3 inches across. Leave 2 to 2½ inches between each cookie.

- Bake the cookies for about 11 minutes, or until they're a very light golden brown around the edges. Cool them on the sheet for 5 minutes, then transfer to a rack to cool completely.

- **To make the white icing:** In a saucepan set over low heat, or in the microwave, melt the white chocolate or confectionery coating, stirring until smooth. Sift the confectioners' sugar into a large bowl and add the corn syrup, hot water, and vanilla, stirring until smooth. Stir in the melted chocolate. If you're using a mixer, set it on low speed so the icing doesn't become too aerated. If the mixture is too thick to pour, reheat it briefly over low heat and stir in 2 to 4 teaspoons additional hot water.

- Spread half of each cookie with the white icing. The easiest way to do this is to pour some icing across the equator of the cookie, then tilt it so it spreads nicely over one half. Place the cookies on a rack and let them set while you make the chocolate icing.

Pour and spread vanilla icing on half of each cookie. Then pour and spread chocolate icing on the unfrosted halves.

- **To make the chocolate icing:** Using the chocolate icing ingredients, follow the directions above for the white icing.

- Spread the other half of each cookie with the chocolate icing (pouring and tilting as you did with the white icing), and place them on a rack to allow the icing to set fully.

Nutrition information per serving (1 cookie, 100 g): 335 cal, 11 g fat, 4 g protein, 17 g complex carbohydrates, 39 g sugar, 1 g dietary fiber, 38 mg cholesterol, 194 mg sodium, 73 mg potassium, 50 RE vitamin A, 1 mg vitamin C, 1 mg iron, 59 mg calcium, 58 mg phosphorus, 3 mg caffeine.

VARIATION

Baltimore's Finest

- Baltimore has long been famous for its vanilla cakelike cookies spread with a thick layer of rich chocolate icing. Spread un-iced Half-Moon Cookies with the Rich Chocolate Icing (opposite) for your own Baltimore treat.

Rich Chocolate Icing

Yield: 4½ cups, enough to thickly ice 2 dozen cookies

3½ cups (21 ounces) chocolate chips
4 ounces unsweetened baking chocolate
2 tablespoons (1⅜ ounces) light corn syrup
4 tablespoons (½ stick, 2 ounces) unsalted butter
1½ cups (12 ounces) heavy cream

● In a large bowl, combine the chocolate chips, baking chocolate, corn syrup, and butter. In a saucepan heat the cream to boiling and pour it over the chocolate mixture. Stir until the chocolate is melted and the mixture is smooth. Let cool to room temperature, then beat with an electric mixer until the icing lightens in color and thickens slightly.

● Use 3 tablespoons icing per cookie (it will feel as if you're piling it on, which is precisely the point!), spreading it in a thick layer. Leave ¼ inch showing around the outside edge of each cookie.

Nutrition information per serving (1 cookie with Rich Chocolate Icing, 108 g): 432 cal, 25 g fat, 5 g protein, 20 g complex carbohydrates, 27 g sugar, 2 g dietary fiber, 63 mg cholesterol, 216 mg sodium, 177 mg potassium, 128 RE vitamin A, 1 mg vitamin C, 2 mg iron, 70 mg calcium, 109 mg phosphorus, 29 mg caffeine.

Kourabiedes

If your heritage is Greek, you'll recognize *Kourabiedes:* they appear in every household at Christmas. Round, soft, and snowy white, with a faint but unmistakable floral aroma and taste, these cookies keep very well, packed in tins. They make wonderful, interesting gift cookies.

Yield: *3½ dozen cookies* ● ***Baking temperature:*** *350°F* ● ***Baking time:*** *15 minutes*

1 cup (1 stick, 4 ounces) unsalted butter
½ cup (2 ounces) confectioners' sugar
1 large egg yolk
2 teaspoons brandy
¼ teaspoon almond extract
½ teaspoon baking powder
¼ teaspoon baking soda
½ cup (2½ ounces) chopped, toasted almonds, blanched or unblanched
1½ cups (6¼ ounces) unbleached all-purpose flour

1 tablespoon (½ ounce) rose water or orange flower water
¾ cup (3 ounces) confectioners' sugar

● In a medium-sized bowl, cream together the butter, sugar, egg yolk, brandy, almond extract, baking powder, and baking soda. Beat the mixture at medium-high speed for 10 minutes or so, until it's very light colored. Stir in the nuts and flour. Cover the bowl and let the dough rest at room temperature for 1 hour.

● Preheat the oven to 350°F. Lightly grease (or line with parchment) two baking sheets.

● Drop the dough by the teaspoonful onto the prepared baking sheets. Use your hands to flatten the balls very slightly. Bake the cookies for 15 minutes, or until they're set and starting to brown.

● Remove them from the oven and sprinkle them lightly with the rose water; simply dip a fork in the water and flick it over the cookies a few times. You don't want to douse them, just give them a very, very light shower, just enough for them to carry the scent of flowers.

● Place the warm cookies in a bag with some confectioners' sugar, 5 or 6 at a time, and very gently toss them to coat with sugar. Remove them from the bag and transfer them to a rack to cool.

Nutrition information per serving *(1 cookie, 12 g):* 57 cal, 3 g fat, 1 g protein, 3 g complex carbohydrates, 3 g sugar, 11 mg cholesterol, 14 mg sodium, 16 mg potassium, 23 RE vitamin A, 1 mg vitamin C, 8 mg calcium, 15 mg phosphorus.

Butterscotch Sundae Cookies

When you think of pecans and butterscotch, does a butterscotch sundae, topped with golden salted nuts, come to mind? The same wonderful combination of flavors translates to this mildly crunchy, deep gold cookie.

Yield: 31/2 dozen cookies ● *Baking temperature: 375°F* ● *Baking time: 13 minutes*

3 tablespoons (1½ ounces) plus ¾ cup (6 ounces) unsalted butter
2 cups (8 ounces) small pecan halves, or use coarsely chopped larger pecans
¾ teaspoon plus ¼ teaspoon salt
1⅓ cups (10⅞ ounces) dark brown sugar
A few drops butter-rum flavor, to taste
2 large eggs
½ teaspoon baking powder
¼ teaspoon baking soda
2 cups (8½ ounces) unbleached all-purpose flour
1 cup (6 ounces) butterscotch chips

● Preheat the oven to 375°F. Lightly grease (or line with parchment) two baking sheets.
● In a medium-sized skillet, melt the 3 tablespoons butter over low heat, and add the pecans. Stir for a couple of minutes, until the nuts begin to brown and smell toasty.
● Sprinkle with ¾ teaspoon of the the salt, stir to combine, and remove the pan from the burner. Transfer the nuts to a small bowl.
● In a medium-sized mixing bowl, cream together the remaining ¾ cup butter, sugar, and butter-rum flavor, then beat in the eggs. Beat in the remaining ¼ teaspoon salt, baking powder, and baking soda, then stir in the flour, reserved pecans, and chips.
● Drop the dough by the tablespoonful onto the prepared baking sheets. Bake the cookies for 13 minutes, until they're a deep golden brown. Remove them from the oven, and transfer to a rack to cool.

Nutrition information per serving (1 cookie, 30 g): 143 cal, 9 g fat, 1 g protein, 5 g complex carbohydrates, 9 g sugar, 1 g dietary fiber, 21 mg cholesterol, 74 mg sodium, 64 mg potassium, 43 RE vitamin A, 1 mg iron, 13 mg calcium, 32 mg phosphorus.

Crisp or chewy?

The chewy-crisp dynamic, which can change depending on how you store cookies, is always an interesting one. Some cookies are crisp when they come out of the oven. Then, stored airtight while still a bit warm, they become chewy as they cool. Some cookies are chewy right out of the oven, then become crisp as they cool. To keep chewy cookies nice and moist, store them in an airtight container with a sugar softener (see page 38) or a slice of raw apple. To keep crisp cookies crisp, store them in an airtight container; add a cracker crisper (see page 33) in very humid weather.

Mocha Mudslides

These deep dark, soft and chewy chocolate cookies come with a significant hit of coffee flavor, thanks to the espresso powder that pairs with the cocoa to make mocha. They aren't subtle; but then, who wants chocolate and coffee to be subtle? Together they're a marriage made in heaven. And the molten chocolate and cappuccino chips don't hurt, either! Cappuccino chips are available via mail order. You can substitute chocolate chips, if desired.

Yield: 4 dozen cookies ● ***Baking temperature:** 375°F* ● ***Baking time:** 8 to 10 minutes*

¾ cup (5¼ ounces) granulated sugar
¾ cup (6 ounces) brown sugar
3 to 5 teaspoons espresso powder
1 cup (2 sticks, 8 ounces) unsalted butter
1 teaspoon baking soda
½ teaspoon salt
1 teaspoon vanilla extract
2 large eggs
2¼ cups (9½ ounces) unbleached all-purpose flour
⅓ cup (1 ounce) unsweetened natural cocoa powder
1 cup (6 ounces) chocolate chips or cinnamon chips*
1 cup (6 ounces) cappuccino chips

● Preheat the oven to 375°F. Lightly grease (or line with parchment) two baking sheets.
● In a medium-sized bowl, beat together the sugars, espresso powder, butter, baking soda, salt, and vanilla. Add in the eggs one at a time, beating well after each addition, then stir in the flour, cocoa, and chips.
● Drop the dough by the rounded tablespoonful onto the prepared baking sheets. Bake the cookies for 8 to 10 minutes, until the cookies have flattened out and their tops are cracked; they'll still be soft inside. You want these baked all the way through, but just barely; additional baking will make them crisp rather than chewy. Remove the cookies from the oven and transfer to a rack to cool completely.

*The chocolate-cinnamon-coffee flavor combination isn't to everyone's liking, but for those of you who can get your head around it, by all means try the cinnamon chips.

Nutrition information per serving *(1 cookie, 27 g):* 121 cal, 6 g fat, 1 g protein, 5 g complex carbohydrates, 10 g sugar, 19 mg cholesterol, 54 mg sodium, 57 mg potassium, 40 RE vitamin A, 1 mg iron, 8 mg calcium, 23 mg phosphorus, 9 mg caffeine.

Frosted Butter-Rum Drops

If butter-rum candy is your cup of tea, you'll enjoy these mildly spiked butter cookies. We find them particularly apropos at the holidays, when folks seem to embrace rum punch, eggnog, rum cake, and similar "spirited" offerings.

Yield: 4 dozen cookies ● ***Baking temperature:** 375°F* ● ***Baking time:** 9 minutes*

DOUGH
- 1 cup (2 sticks, 8 ounces) unsalted butter
- ½ cup (2 ounces) confectioners' sugar
- ½ teaspoon salt
- ½ teaspoon almond extract
- 2 tablespoons (1 ounce) rum
- 2 teaspoons rum extract or a few drops strong rum flavor
- ¼ cup (1⅝ ounces) almond flour
- 2 cups (8½ ounces) unbleached all-purpose flour

FROSTING
- 2½ tablespoons (1¼ ounces) unsalted butter
- 1½ cups (6 ounces) confectioners' sugar
- 1 teaspoon vanilla extract
- 1¼ teaspoons rum, or ½ teaspoon rum extract or a few drops strong rum flavor
- Pinch of salt
- 2 tablespoons (1 ounce) cream or milk

● Preheat the oven to 375°F. Lightly grease (or line with parchment) two baking sheets.

● **To make the dough:** In a medium-sized bowl, cream together the butter, sugar, salt, almond extract, rum, and rum flavor. Beat in the almond flour, then stir in the all-purpose flour.

● Roll or scoop the dough into chestnut-sized (1-inch) balls and flatten them to ¼ inch thick with the bottom of a lightly greased drinking glass dipped in granulated sugar. Bake the cookies for 9 minutes, until they're golden brown. Remove them from the oven, and cool on a rack.

● **To make the frosting:** In a small bowl, cream together the butter and sugar until smooth. Add the vanilla, rum, salt, and enough cream to make a spreadable frosting. Spread the cooled cookies with the frosting.

Nutrition information per serving *(1 cookie, 18 g):* 81 cal, 5 g fat, 1 g protein, 4 g complex carbohydrates, 5 g sugar, 12 mg cholesterol, 34 mg sodium, 13 mg potassium, 43 RE vitamin A, 1 mg vitamin C, 4 mg calcium, 9 mg phosphorus.

Marathon Cookies

Our thanks to Kiera Salkowski, of Tucson, Arizona, for this recipe, which packs all kinds of tasty ingredients into a chocolate chip cookie–type framework. Kiera, a young mother and marathon runner, was looking for a good-tasting cookie that offered a bit more than just sugar and fat to her diet. She says, "Walnuts for omega-3's, chocolate for the antioxidants, oats for fiber, fruit for, well, fruit's sake. These can be easily customized by using different nuts, different dried fruits, even different kinds of chips."

Yield: 5½ dozen cookies ● *Baking temperature: 350°F* ● *Baking time: 10 to 12 minutes*

2½ cups (8¾ ounces) rolled oats
2 cups (8½ ounces) all-purpose flour
¾ cup (2¾ ounces) protein powder*
1 teaspoon baking soda
1 teaspoon baking powder
½ teaspoon salt
1 cup (2 sticks, 8 ounces) unsalted butter
1 cup (8 ounces) brown sugar
½ cup (3½ ounces) granulated sugar
2 large eggs
¼ cup (2 ounces) milk
1 tablespoon vanilla extract
2 cups (12 ounces) chocolate chips, or the flavored chips of your choice
1½ cups (6 ounces) chopped walnuts, lightly toasted (see page 27)
1 cup (4 ounces) dried cranberries

● Preheat the oven to 350°F. Lightly grease (or line with parchment) two baking sheets.
● Toast the oats on a baking sheet for about 15 minutes, until they smell toasty. Remove from oven and let cool.
● In a medium-sized bowl, whisk together the flour, protein powder, baking soda, baking powder, and salt. Set aside.
● In a large bowl, cream together the butter and sugars. Add the eggs one at a time, beating well after each. Combine the milk and vanilla and add to the butter mixture. It will look curdled, which is okay.
● Add the flour mixture to the butter mixture in two or three additions, stirring to combine. Stir in the oats. Mix in the chocolate chips, walnuts, and cranberries.
● Drop the dough by the tablespoonful onto the prepared baking sheets, leaving about an inch between them. Bake the cookies for 10 to 12 minutes, until they start to brown around the edges. For chewier cookies, bake for 10 minutes; for crunchy cookies, bake for 12 minutes. Remove the cookies from the oven. Let them cool on the sheet for a few minutes, then transfer to a rack to cool completely.

* Available in the health food section of some supermarkets, or at a nutrition or vitamin shop. Choose your favorite flavor; vanilla or cappuccino are our choices.

Nutrition information per serving (1 cookie, 30 g): 126 cal, 6 g fat, 3 g protein, 8 g complex carbohydrates, 8 g sugar, 1 g dietary fiber, 14 mg cholesterol, 48 mg sodium, 110 mg potassium, 40 RE vitamin A, 1 mg vitamin C, 1 mg iron, 20 mg calcium, 56 mg phosphorus, 4 mg caffeine.

Chocolate-Walnut Holiday Cookies

These dense, sturdy cookies are good keepers; in fact, the original recipe calls for them to be made for the holidays and left in a tin to "season" for a week or so. Ground walnuts pair nicely with light chocolate here, taking these out of the realm of the usual deep-dark-decadent chocolate cookie to a subtler (yet pleasing) destination.

Yield: 3 dozen cookies ● *Baking temperature:* 325°F ● *Baking time:* 13 minutes

> 2 cups (8 ounces) walnuts, ground
> ½ cup (1 stick, 4 ounces) unsalted butter
> 1 cup (7 ounces) sugar
> ½ teaspoon baking powder
> Heaping ½ teaspoon salt
> 2 large eggs
> 3 ounces unsweetened baking chocolate
> 2 cups (8½ ounces) unbleached all-purpose flour

● Preheat the oven to 325°F. Lightly grease (or line with parchment) two baking sheets.

● In a food processor process the nuts until they're very finely ground, but haven't turned to paste. (Alternatively, grind in a nut grinder or other grinder.) Set aside.

● In a medium-sized mixing bowl, cream together the butter, sugar, baking powder, and salt until light. Add the eggs one at a time, beating well after each addition. Melt the chocolate (a microwave works fine here), and stir it into the butter/sugar mixture. Stir in the ground nuts and the flour.

● Drop the dough by the tablespoonful onto the prepared baking sheets. Bake the cookies for about 13 minutes, until they appear set. Remove them from the oven and transfer to a rack to cool.

Nutrition information per serving (1 cookie, 20 g): 99 cal, 8 g fat, 2 g protein, 1 g complex carbohydrates, 6 g sugar, 1 g dietary fiber, 19 mg cholesterol, 41 mg sodium, 57 mg potassium, 31 RE vitamin A, 1 mg vitamin C, 11 mg calcium, 46 mg phosphorus, 5 mg caffeine.

Chip 'n' Nut Drops

Peanut butter, oats, two kinds of chocolate—what's not to like? You'll want to bake an extra batch of these wonderful cookies to have on hand in the freezer when guests pop in or your teenagers decide late at night that they have to have some cookies.

Yield: 4½ dozen cookies ● *Baking temperature: 375°F* ● *Baking time: 7 minutes*

1 cup (2 sticks, 8 ounces) unsalted butter
1 cup (7 ounces) granulated sugar
1 cup (8 ounces) light brown sugar
2 large eggs
1 teaspoon vanilla extract
2½ cups (8¾ ounces) rolled oats
2 cups (8½ ounces) unbleached all-purpose flour
1 teaspoon baking powder
1 teaspoon baking soda
1 cup (6 ounces) peanut butter chips
1 cup (6 ounces) chocolate chips
4 ounces white chocolate, grated, or substitute ⅔ cup (4 ounces) white chocolate chips, crushed or coarsely ground
1½ cups (6 ounces) chopped walnuts

● Preheat the oven to 375°F. Lightly grease (or line with parchment) two baking sheets.
● In a large bowl, cream together the butter and sugars. Beat in the eggs and vanilla.
● Using a blender or food processor, process the oats until they're finely ground. Transfer the oats to a medium-sized bowl and stir in the flour, baking powder, and baking soda. Add the dry ingredients to the creamed mixture, stirring until blended. Stir in the chips, white chocolate, and walnuts.
● Drop the dough by the tablespoonful, 2 inches apart, onto the prepared baking sheets. Bake the cookies for 7 minutes, or until they appear set and are just beginning to brown. Remove them from the oven and transfer to a rack to cool.

Nutrition information per serving (1 cookie, 35 g): 160 cal, 8 g fat, 3 g protein, 7 g complex carbohydrates, 12 g sugar, 1 g dietary fiber, 17 mg cholesterol, 46 mg sodium, 86 mg potassium, 37 RE vitamin A, 1 mg vitamin C, 1 mg iron, 23 mg calcium, 59 mg phosphorus, 2 mg caffeine.

Raspberry-Fudge Sandwich Cookies

These soft chocolaty cookies, studded with pockets of melting chocolate chips, can be used to sandwich all manner of fillings, from chocolate ganache or melted white chocolate to peanut butter or jam. We've chosen to use raspberry jam here, but let your imagination be your guide.

Yield: *48 sandwich cookies* ● ***Baking temperature:*** *350°F* ● ***Baking time:*** *11 to 12 minutes*

½ cup (1 stick, 4 ounces) unsalted butter
2 cups (14 ounces) sugar
3 large eggs
¼ teaspoon (heaping) salt
1 teaspoon vanilla extract
1 cup (4¼ ounces) unbleached all-purpose flour
¾ cup (2¼ ounces) Dutch process cocoa powder
¾ teaspoon baking powder
2 cups (12 ounces) bittersweet chocolate chips*
A heaping ½ cup (6 ounces) raspberry jam,** for filling

● Preheat the oven to 350°F. Lightly grease (or line with parchment) two baking sheets.
● In a large bowl, beat together the butter and sugar until well combined. Add the eggs one at a time, beating well after each addition. Beat in the salt and the vanilla.
● In a separate bowl, whisk together the flour, cocoa, and baking powder. Gradually blend this mixture into the butter mixture until smooth. Stir in the chocolate chips.
● Drop the dough by the teaspoonful onto the prepared baking sheets, leaving about 1½ inches between each cookie. Bake the cookies for 11 to 12 minutes; they'll feel soft on top. Remove them from the oven and transfer to a rack to cool.
● When the cookies are completely cool, top half of them with a generous spoonful of raspberry jam, or the filling of your choice. Top with the remaining cookies.

*Choose your own favorite chip flavor. Try cinnamon or cappuccino chips, white chocolate, white mint, cherry or peanut butter—just remember, if you're using a filling too, be sure the chips will complement the filling.
**Just plain peanut butter, or the Vanilla Creme (page 470), Chocolate Creme (page 470), or Peanut Butter Fillings (page 466) are other delightful options.

Nutrition information per serving (*1 sandwich cookie, 46 g):* 178 cal, 7 g fat, 27 g complex carbohydrates, 22 g sugar, 2 g protein, 1 g dietary fiber, 30 mg cholesterol, 42 mg sodium, 165 mg potassium, 40 RE vitamin A, 1 mg iron, 17 mg calcium, 47 mg phosphorus, 14 mg caffeine.

Amish Cookies

While none of the mild flavors in this cookie—a touch of vanilla and spice, a wee bit of oats, a scattering of raisins—is assertive, all three together make a happy marriage. The texture of these cookies is surprising, given their earthy appearance—crunchy on the outside, a bit chewy within, and light, light, *light!*

Yield: 4½ dozen cookies ● *Baking temperature:* 375°F ● *Baking time:* 10 minutes

DOUGH
- ½ cup (1 stick, 4 ounces) unsalted butter
- ½ cup (4 ounces) brown sugar
- ½ cup (3½ ounces) granulated sugar
- ½ teaspoon baking powder
- ½ teaspoon salt
- ½ teaspoon baking soda
- 1½ teaspoons vanilla extract
- ¼ teaspoon cinnamon
- ¼ teaspoon nutmeg
- 1 large egg
- 2 tablespoons (1 ounce) milk (regular or low fat, not nonfat)
- 1 cup (4¼ ounces) unbleached all-purpose flour
- 1 cup (3½ ounces) rolled oats
- ½ cup (3 ounces) raisins

COATING
- ½ cup (4 ounces) light brown sugar
- 1 teaspoon cinnamon

● **To make the dough:** In a large bowl, beat together the butter, sugars, baking powder, salt, baking soda, vanilla, cinnamon, and nutmeg. Beat in the egg and milk, then stir in the flour, oats, and raisins. Chill the dough until it's firm, about 1 hour.

● Preheat the oven to 375°F. Lightly grease (or line with parchment) two baking sheets.

● **To make the coating:** Mix the brown sugar and cinnamon together and place it in a shallow bowl, or in a gallon-size or other large plastic bag.

● Shape the dough into 1-inch (2-teaspoon) balls; a teaspoon cookie scoop works well here. Roll each ball in the cinnamon-sugar. Place the coated balls on the prepared baking sheets. Use the tines of a fork to flatten each cookie to about ⅓ inch thick.

● Bake the cookies for 10 minutes, until they're golden brown. Remove them from the oven and cool on a rack.

Nutrition information per serving (1 cookie, 16 g): 59 cal, 2 g fat, 1 g protein, 4 g complex carbohydrates, 6 g sugar, 9 mg cholesterol, 39 mg sodium, 38 mg potassium, 18 RE vitamin A, 1 mg vitamin C, 10 mg calcium, 17 mg phosphorus.

Chip 'n' Chunk Cookies

These crisp cookies are loaded with flavor: coconut, chocolate, cinnamon, and pecans give them their rich taste. Leave out the coconut if the kids object, but we think young and old alike will find these delicious. Toasted coconut gives the cookies better flavor than plain coconut. See directions on page 27 for toasting coconut.

Yield: 3 dozen cookies ● *Baking temperature: 375°F* ● *Baking time: 12 to 15 minutes*

½ cup (1 stick, 4 ounces) unsalted butter
¾ cup (5¼ ounces) sugar
1 teaspoon baking soda
2 teaspoons vanilla extract
½ teaspoon salt
1 large egg
1¼ cups (5¼ ounces) unbleached all-purpose flour
¾ cup (4½ ounces) cinnamon chips
1 cup (6 ounces) chocolate chunks
1½ cups (6 ounces) chopped pecans or walnuts
½ cup (1½ ounces) toasted coconut

● Preheat the oven to 375°F. For easiest cleanup, line two baking sheets with parchment; there's no need to grease them.
● In a large mixing bowl, cream together the butter, sugar, baking soda, vanilla, and salt until they're light and fluffy. Beat in the egg, then stir in the flour, chips, chocolate, nuts, and coconut.
● Shape the dough into ¾-ounce balls (about the size of a walnut), and place them on the prepared baking sheets, leaving about 2 inches between them. Or drop the dough onto the baking sheets with a tablespoon cookie scoop. Flatten the balls slightly, to about ½ inch thick.
● Bake the cookies for 12 to 15 minutes, until they're a light golden brown. Bake them a bit longer if you like extra-crisp cookies; a bit shorter if you prefer chewier cookies. Remove them from the oven and cool on a rack.

Nutrition information per serving (1 cookie, 30 g): 148 cal, 9 g fat, 2 g protein, 7 g complex carbohydrates, 9 g sugar, 1 g dietary fiber, 13 mg cholesterol, 72 mg sodium, 58 mg potassium, 27 RE vitamin A, 1 mg vitamin C, 1 mg iron, 13 mg calcium, 35 mg phosphorus, 4 mg caffeine.

Midnights

These cookies are for those of you for whom the chocolate, only the chocolate, and nothing but the chocolate will do.

Yield: 6 dozen cookies ● *Baking temperature:* 350°F ● *Baking time:* 9 minutes

1⅔ cups (10 ounces) bittersweet or semisweet chocolate chips or chunks
6 ounces unsweetened chocolate
1 cup (2 sticks, 8 ounces) unsalted butter
1⅔ cups (13⅜ ounces) brown sugar
2 large eggs
1 teaspoon vanilla extract
2 teaspoons espresso powder
¾ cup (3 ounces) unbleached all-purpose flour
¾ cup (2¼ ounces) natural cocoa powder
1¼ teaspoons salt
1¼ teaspoons baking soda
1⅔ cups (10 ounces) semisweet chocolate chips

● In a saucepan set over very low heat, or in the microwave, melt together the first two ingredients, stirring frequently until smooth. Remove the chocolate from the heat before it's entirely melted, which will help prevent burning. Set aside.

● In a large bowl, cream together the butter and brown sugar, then beat in the eggs one at a time, scraping the bowl down and beating well after each addition. Add the vanilla, espresso powder, and reserved melted chocolate, mixing until evenly incorporated. Stir in the flour, cocoa powder, salt, and baking soda. Stir in the other 1⅔ cups chocolate chips. Cover the bowl and refrigerate the dough for 1 hour, or until it's firm.

● Preheat the oven to 350°F. Lightly grease (or line with parchment) two baking sheets.

● Drop the dough by the tablespoonful onto the prepared baking sheets. Bake the cookies for 9 minutes, until they appear set. Remove them from the oven, let rest on the baking sheet for 5 minutes, then transfer to a rack to cool completely.

Nutrition information per serving (1 cookie, 22 g): 105 cal, 6 g fat, 1 g protein, 2 g complex carbohydrates, 9 g sugar, 1 g dietary fiber, 13 mg cholesterol, 64 mg sodium, 82 mg potassium, 27 RE vitamin A, 1 mg iron, 11 mg calcium, 31 mg phosphorus, 14 mg caffeine.

VARIATION

● Substitute white chocolate chips or peanut butter chips for the semisweet chocolate chips added at the end of the recipe.

Orange Blossoms

Soft and cakey, pretty, sunny, happy flavor, golden, nice, bright and clear...delicious! These are all words our taste-testers used to describe these butter-colored cookies topped with their orange-flecked icing. Looking for a change from chocolate? These mild but nicely orangey cookies are just the ticket.

Yield: 27 cookies ● *Baking temperature: 400°F* ● *Baking time: 10 minutes*

DOUGH
- 11 tablespoons (5½ ounces) unsalted butter
- ¾ cup (5¼ ounces) sugar
- 1 large egg
- ½ cup (4 ounces) orange juice
- 2 tablespoons grated orange rind (zest)
- ½ teaspoon baking powder
- ½ teaspoon baking soda
- ½ teaspoon salt
- ⅛ teaspoon *Fiori di Sicilia* (optional)*
- 2 cups (8½ ounces) unbleached all-purpose flour

ICING
- 2 cups (8 ounces) confectioners' sugar
- 2 tablespoons (1 ounce) unsalted butter
- 1 tablespoon grated orange rind (zest)
- 3 tablespoons (1½ ounces) orange juice

● Preheat the oven to 400°F. Lightly grease (or line with parchment) two baking sheets.

● **To make the dough:** In a medium-sized mixing bowl, cream together the butter and sugar until light. Beat in the egg, then the orange juice and zest, baking powder, baking soda, salt, and *Fiori di Sicilia.* Stir in the flour.

● Drop the dough by the tablespoonful onto the prepared baking sheets. Bake the cookies for 10 minutes, until they're just beginning to brown. Remove them from the oven and transfer to a rack to cool.

● **To make the icing:** In a medium-sized bowl, cream together the confectioners' sugar, butter, and orange zest, then stir in the orange juice, adding additional juice, if necessary, to make a spreadable icing. Ice the cooled cookies and place them on the rack until set.

* See page 490.

Nutrition information per serving *(1 cookie, 38 g):* 139 cal, 6 g fat, 1 g protein, 7 g complex carbohydrates, 14 g sugar, 23 mg cholesterol, 75 mg sodium, 27 mg potassium, 56 RE vitamin A, 4 mg vitamin C, 1 mg iron, 9 mg calcium, 16 mg phosphorus.

Self-Frosting Licorice Drops

Attention, black-licorice lovers: one bite into these flat, crisp disks, formed in oh-so-easy drop cookie fashion, and you'll recognize your favorite flavor. During the dough's long resting time (8 hours), some of the egg whites and sugar in the mixture rise to the top surface of the cookies to form a smooth "frosting" that's an added bonus for the taste buds. (Hence the "self-frosting" part!) If you don't have an electric stand mixer, you may want to think twice before making this recipe, due to its extra-long beating time.

Yield: 4½ dozen cookies ● *Baking temperature: 325°F* ● *Baking time: 10 to 12 minutes*

3 large eggs, at room temperature
1 cup plus 2 tablespoons (8 ounces) sugar
1¾ cups (7¼ ounces) unbleached all-purpose flour
½ teaspoon baking powder
½ teaspoon salt
2½ teaspoons aniseed

● In the bowl of an electric stand mixer, beat the eggs at medium-high speed until they're light lemon-colored and thick. Add the sugar very gradually, beating all the while. When all the sugar has been added, continue to beat the mixture for 20 minutes. (Yes, this really is necessary!)

● While the egg mixture is beating, in a medium-sized bowl, sift the flour together with the baking powder and salt. Set aside.

● Reduce the speed of the mixer after 20 minutes and gradually add the dry ingredients. Continue beating for 3 more minutes. Add the aniseed and mix thoroughly.

● Drop the dough by the teaspoonful onto the prepared baking sheets, shaping the dough into rounds with a spoon. Let the cookies stand at room temperature, uncovered, for at least 8 hours.

● Preheat the oven to 325°F. Lightly grease (or line with parchment) two baking sheets.

● Bake the cookies for 10 to 12 minutes, until they're a creamy just-golden color, not brown, on the bottom.

Nutrition information per serving (1 cookie, 8 g): 23 cal, 1 g fat, 1 g protein, 2 g complex carbohydrates, 3 g sugar, 8 mg cholesterol, 19 mg sodium, 7 mg potassium, 4 RE vitamin A, 1 mg vitamin C, 3 mg calcium, 7 mg phosphorus.

Ethereal Coconut-Almond Crisps

"Crisp" doesn't begin to describe the texture of these cookies. Light as air, they look like thick, soft cookies; but one bite will disabuse you of that notion. They shatter (pleasantly) into a million delicious crumbs in your mouth. Since it's the leavening that gives these cookies their nearly indescribable texture, don't make them if you can't lay your hands on baker's ammonia; it's available via mail order.

Yield: 10 dozen cookies ● *Baking temperature:* 350°F ● *Baking time:* 12 minutes

1 cup (2 sticks, 8 ounces) unsalted butter
1 cup (6½ ounces) vegetable shortening
2 cups (14 ounces) sugar
1 teaspoon salt
1½ teaspoons almond extract
1 teaspoon baker's ammonia
1 tablespoon boiling water
3 cups (12¾ ounces) unbleached all-purpose flour
1 cup (3 ounces) flaked coconut (unsweetened preferred)

● Preheat the oven to 350°F. Lightly grease (or line with parchment) two baking sheets.
● In a medium-sized bowl, cream together the butter and shortening. Add the sugar, salt, and almond extract and mix on high speed for 10 minutes. Don't skimp on the mixing time; it's responsible for these cookies' light texture, along with the baker's ammonia.
● Dissolve the baker's ammonia in the boiling water and beat this into the butter mixture. Stir in the flour and coconut, mixing well. Drop the cookies by the teaspoonful (a teaspoon cookie scoop works well) onto the prepared baking sheets.
● Bake the cookies for about 12 minutes. They should be set but not brown. Let the cookies cool on the baking sheet for a few minutes before transferring them to a rack to cool completely.

Nutrition information per serving (1 cookie, 11 g): 53 cal, 3 g fat, 1 g protein, 2 g complex carbohydrates, 3 g sugar, 4 mg cholesterol, 20 mg sodium, 7 mg potassium, 14 RE vitamin A, 1 mg calcium, 4 mg phosphorus.

VARIATION

● For Coconut-Lime Crisps, substitute 1 to 2 tablespoons grated lime rind (zest), or ¼ to ½ teaspoon lime oil for the almond extract.

Lemon Coolers

Why coolers? Because these citrusy, slightly tart cookies are a "cool" alternative to the usual heavy, chocolate, sweet confections that cover the bake sale table. Tender but not exactly crisp, soft but not soggy, these cookies melt in your mouth.

Yield: 2½ dozen cookies ● ***Baking temperature:*** *375°F* ● ***Baking time:*** *10 to 12 minutes*

DOUGH
1 cup (2 sticks, 8 ounces) unsalted butter
½ cup (4 ounces) cream cheese
¼ teaspoon salt
½ teaspoon baking powder
1 teaspoon grated lemon rind (zest)*
¼ teaspoon lemon oil*
½ cup (3½ ounces) granulated sugar
½ cup (2 ounces) confectioners' sugar
2 cups (8½ ounces) unbleached all-purpose flour

COATING
1 cup (4 ounces) confectioners' sugar
¾ cup (5¼ ounces) granulated sugar, superfine preferred
2 tablespoons grated lemon rind (zest), or ¼ teaspoon lemon oil

● **To make the dough:** In a medium-sized mixing bowl, beat together the butter, cream cheese, salt, baking powder, lemon zest, and lemon oil. When the mixture is creamy, add the sugars, a bit at a time, beating until fluffy. Finally, mix in the flour. Cover the bowl and refrigerate the dough for 30 minutes.

● Preheat the oven to 375°F. Lightly grease (or line with parchment) two baking sheets.

● Scoop out about 2 level tablespoons of dough for each cookie (a tablespoon cookie scoop works well here) and roll each piece into a ball. Place the balls on the prepared baking sheets and use the bottom of a drinking glass, dipped in confectioners' sugar, to flatten them to a thickness of about ¼ inch, and 1¾ to 2 inches in diameter.

● Bake the cookies for 10 to 12 minutes, until they're lightly browned on the bottom and edges.

● **To make the coating:** While the cookies are baking, make the coating. Combine the sugars in a food processor or blender and add the lemon zest. Process until well blended.

● Allow the cookies to cool on the sheets for about 5 minutes, then dip their tops into the coating. Place the cookies on a rack and let them cool completely. After they have cooled completely, shake more of the lemon sugar over them or, if that's gone, cover them with confectioners' sugar; you want them to be well covered.

*Or substitute 1½ tablespoons grated lemon zest for the 1 teaspoon lemon zest and ¼ teaspoon lemon oil.

Nutrition information per serving (1 cookie, 32 g): 143 cal, 7 g fat, 1 g protein, 6 g complex carbo-hydrates, 12 g sugar, 21 mg cholesterol, 38 mg sodium, 17 mg potassium, 74 RE vitamin A, 1 mg vitamin C, 1 mg iron, 10 mg calcium, 15 mg phosphorus.

VARIATION

● For Raspberry-Lemon Coolers, add 1 teaspoon raspberry flavor to the cookie dough. If you like raspberry lemonade, you'll love these cookies.

Butterscotch Chews

While the name of these cookies does belie their texture somewhat—they're chewy in the center, but crisp around the edges—their flavor is reminiscent of the rich, thick ("chewy") butterscotch sauce you pour over vanilla ice cream.

Yield: 2½ dozen cookies ● *Baking temperature: 375°F* ● *Baking time: 8 to 10 minutes*

½ cup (1 stick, 4 ounces) unsalted butter
1 cup (8 ounces) brown sugar
2 tablespoons (1⅜ ounces) light corn syrup
Gently heaped ½ teaspoon salt
1 teaspoon vanilla extract
⅛ to ¼ teaspoon strong butter-rum or butterscotch flavor
¼ teaspoon baking soda
½ teaspoon baking powder
1 large egg
1 cup (4 ounces) finely chopped pecans
1¾ cups (7¼ ounces) unbleached all-purpose flour

● Preheat the oven to 375°F. Lightly grease (or line with parchment) two baking sheets.
● In a medium-sized mixing bowl, cream together the butter, sugar, syrup, salt, vanilla, butter-rum flavor, baking soda, and baking powder. Add the egg, then stir in the pecans and flour.
● Drop the dough by the tablespoonful onto the prepared baking sheets. Flatten them to ¼ inch thick. Bake the cookies for 8 to 10 minutes, until they're golden brown. Remove them from the oven and transfer to a rack to cool.

Nutrition information per serving (1 cookie, 25 g): 109 cal, 6 g fat, 1 g protein, 6 g complex carbo-hydrates, 8 g sugar, 15 mg cholesterol, 72 mg sodium, 52 mg potassium, 32 RE vitamin A, 1 mg vitamin C, 1 mg iron, 14 mg calcium, 24 mg phosphorus.

Nut Butter Chippers

These tender, crumbly cookies are packed with nut flavor—particularly if you take the time to make your own nut butter (page 313). Almost a peanut butter cookie, kind of a chocolate chip cookie, these cookies bring the best of both worlds to the table.

Yield: 2½ dozen cookies ● ***Baking temperature:*** *350°F* ● ***Baking time:*** *10 to 12 minutes*

½ cup (3¼ ounces) vegetable shortening
½ cup (1 stick, 4 ounces) unsalted butter
1 cup (9½ ounces) peanut butter, cashew butter, almond butter, or hazelnut butter*
1¼ cups (10 ounces) light brown sugar
2 large eggs
1 teaspoon vanilla extract
¼ teaspoon baking powder
½ teaspoon baking soda
½ teaspoon salt*
3 cups (12¾ ounces) unbleached all-purpose flour
1 cup (6 ounces) chocolate chips
1 cup (4 ounces) chopped nuts of your choice

● Preheat the oven to 350°F. Lightly grease (or line with parchment) two baking sheets.
● In a large bowl, cream together the shortening, butter, nut butter, and sugar, beating until fluffy. Add the eggs one at a time, beating well after each addition. Beat in the vanilla, baking powder, baking soda, and salt, then stir in the flour, chips, and nuts.
● Drop the dough by the tablespoonful onto the prepared baking sheets. Bake the cookies for 10 to 12 minutes, until they're beginning to brown. Remove them from the oven and transfer to a rack to cool.

*If the nut butter you use is salted—or if you make your own from salted nuts—start with ¼ teaspoon salt and adjust to taste.

Nutrition information per serving *(1 cookie, 30 g):* 129 cal, 6 g fat, 2 g protein, 6 g complex carbohydrates, 12 g sugar, 13 mg cholesterol, 37 mg sodium, 66 mg potassium, 21 RE vitamin A, 1 mg iron, 16 mg calcium, 34 mg phosphorus, 4 mg caffeine.

Homemade Nut Butter

If you have a food processor, making your own delicious, fresh nut butter is fast and easy. This recipe will make 2 cups; use 1 cup in the preceding cookie recipe and refrigerate the other cup to spread on your breakfast toast.

Yield: 2 cups

2½ cups (10 to 12½ ounces) nuts—peanuts, blanched whole almonds, cashews, or skinned hazelnuts, preferably unsalted
1 to 1½ teaspoons salt*
⅓ cup (2⅝ ounces) light brown sugar
6 to 8 tablespoons (2⅝ to 3½ ounces) vegetable oil

- Preheat the oven to 350°F.
- Place the nuts in a single layer on an ungreased baking sheet and bake for 10 to 15 minutes, until they become a darker gold and you can begin to smell them. Remove the nuts from the oven and let them cool to lukewarm.
- Turn on your food processor (equipped with the blade). Gradually pour in the nuts alternately with the salt, brown sugar, and oil. When the butter is creamy, turn off the machine and adjust the salt to taste.

*This amount of salt is for unsalted nuts. If you're starting with salted nuts, decrease the amount, salting to taste.

Nutrition information per serving (2 tablespoons, 29 g): 171 cal, 14 g fat, 3 g protein, 6 g complex carbohydrates, 4 g sugar, 1 g dietary fiber, 205 mg sodium, 123 mg potassium, 1 mg iron, 13 mg calcium, 94 mg phosphorus.

Coconut Jumbles

These crisp-at-the-edges, soft-in-the-middle cookies are a yummy snickerdoodle/coconut maca-roon hybrid that prompted immediate requests for the recipe from many of our taste-testers. With their bright red candied cherry centers, they'll add a nice celebratory note to any platter of holiday cookies. And if you're not a fan of candied cherries—top each cookie with a whole salted macadamia nut.

Yield: 6 dozen cookies ● *Baking temperature:* 375°F ● *Baking time:* 9 minutes

¾ cup (1½ sticks, 6 ounces) unsalted butter
¾ cup (5¼ ounces) sugar
2 large eggs
1½ teaspoons vanilla extract
⅛ teaspoon strong coconut flavor (optional)
¾ teaspoon salt
1¾ cups (7¼ ounces) unbleached all-purpose flour
¼ teaspoon baking soda
1½ cups (4½ ounces) sweetened flaked coconut
Approximately 36 candied red cherries (10 ounces), cut in half, or 72 macadamia nuts

● Preheat the oven to 375°F. Lightly grease (or line with parchment) two baking sheets.

● In a medium bowl, cream together the butter, sugar, eggs, vanilla, and coconut flavor until light and fluffy.

● Sift the salt, flour, and baking soda together into a small bowl and gradually beat them into the egg mixture. Stir in the coconut until everything is well combined.

● Drop the dough by the teaspoonful onto the prepared baking sheets; use the bottom of a drinking glass dipped in sugar to press each ball down slightly. Bake the cookies for 9 min-utes, or until they're light golden brown and just firm to the touch.

● As soon as the cookies come out of the oven, plunk half a candied cherry (round side up, of course), or a macadamia nut, into the center of each and press down gently. Cool the cook-ies completely on a wire rack.

Nutrition information per serving (1 cookie, topped with half a cherry, 13 g): 54 cal, 2 g fat, 1 g protein, 4 g complex carbohydrates, 4 g sugar, 10 mg cholesterol, 31 mg sodium, 15 mg potassium, 19 RE vitamin A, 2 mg calcium, 7 mg phosphorus.

Spiked Coffee Cookies

Do you like to finish your meal with a shot of coffee liqueur in a cup of cappuccino? This cookie translates that experience from beverage to dessert, as it combines both coffee liqueur and espresso powder in a dark, almost black, chocolate cookie. Soft and tender, spread with a glossy coating of liqueur-spiked chocolate glaze, these cookies go beyond rich to decadent.

Yield: 3 dozen cookies ● *Baking temperature: 350°F* ● *Baking time: 12 minutes*

DOUGH
- ¾ cup (1½ sticks, 6 ounces) unsalted butter
- 1 cup (8 ounces) brown sugar
- ¼ cup (2 ounces) coffee liqueur (such as Kahlúa)
- 1 large egg
- 2 teaspoons baking soda
- ½ teaspoon salt
- 1 teaspoon espresso powder
- ½ cup (1½ ounces) Dutch process cocoa powder
- 1¾ cups (7¼ ounces) unbleached all-purpose flour

GLAZE
- 1 cup (6 ounces) chocolate chips
- 6 tablespoons (3 ounces) heavy cream
- 1 tablespoon (¾ ounce) coffee liqueur

● Preheat the oven to 350°F. Lightly grease (or line with parchment) two baking sheets.

● **To make the dough:** In a large mixing bowl, cream together the butter and brown sugar. Add the liqueur, egg, baking soda, salt, and espresso powder, beating until smooth. Beat in the cocoa and flour.

● Drop the dough by the tablespoonful onto the prepared baking sheets. Bake the cookies for 12 minutes, until they appear set and you can begin to smell the chocolate. Remove them from the oven and transfer to a rack to cool.

● **To make the glaze:** In a microwave-safe measuring cup or bowl, or in a saucepan set over very low heat, heat the chocolate chips and cream, stirring until the chocolate melts. Continue stirring until you've made a smooth glaze, then stir in the liqueur. Spread the tops of the cooled cookies with the glaze.

Nutrition information per serving (1 cookie, 30 g): 126 cal, 6 g fat, 1 g protein, 6 g complex carbohydrates, 9 g sugar, 1 g dietary fiber, 19 mg cholesterol, 106 mg sodium, 70 mg potassium, 48 RE vitamin A, 1 mg vitamin C, 1 mg iron, 12 mg calcium, 26 mg phosphorus, 8 mg caffeine.

VARIATION

● Forgo the glaze and sandwich the cookies around a scoop of softened coffee ice cream. Press just enough to spread the ice cream evenly to the edges of the cookies, wrap in plastic wrap, and freeze until ready to serve.

South Seas Cookies

Samoa cookies, those wonderful, chewy, chocolate-coconut-caramel cookies the Girl Scouts sell every year, seem to evaporate from the cupboard nearly as soon as you've written your check and waved goodbye to the Scout. So, for those times of the year when that Polynesian-named confection is hard to come by, we offer this close relation.

Yield: 32 cookies ● *Baking temperature: 300°F* ● *Baking time: 25 minutes*

DOUGH

4¼ cups (12¾ ounces) sweetened shredded coconut
1 can (14 ounces) sweetened condensed milk
½ teaspoon vanilla extract
3 large egg whites, at room temperature
1 teaspoon lemon juice
¼ teaspoon salt

TOPPINGS

1⅔ cups (10 ounces) semisweet or milk chocolate chips
⅓ cup (3 ounces) caramel (about 10 individual caramels)
2 tablespoons (1 ounce) milk or heavy cream

● Preheat the oven to 300°F. Lightly grease (or line with parchment) two baking sheets.
● **To make the dough:** In a large bowl, combine the coconut, sweetened condensed milk, and vanilla. In a separate bowl, combine the egg whites, lemon juice, and salt and beat at medium speed until medium to stiff peaks form. Fold half of the beaten egg whites into the coconut mixture, then add the remainder.
● Drop the batter by the tablespoonful (a cookie scoop works well here) onto the prepared baking sheets. Bake the cookies for 25 minutes, until they're golden brown. Remove them from the oven and transfer to a rack to cool.
● **To make the toppings:** Melt the chocolate chips in a saucepan set over very low heat, or in the microwave, stirring frequently. When the cookies are completely cool, dip the bottoms into the chocolate and set them on the rack upside down to let the chocolate set up. Keep any leftover chocolate warm.
● In a saucepan set over low heat, or in the microwave, melt the caramel with the milk or cream. Drizzle stripes of caramel over the tops of the cookies. Repeat the stripes with any of the leftover chocolate.

Nutrition information per serving (1 cookie, 45 g): 177 cal, 9 g fat, 3 g protein, 5 g complex carbohydrates, 17 g sugar, 1 g dietary fiber, 9 mg cholesterol, 82 mg sodium, 149 mg potassium, 14 RE vitamin A, 1 mg vitamin C, 74 mg calcium, 82 mg phosphorus, 3 mg caffeine.

Chewy Granola Cookies

Granola bars come in two varieties: crisp and chewy. These moist, "bendy" cookies are a dead ringer for the chewy variety. Have a favorite breakfast granola? Now it can easily go wherever you go, whether you're hiking, picnicking, or simply brown-bagging it at work. If you choose a rather plain granola, one without fruit, feel free to add up to 1 cup of dried fruit, such as raisins, dried cranberries, chopped apricots, etc.

Yield: 3 dozen cookies ● *Baking temperature:* 350°F ● *Baking time:* 12 minutes

6 tablespoons (¾ stick, 3 ounces) unsalted butter
1 tablespoon (½ ounce) vegetable oil
1 cup (8 ounces) brown sugar
½ teaspoon baking soda
½ teaspoon salt
¾ teaspoon cinnamon
¼ teaspoon nutmeg
2 teaspoons vanilla extract
2 large eggs
¼ cup (2 ounces) yogurt, plain or vanilla, regular, low fat, or nonfat
1 cup plus 2 tablespoons (4¾ ounces) unbleached all-purpose flour
2¼ cups (9¼ ounces) granola

● Preheat the oven to 350°F. Lightly grease (or line with parchment) two baking sheets.
● In a large bowl, cream together the butter, oil, brown sugar, baking soda, salt, cinnamon, nutmeg, and vanilla. Add the eggs one at a time, beating well after each addition. Beat in the yogurt. Stir in the flour, then the granola.
● Drop the dough by the tablespoonful onto the prepared baking sheets. Bake the cookies for 12 minutes. They'll still be light tan; don't let them brown or they'll be crisp instead of chewy. Remove them from the oven, let cool on the baking sheet for 5 minutes, then carefully transfer them to a rack; they'll be delicate when warm, then chewy as they cool.

Nutrition information per serving (1 cookie, 25 g): 98 cal, 5 g fat, 2 g protein, 7 g complex carbohydrates, 7 g sugar, 1 g dietary fiber, 17 mg cholesterol, 55 mg sodium, 71 mg potassium, 23 RE vitamin A, 1 mg vitamin C, 1 mg iron, 15 mg calcium, 42 mg phosphorus.

Awesome Chocolate Chunks

This fat, palm-sized, deep-chocolate cookie harbors all kinds of delicious, rich and fattening things: chocolate chips, white chocolate chips, nuts . . . In fact, there's barely enough cookie to hold everything that's in it! This is an impressive cookie for those who couldn't care less about calories or fat, but simply love chocolate cookies.

You may substitute or add most any kind of nut or chip; the options we've given here should be taken as suggestions. The recipe will hold up to about 4 to 5 cups of "additions," so use a generous hand and a free imagination.

Yield: 2 dozen cookies ● *Baking temperature:* 350°F ● *Baking time:* 18 minutes

¾ cup (1½ sticks, 6 ounces) unsalted butter
2 cups (14 ounces) sugar
3 large eggs
1 tablespoon vanilla extract
2 teaspoons espresso powder
1 cup (4¼ ounces) unbleached all-purpose flour
½ teaspoon salt
1 cup (3 ounces) Dutch process cocoa powder
1 cup (6 ounces) chocolate chips
1 cup (6 ounces) white chocolate chips
1 cup (4 ounces) chopped hazelnuts, toasted*
1 cup (4 ounces) chopped pecans, toasted*

● In a large bowl, cream together the butter and sugar. Add the eggs and beat until light, thick, and lemon-colored. Beat in the vanilla and espresso powder.
● Add the flour, salt, and cocoa, stirring to combine. Mix in the chips and nuts. Refrigerate the dough for 1 hour, or until it becomes firm.
● Preheat the oven to 350°F. Lightly grease (or line with parchment) two baking sheets.
● Use a muffin scoop or ¼-cup measure to drop dough onto the prepared baking sheets. Bake the cookies for about 18 minutes, until they appear set and start to smell done. Remove the pans from the oven and transfer the cookies to a rack to cool completely.

*We've also used walnuts, cashews, and even macadamia nuts. Or substitute dried cherries or dried cranberries for some of the nuts or chips.

Nutrition information per serving (1 cookie, 63 g): 300 cal, 18 g fat, 4 g protein, 7 g complex carbohydrates, 24 g sugar, 2 g dietary fiber, 43 mg cholesterol, 63 mg sodium, 162 mg potassium, 69 RE vitamin A, 1 mg vitamin C, 1 mg iron, 38 mg calcium, 83 mg phosphorus, 17 mg caffeine.

Almond Joyfuls

Almond, coconut, and chocolate: does this sound familiar? If you like the candy bar, you'll love these cookies. Soft and tender, glazed with chocolate and topped with toasted almonds . . . it just doesn't get any better than this!

Yield: 39 cookies ● *Baking temperature: 350°F* ● *Baking time: 14 minutes*

DOUGH

1 cup (2 sticks, 8 ounces) unsalted butter, at room temperature

⅔ cup (4¾ ounces) sugar

½ teaspoon salt

1 teaspoon almond extract

1 teaspoon coconut extract, or ¼ teaspoon strong coconut flavor

¼ cup (2¼ ounces) almond paste

1 large egg

1 cup (3 ounces) shredded sweetened coconut

2⅓ cups (10 ounces) unbleached all-purpose flour

ICING

1 cup (6 ounces) chocolate chips

2 tablespoon (1⅜ ounces) corn syrup

2 tablespoons (1 ounce) unsalted butter

TOPPING

1 cup (5 ounces) blanched almonds, chopped and toasted (see page 27)

● Preheat the oven to 350°F. Lightly grease (or line with parchment) two baking sheets.

● **To make the dough:** In a medium-sized mixing bowl, cream together the butter, sugar, salt, almond extract, coconut extract or flavor, and almond paste. Add the egg, beating until fairly smooth, then stir in the coconut. Stir in the flour.

● Drop the dough by the tablespoonful onto the prepared baking sheets. Use your fingers to gently flatten each cookie to about 2 inches in diameter.

● Bake the cookies for 14 minutes, until their edges are a light golden brown. Remove them from the oven and transfer to a rack to cool.

● **To make the icing:** In a small saucepan set over low heat, or in the microwave, melt together the chocolate chips, corn syrup, and butter, stirring until smooth. Dip the top of each cooled cookie in the icing, then transfer them to a rack. Sprinkle each cookie with almonds.

Nutrition information per serving (1 cookie, 32 g): 153 cal, 10 g fat, 2 g protein, 7 g complex carbohydrates, 8 g sugar, 1 g dietary fiber, 20 mg cholesterol, 37 mg sodium, 71 mg potassium, 52 RE vitamin A, 1 mg vitamin C, 1 mg iron, 17 mg calcium, 44 mg phosphorus, 3 mg caffeine.

Chocolate Wakeups

As in, wake up those taste buds! These cookies are a revelation to everyone who tastes them. Ah, chocolate cookies! A bite, another bite, then the eyes widen, the hand to fan the mouth—"What's *in* these?!" It's cayenne pepper, and though it may seem a strange bedfellow with chocolate, the combination of the two, along with the cinnamon, produces an addictive little cookie—to those who like their food hot. Thin, crisp, not too sweet, these are chocolate wafer cookies with an attitude.

Yield: 5 dozen cookies ● *Baking temperature:* 375°F ● *Baking time:* 10 to 11 minutes

½ cup (1 stick, 4 ounces) unsalted butter
1 cup (7 ounces) sugar
½ teaspoon vanilla extract
Pinch* of black pepper
Pinch of cayenne pepper
¾ teaspoon cinnamon
½ teaspoon salt
1 large egg
¾ cup (2¼ ounces) natural cocoa powder
1½ cups (6¼ ounces) unbleached all-purpose flour
Pearl sugar (optional)

● Preheat the oven to 375°F. Lightly grease (or line with parchment) two baking sheets.
● In a large bowl, cream together the butter, sugar, vanilla, peppers, cinnamon, and salt. Beat in the egg. Add the cocoa, then the flour. Stir to combine well; the dough will be very stiff.
● Drop the dough by the teaspoonful onto the prepared baking sheets. Lightly flatten the cookies to ¼ inch thick with the bottom of a drinking glass dipped in sugar. If desired, press some pearl or coarse sugar onto the top of each cookie.
● Bake the cookies for 10 to 11 minutes. They won't look brown and they won't feel done, but that's the correct time and temperature. Remove the cookies from the oven, transfer them to a rack, and let them cool.

*Using your thumb and forefinger, "pinch" up some of the spice. The bigger the pinch, the hotter the cookies. These were made with a moderate pinch, probably about 1/16 teaspoon.

Nutrition information per serving (1 cookie, 10 g): 42 cal, 2 g fat, 1 g protein, 3 g complex carbohydrates, 3 g sugar, 8 mg cholesterol, 20 mg sodium, 24 mg potassium, 16 RE vitamin A, 1 mg vitamin C, 3 mg calcium, 13 mg phosphorus, 3 mg caffeine.

VARIATION

● For a softer cookie with a different look—much like a chocolate Wedding Cookie (page 287)—drop the dough by the tablespoonful onto the prepared baking sheets. Bake the cookies for 10 minutes, and when you take them out of the oven, place them in a bag with confectioners' sugar and shake gently to coat.

Citrus Sizzlers

Like the Chocolate Wakeups (opposite), these innocuous gems can be a source of great surprise to the unsuspecting cookie eater. They look like little lemon tea cookies—only they're not. Cayenne pepper, in whatever amount you choose, can brand these cookies anything from a bit spicy to inedible, except for true devotees of ultrahot food.

When we first made these cookies, we used 1 teaspoon of pepper. On first bite they're okay; pretty spicy, but okay. However, the second bite produces a growing sensation in the back of the throat that soon becomes identifiable as heat, and the third bite definitely separates the men from the boys.

Yield: 5 dozen cookies ● *Baking temperature:* 400°F ● *Baking time:* 10 minutes

1 cup (2 sticks, 8 ounces) unsalted butter
½ cup (3½ ounces) sugar
2 tablespoons (1 ounce) lemon juice or Key lime juice
2 tablespoons grated lemon rind (zest), or ½ teaspoon lemon oil or lime oil
1 large egg
2¼ cups (9½ ounces) unbleached all-purpose flour
¼ to 1½ teaspoons cayenne pepper*
¾ teaspoon salt
¼ teaspoon baking soda

● Preheat the oven to 400°F. Lightly grease (or line with parchment) two baking sheets.
● In a medium-sized bowl, cream together the butter and sugar. Beat in the juice, zest, and egg, then stir in the flour, pepper, salt, and baking soda.
● Drop it by the teaspoonful onto the prepared baking sheets. Flatten each ball of dough slightly, using the bottom of a drinking glass dipped in sugar.
● Bake the cookies for 10 minutes, or until they're light brown around the edges. Remove them from the oven and transfer to a rack to cool.

*¼ teaspoon is mildly hot; ½ teaspoon is moderately hot; 1 teaspoon is *hot!* And 1½ teaspoons is unbearable to all but the stouthearted.

Nutrition information per serving (1 cookie, 12 g): 50 cal, 3 g fat, 1 g protein, 3 g complex carbohydrates, 2 g sugar, 12 mg cholesterol, 33 mg sodium, 9 mg potassium, 31 RE vitamin A, 1 mg vitamin C, 2 mg calcium, 6 mg phosphorus.

Roll-Out Cookies

While drop cookies are by far the most frequently made cookies in America today, it wasn't long ago that roll-out cookies were equally popular. Back when women spent half their day in the kitchen, the drawn-out (though not difficult) process of making roll-out cookies was easily incorporated into the daily routine. Cookie dough was made in the late afternoon, chilled overnight, and rolled out and baked the next morning, once the breakfast dishes were cleared away. By the time the kids came home from school, a plate of gingerbread boys, chocolate sandwiches, or sugar stars was on the table, ready to enjoy with a glass of cold milk.

But these days, speed is by far the most desirable recipe attribute for many home cooks and bakers, so roll-out cookies have become a rainy day project, something to do with the children when you've got a whole day to mix and chill dough, roll it out, bake it, and decorate the cookies. While this "big project" baking is possible occasionally, few of us can make a regular habit of it; it's an activity whose pace was determined in a different, less frenetic era. But roll-out cookies don't have to take all day; if you plan ahead, as you do with yeast-bread baking, they're actually quick and easy.

Just before bed, when the kitchen is quiet, take 15 minutes to whip up a batch of cookie dough; wrap it up and stick it in the fridge overnight. The next day (or the day after, or the day after that), when you find yourself with an hour or so, take the dough out of the fridge, roll it out, cut it (circles are fine; every cutout cookie doesn't have to be a Christmas tree or Halloween pumpkin) and bake. In less than an hour, you'll have lovely, crisp-tender cookies on the cooling rack. Serve them just as they are, sandwich them around creamy filling or ice cream, add a glaze, layer them with pudding and fruit to make a cookie trifle . . . roll-out cookies are the building blocks of the cookie world.

So, while the picture in your head may be of a beaming grandma rolling out cookies on an old wooden table, it doesn't take much imagination to update that picture and put yourself in it. As busy as you are, there's a place in your life for roll-out cookies. Remember, there's more to life than chocolate chips.

Smooth rolling

When you're rolling out cookie dough, don't roll back and forth across the dough; instead, roll from the center toward the outer edge, giving the dough a quarter-turn every few strokes. If you roll the dough in two different directions, the gluten strands in the flour try to stretch two ways at once, and the dough won't roll easily.

Butterscotch Thins

These ultrathin, chewy-crisp butterscotch rounds remind us of the slice-and-bake butterscotch cookies Mom might have made fifty years ago. If you want over-the-top butterscotch flavor, substitute a few drops of strong butterscotch or butter-rum flavor for the vanilla extract. Our thanks to Virginia Matz of Sidney, Ohio, whose old family recipe inspired this one.

Yield: About 5½ dozen cookies ● *Baking temperature: 375°F* ● *Baking time: 6 to 8 minutes*

> 1 cup (6 ounces) butterscotch chips
> ½ cup (1 stick, 4 ounces) unsalted butter
> ⅔ cup (5¼ ounces) brown sugar
> ¼ teaspoon salt
> 1 large egg
> ¾ teaspoon vanilla extract, or a few drops butterscotch or butter-rum flavor
> 1⅓ cups (5¾ ounces) unbleached all-purpose flour
> ¾ teaspoon baking soda
> ½ cup (2 ounces) finely chopped pecans

● In a small saucepan set over low heat, or in the microwave, melt together the chips and butter, stirring until smooth. Remove from the heat and let cool for a couple of minutes. Transfer the mixture to a medium-sized mixing bowl, then beat in the brown sugar, salt, egg, and vanilla. Stir in the flour and baking soda, then the pecans. Flatten the dough into a thick round, wrap it in a plastic wrap or bag (see illustration), and refrigerate overnight.

● Preheat the oven to 375°F. Line two baking sheets with parchment (optional, to save cleanup time; there's no need to grease the sheets). Position the racks in the middle of the oven.

● Remove the dough from the refrigerator, and let it rest at room temperature for 5 to 10 minutes. Then lightly dust both sides of the chilled dough with flour. When you pinch a piece of dough, it should feel pliable, not break off in a chunk. Trying to roll ice-cold dough is like trying to flatten an ice-cold stick of butter; it's more likely to crack and break into pieces than to roll flat and smooth.

● Transfer the dough to a lightly floured, clean work surface. Starting in the middle, and rolling out toward the edges, roll the dough into a ⅛- to ¼-inch-thick circle. Thinner cookies will be crisper; thicker cookies will be sturdier (and appropriate for sandwiching around a scoop of ice cream). Using a round cutter with a diameter of about 2¼ inches, cut out the cookies.

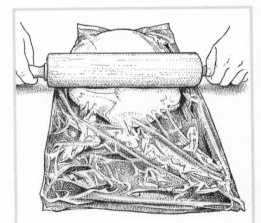

Flattening the dough in a plastic bag allows it to chill more quickly in the refrigerator. When you're ready to roll, it's already partly flattened, and will become pliable quickly and evenly.

- Using a metal turner, transfer the cut cookies to the prepared baking sheets. Here's how: Edge the turner under the cookie, lift slightly, pull away the scraps around the edge, then give your hand a gentle jerk to slip the cookie onto the baking sheet; this is the same motion you'd use for sliding a pancake onto a plate or a hamburger onto a bun.

- Bake the cookies for 6 to 8 minutes (depending on how thin you've managed to roll the dough; if it's a bit thicker than ⅛ inch, bake for the longer amount of time), until they're a very light brown around the edges. Halfway through the baking time, exchange the pans on the racks (top to bottom, bottom to top) and turn each pan around so the cookies that were at the back of the oven are now at the front. This will help counteract any hot spots you may have in your oven.

- Remove them from the oven and let cool for 5 minutes on the baking sheet before transferring them to a rack to cool completely. Use a metal turner to pick up one cookie; if it seems fragile or breaks, let the cookies continue to cool until you can handle them easily. When the cookies are completely cool, store them at room temperature in an airtight container or a plastic bag.

Nutrition information per serving (1 cookie, 11 g): 50 cal, 3 g fat, 1 g protein, 2 g complex carbohydrates, 4 g sugar, 7 mg cholesterol, 27 mg sodium, 21 mg potassium, 15 RE vitamin A, 1 mg vitamin C, 3 mg calcium, 9 mg phosphorus.

Chilling cookie dough

Why do some cookie doughs need to be chilled before you roll them out, and others can be rolled right from the mixing bowl? Usually, cookie dough that's high in fat (and will thus result in a very crisp or very tender cookie, rather than one that's hard or firm) will need to be refrigerated before rolling. This gives a chance for the solid fat in the recipe (butter or shortening), which has been heated and softened by the mixing process, to firm up. Dough in which the fat has softened tends to be quite sticky, making it difficult to roll. Well, just throw more flour onto the rolling surface, right? Wrong. Flour on the work surface will be absorbed by the cookie dough, and change the proportion of fat to flour. This causes the cookie to lose its crisp or tender texture. So chill sticky doughs before rolling; and if you've divided the dough in half, roll half and allow the other half to remain in the refrigerator, chilling out, until the first half is safely rolled and cut.

Chocolate Snaps

Although you can buy chocolate wafer cookies at the grocery store, here's a version you can make yourself that has more flavor, and more body when they're frosted, filled, or become part of a "cake." These not-too-sweet, dark chocolate cookies make wonderful building blocks for all sorts of cookie creations, as you'll soon see.

Yield: 8 to 9 dozen cookies ● *Baking temperature:* 325°F ● *Baking time:* 17 to 18 minutes

> 1½ cups (6¼ ounces) unbleached all-purpose flour
> ¾ cup (2¼ ounces) Dutch-process cocoa powder*
> ½ teaspoon salt
> ½ teaspoon baking powder
> ¾ cup (1½ sticks, 6 ounces) unsalted butter
> 1 cup plus 2 tablespoons (8 ounces) sugar
> 1 large egg
> 1 tablespoon water
> 1 teaspoon vanilla extract

● In a medium-sized mixing bowl, whisk together the flour, cocoa, salt, and baking powder, whisking until no lumps remain. In a separate, larger bowl, beat the butter until light. Add the sugar and continue beating until it's well incorporated. Then add the egg, water, and vanilla and beat for at least 2 minutes, until the mixture has lightened both in color and texture. Gently mix in the dry ingredients.

● Shape the dough into a flattened disk. Wrap in plastic wrap and refrigerate for 3 to 4 hours, or overnight. This dough is very soft, so it's imperative that it's been chilled before you roll it out.

● Preheat the oven to 325°F. Lightly grease (or line with parchment) two or three baking sheets.

● On a clean, heavily floured work surface, roll the dough to a ⅛-inch thickness, and use a round cutter to cut it into 2¼-inch circles. Place the cookies on the prepared baking sheets. They won't expand a great deal, so you don't need a lot of space between them.

● Bake the cookies for 17 to 18 minutes. (Watch them carefully; it's difficult to tell when they're done, as they're so dark you can't see if they're brown, but when you start to smell them they're probably done. If you smell even a whiff of scorching, remove them from the oven immediately.) Transfer the cookies to a rack and cool them completely.

*You may use regular cocoa, but Dutch-process will give you a darker, more chocolaty cookie.

Nutrition information per serving (1 cookie, 7 g): 30 cal, 1 g fat, 1 g protein, 2 g complex carbohydrates, 2 g sugar, 6 mg cholesterol, 14 mg sodium, 14 mg potassium, 14 RE vitamin A, 3 mg calcium, 8 mg phosphorus, 2 mg caffeine.

Can the can!

Do you cut out cookie dough with a recycled can? If so, here are two reasons to ditch the can. First, it's probably not sharp enough to cut cleanly through the dough. Even it you're cutting a very thin dough, it will crush the edges, which will prevent the cookies from rising and becoming light and crisp as they bake. And second—with all the gorgeous shaped cookie cutters out there, who can resist cutting out stars, hearts, or flowers (or a flock of Thanksgiving turkeys, for that matter), in addition to that plain, round circle?

Faux-Reos

"Better than store-bought"—that's what baking at home is all about, right? Though you'll never duplicate exactly the look of an Oreo—Nabisco has it all over us in that respect—this version comes as close as we were able to matching the taste and texture of those wonderful cookies in your home kitchen.

Yield: about 50 sandwich cookies

1 batch Chocolate Snaps (page 327)
1 batch Vanilla Creme Filling (page 470)

● Spread half the cookies with filling, using about 1½ teaspoons for regular faux-reos, more for "double-stuffed." (You'll have some filling left over if you fill the cookies moderately.) Top with the remaining cookies, pressing down gently.

Nutrition information per serving (1 cookie, 19 g): 83 cal, 3 g fat, 2 g protein, 2 g complex carbohydrates, 10 g sugar, 6 mg cholesterol, 15 mg sodium, 15 mg potassium, 14 RE vitamin A, 4 mg vitamin C, 5 mg calcium, 9 mg phosphorus, 2 mg caffeine.

VARIATION

● For a chocolate-stuffed Faux-Reos, fill these cookies with Chocolate Creme Filling (page 470), in place of the vanilla filling.

Mint Dips

Chocolate and mint are a classic flavor combination, appearing in candy, pie, cake, and cookies. This is our version of everyone's favorite Girl Scout cookie.

Yield: *8 to 9 dozen cookies*

1 batch Chocolate Snaps (page 327)

GLAZE

1 cup (8 ounces) heavy cream

1⅓ cups (8 ounces) chopped semisweet or bittersweet chocolate

3 tablespoons (1¼ ounces) vegetable shortening

1½ teaspoons peppermint extract, or a few drops peppermint oil, to taste

- **To make the glaze:** In a small saucepan or microwave-safe bowl, heat the cream to a simmer. Pour it over the chocolate and shortening and stir until smooth. Add the peppermint extract to taste. The glaze will be quite thin.
- **To finish cookies:** Using a pair of tongs or your fingers, dip the cookies in the glaze. Grasp each cookie by an edge and dip it completely into the chocolate, shaking off any excess. Set the cookies on a cooling rack with parchment underneath, to catch any drips.

Nutrition information per serving (1 cookie, 12 g): 52 cal, 3 g fat, 1 g protein, 2 g complex carbohydrates, 3 g sugar, 9 mg cholesterol, 15 mg sodium, 22 mg potassium, 23 RE vitamin A, 1 mg vitamin C, 5 mg calcium, 12 mg phosphorus, 3 mg caffeine.

Ultrapasteurized?

You may have noticed that most of the heavy cream at the supermarket is labeled "ultrapasteurized;" typically, only locally produced cream, the kind you might find in glass bottles right at the dairy, isn't ultrapasteurized. What does this term mean? Ultrapasteurized cream has been heated higher than cream that's simply "pasteurized." This denatures enzymes that can cause cream to sour (and develop flavor), so it increases the cream's shelf life (the American dream, ultimate shelf life). The downside is that because the cream can't develop flavor, it doesn't have much, and it doesn't whip easily. If you find pasteurized cream from a local dairy that hasn't had this treatment, the resulting whipped cream will be significantly "richer." If you can't, ultrapasteurized cream will ultimately whip and work as the binder, but your imagination will have to augment the flavor.

Chocolate Refrigerator Cake

Although this recipe dates back to the 1950s, no matter how often you pull it out, dust it off, and re-create it, it hits a chocolate button that always resonates. It's a "recipe" that's a cinch for kids to make; it can take any shape, so let them use their imaginations. This cake will stand on its own, so you can use a baking sheet as a base for the letters, numbers, or fanciful freeform designs you and your children create.

Yield: 24 servings

1 batch Chocolate Snaps (page 327)
1 pint (16 ounces) heavy cream or whipping cream
¼ cup (1 ounce) confectioners' sugar, or 3 tablespoons (1¼ ounces) granulated sugar, superfine preferred
2 teaspoons vanilla extract

- **To whip the cream:** Choose a mixing bowl with sides that are as vertical as possible. (This keeps most of the cream in the bowl while you're beating it.) Beat the cream until fairly stiff, then fold in the sugar and vanilla.
- **To assemble the cake:** Generously spread one cookie with whipped cream. Stack another on top of it, spread with whipped cream, add another cookie, and continue stacking and spreading until you have a stack of five or six cookies, however many you think you can handle at once. Place the stack on a long serving plate, so the cookies are resting on edge. Continue with the remaining cookies, making one long cake, or making a shorter, wider cake by placing two equal rows of whipped cream–filled cookies side by side. Frost the entire "cake" with the remaining whipped cream.

● After you've finished creating the cake, cover it with plastic wrap and refrigerate it for several hours, or overnight. As the cake rests, the cookies will soften in the cream so that eventually the whole conglomeration becomes a cohesive "cake" composed of wonderful thin layers of chocolate and cream. To serve, sprinkle the top with a few shaved chocolate curls, or even a little cocoa. Cut the cake at about a 45-degree angle, rather than straight up and down; this way the layers of cookies and cream will show.

Nutrition information per serving (*4 cookies with whipped cream, 48 g):* 184 cal, 12 g fat, 4 g protein, 8 g complex carbohydrates, 12 g sugar, 48 mg cholesterol, 64 mg sodium, 68 mg potassium, 128 RE vitamin A, 4 mg vitamin C, 24 mg calcium, 44 mg phosphorus, 8 mg caffeine.

The Best Graham Crackers

If you like graham crackers, you'll love these homemade ones. Their taste and texture goes a step beyond store-bought, from "Hmmm, good" to "WOW!"

Yield: 32 crackers (3½ x 2½ inches) ● *Baking temperature: 325°F* ● *Baking time: 15 minutes*

½ cup (2 ounces) unbleached all-purpose flour
1½ cups (7⅞ ounces) whole wheat flour
¾ cup (3 ounces) confectioners' sugar
1 teaspoon baking powder
½ teaspoon salt
1 teaspoon cinnamon (optional)
½ cup (1 stick, 4 ounces) unsalted butter
2 tablespoons (1½ ounces) honey
2 tablespoons (1 ounce) cold milk (regular or low fat, not nonfat)

● Preheat the oven to 325°F. Tear or cut out two sheets of parchment as large as your baking sheets, or grease two sheets lightly.

● In a medium-sized bowl, whisk together the flours, sugar, baking powder, salt, and cinnamon. With a pastry blender, two knives, or your fingertips, cut the butter into the flour mixture until it is evenly crumbly. In a separate bowl, combine the honey and milk, stirring until the honey dissolves. Add the milk/honey mixture liquid to the dry ingredients and toss lightly with a fork until the dough comes together. Add additional milk, if necessary.

● Turn out the dough onto a well-floured surface and fold it over gently 10 to 12 times, until smooth. Divide the dough in half. Work with half the dough at a time, keeping the remaining dough covered.

● If you're not using parchment, keep your work surface very well floured. Roll one piece of dough into a rectangle a bit larger than 10 x 14 inches; the dough will be about ¹⁄₁₆ inch thick. Trim the edges and prick the dough evenly with a dough docker or fork.

● Use a pizza wheel to cut the dough into 16 rectangles. Transfer the crackers to a baking sheet. If you've used parchment, just pick up the parchment and place it on the sheet. The crackers will bake together, but will break apart easily along the cut lines after cooling slightly. If you haven't used parchment, move the individual crackers carefully, setting them close together on the prepared baking sheet.

Rolling tender dough on parchment

Dough that is quite soft and fragile is deceptively easy to roll out, but once cookies are cut, it may be difficult to transfer them to the baking sheet without stretching or tearing them. We recommend rolling and cutting soft, fragile dough directly on parchment, removing any excess dough between the cookies, then transferring the cut cookies, parchment and all, to your baking sheet.

● Bake the crackers for 15 minutes, or until they're a medium gold color. Remove them from the oven and let cool on the pan for 8 to 10 minutes, until they're just barely warm. Carefully break each cracker along the scored lines (see illustration below) and cool completely on a rack. Store the cooled crackers tightly wrapped.

Nutrition information per serving *(1 cracker, 17 g):* 69 cal, 3 g fat, 1 g protein, 6 g complex carbohydrates, 4 g sugar, 1 g dietary fiber, 8 mg cholesterol, 49 mg sodium, 29 mg potassium, 27 RE vitamin A, 1 mg vitamin C, 11 mg calcium, 28 mg phosphorus.

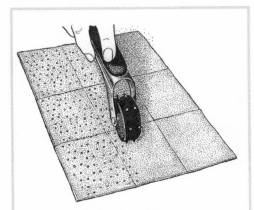

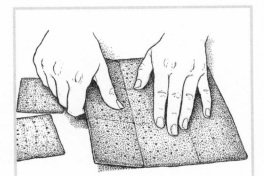

A dough docker looks like an instrument of medieval torture, but it's actually a useful tool for cookie and cracker making. Without docking (pricking) a whole sheet of dough, it would puff irregularly, as the steam created during baking wouldn't have enough avenue for escape.

Leaving the crackers on the pan, set the edge of one hand along a scored line in the crackers. Use your other hand to carefully break the crackers into strips along that line. Repeat with the remainder of the long lines. Then pick up each strip and break off individual crackers.

Graham Cracker Crust

Crushed graham crackers are the basis for graham cracker crust, perfect for cheesecake and all manner of cream pies.

Yield: *1 deep-dish 9-inch piecrust or 9-inch springform pan crust* ● **Baking temperature:** *375°F*
Baking time: *12 to 15 minutes*

1¾ cups (about 8¾ ounces) graham cracker crumbs, regular or chocolate
¼ cup (1 ounce) confectioners' sugar
6 tablespoons (¾ stick, 3 ounces) unsalted butter

● Preheat the oven to 375°F.
● In a medium-sized mixing bowl, stir together the crumbs, sugar, and butter. Press the mixture into the bottom and up the sides of a 9-inch deep-dish pie plate or a 9-inch springform

pan. If you're using a shallower 9-inch pie plate, you'll have crumbs left over; simply sprinkle them over the top of the pie, as a garnish.

● Bake the crust for 12 to 15 minutes, just until it's set and starts to smell toasty. Remove it from the oven and cool completely before adding filling.

Nutrition information per serving (1/8 recipe, 33 g): 168 cal, 11 g fat, 1 g protein, 12 g complex carbohydrates, 6 g sugar, 23 mg cholesterol, 127 mg sodium, 43 mg potassium, 80 RE vitamin A, 6 mg calcium, 16 mg phosphorus.

Chocolate Graham Crackers

Crisp and light, these deep chocolate graham crackers are yummy spread with peanut butter; they also make a wonderful crust for chocolate cream pie.

Yield: 32 crackers (3½ x 2½ inches) ● *Baking temperature:* 325°F ● *Baking time:* 15 minutes

½ cup (2 ounces) unbleached all-purpose flour
¾ cup (3¾ ounces) whole wheat flour
½ cup (1½ ounces) Dutch-process cocoa powder
1¼ cups (5 ounces) confectioners' sugar
1 teaspoon baking powder
½ teaspoon salt
½ cup (1 stick, 4 ounces) unsalted butter
2 tablespoons (1½ ounces) honey
2 tablespoons (1 ounce) cold milk

● Follow the instructions for The Best Graham Crackers (page 331). Roll out the dough and prick it, but don't cut it into rectangles (it will bake together and the scored lines will disappear). Bake as directed, then use a pizza wheel or a sharp knife to cut into rectangles as soon as the crackers come out of the oven. Cool and store as directed.

Chocolate Dipping Sticks

These sturdy little fingers of chocolaty goodness are perfect for dipping into cocoa, marshmallow creme, or (our favorite) the Peanut Butter Icing on page 464.

Yield: 5 dozen ● *Baking temperature:* 350°F ● *Baking time:* 20 to 22 minutes

2½ cups (10½ ounces) unbleached all-purpose flour
¼ cup (¾ ounce) unsweetened cocoa powder, natural or Dutch-process
½ teaspoon baking soda
1 teaspoon salt
½ cup (1 stick, 4 ounces) unsalted butter
½ cup (3¼ ounces) vegetable shortening
2 ounces unsweetened chocolate, melted and cooled
½ cup (3½ ounces) granulated sugar
½ cup (4 ounces) brown sugar
2 large eggs
1½ teaspoons vanilla extract
¾ cup (3 ounces) finely chopped nuts (optional)

● In a medium-sized bowl, whisk together the flour, cocoa, baking soda, and salt; set it aside. In a large mixing bowl, cream together the butter and shortening. Add the melted chocolate and mix to combine. Beat in the sugars, mixing until fluffy. Scrape the bottom and sides of the bowl and add the eggs one at a time, beating well after each addition. Add the vanilla, then the reserved dry ingredients, mixing to combine. Stir in the nuts. Flatten the dough into a thick round, wrap it in plastic, and refrigerate for 4 hours, or overnight.

● Preheat the oven to 350°F. Lightly grease (or line with parchment) one baking sheet.

● Remove the dough from the refrigerator and place it on a piece of parchment. Place a piece of plastic wrap over the top and roll the dough to a ⅜-inch thickness. Transfer the dough and parchment to a rimless cookie sheet or an inverted baking sheet. Using a ruler and a sharp knife or pizza cutter, cut the dough into ½-inch-wide strips. Cut the strips crosswise into 3-inch lengths. There's no need to separate the strips; you'll do that after they're baked.

● Bake the sticks for 20 to 22 minutes. Remove them from the oven and let cool on a rack until firm. The cookies will have a brownie-like texture while warm, and will set up as they cool. Use a knife as necessary to separate into individual sticks. Use for dipping, or frost as desired.

Nutrition information per serving (1 stick, 17 g): 76 cal, 5 g fat, 1 g protein, 4 g complex carbohydrates, 4 g sugar, 1 g dietary fiber, 11 mg cholesterol, 49 mg sodium, 34 mg potassium, 18 RE vitamin A, 1 mg vitamin C, 5 mg calcium, 19 mg phosphorus, 3 mg caffeine.

Hearty Rolled-Oat Cutouts

The following recipe is a departure from the usual butter/flour/sugar interpretation for roll-out cookies; whole wheat flour and rolled oats give these cookies a toasty-brown look and tooth-some, hearty texture. Cookies like these are ideal for kids; you know they're going to consume their fair share of sweets, so why not get some fiber, minerals, and protein into them at the same time? These cookies are especially pretty cut into fanciful shapes, then brushed with beaten egg white and sprinkled with coarse sugar, a large-crystalled sugar available through specialty food stores or catalogues. The sugar makes the cookies sparkle. You may also sprinkle cookies with colored sugars or with chocolate sprinkles.

Yield: 6½ dozen cookies ● *Baking temperature:* 350°F ● *Baking time:* 10 minutes

¾ cup (1½ sticks, 6 ounces) unsalted butter
¾ cup (5¼ ounces) sugar
1 tablespoon milk
1 large egg
1 tablespoon vanilla extract
2½ cups (13 ounces) whole wheat flour*
1 teaspoon baking powder
¾ teaspoon salt
1 cup (3½ ounces) rolled oats

● Preheat the oven to 350°F. Lightly grease (or line with parchment) two or three baking sheets.

● In a large mixing bowl, cream the butter and sugar together until light and fluffy. Beat in the milk, egg, and vanilla. Add the flour, baking powder, salt, and oats to the bowl and stir until well combined.

● Transfer the dough to a lightly floured work surface and roll it to a ⅛-inch thickness. Cut it into whatever shapes you like. Transfer the cookies to the prepared baking sheets.

● Bake the cookies for 10 minutes, or until they're lightly browned. Remove the pans from the oven and transfer the cookies to a rack to cool completely.

*White wheat flour—whole wheat flour ground from white wheat, rather than traditional red wheat—is a good choice here. Its flavor is milder and "sweeter" than red whole wheat flour. You can find it in selected supermarkets, or through The Baker's Catalogue.

Nutrition information per serving (1 cookie, 11 g): 45 cal, 2 g fat, 1 g protein, 4 g complex carbo-hydrates, 2 g sugar, 1 g dietary fiber, 8 mg cholesterol, 28 mg sodium, 22 mg potassium, 18 RE vitamin A, 1 mg vitamin C, 5 mg calcium, 24 mg phosphorus.

Butter-Pecan Crunch

Start with a base of crunchy homemade graham crackers. Add brown sugar, butter, and nuts . . . what's not to like? These few simple ingredients turn a plain graham cracker into a satisfyingly sweet, buttery bar cookie.

Yield: 24 squares ● *Baking temperature:* 375°F ● *Baking time:* 9 minutes

⅓ cup (5⅔ stick, 2¾ ounces) unsalted butter
¼ teaspoon salt
1 teaspoon vanilla extract
½ cup (4 ounces) light brown sugar
1 cup (4 ounces) chopped pecans
About 9¼ whole (5 ounces) graham crackers, homemade preferred (page 332)

● Preheat the oven to 375°F.
● In a medium-sized saucepan, combine the butter, salt, vanilla, and brown sugar, stirring until the butter has melted and the sugar is dissolved; don't let the mixture boil.
● Line the bottom of an ungreased 9 x 13-inch pan with a single layer of graham crackers, breaking them to fit. Pour the sugar syrup over the graham crackers, spreading it to cover with an offset spatula. Sprinkle with the pecans.
● Bake for 9 minutes, until it's bubbly. Remove from the oven and cut into squares immediately. Lift them out of the pan as soon as they're cool enough to handle; if you wait too long, they'll stick.

Nutrition information per serving (1 square, 19 g): 96 cal, 6 g fat, 1 g protein, 5 g complex carbohydrates, 6 g sugar, 7 mg cholesterol, 64 mg sodium, 47 mg potassium, 25 RE vitamin A, 1 mg vitamin C, 6 mg calcium, 23 mg phosphorus.

Gianduja Wafers

Lightly crunchy, tender, and gently nutty, with a creamy mocha-flavored icing, these cookies take their inspiration from *gianduja* (jahn-DOO-yah), a chocolate-hazelnut paste native to the Piedmont region of Italy.

Yield: 27 cookies ● *Baking temperature: 350°F* ● *Baking time: 10 to 12 minutes*

DOUGH
> ½ cup (1 stick, 4 ounces) unsalted butter
> ⅓ cup (2¼ ounces) sugar
> ¾ cup (2½ ounces) ground hazelnuts*
> 1 teaspoon vanilla extract
> ½ teaspoon almond extract
> 1¼ cups (5¼ ounces) unbleached all-purpose flour

ICING
> 1½ cups (6 ounces) confectioners' sugar
> 1 tablespoon Dutch-process cocoa powder
> 1 teaspoon espresso powder
> ½ cup (4 ounces) heavy cream

● **To make the dough:** In a medium-sized bowl, cream together the butter and sugar until light and fluffy. Stir in the hazelnuts and vanilla and almond extracts. Mix in the flour to form a stiff dough. Cover and chill in the refrigerator for at least 1 hour, or overnight.

● Preheat the oven to 350°F. Lightly grease (or line with parchment) two baking sheets.

● On a lightly floured work surface, roll the dough to a ¼-inch thickness, and cut it into 2-inch rounds, gathering the scraps and rerolling the dough as necessary. Place the rounds on the prepared baking sheets.

● Bake the cookies for 10 to 12 minutes, until they're lightly browned. Transfer them to a rack to cool.

● **To make the icing:** Sift or strain the confectioners' sugar, cocoa, and espresso powder into a medium bowl to remove any lumps. Whisk the cream into the dry ingredients a little at a time to make a smooth, spreadable icing, adjusting the amount of cream as necessary, as you may not need all of it. Keep the icing covered until use, to prevent a crust from forming. Spread the icing onto the cooled cookies.

*Grind the hazelnuts (or whirl them in a food processor) until they're about the size of half a rice grain. Don't process them so long that they turn into flour, or become pasty.

Nutrition information per serving (1 cookie, 26 g): 119 cal, 7 g fat, 1 g protein, 5 g complex carbohydrates, 9 g sugar, 15 mg cholesterol, 2 mg sodium, 31 mg potassium, 50 RE vitamin A, 1 mg vitamin C, 10 mg calcium, 20 mg phosphorus, 2 mg caffeine.

Don't scrap the scraps

After you've cut cookies from a rolled-out piece of dough, even if you've cut the cookies very close to one another, you'll have lots of little dough scraps left over. Gather these scraps, brushing off as much flour as possible, and squeeze them into a ball. Flatten the ball and chill it for 15 minutes or so. This will allow the fats to solidify again and the gluten strands in the flour to relax, making the dough easier to roll. If you do this more than once, you may find the resulting cookies just a bit harder and less tender; this is due to the extra flour in the dough, and the extra "excitement" experienced by the gluten, each time you roll. We're betting that you and your guests won't be able to tell the difference, if you've been careful not to add too much flour and if you've handled the dough gently.

Lemon Tea Snaps

These lovely little butter cookies have a refreshing, lemony tang. Sandwich them around Lemon Creme Filling (page 468) to make fancy teatime cookies.

Yield: *6 dozen small cookies* ● ***Baking temperature:*** *350°F* ● ***Baking time:*** *15 to 18 minutes*

> ½ cup (1 stick, 4 ounces) unsalted butter
> ½ cup (3½ ounces) sugar
> ½ teaspoon salt
> ½ teaspoon baking soda
> 1 tablespoon grated lemon rind (zest), or ¼ to ½ teaspoon lemon oil, to taste
> 2 cups (8½ ounces) unbleached all-purpose flour
> 2 tablespoons (1 ounce) lemon juice
> Milk for brushing (optional)
> Coarse sugar for sprinkling (optional)

● Preheat the oven to 350°F.

● In a large mixing bowl, cream together the butter, sugar, salt, and baking soda. Mix in the lemon zest, then half of the flour. Add the lemon juice, then the other half of the flour.

● Roll the dough into a ⅛-inch-thick rectangle on a piece of parchment paper. Transfer the parchment to a baking sheet. Prick the dough all over with a fork or a dough docker (see illustration, page 333), and cut it into 1 x 1½-inch rectangles. There's no need to separate the rectangles; all you need to do is cut the dough.

● Brush the top of the dough with milk and sprinkle with coarse sugar, if desired. Bake the cookies for 15 to 18 minutes, until they're a light golden brown. Remove them from the oven and transfer to a rack to cool. When they're cool, break them apart into individual cookies; they'll separate nicely.

Nutrition information per serving *(1 cookie, 7 g):* 28 cal, 1 g fat, 1 g protein, 2 g complex carbohydrates, 1 g sugar, 3 mg cholesterol, 24 mg sodium, 5 mg potassium, 12 RE vitamin A, 1 mg vitamin C, 1 mg calcium, 3 mg phosphorus.

Alfajores

This Latin American sandwich cookie, a native of Peru, is extra-rich and nutty. It's filled with softened *dulce de leche* (DOOL-say day LAY-chay), a rich, deep gold caramel that spreads like peanut butter. Brazil nuts, while traditional, are not readily available in some places. Try pine nuts instead, which have a similar oil content and texture to Brazil nuts; macadamias stand in well, also. Some *alfajore* recipes substitute unsweetened shredded coconut for the nuts.

Yield: 36 sandwich cookies ● *Baking temperature: 350°F* ● *Baking time: 15 to 20 minutes*

1½ cups (3 sticks, 12 ounces) unsalted butter
¾ cup (5¼ ounces) granulated sugar
½ cup (2 ounces) confectioners' sugar
1 large egg
½ teaspoon almond extract
1 teaspoon vanilla extract
½ teaspoon salt
3 cups (12¾ ounces) unbleached all-purpose flour
½ cup (2½ ounces) Brazil nuts, toasted (see page 27) then ground
1½ cups (about 14 ounces) prepared *dulce de leche*

● In a large mixing bowl, cream together the butter and sugars until fluffy. Add the egg and the extracts and beat to combine, scraping the sides and bottom of the bowl. Mix in the salt, flour, and nuts and blend to make a stiff dough. Wrap in plastic and chill overnight.
● Preheat the oven to 350°F. Lightly grease (or line with parchment) two baking sheets.
● Unwrap the dough and place it on a heavily floured work surface. Working quickly, roll it to a ¼-inch thickness; if it gets too warm, it will be difficult to work with. Use a 2½-inch round cookie cutter, plain or scalloped-edge, to cut cookies, placing them on the prepared baking sheets.

Making your own *dulce de leche*

To make *dulce de leche* at home, place an unopened 14-ounce can of sweetened condensed milk in a deep stockpot. Add water to the pot until it covers the can by at least 3 inches. Bring the water to a boil over medium heat, then reduce the heat and cook the milk, at a strong simmer, for about 3 hours, adding more boiling water if necessary; it's imperative that the can remain covered with water at all times, as it might rupture in dangerous fashion if the water boils away. After 3 hours, turn off the heat, and when the water has cooled to a comfortable temperature, remove the can. When the can is completely cool, open it; you'll find an amazing transformation has taken place—the creamy white milk has turned into a rich, mahogany-brown caramel spread. Scoop the *dulce de leche* out of the can and store it in the refrigerator.

- Bake the cookies for 15 to 20 minutes, until they're just slightly golden brown around the edges. Remove them from the oven and let cool on the baking sheet for 5 minutes before transferring to a rack to cool completely.
- Spread 2 teaspoons of the *dulce de leche* on the bottom of half the cookies and top with the remaining cookies (bottom toward the filling).

Nutrition information per serving (1 cookie, 38 g): 174 cal, 9 g fat, 2 g protein, 7 g complex carbohydrates, 14 g sugar, 26 mg cholesterol, 54 mg sodium, 48 mg potassium, 71 RE vitamin A, 1 mg iron, 17 mg calcium, 34 mg phosphorus.

Pecan-Praline Sandwich Cookies

Pecans, toffee, and chocolate—what's not to like? Tender, shortbread-texture pecan-scented cookies sandwich a filling of toffee and chocolate; as Sue Gray, who heads up our test kitchen, said when she was making them, "Why don't we forget the cookies and just dip our spoons into this filling?" Sue added, "If I need a lot of cookies for the school bake sale, I sometimes make these 'open face' (one layer, not two), and use a star tube to place a dab of filling in the center of each cookie. That method doubles the cookie count. Either way, they're a hit."

Yield: 41 sandwich cookies ● *Baking temperature: 375°F* ● *Baking time: 6 to 8 minutes*

DOUGH
- 1 cup (2 sticks, 8 ounces) unsalted butter, room temperature
- 1 cup (4 ounces) confectioners' sugar
- 1 large egg
- ¼ teaspoon salt
- ½ teaspoon baking powder
- ½ cup (1¾ ounces) pecan meal (or other nut flour)
- 2½ cups (10½ ounces) unbleached all-purpose flour
- ¼ cup (1¾ ounces) granulated sugar (for sprinkling over the dough)

FILLING
- ½ cup (2½ ounces) toffee bits or toffee candy (such as Heath Bar)
- ½ cup (4 ounces) evaporated milk or heavy cream
- 1 cup (6 ounces) chopped bittersweet chocolate

- **To make the dough:** In a medium-sized mixing bowl, cream together the butter and sugar until light. Add the egg, salt, baking powder, and pecan meal. Mix together until well blended, then add the flour and stir until combined. The mixture is a bit heavy, so use your mixer's slow speed, so as not to tax it.
- Divide the dough in half and form each half into a disk. Wrap each disk separately and refrigerate for 1 hour or longer.
- Preheat the oven to 375°F. Lightly grease (or line with parchment) two or three baking sheets.

- **To shape the dough:** Remove one disk from the refrigerator and lightly flour both sides. Roll it out to a ⅛-inch thickness on a lightly floured work surface. If the dough splits when you start rolling, let it rest at room temperature for about 15 minutes to become more pliable. The thinner the dough, the crisper the cookies.
- Cut out the cookies with a 1½- to 2-inch cookie cutter. Sprinkle each cookie with sugar, then place on the prepared baking sheets. Repeat this process with the other dough disk.
- Bake the cookies for 6 to 8 minutes; don't let them brown. Transfer the cookies to a rack to cool.
- **To make the filling:** First, freeze the toffee bits; this makes them easier to crush. If you have a small food processor or blender, process the candy until it's finely ground. If you're doing this by hand, crush the frozen candy with a rolling pin into fine pieces.
- Heat the milk or cream until bubbles form around the edges. Place the toffee and chocolate pieces in a medium-sized mixing bowl and pour the hot milk or cream over them, stirring until smooth. If you've crushed the toffee by hand, there will probably be a few small chunks remaining in the filling, which is okay. Set the mixture aside to cool to room temperature.
- When the filling has cooled but is not yet fully set, spread 1 generous teaspoon of filling on the bottom of half the cookies and top with the remaining cookies. If you're making open-face cookies, use ½ teaspoon of filling on each, piping it through a star tube. Allow the filling to harden for several hours before placing the cookies in air-tight containers.

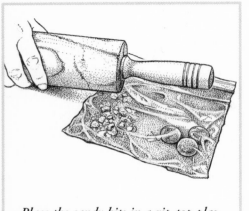

Place the candy bits in a zip-top plastic bag and use a rolling pin to crush them thoroughly.

Nutrition information per serving (1 cookie, 35 g): 148 cal, 9 g fat, 2 g protein, 7 g complex carbohydrates, 8 g sugar, 23 mg cholesterol, 35 mg sodium, 51 mg potassium, 54 RE vitamin A, 1 mg iron, 18 mg calcium, 30 mg phosphorus, 4 mg caffeine.

Leftover makeover

If you happen to have a little praline filling left over after you've made your cookies, it's great melted with a bit more evaporated milk or cream and then served over ice cream. It can also be rolled into small balls, then dusted with cocoa, and voilà! Truffles!

English Digestive Biscuits

English digestive biscuits were developed at the end of the nineteenth century to increase fiber in Victorian diets. They're made with whole wheat flour rather than white flour, but wait, they actually taste good! Based on shortbread, they have a lovely buttery, nutty wheat flavor. They're comforting in a back-to-your-childhood way, like arrowroot cookies or zwieback biscuits.

Yield: 3 dozen cookies ● *Baking temperature:* 350°F ● *Baking time:* 15 minutes

½ cup (1 stick, 4 ounces) unsalted butter
¾ cup (3 ounces) confectioners' sugar
1½ teaspoons vanilla extract
¼ cup (2 ounces) cold milk
2 cups (10 ounces) whole wheat flour
1 teaspoon baking powder

● In a medium-sized bowl, cream the butter, then beat in the confectioners' sugar. Add the vanilla and milk, beating until smooth. Stir in the flour and baking powder. Gather the dough into a ball, flatten it into a disk, wrap it well, and refrigerate for several hours, or overnight.
● Preheat the oven to 350°F. Lightly grease (or line with parchment) two baking sheets.
● On a lightly floured surface, roll the dough to a ⅛-inch thickness. Cut round biscuits (cookies) about 2½ inches in diameter. Place the biscuits on the prepared baking sheets, prick them evenly with a fork, and bake for 15 minutes, or until they're pale gold. Remove them from the oven and transfer to a rack to cool.

Nutrition information per serving (1 biscuit, 15 g): 62 cal, 3 g fat, 1 g protein, 5 g complex carbohydrates, 2 g sugar, 1 g dietary fiber, 7 mg cholesterol, 15 mg sodium, 32 mg potassium, 24 RE vitamin A, 1 mg vitamin C, 10 mg calcium, 33 mg phosphorus.

When a biscuit is a cookie is a biscuit . . .

Aren't biscuits those soft, fluffy baking powder rolls, the ones that go on top of the chicken pie? Not always. In England and Australia, a biscuit is what we call a cookie. From the Latin *bis coctum,* "twice baked," biscuits were originally hard, thin, very dry crackers. For centuries, ship's biscuits were a mainstay on many a sea voyage, due to their good keeping qualities; they were so dry that they'd stay "fresh" for months. While the English continued to refer to any small, thin, dry "cake" as a biscuit, the Dutch called their cookies *koekje*—"small cake." According to legend, cookies were born when cake bakers poured out and baked small amounts of batter as test cakes. The Dutch *koekje* came to America with the Pilgrims in 1620, and eventually morphed into the American cookie. Just to bring the story full circle, one of the earliest mentions of what we now know as cookies was in second-century Rome *(bis coctum).* And what are Italy's best-known cookies today? Biscotti. A biscuit is a cookie is a biscuit . . .

Brambles

This recipe reveals its history with its odd name. Cookie recipes from the early part of the twentieth century often had nonsensical names, like snickerdoodles or jumbles, and brambles date from that era. You'll notice that the cookie part of these filled delights is simply a very flaky, tender pastry crust; the absence of sugar in the cookie allows the sweetness of the raisins and flavor of lemon and vanilla in the filling to shine through.

Yield: 21 sandwich cookies ● *Baking temperature:* 400°F ● *Baking time:* 15 to 18 minutes

DOUGH
> 2¼ cups (9½ ounces) unbleached all-purpose flour
> ¾ teaspoon salt
> 6 tablespoons (¾ stick, 3 ounces) unsalted butter
> ⅓ cup (2¼ ounces) vegetable shortening
> 4 to 6 tablespoons (2 to 3 ounces) ice water

FILLING
> ⅔ cup (4 ounces) raisins, packed
> ¼ cup (⅞ ounce) crushed soda crackers (about 8 square crackers)
> 4 tablespoons (½ stick, 2 ounces) unsalted butter
> ⅔ cup (4¾ ounces) sugar
> 1 teaspoon vanilla extract
> 1 tablespoon lemon juice
> 1 teaspoon grated lemon rind (zest), or a few drops lemon oil

TOPPING
> Milk, for brushing
> Coarse sugar, for sprinkling

● **To make the dough:** In a medium-sized bowl, whisk together the flour and salt. Cut in the butter and shortening, using your fingers, a pastry fork or blender, or a mixer, working the mixture until it's crumbly. Sprinkle in enough of the ice water to make the dough cohesive when you grab a handful. Knead the dough briefly to gather it into a ball, then flatten it into a thick disk, wrap it, and chill for 30 minutes.

● **To make the filling:** In a food processor or blender, process the raisins and crackers together until they're very finely chopped; the mixture will become semi-pasty.

● In a small saucepan set over medium-low heat, melt the butter. Add the sugar, stirring until smooth, then add the raisin/cracker mixture, the vanilla, and the lemon juice and zest, stirring to combine. Cook gently, stirring frequently, for about 3 minutes, or until the filling has started to thicken. Remove the filling from the heat and set it aside.

● Preheat the oven to 400°F. Lightly grease (or line with parchment) two baking sheets.

● **To assemble the cookies:** Remove the dough from the refrigerator and roll it to a ⅛-inch thickness on a lightly floured work surface. Using a biscuit or cookie cutter, cut 2½- to 2¾-inch rounds from the dough. Place half of the rounds on the prepared baking sheets. Top each round with 2 teaspoons of filling. Center the remaining rounds atop the filling, using a

fork to press down the edges to seal. Be sure to press the edges together firmly; you don't want the filling to leak out. Brush each cookie with milk and sprinkle with coarse sugar.
- Bake the cookies for 15 to 18 minutes, until they're golden brown. Remove them from the oven and transfer to a rack to cool.

Nutrition information per serving (1 cookie, 41 g): 165 cal, 8 g fat, 2 g protein, 15 g complex carbohydrates, 7 g sugar, 1 g dietary fiber, 15 mg cholesterol, 94 mg sodium, 65 mg potassium, 51 RE vitamin A, 1 mg vitamin C, 1 mg iron, 7 mg calcium, 20 mg phosphorus.

Eggnog Sandwich Cookies

These buttery rounds, with a touch of eggnog flavor in both the dough and the filling, make delicious linzer cookies (see sidebar, page 346). If you're going to make Linzers, we suggest tinting the filling a light pastel color. If you prefer, instead of using separate ingredients to achieve the eggnog taste, you can substitute ¼ to ½ teaspoon eggnog flavor, to taste, for the vanilla, nutmeg, and rum flavor in the dough, and/or ⅛ to ¼ teaspoon eggnog flavor, to taste, for the vanilla, nutmeg, and rum flavor in the filling.

Yield: 33 sandwich cookies ● *Baking temperature:* 350°F ● *Baking time:* 10 minutes

DOUGH
- ½ cup (3¼ ounces) vegetable shortening
- ½ cup (1 stick, 4 ounces) unsalted butter
- ½ cup (4 ounces) brown sugar
- ½ cup (3½ ounces) granulated sugar
- ¾ teaspoon salt
- 1 teaspoon baking powder
- 2 teaspoons vanilla extract
- 1¼ to 1½ teaspoons nutmeg, to taste
- ¼ teaspoon strong butter-rum flavor, or ½ to 1 teaspoon rum extract
- 1 large egg
- 2½ cups (10½ ounces) unbleached all-purpose flour
- ½ cup (2⅜ ounces) white rice flour or cornstarch

FILLING
- 2 cups (8 ounces) confectioners' sugar
- 1 teaspoon vanilla extract
- ¼ teaspoon nutmeg
- A few drops strong butter-rum flavor or ⅛ teaspoon rum extract
- 3 to 4 tablespoons (1½ to 2 ounces) milk or cream
- Food coloring of your choice (optional)

TOPPING
- Confectioners' sugar

- **To make the dough:** In a large bowl, beat together the shortening, butter, sugars, salt, baking powder, vanilla, nutmeg, and rum flavor. Add the egg, beating until fluffy. Whisk together the flours and stir in. Divide the dough in half, shape into two rounds, wrap in plastic, and refrigerate for 1 hour or longer.
- Preheat the oven to 350°F. Lightly grease (or line with parchment) two baking sheets.
- Remove the chilled dough from the refrigerator and roll it to a ⅛-inch thickness on a lightly floured work surface. Use a cutter to cut 2¼-inch rounds and place them on the prepared baking sheets, leaving about 1 inch between them.
- Bake the cookies for 10 minutes, or until they're very lightly browned around the edges. Remove them from the oven and transfer to a rack to cool.
- **To make the filling:** Mix the filling ingredients in a medium-sized bowl, tinting gently with food coloring, if desired, to make a pastel-colored filling. Spread a thin layer of filling on the bottom of half the cookies. Top with the remaining cookies. Store the cookies in airtight containers for several days, or freeze for longer storage.

Nutrition information per serving (1 cookie, 35 g): 143 cal, 6 g fat, 1 g protein, 8 g complex carbohydrates, 13 g sugar, 14 mg cholesterol, 52 mg sodium, 29 mg potassium, 29 RE vitamin A, 1 mg vitamin C, 1 mg iron, 15 mg calcium, 17 mg phosphorus.

VARIATION

- To make eggnog construction dough, suitable for a cream-colored "gingerbread" house, reduce the amounts of vegetable shortening and butter to ⅓ cup each; increase the eggs to 2; increase the all-purpose flour to 3¼ cups, and delete the rice flour. (If you don't plan on eating the house eventually, feel free to leave out the extracts and flavors.) Roll the chilled dough about ⅓ inch thick, cut it with gingerbread house templates (see page 183), and bake it in a preheated 300°F oven for 25 to 30 minutes, until it's quite firm to the touch.

Lovely Linzers

The linzer cookie, a lovely Austrian sandwich cookie also known as Ischl Tart, is traditionally made with a buttery nut dough rolled thin and cut into circles. Half the circles have another, smaller design cut into their centers. After the cookies are baked, they're sandwiched together with berry jam, the bright jam peeking through the cutout design on top. In this country, linzer cookies have come to mean just about any cookie featuring a cutout design on top. Many varieties of roll-out sugar cookies become linzers, and the filling can vary from jam to flavored icing, or even caramel. As usual, we here in the American melting pot have adapted a classic European recipe to suit our own tastes.

For a recipe very similar to traditional linzer cookie dough, see Zimsterne, page 349.

Stained Glass Cookies

These cookies, with their shimmering crystalline centers, are attractive enough to display as part of a centerpiece, and durable enough to transform into ornaments (simply by looping a piece of ribbon through the baked cookie before the sugar syrup center is poured in). More important, though, they're yummy enough to eat, all the way from their mildly spiced outer edges to their cool, hard middles—shaped, colored, and flavored as you choose. Yes, you must use a candy thermometer to make them, and yes, the effort will be well worth your time when you see the lit-up faces of the children who enjoy them.

Yield: 4 dozen cookies ● *Baking temperature:* 375°F ● *Baking time:* 8 minutes

DOUGH
½ cup (3¼ ounces) vegetable shortening
½ cup (1 stick, 4 ounces) unsalted butter
1½ cups (10½ ounces) sugar
4 ounces (half an 8-ounce package) cream cheese, softened
1 teaspoon vanilla extract
1 large egg
4 cups (17 ounces) unbleached all-purpose flour
½ teaspoon ground ginger
1 teaspoon nutmeg
½ teaspoon baking soda
½ teaspoon salt

CANDY CENTERS
2 cups (14 ounces) sugar
1 cup (11 ounces) light corn syrup
½ cup (4 ounces) water
Food coloring
A few drops strong flavoring of your choice (optional)

● **To make the dough:** In a large bowl, cream together the shortening, butter, and sugar until light and fluffy. Mix in the cream cheese, vanilla, and egg and beat well.

● In a medium-sized bowl, sift together the flour, ginger, nutmeg, baking soda, and salt. Gradually add the dry ingredients to the butter mixture, beating until well combined. The dough will be soft; cover and refrigerate it overnight.

● The next day, remove the dough from the refrigerator and divide it into quarters. Refrigerate three of the pieces until needed. Preheat the oven to 375°F. Lightly grease (or line with parchment) two or three baking sheets.

● Roll each piece of dough to a ⅛-inch thickness on a lightly floured work surface.

● Use a 3½- to 4-inch round cookie cutter to cut the dough, and immediately transfer the rounds to the prepared baking sheets, leaving a bit of space between them. Use another shape cutter if you like; just make sure it leaves enough space in the middle to cut out the space for the candy filling. Use a smaller (1-inch or so) cutter in the shape of a circle, heart, star, diamond or what-have-you to cut out the centers. A bagel or doughnut cutter works well here—it cuts out the cookie and its center hole at the same time. If the dough isn't cold enough, refrigerate the sheets and cut out the centers when the dough is a bit easier to work with. Repeat with the remaining pieces of dough.

● Bake the cookies for 8 minutes, or until they're barely firm and still somewhat pale; they'll be just lightly browned around the outer edges. Let them cool on the baking sheets.

● **To make the candy centers:** Place two or three 1-cup ovenproof glass measuring cups (or any small ovenproof, spouted glass cups) in a 375°F oven to warm. In a medium-sized pan, combine the sugar, corn syrup, and water, and stir over medium heat until the sugar is dissolved. Next, and without stirring, cook the syrup until it reaches 300°F to 310°F (hard-crack stage) on a candy thermometer. Remove the syrup from the heat and take one measuring cup from the oven. Pour one half (or one third) of the syrup into the measuring cup, depending on how many colors of filling you want to make, and stir in the food coloring and flavor of your choice. Leave the remaining syrup in the pan, set over low heat.

● When the syrup in the cup stops bubbling, hold the cup with a very thick potholder and pour the syrup in a thin, gentle stream to fill the cookie centers. Stop pouring just as the syrup comes up to the top level of the cookie. Be careful; this is an extremely hot process and you may need to take a break halfway through to give your hand a rest. Alternatively, you can use a small (teaspoon) cookie scoop to dip syrup out of the cup and deposit it in the cookie centers; fill the scoop about halfway. This prevents the mild discomfort of holding onto a hot glass for a long time.

Use a small cookie scoop to dip hot syrup out of the cup and deposit it into the hole in the center of the cookie. Using a scoop does away with the awkward task of using a bulky mitt to hold onto the hot dish of syrup as you work.

● Use the second and/or third cup and the rest of the syrup, colored and flavored differently, to fill the centers of the remaining cookies. (If you have any leftover syrup, pour it into small rounds on a piece of parchment or aluminum foil to make hard candies.)

● Let the finished cookies cool completely. Using a metal spatula, loosen them carefully and peel them off the baking sheets. If these cookies are for consumption, store them in a cool, dry place in a single layer in an airtight container. (For show, we've left them uncovered for at least 1 month, and they've been just as sturdy as ever. Be sure not to store them near a heat source.)

Nutrition information per serving (1 cookie with unflavored center, 43 g): 157 cal, 5 g fat, 1 g protein, 7 g complex carbohydrates, 20 g sugar, 14 mg cholesterol, 53 mg sodium, 16 mg potassium, 30 RE vitamin A, 18 mg calcium, 13 mg phosphorus.

VARIATIONS

● Some hard candies melt beautifully to form the centers of these cookies; others don't. You'll only know if you try. We used some lovely striped peppermint drops and they melted into a gorgeous design. Crushed Jolly Rancher hard candies were also a winner. On the other hand, LifeSavers didn't melt at all. Add hard candies to the cut-out center of cookies before baking; we suggest baking a few sample cookies first, with the various candies you want to try, to see if they melt.

Zimsterne

This German recipe is traditionally used to make star-shaped cookies for decorating the Christmas tree. Since small children find it irresistible to touch Christmas tree ornaments, we find that edible ornaments are a great solution. Save your grandmother's old-fashioned glass balls for the top of the tree.

Yield: About 8 dozen cookies ● *Baking temperature:* 350°F ● *Baking time:* 12 minutes

4 tablespoons (½ stick, 2 ounces) unsalted butter
1 cup (4 ounces) confectioners' sugar
½ cup (3½ ounces) granulated sugar
2 large eggs
1 teaspoon vanilla extract
1 teaspoon almond extract
2¼ cups (9½ ounces) unbleached all-purpose flour
1 tablespoon baking powder
1½ teaspoons cinnamon
1 cup (3¼ ounces) ground blanched almonds or almond flour
1 large egg white, lightly whisked with a pinch of salt
Granulated sugar, for sprinkling

● In a large bowl, cream together the butter and sugars until they're smooth and light colored. Add the eggs one at a time, beating well after each addition. Stir in the extracts.

● In a separate bowl, whisk together the flour, baking powder, cinnamon, and almonds. Stir this into the butter mixture. Shape the dough into a flattened disk and refrigerate it for at least 1 hour, or overnight.

● Preheat the oven to 350°F. Lightly grease (or line with parchment) two or three baking sheets.

● Sprinkle a clean work surface with confectioners' sugar and roll the cookie dough to a ⅛- to ¼-inch thickness. Continue to sprinkle on confectioners' sugar if the dough sticks to the work surface or the rolling pin. Use a 2-inch star cutter to cut cookies, or use your own favorite size and shape. Place the cookies on the prepared baking sheets; they'll puff and spread, so leave 2 inches between them. Brush the cookies with the beaten egg white. Sprinkle a little granulated sugar on top of each cookie.

● Bake the cookies for approximately 12 minutes, until they're lightly browned. Remove the cookies from the oven. If you plan on using them as ornaments, immediately use a thick skewer to poke a hole in the top of each; for larger holes, use a drinking straw. Transfer the cookies to a rack to cool.

Nutrition information per serving (1 cookie, 20 g): 79 cal, 4 g fat, 4 g protein, 5 g complex carbohydrates, 5 g sugar, 1 g dietary fiber, 16 mg cholesterol, 31 mg sodium, 35 mg potassium, 34 mg calcium, 31 mg phosphorus.

Mailanderli

From Germany's *springerle* and *lebkuchen*, to *pepparkakor* (Sweden's version of American ginger-bread), to Austria's wonderful vanilla *kipferl* and Greece's flower-scented nut cookies, *Koura-biedes*, Christmas cookies are an old and revered tradition in both America and Europe. *Mailanderli*, a not-too-sweet butter cookie with a hint of lemon, is Switzerland's favorite holiday cookie. The egg wash gives the baked cookie a lovely shiny, golden glaze.

Yield: 9 dozen cookies ● *Baking temperature:* 350°F ● *Baking time:* 10 minutes

> 2 sticks plus 2 tablespoons (9 ounces) unsalted butter
> 1¼ cups (8¾ ounces) sugar
> 3 large eggs, at room temperature
> ¾ teaspoon salt
> 1 tablespoon finely grated lemon rind (zest), or ⅛ teaspoon lemon oil
> 4⅓ cups (18½ ounces) unbleached all-purpose flour
> 1 egg yolk plus 1 teaspoon milk, for brushing

- In a large mixing bowl, beat the butter until soft and creamy. Beat in the sugar. Add the eggs one at a time, beating well after each addition; scrape down the sides of the bowl once or twice while adding the eggs. Beat in the salt and the lemon zest.
- Sift the flour and add it, half at a time, to the butter mixture. Mix only until the flour is well incorporated. Gather the dough into a ball, flatten it into a disk, and refrigerate it for 2 to 3 hours, or overnight.
- Preheat the oven to 350°F. Lightly grease (or line with parchment) two or three baking sheets.
- Remove the dough from the refrigerator. If it's very hard, allow it to warm a little before trying to roll it out. It's best to work with small pieces, about one-fourth of the dough at a time; refrigerate the rest until you're ready to roll it out. On a lightly floured work surface, or between two pieces of plastic wrap, roll the dough to a ⅛-inch thickness. Cut out different shapes with cookie cutters dipped in flour. Transfer the dough to the prepared baking sheets.
- Mix the egg yolk and milk in a small bowl. Brush the cookies with the egg wash. If possible, refrigerate the cookies for 10 to 15 minutes before baking.
- Bake the cookies in the middle of the oven for 10 minutes, or until they're an even, pale golden brown. Remove the cookies from the oven. Transfer the baking sheets to a rack to cool almost completely, then transfer to a rack.

Nutrition information per serving (1 cookie, 11 g): 45 cal, 2 g fat, 1 g protein, 4 g complex carbo-hydrates, 2 g sugar, 13 mg cholesterol, 17 mg sodium, 9 mg potassium, 21 RE vitamin A, 1 mg vitamin C, 2 mg calcium, 8 mg phosphorus.

Totenbeinli

These lightly spiced cookies, another Swiss Christmas tradition, feature a nutty crunch in every bite. Dry (but not unpleasantly so), and sturdy without moving over the line to rock-hard, these cookies possess a European aura. We can imagine sitting in front of the Yule log in a cozy chalet, dunking these cookies in tea, or a cup of coffee or Swiss cocoa.

Yield: 6 dozen cookies ● *Baking temperature:* 375°F ● *Baking time:* 18 to 20 minutes

5 tablespoons (2½ ounces) unsalted butter, softened
1 cup (7 ounces) sugar
2 large eggs
1 tablespoon finely grated lemon rind (zest), or ⅛ teaspoon lemon oil
1 teaspoon cinnamon
Small pinch of ground cloves
Pinch of salt
½ cup (1½ ounces) ground hazelnuts (hazelnut flour)
2 cups (8 ounces) chopped hazelnuts
2 cups plus 2 heaping tablespoons (9¼ ounces) unbleached all-purpose flour
1 egg white, lightly beaten, for brushing

● Preheat the oven to 375°F. Lightly grease (or line with parchment) two baking sheets.
● In a large bowl, beat the butter until soft, then add the sugar, beating until smooth. Beat in the eggs one at a time, scraping the sides of the bowl and beating well after each addition. Add the lemon zest and beat the mixture until it's light and fluffy, approximately 3 minutes.
● Beat in the cinnamon, cloves, and salt, then fold in the hazelnut flour and hazelnuts. Gently stir the all-purpose flour into the mixture. Cover the dough and refrigerate it for 30 minutes.
● On a lightly floured work surface, roll the dough to a ¼-inch thickness. Using a sharp knife or a pizza wheel, cut it into 1 x 2½-inch sticks. Transfer the cookies to the prepared baking sheets. Brush them with beaten egg white. Bake the cookies for 18 to 20 minutes, until they're golden brown. Remove the cookies from the oven and transfer them to a rack to cool completely.

Nutrition information per serving (1 cookie, 13 g): 56 cal, 3 g fat, 1 g protein, 3 g complex carbohydrates, 3 g sugar, 8 mg cholesterol, 6 mg sodium, 24 mg potassium, 10 RE vitamin A, 1 mg vitamin C, 8 mg calcium, 17 mg phosphorus.

Shaped Cookies

Remember building sand castles, molding clay animals, and making snowmen when you were young? The desire to shape raw materials—whether Play-Doh, or the mashed potatoes on your dinner plate—begins early, and usually lasts a lifetime. As we get older, our medium of choice becomes more refined: think topiary gardens, or hand-thrown pottery. And, if you're a baker, think cookies: crescents and rings, pinwheels, pretzels, and ribbons, to say nothing of spheres of chocolate stuffed with nuggets of caramel, or tricorner "hats" cradling honey-apricot filling.

When it comes to baking cookies, drop cookies anchor one end of the degree-of-difficulty scale, and shaped cookies hold down the other. All of the following cookies involve a longer process than simply beating together dough and plopping it onto a cookie sheet. But if you're a baker who enjoys the journey just as much as the destination, or a cookie fan who's never lost the desire to build sand castles and make mud pies, then you'll enjoy these recipes. And anyway, what fun is it to lick your fingers if you haven't first plunged them into the dough?

Fudge-Coated Dipsticks

These tender-crisp, butter-scented cookies, shaped into short "fingers," are a delicious teatime treat. Dipped in dark chocolate and sprinkled with toasted pecans, they look lovely arrayed on a serving plate along with imprinted shortbread cookies (see sidebar, page 125).

Yield: 4½ dozen cookies ● *Baking temperature: 325°F* ● *Baking time: 20 minutes*

DOUGH

1 cup (4 ounces) pecans, finely crushed, or pecan meal
1 cup (2 sticks, 8 ounces) unsalted butter
⅓ cup (2⅜ ounces) sugar
1 teaspoon salt
2 teaspoons vanilla extract
2 cups (8½ ounces) unbleached all-purpose flour

TOPPING

1 cup (6 ounces) chocolate chips
1½ tablespoons (¾ ounce) unsalted butter
1½ tablespoons (1 ounce) light corn syrup
⅔ cup (2¾ ounces) chopped pecans, toasted (see page 27)

● Preheat the oven to 325°F.
● Place the pecans in a zip-top plastic bag and crush them thoroughly with a rolling pin, or process in a food processor until very finely chopped but not pasty.
● **To make the dough:** In a medium-sized bowl, cream together the butter, sugar, salt, and vanilla. Add the flour and crushed pecans, stirring to make a cohesive dough.
● Divide the dough into four pieces and roll each piece into a 25-inch rope. Cut each rope into 2½-inch pieces. Shape the dough into logs about the size of your index finger, rolling them on the counter to smooth them. Place the logs about 1 inch apart on ungreased or parchment-lined (for fastest cleanup) baking sheets.
● Bake the cookies for about 20 minutes, until they're a light, golden brown. Remove the cookies from the oven and transfer them to a rack to cool.
● **To make the topping:** In a microwave-safe bowl, melt the chocolate chips, butter, and corn syrup in the microwave, stirring until smooth. Dip about two-thirds of each cookie into the chocolate mixture, then sprinkle with the pecans. Place the cookies back on the rack to set.

Nutrition information per serving (1 cookie, 17 g): 90 cal, 6 g fat, 1 g protein, 4 g complex carbohydrates, 3 g sugar, 10 mg cholesterol, 41 mg sodium, 27 mg potassium, 35 RE vitamin A, 1 mg vitamin C, 3 mg calcium, 16 mg phosphorus, 2 mg caffeine.

Caramel Rocks

These chewy, gooey chocolate cookies feature a caramel candy filling that pokes temptingly through their top crust. Cut the stickiness factor in half, if you wish, by using only half a caramel in each cookie.

Yield: 2 dozen cookies ● *Baking temperature: 375°F* ● *Baking time: 8 to 10 minutes*

DOUGH
6 tablespoons (¾ stick, 3 ounces) unsalted butter
3 ounces unsweetened baking chocolate
1 cup (8 ounces) brown sugar
1 teaspoon vanilla extract
½ teaspoon espresso powder
1 large egg
1 teaspoon baking powder
½ teaspoon baking soda
¼ teaspoon salt
1½ cups (6¼ ounces) unbleached all-purpose flour

FILLING
24 (5⅝ ounces) vanilla caramel candies

TOPPING
¼ cup (1 ounce) confectioners' sugar
1½ teaspoons unsweetened cocoa powder, natural or Dutch process

● Preheat the oven to 375°F. Lightly grease (or line with parchment) two baking sheets.
● **To make the dough:** In a saucepan set over low heat, or in the microwave, heat the butter and chocolate together, stirring until both are melted and the mixture is smooth. Transfer to a medium-sized mixing bowl and allow to cool to lukewarm.
● Add the sugar, vanilla, espresso powder, and egg, beating until smooth. Add the baking powder, baking soda, salt, and flour, mixing to form a smooth, cohesive dough.
● **For the filling:** Wrap about 1 tablespoon of dough around a caramel piece, covering it completely. Roll it in your hands to make a smooth dough ball. Repeat with the remaining caramels.
● **For the topping:** Combine the confectioners' sugar and cocoa in a zip-top bag. Place 5 or 6 dough balls in the bag at a time, and shake gently until they're coated with the sugar. Transfer them to the prepared baking sheets.
● Bake the cookies for 8 to 10 minutes, until they're set around the edges but still soft in the middle. Remove them from the oven and let cool for 5 minutes on the baking sheet before transferring to a rack to cool completely.

Nutrition information per serving (1 cookie, 59 g): 223 cal, 6 g fat, 4 g protein, 23 g complex carbohydrates, 16 g sugar, 2 g dietary fiber, 17 mg cholesterol, 73 mg sodium, 123 mg potassium, 32 RE vitamin A, 1 mg vitamin C, 2 mg iron, 35 mg calcium, 62 mg phosphorus, 8 mg caffeine.

Holiday Bonbons

Okay, so these aren't really bonbons, in the strict sense of the word (a bonbon being a chocolate candy with a filling of fondant and/or fruit and nuts). Neither are they sugarplums, which are fruits or nuts coated with fondant. Nevertheless, if you love the flavor of almonds, visions of these almond-paste-filled, chocolate-dipped cookies will definitely dance in your head long after the holidays are over.

Yield: 27 cookies ● *Baking temperature: 350°F* ● *Baking time: 14 minutes*

DOUGH
1 cup (2 sticks, 8 ounces) unsalted butter
1½ cups (6 ounces) confectioners' sugar
1 tablespoon vanilla extract
¾ teaspoon salt
2½ cups (10½ ounces) unbleached all-purpose flour

FILLING
½ cup (4½ ounces) almond paste, praline paste, or marzipan*
1 tablespoon unsalted butter
⅛ teaspoon almond oil, or ½ teaspoon almond extract (leave this out if you're using praline paste)
¼ cup (1 ounce) confectioners' sugar
½ cup (1⅛ ounce) soft, fresh bread crumbs

GLAZE
1¼ cups (7½ ounces) chocolate chips
2 tablespoons (1 ounce) unsalted butter
2 tablespoons (1⅜ ounces) light corn syrup
Sliced almonds for topping, optional

● Preheat the oven to 350°F. Line two baking sheets with parchment, (for easy cleanup), or leave them unlined; they don't need to be greased.

● **To make the dough:** In a medium-sized mixing bowl, beat the butter until light. Add the sugar, vanilla, and salt and beat until fluffy. Add the flour and stir until a firm dough forms.

● **To make the filling:** Crumble the almond paste into a small bowl. Beat in the butter, almond oil, and sugar. When the mixture is smooth, add the bread crumbs and mix until blended.

● **To shape the cookies:** Roll the filling into grape-sized balls. Break off a piece of dough the size of a table tennis ball and use your thumb to make a deep indentation in the center. Place a ball of filling in the indentation, then bring the dough up and over to enclose it, rolling it in your

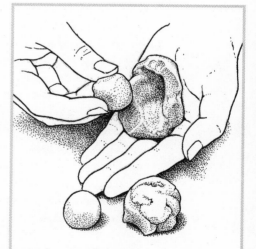

Make an indentation in the dough ball and insert the filling.

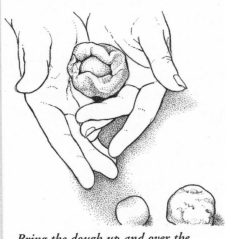

Bring the dough up and over the filling, enclosing it completely.

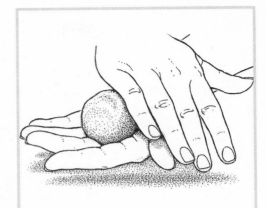

Once the filling is completely enclosed, roll the ball of dough in your hands to smooth it out.

hands to make a smooth ball. Repeat with the remaining filling and dough.

● Place the bonbons on the prepared baking sheets and bake them for 14 minutes. They won't brown, which is okay. Let the bonbons cool on the baking sheet for 10 minutes (they're quite fragile while hot) before transferring to a rack to cool completely.

● **To make the glaze:** Melt the chocolate chips in a microwave, a double boiler, or in a saucepan set over low heat. Add the butter and corn syrup, stirring until smooth and glossy.

● Dip the tops of the cooled bonbons in the glaze. If the glaze thickens, reheat it briefly, then continue dipping. Top each with an almond slice or two, if desired. Let the bonbons sit for several hours until the glaze hardens, then store them in an airtight container.

* If you use marzipan, omit the sugar from the filling.

Nutrition information per serving (1 cookie, 44 g): 208 cal, 12 g fat, 2 g protein, 10 g complex carbohydrates, 14 g sugar, 1 g dietary fiber, 22 mg cholesterol, 67 mg sodium, 72 mg potassium, 75 RE vitamin A, 1 mg vitamin C, 1 mg iron, 17 mg calcium, 42 mg phosphorus, 6 mg caffeine.

Grasp cooled cookies by their edges and dip their tops in glaze.

Over-the-Top Mandelbrot

Mandelbrot (MAHN–dull–brot), originally a crisp, almond-scented, twice-baked cookie, is the Jewish version of Italian biscotti (also originally an almond-scented, twice-baked cookie). Over the years, both biscotti and *mandelbrot* have taken on all manner of nuts, chips, and flavors to morph into the classic loaded-with-sweets American cookie. Our thanks to Mona Shabelman for this recipe.

Yield: 6 dozen cookies ● *Baking temperature:* 350°F, then 300°F
Baking time: 28 minutes, then 25 minutes

3 large eggs
1 cup (7 ounces) vegetable oil
1 cup (7 ounces) sugar
1 teaspoon vanilla extract
1 teaspoon salt
3½ cups (14¾ ounces) unbleached all-purpose flour
1 teaspoon baking powder
2 cups (12 ounces) chocolate chips
1½ cups (7½ ounces) plain toffee bits*

● In a medium-sized bowl, beat together the eggs, oil, sugar, vanilla, and salt at medium-high speed until thick and light-colored, about 5 minutes. Stir in the flour and baking powder, then the chocolate chips and toffee bits. Wrap the dough in plastic wrap, and refrigerate it for at least 3 hours, or overnight.

● Preheat the oven to 350°F. Lightly grease (or line with parchment) two baking sheets.

● Transfer the dough to a lightly floured work surface and divide it into four even pieces, about 13 ounces each. Working with one piece at a time, place the dough on the prepared baking sheet, shaping it into an 8 x 2-inch log. Repeat with the remaining pieces of dough, leaving at least 2 inches between them (there will be 2 logs on each baking sheet).

● Bake the logs for 28 minutes, until they're lightly browned. Remove them from the oven and reduce the oven temperature to 300°F. Allow the logs to cool for 10 minutes, then cut each one into ½-inch slices, on the diagonal. For longer *mandelbrot,* cut at a greater diagonal; for the shortest cookies, cut crosswise, not at a diagonal.

● Return the slices to the baking sheets, standing them upright (see illustration #8, page 135). Bake the cookies for 25 minutes, until they're golden brown. Remove them from the oven and cool on the baking sheets.

* You'll find these in the baking aisle of your supermarket, with the chocolate and other flavored chips. Be sure to get the plain toffee chips, not the ones covered in chocolate.

Nutrition information per serving (1 cookie, 22 g): 103 cal, 6 g fat, 1 g protein, 5 g complex carbohydrates, 6 g sugar, 1 g dietary fiber, 11 mg cholesterol, 49 mg sodium, 32 mg potassium, 4 RE vitamin A, 1 mg iron, 6 mg calcium, 17 mg phosphorus, 2 mg caffeine.

Magic in the Middles

Reminiscent of a chocolate peanut butter cup candy (or a buckeye, if you're into homemade candies), this recipe is one that's been making the rounds for years. We guarantee these will disappear in a snap, whatever the audience—from hungry kids after a soccer game, to your coworkers gathered around the office coffeepot.

Yield: 26 cookies ● *Baking temperature:* 375°F ● *Baking time:* 7 to 9 minutes

DOUGH

1½ cups (6¼ ounces) unbleached all-purpose flour
½ cup (1½ ounces) unsweetened natural cocoa powder
½ teaspoon baking soda
¼ teaspoon salt
½ cup (3½ ounces) granulated sugar (and extra for dipping)
½ cup (4 ounces) brown sugar
½ cup (1 stick, 4 ounces) unsalted butter
¼ cup (2⅜ ounces) smooth peanut butter
1 teaspoon vanilla extract
1 large egg

FILLING

¾ cup (7⅛ ounces) smooth peanut butter
¾ cup (3 ounces) confectioners' sugar

● Preheat the oven to 375°F. Lightly grease (or line with parchment) two baking sheets.
● **To make the dough:** In a medium-sized mixing bowl, whisk together the flour, cocoa, baking soda, and salt. In another medium-sized mixing bowl, beat together the sugars, butter, and peanut butter until light and fluffy. Add the vanilla and the egg, beating to combine, then stir in the dry ingredients, blending well.
● **To make the filling:** In a small bowl, stir together the peanut butter and confectioners' sugar until smooth. With floured hands, roll the filling into 26 one-inch balls.
● **To shape the cookies:** Break off about 1 tablespoon of the dough, make an indentation in the center with your finger, and press one of the peanut butter balls into the indentation. Bring the dough up and over the filling, pressing it closed; roll the cookie in the palms of your hand to smooth it out. Repeat with the remaining dough and filling (see illustrations, pages 356–357).
● Dip the top of each cookie in granulated sugar and place on the prepared baking sheets about 2 inches apart. Grease the bottom of a drinking glass and use it to flatten each cookie to about ½ inch thick.
● Bake the cookies for 7 to 9 minutes, until they're set. Remove them from the oven and cool on a rack.

Nutrition information per serving (1 cookie, 38 g): 171 cal, 9 g fat, 4 g protein, 7 g complex carbohydrates, 13 g sugar, 2 g dietary fiber, 18 mg cholesterol, 98 mg sodium, 132 mg potassium, 37 RE vitamin A, 1 mg iron, 9 mg calcium, 62 mg phosphorus, 6 mg caffeine.

Date Pinwheels

Soft, brown dough, dates bubbling on the stove, the tricky process of rolling the filling inside the dough, and the magical way the refrigerator makes the sticky mass solid and sliceable—that's date pinwheels. Once you've made them, wait for just the right moment—the cookies hot out of the oven but the filling cool enough not to burn—to take your first warm and wonderful bite. Date pinwheels aren't beautiful; in fact, they're usually kind of plain-looking, in their shades of somber brown, their spiral of filling often a bit out of whack. But these homely little gems will strike just the right note on your holiday cookie spread.

Yield: 6 dozen cookies ● ***Baking temperature:*** *400°F* ● ***Baking time:*** *8 to 10 minutes*

DOUGH
- ¾ cup (1½ sticks, 6 ounces) unsalted butter
- 2 cups (16 ounces) light brown sugar
- 3 large eggs
- 4 cups (17 ounces) unbleached all-purpose flour
- 1½ teaspoons salt
- ½ teaspoon baking soda

FILLING*
- 1¾ cups (9¼ ounces) chopped dates
- ¾ cup (5¼ ounces) granulated sugar
- ¾ cup (6 ounces) water
- ⅛ teaspoon salt
- 1½ cups (6 ounces) chopped pecans or walnuts

● **To make the dough:** In a large bowl, cream together the butter and brown sugar. Add the eggs one at a time, beating well after each addition. Stir in the flour, salt, and baking soda. Cover the bowl and chill the dough until it's firm enough to roll out, at least 1 hour.

● **To make the filling:** While the dough is chilling, combine the dates, sugar, water, and salt in a small saucepan set over medium-high heat. Bring to a boil, reduce the heat, and boil gently for 15 minutes, or until the mixture has thickened to about the consistency of soft jam. Stir in the nuts and set aside.

● **To shape the cookies:** Divide the dough in half. Working with one half at a time, roll the dough into a 9 x 12-inch, ¼-inch-thick rectangle. Spread half the filling over the entire surface of the dough. The filling is sticky and stiff, but if you keep wetting your fingers, you can push and spread it around without too much trouble (see sidebar, opposite). Roll up the dough lengthwise to make a foot-long log. It's delicate, but using a baker's bench knife or spatula helps. Repeat with the remaining dough and filling. Wrap each log in waxed paper, parchment, or plastic wrap and chill for several hours, or overnight.

● Preheat the oven to 400°F. Lightly grease (or line with parchment) two baking sheets.

- Remove the dough from the refrigerator and let it rest at room temperature for 10 minutes. If the logs have flattened out while chilling, gently roll back into rounds. They may have cracked in several places; just smooth the cracks closed with your fingers. Cut each log into ⅓-inch slices, (you'll get about 36 cookies from each log) and place the slices 2 inches apart on the prepared baking sheets.
- Bake the cookies for 8 to 10 minutes (the shorter amount of time on a greased baking sheet, the longer time on parchment), or until they're light brown. Remove the cookies from the oven and transfer them to a rack to cool.

* Although this filling is easy enough to make, if you want to use purchased date (or fig) filling, go ahead. You'll need about 2 cups (24 ounces) of filling.

Nutrition information per serving (1 cookie, 28 g): 99 cal, 4 g fat, 1 g protein, 7 g complex carbohydrates, 8 g sugar, 1 g dietary fiber, 14 mg cholesterol, 66 mg sodium, 63 mg potassium, 22 RE vitamin A, 1 mg vitamin C, 1 mg iron, 9 mg calcium, 20 mg phosphorus.

Spreading a sticky filling

When you're trying to spread a sticky filling onto the dough for a filled cookie (or onto the crust of a bar cookie), use your hands instead of a spatula; you'll have a much better feel for how hard to press (hard enough to spread the filling, not so hard that you rip the dough underneath). And don't grease your hands; it's much more effective to simply wet your fingers with lukewarm water, then keep wetting them as the filling begins to stick. The little bit of added water from your fingers won't affect the filling.

Vanilla Kipferl

These Austrian Christmas cookies are a simple mixture of butter, sugar, and flour; but it's the freshly made vanilla sugar they're coated in that gives them their wonderful flavor. If you gravitate to chocolate over vanilla, we urge you to give these a try; until you've tasted vanilla sugar made with ground vanilla beans, you'll never know what you've been missing!

Yield: 57 cookies ● *Baking temperature: 350°F* ● *Baking time: 8 to 10 minutes*

DOUGH
⅞ cup (1¾ sticks, 7 ounces) unsalted butter
½ teaspoon salt
7 tablespoons (3 ounces) granulated sugar
1 teaspoon vanilla extract
1¾ cups (7¼ ounces) unbleached all-purpose flour
Scant 2⅓ cups (7½ ounces) almond flour (ground almonds), preferably toasted

VANILLA SUGAR
¼ cup (1¾ ounces) superfine or castor sugar*
½ to 1 vanilla bean**

● In a medium-sized bowl, beat together the butter, salt, sugar, and vanilla until smooth. Add the flour and almond flour, stirring to make a cohesive dough. Wrap the dough in plastic wrap and refrigerate it for at least 1 hour, or overnight.

● Preheat the oven to 350°F. Lightly grease (or line with parchment) two baking sheets.

● Break off walnut-sized pieces of the dough, and roll them into short (about 2-inch) logs. Shape the logs into crescents, then gently press to flatten them slightly. Place the cookies on the prepared sheets.

● Bake the cookies for 8 to 10 minutes, until they're a light, golden brown. Remove them from the oven and let cool on the pan for 10 minutes.

● While the cookies are cooling, process the sugar and vanilla bean in a food processor or blender until the bean is thoroughly ground. Place the vanilla sugar in a shallow bowl. While the cookies are still warm, gently roll them in the vanilla sugar. Transfer them to a rack to cool completely.

Roll each piece of dough into a log, then shape each log into a crescent.

* Use regular granulated sugar if you can't find superfine.
** Use a whole bean here for the best and strongest vanilla flavor.

Nutrition information per serving *(1 cookie, 13 g):* 67 cal, 4 g fat, 1 g protein, 3 g complex carbohydrates, 2 g sugar, 1 g dietary fiber, 8 mg cholesterol, 19 mg sodium, 31 mg potassium, 26 RE vitamin A, 1 mg vitamin C, 10 mg calcium, 22 mg phosphorus.

Grease, parchment, or silicone?

Does it make a difference whether you grease your baking sheets, line them with parchment, or use a silicone liner? Yes. All have slightly different effects on your cookies as they bake.

Greasing baking sheets is the time-tested way to render them nonstick. Use solid shortening (some folks keep a folded paper towel right in their shortening can, ready for action), or a nonstick vegetable oil spray. If you're using spray, pick one without lecithin, as it tends to darken and become sticky on the baking sheet. Cookies baked on a greased sheet will brown the most on the bottom, compared to the other two methods. If your pans are very dark, or thin, or you usually have difficulty with cookies that overbrown on the bottom, then greasing the sheet isn't your best choice.

Lining a sheet with reusable parchment (page 35) not only keeps your baking sheet perfectly clean, it gives high-fat and/or high-sugar cookies just that slight extra cushion they need to prevent overbrowning on the bottom. In addition, cookies on parchment can be lifted off the baking sheet and set on the counter to cool before being transferred to a rack to cool completely. This frees up the baking sheet for another batch of cookies (let it cool first). Cookie dough can be deposited on parchment, then lifted onto a baking sheet, parchment and all, when one becomes free.

Silicone mats (and nonstick-coated flexible fiberglass mats) are the newer, high-tech answers to the issue of nonstick. Like parchment, they keep your baking sheet clean, and you can shape cookies on them, then transfer them to a baking sheet as you cycle batches in and out of the oven. And unlike parchment, you don't have to discard them after four or five bakes. However, some bakers notice that some cookies don't brown on the bottom as nicely as they'd like on a silicone mat (which is usually thicker than nonstick coated fiberglass and provides a degree of insulation between cookie and pan).

Our personal favorite is parchment. Cookies will slide right off, it's thin enough that it doesn't affect their baking time, and cleanup is nonexistent. When parchment becomes brown and brittle, or greasy and sticky, simply discard it and slip a new piece onto your baking sheet.

Stuffed Butterballs

These coconut-crunchy mounds of tender, buttery cookie come with a surprise in the center: big, tasty toasted nut halves. Or a piece of bittersweet chocolate. Or maybe some dried cherries and white chocolate chips. Use your imagination to come up with your favorite "surprise" filling.

Yield: 2 dozen cookies ● ***Baking temperature:*** *350°F* ● ***Baking time:*** *25 minutes*

1 cup (2 sticks, 8 ounces) unsalted butter
⅔ cup (2¾ ounces) confectioners' sugar
2 teaspoons vanilla extract
¼ teaspoon almond extract
¾ teaspoon salt
2 cups (8½ ounces) unbleached all-purpose flour
½ cup (2-2½ ounces) pecan halves or whole blanched almonds, toasted (see page 27)
1 egg white whisked with 1 tablespoon water, for glaze
1¼ cups (4 ounces) flaked sweetened or unsweetened coconut, for coating

● In a medium-sized mixing bowl, cream together the butter, sugar, vanilla and almond extracts, and salt. Add the flour, stirring to make a smooth dough. If the dough is too soft to shape, cover and refrigerate it, until it stiffens and becomes workable, 1 hour or overnight.

● Preheat the oven to 350°F. Lightly grease (or line with parchment) two baking sheets.

● Shape a piece of dough the size of a table tennis ball (about ⅞ ounce) into a round. Poke a hole in the center with your finger and add a couple of pecan halves or whole almonds. Work the dough over the filling to cover it. Repeat with the remaining dough and nuts.

● Dip the cookies in the egg glaze and roll them in flaked coconut. Place the cookies on the prepared baking sheets.

● Bake the cookies for 25 minutes, until the coconut coating is lightly browned Remove them from the oven and cool on a rack.

Nutrition information per serving *(1 cookie, made with pecans, 31 g):* 152 cal, 11 g fat, 2 g protein, 9 g complex carbohydrates, 4 g sugar, 1 g dietary fiber, 21 mg cholesterol, 71 mg sodium, 40 mg potassium, 72 RE vitamin A, 1 mg vitamin C, 1 mg iron, 4 mg calcium, 23 mg phosphorus.

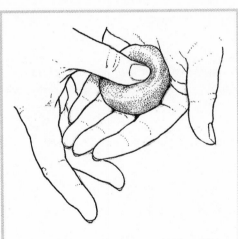

Use your thumb to press an indentation into the ball of dough.

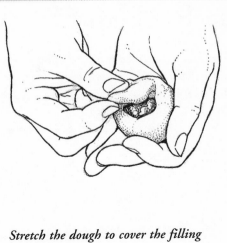

Stretch the dough to cover the filling completely.

After dipping the ball of dough in beaten egg white, coat it with coconut.

Jam-Packeds

These flaky, half-moons harbor a sweet secret: your favorite flavor of jam, be it apricot, raspberry, peach, or (our favorite) pineapple. These resemble bite-sized turnovers, and visually are a nice addition to a cookie gift tin.

Yield: 34 cookies ● *Baking temperature: 375°F* ● *Baking time: 15 minutes*

DOUGH
- ¾ cup (1½ sticks, 6 ounces) unsalted butter
- Two 3-ounce packages (6 ounces) cream cheese (reduced fat [Neufchâtel] or full fat)
- ⅓ cup (1⅜ ounces) confectioners' sugar
- ½ teaspoon almond extract
- ¾ teaspoon salt
- 1¾ cups (7¼ ounces) unbleached all-purpose flour
- 1 large egg, lightly beaten, to seal dough

FILLING
- ¾ cup (8 ounces) jam or preserves
- 1 tablespoon cornstarch
- 2 teaspoons lemon juice
- 2 teaspoons water

● **To make the dough:** In a medium-sized bowl, cream together the butter, cream cheese, sugar, almond extract, and salt. Add the flour, mixing to form a cohesive dough. Gather the dough into a ball, divide it in half, and flatten each half into a round. Wrap in plastic wrap and refrigerate for 1 hour, or overnight. While the dough is chilling, prepare the filling.

● **To make the filling:** Heat the preserves in a small saucepan set over low heat. Stir together the cornstarch, lemon juice, and water. Add this mixture to the jam, increase the heat to medium-low, and bring the mixture to a boil, stirring frequently. Boil and stir for a couple of minutes; the preserves will be thin at first, but will thicken enough that you can see the marks your spoon is leaving on the bottom of the pan as you stir. Remove from the heat and set aside to cool.

● Preheat the oven to 375°F. Lightly grease (or line with parchment) two baking sheets.

● Remove one round of dough from the refrigerator and roll it about ⅛ inch thick. Cut the dough into 3-inch circles. Transfer the cookies to a prepared baking sheet. Top each circle with about 1 level teaspoon of the filling. Brush the edges of the circles with the beaten egg, and fold each in half (making a half-moon shape). Use the tines of a fork to press them closed and to prick the top so steam can escape. Repeat with the remaining dough.

● Bake the cookies for 15 minutes, or until they're golden brown. Remove them from the oven and transfer to a rack to cool.

Nutrition information per serving (1 cookie, 27 g): 101 cal, 6 g fat, 1 g protein, 5 g complex carbohydrates, 5 g sugar, 23 mg cholesterol, 64 mg sodium, 23 mg potassium, 62 RE vitamin A, 1 mg vitamin C, 6 mg calcium, 15 mg phosphorus.

Koulouria

Greece is known for its special Easter breads, such as *tsourekia,* the familiar wreath bread topped with colored eggs. But the celebration doesn't stop there. Cookies are an important part of the holiday, too, in particular these crunchy, light, anise-scented, shaped cookies beloved of Greeks (and Americans of Greek descent) everywhere. Boxes and boxes of these are sent around the country to family and friends during the Easter season. They travel well, and are guaranteed to evoke fond childhood memories from anyone who grew up in a Greek household. This recipe is based on one sent to us by Barbara Mackenzie of Milwaukee.

Yield: 3 dozen cookies ● ***Baking temperature:*** *350°F* ● ***Baking time:*** *15 to 20 minutes*

> 3¼ cups (13¾ ounces) unbleached all-purpose flour
> 1 tablespoon baking powder
> ½ teaspoon salt
> ⅔ cup (4¾ ounces) sugar
> 3 large eggs, two whole, one separated
> ¾ cup (1½ sticks, 6 ounces) unsalted butter, melted and cooled
> 1 to 1½ teaspoons anise extract, a few drops anise oil, or
>   1½ teaspoons ground aniseed*
> 5 tablespoons (1½ ounces) sesame seeds

● In a large mixing bowl, combine the flour, baking powder, salt, and sugar. Add the 2 whole eggs and the yolk of the third to the flour, set aside the egg white; mix until crumbly. Add the melted butter and anise, mixing to combine. The dough should be stiff; add a few table-spoons extra flour if it is very sticky. Cover the bowl with plastic wrap and refrigerate for 1 to 2 hours (or overnight), to make it easier to work with.

● Preheat the oven to 350°F. Lightly grease (or line with parchment) two baking sheets.

● Scoop the dough into 2-tablespoon balls. Roll them into ropes about 8 inches long and the thickness of a pencil. Shape the ropes into S-shaped snakes, pretzels, or letters, and place them on the prepared baking sheets.

● In a small bowl, lightly beat the reserved egg white, then brush it on top of the cookies. Sprinkle the cookies heavily with the sesame seeds.

● Bake the cookies for 15 to 20 minutes; they should be set but not brown. Remove them from the oven and transfer to a rack to cool.

*The classic *koulouria* recipe calls for mastic, the mildly licorice-flavored resin of the *lentisk* bush, sold in Middle Eastern markets in small, pebblelike pieces. Use it if you can find it; pulverize it first, and add 1 teaspoon to the cookie dough. You may also substitute 4 teaspoons ouzo (Greek anise liqueur) for the anise in the recipe.

Nutrition information per serving *(1 cookie, 27 g):* 105 cal, 5 g fat, 2 g protein, 9 g complex carbo-hydrates, 4 g sugar, 1 g dietary fiber, 30 mg cholesterol, 81 mg sodium, 27 mg potassium, 46 RE vitamin A, 1 mg vitamin C, 1 mg iron, 29 mg calcium, 38 mg phosphorus.

Hamantaschen

Hamantaschen, distinctive triangular filled cookies, are a specialty of the Jewish holiday of Purim, which commemorates the rescue of the fifth century BC Persian Jews from Haman, vizier to the Persian king, who had ordered their destruction. Haman's signature tricorner hat is commemorated in hamantaschen, traditionally given as a gift to family and friends. While poppy seed filling (*mohn*) is classic, many kinds of fruits find their way into the center of these buttery cookies. Our version features a mixture of golden raisins, apples, and apricots.

Yield: 33 cookies ● *Baking temperature: 375°F* ● *Baking time: 13 minutes*

DOUGH
- ¾ cup (1½ sticks, 6 ounces) unsalted butter
- ¾ cup (5¼ ounces) sugar
- ¾ teaspoon salt
- 2 tablespoons grated lemon rind (zest)
- 1 teaspoon vanilla extract
- ⅛ teaspoon lemon oil (optional)
- 3½ cups (14¾ ounces) unbleached all-purpose flour
- 3 tablespoons (¾ ounce) cornstarch
- 2 teaspoons baking powder
- 1 large egg plus 1 egg white (reserve the yolk)

FILLING
- ½ cup (3 ounces) golden raisins, packed
- 2 tablespoons (1 ounce) unsalted butter
- 2 tablespoons (1½ ounces) honey
- 1 cup (6 ounces) finely diced dried apricots
- 1 tablespoon grated lemon rind (zest)
- 2 tablespoons (⅞ ounce) sugar
- 1 cup (8 ounces) apple juice
- 1 large apple, cored, peeled, and grated or finely chopped

● **To make the dough:** In a medium-sized mixing bowl, cream together the butter, sugar, salt, zest, vanilla, and lemon oil until light and fluffy. Add the flour, cornstarch, baking powder, egg, and egg white and mix until the dough is cohesive; it will be very stiff. Divide the dough in half, wrap it well, and refrigerate it for at least 1 hour, or overnight.

● **To make the filling:** Place all the filling ingredients in a small saucepan and bring to a boil, stirring constantly. When the mixture thickens, remove it from the heat. Refrigerate until chilled.

● Preheat the oven to 375°F. Lightly grease (or line with parchment) two baking sheets.

● **To shape the cookies:** Lightly flour a clean work surface. Working with half of the dough at a time, flour it thoroughly, and roll it into a 16-inch square approximately ¼ inch thick. Cut the dough into 3½-inch circles. Place the circles on the prepared baking sheets, and place a rounded teaspoonful of filling in the center of each circle.

- Brush the edges of the dough with the reserved egg yolk, which you've beaten with 1 tablespoon water. Now, imagine the circle as a triangle; bring three of the "sides" together to meet in the center, forming what looks like an old-fashioned tricorner hat. Pinch the edges together to seal.
- Bake the cookies for 13 minutes, until they're lightly browned on the bottom and edges. Remove them from the oven and transfer to a rack to cool completely. They'll firm up and become crisp.

Nutrition information per serving (1 cookie, 41 g): 126 cal, 5 g fat, 2 g protein, 13 g complex carbohydrates, 5 g sugar, 1 g dietary fiber, 20 mg cholesterol, 82 mg sodium, 53 mg potassium, 49 RE vitamin A, 1 mg vitamin C, 1 mg iron, 21 mg calcium, 25 mg phosphorus.

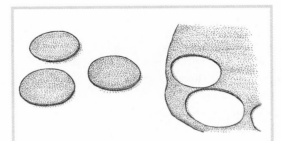

Cut the dough into 3½-inch circles. If you don't have a large cutter, trace around the rim of a large cup or can.

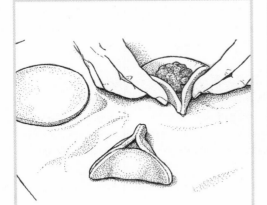

Once you've dropped a dollop of filling in the center of the dough circle, fold it up on three sides.

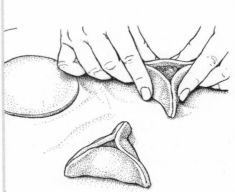

Finish shaping the hamantaschen by gently squeezing all three sides in toward the center, pinching the corners together firmly.

Berlinerkranser

Berlinerkranser, despite the initial impression one gets from their name, are a Christmas specialty of Norway, not Germany. Everyone who sampled our test-kitchen *Berlinerkranser* had the same reaction: "Hey! These are those sugar cookies that come in all different shapes and they're in a round tin and someone always sends them to you at Christmas." And they're right; these light, almost crumbly textured butter cookies, the ones with the coarse white sugar on top, are an integral part of every "Scandinavian butter cookie" gift tin. While they're traditionally formed into bow shapes, *Berlinerkranser* are also great candidates for a cookie press and the various shapes it can produce.

Yield: *4 dozen bows* ● ***Baking temperature:*** *350°F* ● ***Baking time:*** *15 to 17 minutes*

DOUGH
1 cup (7 ounces) sugar
2 cups (4 sticks, 1 pound) unsalted butter
2 large eggs, 1 whole, 1 separated
2 teaspoons vanilla extract*
5 cups (21¼ ounces) unbleached all-purpose flour
¾ teaspoon salt
2 tablespoons milk, as needed

TOPPING
Pinch of salt
Coarse white sugar or pearl sugar

● In a large bowl, cream together the sugar and butter. Beat in the whole egg, egg yolk, and vanilla. Add the flour 1 cup at a time, and the salt, beating until smooth after each addition. Add a couple of tablespoons of milk, if necessary, to make a stiff, cohesive dough. Divide the dough into four pieces, shape each piece into a slightly flattened round, wrap well, and refrigerate overnight.

● Preheat the oven to 350°F. Lightly grease (or line with parchment) two baking sheets.

● Generously flour your work surface. Working with one piece of dough at a time (keeping the others refrigerated), break off a 2-tablespoon piece of dough. Roll it into a 6-inch rope and transfer it to the prepared baking sheet. Shape the rope into a circle whose ends cross and overlap about ½ inch; let the ends hang down, like the ends of a bow. Repeat with the remaining dough.

● For the topping, beat together the egg white and salt. Brush the cookies with this glaze and sprinkle with coarse sugar.

● Bake the cookies for 15 to 17 minutes, until set; the cookies won't brown. Remove them from the oven and transfer to a rack to cool completely.

* Substitute 1 teaspoon almond extract, if desired, or the extract, flavor, or oil of your choice.

Nutrition information per serving (1 cookie, 28 g): 129 cal, 8 g fat, 2 g protein, 9 g complex carbohydrates, 4 g sugar, 30 mg cholesterol, 37 mg sodium, 20 mg potassium, 75 RE vitamin A, 1 mg iron, 3 mg calcium, 17 mg phosphorus.

Iced Spice Rings

Caraway is the surprise flavor in these interesting spice cookies, and semolina the unusual flour. Based on a Middle Eastern cookie, *zaddik*, we've Americanized this recipe to use commonly available ingredients. The result is a cookie for adult tastes: crisp, spicy, and not too sweet, perfect with a cup of coffee or sweet dessert wine.

Yield: 3 dozen cookies ● *Baking temperature:* 350°F ● *Baking time:* 20 minutes

DOUGH
1 cup (2 sticks, 8 ounces) unsalted butter
⅔ cup (4¾ ounces) sugar
½ teaspoon nutmeg
½ teaspoon cinnamon
½ teaspoon ground cloves
2 teaspoons caraway seeds
1 teaspoon salt
2 tablespoons (⅞ ounce) vegetable oil
1 teaspoon baking powder
⅓ cup (2 ounces) semolina
2¾ cups (11½ ounces) unbleached all-purpose flour
½ cup (4 ounces) milk (regular or low fat, not nonfat)

GLAZE
1 cup (4 ounces) confectioners' sugar
¼ cup (2 ounces) heavy cream
1 teaspoon vanilla extract

● **To make the dough:** In a medium-sized bowl, beat together the butter, sugar, spices, caraway seeds, salt, and vegetable oil. Add the baking powder and semolina, then 1 cup of the flour, beating until smooth. Mix in the milk, then the remaining 1¾ cups flour. Refrigerate the dough for at least 1 hour, or overnight.

● Preheat the oven to 350°F. Lightly grease (or line with parchment) two baking sheets.

● Break off heaping-tablespoon chunks of dough and roll each into a 6-inch rope. Bring the ends of each rope together to form a ring. Place the rings on the prepared baking sheets. If any rings crack around the edges, simply smooth out the cracks with your fingers.

● Bake the rings for 20 minutes, until they're golden brown. Remove them from the oven and let them rest on the pan for 5 minutes before transferring to a rack to cool completely.

● While the cookies are cooling, prepare the glaze by whisking together the sugar, cream, and vanilla. Dip the tops of the cooled cookies in the glaze. Allow the glaze to harden before packing the cookies for storage.

Nutrition information per serving (1 cookie, 30 g): 124 cal, 7 g fat, 1 g protein, 8 g complex carbohydrates, 7 g sugar, 16 mg cholesterol, 76 mg sodium, 24 mg potassium, 55 RE vitamin A, 1 mg vitamin C, 1 mg iron, 16 mg calcium, 19 mg phosphorus.

Cherry-Nut Rugelach

A *rugelach* (RUHG-uh-lukh) is a crescent-shaped cookie with filling, traditionally baked for Jewish holidays, Hanukkah and Shabbat in particular. Originally brought over from Eastern Europe, *rugelach* is now baked as a dessert treat anytime; it's even sold online. The name has evolved into many spelling variations: roggles, ruggles, rogulah, and rugula (which is Latin for "small fold"). The Yiddish translation for these cookies is "little twists." Whatever you call them, they're tasty, bite-sized treats.

Traditional fillings include raisins, apples, and nuts, but a quick survey reveals a wide variety of fillings: peanut butter–chocolate, apple strudel, apricot–almond and cranberry–walnut. While the filling types vary, *rugelach's* "staple" is its cream cheese dough.

Yield: 64 cookies ● *Baking temperature: 350°F* ● *Baking time: 20 minutes*

DOUGH
1 cup (2 sticks, 8 ounces) unsalted butter
One 8 ounce package cream cheese (reduced fat [Neufchâtel] or full fat)
½ cup (3½ ounces) sugar
1¼ teaspoons salt
3 cups (12¾ ounces) unbleached all-purpose flour

FILLING
1 cup (4⅝ ounces) dried cherries
¾ cup (3 ounces) walnuts, toasted (see page 27)
1 cup (7 ounces) sugar
¼ cup (2 ounces) unsalted butter, melted
2½ teaspoons cinnamon
¼ teaspoon salt

TOPPING
1 large egg beaten with 2 teaspoons water
Granulated, coarse, or pearl sugar

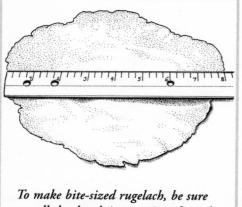

To make bite-sized rugelach, be sure to roll the dough into an 8-inch circle to start.

● **To make the dough:** In a large bowl, beat the butter and cream cheese until light. Add the sugar and salt and beat until fluffy. Stir in the flour, then gather the dough into a ball and knead it until it's smooth and all the flour is incorporated.

● Divide the dough into 8 equal pieces, roll each piece into a ball, then flatten each slightly into thick disks. Wrap each in plastic wrap and refrigerate for 1 hour or longer.

● Preheat the oven to 350°F. Lightly grease (or line with parchment) two baking sheets. Parchment is preferred, as it will shorten the cleanup time necessitated by some of the inevitable oozing of the filling as these cookies bake.

- **To make the filling:** Combine all the filling ingredients in a food processor and pulse a few times (or finely dice the cherries and walnuts, add the remaining filling ingredients and blend well).
- **To shape the cookies:** Work with one dough disk at a time, and keep the others refrigerated. On a piece of parchment or a lightly floured work surface, roll the dough into an 8-inch circle. Place a small round lid (from a film canister, a salad dressing bottle, or something similar-sized) in the center of the circle. Spread ¼ cup of the filling over the dough, leaving ½ inch uncovered around the outside edge of the circle.
- Remove the lid and use a sharp knife or a pizza wheel to cut the circle into 8 equal wedges. Starting at the wide (outside) edge of each wedge, roll it toward its narrow edge, as you would a crescent roll. Place the rolled wedges, tip down, on the prepared baking sheets.

Curve each cookie into a crescent shape. Repeat this process with the remaining dough.

Leave space around the outside edge when you spread on the filling.

Roll each of the eight wedges from their wide outer edge to their point in the center.

- Brush each cookie with some of the beaten egg mixture and sprinkle with sugar. Bake the *rugelach* for 20 minutes, or until they're golden brown. Remove them from the oven and transfer to a rack to cool.

Nutrition information per serving (1 cookie, 23 g): 97 cal, 6 g fat, 1 g protein, 5 g complex carbohydrates, 1 g sugar, 17 mg cholesterol, 64 mg sodium, 42 mg potassium, 60 RE vitamin A, 1 mg vitamin C, 1 mg iron, 7 mg calcium, 19 mg phosphorus.

What's with the lid in the center of the dough?

Did you wonder why you placed a bottle lid in the center of the dough to keep it free of filling? As you roll a wedge, the filling is pushed toward the wedge's point and it will fill in that empty space. If the space already had filling, it would simply be forced out and make a mess.

Easter Doughnut Cookies

These crunchy, dense cookies, iced in soft pastels, appear in Italian-American households the day before Easter—and they're usually gone well before the Easter egg hunt. Their name comes from the fact that they're shaped into rings before baking.

Yield: 3½ *dozen cookies* ● *Baking temperature:* 350°F ● *Baking time:* 18 *minutes*

DOUGH

- 2 tablespoons (⅞ ounce) vegetable oil
- 3 tablespoons (1½ ounces) unsalted butter, melted
- 2 large eggs
- 2 teaspoons vanilla extract
- ¾ teaspoon salt
- 2 teaspoons baking powder
- 1 cup (4 ounces) confectioners' sugar
- 2½ cups (10½ ounces) unbleached all-purpose flour

ICING

- 1 cup (4 ounces) confectioners' sugar
- 4 teaspoons milk (regular or low fat, not nonfat)
- 4 teaspoons light corn syrup
- Food colors

● **To make the dough:** In a medium-sized bowl, beat together the oil, butter, eggs, vanilla, salt, baking powder, and confectioners' sugar until smooth. Add the flour, beating until smooth. Cover the bowl with plastic wrap and refrigerate for at least 1 hour, or overnight.

● Preheat the oven to 350°F. Lightly grease (or line with parchment) two baking sheets.

● Scoop the dough into 2-teaspoon balls; a teaspoon cookie scoop works perfectly here. Roll the balls into ropes about 4 inches long and about ½ inch in diameter (about the size of your finger, if you have long, thin fingers). Coil the ropes into round doughnut shapes, leaving a very small hole in the middle.

● Place the cookies on the prepared baking sheets about 1 inch apart. Bake for about 18 minutes. They may have the merest hint of golden color on top, but definitely won't be brown. Remove them from the oven and transfer to a rack to cool completely before icing.

● **To ice the cookies:** Put ¼ cup confectioners' sugar into each of four tiny bowls or condiment cups. Add 1 teaspoon milk and 1 teaspoon corn syrup to each bowl. Stir until you've made a soft, spreadable icing, adding more milk if necessary. Tint the icing in each bowl a different color. If you're using strong gel or paste food colors, mix 1 drop with a teaspoon of milk, then dribble it into the uncolored frosting by the ¼ teaspoonful, until icing is the shade you want.

● Dip the top of each cookie in one of the icings. Or make these cookies all one color, if you don't feel like fussing. Allow the frosting to harden before storing the cookies.

Nutrition information per serving (1 cookie, 19 g): 66 cal, 2 g fat, 1 g protein, 5 g complex carbohydrates, 6 g sugar, 12 mg cholesterol, 66 mg sodium, 13 mg potassium, 12 RE vitamin A, 1 mg vitamin C, 15 mg calcium, 16 mg phosphorus.

Wine Biscuits

Wine, as in containing wine? Or as in to serve with wine? Well, both, actually. These sweet, peppery-hot biscuits are a variation on a traditional Italian favorite, *biscotti di vino,* which are hard, semisweet biscuits served with an after-dinner cheese, or as an appetizer, along with wine. We like them served on the porch, after a hard day at work in a hot kitchen. Sangria, that Spanish concoction of mild wine and fruit, is a perfect accompaniment to these biscuits. But they're fine with a grape juice spritzer, too, or lemon-scented club soda. By the way, the term "biscuit," as it's used here, refers to a hard, fairly dense cookie, rather than the biscuit Americans know—a soft white-bread roll.

Yield: 27 cookies ● ***Baking temperature:** 350°F* ● ***Baking time:** 35 to 40 minutes*

> 2½ cups (10½ ounces) unbleached all-purpose flour
> 2 teaspoons coarsely ground black pepper (or to taste; this amount makes a very spicy cookie)
> 4 to 6 tablespoons (1¾ to 2⅝ ounces) sugar, to taste*
> 1 teaspoon salt
> 2 teaspoons baking powder
> ½ cup plus 2 tablespoons (9 ounces) dry red wine, such as Cabernet Sauvignon (nonalcoholic is fine)
> ⅓ cup (2½ ounces) vegetable oil

● In a medium-sized mixing bowl, combine the flour, pepper, sugar, salt, and baking powder. In a separate bowl, whisk together the wine and vegetable oil. Add the liquid ingredients to the dry ingredients and beat vigorously until the mixture is smooth, about 1 minute. Cover the bowl and refrigerate the dough for at least 1 hour, or overnight.

● Preheat the oven to 350°F. Lightly grease (or line with parchment) one large or two smaller baking sheets.

● Break off a piece of dough about the size of a walnut and roll it into a ball. Poke a hole in the middle of the ball to make a small bagel-shaped cookie. Place it on the prepared baking sheet. Repeat with the remaining dough.

● Bake for 35 to 40 minutes, or until they're golden brown (they'll look kind of purple, which is okay). Remove them from the oven and transfer to a rack to cool.

* The greater amount of sugar will make a biscuit that's just about as sweet as a regular cookie; the lesser amount will yield a more savory-type cookie.

Nutrition information per serving *(1 cookie, 23 g):* 76 cal, 3 g fat, 1 g protein, 8 g complex carbohydrates, 3 g sugar, 115 mg sodium, 22 mg potassium, 1 mg iron, 21 mg calcium, 18 mg phosphorus.

Mini-Elephant Ears

These flat, crunchy, sweet spirals are a delicious accompaniment to fresh berries. Often appearing as palm-sized pastries in the bakery case, when downsized they become cookies, as they are here. The classic dough for these cookies is a laboriously made puff pastry dough. Our version, based on one developed by author and King Arthur Flour friend Lora Brody, is much easier to prepare and yields sublime results.

Yield: 4 dozen cookies ● *Baking temperature:* 425°F ● *Baking time:* 19 minutes

2¼ cups (9½ ounces) unbleached all-purpose flour
1 tablespoon dough relaxer (optional, but very helpful, see page 494)
¼ teaspoon salt
½ teaspoon baking powder
¾ cup (1½ sticks, 6 ounces) unsalted butter, cut into ¼-inch dice and frozen for 30 minutes
¾ cup (6 ounces) sour cream (regular or low fat, not nonfat)
½ to ¾ cup (3½ to 5¼ ounces) sugar, for coating

● In a medium-sized bowl, combine the flour, dough relaxer, salt, and baking powder. Using your fingers or a pastry blender, work in the frozen butter, mixing until even crumbs form. Stir in the sour cream, gather the dough into a ball, and knead it briefly to make it cohesive.

● Flatten the dough into an oval and fold it like a letter (first one side into the middle, then the other side over the first side). Give the dough a quarter turn, flatten it, and fold it again.

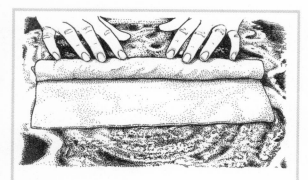

Be sure to use lots of sugar when rolling the elephant ear dough. Since there's no sugar in the dough itself, these cookies rely on the sugar topping for sweetness.

Divide it in half, wrap in plastic wrap, and refrigerate for at least 1 hour, or overnight.

● Sprinkle your work surface with sugar. Remove one piece of the dough from the refrigerator, and roll it into a 12 x 10-inch rectangle. Sprinkle sugar over the dough, gently pressing it on with a rolling pin. Starting with a long side, roll the pastry into a log. Repeat with the other piece of dough. Wrap the logs in plastic wrap, and refrigerate them for at least 1 hour (or freeze for 30 minutes).

● Preheat the oven to 425°F. Lightly grease (or line with parchment) two baking sheets.

● Using a sharp knife, gently cut each log into ⅓-inch-thick slices and lay the slices on the prepared baking sheets.

● Bake the cookies for about 13 minutes, or until the sugar on the bottom has begun to brown. Turn them over and bake for an additional 6 minutes, or until the sugar is lightly browned on the other side. Watch closely—these go from golden brown to inedibly scorched in nothing flat. Remove the cookies from the oven and transfer to a rack to cool completely.

Nutrition information per serving (1 cookie, 16 g): 64 cal, 4 g fat, 1 g protein, 4 g complex carbo-hydrates, 3 g sugar, 9 mg cholesterol, 18 mg sodium, 13 mg potassium, 34 RE vitamin A, 1 mg vitamin C, 8 mg calcium, 10 mg phosphorus.

VARIATIONS

● To make cinnamon spirals, add 4 teaspoons cinnamon to the sugar for coating.

● To make *palmiers,* a classic French pastry, prepare the dough as directed up to the step where you roll up the rectangles. Then start at one long edge and instead of rolling the dough into logs, roll it only until you reach the center of the dough. Then do the same starting with the other long edge. You'll now have two cylinders that have met in the middle. Wrap, freeze, slice, and bake as directed in the elephant ears recipe.

Starting from opposite edges, roll the dough into two cylinders that meet in the center.

Ossi da Morto (Bones of the Dead)

These gnarly, crunchy, almond-scented cookies are traditionally baked and eaten in Italy on November 2, the day after All Saints Day, in honor of family members who've passed away. There are as many different combinations of ingredients and different shapes for these cookies as there are villages in Italy. This recipe combines versions from several different locales. It calls for almond oil, but almond is only one of the flavors associated with *Ossi da Morto*. Other versions call for lemon, anise, cinnamon, or cloves. Feel free to substitute your favorite extract, oil, or spice.

Yield: *3½ dozen cookies* ● **Baking temperature:** *300°F* ● **Baking time:** *15 to 25 minutes*

> 2½ cups (10 ounces) confectioners' sugar
> 2 teaspoons baking powder
> 2 cups (8½ ounces) unbleached all-purpose flour
> ½ cup (1⅝ ounces) almond flour (finely ground blanched almonds)*
> ½ teaspoon salt
> 2 large eggs
> ½ to 1 teaspoon almond extract, or a few drops almond oil, to taste
> 1½ to 2 tablespoons (¾ to 1 ounce) milk (regular or low fat, not nonfat)

● Lightly grease (or line with parchment) two baking sheets.
● In a medium-sized bowl, whisk together the sugar, baking powder, flour, almond flour, and salt. Beat in the eggs, almond extract, and enough milk to make a smooth, soft (but not sticky) dough. The dough will seem dry at first; keep beating until it comes together.
● Transfer the dough to a heavily floured work surface and divide it into 8 pieces. Roll each piece into a long rope about ¾ inch in diameter. Cut each rope into 4-inch pieces. Working with one piece at a time, pinch the center, giving it a slender "waist" about ½ inch thick. Plump the ends into knobs so the whole thing resembles a bone. Don't worry about them being straight, smooth, and even; these are supposed to be fairly gnarly looking.
● Transfer the "bones" to the prepared baking sheets and refrigerate, uncovered, overnight.
● The next day, remove the cookies from the refrigerator. Allow them to rest at room temperature for 1 hour.
● Meanwhile, preheat the oven to 300°F.
● Bake the cookies for 15 minutes to make a cookie that's lightly crunchy on the outside and chewy within. Bake for 20 minutes for a cookie that has less of a chew in the center. Bake for 25 minutes if you want a cookie that's downright hard, like biscotti. These will be rather pale-looking, which is okay. Remember, they're supposed to be bones! Remove the cookies from the oven and transfer them to a rack to cool. Store the cookies tightly wrapped.

* Substitute ½ cup unbleached all-purpose flour if you don't have almond flour. The almond flour is more traditional, but the all-purpose will do just fine.

Nutrition information per serving (1 cookie, 17 g): 58 cal, 1 g fat, 1 g protein, 5 g complex carbohydrates, 7 g sugar, 10 mg cholesterol, 52 mg sodium, 21 mg potassium, 5 RE vitamin A, 1 mg vitamin C, 18 mg calcium, 22 mg phosphorus.

Golden Lemon Rings

Inspired by a cookie native to southern Italy, *anginetti,* the texture of these lemony rings is similar to that of many Italian cookies (other than biscotti): fine-grained and firm, but nicely crumbly once you take a bite. These would partner well with fresh fruit or a cup of tea.

Yield: 3 dozen cookies ● *Baking temperature:* 350°F ● *Baking time:* 20 minutes

DOUGH

- 6 tablespoons (¾ stick, 3 ounces) unsalted butter
- ½ cup (3½ ounces) sugar
- 2 teaspoons vanilla extract
- 1 tablespoon grated lemon rind (zest)
- ½ teaspoon salt
- 3 large eggs
- 2 cups (8½ ounces) unbleached all-purpose flour
- 1½ teaspoons baking powder

GLAZE

- 1 tablespoon (½ ounce) unsalted butter
- ¼ cup (2 ounces) lemon juice, freshly squeezed preferred
- 1 tablespoon (½ ounce) water
- 2 teaspoons grated lemon rind (zest)
- 1 teaspoon vanilla extract, or ⅛ teaspoon *Fiori di Sicilia* flavor
- 3 cups (12 ounces) confectioners' sugar

● Preheat the oven to 350°F. Lightly grease (or line with parchment) two baking sheets.

● **To make the dough:** In a medium-sized bowl, cream together the butter, sugar, vanilla, lemon zest, and salt. Beat in the eggs, scraping the bottom and sides of the bowl. The mixture may look curdled, which is okay. Add the flour and baking powder, beating until smooth.

● Spoon the soft dough into a pastry bag fitted with a plain ⅜-inch round tip. Pipe rings, 2 inches in diameter, onto the prepared baking sheets. Wet your fingers and smooth over the place where the rings meet. If you don't have a pastry bag and tip, spoon the dough into a zip-top plastic bag, snip off one corner, and squeeze the dough out into rings.

● Bake the cookies for 15 to 20 minutes, until they're golden brown. While the cookies are baking, make the glaze.

● **To make the glaze:** In a small saucepan set over low heat, melt the butter, then stir in the lemon juice, water, lemon zest, and vanilla. Add the confectioners' sugar, stirring to make a smooth glaze. Heat and stir until the mixture is smooth and soft enough to brush on the cookies; if it's too thick, stir in additional water. Remove the glaze from the heat.

● Remove the cookies from the oven and immediately brush them with the warm glaze. Transfer them to a rack set over parchment or waxed paper, and let them cool completely.

Nutrition information per serving (1 cookie, 29 g): 97 cal, 3 g fat, 1 g protein, 5 g complex carbohydrates, 12 g sugar, 24 mg cholesterol, 56 mg sodium, 16 mg potassium, 29 RE vitamin A, 1 mg vitamin C, 15 mg calcium, 19 mg phosphorus.

Students' Biscuits

János Dyall, a member of what we call our King Arthur international baking community, has traveled the world throughout his life, and has been kind enough to send us many, many recipes over the years. He sent us this one in response to our published plea, on behalf of another reader, for a cookie she remembered from her childhood—a "kind of crispy almond-flavored shortbread round, 5 inches across, with a big chocolate dot in the middle and a dusting of grated chocolate or cocoa around the edge." Mr. Dyall wrote us, "We used to call these 'Students' Biscuits' years ago. Now I have not seen them for years. Our biscuits were good and indeed quite large, and I still have the recipe so am sending it herewith. I am sorry I use the word biscuit, but I learned England English; of course I mean cookie."

We're glad Mr. Dyall chose to share the recipe for these big, thick, tender-crunchy almond-flavored cookies with us. All of the taste-testers here at King Arthur Flour gave them the thumbs-up.

Yield: *16 cookies* ● **Baking temperature:** *325°F* ● **Baking time:** *20 to 23 minutes*

DOUGH
2¼ cups (9½ ounces) unbleached all-purpose flour
1¾ cups (5¾ ounces) almond flour (ground almonds*)
Heaping ½ teaspoon salt
1¼ cups (2½ sticks, 10 ounces) unsalted butter
1¼ cups (8¾ ounces) sugar
1 teaspoon almond extract

COATING
¼ cup (1 ounce) confectioners' sugar
2 teaspoons unsweetened cocoa, natural or Dutch process
1 egg white beaten with 1 tablespoon water (optional, to give cookies a shiny-crackly look)

FILLING
1⅓ cups (8 ounces) chocolate chips
2 tablespoons (1 ounce) unsalted butter
2 tablespoons (1⅜ ounces) corn syrup

● **To make the dough:** In a small bowl, whisk together the flour, almond flour and salt. Set aside. In a medium-sized mixing bowl, cream together the butter, sugar, and almond extract. Add the dry ingredients and beat until smooth and cohesive. Shape the dough into a log about 2½ inches in diameter and 9 inches long.

● **For the coating:** Whisk together the confectioners' sugar and cocoa and sprinkle it on a clean work surface or, better, on a piece of parchment. Roll the log in it to coat. To make the log nice and round, roll it in the parchment using a straight edge (see illustrated technique on page 25). Wrap the log in plastic wrap and place it in the freezer overnight.

● Remove the dough from the freezer and let it thaw, still wrapped, for 45 minutes.

● Preheat the oven to 325°F. Lightly grease (or line with parchment) two baking sheets.

- Remove the plastic and cut the log into ¾-inch slices. Lay the slices on the prepared baking sheets, about 2 inches apart. Brush with the beaten egg white, if desired.
- Bake the cookies for 20 to 23 minutes, until they're just barely beginning to brown. Remove them from the oven and, using the top of a salad dressing bottle or other round, flat object about 1½ inches in diameter, make a deep indentation in the center of each warm cookie. Transfer the cookies to a rack to cool.
- **To make the filling:** In a small saucepan over very low heat, or in a microwave-safe bowl, combine the chocolate chips, butter, and corn syrup, stirring until the mixture is smooth.
- Using a teaspoon-sized cookie scoop (or a teaspoon), drop a ball of the filling onto the center of each cookie. Wet your fingers and flatten the chocolate slightly. Allow the chocolate to cool before storing the cookies in an airtight container.

* You may process whole blanched almonds in a food processor or blender to make almond flour, but be sure to process just until they're finely ground; a second too long and you'll have oily almond paste.

Nutrition information per serving (1 cookie, 88 g): 423 cal, 24 g fat, 5 g protein, 17 g complex carbohydrates, 29 g sugar, 3 g dietary fiber, 43 mg cholesterol, 79 mg sodium, 155 mg potassium, 147 RE vitamin A, 1 mg vitamin C, 2 mg iron, 34 mg calcium, 97 mg phosphorus, 11 mg caffeine.

Springerle

Springerle (SPRING-er-lee), perhaps the most traditional of German Christmas cookies, are made from a simple dough of eggs, sugar, and flour, usually seasoned with anise or lemon. These very hard cookies are extremely long-lasting and ship very well. They're ideal served with coffee or tea. Originally, *springerle* were made using individual, hand-carved molds, often very intricate in design. In the area around Germany's Black Forest, where *springerle* originated, these molds sometimes developed into giant, 2- to 3-foot high affairs featuring costumed revelers and animals. More commonly, *springerle* molds were cookie-sized and featured Christmas scenes, such as fir trees, St. Nicholas, and angels. These days, a *springerle* pin—a rolling pin imprinted with *springerle* designs—is as commonly used as individual molds. Both molds and pins are available via mail order.

Although this recipe is a bit time-consuming, we think the investment is worth it. Keep in mind that the baked cookies will be very hard when they cool, and will be a pale tan color, not brown at all. If this is what you end up with, you did it the right way—the traditional way.

Yield: 2½ to 3 dozen small cookies ● *Baking temperature: 275°F*
Baking time: 25 to 30 minutes, plus a day of waiting time

3 large eggs
½ teaspoon salt
3½ cups (14 ounces) confectioners' sugar
¼ to ½ teaspoon anise oil, lemon oil, or flavor of your choice
3½ cups (14¾ ounces) unbleached all-purpose flour
Anise seed (optional)

● Lightly grease (or line with parchment) two baking sheets.

● In a large bowl, beat together the eggs, salt, confectioners' sugar, and flavor. Beat for 5 to 6 minutes, until the mixture is very light and falls in thick ribbons from the beater. Gradually beat in the flour to form a stiff dough. Transfer the dough to a well-floured work surface and knead with your hands for several minutes—it will seem very dry at first, but will become smooth as you work with it. Wrap the dough in plastic wrap and let it rest at room temperature for 30 minutes or so.

● **To shape cookies using a *springerle* pin:** Dust your work surface lightly with flour. Divide the dough in half and work with one piece at a time, keeping the other piece covered. Use a regular rolling pin to roll the dough into a ¼-inch-thick rectangle, roughly the same width as your *springerle* pin. Use a pastry brush to brush a very light coating of flour onto the dough. Flour your *springerle* pin, then give it a couple of sharp raps to knock off the excess. Slowly roll the *springerle* pin over the dough, pressing down hard enough to leave a good impression. Cut the cookies apart on the lines, with a pizza wheel or sharp knife.

● **To shape cookies using a *springerle* mold:** Lightly flour your work surface. Dust the mold with flour, then tap it firmly to remove the excess. Divide the dough in half and work with one piece at a time, and keeping the other piece covered. Roll the dough into a ¼-inch-thick square or rectangle, then press the lightly floured mold firmly into the dough. Remove the mold and cut around the design with a knife. Repeat until all the dough is cut.

- Transfer the cookies to the prepared baking sheets. If you're using aniseed, sprinkle it on the cookie sheet or the parchment before laying down the cookies. Some of the seeds will stick to the bottom of the cookies, giving them extra flavor. They'll also raise the cookies just a bit, allowing air to circulate around the bottom, drying them thoroughly. Set the unbaked cookies aside to rest at room temperature, uncovered, for 24 hours.
- Preheat the oven to 275°F.
- Bake the cookies for 25 to 30 minutes, until they're firm but not brown. (If the cookies are a bit puffy, and the design isn't as sharp as you'd like, bake the next batch at 250°F for 35 to 40 minutes.) Remove them from the oven and transfer to a rack to cool completely.
- Store the cookies in an airtight container. To keep them from becoming rock hard, we suggest placing a piece of soft bread, a slice of apple, or a cookie softener in the container with them.

Nutrition information per serving (*1 cookie, 27 g*): 89 cal, 1 g fat, 2 g protein, 8 g complex carbohydrates, 11 g sugar, 18 mg cholesterol, 35 mg sodium, 20 mg potassium, 8 RE vitamin A, 1 mg iron, 2 mg calcium, 18 mg phosphorus.

Speculaas

In their packaged form, *speculaas* (SPEC-you-lahss) are familiar to all of us as the thin, crisp, dark brown windmill-shaped cookies you can find in the cookie aisle of your supermarket. In fact, this windmill design, imprinted on the cookies via a *speculaa* mold, is the classic form these cookies take in the Netherlands, their home. *Speculaas* are also molded into Christmas-motif shapes, as they're a favorite during St. Nicholas season, which stretches from late November through December 6 in Holland. In Germany, these intricately shaped ginger cookies are called *speculatius,* and are very much like *springerle* (page 382) in appearance, save for their dark color.

 Speculaa molds are available via mail order. But you don't need a mold to enjoy these snapping crisp, delightfully spicy cookies. You can simply drop balls of dough onto a baking sheet and press them flat, or roll the dough out and cut it into circles or rectangles. Whatever their shape, they're wonderful enjoyed with a glass of cold milk, or dipped in hot coffee.

Yield: 4 dozen small cookies ● *Baking temperature: 325°F* ● *Baking time: 15 to 20 minutes*

½ cup (1 stick, 4 ounces) unsalted butter
¾ cup (6 ounces) brown sugar
1 teaspoon vanilla extract
½ teaspoon ground cardamom
½ teaspoon ground cloves
½ teaspoon ground mace (or substitute ½ teaspoon nutmeg)
1½ teaspoons cinnamon
½ teaspoon salt
1½ cups (6¼ ounces) unbleached all-purpose flour
½ cup (1⅝ ounces) almond flour (toasted preferred)
1 teaspoon baking powder
2 to 4 tablespoons (1 to 2 ounces) milk (regular or low fat, not nonfat)
Additional milk, to glaze

● In a large mixing bowl, cream together the butter, sugar, vanilla, spices, and salt. Stir in the flour, almond flour, and baking powder, then enough of the milk to make a stiff dough. Flatten the dough into a disk, wrap it in plastic wrap, and refrigerate for 1 hour, or overnight.

● Preheat the oven to 325°F. Lightly grease (or line with parchment) two baking sheets.

● **To make *speculaas* with a mold:** Lightly dust the mold with cornstarch. Break off a chunk of dough large enough to cover the design cut into the mold. Press the dough into the mold, gently rolling it flat. Trim off any excess by scraping a baker's bench knife across the mold. Unmold the cookie onto the prepared baking sheets. Repeat with the remaining dough.

● **To make *speculaas* without a mold:** Drop the dough by 2-teaspoonfuls onto the prepared baking sheets. Use the bottom of a drinking glass dipped in sugar to press each ball of dough to ¼ inch thick. Or, if you have a cookie stamp, use that. (Alternatively, roll the dough ¼ inch thick and cut it into rectangles; or roll a *springerle* rolling pin across it, using a knife to cut the cookies apart once they're rolled.)

● Bake the cookies for 15 to 20 minutes, until they're lightly browned around the edges. Remove them from the oven and transfer them to a rack to cool. As they cool, they'll become quite hard.

Nutrition information per serving (*1 cookie, 13 g*): 52 cal, 3 g fat, 1 g protein, 3 g complex carbohydrates, 3 g sugar, 5 mg cholesterol, 35 mg sodium, 30 mg potassium, 18 RE vitamin A, 1 mg vitamin C, 15 mg calcium, 15 mg phosphorus.

For an even bake

When baking cookies, even if you're only baking one sheet at a time, it helps to rotate the baking sheets through the oven during their bake. What does this mean? If you're baking one sheet of cookies, start it on the lower-middle oven shelf. Midway through its bake time, take the sheet out of the oven, reverse it so the cookies that were in back are now in front, and place it back on the upper-middle rack in your oven. Do the same thing with two sheets, simply reversing them back to front and exchanging their positions on the racks. This ensures that cookie tops and bottoms are both nicely baked and the effects of any hot spots in your oven are minimized.

Amaretti

These almond-scented macaroon-type cookies, native to Italy, are simple to make and very versatile: they're great crunched up as a topping for custard- or mascarpone-filled desserts, or as a cookie crust base. They're also great keepers, either in the form of unbaked dough (up to three weeks in the refrigerator), or as finished morsels (stored in an airtight container). When warm from the oven, they're crunchy on the outside and ever-so-slightly chewy on the inside. For festive presentation at the holidays, wrap individually in mini-muffin papers, or in colored foil or tissue paper squares, and layer in a cookie tin.

Yield: 26 cookies ● *Baking temperature:* 350°F ● *Baking time:* 25 to 28 minutes

> 1¾ cups (12¼ ounces) sugar
> One 15-ounce can almond paste
> 4 large egg whites (5 ounces)
> 2 tablespoons (1 ounce) amaretto liqueur, or 2 teaspoons almond extract
> 1 teaspoon salt
> Sliced almonds or coarse sugar, for topping

● In a large bowl, beat together the sugar, almond paste, egg whites, amaretto, and salt at medium speed for 5 minutes. Stop the mixer, scrape down the sides of the bowl, and continue beating for an additional 5 to 10 minutes, until the mixture is completely smooth. Cover the bowl and refrigerate the dough overnight.

● The next day, preheat the oven to 350°F. Lightly grease (or line with parchment) two baking sheets.

● Remove the dough from the refrigerator and fill a disposable pastry bag three-quarters full. Pipe it into 2-teaspoon mounds, no more than ½-inch high, on the prepared baking sheets (see illustrations, opposite). Decorate the tops of the amaretti with sliced almonds or coarse sugar.

● Bake the cookies for 25 to 28 minutes. They should be an even, deep beige color, and firm to the touch on top. Remove the amaretti from the oven and cool for 15 minutes before transferring them to a rack to cool completely. The cookies will crisp up as they cool.

Nutrition information per serving (1 cookie, 36 g): 129 cal, 3 g fat, 3 g protein, 3 g complex carbohydrates, 15 g sugar, 1 g dietary fiber, 93 mg sodium, 114 mg potassium, 39 mg calcium, 75 mg phosphorus.

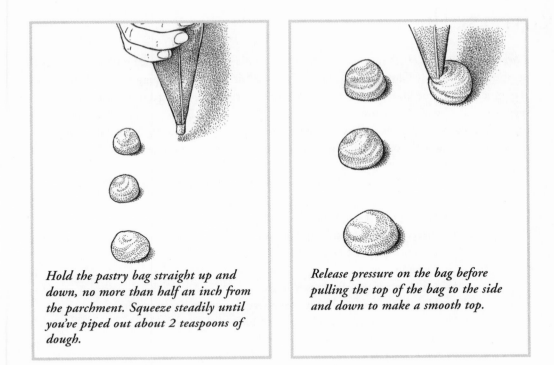

Hold the pastry bag straight up and down, no more than half an inch from the parchment. Squeeze steadily until you've piped out about 2 teaspoons of dough.

Release pressure on the bag before pulling the top of the bag to the side and down to make a smooth top.

Garnish the tops of the cookies before baking.

Chrusciki

Chrusciki (khroosh-CHEE-kee), a crisp, deep-fried cookie, is a Polish specialty served on special occasions, particularly Christmas and Easter. Though fairly time-consuming to make (and, alas, very quickly consumed!), if you have fond memories of these cookies and find yourself craving them when the holidays roll around, this is a good recipe to try. By the way, these are nearly identical to Norway's *fattigmann,* also served at the holidays. Note that the small bit of alcohol called for is traditional, you can substitute apple juice or water, if you like.

Yield: 4 dozen cookies ● *Frying temperature: 375°F* ● *Frying time: 60 to 90 seconds*

1 large egg plus 1 egg yolk
1 tablespoon rum, brandy, or whiskey
1 teaspoon vanilla extract
½ teaspoon salt
¼ cup (1 ounce) confectioners' sugar
2 tablespoons (1 ounce) sour cream (regular or low fat, not nonfat)
1½ cups (6¼ ounces) unbleached all-purpose flour
Vegetable oil or solid shortening for deep frying
¼ cup (1 ounce) confectioners' sugar, for coating

● In a medium-sized bowl, beat together the egg, egg yolk, liquor, vanilla, salt, sugar, and sour cream until smooth. Stir in the flour to make a soft dough. Divide the dough in half, shape each half into a slightly flattened log, and refrigerate for at least 30 minutes, or overnight.

● Remove one piece of dough from the refrigerator and place it on a well-floured work surface. Roll it into a 12 x 10-inch rectangle, ⅛ inch thick. If the dough shrinks back as you roll, simply cover it with a piece of plastic wrap and let it rest for 10 minutes. Cut the rectangle into two 5 x 12-inch pieces, then cut each piece crosswise into twelve 5 x 1-inch strips.

● Cut a vertical 1-inch slit in the center of each strip (see illustrations). Carefully poke one end through the slit and twist it gently once it's through. Repeat with the remaining dough strips, gently laying the shaped cookies onto a baking sheet. Repeat with the remaining dough. If your kitchen is very hot, refrigerate the cookies until all the dough has been shaped and you're ready to start frying.

● Heat the vegetable oil to 375°F in a large, deep saucepan, or an electric frying pan. Fry the cookies 5 or 6 at a time by dropping them into the oil and frying for 60 to 90 seconds, turning them with a fork midway through. The cookies should be golden brown when fully cooked. If you've rolled the dough thicker than ⅛ inch you'll need to fry them a bit longer to make them crisp.

● Remove the cookies from the oil and immediately sprinkle them with confectioners' sugar. Transfer to a rack to cool.

Nutrition information per serving (1 cookie, 10 g): 43 cal, 3 g fat, 1 g protein, 3 g complex carbohydrates, 1 g sugar, 9 mg cholesterol, 24 mg sodium, 7 mg potassium, 5 RE vitamin A, 1 mg vitamin C, 2 mg calcium, 8 mg phosphorus.

SHAPING *CHRUSCIKI*

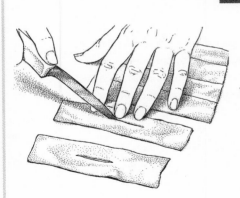

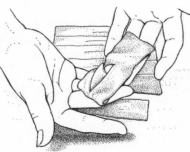

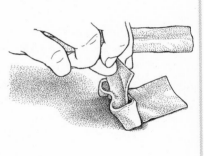

Make a vertical, 1-inch slit in the strip of dough.

Gently grasp one end of the dough strip and poke it through the slit.

Give the chrusciki *a single twist.*

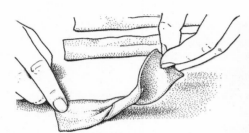

The shaped chrusciki *will look like a loosely tied bowtie.*

Use a shaker to sprinkle the chrusciki *generously with confectioners' sugar as soon as they come out of the hot oil.*

Testing *chrusciki* for crispness

Though it extends the process a bit, test-fry one *chrusciki* first. Remove it from the oil, allow it to cool for several minutes, and take a bite. Is it crisp? Then proceed with the remaining cookies. Is it chewy or leathery? You haven't fried it long enough, or the oil temperature is too low; try another test cookie. If *chrusciki* are a very deep, golden brown, yet still not crisp, reduce the temperature of the frying oil by 10°F.

Zwieback

When you think comfort food, do you think chicken-noodle soup, creamy macaroni and cheese, or a silky chocolate pudding? Well, how about zwieback? Those ultradry, lightly spiced, faintly sweet and invariably satisfying toasts on which kids everywhere cut their teeth are a quintessential childhood (read: comfort) food. Note that this is a two-day process, as the loaf the zwieback are made from needs to rest overnight—so plan accordingly.

Yield: 4 dozen zwieback ● *Baking temperature:* 350°F for the bread; 250°F for the zwieback ● *Baking time:* 25 minutes for the bread; 90 minutes for the zwieback

4 tablespoons (½ stick, 2 ounces) unsalted butter
⅓ cup (2⅜ ounces) sugar
¾ cup (6 ounces) milk (regular or low fat, not nonfat)
¼ teaspoon cinnamon
¼ teaspoon nutmeg
¾ teaspoon salt
1¼ teaspoons instant yeast
1 large egg
3 cups (12¾ ounces) unbleached all-purpose flour

● Lightly grease (or line with parchment) a large baking sheet.
● **To make the zwieback bread:** In the microwave, or in a small saucepan set over low heat, stir together the butter, sugar, and milk just until the butter melts. Remove from the heat and let the mixture cool to 100° to 105°F, or until barely warm.
● Combine the milk mixture and the cinnamon, nutmeg, salt, yeast, egg, and flour in the bowl of an electric mixer, or in the bucket of a bread machine. This dough may be prepared up through its first rise in a bread machine set on the dough or manual cycle. Mix and knead to form a smooth, elastic dough that's quite soft; this will take about 5 minutes in an electric mixer.
● Lightly grease a large bowl, place the dough inside, cover it with plastic wrap, and let it rise for 60 to 90 minutes. The rising time is flexible, since it won't rise quickly. It should just become a bit puffy.
● Gently deflate the dough and divide it in half. Roll the pieces with your hands to form two 14-inch-long cylindrical loaves. If the dough resists rolling, let it rest, covered, for several minutes. When you return, you should find the gluten relaxed and the task much easier.
● Place the loaves on the prepared baking sheet. Use the palms of your hands or a rolling pin to flatten them so they're about 3½ inches wide. Cover the loaves with plastic wrap and let them rise until they're puffy, about 90 minutes.
● Preheat the oven to 350°F.
● Bake the bread for 25 minutes, until it's golden brown and an instant-read thermometer inserted in the center of the loaves reads 190°F. Remove the loaves from the oven and transfer to a rack to cool overnight, uncovered.
● **To bake the zwieback toast:** The next day, preheat the oven to 250°F.

- With a serrated knife, cut the loaves on a slight diagonal into ½- to ¾-inch slices. Place the slices upright on ungreased or parchment-lined baking sheets (see illustration #8, page 135). Bake the zwieback until they're completely dry and beginning to turn golden, about 90 minutes, depending on the weather and the vagaries of your oven.
- Remove the zwieback from the oven and transfer to a rack to cool. When thoroughly cooled, these will keep for many weeks in an airtight container.

Nutrition information per serving (1 zwieback, 21 g): 56 cal, 1 g fat, 2 g protein, 8 g complex carbohydrates, 1 g sugar, 9 mg cholesterol, 27 mg sodium, 27 mg potassium, 14 RE vitamin A, 1 mg iron, 27 mg calcium, 19 mg phosphorus.

VARIATION

These cinnamon-sugar zwieback taste like extra-crunchy cinnamon toast.

> 1 batch zwieback bread, sliced
> 4 tablespoons (½ stick, 2 ounces) unsalted butter, melted
> ¼ cup (1¾ ounces) sugar
> ¼ teaspoon cinnamon

- Prepare, bake, and cut the zwieback bread as directed in the recipe.
- Brush melted butter on one side of each of the slices. Combine the sugar and cinnamon and sprinkle it over the butter.
- Bake the zwieback as directed for 90 minutes.

Brattleboro Bonbons

With their rim of diced pecans, these tender-crunchy butter cookies are as pretty as they are tasty. They were a specialty of King Arthur Flour's head baker, Jeffrey Hamelman, at his former bakery in Brattleboro, Vermont.

Yield: **5½ dozen cookies** ● ***Baking temperature:*** *375°F* ° ***Baking time:*** *12 to 15 minutes*

¾ cup plus 1 tablespoon (1½ sticks plus 1 tablespoon, 6½ ounces) unsalted butter
½ cup (3½ ounces) sugar
Heaping ½ teaspoon salt
1 large egg plus 1 large egg yolk
1 teaspoon vanilla extract
½ cup (2 ounces) chopped pecans plus ½ cup (2 ounces) finely diced pecans
2 cups (8½ ounces) unbleached all-purpose flour

● In a medium-sized bowl, cream together the butter, sugar, and salt. Beat in the egg, egg yolk, and vanilla, scraping the bottom and sides of the bowl. Stir in the ½ cup chopped pecans and flour, mixing until cohesive.
● Shape the dough into a 17 x 2-inch log and roll the log in the finely diced pecans. Wrap the log in plastic wrap and place in the freezer for about an hour.
● Preheat the oven to 375°F. Lightly grease (or line with parchment) two baking sheets.
● Remove the dough from the freezer, slice it into ¼-inch-thick patties, and place them on the prepared baking sheets. Bake the cookies for 12 to 15 minutes, until they're a deep, golden brown and they feel set. Remove them from the oven and transfer to a rack to cool.

Nutrition information per serving (1 cookie, 10 g): 46 cal, 3 g fat, 1 g protein, 3 g complex carbohydrates, 2 g sugar, 13 mg cholesterol, 18 mg sodium, 10 mg potassium, 24 RE vitamin A, 1 mg vitamin C, 2 mg calcium, 9 mg phosphorus.

CREATE-A-COOKIES • • • • • • •

Did you enjoy playing with modeling clay as a child? Then you'll love creating these stunning-looking cookies, which range from square checkerboards and round pinwheels to pretzels and peppermint sticks. These "do it all" doughs, in three flavors—vanilla, fruit, and chocolate—can be combined or used separately to make any number of fanciful cookies.

For these recipes, we recommend using extra-fine salt. Diamond Crystal table salt is much finer-grained than everyday table salts, and is a good choice for this recipe; check for it at your supermarket.

Vanilla Cookie Dough

This is your basic building-block dough, from which all others are created. It's easy to make, easy to work with, and yields a crisp, buttery cookie.

> ½ cup (2 ounces) confectioners' sugar
> ¾ cup (1½ sticks, 6 ounces) unsalted butter
> ½ teaspoon salt, extra-fine preferred
> 1½ teaspoons vanilla extract
> 1½ cups (6¼ ounces) unbleached all-purpose flour

● In a medium-sized mixing bowl, cream together the sugar, butter, salt, and vanilla. Add the flour, stirring to make a cohesive dough. Flatten the dough into a disk, wrap it in plastic wrap, and refrigerate until you're ready to use it.

Nutrition information per serving (1 cookie, 1/36 of recipe, 12 g): 57 cal, 4 g fat, 1 g protein, 4 g complex carbohydrates, 2 g sugar, 10 mg cholesterol, 30 mg sodium, 7 mg potassium, 36 RE vitamin A, 1 mg calcium, 5 mg phosphorus.

Fruit-Flavored Cookie Dough

For added color in your creations, try this dough. The fruit flavor is mild but the bright colors are striking—raspberry, cherry, strawberry, and orange are particular favorites.

> 3 tablespoons (¾ ounce) confectioners' sugar
> 1 package (3 ounces) fruit-flavored gelatin powder (not sugar-free)
> ¾ cup (1½ sticks, 6 ounces) unsalted butter
> ½ teaspoon salt, extra-fine preferred
> 1½ teaspoons vanilla extract
> 1½ cups (6¼ ounces) unbleached all-purpose flour

● In a medium-sized mixing bowl, cream together the sugar, gelatin powder, butter, salt, and vanilla. Add the flour, stirring to make a cohesive dough. Flatten the dough into a disk, wrap it in plastic wrap, and refrigerate until you're ready to use it.

Nutrition information per serving (1 cookie, 13 g): 62 cal, 4 g fat, 1 g protein, 4 g complex carbohydrates, 2 g sugar, 10 mg cholesterol, 31 mg sodium, 8 mg potassium, 36 RE vitamin A, 1 mg calcium, 5 mg phosphorus.

Fanciful shapes

Any of these base doughs (see pages 393–395) are great candidates for making spritz cookies, Scandinavian cookies whose dough is shaped by being forced through a cookie press. You'll often see these cookies for sale during the Christmas holidays, packed in a pretty tin.

A cookie press is a useful tool for making all kinds of shaped cookies, but don't think you can force just any cookie dough through a press. In order for the cookies to maintain their shape as they bake, they need to have the correct fat to flour ratio, and they need to be unleavened.

Chocolate Cookie Dough

This deep dark chocolate dough makes a striking contrast, both in flavor and color, to the vanilla dough.

> ½ cup (2 ounces) confectioners' sugar
> ¾ cup (1½ sticks, 6 ounces) unsalted butter
> ½ teaspoon salt, extra-fine preferred
> 1½ teaspoons vanilla extract
> ¼ cup (¾ ounce) unsweetened cocoa, Dutch process preferred
> 1¼ cups (5¼ ounces) unbleached all-purpose flour

● In a medium-sized mixing bowl, cream together the sugar, butter, salt, and vanilla. Add the cocoa and flour, stirring to make a cohesive dough. Flatten the dough into a disk, wrap it in plastic wrap, and refrigerate until you're ready to use it.

Nutrition information per serving (1 cookie, 1/36 of recipe, 11 g): 56 cal, 4 g fat, 1 g protein, 3 g complex carbohydrates, 2 g sugar, 10 mg cholesterol, 30 mg sodium, 37 mg potassium, 36 RE vitamin A, 2 mg calcium, 10 mg phosphorus, 1 mg caffeine.

Egg White Glaze

This glaze will serve as the "glue" that binds your various creations together as they bake.

> 1 large egg white
> 1 tablespoon water

● Whisk together the egg white and water until very slightly foamy. Refrigerate until ready to use.

Pretzels

The pretzel shape in baking has a very long history; a northern Italian monk is credited with inventing the shape (said to mimic arms crossed over chest, in an attitude of prayer) for his unleavened bread nearly fourteen hundred years ago. Today, this distinctive shape appears in cookies, in crunchy snacks, and in soft breads—including the foot-wide New Year's pretzel made famous by bakers in Sandusky, Ohio. These crunchy cookies look especially luscious when made with chocolate dough and sprinkled with pearl sugar.

Yield: 3 dozen pretzels ● *Baking temperature: 350°F* ● *Baking time: 12 minutes*

1 recipe Vanilla Cookie Dough (page 393) or Chocolate Cookie Dough (page 395), chilled
Egg White Glaze (page 395)
Coarse sugar or pearl sugar

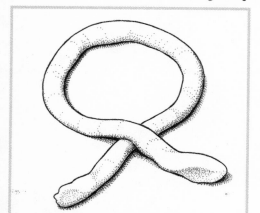

Take the rope of dough and cross one end over the other to make a large loop with short "tails."

● Preheat the oven to 350°F. Lightly grease (or line with parchment) two baking sheets.
● Break off a piece of dough the size of a table tennis ball. On a very lightly floured work surface, shape it into a rope about 10 inches long. Form the rope into a pretzel, as illustrated, and place it on the prepared baking sheet, Repeat with the remaining dough. Brush each pretzel with the egg white glaze and sprinkle with coarse or pearl sugar.
● Bake the cookies for 12 minutes, until they feel firm. Remove them from the oven and transfer to a rack to cool.

Nutrition information per serving (1 pretzel, made with chocolate dough, 24 g): 114 cal, 8 g fat, 1 g protein, 7 g complex carbohydrates, 3 g sugar, 21 mg cholesterol, 62 mg sodium, 45 mg potassium, 71 RE vitamin A, 1 mg iron, 3 mg calcium, 15 mg phosphorus, 1 mg caffeine.

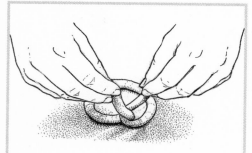

Grab one end of the loop in each hand and bring them to the far end of the loop.

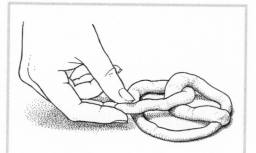

Squeeze the ends to the loop, then gently straighten the whole thing out to make a nice even pretzel.

Cinnamon Bun Cookies

These cookies mimic the classic cinnamon bun—a swirl of cinnamon inside buttery dough. But in this case, the dough bakes into a crisp cookie.

Yield: 2 dozen cookies ● ***Baking temperature:*** *350°F* ● ***Baking time:*** *12 to 15 minutes*

1 recipe chilled Vanilla Cookie Dough (page 393)
¼ cup (1¾ ounces) sugar
1½ teaspoons cinnamon
Egg White Glaze (page 395)
Vanilla Glaze (page 458) or Cinnamon Glaze (page 459)

● Transfer the dough to a piece of parchment or waxed paper. Roll it into a 9 x 12-inch rectangle. Brush it with the egg white glaze,

● In a small bowl, whisk together the sugar and cinnamon. Sprinkle it evenly over the dough. Starting with a long edge, roll the dough into a log, sealing the edge. Wrap it in plastic wrap or parchment, and freeze until firm.

● Preheat the oven to 350°F. Lightly grease (or line with parchment) one large or two smaller baking sheets.

● Remove the dough from the freezer and unwrap it. Using a sharp knife, gently cut it into ½-inch slices. Transfer them to the prepared baking sheets.

● Bake the cookies for 12 to 15 minutes, until they're a light golden brown. Remove them from the oven and transfer to a rack to cool. When cookies are completely cool, drizzle them with Vanilla Glaze or Cinnamon Glaze.

Nutrition information per serving (1 cookie, 21 g): 95 cal, 6 g fat, 1 g protein, 5 g complex carbohydrates, 4 g sugar, 16 mg cholesterol, 47 mg sodium, 14 mg potassium, 53 RE vitamin A, 1 mg vitamin C, 4 mg calcium, 8 mg phosphorus.

Try dental floss for slicing cookie dough

Pressing down on a log of cookie dough to slice it into cookies often results in a misshapen log (and wobbly-edged cookies). For smoothest slicing, try dental floss. Simply loop the floss under the log of dough, cross the ends of the floss, and pull; it will cut right through the dough without altering its shape.

Pinwheels

Make two batches of dough in contrasting colors for these attractive pinwheel cookies. Vanilla and raspberry make a festive holiday cookie, while vanilla and chocolate are a classic combo.

Yield: 4 dozen cookies ● *Baking temperature:* 350°F ● *Baking time:* 12 to 14 minutes

2 recipes chilled cookie dough (two different flavors: Vanilla, page 393; Fruit-Flavored, page 394; or Chocolate, page 395)
Egg White Glaze (page 395)

● Place a piece of parchment or waxed paper on your work surface. Lay one piece of dough on the parchment and roll it into a 9 x 12-inch rectangle. Set it aside.

● Using another piece of parchment or waxed paper, roll the other piece of dough just slightly smaller than the first, into an 8½ x 11½-inch rectangle. Brush the egg white glaze over the larger piece of dough. Place the smaller piece of dough on top of the larger piece, using the parchment to transport.

● Starting with a long edge, use the parchment to help you gently roll the stacked doughs into a tight log, with no gaps. Press the edge to seal, then wrap the log in plastic wrap or parchment, and freeze until firm.

● Preheat the oven to 350°F. Lightly grease (or line with parchment) two baking sheets.

● Remove the dough from the freezer, unwrap it, and place it on a clean work surface. Let it thaw for 15 minutes. Use a sharp knife to gently cut the log into ¼-inch slices. If the dough becomes too soft to handle, place it back in the freezer briefly. Transfer the cookies to the prepared baking sheets.

● Bake the cookies for 12 to 14 minutes, or until they feel firm. Remove them from the oven and transfer to a rack to cool.

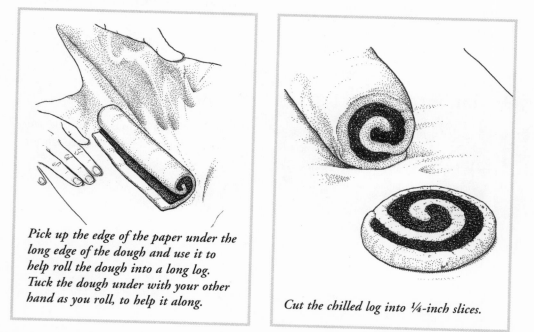

Pick up the edge of the paper under the long edge of the dough and use it to help roll the dough into a long log. Tuck the dough under with your other hand as you roll, to help it along.

Cut the chilled log into ¼-inch slices.

Nutrition information per serving (1 cookie, made with vanilla and chocolate dough, 18 g): 86 cal, 6 g fat, 1 g protein, 5 g complex carbohydrates, 2 g sugar, 16 mg cholesterol, 47 mg sodium, 34 mg potassium, 53 RE vitamin A, 1 mg iron, 2 mg calcium, 11 mg phosphorus, 1 mg caffeine.

VARIATION

Marble Cookies

- Prepare Pinwheels up to the point where you've rolled out both pieces of dough and glazed the larger one. Tear the smaller piece of dough into irregular shapes and place them haphazardly onto the glazed dough. Fold the dough in half crosswise, give it a quarter turn, then fold in half again. On the second fold, gently twist the dough as you fold, as if you were wringing out a cloth; this will increase the marbling effect.
- Roll the dough into a log, smoothing the outside, wrap it in plastic wrap or parchment, and freeze until firm. Slice and bake as directed in the Pinwheels recipe.

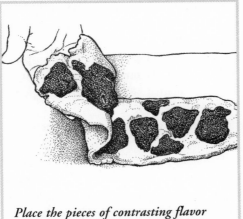

Place the pieces of contrasting flavor dough onto the glazed dough and fold it in half crosswise.

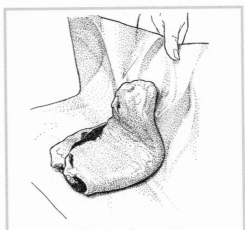

Give the folded dough a quarter turn and fold it again, giving it a twist.

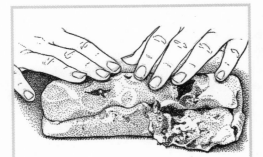

The folded dough will be messy looking, which is okay. Just shape it into a 12-inch log, smoothing it with your fingers.

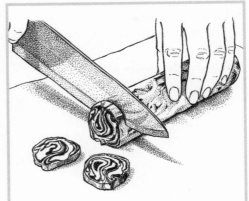

The beautiful marbled effect is revealed when you slice the log.

Checkerboards

While making these cookies isn't for the faint of heart assembly-wise, they do have an amazing look. Your friends will think you worked on them for hours; they'll be right.

Yield: 3 dozen square cookies ● *Baking temperature:* 350°F ● *Baking time:* 12 to 14 minutes

> 2 recipes chilled cookie dough (two different flavors: Vanilla, page 393; Fruit-Flavored, page 394; and Chocolate, page 395)
> Egg White Glaze (page 395)

● Working with one piece at a time, place the dough on a piece of parchment or on a lightly floured work surface. Roll it into an 8½ x 10½-inch rectangle, ½ inch thick. Brush the egg white glaze on one piece of dough, then stack the other piece on top of it, gently pressing them together. Trim the edges of the dough to make an 8 x 10-inch rectangle. Cut the dough in half lengthwise (see illustration, left) to make two 4 x 10-inch rectangles. Wrap one in plastic wrap and refrigerate it while you work on the other.

● Cut the dough rectangle in half lengthwise to make two 2 x 10-inch layered dough strips. Brush the top of one strip with the egg white glaze and stack the other strip atop it. You should now have a 2 x 10-inch strip of dough with four alternating colored layers. Repeat with the remaining dough rectangle.

● Wrap both pieces and freeze for at least 2 hours. Remove the stacked dough from the freezer and let it thaw for 15 minutes.

● Cut each stack into four ½ x 10-inch slices (see illustrations, next page). Turn the slices on their sides. Brush one slice with the glaze, then stack a second atop it, being sure to alternate the light and dark doughs in a checkerboard pattern. Brush the top slice with glaze, and add another slice. Brush that slice with glaze and top it with the fourth and final slice. Repeat with the remaining piece of stacked dough.

● Wrap both pieces of dough, and freeze for 1 hour.

● Preheat the oven to 350°F. Lightly grease (or line with parchment) two baking sheets.

● Remove the dough from the freezer and cut it into ½-inch cookies.

● Place the cookies on the prepared baking sheets and bake for 13 to 15 minutes, until they're firm to the touch. Remove them from the oven and transfer to a rack to cool.

Nutrition information per serving (*1 cookie, made with vanilla and chocolate dough, 22 g):* 103 cal, 7 g fat, 1 g protein, 6 g complex carbohydrates, 3 g sugar, 19 mg cholesterol, 56 mg sodium, 41 mg potassium, 64 RE vitamin A, 1 mg iron, 3 mg calcium, 14 mg phosphorus, 1 mg caffeine.

SLICING AND STACKING CHECKERBOARDS

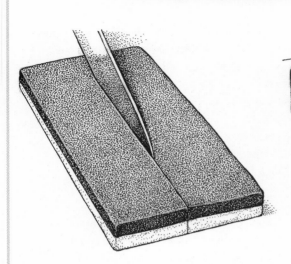

Cut the stacked, trimmed dough in half lengthwise.

Use a sharp knife to cut four even, straight, lengthwise slices from the stacked dough.

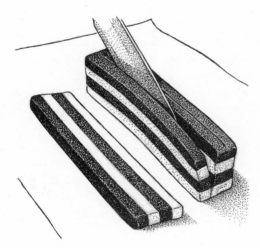

Turn the slices on their sides.

Stack the slices so the dough colors alternate.

Neapolitans

While the term Neapolitan originally referred to a layered brick of vanilla, chocolate, and straw-berry ice cream, it's now come to mean any dessert made in three distinct layers. These cookies bear close resemblance to that classic ice cream, both in appearance and flavor.

Yield: *54 cookies* ● **Baking temperature:** *350°F* ● **Baking time:** *12 to 14 minutes*

1 recipe Vanilla Cookie Dough (page 393)
1 recipe Chocolate Cookie Dough (page 395)
1 recipe Fruit-Flavored Cookie Dough (page 394), raspberry flavor
Egg White Glaze (see page 395)

● Line a 9 x 5-inch loaf pan with plastic wrap, using a piece big enough to overlap on all four sides. Pat the vanilla dough into the bottom of the pan. Use your wet fingers, then a wet bowl scraper, to smooth it flat; the bowl scraper is exactly the right size and shape to smooth dough in this size pan. Brush with the egg white glaze, then layer on the chocolate dough, smoothing it out. Brush with glaze again and add the rasp-berry dough, smoothing the top. Fold the plastic wrap over the top and freeze for 4 hours, or overnight.

● Preheat the oven to 350°F. Lightly grease (or line with parchment) two baking sheets.

● Remove the dough from the freezer and turn it out of the pan. Unwrap it and cut it in half lengthwise. Trim any ragged edges. Cut ⅓-inch crosswise slices from each piece. Transfer the cookies to the prepared baking sheets.

● Bake the cookies for 12 to 14 minutes, until the vanilla layer is a very light golden brown. Remove them from the oven and transfer to a rack to cool.

Nutrition information per serving (1 cookie, 19 g): 94 cal, 6 g fat, 1 g protein, 6 g complex carbohydrates, 3 g sugar, 17 mg cholesterol, 50 mg sodium, 29 mg potassium, 58 RE vitamin A, 1 mg iron, 2 mg calcium, 11 mg phosphorus, 1 mg caffeine.

Cut each strip of layered dough into crosswise slices.

Neon cookies for the kids

Want to make some incredibly bright, neon-colored cookies for the kids? The Fruit-Flavored Cookie Dough (page 394) takes on screamingly vibrant colors from whatever gelatin it's flavored with. Bright red, blue, orange, green, purple . . . take your pick. Simply prepare the dough, drop it by the tablespoonful onto lightly greased or parchment-lined baking sheets, and flatten each ball of dough slightly. Bake in a preheated 350°F oven for about 17 minutes, until they're a very light, golden brown around the edges. Transfer them to a rack to cool. Don your sunglasses, and serve.

Peppermint Sticks

What a great Christmas cookie! The combination of peppermint and chocolate in this "stick" cookie is a beloved flavor duo.

Yield: 2 dozen cookies ● *Baking temperature:* 350°F ● *Baking time:* 12 to 15 minutes

> 1 recipe chilled Chocolate Cookie Dough (page 395) or Vanilla Cookie Dough (page 393)
> GLAZE
> ¾ cup (4½ ounces) chocolate chips
> 1 tablespoon (½ ounce) unsalted butter
> 1 tablespoon (¾ ounce) corn syrup
> TOPPING
> ½ cup (3½ ounces) crushed hard red and white peppermint candies
> or candy canes

● Preheat the oven to 350°F. Lightly grease (or line with parchment) a baking sheet.
● **To make the cookies:** Transfer the dough to a lightly floured work surface and roll it into an 8 x 6-inch rectangle, trimming the edges so they're straight. Divide the rectangle in half lengthwise to make two 8 x 3-inch strips of dough. Cut each strip of dough into ¾ x 3 inch slices. Place the slices on the prepared baking sheet.
● Bake the sticks for 12 to 15 minutes, until they feel firm when pressed. Remove them from the oven and transfer to a rack to cool.
● **To make the glaze:** In a small microwave-safe bowl, or in a small saucepan set over very low heat, melt the chocolate chips and butter together, stirring constantly. Stir in the corn syrup.
● Drizzle the glaze over the cooled cookies and sprinkle them with the crushed peppermints. Place them on a rack to allow the glaze to set.

Nutrition information per serving (1 cookie, made with chocolate dough, 29 g): 147 cal, 9 g fat, 2 g protein, 7 g complex carbohydrates, 8 g sugar, 1 g dietary fiber, 18 mg cholesterol, 53 mg sodium, 85 mg potassium, 61 RE vitamin A, 1 mg iron, 3 mg calcium, 25 mg phosphorus, 6 mg caffeine.

Yin-Yang Cookies

Yin and yang, in Chinese philosophy, represent dark/feminine and bright/masculine. In this case, they represent chocolate and vanilla. Those two doughs are shaped and sliced to resemble the traditional yin-yang figure.

Yield: 4 dozen cookies ● *Baking temperature:* 350°F ● *Baking time:* 12 minutes

1 recipe chilled Vanilla Cookie Dough (page 393)
1 recipe chilled Chocolate Cookie Dough (page 395)
Egg White Glaze (page 395)

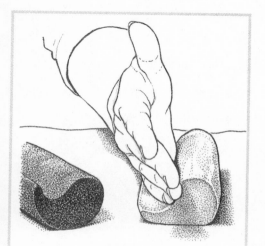

Use the edge of your hand to flatten one side of each log of dough.

● Transfer both pieces of dough to a lightly floured work surface. Shape each into a 12-inch log.
● Use your fingertips to make an indentation down the length of one piece of dough, then press that indentation with the side of your hand to flatten. The dough should look like a big quotation mark in cross section. Brush the inner side of the dough—the flattened half—with the egg white glaze.
● Shape the remaining piece of dough just as you did the first piece, turn it over, and press it onto the first piece. Roll into a smooth cylinder.
● Wrap the dough cylinder in parchment or plastic wrap and freeze it until firm.
● Preheat the oven to 350°F. Lightly grease (or line with parchment) two baking sheets.
● Remove the dough from the freezer and let it thaw for 15 minutes. Slice it into ¼-inch rounds and place them on the prepared baking sheets.
● Bake the cookies for 12 minutes, until the vanilla part is a light golden brown. Remove them from the oven and transfer to a rack to cool.

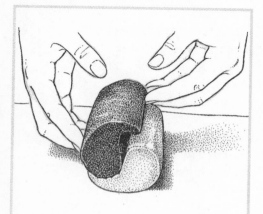

Press the two pieces of dough together so they make a nice round cylinder.

Nutrition information per serving (1 cookie, 18 g): 86 cal, 6 g fat, 1 g protein, 5 g complex carbohydrates, 2 g sugar, 16 mg cholesterol, 47 mg sodium, 34 mg potassium, 53 RE vitamin A, 1 mg iron, 2 mg calcium, 11 mg phosphorus, 1 mg caffeine.

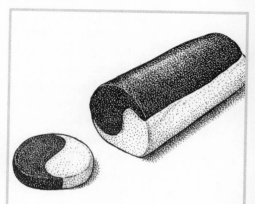

Slice the dough cylinder to reveal the yin-yang shape.

Cookie Wheels

These cookies feature concentric rounds of alternating flavors. Try orange-flavored and vanilla doughs for a cookie reminiscent of a Creamsicle.

Yield: 4 dozen cookies ● *Baking temperature: 350°F* ● *Baking time: 12 to 14 minutes*

> 1 recipe chilled Vanilla Cookie Dough (page 393)
> 1 recipe chilled Chocolate Cookie Dough (page 395) or Fruit-Flavored Cookie Dough (page 394)
> Egg White Glaze (page 395)

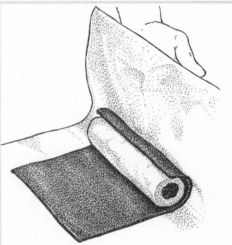

Use the parchment to help you roll the dough into a round log.

● Divide one batch of cookie dough into two pieces—one third of the dough, and two thirds. Roll the smaller piece into a 9-inch rope. Working on a piece of parchment or waxed paper, roll the larger piece into a rectangle about ¼ inch thick, and 9 inches along a short side.

● Roll the alternate flavor cookie dough into a rectangle that's 9 inches along a short side and ½ inch thick. Trim the edges neatly.

● Brush the ½-inch-thick dough with the egg white glaze. Lay the dough rope along one short edge and starting with a short edge, roll the two together into a log, pressing the edges of the outside dough together to seal the rope inside. Trim any excess dough before you seal the edges; the edges should just meet, not overlap.

● Brush the third flat piece of dough with glaze. Lay the rolled log along a short edge and roll it up, sealing the edges neatly. Again, the edges should just meet, not overlap. Roll the log until it's about 12 inches long. Wrap it in plastic and freeze until firm.

● Preheat the oven to 350°F. Lightly grease (or line with parchment) two baking sheets.

● Using a sharp knife or dental floss (see sidebar page 397), slice the dough into ¼-inch slices.

● Place the cookies on the prepared baking sheets and bake for 12 to 14 minutes, until they're firm to the touch. Remove from the oven and transfer to a rack to cool.

Slice the log, giving the dough a quarter turn with each slice to avoid flattening one side.

***Nutrition information per serving** (1 cookie, made with vanilla and chocolate dough, 18 g):* 86 cal, 6 g fat, 1 g protein, 5 g complex carbohydrates, 2 g sugar, 16 mg cholesterol, 47 mg sodium, 34 mg potassium, 53 RE vitamin A, 1 mg iron, 2 mg calcium, 11 mg phosphorus, 1 mg caffeine.

Batter Cookies

Convention in cookie making is to mix the dough, drop it in balls on a cookie sheet, and bake in the oven. However, not all cookies follow this familiar process. Some cookies begin life as a loose batter rather than a stiff dough. And because of their extremely high liquid-to-flour ratio, they spread to an ultrathin crisp wafer as they bake, requiring little or no chemical leavening for their texture. Other cookies begin as a slightly stiffer batter, and boosted by baking powder, become a tender, moist confection, halfway between cookie and cake.

Either way, batter cookies are cookies of a different stripe. When you think batter cookies, think Italian *pizzelle*, Norwegian *krumkake*, British brandy snaps, and Dutch *stroopwafels*. Even American whoopie pies fall into this category. Though their ethnic origins are diverse, these cookies share a common characteristic: they're all longtime favorites in their native country, having built their enduring reputations through years and years of happy repetition.

Some of these cookies require an iron to prepare—a waffle iron or a cookie-specific type of iron. Note that *pizzelle, krumkake,* and *stroopwafels* each have their own traditional iron, yet each can be baked in the other's iron as well, if you don't mind slight variations in size and imprint pattern. For these three types of cookies, if you don't have one of these special irons, don't attempt to bake them. There's no other way to give them their distinct texture and look.

For the main part, though, you won't need any special equipment for batter cookies. A bowl and a mixer, a cookie scoop and a baking sheet—the normal tools of the trade—will take you just about anywhere you want to go in this chapter, from delicate Lace Cookies to ultrarich, deep dark chocolate Fudgies, with a satisfying stop along the way for three different whoopie pies. Batter up!

Lace Cookies

These gossamer cookies, whose texture has the delicate snap of skim ice on a November pond, contain just enough flour to keep them from flowing off the cookie sheet. Be sure to leave lots of space between them when you drop the batter onto the baking sheet—they spread enormously, acquiring their lacy look in the process. Like snowflakes, lace cookies should be a winter phenomenon in the North, as they tend to become limp in any but the driest weather. Don't try making these when it's rainy or humid; they just won't become crisp.

Yield: 70 cookies ● *Baking temperature:* 375°F ● *Baking time:* 5 to 7 minutes

> 3 tablespoons (¾ ounce) unbleached all-purpose flour
> 2¼ cups (7⅞ ounces) rolled oats
> 2¼ cups (18 ounces) light brown sugar
> 1 teaspoon salt
> 1 cup (2 sticks, 8 ounces) unsalted butter
> 1 large egg
> 1 teaspoon vanilla extract

● Preheat the oven to 375°F. Line 2 baking sheets with parchment, or a nonstick liner.

● In a large bowl, stir together the flour, oats, brown sugar, and salt. In a small saucepan, or in the microwave, warm the butter until it has just melted. Stir it into the dry ingredients.

● In a small bowl, beat the egg with the vanilla and stir it into the oat mixture.

● Drop the batter by the teaspoonful (a teaspoon cookie scoop works well here, see page 32) onto the prepared baking sheets, allowing plenty of room for cookies to spread; test-bake one cookie first to see how much it spreads, then space the remaining cookies on the sheet accordingly.

● Bake the cookies for 5 to 7 minutes, until they're light brown around the edges. Remove the cookies from the oven and let cool just enough on the parchment so you can get a metal spatula under them without tearing them. (If you wait any longer, they'll stick tenaciously.) Transfer them to a rack to cool. Store in a dry, airtight container in a cool place.

Nutrition information per serving (1 cookie, 15 g): 65 cal, 3 g fat, 1 g protein, 2 g complex carbohydrates, 7 g sugar, 10 mg cholesterol, 35 mg sodium, 38 mg potassium, 26 RE vitamin A, 9 mg calcium, 19 mg phosphorus.

Honey Crisps

These whisper-thin cookies, light as a handful of popcorn, can take any shape you like. Drape them over a custard cup or ramekin while still warm and pliable and they'll make an elegant container for fruit or mousse, or leave them flat, to layer with whipped cream and berries. They also make wonderful, delicate fortune cookies, cookies you'll actually want to eat, not just break apart to read the fortune. Have all your fortunes (or love notes) ready ahead of time, and tuck them inside when you're shaping the warm-from-the-oven cookies.

Yield: 55 to 60 cookies ● *Baking temperature:* 425°F ● *Baking time:* 4 to 6 minutes

> 4 tablespoons (½ stick, 2 ounces) unsalted butter
> ⅔ cup (2¾ ounces) confectioners' sugar, sifted
> 3 tablespoons (2¼ ounces) honey
> ¾ teaspoon ground ginger*
> ⅔ cup (2¾ ounces) unbleached all-purpose flour, sifted
> 3 large egg whites, whisked briefly

● Preheat the oven to 425°F. Lightly grease two baking sheets. (Don't use parchment to bake these cookies.) If you spread the circles of batter on the (clean) back of a baking sheet, rather than inside, the lack of a pan rim to interfere with your spatula work means they'll be easier to lift off once they're baked.

● In a medium-sized bowl, cream together the butter and confectioners' sugar. Add the honey and mix until smooth. Add the ginger and half the flour and stir to combine, then mix in half the egg whites. Repeat with the remaining flour and egg whites, mixing until a smooth batter forms.

● Drop the batter by the teaspoonful on the prepared pan. Spread the batter out to about 3 inches in diameter with the back of a wet spoon or a small offset spatula, until it's so thin you can almost see through it.

● Bake for 4 to 6 minutes, until the cookies are an even golden brown. The edges will take on color first, then the center. Remove the cookies from the oven and let them sit on the baking sheet for about a minute, until you can move them without them wrinkling.

● Shape the cookies as desired while they are still warm (to shape into fortune cookies, see illustrations opposite). If you choose to keep the cookies flat, let them cool for 5 minutes before removing them from the baking sheet. Store cookies in a single layer in an airtight container.

Use a wet spoon or offset spatula to spread the cookie batter until it's nearly see-through thin.

* For traditional-style fortune cookies, substitute ¾ teaspoon almond extract for the ginger.

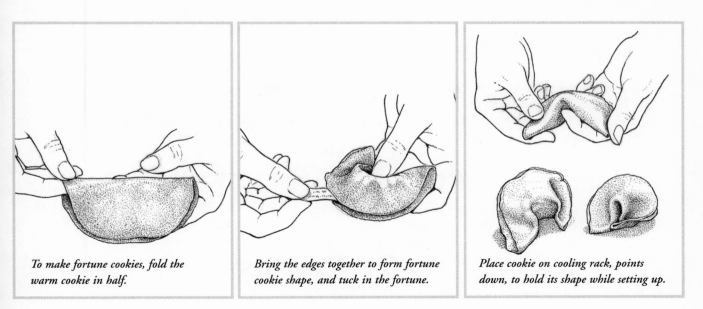

To make fortune cookies, fold the warm cookie in half.

Bring the edges together to form fortune cookie shape, and tuck in the fortune.

Place cookie on cooling rack, points down, to hold its shape while setting up.

Nutrition information per serving *(1 cookie, 6 g):* 20 cal, 1 g fat, 1 g complex carbohydrates, 2 g sugar, 2 mg cholesterol, 3 mg sodium, 5 mg potassium, 7 RE vitamin A, 2 mg phosphorus.

Brandy Snaps

These shiny, mahogany-brown cookies are a British specialty; English bakers serve them filled with brandy-spiked whipped cream. The brandy in these ultracrisp, buttery cookies is much more a hint than a distinct flavor, so don't fret if you're not a fan of the taste of alcohol in your baked goods.

Yield: 42 cookies ● *Baking temperature: 375°F* ● *Baking time: 7 to 8 minutes*

½ cup (1 stick, 4 ounces) unsalted butter
½ cup (3½ ounces) sugar
⅓ cup (4 ounces) molasses
1 cup plus 2 tablespoons (4¾ ounces) unbleached all-purpose flour
¼ teaspoon salt
1 teaspoon ground ginger
1 teaspoon brandy
1 teaspoon vanilla extract

● Preheat the oven to 375°F.
● In a medium-sized saucepan set over medium heat, or in the microwave, heat the butter, sugar, and molasses, stirring until the butter has melted. Remove the mixture from the heat and cool slightly.
● Add the flour, salt, ginger, brandy, and vanilla, stirring until smooth. The batter will look like melted caramel.
● Using a teaspoon cookie scoop, drop the batter in walnut-sized balls onto ungreased baking sheets about 3 inches apart; they'll spread quite a bit.

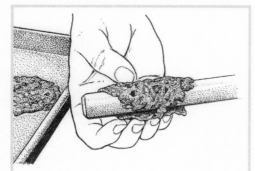

Wrap the hot brandy snaps one by one around the neck of a wine bottle or the handle of a fat wooden spoon. Wrap them just till their ends meet; if you wrap them tightly, they'll stay soft in the middle.

● Bake the cookies for 7 to 8 minutes, until they're brown. Remove from the oven, wait about 15 seconds, then use a thin-bladed metal spatula, or the tip of a knife, to lift them off the baking sheet. Working quickly, roll each cookie loosely (so the ends just meet) around the neck of a bottle or the handle of a fat wooden spoon, to shape it into a tube (see illustration, left).
● Remove the cookies from the bottle or spoon as soon as they set (about a minute). Transfer them to a rack to cool completely. If desired, fill with lightly sweetened, brandied whipped cream just before serving, piping it into the snaps with a pastry bag. Store unfilled cookies in a single layer in an airtight container; if you need to layer them, separate the layers with parchment.

Nutrition information per serving *(1 unfilled cookie, 11 g):* 49 cal, 2 g fat, 1 g protein, 2 g complex carbohydrates, 5 g sugar, 6 mg cholesterol, 17 mg sodium, 18 mg potassium, 20 RE vitamin A, 4 mg calcium, 5 mg phosphorus.

They're HOT!

Clearly, a high-sugar cookie, like a brandy snap, will be very hot right out of the oven. *Tuiles* and *krumkake,* though they don't get as hot as brandy snaps, are still quite warm to the touch. For safety's sake, you'd want to let them cool before handling. But to shape the cookies, you can't wait; once they cool, they're brittle and can't be shaped. Pay close attention once you take the cookies out of the oven. Start poking them with a fingertip within seconds, and as soon as you feel you can handle them without burning yourself, start rolling. If the cookies cool before you can shape them, simply put them back into the oven for 15 to 30 seconds; they'll soften up again.

Tuiles (French Tile Wafers)

This traditional French cookie is named after the curved roof tiles typical of ancient seaside villas along France's Mediterranean coast—for an American reference, think of those potato chips that come stacked in cans. Often served alongside ice cream or sorbet, tuiles can be flavored to taste; almond is traditional, but orange, lemon, and vanilla are other options. Try a more exotic flavor, like coconut, amaretto, or butter-rum. Just a few drops of any of these strong flavors are all you'll need.

Yield: 2 dozen cookies ● *Baking temperature:* 350°F ● *Baking time:* 7 to 8 minutes

2 large egg whites
Heaping ¼ teaspoon salt
¾ cup (3 ounces) confectioners' sugar
¼ teaspoon almond extract
½ cup (2 ounces) unbleached all-purpose flour
7 tablespoons (3½ ounces) butter, melted and cooled to lukewarm
½ to ⅔ cup (2 to 2¾ ounces) sliced unblanched almonds

Use a wet spatula or knife to spread the batter in 3-inch rounds. Sprinkle each generously with sliced almonds.

- Preheat the oven to 350°F. Grease (or line with parchment) two baking sheets.
- Place the egg whites and salt in a medium-sized bowl. Using a wire whisk, or the whisk attachment of your electric mixer, whisk until the egg whites are foamy and starting to thicken. Sprinkle in the confectioners' sugar, whisking until smooth, then stir in the almond extract. Sprinkle the flour over the mixture and whisk it in. Finally, add the melted butter, whisking until smooth and thickened.
- Using a teaspoon cookie scoop, drop walnut-sized balls of the batter onto the prepared baking sheets, leaving 2 inches between them. Use a wet offset spatula or knife to spread the batter into thin 3-inch rounds (see illustration). Sprinkle with the almonds.
- Bake the cookies for 7 to 8 minutes, until they're thoroughly browned around the edges. Once they come out of the oven you'll drape them over a curved surface to cool into their distinctive shape, so while they're baking, set out a pastry pin, wine bottle, or other similar-sized cylin-

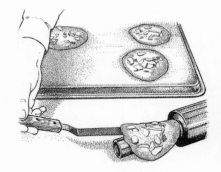

Gently press the hot tuile onto the curved surface of your choice, allowing it to set before moving it onto a rack.

der. A pastry pin is smaller in diameter than a rolling pin, 1½ inches to 2 inches. It's longer, too, so by the time you wrap the cookies from one end to the other, the first cookie will be cool enough to transfer, and so on.

- Remove the cookies from the oven and immediately press them onto the cylinder to shape them (see illustration). Once they're set and fairly cool (about a minute), transfer them to a rack to cool completely. Store the cookies in an airtight container.

Nutrition information per serving *(1 cookie, 16 g):* 70 cal, 5 g fat, 1 g protein, 2 g complex carbohydrates, 4 g sugar, 9 mg cholesterol, 28 mg sodium, 30 mg potassium, 31 RE vitamin A, 1 mg vitamin C, 9 mg calcium, 19 mg phosphorus.

VARIATION

Cigarette Cookies

Sometimes called Russian cigarettes, these cookies are simply a shaping variation on *tuiles*. You'll see where they got their rather unappetizing name once you've made them.

● Prepare and bake the *tuiles* as directed in the recipe, but don't sprinkle with almonds. When you remove the cookies from the oven, roll each around the handle of a wooden spoon to make a thin tube. Immediately remove the cookies from the spoon handle and cool on a rack. Store cookies in an airtight container.

Nutrition information per serving *(1 cookie, 13 g):*
53 cal, 3 g fat, 1 g protein, 2 g complex carbohydrates,
4 g sugar, 9 mg cholesterol, 27 mg sodium, 8 mg potassium,
31 RE vitamin A, 1 mg calcium, 3 mg phosphorus.

An engineer's guide to shaping round wafer cookies

If precision and symmetry are qualities you admire, you might want to make your own *tuile* form. Take a piece of food-safe silicone, with a maximum thickness of 1/16 inch. Trace a 3-inch diameter circle in the center (a jar opener or one of those flat, circular garlic clove peelers works well) and cut out the circle, using a craft knife to get it started and a pair of scissors to finish the job. Discard the circle. To shape *tuile* batter, set the silicone form on the prepared baking sheet, drop the batter in the center of the hole, and spread to the edges. Remove the form and repeat with the remaining batter. Depending on the size of the silicone, you may want to trim the edges so it doesn't disturb any already shaped cookies. Be sure to remove the form from the sheet before baking the cookies.

Florentines

This unusual confection, a cross between cookie and candy, is originally credited to Austria's pastry chefs, who for some reason gave the cookie an Italian name—perhaps because of the Mediterranean fruit that is its main ingredient. The dark chocolate glaze on the bottom of these cookies nicely complements the orange (or apricot, or ginger) in the interior. The fruit and almonds for Florentines can be very finely chopped, so that they're the texture of coarse sand, or they can be more coarsely chopped, into BB-sized pieces. Or go for a combination of the two sizes; there are no hard and fast rules here, it's up to you.

Yield: 30 cookies ● *Baking temperature: 350°F* ● *Baking time: 11 to 12 minutes*

BATTER
- ½ cup (4 ounces) whipping cream
- ⅔ cup (4¾ ounces) sugar
- ½ cup (1 stick, 4 ounces) unsalted butter
- 2 cups (10 ounces) very finely chopped unsalted toasted blanched almonds (see page 27)
- ¼ cup (1 ounce) unbleached all-purpose flour
- 1 cup (5 ounces) finely diced candied orange peel
- ½ teaspoon almond extract

GLAZE
- 1⅓ cups (8 ounces) chocolate chips or semisweet chocolate pieces

● Preheat the oven to 350°F. Lightly grease (or line with parchment) two baking sheets.

● **To make the batter:** In a medium saucepan set over medium heat, combine the cream, sugar, and butter, cooking and stirring until the butter melts. Turn the heat to medium-high and bring the mixture to a boil. Remove it from the heat and add the almonds, flour, orange peel, and almond extract.

● Drop the batter by the tablespoonful, at least 2 inches apart, on the prepared baking sheets. Using the back of a spoon dipped in water or a wet table knife, flatten each cookie until it's evenly smooth.

● Bake the cookies for 11 to 12 minutes, until their edges are lightly browned. Remove them from the oven, cool them for a minute on the pan, then transfer them to a rack, or a rack topped with parchment paper, to cool completely.

● **To make the glaze:** Melt 1 cup (6 ounces) of the chocolate in a saucepan over low heat, or in a microwave, stirring until the chocolate melts. Remove it from the heat and add the remaining ⅓ cup chocolate, stirring until melted and smooth.

● Spread the bottom of each cookie with the glaze. Run the tines of a fork through the chocolate in a wavy pattern (see illustration, right), and place the cookies back on the rack, chocolate side up, to set. To make them set faster, you may refrigerate them.

Nutrition information per serving (1 cookie, 45 g): 199 cal, 14 g fat, 3 g protein, 5 g complex carbohydrates, 13 g sugar, 1 g dietary fiber, 13 mg cholesterol, 3 mg sodium, 139 mg potassium, 47 RE vitamin A, 8 mg vitamin C, 1 mg iron, 43 mg calcium, 75 mg phosphorus, 12 mg caffeine.

Once you've spread the bottom of the Florentines with chocolate, use a fork to give them their signature wavy stripes.

VARIATIONS

● For apricot florentines, substitute 2 cups (12 ounces) slivered dried apricots for the orange peel; reduce the almonds to 1 cup.

● For ginger florentines, substitute ½ cup (3¼ ounces) finely diced crystallized ginger for the orange peel. Substitute 2 cups (8 ounces) finely chopped toasted pecans for the almonds.

Dicing sticky fruit

Sticky fruits and candied peel can be difficult to dice. A good solution is to combine part of the flour in the recipe with the fruit in a blender or food processor and process until the fruit is chopped to the size you like. The flour coats the pieces of fruit, preventing them from turning into a sticky wad. In this Florentine recipe, combine the peel with all of the flour, then blend or process.

Chocolate Whoopie Pies

If you're not from a particular pocket of America (northern New England, Amish-country Pennsylvania, parts of the Midwest) you may never have heard of whoopie pies—more's the pity! These cakelike cookies, sandwiched around a layer of creamy filling, are ubiquitous at bake sales, where an individually wrapped, overstuffed pie will command a premium price, much more than a cookie or muffin. It's all about supply and demand—the demand usually outstrips the whoopie pie supply, particularly at sporting events, where hungry athletes (and their bored siblings) have been known to strip the whoopie pie section clean in minutes.

Yield: 7 or 8 large (4½-inch) whoopie pies ● **Baking temperature: 350°F** ● **Baking time: 15 minutes**

COOKIES
- ½ cup (3¼ ounces) vegetable shortening
- 1 cup (8 ounces) brown sugar
- 1 large egg
- ¼ cup plus 2 tablespoons (1⅛ ounces) Dutch process cocoa powder
- 2 cups (8½ ounces) unbleached all-purpose flour
- 1 teaspoon baking powder
- 1 teaspoon baking soda
- 1 teaspoon salt
- 1 teaspoon vanilla extract
- 1 cup (8 ounces) milk (regular or low fat, not nonfat)

FILLING
- 1 cup (6½ ounces) vegetable shortening
- 1 cup (4 ounces) confectioners' sugar
- 1⅓ cups (4 ounces) Marshmallow Fluff or marshmallow creme
- ¼ teaspoon extra-fine salt, or ¼ teaspoon table salt dissolved in 1 tablespoon water
- 1½ teaspoons vanilla extract

● Preheat the oven to 350°F. Lightly grease (or line with parchment) two baking sheets.
● **To make the cookies:** In a large mixing bowl, cream together the shortening, brown sugar, and egg. In a separate bowl, whisk together the cocoa, flour, baking powder, baking soda, and salt. In a small bowl, stir the vanilla into the milk.

Measuring marshmallow

Sticky, gooey, clinging—supply whatever adjective suits you, but we all know that marshmallow creme (or shortening, or peanut butter) is challenging to measure. The best solution, by far, is a Wonder Cup (page 34). Barring that, if your recipe calls for oil, measure that first in your measuring cup, then measure the marshmallow creme. It will slide right out. Or spray your measuring cup with a vegetable oil spray. As a last resort, try rinsing your measuring cup with cold water before adding the marshmallow. The water will help it (somewhat) to slip out of the cup.

- Alternate adding the dry ingredients and the milk mixture to the shortening mixture, beating until smooth. Drop the stiff batter by the ¼-cupful onto the prepared baking sheets, about 2 inches apart.
- Bake the cookies for about 15 minutes, until they're firm to the touch. Remove them from the oven and transfer to a rack to cool completely.
- **To make the filling:** In a medium-sized bowl beat all the filling ingredients together.
- **To assemble:** Spread half of the cookies with the filling, using about ¼ cup for each; top with the remaining cookies. For best storage, wrap each pie individually.

Nutrition information per serving (*1 whoopie pie, 171 g*): 675 cal, 34 g fat, 7 g protein, 25 g complex carbohydrates, 58 g sugar, 2 g dietary fiber, 30 mg cholesterol, 599 mg sodium, 261 mg potassium, 21 RE vitamin A, 1 mg vitamin C, 3 mg iron, 101 mg calcium, 115 mg phosphorus, 10 mg caffeine.

Cradling one cookie in your hand, flat side up, use a cookie scoop to dollop on filling, and a table knife or offset spatula to spread it.

Pumpkin Whoopie Pies

Although 99 percent of the whoopie pies you'll see at bake sales are chocolate, there's no reason to stop there. A commercial whoopie pie baker in northern Maine distributes all manner of luscious "pies" (strawberry, lemon, vanilla) to convenience stores around Maine and New Hampshire. Believe us, these big, fat cookies, oozing their creamy filling, are comfort for the bruised psyche after a white-knuckle car ride through New Hampshire's White Mountains on a snowy winter night!

Yield: 1 dozen 4-inch whoopie pies ● *Baking temperature:* 375°F ● *Baking time:* 10 to 12 minutes

COOKIES
    1½ cups (15-ounce can) **pumpkin**
    2 large **eggs**
    2 cups (16 ounces) **brown sugar**
    1 cup (7 ounces) **vegetable oil**
    2 tablespoons (1½ ounces) **molasses or dark corn syrup**
    1 teaspoon **salt**
    1 teaspoon **ground cloves**
    1 teaspoon **ground ginger**
    1 teaspoon **cinnamon**
    1 teaspoon **baking powder**
    1 teaspoon **baking soda**
    3 cups (12¾ ounces) **unbleached all-purpose flour**

FILLING

1 tablespoon unflavored gelatin
2 tablespoons (1 ounce) cool water
½ cup (1 stick, 4 ounces) unsalted butter
½ cup (4 ounces) cream cheese (reduced fat [Neufchâtel] or full fat)
2¼ cups (9 ounces) confectioners' sugar
2 tablespoons (⅞ ounce) finely chopped crystallized ginger

- Preheat the oven to 375°F. Lightly grease (or line with parchment) two large baking sheets.
- **To make the cookies:** In a large bowl, beat together the pumpkin, eggs, brown sugar, oil, and molasses. Scrape down the bottom and sides of the bowl, then beat in the salt, spices, baking powder, and baking soda.
- Add the flour to the wet ingredients and beat for 1 minute, until the mixture is well combined. Scrape the bottom and sides of the bowl, then beat for a short time just to make sure everything is thoroughly mixed. Use a muffin scoop, or a ¼-cup measure, to drop the batter onto the prepared baking sheets, 2 inches apart to allow for spreading.
- Bake the cookies for 10 to 12 minutes, until they feel firm to the touch; a slight indentation will remain when you press your finger in the center. Remove the cookies from the oven and transfer to a rack to cool while you prepare the filling.
- **To make the filling:** In a small heatproof bowl, combine the gelatin and water and set aside for the gelatin to soften. In a large mixing bowl, beat together the butter and cream cheese until fluffy. Heat the gelatin and water very gently (in a larger bowl of hot water, or at low power in the microwave), stirring to dissolve the gelatin. Set it aside.
- Add half the confectioners' sugar to the butter/cream cheese mixture, beating well. Add the gelatin and mix to combine. Add the remaining confectioners' sugar, mixing until blended, then stir in the ginger.
- **To assemble:** Spread the flat side of half the cookies with the filling, using 2 generous tablespoons of filling for each cookie. Top with the remaining cookies. For best storage, wrap each pie individually in plastic wrap.

Nutrition information per serving (1 whoopie pie, 180 g): 633 cal, 30 g fat, 6 g protein, 26 g complex carbohydrates, 63 g sugar, 2 g dietary fiber, 66 mg cholesterol, 387 mg sodium, 289 mg potassium, 910 RE vitamin A, 2 mg vitamin C, 3 mg iron, 87 mg calcium, 85 mg phosphorus.

Oatmeal Whoopie Pies

These cookies are similar to the snack cake oatmeal pies—two oatmeal cookies sandwiched around creme filling—that you find at the grocery store. But instead of creme filling, we developed a rich, thick homemade marshmallow filling, which can be left plain, or flavored however you like (do we hear cinnamon?).

Yield: 20 whoopie pies ● *Baking temperature:* 350°F ● *Baking time:* 8 to 10 minutes

COOKIES

1½ cups (12 ounces) brown sugar

½ cup (3¼ ounces) vegetable shortening

4 tablespoons (½ stick, 2 ounces) unsalted butter

1 teaspoon salt

1 teaspoon cinnamon

⅛ teaspoon nutmeg

1 teaspoon baking powder

1 teaspoon baking soda

1 teaspoon vanilla extract

2 large eggs

3 tablespoons (1½ ounces) milk (regular or low fat, not nonfat)

2½ cups (10½ ounces) unbleached all-purpose flour

2 cups (7 ounces) rolled oats

MARSHMALLOW FILLING

1½ cups (12 ounces) cold water

4 packages (¼ ounce each) unflavored gelatin

3 cups (21 ounces) granulated sugar

¼ cup (2¾ ounces) light corn syrup

¼ teaspoon salt

1 tablespoon vanilla extract

½ cup (2 ounces) confectioners' sugar (if making marshmallows)

● Preheat the oven to 350°F. Lightly grease (or line with parchment) two baking sheets.

● **To make the cookies:** In a large bowl, cream together the sugar, shortening, butter, salt, spices, baking powder, baking soda, and vanilla extract. Beat in the eggs and milk, beating until smooth but not fluffy. Stir in the flour and oats. Drop the stiff batter by the tablespoonful onto the prepared baking sheets.

● Bake for 8 to 10 minutes, until the cookies are set and not wet-looking in the center. Remove them from the oven and let cool for 5 minutes on the pan before transferring to a rack to cool completely.

● **To make the filling:** Pour ¾ cup of the water into the bowl of an electric stand mixer. Sprinkle the gelatin on top and let it soften for 5 minutes.

- Bring the remaining ¾ cup water, the granulated sugar, corn syrup, and salt to a boil in a medium saucepan set over high heat. Cook, without stirring, until the mixture reaches soft-ball stage (234°F to 240°F), about 10 minutes.
- Using your mixer's whisk attachment, beat the hot syrup into the gelatin mixture at low speed. Gradually increase the speed to high and beat until soft peaks form, 3 to 5 minutes. Beat in the vanilla. While the marshmallow is beating, line up half the cookies, flat side up, so you can spread them with frosting quickly.
- Spread half the cookies with a generous 2 tablespoons marshmallow. Top with the remaining cookies. Wrap the pies individually, or store in an airtight container.

The marshmallow will increase in volume greatly as you beat it.

Nutrition information per serving *(1 whoopie pie, 113 g):* 366 cal, 8 g fat, 5 g protein, 18 g complex carbohydrates, 52 g sugar, 2 g dietary fiber, 28 mg cholesterol, 244 mg sodium, 124 mg potassium, 33 RE vitamin A, 1 mg vitamin C, 2 mg iron, 41 mg calcium, 81 mg phosphorus.

Homemade Marshmallows

The filling recipe makes enough for you to have some left over once all the cookies are filled. This is easily made into impress-your-friends homemade marshmallows.

- To make marshmallows from the leftover filling, you'll need to have a pan prepared for them before you start. Spray an 8 x 8-inch square (or 9-inch round) cookie pan with nonstick vegetable oil spray. Line the pan with parchment, leaving enough overhang so it comes up over the edge of the pan. Spray the parchment with nonstick spray.
- Prepare the marshmallow filling as directed in the recipe (opposite). After frosting the cookies, beat the remaining marshmallow in the bowl for about a minute to soften it. Immediately spoon the marshmallow into the prepared pan, smoothing it with an offset spatula dipped in water. It won't become totally smooth on top, but will continue to settle and smooth out as it cools. Let it set, uncovered, until it's firm, about 3 hours at room temperature.
- Sift a thin layer of confectioners' sugar onto a clean work surface, making a square or circle about the same size as your pan of marshmallows. Invert the marshmallows onto the sugar and peel off the parchment. Sift more sugar over the uncoated surface.

Gently roll the marshmallows in confectioners' sugar, being sure to coat all the cut sides.

- Cut the marshmallow into squares, using a bench knife sprayed with nonstick vegetable oil spray (or whatever shape you like, using a well-oiled cutter). Roll the cut surfaces in additional confectioners' sugar.
- Store the marshmallows in a plastic bag.

Fudgies

For those of you who love dark chocolate, these cookies are a simple-to-make, satisfying, deep dark chocolate treat. They develop an attractive shiny, cracked top surface as they bake, just like a fudge brownie. Be sure to allow them to cool before moving them off the baking sheet, as they're very delicate while hot. Our immediate thought when sampling them was that they'd be dynamite as the cookie part of an ice cream sandwich. Our ice cream flavor of choice would be something in the coffee family, to complement the faint espresso flavor in the cookies.

Yield: 2 dozen cookies ● *Baking temperature: 325°F* ● *Baking time: 10 to 12 minutes*

1⅓ cups (8 ounces) **chopped bittersweet or semisweet chocolate***
3 tablespoons (1½ ounces) **unsalted butter**
1 cup (7 ounces) **sugar**
3 large **eggs**
1 teaspoon **espresso powder**
1 teaspoon **vanilla extract**
1 cup (4¼ ounces) **unbleached all-purpose flour**
¼ teaspoon **baking powder**
½ teaspoon **salt**

● In a double boiler, or in the microwave, gently melt together the chocolate and butter, stirring until the chocolate has melted.

● In a separate bowl, beat together the sugar and eggs until they're thoroughly combined. Add this mixture to the melted chocolate, then stir in the remaining ingredients. The mixture will be liquid, like brownie batter. Cover and refrigerate for 60 minutes; it will become stiff enough to handle easily.

● Preheat the oven to 325°F. Lightly grease (or line with parchment) two baking sheets.

● Drop the batter in round blobs (a bit larger than a table tennis ball) onto the prepared baking sheets about, 2 inches apart. Using a cookie scoop (or a small ice cream scoop that will hold about 2 level tablespoons of liquid) makes this task extremely simple.

● Bake the cookies for 10 to 12 minutes, until their tops are shiny and cracked. You want them baked all the way through, but just barely; additional baking will make them crisp rather than chewy. To make sure they're done, take the sheet out of the oven and use a spoon or fork to gently cut into one; it shouldn't have any raw-appearing or liquidlike batter in the center.

● Remove the cookies from the oven, wait 5 minutes, and transfer them to a rack to cool. Store cookies in an airtight container.

* You may use semisweet chocolate chips, but we prefer the flavor of bittersweet chips or bittersweet chocolate. If you're using bar chocolate (as opposed to chips), chop it into irregular ½- to ¾-inch chunks.

Nutrition information per serving (*1 cookie, 31 g*): 120 cal, 5 g fat, 2 g protein, 18 g complex carbohydrates, 13 g sugar, 31 mg cholesterol, 36 mg sodium, 45 mg potassium, 26 RE vitamin A, 1 mg iron, 9 mg calcium, 27 mg phosphorus, 10 mg caffeine.

Madeleines

Madeleines, tender, cakelike, shell-shaped cookies, are famed for their starring role in Marcel Proust's epic novel, *Remembrance of Things Past*. They're a bit fussy to make (the butter has to be browned first, and they require a special pan), but the result is a cookie perfect for dunking in tea, dipping in chocolate, or just enjoying in all its simple splendor. You may also choose to dip madeleines halfway in melted chocolate (as illustrated below); drizzle them with a flavored glaze; or brush plain madeleines with Lemon-Honey Butter (recipe opposite).

Yield: 24 cookies ● ***Baking temperature:*** *375°F* ● ***Baking time:*** *12 to 14 minutes*

10 tablespoons (1 stick plus 2 tablespoons, 5 ounces) unsalted butter
⅔ cup (4¾ ounces) sugar
3 large eggs, at room temperature
½ teaspoon salt
2 teaspoons vanilla extract
1 cup (4¼ ounces) unbleached all-purpose flour, sifted or whisked to aerate
Confectioners' sugar, for sifting over cookies

● In a saucepan set over medium heat, melt the butter, then simmer it gently for 5 to 6 minutes, until small brown particles appear around the edges of the pan and the butter changes color slightly. Set it aside to cool to room temperature.

● In a medium-sized mixing bowl, beat the sugar, eggs, and salt until they're light yellow and very thick. Stir in the vanilla.

● Add the flour and brown butter alternately to the egg mixture, using a folding motion (be gentle!), so the batter loses as little volume as possible. Refrigerate the batter, covered, for 45 minutes or so, until it's thick.

● Preheat the oven to 375°F. Lightly grease your madeleine pan or pans, using melted butter or nonstick vegetable oil spray. (This recipe requires 24 full-sized cups; bake in batches if necessary.)

● Fill the prepared pans, using 1 slightly rounded tablespoon of batter for each cookie. Bake the madeleines for 12 to 14 minutes, until they're light brown at the edges. Cool in the pan for several minutes, then remove from the pan and cool completely on a rack.

● Sift a light coating of confectioners' sugar over the madeleines just before serving. Store in an airtight container.

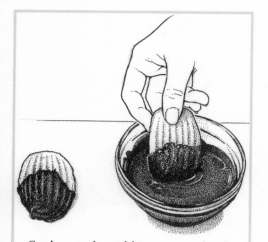

Gently grasp the madeleine at one end and dip the other end in the chocolate. Set on a rack (over parchment paper, to catch any drips) until the chocolate hardens.

Nutrition information per serving *(1 plain cookie, 24 g):* 94 cal, 6 g fat, 1 g protein, 4 g complex carbohydrates, 6 g sugar, 40 mg cholesterol, 53 mg sodium, 16 mg potassium, 59 RE vitamin A, 5 mg calcium, 17 mg phosphorus.

Lemon-Honey Butter

2 tablespoons (1 ounce) unsalted butter, melted
2 tablespoons (1½ ounces) honey
1 teaspoon fresh lemon juice

● Mix all the ingredients together, stirring until smooth.

VARIATIONS

Chocolate Madeleines

● Place 3 tablespoons unsweetened cocoa powder (we prefer Dutch process) into a 1-cup measuring cup. Spoon unbleached all-purpose flour into the cup until it's full; level it off. Whisk or sift the flour and cocoa together. Use this mixture in place of the flour in the basic recipe. Add 1 teaspoon chocolate extract to perk up the cookies' flavor, and/or ¼ to ½ teaspoon cinnamon.

Almond Madeleines

● Substitute ¾ cup unbleached all-purpose flour plus ½ cup almond flour (finely ground almonds) for the flour in the basic recipe. In addition to the vanilla extract, add ¼ teaspoon almond extract.

Lemon-Poppy Seed Madeleines

● Add 1 tablespoon fresh lemon juice and the zest from 1 lemon to the eggs and sugar when beating. Add a drop or two of lemon oil for extra-strong flavor. Whisk 2 tablespoons poppy seeds into the flour before folding it in.

Rose Water Madeleines

● Reduce the vanilla extract to 1 teaspoon, and add 2 to 3 teaspoons rose water or 1 teaspoon rose extract. Rose water varies greatly in aroma and strength, so begin with the lesser amount—you want a very light aroma and taste.

Ginger-Orange Madeleines

● Add 3 tablespoons finely minced crystallized ginger to the eggs and sugar once they've been beaten until thick. Whisk 1 tablespoon orange zest into the flour, and add ⅛ teaspoon orange oil to the finished batter, for extra flavor.

Cat's Tongues

The French call these puffy-crisp ovals *langues de chat*—cat's tongues, though finding a housecat with a tongue this size would be a bit of a stretch. Enjoy these with a cup of coffee or tea. They're also the perfect vehicle for sandwich cookies, filled with Lemon Creme (page 468), or Vanilla or Chocolate Creme Fillings (page 470).

Yield: 45 to 50 cookies ● *Baking temperature:* 425°F ● *Baking time:* 7 to 8 minutes

¾ cup (1½ sticks, 6 ounces) unsalted butter
1 cup (7 ounces) sugar
2 teaspoons vanilla extract
½ teaspoon salt
3 large egg whites
2 cups (8½ ounces) unbleached all-purpose flour

● Preheat the oven to 425°F. Line two baking sheets with parchment (baking these on a parchment-lined baking sheet, rather than on a greased sheet, will produce a puffier, lighter cookie).

● In a medium-sized bowl, beat together the butter, sugar, vanilla, and salt. In a separate large bowl, beat the egg whites until they're stiff, but not dry.

● Sift the flour over the butter mixture. Spoon the beaten egg whites on top and gently mix everything together. The mixture will seem very dry at first, but will eventually come together.

● Spoon the batter into a pastry bag fitted with a large (⅜-inch or so) plain tube, or into a zip-top plastic bag. If you're using a plastic bag, snip off a tiny bit of one corner to make an opening about ⅜ inch in diameter. Pipe strips of dough about 3 inches long onto the prepared baking sheets, leaving at least 1 inch between the cookies (side to side), so they have room to spread.

● Bake the cookies for 7 to 8 minutes, until they're a very light brown around the edges but not brown on top. Remove them from the oven and transfer to a rack to cool.

Nutrition information per serving (1 cookie, 16 g): 64 cal, 3 g fat, 1 g protein, 4 g complex carbohydrates, 4 g sugar, 8 mg cholesterol, 28 mg sodium, 11 mg potassium, 29 RE vitamin A, 1 mg calcium, 6 mg phosphorus.

Ladyfingers

Ladyfingers, very similar in size and shape to Cat's Tongues (opposite) are soft and elegantly dry, much like an airy sponge cake. In fact, they're made much the same way, with the addition of extra flour to make them easy to shape. Their texture makes them the perfect building block for layered desserts such as *tiramisu*, that classic combination of espresso-, mascarpone- and liqueur-enriched cream filling and cookies. *Savoiardi,* Italy's version of ladyfingers, are the basis for tiramisu. A classic trifle is also delicious made with ladyfingers, which are able to soak up both cream and fruit juice and still hold their shape (unlike the rest of us).

Yield: About 40 cookies ● *Baking temperature: 350°F* ● *Baking time: 8 minutes*

> 3 large eggs, separated
> Generous ⅓ cup (2⅝ ounces) granulated sugar, superfine preferred
> ½ teaspoon vanilla extract or a few drops orange-flower water
> ¾ cup (3 ounces) cake flour
> ¼ teaspoon salt
> Confectioners' sugar, for sprinkling

● Preheat the oven to 350°F. Line two baking sheets with parchment (baking these on a parchment-lined baking sheet, rather than on a greased sheet, will produce a puffier, lighter cookie).

● Beat the egg whites with an electric mixer until soft peaks form. Gradually beat in 2 tablespoons of the granulated sugar and continue beating until stiff peaks form; the meringue will be glossy and smooth.

● In a separate bowl, beat the egg yolks with the remaining sugar and the vanilla, beating until thick and lemon-colored.

● Sift the flour and salt over the egg yolk mixture. Spoon the meringue on top. Gently fold everything together.

● Spoon the batter into a pastry bag fitted with a large (⅜-inch or so) plain tube, or into a zip-top plastic bag. If you're using a plastic bag, snip off a tiny bit of one corner to make an opening about ⅜ inch in diameter. Pipe strips of dough about 3 inches long onto the prepared baking sheets, leaving at least 1 inch between the cookies (side to side), so they have room to spread. Sprinkle the cookies lightly but thoroughly with confectioners' sugar; wait 5 minutes, then sprinkle again.

● Bake the cookies for 8 minutes, until their edges are barely beginning to brown, but they're still soft and very light-colored in the center. Remove the cookies from the oven and transfer to a rack to cool. Wrap tightly once they're cool. They'll become stale quickly, so eat them or use in a dessert immediately, or freeze for up to 2 weeks, tightly wrapped.

Nutrition information per serving (1 cookie, 8 g): 21 cal, 1 g fat, 1 g protein, 2 g complex carbohydrates, 2 g sugar, 1 g dietary fiber, 16 mg cholesterol, 18 mg sodium, 7 mg potassium, 7 RE vitamin A, 2 mg calcium, 9 mg phosphorus.

Cake Cookie Cutouts

There's more than one way to make cutout cookies . . . and who says they have to be crisp, anyway? Children love these baby-soft cookies. A thin layer of cakelike batter is poured into a pan, baked, then cut into any fanciful shapes you like. For a final touch, frost with a complementary icing. We recommend Chocolate Ganache (page 460) or Caramel Icing (page 463).

Yield: 2 dozen 4½-inch cookies ● *Baking temperature: 400°F* ● *Baking time: 15 minutes*

> ¾ cup (1½ sticks, 6 ounces) unsalted butter
> 1½ cups (10½ ounces) sugar
> 3 large eggs, lightly beaten
> 2⅔ cups (10¾ ounces) cake flour
> 1½ teaspoons baking powder
> ¾ teaspoon salt
> ¾ cup (6 ounces) milk (regular or low fat, not nonfat)
> 2 teaspoons vanilla extract
> ½ teaspoon almond extract
> 1½ cups (9 ounces) chocolate chips
> Chocolate Ganache (page 460), or Caramel Icing (page 463)

● Make sure the butter and eggs are at cool room temperature, 68°F to 72°F depending on the temperature of your kitchen. Plan on removing them from the refrigerator 45 minutes to 2½ hours before you begin to prepare the cookies.

● Preheat the oven to 400°F. Lightly grease an 18 x 13-inch half-sheet pan (or line the bottom of the pan with parchment and grease the sides). You may also use two 9 x 13-inch pans.

● In a large mixing bowl, beat the butter, at medium speed of an electric stand mixer or high speed of an electric hand mixer, for 1 minute. Add the sugar and continue to beat for 5 minutes. Dribble in the eggs very gradually, beating all the while, and beat until the mixture is light colored; this will take 5 minutes. Be sure to stop once to scrape down the sides of the bowl.

● In a small bowl, sift together the flour, salt, and baking powder; set aside. Whisk together the milk, vanilla, and almond extract in a cup; set aside.

● Using a spatula or large spoon (or an electric mixer on low speed), alternate stirring the flour mixture and the milk mixture into the butter mixture, beginning and ending with the flour. Stir only until the batter is completely mixed. Stir in the chocolate chips.

● Spread the batter in the prepared pan. Bake for 15 minutes, or until it springs back lightly and doesn't leave a fingerprint when you gently press the center. (If you're baking in two 9 x 13-inch pans, start checking for doneness several minutes sooner.)

- Remove the baked batter from the oven and allow it to cool. Carefully turn it out onto a large rectangular rack by placing the rack upside-down on top of it, then flipping the whole thing over, so the cake is upside down on the rack. Use the cookie cutters of your choice to cut cookies, leaving them in place on the rack after you've cut them. When all the cookies are cut, pick out the scraps; you can simply nibble on them, or layer them with instant pudding to make an easy trifle.
- Drizzle the icing over the cookies, or spread each with icing individually. Store the cookies in a single layer, tightly wrapped.

Nutrition information per serving (1 cookie, 58 g): 216 cal, 10 g fat, 3 g protein, 12 g complex carbohydrates, 18 g sugar, 43 mg cholesterol, 110 mg sodium, 66 mg potassium, 68 RE vitamin A, 1 mg vitamin C, 1 mg iron, 35 mg calcium, 48 mg phosphorus, 8 mg caffeine.

VARIATIONS

- Substitute different flavored chips (cappuccino, butterscotch, mint chocolate) for the chocolate chips, and substitute a complementary flavor for the almond extract.
- Substitute dried fruit (chopped apricots, cherries, chopped dates, blueberries, cranberries), or a combination of dried fruit and nuts, for the chips.
- Omit the chips and the almond extract and flavor to taste with ¼ to ½ teaspoon citrus oil, or ⅛ to ¼ teaspoon of the extra-strong flavor of your choice (maple, coconut, hazelnut, raspberry, etc.).

Krumkake

Norwegian *krumkake* are thin, waffle-like cookies very similar, in shape, size, and consistency, to Italian *pizzelle* (see page 432). A favorite way to serve *krumkake* is to roll them into a fat cylinder, hot off the iron while they're still pliable; a metal cannoli tube is ideal for this task. When they're cool, fill them with lightly sweetened whipped cream and serve with fresh berries. *Krumkake* can also be shaped around a wooden cone, to make a delicate waffle cone for ice cream; or they can be pressed into individual muffin cups to make crisp edible serving bowls for pudding or other sweets. Alternatively, leave them flat and dust with confectioners' sugar just before serving.

Yield: *15 krumkake*

½ cup plus 2 tablespoons (4½ ounces) sugar
2 large eggs
½ cup (1 stick, 4 ounces) unsalted butter, melted
1 cup (4¼ ounces) unbleached all-purpose flour
½ teaspoon salt
½ teaspoon ground cardamom

- Preheat a *krumkake* iron and spray it with non-stick vegetable oil spray. (See page 34 for information about the *krumkake* iron.)
- In a medium-sized bowl, mix the sugar and eggs until thoroughly combined, but don't beat them. Stir in the butter, then the flour, salt, and cardamom.
- Drop the batter, by the tablespoonful, just back of center on the circles etched into the bottom plate of the *krumkake* iron; the iron will push the batter forward a bit as it closes, so you don't want to center it exactly.
- Bake the *krumkake* for about 75 seconds; you'll need to test a few to get the exact time right. Remove them from the iron and roll immediately, or let them cool flat on a rack. Repeat with the remaining batter. Store *krumkake* in an airtight container, or on a plate, well wrapped.

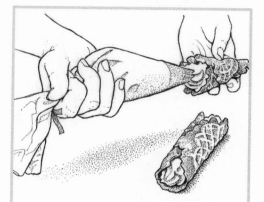

Using a pastry bag fitted with the star tip, pipe whipped cream into the rolled krumkake *just before serving. If you don't have a pastry bag, fill a plastic zip-top bag with whipped cream, snip off one corner, and squeeze cream into the* krumkake.

Nutrition information per serving *(1 cookie, 31 g):* 125 cal, 7 g fat, 2 g protein, 6 g complex carbohydrates, 9 g sugar, 45 mg cholesterol, 80 mg sodium, 21 mg potassium, 70 RE vitamin A, 1 mg iron, 5 mg calcium, 21 mg phosphorus.

VARIATIONS

Chocolate Krumkake

This nontraditional but delightful chocolate *krumkake* makes a tasty bowl for a mini ice cream sundae.

¼ cup (¾ ounce) unsweetened cocoa powder, Dutch process preferred
2 tablespoons (1 ounce) unsalted butter, melted
2 teaspoons vanilla extract
1 recipe *krumkake* batter

• Mix together the cocoa, butter, and vanilla, and stir it into the prepared batter. Bake as directed in the *krumkake* recipe. Drizzle the finished *krumkake* with Chocolate Ganache (page 460), if desired.

Mocha Krumkake

• Make the chocolate krumkake batter (above), reducing the vanilla extract to 1½ teaspoons and adding 1 teaspoon espresso powder.

Krumkake Stack Cake

• Remember the famous Chocolate Refrigerator Cake (page 330), made by sandwiching thin chocolate wafer cookies with whipped cream in a long roll? Try the same thing with chocolate or mocha *krumkake*. Spread one with about ¼ cup lightly sweetened whipped cream, add another *krumkake*, spread with whipped cream, and so forth until you've made a stack as tall as you like. Refrigerate for several hours to allow the cookies to soften. Cut in half (for large servings) or in four wedges to serve.

What if I don't have a *krumkake* iron?

Traditional *krumkake* require an iron—however, it doesn't have to be a *krumkake* iron. Substitute a *pizzelle* iron, if you have one; the imprint on the cookies will be different (traditional Italian rather than traditional Norwegian), but other than that it performs the same function: baking a very thin, very crisp cookie. If you don't have an iron of any kind, then you should bypass these cookies.

A time-tested formula for *krumkake*

The traditional recipe for pound cake calls for a pound each of butter, sugar, flour, and eggs. *Krumkake*, probably the most beloved of Norwegian cookies, has a similar traditional formula: for the weight of each egg (weighed in its shell), the baker is directed to use twice that weight of sugar, butter, and flour, then to season to taste with salt and cardamom. This kind of formula makes it possible for a baker to easily increase (or reduce) the size of the recipe. Just to demonstrate once again that old ways are often the best, the recipe printed here follows almost exactly that traditional way of stirring up *krumkake*.

Pizzelle

In Italy, these flat, crisp, imprinted wafer cookies are typically street food, hawked by vendors, especially during the various saints' days festivals for which that country is famous. In America, they've become a holiday specialty, appearing regularly at Christmas and Easter—as well as any other time the craving for *pizzelle* strikes the fortunate owner of a *pizzelle* maker.

Yield: *23 pizzelle*

½ cup (1 stick, 4 ounces) unsalted butter
½ teaspoon salt
3 large eggs
⅞ cup (¾ cup plus 2 tablespoons, 6⅛ ounces) sugar
1¾ cups (7¼ ounces) unbleached all-purpose flour
1½ teaspoons baking powder
1 tablespoon vanilla extract*
Confectioners' sugar, for dusting (optional)

● Spray a *pizzelle* maker with nonstick vegetable oil spray. Preheat the iron (see page 36 for information about the *pizzelle* maker).

● In a very small saucepan, or in a microwave, heat the butter and salt until the butter melts. Set aside to cool to lukewarm.

● In a medium-sized mixing bowl, beat together the eggs and sugar until well combined. Stir in the cooled butter, then the flour and baking powder. Add the vanilla or flavor of your choice.

● Use a tablespoon cookie scoop or ice cream scoop, to drop a ball of dough just back of center of each imprint on the *pizzelle* maker; the iron will push the batter forward a bit as it closes, so you don't want to center it exactly. Close it and lock it closed, if it has a locking mechanism.

● Bake the *pizzelle* for 45 to 75 seconds; time will vary from iron to iron. Generally, when they stop steaming, they're done. Open the *pizzelle* maker and check; *pizzelle* should be a medium-to-deep golden brown all over.

● Use the tip of a table knife or a thin-bladed offset spatula, to lift each *pizzelle* off the iron and place it flat on a rack to cool. If desired, trim off any ragged edges while the *pizzelle* are still hot; you can do this with your fingers, or use a pair of scissors. Repeat with the remaining batter. Cool the *pizzelle* completely.

● Just before serving, dust the *pizzelle* with confectioners' sugar. Store in an airtight container, or stacked on a plate, tightly wrapped.

* Or substitute 2 teaspoons of the extract of your choice, or up to ¼ teaspoon extra-strong flavor or oil. Anise, rum, and orange are traditional flavors; we like hazelnut, butterscotch, and cinnamon, too.

Nutrition information per serving (1 cookie, 29 g): 106 cal, 5 g fat, 2 g protein, 7 g complex carbohydrates, 8 g sugar, 39 mg cholesterol, 87 mg sodium, 20 mg potassium, 50 RE vitamin A, 1 mg iron, 22 mg calcium, 27 mg phosphorus.

VARIATION

Confetti Pizzelle

Adding multicolored nonpareils to the *pizzelle* batter produces festive-looking rainbow *pizzelle*. Our thanks to author and television personality Mary Ann Esposito for the inspiration behind this recipe.

> **1 recipe *Pizzelle* batter**
> **¼ cup (2 ounces) nonpareils, multicolored or single color**

● Add the nonpareils to the prepared batter. Bake as directed in the basic recipe.

What's the difference between *pizzelle* and *krumkake*?

Not a whole lot, truthfully. *Pizzelle* are leavened with baking powder and are generally a bit thicker, a bit less crisp, and typically flavored with rum, anise, orange, or vanilla extract. Unleavened *krumkake,* thinner and crisper, are traditionally flavored with cardamom. Both are baked in an iron. Irons used to sport traditional patterns, often quite intricate; these days, the patterns are simpler and more generic.

Stroopwafels

These caramel-cinnamon treats, native to the Netherlands, elevate the term "sandwich cookie" to new heights. To serve them as they do in Amsterdam, set a cookie atop your mug of steaming coffee; it will act as a lid to keep the coffee warm and will soften a bit in the process. Note: You must have a *pizzelle* (or *krumkake,* or waffle cone) maker, preferably a "mini," to prepare these.

Yield: 32 sandwich cookies

BATTER
- ½ cup (1 stick, 4 ounces) unsalted butter
- ¾ cup (6 ounces) brown sugar
- 3 large eggs
- 2 teaspoons vanilla extract
- 1¾ cups (7¼ ounces) unbleached all-purpose flour
- ¼ teaspoon salt
- ½ teaspoon cinnamon
- 2 teaspoons baking powder

FILLING
- 2 tablespoons (1 ounce) water
- 1 cup (8 ounces) brown sugar
- 6 tablespoons (¾ stick, 3 ounces) unsalted butter
- ¼ cup (2¾ ounces) dark corn syrup
- 1 teaspoon cinnamon

- Preheat a mini-waffle cone iron or mini-*pizzelle* iron. If you don't have a mini-iron, use a regular-sized one; your *stroopwafels* will just be larger than normal.
- **To make the batter:** In a medium-sized bowl, or in a saucepan set over low heat, melt the butter; let it cool slightly. Whisk in the brown sugar, eggs, and vanilla. In a separate bowl, whisk together the flour, salt, cinnamon, and baking powder and stir into the butter mixture.
- Drop the batter by the teaspoonful onto the lightly greased, heated iron. Close the lid and bake until golden brown. Irons vary, so try a test cookie first to determine baking time. Remove the cookie from the iron and place on a rack to cool completely before filling.
- **To make the filling:** In a medium-sized saucepan set over low heat, combine the water, sugar, butter, and corn syrup, stirring until the sugar is dissolved. Cover the pan and bring to a boil. Boil for 3 minutes.
- Remove the lid and stir in the cinnamon. Boil until the syrup reaches the soft-ball stage, 234°F to 240°F. Remove from the heat and let cool for about 10 minutes.

In the Netherlands, a **stroopwafel** *often serves as the lid for a mug of hot coffee.*

● Place about ½ teaspoon of syrup onto each cookie. Sandwich pairs of cookies, pressing them together to spread the filling. Be careful, as the caramel is very hot. If it cools too much, making it hard to spread, rewarm slightly. Store cookies in an airtight container.

Nutrition information per serving (*1 sandwich cookie, 33 g*): 128 cal, 6 g fat, 1 g protein, 5 g complex carbohydrates, 14 g sugar, 34 mg cholesterol, 62 mg sodium, 59 mg potassium, 56 RE vitamin A, 1 mg vitamin C, 1 mg iron, 33 mg calcium, 25 mg phosphorus.

VARIATION

● If you're one of those folks who think a cookie just isn't a cookie without chocolate, try this rich chocolate-hazelnut filling.

> **½ cup (about 5 ounces) praline paste**
> **6 ounces bittersweet chocolate, chopped or, 1 cup bittersweet chocolate chips**

Melt the praline paste and chocolate together in a double boiler, or in a microwave on low power. Place about ½ teaspoon of filling onto each cookie. Sandwich pairs of cookies, pressing them together gently. Allow to stand until the filling is set, several hours at (cool) room temperature or 2 to 3 hours in the refrigerator. Store cookies in an airtight container.

That rainy day feeling

Humid weather can wreak havoc with crisp cookies, especially some of the ultrathin ones found in this chapter. To keep crisp cookies crisp, store them in an airtight container with a moisture absorber (sometimes called a cracker crisper). If unprotected cookies become soggy, lay them in a single layer on an ungreased baking sheet and refresh them in a preheated 350°F oven for 5 to 10 minutes. (Thinner cookies will need less time, thicker, a little more.) Remove them from the oven and cool them on a rack; this process should restore them to their former splendor.

Rosettes

The fried dough stand is a favorite stop along the midway for many a county fairgoer. Take fried dough one step further—make it ultrathin and crisp, and form it into a star, a heart, or something other than its usual unappetizing blob shape—and you've got rosettes. A special dipping iron is required to make these deep-fried batter cookies, but once you taste them you'll gladly add that one extra piece of equipment to your pantry. Rosettes can easily be flavored to taste. Use 1 teaspoon regular-strength extract, or a few drops to ⅛ teaspoon extra-strong flavor.

Yield: 3 dozen rosettes

1 large egg
1 cup (8 ounces) milk (regular or low fat, not nonfat)
2 tablespoons (⅞ ounce) sugar
⅛ teaspoon salt
1 teaspoon vanilla extract
1 cup (4¼ ounces) unbleached all-purpose flour
Vegetable oil
Confectioners' sugar, for dusting

- In a medium-sized bowl,* whisk together all the ingredients until smooth. For the crispiest rosettes, refrigerate the batter for 2 hours before using.
- Heat 1½ to 2 inches of vegetable oil in a wide saucepan or kettle; a deep electric frying pan is ideal, as you can control the temperature so easily. Heat the oil to 365°F to 375°F.
- Attach the rosette iron to its handle and immerse the iron in the hot oil briefly (about 5 seconds) to heat it. Remove it from the oil, shake off any excess, and dip it into the batter, allowing the batter to come close to, but not over the top edge of the iron; if it goes all the way over the top, you'll have a hard time getting the rosette off. Hold the iron in the batter for about 5 seconds, then lift it out and shake off any excess. The batter on the iron will

Dip the batter-covered rosette iron into the hot oil just to cover.

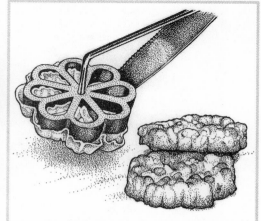

Peel the rosette off the iron with a table knife.

seem very thin, which is okay.

● Plunge the iron into the hot oil far enough to cover it. When the rosette is golden brown and the oil starts to bubble more gently, use a table knife to gently coax the rosette off the iron into the oil. Turn it over, grab a pair of tongs, and lift it out of the oil onto a paper towel–lined baking sheet to drain. Repeat with the remaining batter.

● Just before serving, dust the rosettes with confectioners' sugar. Store them in an airtight container.

* Use a bowl that's rather flat-bottomed, and at least as wide as the diameter of your rosette iron.

Nutrition information per serving (1 cookie, 17 g): 62 cal, 5 g fat, 1 g protein, 3 g complex carbohydrates, 1 g sugar, 7 mg cholesterol, 12 mg sodium, 15 mg potassium, 5 RE vitamin A, 1 mg vitamin C, 8 mg calcium, 11 mg phosphorus.

Belgian Sugar Waffles

Sweet, crunchy-soft, buttery. These waffle cookies are a traditional treat in Belgium, where street vendors cook and serve them to delighted aficionados. They'll be crisp-crunchy once they're cool; store them lightly covered to retain that texture.

Yield: 35 cookies

1 cup (2 sticks, 8 ounces) unsalted butter, melted and cooled to room temperature
4 large eggs
½ cup (3½ ounces) granulated sugar*
1 tablespoon vanilla extract
1½ cups (6¼ ounces) unbleached all-purpose flour
1½ teaspoons baking powder
½ teaspoon salt
½ cup (4⅜ ounces) coarse white sugar crystals

● Preheat a greased American-style waffle iron. If your waffle iron has a browning dial, turn it to the darkest setting. A heart-pattern iron makes attractive cookies, but any kind of American-style waffle iron, one that makes thin waffles (as opposed to a deep-pocketed Belgian iron), will do.

● In a medium-sized mixing bowl, beat together the butter, eggs, sugar, and vanilla until smooth. In a separate bowl, whisk together the flour, baking powder, and salt. Add the dry ingredients to the wet ingredients, beating until well combined. Stir in the coarse sugar.

● Pour ½ cup of batter onto the preheated waffle iron. Bake the cookie until it's a deep golden brown (don't underbake, or it won't be crisp). Open the waffle iron and use a flat spatula or a couple of forks to transfer the cookie—it will be quite tender—to a wire rack to cool.

● While the cookies are still warm, use a pair of scissors to cut them into pieces. If you used a heart iron, cut out the hearts. For a plain square iron, cut the cookies into 2- to 2½-inch squares. Allow them to cool completely, for maximum crispness. Store in an airtight container.

* The traditional sugar waffle is very sweet; we prefer this slightly less sweet Americanized version, but increase the sugar to ¾ cup for a more traditional Belgian treat.

Nutrition information per serving (1 cookie, 24 g): 97 cal, 6 g fat, 1 g protein, 4 g complex carbohydrates, 6 g sugar, 38 mg cholesterol, 45 mg sodium, 15 mg potassium, 60 RE vitamin A, 8 mg calcium, 18 mg phosphorus.

No~Bake Cookies

Here at King Arthur Flour, we do everything we can think of to get you to bake. So why are we offering recipes for no-bake cookies? We know any lifelong journey begins with a single step, or in this case, a bowl and a spoon. Once you've seen how easy it is to stir up a batch of treats that please people without even turning on the oven, we think you'll come back to the kitchen (and *real* baking) again and again. Making these cookies is a wonderful way for kids to develop the habit of mixing different ingredients to create their own examples of culinary magic. And the finished cookies are a great reminder for grownups of how simple life used to be.

We all know there are times when heating up the kitchen isn't a desirable option. That's when no-bake cookies can come to the rescue. Or maybe there just isn't an oven around; who says you can't make cookies on a camping trip?

Your camp stove, a cooking pot, and a spoon are all you need to make many of these recipes.

No-bake cookies are simply crunchy things bound together with gooey things. Crunchy things can be nuts, oats, any kind of cereal, cookie crumbs, even chow mein noodles for the butterscotch haystacks we all remember from childhood. Ingredients that bind (the gooey things) run the gamut from combinations of dried milk and corn syrup, to melted chocolate, peanut butter, or marshmallows. Many of these cookies benefit from a little time in the refrigerator, to help them set up.

If you're looking for a simple way to recapture some of the memories and flavors you've cherished from childhood, read on.

Crispy Rice Treats

This is the one that started it all. The marriage of melted marshmallows and crisp rice cereal is the ultimate example of opposites blending to make an irresistible combination. The play of crispy against chewy has been pleasing kids of all ages for years. It's an immensely versatile recipe, both for the shapes it can take and the other flavor variations is can accommodate.

Yield: *24 bars*

3 tablespoons (1½ ounces) unsalted butter
½ teaspoon salt
1 package (10 ounces) miniature or regular marshmallows
½ teaspoon vanilla extract
6 cups (6¼ ounces) crisp rice cereal

● Lightly grease a 9 x 13-inch pan.
● In a large saucepan set over low heat, combine the butter, salt, marshmallows, and vanilla. Cook, stirring frequently, until the marshmallows melt and the mixture is smooth. Remove the pan from the heat and add the cereal, stirring until it's completely coated. Press the mixture into the prepared pan using a buttered spatula or your lightly greased hands (see illustration next page). Allow the mixture to cool to room temperature before cutting.

Nutrition information per serving (one 2 x 2¼-inch bar, 21 g): 77 cal, 1 g fat, 1 g protein, 6 g complex carbohydrates, 10 g sugar, 4 mg cholesterol, 139 mg sodium, 10 mg potassium, 50 RE vitamin A, 4 mg vitamin C, 1 mg iron, 1 mg calcium, 10 mg phosphorus.

VARIATIONS

● This recipe can be molded into any number of shapes. Try pressing the warm mixture onto the bottom and up the sides of the greased well of a muffin tin or a small bowl. Once the mixture cools and sets, these edible bowls can be vessels for pudding, ice cream, or mousse.

● In Vermont, in the dead of winter, we desperately need a breath of tropical air. These bars are a worthy substitute.

> **1 cup (5½ ounces) mixed dried tropical fruits, such as mango, pineapple, and papaya**
> **1 cup (3 ounces) sweetened flaked coconut**
> **½ teaspoon coconut extract, or a few drops strong coconut flavor (optional)**

Prepare the bars as directed, substituting coconut extract or flavor for the vanilla, and stirring the fruit and coconut into the mixture before pressing it into the pan.

● For butterscotch or chocolate crispy rice treats it's easy to add another flavor to these bars in the form of chips, chocolate or otherwise. Prepare the bars as directed, adding 1 cup (6 ounces) butterscotch or chocolate chips to the marshmallow mixture in the saucepan, before removing from the heat. Stir until the chips have melted completely and the mixture is smooth.

If you're pressing the bars into the pan by hand and don't want to get too messy, put your hand inside a plastic bag and spray the outside of the bag with nonstick spray.

Butterscotch Haystacks

We all remember our first encounter with these cookies—it might have been a grade school bake sale, or a rainy afternoon project with Mom. Peanut butter and butterscotch seem like an unlikely combination, but after our first taste of this crunchy confection, it's one that most of us never forget.

Yield: *36 cookies*

¾ cup (7⅛ ounces) smooth or chunky peanut butter
1 cup (6 ounces) butterscotch chips
1 cup (3 ounces) sweetened or unsweetened coconut (optional)
5 cups (8¾ ounces) dry chow mein noodles (canned)

● In a large saucepan set over low heat, or in the microwave, melt together the peanut butter and butterscotch chips, stirring until smooth. Add the coconut and chow mein noodles, stirring until they're well coated. Drop the mixture by the tablespoonful onto waxed paper or greased parchment. Chill until set.

Nutrition information per serving (1 cookie, 20 g): 107 cal, 7 g fat, 2 g protein, 5 g complex carbohydrates, 4 g sugar, 1 g dietary fiber, 67 mg sodium, 62 mg potassium, 1 RE vitamin A, 1 mg vitamin C, 1 mg iron, 2 mg calcium, 35 mg phosphorus.

Bird's Nests

These are great treats for Easter or birthdays, filled with a child's favorite candy, or with a little marshmallow chick peering out.

Yield: *8 nests*

> 3 cups (6 ounces) miniature marshmallows
> 3 tablespoons (1½ ounces) unsalted butter
> ½ teaspoon vanilla extract
> 4 cups (7 ounces) dry chow mein noodles (canned)
> Small jelly beans, gumdrops, pastel candy-coated almonds, or candy-coated chocolates

- In a saucepan set over low heat, or in the microwave at low power, melt the marshmallows with the butter. Stir in the vanilla and add the chow mein noodles. Stir until the noodles are coated.
- Shape into tennis-ball-sized clumps on parchment or waxed paper. With greased or buttered hands, shape the mixture into bird's nests. Allow the nests to cool, then fill with the brightly colored candy of your choice.

Nutrition information per serving (1 nest, without filling, 45 g): 211 cal, 11 g fat, 2 g protein, 13 g complex carbohydrates, 13 g sugar, 1 g dietary fiber, 12 mg cholesterol, 106 mg sodium, 29 mg potassium, 42 RE vitamin A, 1 mg iron, 9 mg calcium, 39 mg phosphorus.

Form the bird's nest by pressing into the center with your thumbs.

VARIATION

- For coconut bird's nests, increase the marshmallows to 4 cups and the butter to 4 tablespoons. Stir in 3 cups sweetened shredded coconut before shaping.

Butter-Pecan Rum Balls

These chewy rounds are perfect for holiday gatherings, and go together very quickly. The butter and rum flavors become pleasantly mellow with a little aging. If you're looking for a good cookie to ship to someone far away, this is an excellent choice.

Yield: 32 cookies

One 12-ounce box (3 cups) vanilla wafer cookies, crushed, or Brown-Edge Cookies (page 63)
2 cups (8 ounces) finely chopped pecans
½ teaspoon salt
4 tablespoons (½ stick, 2 ounces) unsalted butter, melted
½ cup plus 2 tablespoons (7 ounces, ½ large can) sweetened condensed milk
1 teaspoon vanilla extract, or a few drops to ⅛ teaspoon butter-pecan flavor
¼ cup (2 ounces) dark or spiced rum, or caramel syrup
Confectioners' sugar, for coating

- In a large bowl, stir together the crushed cookies, pecans, and salt. Stir in the butter, condensed milk, vanilla, and rum. Mix until smooth and evenly moistened.
- Scoop the mixture by the tablespoonful and roll into balls. Roll the balls in confectioners' sugar to coat. Store in an airtight container.

Nutrition information per serving (1 ball, 28 g): 141 cal, 9 g fat, 2 g protein, 6 g complex carbohydrates, 6 g sugar, 1 g dietary fiber, 14 mg cholesterol, 82 mg sodium, 64 mg potassium, 16 RE vitamin A, 1 mg vitamin C, 19 mg calcium, 38 mg phosphorus.

VARIATION
- For chocolate bourbon balls, substitute crushed chocolate wafer cookies for the vanilla cookies, (or Chocolate Snaps, page 327) and substitute bourbon for the rum.

Chocolate-Hazelnut Crisps

Europeans are familiar with the delights of chocolate-hazelnut spread. It's a great addition to these crunchy cookies, which are best stored in the refrigerator.

Yield: *26 cookies*

1 cup (6 ounces) semisweet or bittersweet chocolate chips
¾ cup (8¾ ounces) chocolate-hazelnut spread (such as Nutella)
3 cups (3½ ounces) crisp rice cereal
½ cup (2 ounces) hazelnuts, toasted (see page 27) and chopped

- In a medium-sized microwave-safe bowl, or in a small saucepan set over low heat, melt the chocolate chips and hazelnut spread, stirring until no lumps remain. In a medium-sized bowl, pour the mixture over the rice cereal, stirring until the cereal is coated.
- Drop the batter by the tablespoon onto lightly greased parchment or waxed paper, flattening it into rounds with the back of a wet spoon. Sprinkle the tops of the cookies with the hazelnuts. Chill until set.

Nutrition information per serving (1 cookie, 20 g): 105 cal, 6 g fat, 3 g protein, 5 g complex carbohydrates, 5 g sugar, 1 g dietary fiber, 31 mg sodium, 89 mg potassium, 26 RE vitamin A, 2 mg vitamin C, 1 mg iron, 16 mg calcium, 47 mg phosphorus, 7 mg caffeine.

Dip a spoon in some water, shake off the excess, and use the back of it to spread the cookie batter into a flat, round shape.

Peanut Butter Graham Squares

These rectangles sport crispy graham cracker bottoms, a wonderfully smooth and creamy peanut butter middle, and just the right touch of chocolate on top. They look very grown up when cut and arranged on a plate, but the flavor appeals to children (of *all* ages).

Yield: 24 bars

11 whole graham crackers (6 ounces)
1½ cups (7½ ounces) graham cracker crumbs
1 cup (2 sticks, 8 ounces) unsalted butter
2½ cups (10 ounces) confectioners' sugar
¾ cup (7⅛ ounces) smooth or chunky peanut butter
1 teaspoon vanilla extract
½ teaspoon salt
1¼ cups (7½ ounces) chocolate chips

- Line a 9 x 13-inch pan with the graham crackers. In a medium-sized mixing bowl, combine the graham cracker crumbs, butter, sugar, peanut butter, vanilla, and salt, stirring until smooth. Spread the mixture evenly over the graham crackers and chill for 1 hour.
- When the mixture is chilled, melt the chocolate chips over low heat, stirring until smooth. Pour the chocolate over the peanut butter filling, spreading it evenly over the top. Allow the chocolate to cool until set. Cut into bars to serve.

Nutrition information per serving (one 2 x 2¼-inch bar, 52 g): 266 cal, 16 g fat, 3 g protein, 8 g complex carbohydrates, 21 g sugar, 1 g dietary fiber, 22 mg cholesterol, 164 mg sodium, 109 mg potassium, 75 RE vitamin A, 1 mg iron, 11 mg calcium, 49 g phosphorus, 7 mg caffeine.

Crunchy Peanut Butter Bars

These bars are for the peanut-butter purist, who doesn't want any marshmallow getting in the way.

Yield: 35 bars

1½ cups (14¼ ounces) smooth peanut butter
1 can (14 ounces) sweetened condensed milk
¼ cup (2¾ ounces) corn syrup
6 cups (6¼ ounces) crisp rice cereal
1 cup (6 ounces) chocolate chips (optional)

- Line a 10 x 15-inch jelly roll pan with parchment or waxed paper. Spray the paper lightly with nonstick spray.
- In a medium-sized saucepan set over low heat, combine the peanut butter, sweetened condensed milk, and corn syrup, stirring until smooth. Remove the pan from the heat.
- Place the cereal in a large bowl. Pour the warm peanut butter mixture over the cereal, stirring until evenly combined. Use a flexible spatula to press the mixture into the prepared pan. Sprinkle the chocolate chips over the bars while they're still warm. Let the pan sit for 5 minutes and chill until set, then cut into bars.

Nutrition information per serving (one 2 x 2¼-inch bar, with chocolate, 35 g): 153 cal, 8 g fat, 4 g protein, 7 g complex carbohydrates, 11 g sugar, 1 g dietary fiber, 5 mg cholesterol, 128 mg sodium, 131 mg potassium, 29 RE vitamin A, 3 mg vitamin C, 1 mg iron, 31 mg calcium, 66 mg phosphorus, 4 mg caffeine.

VARIATION

- Sprinkle the chocolate chips over the bars while they're still warm and spread the softened chips over the top.

Butterscotch-Oatmeal Stovetop Cookies

Oatmeal and butterscotch chips keep each other company in this quick stir-together cookie. The comforting chew of the oatmeal is nicely complemented by crisp cereal and delicious pockets of butterscotch.

Yield: 26 cookies

1½ cups (5¼ ounces) rolled oats (not quick-cooking)
1 cup (8 ounces) brown sugar
1 small can (5 ounces) evaporated milk
½ teaspoon salt
1 teaspoon vanilla extract
1 cup (1 ounce) crisp cereal of your choice
1 cup (6 ounces) butterscotch chips
½ cup (2 ounces) chopped walnuts (optional)

- Place the oats in a large bowl and set aside.
- In a medium-sized saucepan set over low heat, combine the brown sugar, evaporated milk, salt, and vanilla. Bring the mixture to a boil, then pour it over the oats and stir to combine. Allow the mixture to cool to room temperature.
- Stir in the cereal and butterscotch chips. Drop by the tablespoonful onto waxed or lightly greased parchment paper, pressing to flatten slightly with wet fingers. Chill until set.

Nutrition information per serving (1 cookie, 30 g): 114 cal, 4 g fat, 2 g protein, 6 g complex carbo-hydrates, 13 g sugar, 1 g dietary fiber, 2 mg cholesterol, 67 mg sodium, 92 mg potassium, 9 RE vitamin A, 1 mg vitamin C, 1 mg iron, 26 mg calcium, 56 mg phosphorus.

Chocolate-Oatmeal Drops

These cookies have a rich, fudgy texture, flecked with chewy oats and crunchy nuts.

Yield: *36 cookies*

3 cups (10½ ounces) rolled oats
1 cup (6 ounces) chocolate chips
1 cup (4 ounces) chopped nuts (optional)
1 teaspoon vanilla extract
½ cup (1 stick, 4 ounces) unsalted butter
½ cup (4 ounces) milk
2 cups (14 ounces) sugar
½ teaspoon salt

- In a large mixing bowl, combine the oats, chocolate chips, nuts, and vanilla.
- In a saucepan, combine the butter, milk, sugar, and salt, and bring to a rolling boil. Boil for 4 to 5 minutes, until the bubbles make a snapping sound. Carefully pour the hot mixture over the oatmeal mixture, stirring to combine.
- Drop by the tablespoonful onto waxed paper or parchment, then chill until the cookies set up.

Nutrition information per serving (1 cookie, 26 g): 111 cal, 6 g fat, 1 g protein, 1 g complex carbohydrates, 14 g sugar, 7 mg cholesterol, 32 mg sodium, 37 mg potassium, 26 RE vitamin A, 1 mg vitamin C, 8 mg calcium, 23 mg phosphorus, 4 mg caffeine.

VARIATIONS

- For chocolate–peanut butter drops, add 1 cup smooth or chunky peanut butter to the mixing bowl with the oat mixture.
- Press miniature marshmallows into the tops of the cookies while they're still warm, to make domino designs.

Oatmeal Fruit Cookies

These cookies are packed with plenty of nutrition and are relatively low in fat. If you like your cookies soft and chewy, these will fill the bill. If you'd like squares instead of cookies, the batter can be pressed into a greased 8 x 8-inch baking pan, allowed to cool, and cut into squares.

Yield: 2 dozen cookies

2 cups (7 ounces) rolled oats
3 tablespoons (1½ ounces) unsalted butter
1 cup (8 ounces) brown sugar
½ cup (4 ounces) frozen apple juice concentrate, thawed
1 teaspoon cinnamon
¼ teaspoon nutmeg
½ teaspoon salt
1¼ cups (6¼ ounces) nonfat dry milk
1½ cups (4½ to 9 ounces) dried apples, cranberries, raisins, or any combination
¾ cup (3 ounces) chopped walnuts (optional)

- Place the oats in a large mixing bowl and set aside.
- In a medium-sized saucepan set over low heat, combine the butter, brown sugar, apple juice concentrate, spices, and salt. Bring to a boil, stirring until the sugar dissolves. Pour this mixture over the oats, stirring to combine. Stir in the dry milk and the fruit.
- Drop by the tablespoonful onto lightly greased parchment or waxed paper. Press to flatten slightly.

Nutrition information per serving (1 cookie, 39 g): 96 cal, 2 g fat, 1 g protein, 9 g complex carbohydrates, 10 g sugar, 1 g dietary fiber, 4 mg cholesterol, 53 mg sodium, 97 mg potassium, 15 RE vitamin A, 1 mg iron, 15 mg calcium, 37 mg phosphorus.

Rocky Road No-Bakes

Rocky road, an ever-popular ice cream type, is a great combination of flavors for cookies, too. These cookies combine chocolate with grace notes of lightly salted almonds and miniature marshmallows.

Yield: 30 cookies

> 3 cups (5⅝ ounces) crisp rice cereal
> 1 cup (6 ounces) chocolate chips
> ¾ cup (8¾ ounces) chocolate-hazelnut spread (such as Nutella)
> 1 cup (4 ounces) sliced almonds, sprinkled lightly with salt and toasted (see page 27)
> 1 cup (2 ounces) miniature marshmallows

- Place the rice cereal in a large bowl and set aside.
- In a small saucepan set over low heat, or in a small bowl in the microwave, melt the chocolate chips and hazelnut spread together, stirring until no lumps remain. Pour the melted mixture over the cereal and let cool slightly. Stir in the toasted almonds and marshmallows. Drop by the tablespoonful onto waxed paper or lightly greased parchment paper and chill until set.

Nutrition information per serving (1 cookie, 22 g): 115 cal, 7 g fat, 3 g protein, 5 g complex carbohydrates, 5 g sugar, 1 g dietary fiber, 28 mg sodium, 100 mg potassium, 23 RE vitamin A, 2 mg vitamin C, 1 mg iron, 22 mg calcium, 57 mg phosphorus, 6 mg caffeine.

The Finishing Touch

Many cookies are sublime in their simplicity—the combination of flour, sugar, salt, and butter undergoes a magical transformation in the oven to become shortbread; add chocolate, eggs, and a bit of leavening, and you have America's best-loved cookie, chocolate chip.

Other cookies generate delight not from their simple ingredients, but from their appearance. Think of a fat gingerbread boy, with iced blue trousers and a red-buttoned shirt. Or a cutout heart, I Love You written across its pink-iced face. Then, there are simple cookies that assume a fancy, downtown aura when you add filling, or top them with a generous layer of dark chocolate ganache (see Baltimore's Finest, page 294). Take a couple of cut-out sugar cookies, spread on a tasty layer of jam or preserves, and what do you have? That Christmas classic, the linzer cookie.

This chapter focuses on adding panache to your cookies, with icing, with filling, and even with some special cookie dips. Throughout this book you'll find icings and fillings that have been formulated to go with specific cookie recipes. Feel free to apply them (liberally!) to other cookies; as always, baking is as much art as science—don't be afraid to color outside the lines. In this chapter, we've gathered a variety of all-purpose glazes, icings, fillings, and dips, a wonderful buffet of possibilities that can be applied to the cookie of your choice. Imagination is key; it unlocks many doors. Two crisp oatmeal cookies sandwiched around golden, smooth caramel filling? Reach for the sky—that's where you'll find Cookie Heaven.

GLAZES AND ICINGS • • • • •

From a hard, smooth, shiny coating, perfect for adding a written message or painted design, to the unctuous luxury of ganache, the ne plus ultra of creamy frostings, there's all kinds of magic you can make in topping your baked cookies. Just be sure cookies are totally cool before spreading on any kind of topping, otherwise, it's likely to melt and slide right off.

Hard Glaze for Cookies

This smooth, shiny glaze is ideal for cookies that will be decorated with food-safe pens or other writers. It covers cookies very well (the color of your dark gingerbread won't show through), and dries to a hard enough finish that iced cookies can be stacked on top of each other, perfect for storage or assembly of a holiday gift basket. Try building on the base layer of coating with an outline or decorations in a contrasting color.

Yield: 1¼ *cups glaze*

> ¼ cup (1 ounce) meringue powder*
> ¼ teaspoon salt
> 3 to 4 cups (12 to 16 ounces) confectioners' sugar
> ⅓ to ½ cup (2⅝ to 4 ounces) cool water
> 1 teaspoon vanilla extract
> Food color or coloring paste

- In a medium-sized mixing bowl, whisk together the meringue powder, salt, and confectioners' sugar. Add ⅓ cup cool water and the vanilla, and stir, or beat on slow speed. The mixture will seem hard and lumpy, but the sugar will dissolve after 4 or 5 minutes and everything will smooth out. Add more water, 1 tablespoon at a time, mixing well after each addition to achieve a spreadable consistency. For a very smooth, shiny glaze, the icing should be the consistency of corn syrup or molasses. For colored icing, add food color or coloring paste a drop at a time.
- Dip the tops of cooled cookies in the glaze, then sweep a spatula over them to remove the excess. Place cookies on a rack for several hours for the glaze to harden and dry. This may take as long as overnight, depending on the humidity of your kitchen and the consistency of the glaze.

* Available at cake decorating specialty stores and via catalogs and web sites that sell baking ingredients.

Nutrition information per serving (2 teaspoons coating, 14 g): 37 cal, 9 g sugar, 16 mg sodium, 3 mg potassium.

VARIATION

Royal Icing

- To make a thick, fluffy, hard-drying royal icing (the type of icing you use as mortar in a gingerbread house, or to pipe decorations), add ½ cup cool water to the dry ingredients in the hard glaze recipe. Omit the vanilla. Stir slowly to allow the sugar to dissolve. Mix on low speed, increasing to high speed over several minutes. Beat until the icing is fluffy. Add food color as desired; we recommend gel paste colors because they're so strong you only need to use a drop or two for brilliantly vibrant colors. If you're icing a lot of cookies and the icing in the bowl starts to develop a crust, cover it with plastic wrap or a damp cloth to prevent it from drying out.

Yield: A generous 3 cups fluffy icing

Simple Cookie Glaze

This glaze, though slightly less opaque than hard glaze made with meringue powder, dries hard and shiny, and uses ingredients you're likely to have in your pantry. It stirs up in a jiffy. Be sure you measure accurately: too little milk and the glaze won't spread well; too much and it will be thin and spotty. The goal is a glaze that isn't perfectly smooth when you apply it, but that settles into a smooth surface within half a minute or so. Glaze one cookie and set it aside for a minute; if the glaze smoothes out it's the right consistency. And remember, it's easier to add more liquid than to stir in more sugar, so start with a glaze that's thicker than you think it should be, then add milk by the teaspoonful to adjust its consistency.

Yield: ⅔ cup glaze

2¼ cups (9 ounces) **confectioners' sugar**
2 tablespoons (1⅜ ounces) **light corn syrup**
2 tablespoons plus 1 teaspoon (1¼ ounces) **milk**

• In a small bowl, whisk together the sugar, corn syrup, and milk. The coating should be the consistency of thick, cold honey. Use an offset spatula or table knife to spread glaze on the cookies. This amount of coating will cover about 2½ dozen 2-inch cookies. Double the recipe, if you like, for more and/or larger cookies.

Nutrition information per serving (1 teaspoon, 11 g): 37 cal, 9 g sugar, 2 mg sodium, 2 mg potassium, 1 RE vitamin A, 2 mg calcium, 1 mg phosphorus.

Vanilla Glaze

This is the quickest, simplest, most versatile glaze you can make for a cookie. Not as hard or as shiny as the Hard Glaze for Cookies on page 457, it's a nice choice for where you're after added flavor rather than creating a blank canvas suitable for decorating. Drizzle the glaze atop cookies, paint it on with a pastry brush, spread it with a spatula, or serve it in a bowl for dipping. It dries to a smooth, satiny finish and can be tinted any color you choose. Looking for another flavor? Start here, and vary the extract or flavor as you please.

Yield: 1 cup glaze

1 cup (4 ounces) **confectioners' sugar**
¼ cup (2 ounces) **heavy cream**
1 teaspoon **vanilla extract**

• Sift or strain the confectioners' sugar into a medium-sized bowl to remove any lumps. Whisk the cream into the sugar to make a smooth glaze. Stir in the vanilla. Keep the glaze covered until ready to use, to prevent a crust from forming.

Nutrition information per serving (1 teaspoon, 4 g): 19 cal, 1 g fat, 3 g sugar, 2 mg cholesterol, 1mg sodium, 1 mg potassium, 7 RE vitamin A, 1 mg calcium, 1 mg phosphorus.

VARIATIONS

Mint Glaze

● Substitute ¼ to ½ teaspoon peppermint extract for the vanilla extract.

Coconut Glaze

● Substitute ½ teaspoon coconut extract (or a few drops strong coconut flavor) for the vanilla extract.

Orange or Lemon Glaze

● Reduce the cream to 2 tablespoons and add 2 tablespoons orange or lemon juice. Add 2 teaspoons orange or lemon zest (or a few drops orange or lemon oil), if desired.

Cappuccino Glaze

● Add 2 teaspoons espresso powder.

Maple Glaze

● Reduce the cream to 3 tablespoons, and add 1 tablespoon maple syrup. Substitute ½ teaspoon maple flavor for the vanilla extract.

Cinnamon Glaze

● Add 1 teaspoon ground cinnamon, or a few drops cinnamon oil.

Chocolate Glaze

● Reduce confectioners' sugar to ¾ cup and increase the cream to 6 tablespoons. Add ¼ cup unsweetened cocoa powder (regular or Dutch process) to the confectioners' sugar before sifting.

Brandy, Frangelico, or Sherry Glaze

● Reduce the cream to 2 tablespoons and add 2 tablespoons brandy, or the liqueur of your choice.

Milk or heavy cream for glaze?

Many of us grew up with recipes that call for a quick combination of milk and confectioners' sugar for glazing baked goods. So why are we calling for heavy cream? While it's a bit more expensive, we feel the results are worth the investment. Heavy cream makes a glaze that's richer, naturally, but it also spreads better and dries to a smoother, shinier surface.

Chocolate Ganache

The name rhymes with panache, with good reason. What could be more sophisticated than the glossy sheen of a perfectly coated chocolate confection, or the je ne sais quoi of an artfully drizzled design? Flavor this rich chocolate concoction with anything from vanilla extract to flavored liqueurs, such as hazelnut, raspberry, or Grand Marnier.

Yield: 2 cups ganache

1⅓ cups (8 ounces) chopped semisweet or bittersweet chocolate (see sidebar on page 462)
¾ cup (6 ounces) heavy cream
1 teaspoon extract or flavor, or more or less to taste; or up to 6 tablespoons liqueur

● Place the chocolate in a medium-sized heatproof bowl. In a small saucepan, over medium heat, bring the cream to a simmer, then pour it over the chocolate. Stir until the mixture is completely smooth, with no lumps (see illustrations 1–4). Stir in the flavor or the liqueur. If you're using a significant amount of liqueur, you may need to add additional cream to provide sufficient fat to keep the ganache smooth.

Nutrition information per serving (1 tablespoon, 13 g): 55 cal, 4 g fat, 1 g protein, 1 g complex carbohydrates, 4 g sugar, 8 mg cholesterol, 2 mg sodium, 26 mg potassium, 23 RE vitamin A, 1 mg vitamin C, 6 mg calcium, 11 mg phosphorus, 6 mg caffeine.

Pour simmering cream over the chopped chocolate.

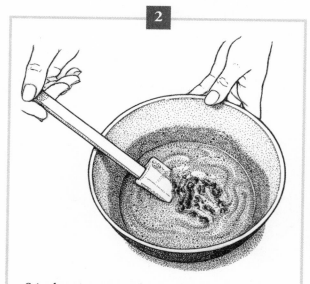

Stir the mixture together; at first it will look gloppy and fragmented, but that's normal.

White Chocolate Ganache

White chocolate has different qualities than dark, since it's made of the cocoa butter that remains after the chocolate "liquor" (chocolate solids) has been extracted from the crushed cacao bean. It's sensitive to scorching, and needs less liquid to form a workable ganache. White chocolate ganache won't set up as firmly as its dark chocolate sibling; the surface stays slightly tacky to the touch, even after it's cooled and set. One last thing to note: white chocolate ganache is somewhat translucent, so if you're to trying encase something dark, be aware that it will show through faintly, like the outline of a nearby island on a foggy day at sea.

Yield: *1¾ cups ganache*

1⅓ cups (8 ounces) chopped white chocolate (see sidebar on page 462)
¼ to ⅓ cup (2 to 2⅝ ounces) heavy cream

● Place the chocolate in a medium-sized heatproof bowl (see illustrations 1–4). Heat ¼ cup of heavy cream to a simmer and pour it over the white chocolate. Stir until the mixture becomes completely smooth, with no lumps. If the mixture is too thick to pour easily, add another tablespoon or two of the hot cream, as needed.

Nutrition information per serving (1 tablespoon, 11 g): 55 cal, 4 g fat, 1 g protein, 1 g complex carbohydrates, 5 g sugar, 4 mg cholesterol, 8 mg sodium, 25 mg potassium, 11 RE vitamin A, 1 mg vitamin C, 19 mg calcium, 2 mg phosphorus.

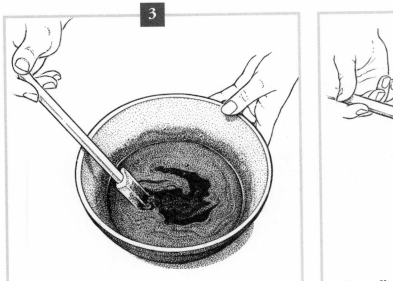

As you continue to stir, the chocolate will begin to melt and smooth out.

Once all the cream is incorporated, the mixture will be smooth and shiny, with no lumps. The ganache is now ready to use.

Chunk chocolate or chocolate chips in ganache?

Why should you go to all the trouble of chopping up an expensive bar of chocolate to make your ganache, when it's just as easy to open a bag of semisweet chips? Because better chocolate means better results. Chocolate chips are made with stabilizers, which help the chips hold their distinctive pointy shape when they're baked. These stabilizers affect the chips' ability to melt smoothly, and also make their chocolate flavor less intense. In addition, ganache made with chocolate chips won't set as firmly or look as shiny and smooth as ganache made with chopped chocolate. But don't worry, whichever one you use, you'll still get lots of oohs and aahs when people see your beautiful cookies.

Fondant Icing

This thick, soft icing is a pleasure to pour or paint over cookies. It can be colored any hue of the rainbow, and reheated again and again without getting grainy. When cooled, it sets to a beautiful satiny shine without being stiff or hard. Note that any fondant that runs off the cookies may be reheated and used again; if it's full of crumbs, strain it through a fine-mesh strainer. Leftover fondant also may be made into wafer candies; drop it by the teaspoonful onto parchment-lined or lightly greased baking sheets.

Yield: 2¼ cups icing

> 1 cup (6 ounces) white confectionery coating or white chocolate pieces
> 4 cups (1 pound) confectioners' sugar
> ¼ cup (2¾ ounces) light corn syrup
> ½ cup (4 ounces) hot water
> 1 teaspoon vanilla extract
> Food coloring (optional)

- **To make the icing:** Sift the confectioners' sugar into a large bowl, then whisk in the corn syrup and hot water, stirring until smooth. In a saucepan set over very low heat, or in a double boiler or the microwave, melt the white coating or chocolate, stirring until smooth.
- Add the melted coating to the sugar mixture, then add the vanilla and color. If the icing is too thick to pour, reheat it briefly over low heat and stir in 1 to 3 tablespoons additional water. The icing is easiest to work with, and coats smoothly, at about 100°F. Keep it warm and covered, laying a lightly greased piece of plastic wrap on the surface to keep it from drying out and forming lumps.
- **To ice the cookies:** Place cooling racks over parchment paper or baking sheets. Dip the cookies into the icing, or drizzle the icing with a spoon, coating the tops. Place the cookies on the racks, allowing the extra icing to drip off onto the parchment.

- You can decorate the top of each cookie with sugar decorations, jimmies, or Royal Icing flowers (see page 457) while the fondant is still soft. Decorations may also be added after the icing hardens; you'll just need to use a bit of softened icing to hold them on.

Nutrition information per serving (1 tablespoon, 24 g): 86 cal, 2 g fat, 1 g protein, 18 g sugar, 7 mg sodium, 12 mg potassium, 1 mg iron, 9 mg calcium, 1 mg phosphorus.

VARIATION
- For chocolate icing, replace the white confectionery coating with chopped unsweetened (baking) chocolate.

Caramel Icing

This is a quick and easy way to put a golden caramel finish on your cookies. This icing is thin enough to be spread with a pastry brush, but also has enough body that you can use a small spatula.

Yield: 3 cups icing

½ cup (1 stick, 4 ounces) unsalted butter
¼ teaspoon salt
1 cup (8 ounces) brown sugar
¼ cup (2 ounces) milk (regular or low fat, not nonfat)
1 teaspoon vanilla extract
4 cups (1 pound) confectioners' sugar

- Melt the butter in a heavy 2-quart saucepan. Stir in the salt and brown sugar and heat the mixture to boiling, stirring just until the sugar is totally dissolved. Cook over low heat for 2 minutes. Stir in the milk and return to a full boil, without further stirring. Remove the pan from the heat and cool to lukewarm.
- Stir in the vanilla, then gradually stir in the confectioners' sugar. Adjust the consistency with a little more milk if necessary.

Nutrition information per serving (2 teaspoons, 12 g): 50 cal, 1 g fat, 1 g protein, 1 g complex carbohydrates, 10 g sugar, 4 mg cholesterol, 9 mg sodium, 13 mg potassium, 12 RE vitamin A, 1 mg vitamin C, 4 mg calcium, 2 mg phosphorus.

Mocha Glaze

A coffee-lover's dream, this glaze can work overtime as cookie or cake frosting, too.

Yield: 1¼ cups glaze

5 tablespoons (2½ ounces) unsalted butter
2 tablespoons (⅜ ounce) unsweetened cocoa (Dutch process or natural)
4 teaspoons espresso powder, or 2 tablespoons instant coffee
¼ cup (2 ounces) boiling water*
½ teaspoon salt
2 cups (8 ounces) confectioners' sugar

● In a small bowl, cream together the butter and cocoa. In another small bowl, combine the espresso powder with the boiling water and salt, then stir it into the butter mixture. Add the confectioners' sugar and stir until smooth.

* For frosting, decrease the water to 2 tablespoons. Beat the mixture until fluffy, adding a teaspoon or two of water if the frosting seems stiff.

Nutrition information per serving (2 teaspoons, 13 g): 48 cal, 2 g fat, 1 g protein, 1 g complex carbohydrates, 8 g sugar, 5 mg cholesterol, 36 mg sodium, 15 mg potassium, 18 RE vitamin A, 2 mg calcium, 4 mg phosphorus, 8 mg caffeine.

Peanut Butter Icing

This is a very peanut-buttery icing that dries to a smooth finish. It won't become totally hard, so be careful not to stack iced cookies on top of each other.

Yield: 2 cups icing

1 cup (9½ ounces) smooth peanut butter
¼ cup (2¾ ounces) corn syrup
½ cup (4 ounces) milk (regular or low fat, not nonfat)
1 cup (4 ounces) confectioners' sugar
1 teaspoon vanilla extract

● In a small saucepan set over low heat, or in the microwave, heat the peanut butter, corn syrup, and milk together, stirring until smooth. Remove from the heat and stir in the confectioners' sugar and vanilla.

Nutrition information per serving (2 teaspoons, 6 g): 24 cal, 1 g fat, 1 g protein, 1 g complex carbohydrates, 2 g sugar, 1 mg cholesterol, 15 mg sodium, 20 mg potassium, 1 mg vitamin C, 1 mg calcium, 10 mg phosphorus.

FILLINGS • • • • • • • • • • • • • • • •

Take two cookies. Add filling. Sandwich together. Voilà! A whole that's ever so much more wonderful than its parts. Fillings give you an opportunity to play with complementary tastes—add cinnamon to marshmallow and use it to sandwich two oatmeal cookies; sugar cookies sing when you pair them with caramel filling. Go ahead, experiment, it's very difficult to come up with anything less than tasty here.

Creme Filling

This filling has the same texture as store-bought snack cake fillings, but tastes a whole lot better, mostly because of the butter. It pipes and spreads very easily and has just a hint of toasted-marshmallow flavor.

Yield: 2 cups filling

4 tablespoons (¼ cup, 2 ounces) unsalted butter
½ cup (3¼ ounces) vegetable shortening
½ teaspoon salt, dissolved in 2 teaspoons water
1 teaspoon vanilla extract
2 cups (8 ounces) confectioners' sugar
½ cup (2½ ounces) marshmallow creme

● In a large bowl, cream together the butter and shortening, then beat in the salt water, vanilla, and sugar. Beat until the mixture becomes fluffy, scraping the bowl at least once. Add the marshmallow creme and beat until incorporated.

Nutrition information per serving (1½ tablespoons, 21 g): 113 cal, 7 g fat, 13 g sugar, 6 mg cholesterol, 52 mg sodium, 2 mg potassium, 22 RE vitamin A, 1 mg calcium, 1 mg phosphorus.

VARIATION
● For malted milk filling, add 2 tablespoons unsweetened cocoa powder and 6 tablespoons malted milk to the confectioners' sugar before adding it to the butter mixture.

Peanut Butter Filling

This filling is fairly stiff; it's most suitable for sandwiching between sturdy roll-out cookies, or spreading on top of a crisp or crunchy cookie before covering with chocolate ganache. For a more spreadable filling, add up to an additional ½ cup milk.

Yield: 3 cups filling

1 cup (9½ ounces) peanut butter
1½ teaspoons vanilla extract
2½ cups (10 ounces) confectioners' sugar
6 to 8 tablespoons (3 to 4 ounces) milk (regular or low fat, not nonfat)

● In a medium-sized bowl, beat the peanut butter and vanilla at medium speed. Add the confectioners' sugar and beat until the mixture smooths out. Add the milk as necessary to make a pliable but relatively stiff filling.

Nutrition information per serving (2 teaspoons, 10 g): 38 cal, 2 g fat, 1 g protein, 5 g sugar, 18 mg sodium, 26 mg potassium, 1 RE vitamin A, 2 mg calcium, 13 mg phosphorus.

Marshmallow Filling

Moon Pies have it. Mallomars have it. Where would we be without marshmallow filling? This recipe makes nearly a lot (2 quarts) of smooth, creamy marshmallow, tastier by far than the marshmallows you buy at the supermarket. Don't worry, we give instructions for making your own individual s'more-friendly marshmallows out of any leftovers.

Yield: 7 cups

1½ cups (12 ounces) cold water
4 packages (¼ ounce each) unflavored gelatin
3 cups (21 ounces) granulated sugar
¼ cup (2¾ ounces) light corn syrup
¼ teaspoon salt
1 tablespoon vanilla extract*
½ cup (2 ounces) confectioners' sugar (if making marshmallows)

● Pour ¾ cup of the water into the bowl of an electric stand mixer. Sprinkle the gelatin on top and let it soften for 5 minutes.
● Bring the remaining ¾ cup water, granulated sugar, corn syrup, and salt to a boil in a medium-sized saucepan set over high heat. Cook, without stirring, until the mixture reaches the soft-ball stage (234°F to 240°F), about 10 minutes.
● Using your mixer's whisk attachment, beat the hot syrup into the gelatin mixture at low

speed. Gradually increase the speed to high, and beat until the mixture forms soft peaks, 3 to 5 minutes. Beat in the vanilla. (While the marshmallow is beating, line up half the cookies to be filled, flat side up, so you can spread them with filling quickly.)

● Spread half the cookies with a generous dollop of marshmallow. Top with the remaining cookies.

* Substitute your favorite flavor for the vanilla extract, adding to taste; use 2 to 3 teaspoons extract; much less (a few drops to perhaps 1 teaspoon) of a strong flavor or oil.

Nutrition information per serving (¼ cup, 37 g): 92 cal, 1 g protein, 23 g sugar, 21 mg sodium, 1 mg potassium, 1 mg calcium.

Homemade Marshmallows

The filling recipe makes enough for you to have some left over once all the cookies are filled; this is easily made into impress-your-friends homemade marshmallows.

● To make marshmallows from the leftover filling, you'll need to have a pan prepared for them before you start. Spray an 8 x 8-inch square (or 9-inch round) cookie pan with nonstick vegetable oil spray. Line the pan with parchment, leaving enough overhang so it comes up over the edge of the pan. Spray the parchment with nonstick spray.

● Prepare the marshmallow filling as directed in the recipe (opposite). After frosting the cookies, beat the remaining marshmallow for about a minute to soften it. Immediately spoon it into the prepared pan, smoothing it with an offset spatula dipped in water. It won't be totally smooth on top, but will continue to settle and smooth out as it cools. Let it set, uncovered, until it's firm, about 3 hours at room temperature.

● Sift a thin layer of confectioners' sugar onto a clean work surface, making a square or circle about the same size as your pan of marshmallows. Invert the marshmallows onto the sugar and peel off the parchment. Sift more sugar over the uncoated surface.

● Cut the marshmallow into squares, using a bench knife sprayed with nonstick vegetable oil spray (or whatever shape you like, using a well-oiled cutter). Roll the cut surfaces in confectioners' sugar.

● Store the marshmallows in a plastic bag.

Jams and jellies—you can't beat this spread!

One of the best fillings you can use is your favorite jam or jelly. Apricot, raspberry, and strawberry are flavors most frequently used with cookies, but if you're an orange marmalade fan, by all means, have at it! If you want to use jam or jelly to fill a cookie, here are some tips to make it easier.

● Jam will spread or pipe better if it's warmed first. You can do this at medium power in the microwave, or over low heat on the stove.

● After adding a dollop of jam as a topping, or coating a cookie with jam, let it air-dry overnight. This will remove enough of the jam's water to give you a clear, nonsticky surface.

● We like seedless preserves for our fillings, but if you can't find them, you can strain the seeds out of your jam after warming it. A flexible spatula is helpful with this, to push the jam through a strainer.

Lemon Creme Filling

Use this smooth creme filling with its bright, sunny flavor to make sandwich cookies. Thinly rolled shortbread, or the Lemon Snaps on page 339, are an ideal place to start.

Yield: 1½ cups filling

1 teaspoon unflavored gelatin
2 tablespoons (1 ounce) freshly squeezed lemon juice
½ cup (3¼ ounces) vegetable shortening
2½ cups (10 ounces) confectioners' sugar
2 teaspoons grated lemon rind (zest), or ⅛ teaspoon lemon oil

- Combine the gelatin and lemon juice in a small cup. Place the cup in a larger dish of hot water and leave it there until the gelatin is completely dissolved and the liquid is transparent. Remove the cup from the hot water and let the liquid cool until it's room temperature, but hasn't begun to set. This should take about 5 minutes.
- In a medium-sized mixing bowl, cream the shortening, then beat in the confectioners' sugar a little at a time, beating until the mixture is light and creamy. Beat in the lemon zest, then the gelatin.

Nutrition information per serving (1½ teaspoons, 9 g): 40 cal, 2 g fat, 1 g protein, 1 g complex carbohydrates, 6 g sugar, 1 g dietary fiber, 1 mg sodium, 1 mg potassium, 1 mg vitamin C, 1 mg iron, 1 mg calcium, 1 mg phosphorus.

Cream Cheese and Ginger Filling

We used this filling to devastating effect in the Pumpkin Whoopie Pies on page 419. It would do just as nicely layered between the Honey Crisps on page 410 for a quick Napoleon-style dessert.

Yield: 2 cups filling

1 tablespoon unflavored gelatin
2 tablespoons (1 ounce) cool water
½ cup (1 stick, 4 ounces) unsalted butter
½ cup (4 ounces) cream cheese (reduced fat [Neufchâtel] or full fat), softened
2¼ cups (9 ounces) confectioners' sugar
2 tablespoons (⅞ ounce) finely chopped crystallized ginger

- In a small bowl, combine the gelatin and water to soften the gelatin, and set aside.
- In a large bowl, beat together the butter and cream cheese until fluffy. Place the bowl of gelatin and water over hot water, or heat it at low power in the microwave, until the gelatin dissolves completely. Set aside.

● Add half the confectioners' sugar to the butter mixture, beating thoroughly. Add the gelatin, stirring to combine. Mix in the remaining sugar, then stir in the ginger.

Nutrition information per serving (2 tablespoons, 35 g): 148 cal, 8 g fat, 1 g protein, 1 g complex carbohydrates, 18 g sugar, 23 mg cholesterol, 24 mg sodium, 12 mg potassium, 84 RE vitamin A, 1 mg vitamin C, 9 mg calcium, 9 mg phosphorus.

Caramel Filling

This caramel filling is great on chocolate shortbread, or sandwiched between your favorite roll-out cookies. It stays pliable at room temperature, but is thick enough to slice. The recipe is easily halved for a smaller batch.

Yield: 4 cups soft caramel

2 cups (16 ounces) brown sugar
1 cup (11 ounces) light corn syrup
½ cup (1 stick, 4 ounces) unsalted butter
1 cup (8 ounces) cream (light, heavy, or whipping), or evaporated milk
2 teaspoons vanilla extract

● In a large (3½- to 4-quart) heavy-bottomed saucepan combine the sugar and corn syrup. If you have a large nonstick saucepan, now's the time to use it. Bring the mixture to a boil, stirring constantly. Cover the pan and boil for 3 minutes without stirring, to wash off any sugar crystals from the insides of the pan.
● Uncover the pan, stir in the butter, and continue to boil, stirring often, until the caramel reaches the soft-ball stage, 234°F to 240°F on a candy thermometer. While the syrup is boiling, gently heat the cream or evaporated milk in a saucepan over medium heat until it's hot but not boiling.
● Remove the syrup from the heat and slowly stir in the hot cream and the vanilla. Return the mixture to the burner and cook without stirring until the mixture reaches the firm-ball stage, 245°F to 248°F. Pour the caramel into an 8-inch square pan and cool for 30 minutes, or until it's cool enough to work with.

Nutrition information per serving (2 teaspoons, 16 g): 59 cal, 3 g fat, 9 g sugar, 8 mg cholesterol, 9 mg sodium, 21 mg potassium, 27 RE vitamin A, 8 mg calcium, 4 mg phosphorus.

Vanilla Creme Filling

You know those rows and rows of sandwich cookies you see lined up on the supermarket shelves? This is our take on the white filling that's the center of those sweet sandwiches. While we're always happy to duplicate a store-bought favorite, in this case we think our version is better!

Yield: 1½ cups

1 teaspoon plus a heaping ¼ teaspoon unflavored gelatin
2 tablespoons (1 ounce) cold water
½ cup (3¼ ounces) vegetable shortening
1 teaspoon vanilla extract
2½ cups (10 ounces) confectioners' sugar

- Combine the gelatin and water in a small cup. Place the cup in a larger dish of hot water and leave it there until the gelatin is completely dissolved and the liquid is transparent. Remove the cup from the hot water and let the liquid cool until it's room temperature, but hasn't begun to set. This should take about 5 minutes.
- In a medium-sized mixing bowl, cream the shortening, then beat in the vanilla and sugar a little at a time, beating until the mixture comes together. Be sure to scrape the bowl once. Beat in the gelatin. Use immediately, or store, well-wrapped, at room temperature.

Nutrition information per serving (2 teaspoons, 12 g): 53 cal, 2 g fat, 1 g protein, 8 g sugar, 1 mg sodium, 1 mg potassium, 1 mg iron, 1 mg calcium, 1 mg phosphorus.

VARIATION

Chocolate Creme Filling

Vanilla filling for chocolate cookies? Here's chocolate filling for vanilla cookies, or, for you true chocoholics, for chocolate-on-chocolate cookies.

Yield: 2 cups

- Prepare Vanilla Creme Filling, adding ½ cup (1½ ounces) Dutch-process cocoa, 2 tablespoons (¾ ounce) vegetable shortening, and 1 tablespoon (½ ounce) water. Add up to 2 teaspoons espresso powder, if desired, to make mocha filling. Use immediately, or store, well-wrapped, at room temperature.

Nutrition information per serving (2 teaspoons, 10 g): 47 cal, 2 g fat, 1 g protein, 1 g complex carbohydrates, 6 g sugar, 1 mg sodium, 15 mg potassium, 1 mg calcium, 7 mg phosphorus, 2 mg caffeine.

Dips ● ● ● ● ● ● ● ● ● ● ● ● ● ● ● ● ●

What, you never heard of cookie dip? We hadn't either, but why not? If you

can heighten the potato chip experience by dipping them into something savory,

why not do the same with cookies and sweet dip?

Chocolate-Caramel Dip

If you were one of those kids who had a hard time deciding whether to go with the chocolate or the caramel sauce on your ice cream sundae, this one's for you. Here they're stirred together, making a warm, smooth, unforgettable combination, perfect for scooping up with a crisp cookie.

Yield: 1½ cups dip

½ cup (3 ounces) chocolate chips
½ cup (5 ounces) caramel*
⅓ cup (2¾ ounces) heavy cream or evaporated milk
2 tablespoons (1 ounce) butter
⅛ teaspoon salt

● Place all the ingredients in a small, heavy saucepan and cook over low heat, stirring just until everything is melted and the dip is smooth. Remove from the heat and pour into small bowls for dipping. Serve warm. Store any leftovers in the refrigerator, heating briefly in the microwave to soften.

* Use homemade Caramel Filling (page 469), purchased block caramel, or individual vanilla caramels. If you use individual caramels, unwrap them and pack them tightly into the measuring cup.

Nutrition information per serving *(2 tablespoons, 26 g):* 112 cal, 7 g fat, 1 g protein, 1 g complex carbohydrates, 11 g sugar, 15 mg cholesterol, 48 mg sodium, 47 mg potassium, 46 RE vitamin A, 1 mg vitamin C, 20 mg calcium, 23 mg phosphorus, 5 mg caffeine.

Raspberry-White Chocolate Dip

The right cookie at the right time makes for a happy moment. If you're feeling playful, any rollout or shortbread cookie is suitable for swirling through this classic combination of flavors.

Yield: ¾ cup of each dip, 1½ cups total

RASPBERRY DIP
¾ cup (8¾ ounces) seedless raspberry preserves
2 tablespoons (1 ounce) water

WHITE CHOCOLATE DIP
¾ cup (4½ ounces) white chocolate, chopped or chips
2 tablespoons (1⅜ ounces) light corn syrup
2 tablespoons (1 ounce) water

- **For the raspberry dip:** In a saucepan set over low heat, or in the microwave, heat the raspberry preserves with the water, stirring until smooth. Remove from the heat.
- **For the white chocolate dip:** Melt the white chocolate, corn syrup, and water together over low heat, or in the microwave, stirring until the mixture is smooth.
- **To serve:** Pour the raspberry dip into one side of a bowl, and pour the white chocolate dip into the other side. Swirl the two together as much or as little as you like.

Nutrition information per serving for raspberry dip (1 teaspoon, 7 g): 14 cal, 1 g fat, 1 g protein, 1 g complex carbohydrates, 3 g sugar, 2 mg sodium, 4 mg potassium, 1 mg vitamin C, 1 mg iron, 1 mg calcium, 1 mg phosphorus.

Nutrition information per serving for white chocolate dip (1 teaspoon, 4 g): 16 cal, 1 g fat, 1 g protein, 2 g sugar, 3 mg sodium, 6 mg potassium, 1 mg iron, 5 mg calcium, 1 mg phosphorus.

Pour the two dips into a bowl, side by side.

Swirl them together to make a pretty pattern.

Dip your favorite cookie into the combination.

Hot Fudge Dip

This makes a dip that's nicely pourable when hot, but thick like peanut butter after it's been refrigerated—all the better to spoon it directly from the fridge into your mouth on those late-night food forays. To serve the dip hot, as soon as it's made, boil it for 3 minutes; this will thicken it without it having to cool first.

Yield: 1½ cups dip

¾ cup (5¼ ounces) granulated sugar
¼ cup (¾ ounce) unsweetened cocoa powder*
Dash of salt
4 tablespoons (½ stick, 2 ounces) unsalted butter
1½ ounces unsweetened baking chocolate
½ cup (4 ounces) light cream or evaporated milk
1 teaspoon vanilla extract

- In a small bowl, whisk together the sugar, cocoa, and salt.
- In a small saucepan set over medium-low heat, melt the butter with the chocolate, stirring until smooth. Stir in the cream—the mixture will look streaky and curdled, which is okay.
- Stir the dry ingredients into the chocolate mixture. Stirring constantly, heat the mixture until it's boiling vigorously around the edges; boil for 1 minute and remove it from the heat. Stir in the vanilla.
- Cool the dip to room temperature. Store any leftovers in the refrigerator. Reheat over low heat or in the microwave.

* Use either Dutch-process or natural cocoa; we prefer the smoother taste of Dutch-process. Whisking the cocoa with the other ingredients prevents it from forming lumps in the sauce.

Nutrition information per serving (2 tablespoons, 32 g): 124 cal, 8 g fat, 1 g protein, 2 g complex carbohydrates, 12 g sugar, 1 g dietary fiber, 18 mg cholesterol, 5 mg sodium, 88 mg potassium, 56 RE vitamin A, 1 mg iron, 16 mg calcium, 37 mg phosphorus, 9 mg caffeine.

Ingredients

If bakers communicate via recipes, then surely a recipe's ingredients are the heart of that communication. Cookbooks from the turn of the twentieth century often list a recipe's ingredients, without providing any directions; apparently cooks and bakers back then were more knowledgeable about basic techniques than we are today. But these days, you will never find a baking book that lists directions without specifying ingredient amounts; while cooks may "add a little of this and a little of that," bakers have to stick to prescribed parameters for the food chemistry to work.

We always maintain that there are no failures in baking (only more food for the birds), but there are ways to ensure that you reach your baking goals: tasty treats that look good, taste great, and please your audience. The following survey of baking ingredients will help you understand what role each plays in your cookies, and how you can (sometimes, carefully) interchange and substitute ingredients.

WHEAT FLOUR ● ● ● ● ● ● ● ● ● ●

The basic building block of almost any cookie is flour. But not just any flour: wheat flour, specifically *all-purpose flour,* is the cookie flour of choice. With its moderate protein level (10.5% to 11.7%), it has the perfect combination of strength and tenderness. While high-protein bread flour helps yeast bread hold its structure as it rises, and low-protein pastry flour makes an ultratender piecrust, all-purpose flour, as its name connotes, is a wonderful combination of both of those attributes. When used in cookies, this means your chocolate chippers will be tender and light, yet will still be able to achieve and hold their desired shape (rise a bit, spread a bit) as they bake.

There's been some buzz in recent years about *cake flour* and its role in cookie baking. Cake flour is a low-protein (8.0%) flour that's bleached with chlorine gas. This bleaching process makes the starch in the cookie better able to link with the fat and sugar in the recipe. Why is this important? Because cookies have a very high ratio of sugar and fat to flour, both of which tend to make cookies spread. In order to control spread, it's important that the flour help "carry" the fat and sugar, and this is better accomplished by cake flour, or by pastry flour, with its finer granulation.

Cake flour's effect won't be apparent in all cookies, but cookies such as *springerle,* patterned shortbreads, stamped cookies, thumbprints, or cutout cookies may hold their shape better, retaining the sharpness of their design, when made with cake flour.

Clearly, we couldn't test every cookie recipe in existence with cake flour. But if you have a cookie recipe that aggravates you by spreading too much, try substituting cake flour for all-purpose, as well as trying some of the solutions on page 54.

Should you try cake flour in cookies? Sure, if you like. But be aware the cookies may be lighter-colored and you may be able to detect a slight chemical aftertaste. Our advice? Stick with all-purpose flour for your cookie baking, unless your recipe specifically calls for another type of flour or you're not happy with the cookie's degree of spread.

Whole wheat flour—flour milled from the entire wheat berry, including the germ and bran—can be used successfully for cookie baking if you want to add fiber to those sugar-, butter-, and chocolate-filled gems issuing from your oven. Try substituting whole wheat flour for one third of the all-purpose flour in your recipe. If you like the result and want to venture further down this road, go for it. Cookies made with whole wheat flour tend to be denser, harder, and drier. To avoid the somewhat astringent aftertaste whole wheat sometimes has, try 100% white whole wheat flour, a flour that's nutritionally identical to traditional red whole wheat flour, but lacking the chemical in the bran layer that produces that signature "whole-wheaty" taste—which some like, and some don't.

OTHER FLOURS AND GRAINS ● ● ● ● ●

CORN

Cornstarch, milled from the starchy endosperm of the corn kernel, is used primarily as a thickening agent. However, it can also be added sparingly to all-purpose flour to lower its protein just a bit, producing a more tender (but also more spreadable) cookie. The classic Sugar Puffs (page 64), an extremely tender, fragile cookie, contain a high percentage of cornstarch.

Cornmeal is sometimes added to cookies to give them a pleasantly gritty crunch. If you're making a crunchy cookie (no sense doing this with chewy or soft cookies), substitute cornmeal for an eighth to a quarter of the all-purpose flour in your recipe, and see what happens.

OATS

Old-fashioned rolled oats (thick oat flakes)—the familiar breakfast oatmeal you find in a canister at the supermarket—are made by husking oat berries, steaming to soften them, then rolling them flat. Quick-cooking oats are made the same way, but the berries are sliced before being steamed, producing thinner (quicker-cooking) rolled oats. Rolled oats are, of course, the key ingredient in oatmeal cookies (one of our Essentials—see pages 73–83). They're also sometimes found in traditional shortbread (page 117), and often in the base or topping for bar cookies. The nutty taste and chewy/tender texture of oats are welcome additions wherever you find them, but we don't recommend adding them unbidden to a recipe unless you're an experienced baker. You have to increase the amount of liquid, which gets tricky when the only liquid in the cookie comes from its fat and eggs.

To add a hint of oat flavor to your cookies without having to adjust the recipe, try substituting *oat flour* (or finely ground rolled oats) for a quarter of the wheat flour in your recipe.

RICE

Rice flour is milled two ways: white rice flour is hulled before milling, while brown rice flour (the equivalent of whole wheat flour) is not. White rice flour is often used in traditional shortbread, to give it its signature tender, "sandy" mouthfeel. However, since it's a gluten-free flour and is incapable of building structure, it is rarely used beyond shortbread.

SWEETENERS ● ● ● ● ● ● ● ● ● ● ● ● ●

How sweet it is! We can truthfully make this claim for just about any cookie out there. In many cookies, sugar is the main ingredient, but even when its presence is somewhat less, it's always a leading player.

Sugar plays many roles in cookie baking. First, since it's hygroscopic (attracts and holds liquid), it helps keep cookies soft and tender. And, since cookies become stale by losing their liquid, sugar helps keep them fresh. Second, sugar crystals melt and migrate to the cookie's surface as it bakes, and there they caramelize and help turn the cookie brown. (This is called the Maillard Reaction, for those of you who want to impress your friends with your copious knowledge of baking science.) And third, and probably most important, sugar gives cookies a lot of their delightful taste. Studies done with newborn infants have shown that even in our first days on earth, sugar is a pleasurable experience; it's no wonder we continue to crave it throughout our lives.

DRY SUGARS

Granulated sugar: By far the most commonly used sweetener in baking, granulated sugar is milled from sugarcane or sugar beets, and is highly processed. It's a good sugar to choose for baking because its flavor is pure, unadulterated sweetness: no other flavors fight for attention, as they do in brown sugar, honey, or maple syrup.

About 70 percent of the world's granulated sugar supply comes from sugarcane, while the remainder comes from sugar beets. There are those who maintain that beet sugar has a slightly different flavor than cane sugar, but to us it's indistinguishable. When you purchase granulated sugar, be sure it's sucrose; most bags of granulated sugar will list cane sugar as their only ingredient. There are some sugar blends on the market that look like granulated sugar, but are actually a blend of dextrose and sucrose. Caveat emptor! This sugar doesn't work consistently well in baking. If you've purchased it by mistake, save it for your coffee.

Superfine sugar: Granulated sugar milled to a much finer crystal is called superfine, bar, or castor sugar. It's useful due to its ability to dissolve very quickly and thoroughly. Use it in fudgy brownies, when you want them to exhibit a shiny, ultrathin crust on top, or in meringues, where superfine sugar dissolves quickly, making a smoother meringue.

Confectioners' sugar: Called icing sugar in Britain and sucre glace in France, this is the finest grind of granulated sugar, combined with about 3 percent cornstarch to prevent it from clumping. It ranges in crystal size from 10X (the finest crystal, the kind found in supermarkets) to less expensive 6X, used in institutional baking. Cookies are often dusted with confectioners' sugar, or iced with confectioners' sugar frosting, but unless your recipe calls for it as an ingredient in the dough, don't substitute—it won't work well. ***Glazing sugar,*** finer than confectioners' sugar and mixed with maltodextrin rather than cornstarch, has a truer sweet flavor; use it in place of confectioners' sugar if you can find it.

Decorating sugars: Sanding sugar, coarse sugar, decorating sugar, sparkling sugar—these are all granulated sugars that have been tinted in different shades (or left white) to sprinkle atop cookies and other baked goods as decoration. Most of these sugars come in crystals about four times larger than granulated sugar crystals, although it's also possible to find "fine sparkling sugars," whose crystals are similar in size to the grains of sand found in an hourglass.

Pearl sugar, often imported from Sweden, is granulated sugar that's been processed into bright-white grains that range from about six times larger than one granulated sugar crystal, to nuggets about the size of peas (or sometimes even larger). This is a wonderful sugar to sprinkle atop cookies before they bake, as it won't melt in the oven.

Flavored sugars: Granulated sugar is the perfect blank canvas for imaginative flavoring. Combine 1 cup granulated sugar with 2 tablespoons cinnamon for cinnamon sugar (the topping that makes a sugar cookie into a snickerdoodle); with ¼ teaspoon citrus oil for citrus sugar; with 1 or 2 chopped vanilla beans for vanilla sugar; or with a few drops of highly concentrated flavor (apricot, coconut, creamy hazelnut, peppermint . . .) for just about any flavor sugar you can imagine. In all cases, put the sugar and add-in into a jar, screw on the lid, and shake vigorously. All except the cinnamon sugar will benefit by resting a few days before using, for the flavor to be fully absorbed by the sugar.

Brown sugar: Originally, brown sugar was granulated sugar that hadn't been highly processed, with some of the molasses (a by-product of sugar processing) left in. Nowadays, brown sugar is granulated sugar with molasses added back in (more for dark brown, less for light brown.) Brown sugar has a deeper, more complex flavor than granulated sugar

Can I use brown sugar and granulated white sugar interchangeably?

If you're making a cookie without any chemical leavening (such as shortbread, or some roll-out cookies), yes, you can. The finished product will be a bit darker in color; have that distinctive molasses–brown sugar taste, may spread more, and be a bit softer. Using white sugar in place of brown will give you the opposite results: the flavor will be less complex, the cookie will be lighter-colored, and it may be a bit crisper and spread less.

However, if you're making a brown sugar cookie with leavening, be aware that the leavening—most likely baking soda—is there to help balance the acidity in the brown sugar, acidity that's mostly missing in granulated sugar. If you've run out of brown sugar, add 1 to 4 tablespoons molasses to 1 cup granulated sugar (the lesser amount to approximate light brown sugar). Stir until the mixture is well combined and looks like store-bought brown sugar; don't give up, this takes a few minutes. The result? A generous 1 cup of brown sugar.

and, because it contains more liquid, will make a softer cookie. As brown sugar ages, its moisture evaporates and it can become rock-hard. To keep it soft, put it in an airtight container with a terra cotta sugar softener, or with a slice of apple that you exchange for a fresh slice every few days.

What's the difference between light brown and dark brown sugar? Simply the amount of molasses added to it in the production process. Use them interchangeably, to taste; dark brown sugar has a more pronounced molasses flavor and will yield a darker cookie.

Barbados (Muscovado) sugar, most commonly found in England, is very similar to American brown sugar in appearance, but it's more strongly flavored. It's a less processed form of granulated sugar.

Turbinado and Demerara sugars: Used as cookie toppings, these are less processed granulated sugars, with some of the molasses left in. Demerara is a coarser grind of turbinado.

Maple sugar: Pure maple syrup from which almost all of the liquid has been removed becomes maple sugar. It's available in two forms: one has the soft, somewhat moist consistency of brown sugar, while the other looks exactly like the "pourable" brown sugar (Brownulated) you'll find at the supermarket. Recipes in this book that call for maple sugar are referring to this second, more easily obtainable type.

LIQUID SWEETENERS

The majority of cookies rely on dry sugar as their sweetener. However some, such as molasses cookies, use a liquid sweetener. Why use a liquid sweetener instead of plain sugar? First, for flavor: molasses, dark corn syrup, maple syrup, sorghum syrup, golden syrup, refiner's syrup, and honey all have their own distinctive taste. And second, if you're making a soft, moist, chewy cookie, a liquid sweetener adds water to the cookie dough, which will result in a softer cookie with better keeping qualities. The following liquid sweeteners are the ones most likely to appear in cookie recipes.

Corn syrup (Karo syrup) is 25 percent water, the remainder glucose, corn solids, salt, and vanilla. It comes in light (clear) and dark varieties, the dark is more strongly flavored. Corn syrup is less sweet than other liquid syrups.

Can I substitute a liquid sweetener for a dry one to make my cookies softer?

As with many baking-related issues, the answer is: sometimes. Don't substitute 1 cup liquid sweetener for 1 cup granulated sugar; you'll have soupy cookie dough. Also, the texture of some cookies comes from the air trapped by sugar crystals when they're creamed with butter;

liquid sweeteners are unable to trap air effectively.

Try substituting a couple of tablespoons of corn syrup, molasses, honey, or maple syrup for an equal amount of granulated sugar in your recipe. See where that takes you, softness-wise, and go from there.

Is Splenda the answer to lower-calorie baking?

Maybe. Sometimes. Splenda is sucralose, a type of sugar. In its initial form it's 600 times sweeter than sugar, but it's been formulated into Splenda Granular, which measures cup-for-cup like sugar.

Splenda has no calories, which is a tempting attribute for some bakers. However, it doesn't bake exactly like granulated cane sugar. Splenda is best when it's used for sweetening rather than for struc- ture; a recipe that calls for creaming sugar and fat together will result in a denser cookie when made with Splenda. In addition, Splenda won't brown like cane sugar, so cookies made with it will remain pale. Finally, cookies made with Splenda will bake more quickly than those made with sugar, so check them several minutes before the end of the baking time to see if they're set (remember, they won't be brown).

Molasses is a by-product of granulated sugar production, what's left over after all the sucrose has crystallized. Golden or light molasses is lighter in color and flavor than dark molasses, which is the result of repeated boiling and extraction. The very darkest molasses, blackstrap, is only 50 percent sugar and is unsuitable for most baking because of its bitter flavor. Use it only if it is specifically called for in a recipe.

If sulfur is used in processing (very rare these days), molasses is labeled sulfured; sul- fured molasses generally has a stronger flavor, and is suitable only for dark, spicy cookies such as gingerbread or molasses.

Honey is the only syrup that can be used without any processing, once it's removed from the beehive and strained of any waxy comb, it's ready to eat. Honey is a popular liq- uid sweetener due to its unique flavor, but be aware that it's sweeter than sugar, and also browns much more quickly. Watch cookies made with honey carefully because they tend to burn.

Maple syrup, the sap of maple sugar trees boiled down until it's thick and golden, can be used interchangeably with molasses. For the best flavor in baking, choose Grade B, the darkest syrup; it's boiled from the very end of the sap run and makes a strong-fla- vored syrup.

SALT ● ● ● ● ● ● ● ● ● ● ● ● ● ● ●

Salt is food's greatest flavor enhancer. Without salt, many prepared foods taste insipid. Even sweet foods, like cookies, need a dose of salt to intensify their other flavors. Salt, like sugar, is hygroscopic, and attracts and holds water; however, its presence in cookies is so minimal compared to sugar that its role in balancing the amount of liquid in cookie dough is inconsequential. In baking, salt is present strictly for flavor.

If what you've baked tastes flat or lifeless, lack of salt may be the problem. Since sodium (the chemical responsible for salt's saltiness) is present in both baking soda and baking powder, as well as in salted butter, it's difficult to give a ratio of salt to flour that will work for every recipe; the amount of salt will vary with the amount present in the other ingredients. However, between ¼ teaspoon and ½ teaspoon salt per cup of flour (with the ½ teaspoon reserved for recipes without chemical leaveners or other sources of salt) should yield satisfactory results.

FAT ● ● ● ● ● ● ● ● ● ● ● ● ● ●

Without fat in the dough, cookies would be unpleasantly tough and hard. Fat coats and separates the particles in the flour, leaving them unable to bond tightly, and thus making a cookie that's crisp, tender, or soft, rather than brick-hard. In addition, fat contributes to the texture of some cookies by trapping air when it's creamed together with sugar, thus helping to leaven the cookies and make them light. Fat is also an emulsifier and a flavor carrier; it moves easily throughout cookie dough (emulsifies), carrying flavor molecules with it, much like alcohol does. Finally, when the fat is butter, it lends its own compelling taste.

Shortening: In the completely literal sense, shortening refers to all fats and oils. Since they have the ability to break up and weaken the gluten connections in dough, they're said to "shorten" the dough. In this book, shortening refers to ***hydrogenated vegetable oil shortening*** (such as Crisco).

What is hydrogenated vegetable oil shortening, exactly? Hydrogenation is a chemical process whereby some of the polyunsaturated fatty acids in vegetable oil are changed to saturated fats, thus changing the oil from a liquid to a solid and making it suitable for many cakes and cookies (which rely on solid fat for their structure). Current medical knowledge has labeled these altered fats trans fatty acids and condemned them for a negative effect on human cholesterol levels. There is currently no exact substitute for hydrogenated vegetable shortening; bakers wishing to attain a certain specific texture in their sweet baked goods have no choice but to use it. Manufacturers are working on produc-

At the risk of sounding like shills...

We have to say, Crisco is the shortening of choice in our King Arthur test kitchen. It gives the baker noticeably better results than competing store brands we've tested against it.

ing a shortening substitute. Luckily, only a few cookie recipes benefit from the use of shortening rather than butter.

In addition, bakers were making cookies long before the invention of hydrogenated shortening, using butter, lard, or other animal fats. You can substitute an equal amount of unsalted butter for the shortening called for in any cookie recipe, usually with no effect on the taste or texture of the final product, and sometimes with minimal effect: the cookie may be slightly less crisp, may spread a tiny bit more, or may not be quite as white (in the case of sugar cookies). But, if you're trying to avoid trans fatty acids in your diet, you may want to make this switch.

When creamed (beaten) with sugar, shortening traps air molecules, which helps to leaven cookies and make them tender. Shortening's other important role is to help create the cookie's structure in the oven. Shortening has a fairly high melting point, which allows cookie dough to rise and set (harden) while being supported by the solid shortening. Eventually the shortening melts, but the cookie's structure is firm enough by then that it doesn't collapse. Finally, shortening, like all fat, makes cookies tender by preventing long strands of gluten from forming in the dough.

Shortening will keep, tightly covered at room temperature, for about three months. If you plan on storing it longer than that, refrigerate it.

Butter: Ah, one of the four basic food groups (sugar, butter, flour, and eggs) of cookie baking! A fresh, buttery cookie, hot from the oven, is right up there on the comfort-food scale with warm bread or chocolate. Only butter among the baking fats, with its unmatched flavor, provides this kind of pleasure. In addition, butter's melting point—98.6°F—exactly mimics our body temperature; thus butter's satisfying "melt in your mouth" quality.

Contrary to popular belief, butter isn't 100 percent fat; it's "only" 80 percent fat, with the remainder being water and milk solids. This refers to a typical American supermarket butter. European butters (such as Plugrá), some of which are now available in this country, can range up to 88 percent fat. That extra 8 percent is evident in butter-heavy pastries (those made with laminated dough, such as croissants), and less evident in cookies, although when using a

Greasing pans with vegetable oil spray

Remember how your mom used to grease cookie sheets with a piece of paper towel she kept folded inside the shortening can? You can choose to do the same, but an easier, more thorough method, with probably fewer fat grams, is to spray the cookie sheet with a nonstick vegetable oil spray. Beware of sprays that contain gums (carrageenan, guar) or lecithin; these tend to leave a dark, sticky residue on your pans over time.

European high-fat butter, you may want to cut back on the butter a bit to avoid a greasy texture.

The recipes in this book are written for unsalted butter, unless otherwise indicated. (To substitute salted butter for unsalted, reduce the amount of added salt in your recipe by ¼ teaspoon per ½ cup—4 ounces, 1 stick—of butter.) Butter is salted to help preserve it; salt masks any "off" tastes. Salted butter will keep in the freezer for about 6 months, while unsalted is good for about 3 months. We prefer unsalted butter, as it allows us to adjust the amount of salt in the recipe to exactly our taste. In addition, unsalted butter is generally fresher than salted. Either way, we suggest buying butter as you need it, rather than stocking up; butter is best at its freshest.

Soft Baking Butter is a Land O Lakes blend of canola oil and butter and is wonderful for roll-out cookies, as the refrigerated dough can be rolled directly upon coming out of the refrigerator, with no waiting period for the butter to soften. It's also ideal for

I'm watching my cholesterol, can I use margarine in place of butter?

It used to be a fairly straightforward procedure to substitute margarine for butter in your baked goods: margarine, like butter, was 80 percent fat, so the two acted similar to one another in baking, even though they don't taste alike. Now, however, margarine comes in all kinds of low-fat versions, some of which can contain less than 50 percent fat. This will definitely affect your baked goods, both by reducing the effect of fat's good qualities (flavor, tenderizing), and adding water, which affects the flour/liquid ratio and may make

cookies spread too much.

Margarine has lost popularity due to its reliance on hydrogenation and the resulting trans fatty acids (deemed a nutritional no-no) to give it its structure. However, if you really want to use it, be sure you purchase plain, full-fat stick margarine, not a low-fat substitute or margarine in a tub. And if you're following one of the recipes in this book— all of which call for unsalted butter, when butter is used—reduce the salt in the recipe by ¼ teaspoon, because nearly all margarine is salted.

...Or how about shortening in place of butter?

Using shortening in place of butter (or butter in place of shortening) will yield results that aren't identical, but probably acceptable. Because shortening's melting point is higher than butter's (119°F vs. 98.6°F), cookies made with shortening won't spread as much. So if you're having issues with cookies spreading, try substituting shortening. You'll lose some of butter's rich flavor, but may solve your spreading problem. You may also choose to substitute butter for short-

ening; while shortening is 100 percent fat to butter's 80 percent, the difference isn't appreciable enough in most cookies. However, you may notice the obverse of the behavior above: cookies made with butter will spread more than cookies made with shortening. So if you have a cookie you'd like to have relax a bit on the pan, try substituting butter for half the shortening (for a little more spread), or for all of the shortening (for a lot more spread).

bar cookie crusts that call for the butter to be cut into the flour; the process is much easier with this softer, more "plastic" butter. Soft baking butter retains butter's wonderful flavor, but adds shortening's ease of use.

Margarine (oleo) is actually closer to vegetable shortening than it is to butter. Made from hydrogenated vegetable oil, sometimes with added milk solids, margarine has neither butter's flavor nor shortening's high melting point. We consider it an inferior substitute for either, and we prefer to use butter or vegetable shortening.

Oils that come primarily from plants—vegetables, seeds, and nuts—are 100 percent liquid fat. Thus they mimic neither butter (80 percent fat), nor shortening (100 percent solid fat) in their baking quality. *Vegetable oil* will sometimes be used in cookies where the flavor of butter isn't key, and the structure provided by a solid fat isn't necessary, e.g., a soft, flat, chewy cookie. If your recipe calls for vegetable oil, use one with mild flavor, such as canola, vegetable (a blend), sunflower, or safflower; highly flavored oils, like olive, corn, sesame, and peanut, should be saved for salads and sautés.

Eggs and dairy ● ● ● ● ● ● ● ● ● ● ●

Good sources of both protein and fat, eggs and dairy products enhance cookies in a variety of ways. Structure, flavor, leavening, browning—in most cookies, all of these rely at least in part on eggs, and somewhat less on other dairy products.

Eggs are made up of fat (the yolk), and protein (the white). Egg yolks add some of fat's characteristics to cookies: tenderness and crispness. They help cookies brown when they're in the dough or brushed on top before baking. Egg whites enhance structure, both by capturing air that's beaten into the dough and by contributing to the protein building blocks that allow a cookie to rise and stay risen. (Meringue cookies and macaroons rely entirely on egg whites for their structure.) Finally, the liquid in eggs helps keep cookies moist and fresh.

The recipes in this book call for large eggs, which weigh about 2 ounces each. Volume-wise, it takes about 5 eggs to fill a cup. As it takes about 3 medium eggs to yield 2 large eggs, you can see it's important to use the size of eggs the recipe calls for.

Although it's not always crucial, it's good practice to bring eggs to room temperature before using them. If you're adding eggs to butter that's been creamed with sugar, cold eggs are liable to chill the butter enough that it "breaks," releasing all the air you've just beaten into it. The best way to bring eggs to room temperature is to remove them from the refrigerator an hour or so before you want to use them. Another way, and one we use here often (being both busy and forgetful!), is to place eggs in their shells in a bowl of warm water for 10 to 15 minutes.

A useful shortcut ingredient is *meringue powder,* a mixture of dried egg whites, sugar, and edible gum. Meringue powder is a key ingredient in royal icing, one of the staples of the icing world, as well as in buttercream frosting, and in the "construction" icing used to make a gingerbread house.

While dairy products don't play as integral a part in most cookies as eggs do, they're sometimes added for flavor and structure. All **milk products** contain protein, which can contribute to a cookie's structure. And most milk products contain fat, which enhances texture. In addition, the lactose (sugar) in milk helps cookies brown nicely as they bake; and the water in milk jump-starts gluten development, thus contributing even more to the cookie's structure and final shape.

Usually the amount of milk (or cream) in cookies (as compared to the amount of milk served *with* cookies) is so small that these effects are minimal, but if your recipe calls for milk, don't think you can substitute water without consequences.

Buttermilk, sour cream, or **yogurt,** being acidic, help tenderize gluten strands in the cookie dough, thus producing a cookie that's soft and tender, or snapping-crisp, but never rock-hard. In addition, they lend an elusive but delightful tang: the flavor of sugar cookies made with sour cream or buttermilk is much more complex, and richer, than that of "plain" sugar cookies.

Cream cheese looks like butter, tastes somewhat like sour cream, and brings to cookies some of the attributes of both. Cookies made with cream cheese will have wonderful flavor, and the fat in the cheese will keep them soft or crisp. In addition, the milk protein will help with structure. Cream cheese begins with cream that's about 33 percent butterfat, so it doesn't bring as much fat to cookies as butter, but it's a wonderful addition to butter in many recipes.

Sweetened condensed milk, seldom used in cookie dough, sometimes appears as a topping for bar cookies. One cup of condensed milk began as 2½ cups of whole milk and ½ cup sugar. Don't substitute sweetened condensed milk for any other kind of milk, use it only where called for.

Can I use yogurt instead of sour cream or buttermilk in my cookies?

Yes, though the results won't be exactly the same. The closest match to sour cream is plain full-fat yogurt; low-fat or nonfat (don't go there!) yogurts will yield a somewhat less tender product, due to their reduced fat. In addition, their taste will be a bit more acidic. As for buttermilk, it's similar enough to both yogurt and sour cream in acidity that you can substitute it for either. However, keep in mind that buttermilk includes a greater percentage of water; you'll want to reduce the amount you use by about 25 percent.

LEAVENING ● ● ● ● ● ● ● ● ● ● ● ●

Where would the cookie baker be without baking powder and baking soda? Stuck with shortbread, that's where. There are very few cookies that don't use some form of chemical leavening to give them their light, crisp (or chewy) texture.

How do chemical leavens work? First, they dissolve in whatever liquid is in the dough. Next, they release carbon dioxide as they dissolve; the CO_2, in turn, is absorbed into the dough's liquid, and then into the air bubbles that you've beaten into the dough as you prepared it. Once the cookies begin to bake, the carbon dioxide in these air bubbles causes them to expand, and they keep expanding until the dough becomes hot enough to set and become firm—to be fully baked. Thus chemical leavens are the agent mainly responsible for how high a cookie rises as it bakes. Without leavening, sugar cookies would be shortbread, chocolate chip cookies would be flat puddles of dough with chocolate chip islands, and crisp oatmeal cookies would be as hard and dense as a piece of granite. Here are the most common (and important) chemical leavens:

Baking soda (sodium bicarbonate, or sodium acid carbonate) is a natural alkaline. In this country, it's manufactured from ore mined in Wyoming by the makers of Arm and Hammer baking soda. Baking soda is the key component in baking powder; when mixed with liquid and an acid, it immediately releases carbon dioxide, and the leavening process begins.

Any recipe leavened with baking soda must also include an acidic ingredient; these can range from the obviously acidic (sour cream, lemon juice) to the less apparent (chocolate, brown sugar, honey). If there's not enough acid in the recipe to neutralize baking soda's alkalinity, your cookie may have a soapy taste, or a brownish-yellow cast. In the absence of any other acidic ingredients, ½ teaspoon baking soda will be neutralized by 1 cup yogurt, buttermilk, sour cream, or citrus juice; or ¾ cup brown sugar, honey, or molasses; or ½ cup natural cocoa powder.

Baking powder is composed of baking soda (an alkaline or base), sodium acid pyrophosphate (an acid), and a neutral medium (usually cornstarch) to keep the two from reacting too soon. Baking powder takes baking soda a step further. Since the acid/alkaline content in baking powder is already perfectly balanced, the baker need not think about the acidity of other ingredients. In addition, double-acting baking powder—the type found most often in the market today—begins to react when it meets liquid, and again when it's heated, giving cookie bakers a double shot of leavening power.

Cream of tartar (acid sodium pyrophosphate) and **Maine Bakewell Cream** (tartaric acid) are both acids that react with baking soda to make it work. These ingredients are never used on their own in cookie baking, except for in meringues, where cream of tartar helps stabilize the egg whites' protein, allowing them to trap more air as they're beaten.

What's the difference between baking soda and baking powder?

They look alike, they do the same thing . . . well, not quite. Baking soda is the basic component in baking powder, thus baking powder is a more "advanced" form of chemical leaven. Where baking soda needs both liquid and acid to begin its work, baking powder includes acid right in its composition. In addition, double-acting baking powder includes two different acids: one that works as soon as it meets liquid, and one that doesn't start working until it's heated. For this reason, cookie dough that must be refrigerated before being used will produce a lighter cookie when it's leavened with baking powder, since even if the liquid-activated acid starts to lose its oomph in the fridge, the heat-activated one will kick in nicely in the oven.

What if I run out of baking powder?

Since cream of tartar and baking soda are the key elements in baking powder and, unlike baking powder, they're shelf stable indefinitely, it's useful to keep them both on hand. If you run out of baking powder, ½ teaspoon cream of tartar (or Maine Bakewell Cream, generally less expensive) mixed with ¼ teaspoon baking soda makes the equivalent of 1 teaspoon baking powder. Since this will be a single-acting rather than double-acting baking powder (see above), it shouldn't be substituted in recipes that are refrigerated or left to rest at room temperature before baking; the leavening will lose its oomph shortly after the batter or dough is made, so it needs to be baked right away.

Help! This recipe doesn't have any baking powder...

Most cookie recipes—aside from short-bread, some roll-out cookies, and molded cookies—use either baking soda or baking powder. But mistakes get made. If you run across a recipe with neither—this often happens in the haste of one baker copying down a recipe for another—keep this rule of thumb in mind: for every cup of flour in the recipe, use ½ to 1 teaspoon baking powder (the more you use, the higher-rising and puffier the cookie will be). If the cookie contains a liquid sweetener, such as molasses, honey, or maple syrup, add ¼ teaspoon baking soda for each ½ cup of sweetener.

Baker's ammonia, the common name for ammonium carbonate or ammonium bicarbonate, is an old-fashioned chemical leaven, one that predates both baking powder and baking soda. It produces incredibly crisp cookies. Originally made from hartshorn, the antler of a red deer, baker's ammonia works fast when it meets liquid. The telltale smell of ammonia it produces is unpleasant, but dissipates completely by the time the cookie is baked. However, due to its somewhat tricky nature, baker's ammonia should only be used in recipes where it's specified.

Yeast appears very seldom in cookie recipes. Though long ago all leavening was done with some form of yeast, the advent of easy-to-use, fast-acting chemical leavens pretty much relegated yeast to yeast breads. The occasional cookie will rely on this live, one-cell organism for its leavening; Crystal Diamonds (page 66), and Zwieback (page 390) are the only recipes in this book calling for yeast. Because of its ease of use, fast action, and strength, we recommend using instant yeast; SAF is a reliable brand.

FLAVORS AND EXTRACTS ● ● ● ● ● ●

Vanilla extract, beloved ingredient of cookie bakers, is but one of a host of flavors and extracts that can lend amazing taste to your cookies. From vanilla, almond, and peppermint to the more exotic butter-rum, coconut, hazelnut, and apricot, flavors and extracts are often the smallest part of your cookie volume-wise, but giants in the taste department.

Vanilla, the most expensive spice in the world after saffron, comes from the bean pod of an orchid plant, *vanilla planifolia.* It takes more than sixteen months to produce vanilla from an immature pod, in a very labor-intensive process. Seventy-five percent of the world's vanilla is produced in Madagascar (formerly called the Bourbon Islands, whence comes the term Bourbon vanilla), with the remainder coming from Tahiti, Indonesia, and Mexico. Each vanilla has its own particular flavor; Tahitian vanilla is described as flowery, Mexican as interesting and complex. But all share that wonderful, comforting vanilla scent and taste we've loved since childhood.

Almond extract, next to vanilla the most commonly used extract in baking, is made from bitter almonds (cousin to the sweet almonds we consume as nuts). Oil from these almonds contains prussic acid, a highly toxic substance that can actually be fatal if consumed in quantity. However, prussic acid is destroyed during processing, and the remaining oil is either sold as is (bitter almond oil) or combined with alcohol to make almond extract. Bitter almond oil is prized by bakers for its "true" almond flavor, though the much more commonly available almond extract is the product used most often.

Can I make my own vanilla?

Sure. It won't be as rich and full-flavored as vanilla manufactured the traditional way, but shortcut vanilla is easy to make, and works fine in most applications where vanilla doesn't play a starring role. To make vanilla, combine 2 or 3 vanilla beans, slit open and snipped into 1-inch pieces, with 1 pint vodka (organic is excellent) or unflavored brandy in a glass jar with tight-fitting lid. Allow the mixture to sit for at least two weeks, preferably four, before using.

What's the difference between an extract, an oil, and a flavor?

Extracts (vanilla, almond) are made from an essential oil (or flavoring components) of natural ingredients, dissolved in alcohol, or glycerin and water. You'll generally add 1 to 2 teaspoons extract to a typical cookie recipe.

Oils (orange, lemon, anise, cinnamon, and others) are extracted from natural products. Their intense flavor means you need add only a few drops to ¼ teaspoon to a cookie recipe. Included in this category is *Fiori di Sicilia,* a blend of citrus and vanilla flavors that's a widely used specialty ingredient in Italian baking.

Flavors—or flavoring oils, or candy flavoring—are highly concentrated compounds that may or may not include natural ingredients. Food scientists are able to chemically match the natural flavors in a variety of sources, and blend and package these compounds for use in baking. While they're not all-natural, we've derived great pleasure from the huge array of flavors—butter-pecan, pineapple, eggnog—that wouldn't otherwise be available to us. Add flavor oils to cookie dough drop by drop, to taste. Finally, flower waters, which are used in many Middle Eastern confections, including cookies, are the mildest of the extract-flavor-oil group. Rose water and orange flower water can be added to cookie dough, but because of their unassertive flavor, which in truth is based mostly on their aroma, we feel they're more effective when very lightly sprinkled onto baked cookies.

How can I gauge the strength of a flavor or extract?

You'll notice that many of the recipes in this book call for "strong" flavors or extracts. There are two basic strengths of flavor available to the home baker: regular, such as those purchased at the supermarket (think almond extract, vanilla extract, lemon extract); or strong, flavors that are often classified as "flavor oils" or just plain "flavors," rather than extracts. These flavors usually come in small bottles and are often called candy-flavoring oils; the label will read "highly concentrated." Compared to extracts, they come in a huge variety of flavors, everything from butter-rum to blackberry to pralines and cream. And they're very strong, usually requiring only a few drops in your dough or batter to make their presence known.

How can you tell if a flavor is strong enough to warrant using only a few drops? First, take a cautious whiff; if it tickles your nose in an almost unpleasant way, it's strong. (In comparison, a whiff of vanilla is pleasurable, inviting you to smell it again.) Second, add the flavor or extract to your dough a few drops at a time, to taste; if, after adding ⅛ teaspoon or so, you still can't taste it, it probably isn't a strong flavor.

SPICES ● ● ● ● ● ● ● ● ● ● ● ● ● ●

Cinnamon, ginger, nutmeg, allspice, cloves . . . where would we be without these aromatic spices? Spices have long been a vital part of the world's economy. Arabs had a monopoly on their trade more than three thousand years ago, when "all the spices of the Orient" were arduously trekked by camel from the Far East to what is today's Middle East.

Spices, like flavors and extracts, are used in tiny quantities in baking, yet lend tremendous flavor. A snickerdoodle without cinnamon is just a sugar cookie, while gingersnaps sans ginger are mere molasses cookies.

For ease of use, most bakers purchase ground spices. However, try to purchase them in small quantities that you can use in a reasonable amount of time; ground spices gradually lose their pep, no matter how carefully you store them. Another option is to purchase whole spices, which have a much longer shelf life, and grind them yourself.

Here are some of the key spices used in cookie baking:

Allspice, the dried berry of a tree in the myrtle family, is grown mainly in Jamaica. Its taste is reminiscent of cinnamon and cloves, with a touch of nutmeg. It's often used in molasses or other spice cookies.

Cardamom, the third most expensive spice in the world (after saffron and vanilla), is the seeds and pod of a tropical herb. Cardamom is available green (dried in the oven), white (bleached), or brown (dried in the sun); green is considered the most aromatic. It's crushed, pod and all, to add to northern European baked goods, particularly Scandinavian cookies. Cardamom seeds crushed, without the pod, have stronger flavor.

Cinnamon, perhaps the most beloved and widely used of all spices, adds a distinctive and compelling aroma to baked goods; indeed, tests show that cinnamon is one of the top male aphrodisiacs. There are two types of cinnamon grown: Ceylon cinnamon, native to Sri Lanka and India, and cassia cinnamon, which grows in Southeast Asia. Cinnamon is the bark of either of these two trees. To tell the two apart, whole *Ceylon cinnamon* looks like a rolled-up paper tube, while *cassia cinnamon* curls inward from both ends, like a scroll. Cassia cinnamon is the type most often sold in the United States; it's richer in flavor and has a higher oil content than Ceylon cinnamon. Of all the cassia cinnamon grown, the best comes from North Vietnam; bakers rejoiced when America finally reopened trade relations with that country.

> ## What's the difference between a spice and an herb?
>
> Herbs usually come from the leafy green part of a plant, while spices come from its roots, bark, seeds, buds, or stems.

Cloves are the unopened flower bud of a tropical evergreen shrub. Cloves have a strong, pungent flavor and are best used in very small quantities to enhance the flavor of other spices, rather than standing on their own.

Ginger, native to Southeast Asia, spread across the world in ancient times. Ginger and black pepper were two of the most widely used spices in medieval England; in those days, gingerbread held the exalted culinary position that chocolate holds for us today. The mature root of the ginger plant, dried and ground, yields the spice that lends its name to gingersnaps and gingerbread men. This same root, harvested when immature, is diced, simmered in sugar syrup, and dried to produce crystallized or candied ginger, a moist, sweet-hot addition to many kinds of chewy spice cookies.

Nutmeg and *mace* both come from a tree native to Indonesia. This tree bears fruit whose pit (nutmeg) is covered by a thin, lacy, leathery reddish tissue (mace). Ground nutmeg is a key ingredient in eggnog cookies, and also adds its distinctive flavor to other sugar-type cookies.

CHOCOLATE ● ● ● ● ● ● ● ● ● ● ● ● ● ●

Can you imagine life without chocolate? (If your answer is yes, turn the page!) Chocolate, like vanilla, is a flavor that we embrace early, and carry like a first love in our hearts forevermore.

Chocolate, theobroma cacao ("food of the gods") is one of the greatest gifts given by the New World to the Old. A native of South America, where it was prized by both the Aztec and Mayan civilizations, chocolate is produced today around the world between the tropics of Cancer and Capricorn (20° above and 20° below the equator). Most of the world's chocolate, however, comes from Ghana, in Africa, which produces half a million tons a year.

Chocolate is made from the seeds (beans) of the fruit of the cacao tree. As with vanilla, making chocolate from cacao beans is a labor-intensive process. First the pods are harvested, split open with a machete, then left to dry for twenty-four hours. The seeds are removed from the pulp and allowed to "sweat" and ferment for several days. Then they're dried, their husks removed, and ground. During grinding, heat is applied to liquefy the beans' cocoa butter, thus producing a soft, rich-brown mass called chocolate liquor, which consists of 47 percent chocolate solids and 53 percent cocoa butter.

Chocolate liquor can be made into unsweetened baking chocolate simply by molding it into cakes and chilling it. For eating chocolate (bittersweet, semisweet, milk, etc.), additional cocoa butter and sugar (and milk solids) are added, then the liquor is kneaded ("conched") for up to three days, to aerate its texture and mellow its flavor. After conching, it's molded into bars or blocks and cooled. Finally, chocolate liquor can be made into cocoa by pressing it to remove a certain percentage of the cocoa butter; the remaining chocolate solids are ground into cocoa. From these three types of chocolate spring the myriad variations we see around us, from Hershey Bars to Godiva truffles.

Certainly the most familiar chocolate in the cookie baker's world is the chocolate chip; after all, more than half the cookies consumed annually in the United States are chocolate chip cookies. But cocoa and unsweetened baking chocolate have significant roles as well—think brownies. And chocolate crinkles. It's useful to understand the various types of chocolate, what to look for in each, and how to use them.

Unsweetened chocolate (baker's chocolate) contains no sugar. It commonly comes in 1-ounce squares, which are melted before using. It can also come pre-melted, in 1-ounce pouches. Use this chocolate in any recipe calling for unsweetened chocolate.

Bittersweet or semisweet chocolate must, by law, contain a minimum of 35 percent chocolate liquor (though most excellent-quality bittersweet chocolate contains up to 70 percent or so chocolate liquor). After that, the amount of added sugar determines whether a chocolate is labeled bittersweet or semisweet. And, since there's no agreement worldwide on what percentage of added sugar makes chocolate semisweet vs. bittersweet, labeling of chocolates is unofficial and left to the individual manufacturers. In addition to sugar, most chocolate will also contain vanilla, which enhances its flavor. Beyond that, some chocolates contain salt, added vegetable fat, and sometimes spices.

Bittersweet or semisweet chocolate comes in bars, blocks, chunks, and chips. Chocolate chips usually have soy lecithin added to keep them from melting and spreading too much as they bake; but some imported chips are lecithin-free. When a recipe calls for melting bittersweet or semisweet chocolate, it's best to choose a block or bar chocolate, as the lecithin in chips may affect the chocolate's melting ability.

Milk chocolate—and milk chocolate chips— substitute 15 to 20 percent milk solids for an equal amount of the chocolate liquor. Most bakers eschew the use of milk chocolate, considering it much better for eating than for baking.

The term *white chocolate* has been batted around by the FDA and chocolate manufacturers for years. Until recently, white chocolate wasn't permitted to be labeled chocolate, as it contains no chocolate liquor. However, FDA officials recently declared it legal to call white chocolate white chocolate. (Whew! Aren't you relieved?) At any rate, white chocolate, that luscious, creamy-white, rich confection, consists of cocoa butter, sugar, milk solids, and vanilla. *Confectionery* coating, which often masquerades as true white chocolate, is in fact not chocolate at

Substituting cocoa for baking chocolate

If you find yourself without any unsweetened baking chocolate on hand, but with plenty of unsweetened cocoa powder, you're in luck. For recipes that call for 1 square (1 ounce) of unsweetened baking chocolate, substitute 3 tablespoons cocoa powder plus 1 tablespoon solid fat, either vegetable shortening or butter.

all. A blend of vegetable fat (not cocoa butter), milk solids, sugar, and flavorings, confectionery coating melts nicely and doesn't need tempering, so it's often used to coat candy. However, it doesn't have the rich taste of true chocolate.

Chocolate ganache is a versatile blend of chocolate and hot cream, stirred to a smooth consistency. It's used to coat cakes, frost brownies, or dip cookies. It can also be flavored with liqueurs, then cooled and whipped to form chocolate truffle centers. See page 460 for a recipe.

Cocoa (unsweetened cocoa powder) is manufactured with two different amounts of fat. Baking cocoa is 12 to 16 percent cocoa butter; high fat ("breakfast") cocoa is 22 to 24 percent cocoa butter. We prefer to use high-fat cocoa for baking, as fat is a flavor carrier, and we feel high-fat cocoa has a better, stronger taste.

In addition, cocoa is manufactured either as *natural* (just the pressed, ground chocolate liquor), or *Dutch-process* (natural cocoa treated with alkali to reduce its acidity). Many consider Dutch-process cocoa a superior baking cocoa due to its less-sharp taste, richer, redder, darker color, and the fact that it doesn't need to be balanced in the recipe with something alkaline (e.g., baking soda).

The very darkest cocoa (think the color of Oreo cookies) is called *black cocoa*. It's treated with even more alkali than regular Dutch-process cocoa. Use it as is for the blackest chocolate cookies you've ever made, or in conjunction with regular Dutch-process cocoa, for a cookie somewhat darker than normal.

FOOD COLORS

Food colors are a wonderful addition to cookie icings and glazes. Add them to icing, by the drop, to attain the exact color you want—from palest pink to midnight black. For the most intense color, use food color paste or gel, rather than liquid; you can find these specialty colors in stores carrying cake decorating supplies, or by mail order.

DOUGH RELAXER

When added to roll-out cookie dough, dough relaxer takes the "fight" out of gluten; it makes rolling out the dough a much easier task, and results in cookies that are tender, not tough. Our favorite version of this helpful ingredient is Lora Brody All-Natural Dough Relaxer, available in gourmet stores and via mail order.

ADD-INS ● ● ● ● ● ● ● ● ● ● ● ● ● ●

Want to go stir-crazy? There are any number of tasty ingredients you can add to cookie dough to liven up your cookies. The following are just some of the options.

Nuts. Pecans, walnuts, almonds, peanuts, cashews, pine nuts… Any nut you enjoy eating out of hand is a good choice to add to cookie dough. You may choose to leave nuts whole in some cases—a plain sugar cookie looks lovely with a whole almond, pecan half, or walnut half placed in its center. However, keep in mind that some whole nuts may look peculiar in your finished cookie if it's not large enough to support their outsized presence. In addition, whole nuts in cookies tend to give you just one bite of nut; for this reason, we usually suggest dicing nuts.

Be aware that some nuts burn more quickly than others. The higher the oil in a nut, the more likely it is to scorch. Pine nuts, in particular, may burn if they're exposed to heat that's too high or baked too long.

Nut flours are simply nuts that have been very finely ground. Typical nut flours include hazelnut, almond, and pecan (often called pecan meal). Nut flours are usually available in both plain and toasted versions; toasted nut flour has a bit more flavor. Substitute nut flour for ¼ to ⅓ of the regular flour in your recipe, for a delicate, sandy texture and added flavor.

Nut pastes, including almond, hazelnut (praline), and pistachio, are a mixture of ground nuts and sweetening. They are sometimes used as a cookie ingredient, but more often used to fill pastries. Marzipan takes almond paste one step further—it includes unbeaten egg whites, to make it pliable. While it's sometimes used as an ingredient, marzipan is most often made into edible decorations, particularly for cakes.

Dried fruit is a wonderful addition to chewy cookies; think hermits with raisins, or chewy oatmeal cookies with chopped dates or dried cranberries. In general, it's not a

Should I add those nuts, or not?

If you're unsure whether nuts will burn in your cookie, or whether those malted milk balls will melt into puddles, or whether the currants will dry out and you should use raisins instead, do a test before committing yourself. Make the dough without the add-ins. Then break off enough for a single cookie, add whatever ingredient(s) you're questioning, and bake. If you're happy with the results, stir the additional ingredients into the dough. If not, try something else.

This is also a good test when you're questioning whether your cookies will spread too much. Test-bake one first; if it spreads more than you like, add some flour and test again. If you want more spread, rather than less, add vegetable oil or water. Either way, make adjustments in small increments; sure, it takes a little time, but it's better than being disappointed with an entire batch of cookies.

good idea to add dried fruit to crisp cookies; the fruit tends to dry out and become unpleasantly hard or, if there's enough of it, it makes the crisp cookies soft.

Adding fresh fruit to cookies is usually a no-no, given the amount of liquid it will exude as the cookies bake. Possible exceptions are finely diced apples or pears, which can add nice moisture and flavor to an already soft, chewy cookie.

The zest (grated rind) of citrus fruits adds wonderful flavor to a plain sugar cookie or shortbread.

Seeds. Sunflower, poppy, caraway, anise, and sesame seeds all make appearances in cookie recipes, particularly those from cultures other than our own. Use them for added crunch and flavor, and treat them like nuts—they may burn, so if you're unsure, test first (see Toasting Nuts page 000).

Candy. Cookies and candy—what could be a more natural pairing? Chocolate chips are the dowager queen of cookie add-ins, but chocolate isn't the only flavor chip you can use. Try peanut butter, butterscotch, raspberry-chocolate, white chocolate, mint, or any of the gourmet flavors (cappuccino, lemon, cherry) available from specialty retailers.

How about jelly beans, or gumdrops? Chopped peppermint patties, hard candies, or a chopped Snickers bar? It's worth it to test-bake one cookie with the desired add-in first (see page 499). If you're trying something like a chopped chocolate bar and you think it might melt, try chopping, then freezing the chopped bits before adding them to the cookie dough; being frozen when they hit the oven might just give them enough time to remain fairly firm throughout the bake.

If marshmallows are one of your favorite ingredients, no doubt you'll be tempted to add them to that fudgy cookie recipe. Don't! Marshmallows melt and disappear way before the cookie is done baking, leaving only a moist, creamy-colored hint of their presence. Your best bet with marshmallows is to halve large marshmallows and plop them onto your nearly baked cookies (sticky side down). Bake for an additional minute or two, just until the marshmallow starts to soften and/or brown, but before it melts.

Index

A

Alfajores, 340
All-purpose flour, 476
Almond
  and apricot squares, 218
  bars, lemony, 210
  and cardamom cookies, 285
  clouds, 268
  and coconut crisps, 309
  cookies, Chinese, 290
  crisps, 286
  extract, 489
  flour, 381
  joyfuls, 319
  and lemon biscotti, 149
  madeleines, 425
  pennies, 277
  and raspberry bars, 238
  See also: Biscotti
Amaretti, 386
Amish cookies, 304
Anise chews, 275
Anzac biscuits, 83
Apple
  bars, caramel, 222
  pie bars, Dutch, 246
Apricot
  and almond squares, 218
  squares, classic, 206

B

Baker's ammonia, 488
Baking pans, 28–30
  cutting cookies in, 247
Baking powder, 487, 488
Baking sheets
  greasing, 21, 43, 363, 483
  lining with parchment, 21
  rotating, 385
Baking soda, 487, 488
Baltimore's finest, 294
Barbados sugar, 480
Bar cookies
  about, 187–188
  avoiding a hard crust, 226
  cutting, 18, 190, 247
  piping jam, 241
  preventing sticking, 213
spreading batter, 192
  spreading jam smoothly, 229
  vs. cookies, 197
Batter cookies
  about, 407–408
Belgian sugar waffles, 438
Bench knife, 31
  to cut bars, 190
Benne wafers, 279
Berlinerkranser, 370
Berry crumble bars, 212
Bird's nests, 445

Biscotti
  about, 132–135
  adding flavor, 141
  American-style, 136
  black forest, 148
  brown sugar–cinnamon, 143
  butter-pecan, 140
  chocolate-chocolate chip, 148
  chocolate-coconut, 146
  cinnamon-raisin, 151
  classic Italian, 149
  cranberry-orange, 141
  creamy orange, 145
  dipping, 150
  Dutch chocolate–almond, 144
  freshness, maintaining, 153
  gianduja, 139
  gingerbread, 152
  granola, 142
  hazelnut-cappuccino, 150
  honey-sesame, 153
  Italian-style, 134
  lemon-almond, 149
  maple-walnut, 151
  Mexican mocha, 138
  mini, 151
  orange-cashew, 145
  piña colada, 147
  pine nut, fennel, and raisin, 142

(Biscotti, *cont.*)
  pistachio-cherry, 138
  rum-raisin, 152
  very vanilla, 147
Biscuits
  Anzac, 83
  defined, 343
  digestive, English, 343
  students', 380
  wine, 375
Black forest biscotti, 148
Black and white short-
  bread, 125
Bonbons
  Brattleboro, 392
  holiday, 356
Bones of the dead (*Ossi da
  morto*), 378
Bourbon balls, chocolate,
  446
Bowl(s)
  about, 30
  scraper, 31
Brambles, 344
Brandied cherry–nut
  cookies, 265
Brandy snaps, 412
Brattleboro bonbons, 392
Breakfast crunch bars,
  224
Brickle 'bread, 124
Brody, Lora, 376
  dough relaxer, 494
Brown-edge cookies, 63
Brownies
  about, 154–155, 159
  cakey, 157
  cheesecake swirl, 161
  chocolate mint, 160

fudgy, 156
Irish Cream cheesecake,
  162
macaroon, 163
on-the-fence, 158
peanut-mallow, 164
raspberry truffle, 164
toffee-coffee, 162
triple play, 167
whoopie, 165
with spirit, 166
Brown sugar
  about, 479
  biscotti, 143
  cookies, 72
  crinkles, 273
Build-a-bars, 220
Butter
  about, 483–485
  lemon-honey, 425
  nut, homemade, 313
  and rum drops, 299
Butterballs
  stuffed, 363
  walnut, 282
Buttermilk, 486
Butter-pecan
  biscotti, 140
  crunch, 337
  fantasies, 253
  rum balls, 446
  shortbread, 115
Butterscotch
  bars, vintage, 190
  chews, 311
  granola chippers, 47
  haystacks, 444
  oatmeal stovetop cookies,
    450

sundae cookies, 297
thins, 325

C

Café au lait bars, 199
Cake cookie cutouts, 428
Cake flour, 476
Cake tester, 31
Camden Home Bakery,
  291
Camelot dream bars, 211
Candy bar cookies, 49
Candy thermometer, 31
Cannoli forms, 31
Cape Cod cranberry bars,
  227
Cappuccino
  bars, double-shot, 232
  biscotti, hazelnut, 150
  glaze, 459
Caramel
  apple bars, 222
  candy bars, 208
  and chocolate dip, 471
  and coconut bars, 226
  filling, 469
  homemade, 223
  icing, 463
  macciato bars, 233
  rocks, 355
  swirl shortbread, 130
Cardamom-almond
  cookies, 285
Carrot drops, 272
Cashew
  bars, and white chocolate,
    242
  and orange biscotti, 145

Cat's tongues, 426
Chai shortbread, 122
Checkerboards, 400
Cheesecake
    bars, strawberry, 240
    Irish Cream, brownies,
        162
    swirl brownies, 161
Cherry
    brandied, and nut
        cookies, 265
    chocolate chip cookies,
        49
    and nut *rugelach*, 372
    and pistachio biscotti,
        138
    squares, 207
Chinese restaurant cookies,
    290
    Americanized, 291
Chip 'n' chunk cookies,
    305
Chip 'n' nut drops, 302
Chippers
    butterscotch-granola, 47
    mega-, 46
    nut butter, 312
    orange-pistachio, 48
Chocolate
    about, 492–494
    and almond biscotti, 144
    bourbon balls, 446
    for brownies, 161
    and caramel dip, 471
    and chocolate chip
        biscotti, 148
    chunks, awesome, 318
    and coconut biscotti, 147
    cookie dough, 395

creme filling, 470
crinkles, 254
crunch bars, 204
dipping sticks, 335
dipsticks, 354
faux-reos, 328
ganache icing, 159, 460
glaze, 459
graham crackers, 334
grating, 50
hazelnut crisps, 447
icing, rich, 295
krumkake, 431
madeleines, 425
melting, 23,146
midnights, 306
mint dips, 329
oatmeal drops, 451
peanut butter drops, 451
and peanut half-moons,
    106
and raspberry bars, 203
refrigerator cake, 330
shortbread, 113
snaps, 327
toffee rounds, 251
wakeups, 320
and walnut holiday
cookies, 301
whoopie pies, 418
    See also: Cocoa,
        Brownies, and
        Chocolate chip
        cookies
Chocolate chip cookies
    about, 42–43
    bars, 189
    butternut, 50
    butterscotch-granola, 47

candy bar, 49
cherry-almond, 49
classic crunchy, 45
and chocolate biscotti,
    148
essential chewy, 44
gianduja delights, 48
good-as-store-bought, 51
mega-chippers, 46
oatmeal, 78
orange-pistachio, 48
peppermint snaps, 52
shortbread, 114
white chocolate
    macadamia, 47
Chrusciki, 388
Cigarette cookies, 415
Cinnamon
    biscotti, and raisin, 151
    bun cookies, 397
    and caramel shortbread,
        130
    glaze, 459
    and raisin rounds, 292
Citrus sizzlers, 321
Cocoa
    about, 492
    for baking, 161
    straining unsweetened,
        27
Coconut
    and almond crisps, 309
    bars, golden, 225
    bird's nests, 445
    brownie macaroons, 163
    and caramel candy bars,
        226
    and chocolate biscotti,
        147

(Coconut, *cont.*)
  glaze, 459
  jumbles, 314
  lime crisps, 309
  macaroons, classic, 262
  stuffed butterballs, 364
  toasting, 27
  two-bit wonders, 255
Coconutties, 78
Coffee
  brownies, toffee, 162
  cookies, spiked, 315
Confectioners' sugar, 478
Confetti *pizzelle*, 433
Cookie cutters, 32
Cookie dough
  chilling, 16, 326
  chocolate, 395
  cutting out, 328
  docker for, 19, 33, 333
  doneness, 19
  flattening in plastic bag,
    325
  fruit-flavored, 394
  how to roll out, 324
  piping, 387
  relaxer, 494
  rolling on parchment,
    332
  rolling scraps, 339
  scooping, stick-free, 52
  slicing with floss, 397
  vanilla, 393
Cookie molds, 32
Cookie press, 32, 394
Cookie scoops, 32, 52
Cookie wheels, 405
Cooling rack, 33
Cornmeal, 477

Cornstarch, 477
Corn syrup
  about, 480
  dark vs. light, 98
Cranberry
  bars, Cape Cod, 227
  biscotti, and orange, 141
  chews, 78
Cream, about, 330
Cream cheese filling, 468
Creaming sugar and fat, 17
Cream of tartar, 487
Creme filling, 465
Crinkles
  brown sugar, 273
  chocolate, 254
Crisps
  almond, 286
  chocolate-hazelnut, 447
  coconut-almond, 309
  coconut-lime, 309
  ginger, 93, 94
  honey, 410
  maple-walnut, 276
Crystal diamonds, 66
Cutout cookies
  cake, 428
  peanut butter, 100
  tips, 60
Cutting in fat and flour, 17

D
Daisies, 266
Date
  and ginger molasses
  cookies, 90
  nut bars, chewy, 195
  oatmeal sandwiches, 79

pinwheels, 360
squares, bakery, 228
stuffed cookies, 274
Decorated cookies
  about, 168–170
  colors, 179
  decorator's dream, 171
  gingerbread, 173
  gingerbread house,
    182–184
  icing, 180
  light spice, 172
  outlining and filling, 178
  rolling and cutting, 170
  tools for, 176
  working with fondant,
    181
Decorating sugar, 479
Decorator's dream cookies,
  171
Demerara shortbread, 126
Demerara sugar, 480
Digestive biscuits, English,
  343
Dipping sticks, chocolate,
  335
Dips
  chocolate-caramel, 471
  hot fudge, 473
  raspberry–white
    chocolate, 472
Dipsticks, fudge-coated,
  354
Docking, 19
Double-butter bars, 230
Double-shot cappuccino
  bars, 232
Doughnut cookies, Easter,
  374

Drop cookies
  about, 249–250
  adjusting size, 258
Dulce de leche, 340
Dutch-process cocoa
  about, 494
  for baking, 161
Dyall, János, 380

E

Easter doughnut cookies, 374
Eggnog
  construction dough, 346
  sandwich cookies, 345
Eggs
  about, 485
  separating, 24
Egg white(s)
  beating, 16
  folding in, 20
  glaze, 395
Elephant ears, mini, 376
Esposito, Mary Ann, 433
Essential cookie recipes
  American-style biscotti, 136
  cakey brownies, 157
  chewy chocolate chip, 44
  chewy oatmeal, 74
  chewy sugar, 55
  crisp molasses, 87
  crisp oatmeal, 76
  crisp sugar, 58
  crunchy chocolate chip, 45

crunchy oatmeal, 75
crunchy sugar, 56
decorator's dream, 171
fudgy brownies, 156
gingerbread, 173
Italian-style biscotti, 134
light spice, 172
on-the-fence brownies, 158
on-the-fence molasses, 88
peanut butter, 97
shortbread, 110
soft molasses, 86
soft oatmeal, 77

F

Fattigmann, 388
Faux-reos, 328
Fig
  filling, 207, 229
  squares, 207, 229, 244
Filling
  caramel, 469
  cherry, dried, 207
  chocolate creme, 470
  cream cheese and ginger, 468
  creme, 465
  fig, 207, 229
  lemon creme, 468
  malted milk, 465
  marshmallow, 466
  mincemeat, 207
  mint, 160
  peanut butter, 466
  quantity for, 105
  raspberry, 229

spreading, 361
vanilla creme, 470
Finishing touch
  about, 455–456
  dips, 471–473
  fillings, 465–470
  glazes and icings, 456–464
Fiori di sicilia, 289, 490
Flavored sugar, 479
Florentines, 416
Flour
  about, 476
  sifter, 33
Flourless oatmeal drops, 81
Fondant
  icing, 462
  working with, 181
Food colors, 494
Fortune cookies, 410–411
Framboise, brownies, 166
Frangelico brownies, 166
Freckled fruit shortbread, 120
Frosted delights, 231
Fruit
  cookies, and oatmeal, 452
  dicing, 417
  flavored cookie dough, 394
  squares, 200
  See also: specific kinds
Fudge
  coated dipsticks, 354
  sandwich cookies, 304
Fudgies, 423

G

Ganache
  chocolate, icing, 159, 460
  chunk or chips for, 462
  white chocolate, 461
Gianduja
  biscotti, 139
  delights, 48
  wafers, 338
Ginger
  crisps, 93
  and orange madeleines, 425
  shortbread, 120
  squares, hot and sweet, 234
Gingerbread
  biscotti, 152
  building a house, 182–184
  cookies, 173
Glaze
  brandy, 459
  cappuccino, 459
  chocolate, 459
  cinnamon, 459
  coconut, 459
  egg white, 395
  hard, for cookies, 457
  maple, 459
  milk or cream for, 459
  mint, 459
  mocha, 464
  orange or lemon, 459
  simple cookie, 174, 458
  vanilla, 458
Glazing sugar, 479

Go-anywhere shortbread, 112
Golden crunch cookies, 257
Graham
  crackers, the best, 332
  crackers, chocolate, 334
  cracker crust, 333
  squares, peanut butter, 448
Grand Marnier brownies, 166
Granola
  bars, Vermont, 202
  biscotti, 142
  cookies, chewy, 317
  s'more, bars, 243
Granulated sugar, 478
Graters, 33
Gray, Sue, 341
Greenwald, Nora, 274

H

Half-moon cookies, 293
  peanut-chocolate, 106
Hamantaschen, 368
Hamelman, Jeffrey, 392
Harvest moons, 278
Hazelnut
  biscotti, cappuccino, 150
  crisps, chocolate, 447
Hermit bars, very best, 196
High-altitude baking, 22
Hobnails, 252
Holiday cookies
  bird's nests, 445
  black and white short-bread, 125

bonbons, 356
cherry-nut *rugelach*, 372
chocolate-walnut, 301
chrusciki, 388
decorator's dream, 171
Easter doughnut, 374
gingerbread, 173
ginger crisps, 93
hamantaschen, 368
hot and sweet ginger, 234
koulouria, 367
kourabiedes, 296
lebkuchen, 198
light spice, 172
mailanderli, 350
ossi da morto (bones of the dead), 378
peppermint sticks, 403
pizzelle, 432
rum balls, 496
speculaas, 384
springerle, 382
totenbeinli, 351
vanilla *kipferl*, 362
Honey
  about, 481
  crisps, 410
  and lemon butter, 425
  and sesame biscotti, 153
Hot fudge dip, 473

I

Iced spice rings, 371
Icing
  caramel, 463
  chocolate ganache, 159, 460

fondant, 462
peanut butter, 464
rich chocolate, 295
royal, 175, 457
Irish Cream cheesecake
brownies, 162
Italian biscotti, classic, 149

J

Jam
piping, 241
spreading, 229
Jam-packeds, 366
Jammies, your favorite,
131
Joe Froggers, 89
Jumbles
coconut, 314
trail mix, 78

K

Kahlúa brownies, 166
Key lime bars, 235
King Arthur's sugar
cookies, 59
Kipferl, vanilla, 362
Kisses, sparkling sugar,
260
Kitchen scale, 37
Knives, 33–34
Koulouria, 367
Kourabiedes, 296
Krumkake, 430
iron, 34

L

Lace cookies, 409
Ladyfingers, 427
Langues de chat (Cat's
tongues), 426
Lavender cookies, 284
Lebkuchen, 198
Lemon
and almond biscotti,
149
coolers, 310
creme filling, 468
drops, 69
essences, 116
glaze, 459
and honey butter,
425
madeleines, 425
rings, golden, 379
squares, 236
to squeeze, 268
tea snaps, 339
and zucchini drops,
280
Licorice drops, 308
Lime crisps, coconut, 309
Linzer cookies
about, 346
bars, 215

M

Macaroons, brownie, 163
Mackenzie, Barbara, 367
Madeleines, 424
Magic in the middles,
359
Mailanderli, 350

Malted milk filling, 465
Mandelbrot, over-the-top,
358
Maple
cookies, Vermont, 258
glaze, 459
meringues, 260
shortbread, 121
snaps, 92
sugar, about, 480
syrup, about, 481
Maple-walnut
biscotti, 151
crisps, 276
Marathon cookies, 300
Marble cookies, 399
Margarine, 484–485
Marmalade morsels, 289
Marshmallow(s)
brownies, and peanut,
164
filling, 466
homemade, 422, 467
measuring, 418
Matz, Virginia, 325
Mega-chippers, 46
Meringue powder, 485
Meringues
about, 261
classic coconut, 262
kisses, sparkling sugar,
260
maple, 260
Mexican mocha biscotti,
138
Midnights, 306
Mincemeat
filling, 207
squares, 207

Mint
  dips, 329
  filling, 160
  glaze, 459
Mocha
  biscotti, Mexican, 138
  chip oatmeal cookies, 78
  glaze, 464
  krumkake, 431
  mudslides, 298
  walnuts, 264
Mochachino bars, 199
Molasses
  about, 481
  choosing, 90
  measuring, 85
Molasses cookies
  about, 84–85
  crisp, 87
  extra-spicy, 90
  ginger crisps, 93, 94
  Joe Froggers, 89
  on-the-fence, 88
  snaps, 92
  soft, 86
Monster cookies, 256

N

Nanaimo bars, 237
Neapolitans, 402
Neon cookies, 403
No-bake cookies
  about, 441
  bird's nests, 445
  bourbon balls, chocolate,
    446
  butter-pecan rum balls,
    446

butterscotch haystacks,
    444
chocolate-hazelnut
  crisps, 447
chocolate-oatmeal drops,
    451
crispy rice treats, 442
crunchy peanut bars, 449
oatmeal fruit, 452
peanut butter graham,
    448
rocky road, 453
stovetop, 450
Nut(s)
  butter chippers, 312
  chopping, for biscotti,
  homemade butter, 313
  toasting, 27
  See also: specific kinds

O

Oatcakes, sweet, 117
Oat flour, 477
Oatmeal
  about, 79
  whoopie pies, 421
Oatmeal cookies
  about, 73
  Anzac, 83
  chewy, essential, 74
  chocolate chip, 78
  coconutties, 78
  cranberry chews, 78
  crisp, essential, 76
  crunchy, essential, 75
  date-stuffed, 79
  drops, chocolate, 451
  flourless, 81

fruit, 452
mocha chip, 78
old-fashioned, 80
piña colada, 78
salty, 82
scotchies, 78
soft, essential, 77
stovetop, butterscotch,
    450
trail mix jumbles, 78
very vanilla, 78
On-the-fence brownies, 158
On-the-fence molasses
  cookies, 88
Orange
  biscotti, creamy, 145
  blossoms, 307
  and cashew biscotti, 145
  chippers, and pistachio,
    48
  and cranberry biscotti,
    141
  glaze, 459
  madeleines, and ginger,
    425
Ossi da morto (Bones of
  the Dead), 378

P

Pastry bag
  about, 35
  filling, 20
  how to use, 176–177
  piping dough, 387
  piping jam, 241
  piping whipped cream,
    430
Pastry blender, 35

Pastry brushes, 35
Pastry tips and couplers, 35
Pastry wheel, 36
PB&J cookies, 101
Peanut brittle bars, 193
Peanut butter
  filling, 466
  icing, 464
  store-bought, 96
Peanut butter cookies
  about, 95–97
  blossoms, 102
  chews, 98
  crisscrosses, 97
  cutouts, 100
  double-butter bars, 230
  drops, chocolate, 451
  essential, 97
  graham squares, 448
  half-moons, 106
  and jelly, 101
  and mallow brownies, 164
  old-fashioned, 99
  1-2-3-4, 108
  pick-me-ups, 107
  scout's honor, 104
  smoothies, 192
  spritz, 101
  squares, fudgy, 216
  triple-play, 103, 167
Pearl sugar, 479
Pecan
  fudge shortbread, 127
  pie bars, rich, 217
  praline sandwich
    cookies, 341
  puffs, 283

Pennies, almond, 277
Peppermint
  snaps, chocolate, 52
  sticks, 403
Persons, Amy, 58
Petticoat tails, 128
Pignoli cookies, 267
Piña colada
  biscotti, 147
  oatmeal cookies, 78
Pine nut biscotti with
  fennel, 142
Pinwheels, 398
  date, 360
Pistachio
  and cherry biscotti, 138
  cookies, St. Patrick's Day, 288
Pizzelle, 432–433
Pizza wheel
  for decorated cookies, 170
  for shortbread, 111
  for sugar cookies, 67
Poppy seed madeleines, 425
Potato chip(s)
  canisters for shipping, 281
  crispy cookies, 271
  to crush, 271
Pretzels, 396
Puffs
  pecan, 283
  sugar, 64
Pumpkin
  bars, harvest, 194
  whoopie pies, 419

R

Raisin
  and cinnamon rounds, 292
  and ginger crisps, 94
  sugar cookies, 71
Raspberry
  and almond bars, 238
  and chocolate bars, 203
  fudge sandwich cookies, 303
  lemon coolers, 311
  squares, bakery, 229
  truffle brownies, 164
  and white chocolate dip, 472
Refrigerator cake, 330
Rhubarb dreams, 239
Rice flour, 477
Rice treats, crispy, 442
Rocky road
  bars, 201
  no-bakes, 453
Rolled oat(s)
  cutouts, 336
  old-fashioned, 477
Rolling pins, 36
Rosette(s), 436
  iron, 37
Rose water madeleines, 425
Royal icing, 175, 457
Rugelach, cherry-nut, 372
Rum
  balls, butter-pecan, 446
  drops, butter, 299
  and raisin biscotti, 152

S

St. Patrick's Day pistachio
cookies, 288
Salkowski, Kiera, 300
Salt
about, 482
extra-fine, 64
Salty oatmeal drops, 82
Savoiardi (*see* ladyfingers)
Scandinavian blondies,
191
Scotchies, oat, 78
Scout's honor sandwiches,
104
Sesame
benne wafter, 280
biscotti, 153
Shabelman, Mona, 358
Shaped cookies
about, 353, 369
crescents, 362
filling, 356–357, 361
rolling dough, 376
stuffing, 365
Sherry cookies, 270
Shipping cookies, 25–26
canisters for, 281
Shortbread
about, 109
bite-sized, 123
black and white, 125
brickle, 124
butter-pecan, 115
chai, 122
chocolate, 113
chocolate chip, 114
cinnamon-caramel swirl,
130

Demerara, 126
essential, 110
filled double, 118–119
freckled fruit, 120
ginger, 120
go-anywhere, 112
jammies, 131
lemon essences, 116
maple, 121
mold, 37
petticoat tails, 128
sweet oatcakes, 117
toasted pecan fudge, 127
tweed cakes, 123
Shortening, 482-483
S'more granola bars, 243
Snaps
brandy, 412
chocolate, 327
chocolate-peppermint,
52
maple, 92
molasses, 92
tea, lemon, 339
Snickerdoodles, 60
South Seas cookies, 316
Spatulas, 37–38
Speculaas, 384
Spice cookies
iced, 371
light, 172
Spices, 491–492
Splenda, 481
Spreading (flattening), 54
Springerle, 382
Spritz cookies, 394
Squares (*See* Bar cookies)
Stained glass cookies, 347
Storing cookies, 27

Stovetop cookies, 450
Strainers, 38
Strawberry
cheesecake bars, 240
rhubarb dreams, 239
Stroopwafels, 434
Students' biscuits, 380
Sugar, about, 478–480
Sugar cookies
about, 53–54
brown-edge, 63
chewy, essential, 55
crisp, 58
crunchy, essential, 56
crystal diamonds, 66
lemon drops, 69
light-as-air, 65
puffs, 64
raisin, old-fashioned, 71
roll-out, King Arthur, 59
snickerdoodles, 60
soft cakes, 68
sparkling kisses, 260
tea sandwiches, 70
vanilla dreams, 62
Summer berry crumble
bars, 212
Superfine sugar, 478

T

Tea
sandwiches, 70
snaps, lemon, 339
and spice squares, 200
Thermometers, 38-39
Thorne, John, 66
Thumbprint cookies, 269
Timers, 39

Toasting
  coconut, 27
  nuts, 27
Toffee
  chocolate rounds, 251
  coffee brownies, 162
  crunchers, 263
Toll House Cookbook, 189
Tongs, 39
Totenbeinli, 351
Trail mix jumbles, 78
Triple play
  brownies, 167
  peanut butter cookies,
    103
Tropical paradise bars, 214
Tuiles, 414
Turbinado sugar, 480
Tweed cakes, 123
Two-bit wonders, 255

U/V

Ultrapasteurized cream,
  330

Vanilla
  biscotti, very, 147
  cookie dough, 393
  creme filling, 470
  dreams, 62
  extract, 489
  glaze, 458
  kipferl, 362
  oatmeal cookies, 78
Vegetable oil
  about, 485
  spray, 483
Vermont granola bars, 202

Vermont maple cookies,
  258
Vieira, Marlita, 203, 270

W

Wafers
  benne, 279
  French tile, 414
  gianduja, 338
  shaping, 415
Waffles, Belgian sugar, 438
Wakefield, Ruth, 189
Walnut butterballs, 282
Wedding cookies, 287
Whisk, 39
White chocolate
  and cashew bars, 242
  chocolate chip cookies,
    47
  ganache, 461
  and raspberry dip, 472
Whole wheat flour, 476
Whoopie brownies, 165
Whoopie pies
  chocolate, 418
  oatmeal, 421
  pumpkin, 419
Wine biscuits, 375

Y/Z

Yin-yang cookies, 404
Yogurt, 486

Zester, 39
Zimsterne, 349
Zucchini drops, lemon,
  280

Zwieback, 390
  cinnamon-sugar, 391